Contents

PATRICK O'NEIL

DATABASE

Principles
Programming
Performance

MORGAN KAUFMANN PUBLISHERS
SAN FRANCISCO, CALIFORNIA

Executive Editor Bruce M. Spatz
Production Manager Yonie Overton
Assistant Editor Douglas Sery
Production Coordinator Julie Pabst
Composition Nancy Logan
Text and Cover Design Carron Design
Copyeditor Jessie Wood
Proofreaders Gary Morris and Nancy Riddiough
Printer Courier Companies, Inc.

Editorial Offices
Morgan Kaufmann Publishers, Inc.
340 Pine Street, Sixth Floor
San Francisco, CA 94104

© **1994 by Morgan Kaufmann Publishers, Inc.**

Library of Congress Cataloging-in-Publication Data is available for this book.

ISBN 1-55860-219-4

Contents

Contents

Preface

The database field has changed dramatically in the 40-odd years of its existence, and the fast pace of change continues today. The relational approach was invented only about 25 years ago, and relational database products have only been available commercially for about 15 years. Almost as soon as new database standards and products are announced, newer ones—promising improved features—take their place. Without a firm grounding in the principles upon which the database field is based, combined with an understanding of the connections (and gaps) between current theory and practice, it is impossible for today's professional to keep up.

This book introduces these fundamental principles to anyone interested in learning about database systems. To support the presentation, we provide an up-to-date introduction to SQL and practical applications created in real commercial database systems. Whether you are currently an SQL user, an application programmer, a database administrator, or a student interested in learning about the field, this book was written with you in mind. Throughout the book we emphasize database programming and the relationships between principles, programming, and performance. The combination of practical information with underlying principles presents a more complete introduction to database systems than what has been available up to now in textbooks and manuals.

Practitioners need an introduction to database application programming that is more than the simple listing of Embedded SQL features so often seen in texts. Vendor manuals sometimes give an excellent introduction to SQL and database programming, but lack the intellectual grounding in fundamental principles that students and professionals need to adapt to future changes in database systems and languages. Some principles that are not well covered in introductory database texts or manuals are these: implication of deadlock aborts (the need to retry), entity-relationship modelling and normalization (as well as the translation of database design into actual tables), and problems of user interaction during transactions that access popular data.

This book can be thought of as a solid introduction to the skills needed by a database administrator, application programmer, or sophisticated SQL user. Although the needs of a database administrator may be broader than those of an application programmer, programmers are more effective when they have a grasp of the general concepts that are essential to a DBA. The same can be said for serious SQL users. In addition to a knowledge of SQL, an understanding of logical database design, physical layout of data, indexing, security, and cost-performance will benefit anyone working with database systems.

An important tenet of this book is that while theoretical concepts will always be valid, many concepts become less relevant with changes in the field. For example, databases vendors often build successful systems by breaking the rules of the relational paradigm. With the recent release of extended or post-relational products, it may even be necessary for relational algebra and existing logical design methodologies to adapt significantly to accommodate the new possibilities. Further revolutionary changes are on the horizon as the object-oriented approach tries to deal with nested hierarchies, and the relational model is extended to handle information with less structure, such as that found in text retrieval applications.

Use of this Book

If you are new to databases, this book will give you a comprehensive introduction. If you are already experienced as a user or programmer, the discussions will enhance your effectiveness and efficiency. The goal is to provide you with a grounding in the fundamentals of database theory, but within the context of the practical details of commercial database standards and products.

The notes that led to this book were developed over a period of several years for the introductory database course and a subsequent, more advanced course offered at the University of Massachusetts at Boston. The first course was an introduction to database design principles. Roughly the first six chapters of the text contain the material from that course. The second course dealt with more advanced database concepts, with a focus on cost-performance concerns. This material is covered in Chapters 7–10.

It is not necessary to proceed through the book sequentially, and the chapters have been prepared to accommodate a variety of reader interests and course plans. Depending on your experience and objectives, chapters can be read briefly or in a different sequence from the order offered by the book. For example, readers who have a familiarity with basic concepts may want to begin with their specific interest in the later chapters, referring to Chapters 1–5 only when needed. The book has been written so that new concepts are only introduced when previous concepts have been mastered. For this reason, experienced readers can begin with the subject most appropriate to their needs.

We've intended this book either as a tutorial and reference for the professional, or as a one- or two-term introductory course in colleges and universities. The presentation moves from basic theory and concepts to the most recent developments in the field. The text introduces basic SQL simultaneously with the fundamentals of relational databases. Examples from ORACLE, INGRES, DB2, Montage, and others are used to illustrate the concepts, and to clarify the cost-performance issues by comparing the differing approaches used in these successful systems. The key issues in each chapter are reinforced by programming examples and exercises. Three appendices provide additional background. For anyone using the book for self-study, solutions to selected exercises are included in the back of the book.

Overview of the Chapters

Chapter 1 introduces the fundamental concepts of databases and gives an overview of what is to come. Chapter 2 provides a grounding in many abstract concepts of the relational model. It identifies the parts of a database and explains the basics of relational algebra. Starting with Chapter 3, the presentation is enriched with examples from commonly used database products. Chapter 3 introduces SQL, describing its capabilities and covering the statements and functions of the programming language. Chapter 4 is relatively unique. It gives an introduction to Embedded SQL (including Dynamic SQL) that is sufficiently detailed to enable students to immediately begin writing database programs. The C language is used for this purpose, but every attempt is made to provide enough examples so that students with good programming backgrounds in other languages will be able to compose C programs by copying the style of the examples provided. Logical database design is presented in Chapter 5. E-R concepts and modeling are detailed, followed by a well-motivated and rigorous introduction to normalization. After this, a case study is presented to reinforce the principles discussed. The database design principles of Chapter 5 have immediate application in Chapter 6, where standard and non-standard integrity capabilities of the various products and standards are covered. This sequence concludes with a careful examination of database views and security in various products.

Chapters 1–6 present a comprehensive introduction to the concepts used by a DBA. Chapter 2 is fundamental to modern database management systems and defines many concepts that will be used later. While Chapter 3 doesn't rely heavily on Chapter 2, it is essential to what follows in Chapter 4. Together, Chapters 2, 3, and 4 develop a general intuition about databases that is useful before reading Chapter 5. Chapter 5 also expands on some concepts from Chapter 2 and is used in Chapter 6 to motivate the discussion of constraints and values.

The final chapters build on some of the capabilities already mastered in the earlier chapters. But they can also stand alone, so that instructors can dip into some of these topics with students who have not previously used the text. The database standards give very little guidance for some of these topics. A number of concepts in physical database design are introduced in Chapter 7. Data storage and indexing issues are related to actual database systems in this chapter. Chapter 8 covers essentially all the features of the DB2 query optimizer, the most sophisticated available, and concludes with coverage of results from the Set Query benchmark to illustrate the concepts presented. Chapter 9 introduces the ACID properties of transactions, including serializability theory and recovery, with various types of checkpointing. The chapter concludes with cost-performance considerations: the five-minute rule and the TPC-A benchmark. Chapter 10 introduces some of the motivations for database systems spanning multiple CPUs, including client-server and distributed transactions. All of these later chapters focus on quantitative aspects of performance. How does performance degrade as a hash index fills up? Why is the multi-page read in DB2 so cost effective? How can we predict the elapsed time for specific DB2 queries?

Chapter 7 relies most heavily on Chapters 3, 4, and 6, and is important grounding for the remaining chapters of the book. Chapter 8 depends on Chapters 3, 4, 6, and 7: it can be thought of as giving all the query optimizer concepts needed to understand the Set Query benchmark results on DB2. Chapter 9 depends mainly on Chapters 4, 6, and 7, and it provides the basic transactional theory needed to understand the TPC-A benchmark. Chapter 10 assumes a good understanding of basic database concepts.

There is much in these topics that is both practical and theoretical. Yet it is well within the grasp of beginners, and the sooner it is learned, the sooner it can be applied. A consistent attempt is made throughout the book to point out disparity between theory and practice, unsatisfactory aspects of current standards, and important differences between database products and their varying SQL dialects and architectural assumptions. We hope that what you learn from this book will serve you for many years to come.

Acknowledgments

A number of people provided detailed comments and advice in reviewing earlier versions of this book:

Shu-Wie Chen at Columbia University
Henry Etlinger at Rochester Institute of Technology
Goetz Graefe at Portland State University
Jim Gray at Digital Equipment Corporation
Fred Korz at Columbia University
Jim Melton at Digital Equipment Corporation
Edward Omiecinski at Georgia Institute of Technology
Yonie Overton at Morgan Kaufmann
Julie Pabst at Morgan Kaufmann
Bryan Pendleton at INGRES Corporation
Donald Slutz at Tandem Computer
Bruce Spatz at Morgan Kaufmann
David Spooner at Rensselaer Polytechnic Institute
Toby Teorey at the University of Michigan at Ann Arbor
Gottfried Vossen at Universitaet Muenster
Yun Wang at IBM Santa Teresa Laboratory
Gerhard Weikum at ETH, Zurich

I particularly thank my wife, Elizabeth J. O'Neil, also of UMass/Boston, who contributed a great deal of time and compiled the final version of the exercises and solutions. My son, Eugene O'Neil, currently at Computervision, provided early programming support for examples and exercises in ORACLE and INGRES. In addition, several generations of students at UMass/Boston gave numerous comments for improving the text. Thank you.

Patrick O'Neil

Introduction

This chapter introduces the central ideas and definitions covered in the text. We describe basic database concepts and profile the typical database users. Then we give an overview of the concepts and features of a relational database management system.

1.1 Fundamental Database Concepts

A *database management system*—or, simply, a *database system* or a *DBMS*—is a program product for keeping computerized records about an enterprise. For example, a wholesale business would normally use a DBMS to keep records about its sales (the *operational data* of the business), and a university would use a DBMS to keep student records (tuition payments, grade transcripts, and so on). Many libraries use a database system to keep track of library inventory and loans, and to provide various types of indexing to material by subject, author, and title. All airlines use database systems to manage their flights and reservations, and state motor vehicle departments use them for drivers' licenses and car registrations. Tower Records has a database system to keep track of its stock, as well as all records and CDs in print, and to provide a query facility to customers searching for specific recordings. The collection of records kept for a common purpose such as these is known as a *database;* the records of the database normally reside on *disk* (a slow access medium where information will persist through power outages), and the records are retrieved from disk into computer memory only when they are accessed.

A DBMS may deal with more than one database at a time. For example, a university might maintain one database for enrolled students and a second database to keep track of the books in its library. The library database contains no records in common with the student records database (although there might be some duplication of information, since some library borrowers are also students), but both databases can be accessed, by different users, through the same DBMS.

A number of different approaches have been developed for structuring access to information in a database. Historically, two early products provided what were later recognized as distinct *data models* for structuring information: IBM's IMS (Information Management System), released in 1968, and Cullinet Software's IDMS, released in the early 1970s. IMS provided what came to be known as the *hierarchical data model*, where different kinds of records relate to one another in a hierarchical form. For example, a database for a bank might place a corporate entity record at the top, with information such as the corporate headquarters' address and telephone number; below that the bank might place records for the banking branches; and below that records for tellers and other employees at each branch. To process information about a particular teller, a program would normally navigate down through the appropriate hierarchical layers. The IDMS product, on the other hand, was conceived as a result of the 1971 CODASYL report of an industry database task group and provided what came to be known as the *network data model*, a generalization of the hierarchical model where a set of records in one layer might have two different containing hierarchies at the next layer up.

Naturally both the IMS and IDMS products had a variety of features that we are not mentioning. To oversimplify somewhat, the hierarchical model structured data as a directed tree, with a root at the top and leaves at the bottom, while the network model structured data as a directed graph without circuits, a slight generalization that allowed the network model to represent certain real-world data structures more easily than was possible in the hierarchical model. The main drawback with these products was that queries against the data were difficult to create, normally requiring a program written by an expert programmer who understood the complex navigational structure of the data. Both products are still in use at a large number of companies, and IMS in particular is still an important source of revenue for IBM.

By far the most commonly used data model for database system products being purchased today is the *relational mode*l, which provides a flexible capability to allow non-programmers to pose general queries quickly and easily. A DBMS that utilizes the relational model is known as a relational DBMS, or *RDBMS*, but we will often just say DBMS or database system to mean RDBMS. In this book we will study a body of concepts and techniques that has been developed to create, maintain, and use a relational database within a database system. The techniques covered are surprisingly general in application. Most new concepts are illustrated with detailed commands from a number of different commercial RDBMS products and standards. While we see that the command syntax for the more complex features will change from one product to another, most of the basic capabilities provided by any one DBMS are shared by the others. Three of the major products considered are **INGRES**, **ORACLE**, and **DB2**. We will see some examples of commands from these products a bit later in this chapter.

To begin to illustrate some fundamental concepts, Figure 1.1 shows an example of a relational database representing student enrollment records in a university. The database is quite small for simplicity of illustration. A more realistic university enrollment database would contain tens of thousands of records, with more information in each record.

students

sid	sname	class	telephone
1	Jones	2	555-1234
2	Smith	3	555-4321
3	Brown	2	555-1122
5	White	3	555-3344

enrollment

cno	sid
101	1
101	3
102	5
105	2
105	5
108	1
108	3

courses

cno	cname	croom	time
101	French I	2-104	MW2
102	French II	2-113	MW3
105	Algebra	3-105	MW2
108	Calculus	2-113	MW4

Figure 1.1 Student Enrollment Database

In a relational database, all information is represented in the form of named tables with labeled columns. For example, the *students* table of Figure 1.1 has the following column names: *sid*, which is a unique student ID number; *sname,* which is the last name of the student (in a full-sized database, the entire name would be represented, probably in more than one column: *lastname, firstn_midin); class* is the student year, 1 for freshman through 4 for senior; and *telephone* is the student's home telephone number. The student records in this table are the individual rows of the *students* table—for example, the first row (just below the column names) represents a student named Jones in the sophomore year, whose student ID is 1 and home telephone number is 555-1234. A table can be roughly pictured as a disk file of records, although many database specialists stress important differences between a table and a disk file. For intuitive presentation we use the following terms interchangeably: disk file and table, rows and records, columns and fields.

The *courses* table in Figure 1.1 lists the set of courses offered, with course number given by *cno*, course name by *cname*, the room where the course meets by *croom*, and the days and period it meets by *time*. The *time* column values are encoded, for example, MW2 means Monday and Wednesday during period 2. The *enrollment* table has only two columns: each row of the table pairs up a student with given student ID, *sid*, and a course that the student is taking, represented by *cno*. The three tables of Figure 1.1 together represent a relational database. Note that we use lowercase names (in monofont type) for tables and column names, but many other texts use uppercase names. A number of other concepts governing the tabular representation of data in the relational model will be covered starting in Chapter 2; for the remainder of this introduction, however, we will simply depend on the reader's intuitive understanding of tables such as these.

1.2 Database Users

One of the most important features of a DBMS is that relatively inexperienced users, called *end users*, are empowered to retrieve information from the database. The user poses a *query* at the terminal keyboard, requesting the database system to display the answer on a terminal screen or on a printed sheet. At Tower Records, for example, the customers attempt to locate desired recordings through a sequence of menu interaction queries. As a result of these queries, lists of recordings appear on a terminal screen. A paper list can be printed to help the customers locate the items in the store.

This easy accessibility to data requires a good deal of work by specialists before end users can pose their queries. Unlike some other program products, a database system is not ready for use as soon as it is operational on the computer platform. The database of interest must still be designed and loaded (and later kept up to date), then application programs must be written to provide a simple menu interface to inexperienced end users. The specialists who perform these tasks can also be thought of as *users* of the database system. The idea of *user friendliness* in a relational database management system must be conditioned by the understanding that there are several types of users. The specialist users are responsible for providing an environment in which higher-level users can work, and each type of user has demands for ease of use. Here is a list of common terms describing the different types of users, followed by a description of each user type.

- End users   —Terminal users
     Casual users   —Users accessing the DBMS with SQL queries
     Naive users   —Users accessing the DBMS through menus
- Application
  programmers   —Programmers who write menu applications
- Database
  administrators   —Specialists who supervise the DBMS

End users. A *casual user* is expected to have some facility with the *SQL* language, the standard query language for relational database systems. Facility with SQL is not a trivial skill, as we shall see in later sections. The term *casual* as used here implies that the user has changing requirements from one session to the next, so that it is not economical to try to write a menu-based program application for each such (casual) use. Queries that are formulated on the spot to answer some immediate need are known as *interactive queries* or *ad hoc queries*. (Ad hoc is a Latin term, meaning roughly "for this specific purpose.") A *naive user* is one who performs all database applications through menu applications, and thus avoids having to construct queries in SQL syntax. Bank clerks and airline reservation specialists use such applications to perform their duties, but the term *naive* is perhaps misleading. Even database system implementers, perfectly capable of constructing SQL queries at need, would use menu applications to retrieve (say) bug report records fitting various criteria while performing program maintenance. The mental effort required to keep track of all the tables and column names and to write valid SQL query syntax introduces inappropriate complexity that detracts from a specialist's concentration on the real work to be performed.

Application programmers. An *application programmer,* in the sense used with database management systems, writes the menu applications used by naive users. The programs must foresee the needs of the users and be able to pose SQL queries during execution to retrieve desired information from the database. Note that programmers are experienced at dealing with complex concepts and difficult problems of syntax—it is appropriate for the application programmer to spend long periods deriving the correct query syntax to answer some question that might be posed by a naive user. In addition to saving the user effort, the programs provide more confidence that there is no subtle mistake in the query that might make it give the wrong answer. As we will see, the more complex SQL queries are difficult to construct in an ad hoc fashion without some risk of error.

Database administrators. The final type of DBMS user listed is known as a *database administrator,* or *DBA.* A DBA is a computer professional responsible for the design and maintenance of the database. Typically the DBA decides how the data is to be broken down into tables, creates the database, loads the tables, and performs a large number of behind-the-scenes tasks to implement various policies about data access and update. These policies include areas such as security (which users are empowered to access what data) and integrity constraints (for example, a savings account balance should not be allowed to fall below $0.00). In addition, the DBA is responsible for the physical layout of the database on secondary storage (disk) and the index structures to achieve best performance.

In this book, our goal is to give a basic grounding in the skills necessary to be a sophisticated casual user, a good application programmer, or a DBA. A sophisticated end user of SQL does not need to know how to write programs, but can benefit from many of the other topics covered in this text. A lead application programmer should understand all the skills required by the DBA to be able to plan efficient programs and to give the feedback that the DBA needs to provide appropriate tuning. The topics that make up the duties of a database administrator are the most all-embracing and form the subjects of most of the chapters that follow. The DBA deals with some of the most advanced features of a DBMS and must be fully conversant with the needs of other users on the scene, ideally having the ability to follow the technical details of applications programs. The decisions made by the DBA will affect these programs in many ways, including the forms of SQL statements and program performance.

Note that another type of specialist is associated with databases, known as a *database system implementer*. This is a systems programmer who writes the programs that perform the internal work by which a DBMS provides its features. Some of the more advanced database textbooks concentrate on concepts of database internals. Because the database field is a large one, this text concentrates on understanding how a database system is used, a crucial goal before embarking on the task of implementing a system. In any event, a good database administrator understands the workings of the DBMS at quite a deep level of detail. As we shall see, such detail is sometimes necessary to properly tune system performance.

1.3 Overview of a Relational DBMS

Up until now, we have discussed only one major feature of an RDBMS—the ability to pose queries to retrieve information from a database. Many other features are commonly supplied, some of them sufficiently specialized that it is difficult to appreciate their value without having first had a certain amount of experience in use. Nevertheless we attempt to give some idea of these features and their significance. In this way, the details to come will be more easily placed in a global context.

In the sections that follow, we provide a short explanation of topics in the order that they are presented in the text. This is a good time to note that some of the smaller and less expensive database management systems provided for personal computers will not have all of the features outlined below. For example, the concerns that arise in multi-user systems are often of no interest on a PC database system that is meant to be accessed by only a single user.

8

The Relational Model and Query Capabilities

Chapter 2,
The
Relational
Model

Starting in Chapter 2, we cover a number of concepts and rules of the relational model that govern the representation of data. A rather careful definition is useful, to make it clear what features a user can expect and when a commercial product is offering a feature that is not a standard part of the model. For example, there is a rule that a value of a table cannot be multi-valued. Thus a hobby column in the students table cannot have several values (chess, hiking, skeet shooting) on the same row of the table. Such a multi-valued column was offered in some earlier data models, a feature known as repeating fields, but it is forbidden in relational tables. Relational rules serve an important purpose of standardizing the various product offerings so that issues of database design are the same in all cases. Even so, as we will see, certain rules are frequently broken without grave harm.

Following this, we characterize the relational model from a different aspect, the standard query power inherent in the *relational algebra*. This algebra consists of a set of operations performed on tables to produce other tables (much as multiplication or addition of real numbers produce other real numbers). The concepts of relational algebra are valuable in later chapters, since answers to many database queries can be represented as relational algebra expressions—query answers always have table form in the relational model. Relational algebra is not available to answer computerized queries on commercial DBMS products, which provide the SQL language for that purpose. However, the relational algebra has a virtue when compared with SQL. It has only a small number of operations, and they are extremely simple to describe and transparent in their effect. All operations of relational algebra must be possible in any acceptable query language such as SQL, and a study of the algebraic operations is thought to be valuable because it offers important insights in a much simpler form than SQL.

Chapter 3,
Query
Language
SQL

In Chapter 3, the industry standard query language SQL is covered in a good deal of depth. An example of an SQL query posed on the student records database of Figure 1.1, together with the tabular form of the answer retrieved, is given in Figure 1.2.

Retrieve the sid and sname for all sophomores.

SQL: select sid, sname from students where class = 2;

answer

sid	sname
1	Jones
3	Brown

Figure 1.2 An SQL Query on the Student Records Database

It is easy to validate the answer in Figure 1.2 by looking at the students table in Figure 1.1 and checking the names and student IDs of rows with class equal to 2. Figure 1.3 shows a somewhat more complex query.

Retrieve the sid and sname of students taking course number 101.

SQL: select sid, sname from students, enrollment
      where students.sid = enrollment.sid
      and enrollment.cno = 101;

answer

sid	sname
1	Jones
3	Brown

Figure 1.3 A Second SQL Query on the Student Records Database

Looking at Figure 1.1, it should be clear that we need information from both the students and enrollment tables to answer the query of Figure 1.3. If we look at students alone, we don't know what courses students take, and if we look at enrollment alone, we don't know student names. We can look at the enrollment table and note the sid values matched with cno 101, then look up the names for these sid values in the students table. The SQL statement in Figure 1.3 reflects this approach.

The fact that the answers to the two queries of Figures 1.2 and 1.3 are identical does not, of course, imply that the two queries have the same meaning. There is no reason to believe that the set of students taking French 1 (course number 101) is always identical with the set of sophomores in the school. Rather we see it as an accident that these two queries happen to have the same answer for the current term—the answers would very likely be different for the two queries with a different enrollment table of a new term. This illustrates an important concept: the columns of a table are designed by the person creating the database and are expected to be stable over time, whereas the rows of the table, which correspond to the data records held in the table, are expected to change without warning. Two query forms represent the same concept only if they can be shown to have the same result for *all possible* row contents of the tables involved.

The SQL language also contains statements to insert new rows into a table, delete existing rows from a table, and update some column values of existing rows in a table (see Figure 1.4). It is perhaps inaccurate to refer to the SQL language as simply a *query language*, and to refer to SQL statements as *queries* when they are really Update, Insert, and Delete statements, but it is commonly accepted to use this broad meaning for the term "query." (Some authors try to be more accurate by referring to SQL as a *data manipulation language*, or simply as a *database language*.) Another common practice is to group SQL Update, Insert, and Delete statements under the single term, *update statements*. We will follow these rather loose conventions, becoming more specific only when a distinction is important.

Insert the row (6, Green, 1, 555-1133) into the `students` table.

    `SQL: insert into students values (6, Green, 1, 555-1133);`

Delete all junior class members from `students`.

    `SQL: delete from students where class = 3;`

Change room number 2-113 to 2-121 where it appears in `courses`.

    `SQL: update courses set croom = '2-121' where croom = '2-113';`

Figure 1.4 SQL Statements to Delete, Insert, and Update

Programs to Access a Database

Chapter 4, Programs to Access a Database

In our examples of SQL queries so far, we have concentrated on the situation where a user interactively types an SQL query into the database system (a query interface), and then the system prints the resulting answer table to the user's terminal screen. This is indeed one approach for queries to be answered, but it is not the only one. As we discuss in Chapter 4, most queries, in fact, are posed through an application program interface. Here an application programmer writes a program in some higher-level language such as C or PASCAL or sometimes a special type of *forms language* provided with the DBMS. When the program is executed, it interacts with a terminal user (there may be many users executing the program simultaneously), usually by displaying a menu form. The terminal user performs some menu selections, after which the program may respond by performing one or more SQL queries to execute tasks posed by the menu selection. All activity is controlled by the terminal user through selections from one terminal form or another—at no time does the terminal user actually construct an SQL query. We give an example of such a menu interaction in Figure 1.5.

Library Database Selector Menu
    Author last name: Asimov
    Author first name: Isaac
    Title:
    Subject: robotics

Figure 1.5   An Example of a Menu Interaction for Database Lookup

In this figure, the user is trying to locate all books written by the author Isaac Asimov on the subject of robotics. For ease of use, various wildcard characters provided by the SQL language might also be used. For example "Asim%" might retrieve either "Asimov" or "Asimoff" if the user is unsure of the spelling. The keyword choice in the **Subject** category might be provided as a list in alphabetical order. This means extra work for the application, but how else would the user know whether to use "robotics" or "robot" or "robots"?

Note a crucial point here: an SQL query (or other type of SQL statement) can be written to execute inside a program. However, an SQL query is not a valid statement in most types of higher-level language such as C or PASCAL, so a special form is used (in the C program of Figure 1.6 an initial code phrase *exec sql*) to designate such SQL statements. The program is then run through a preprocessor, where these special forms are turned into valid calls to C functions in the database function library, and after this the C compiler produces a working program.

```
exec sql begin declare sections;    /* C variables known to SQL        */
    char alnamev[18];               /* author last name variable       */
    char afnamev[14];               /* author first name variable      */
    char titlev[20];                /* book title variable             */
    char subjectv[24];              /* book subject variable           */
exec sql end declare section;

exec sql declare c1 cursor for      /* define cursor for retrieval query*/
    select alname, afname, title, subject from library
        where alname = :alnamev and afname = :afnamev
        and title = :titlev and subject = :subjectv;

menu(alnamev,afnamev,
    titlev, subjectv);              /* function to display menu        */
exec sql open c1;                   /* begin query, start cursor       */
while (TRUE)                        /* row by row printout             */
{
    exec sql fetch c1 into :alnamev,:afnamev,
        :titlev,:subjectv;          /* get row values                  */
    displayrow(alnamev, afnamev, titlev,
        subjectv);                  /* exit if out of rows             */
}
```

Figure 1.6   A (Simplified) Program Fragment for Database Access

The practice of placing SQL statements inside a higher-level language program is known as *Embedded SQL programming*. Anyone who has created programs to write PASCAL records or C structs to a disk file and then retrieve them again must be extremely struck by how much simpler this becomes with SQL. In particular, Embedded SQL makes it relatively easy to perform one of the most difficult tasks programmers encounter: to look up information in a file following retrieval prescriptions that users find easy and flexible to pose. As we will see, the DBMS uses a number of disk-based data structures to make access to the data efficient, but the program logic can remain unaware of this, referencing only the structure of the tables and the column values they contain. It is also not necessary for the program logic to keep track of modes of access, positions in files, record structure, and so on. All of this detail is handled by the DBMS, a feature known as *program-data independence*. The value of program-data independence becomes particularly apparent as changes in table structure occur with the passage of time. Columns may be added to some tables, the number of rows in a table may grow to a point that it no longer fits on a single disk and must be split over several disks, and such growth can entail the need for new data structures to speed access to rows by some column values (comparable to looking up library books through a card catalog). None of this needs to affect application program logic on a properly designed database. In fact, the property of program-data independence is important enough that we offer the only formal definition of this overview.

Definition 1.4.1. *Program-data independence* is a feature of a properly constructed database that makes application logic immune to changes in storage structure and access methods.

Logical Database Design

A DBA deals with a database in every aspect of its creation and subsequent life. To begin with, it is the function of the DBA to make a study in depth of the enterprise to be represented in a relational database. The DBA studies basic properties and interrelationships between data objects in the real world that are part of the enterprise to be modeled. The aim is to provide a faithful representation of such objects as columns in relational tables. As part of this representation, the DBA creates rules, known as *integrity constraints*, that limit possible updates that can be performed on the data. This early phase of DBA responsibility is known as *logical database design,* or simply *database design.* Database design is an extremely complex field of study, in that it requires the DBA to recognize many different types of data relationships that reflect reality, an almost philosophical approach to taxonomy of data classes with an intensely practical aim. We study two basic design approaches in this text. One is based on intuitive recognition of certain real-world data classifications and is known as the *entity-relationship model,* or the *E-R model.* The second approach, which complements the first, is known as *database normalization.* These design approaches are covered in detail in Chapter 5.

Chapter 5, Database Design

Analyzing a large enterprise such as a university, we identify numerous pieces of data that must be represented as column names in tables. We clearly need some guiding principle to decide how these column names might be related, when they should be placed together in the same table, and when they should be placed in distinct tables. This is the basic problem of logical design. To begin, we try to distinguish objects known as *entities.* An *entity,* sometimes referred to as an *entity set* or an *entity type,* is a class of objects that really exist and are distinguishable among themselves. As an example, we consider the set of students at the university and name this entity "Students". Associated with each entity is a set of *attributes* that describe and distinguish the objects. In Figure 1.1 we materialized the Students entity as a relational table (which we named students), containing a group of column names (attributes) that describe a student: sid, sname, class, and telephone. A second differentiable class of objects that clearly must be kept track of in a university is the Courses entity, and Figure 1.1 contains a courses table, with attributes describing individual courses: cno, cname, croom, and time.

The third table, enrollment, that appears in Figure 1.1 does not represent an entity, but rather a *relationship* between entities, named as a verb form, enrolls_in, in the entity-relationship diagram of Figure 1.7. Each student takes a number of courses, and conversely each course contains some number of students. In the E-R diagram of Figure 1.7, an entity is represented as a rectangle, an attribute by an oval, and a relationship between entity sets as a diamond. Lines connect entities with their associated attributes, and relationships with the entities to which they relate.

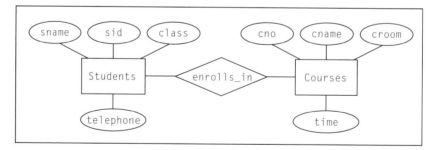

Figure 1.7 An E-R Diagram of a Student Records Database

The entity-relationship viewpoint allows a designer to make sense of the collection of data items encountered in designing a new database for a large enterprise. As each entity is identified, it becomes clear that a number of data items are simply attributes describing this entity. Thus a relational table and a number of columns are identified. As the DBA studies this entity further, additional attributes to model the enterprise may be identified that had not been obvious before. Designing tables associated with relationships is somewhat more complex, since relationships have a number of important properties that are outside the scope of this overview. It turns out that some relationships do not translate into tables of their own, but are represented rather as columns known as "foreign keys" in entity tables. There are many details of logical design from an E-R viewpoint that we put off until Chapter 5.

Database Administration

After the DBA has performed the logical design of a database, there are a number of physical actions required to translate the design into a computerized representation that users can access. Below we explain a number of SQL commands and other database utilities used by the DBA to create database tables, then to load the tables with data contained in operating system input files, and finally to maintain the database under changing conditions. Most aspects of these commands are quite straightforward. The student is expected to master a simple version of the Create Table command at an early stage, preparatory to performing SQL queries. However, the tables created at this early stage are quite simple default forms, without any of the properties introduced in later chapters, such as integrity constraints, data views, security restrictions, and index structures to facilitate high performance access. In the following paragraphs we give a short description of the values of some of these properties. They are detailed further in Chapter 6.

Chapter 6,
Integrity,
Views,
Security,
and Catalogs

Integrity Constraints

As part of the process of logical design, the DBA has identified a number of *integrity constraints* on the data. These are rules that are considered important for the database to obey at all times. For example, there might be a rule that every row of the courses table has a unique cno value (the same course number cannot be used by two different courses). Other examples are that the sid column in the enrollment table must reference a real sid on some row of the students table (what we call a referential integrity constraint), or that the balance column in a row of a savings_accounts table cannot fall below $25.00 (minimum account balance). It is clear that, if these integrity constraints originally hold for a table, then the only way they can later fail is as a result of some SQL update statement—for example, an SQL statement that inserts a new row into the courses table with a duplicate cno value.

If we make an agreement that ad hoc SQL updates to the data are not permitted, then we could presumably guarantee all these integrity rules by careful enforcement of guidelines within our application program logic (". . . the programmer should always check that cno is not duplicated before inserting a new courses row . . ."). However, leaving the enforcement to the programmer is *not* the approach that is taken by relational database management systems. Instead, the constraints are created as distinct entities by the DBA, and they are thereafter enforced automatically by the DBMS, so that it is actually impossible for any constraint to be unwittingly broken. This has the advantage that even ad hoc updates or bad application logic created by an inexperienced programmer cannot harm the validity of the data. In Figure 1.8, an example is given of the syntax used to impose an integrity constraint in the SQL dialect of the **ORACLE** database product.

Add an integrity constraint to the students table to assure that the class column always has a value between 1 and 4 inclusive. Note that this is an SQL statement valid on the **ORACLE** database product.

```
SQL: alter table students modify
    (class smallint check(class >= 1 and class <= 4);
```

Figure 1.8 A Command to Create a New Integrity Constraint in **ORACLE**

Centralized Control of Data and Database Security

It is important to realize that the decision to place information in two different databases has a significant effect: a query cannot retrieve data from two databases at once. Consider, for example, the separate student records database and university library database mentioned earlier. If a student is holding an overdue book, the program that prints a reminder letter and mailing label for the library cannot make use of the student address kept in the student records database. This means that the university library database must keep *its own copy* of the student address. This is known as *data redundancy* (duplication of data—possibly unnecessarily). It is not a very good alternative, since it is easy for the library version of the student address to become out of date, even while the registrar's version in the student records database is methodically updated. To put it another way, there

are ways of keeping addresses up to date by requesting change of address information from the post office with relatively frequent mailings and having a clerk maintain records based on these corrections. Given that this expense has been entailed by the registrar's office, it seems a shame that the library has to forego this information or else duplicate the expense, simply because it has structured its tables in a separate database.

This discussion points out the advantages to be gained in asking a DBA to combine databases with related information, imposing *centralized control of data* to reduce data redundancy, a well-known database principle. But it would seem that there are some disadvantages to centralization as well. For example, we might not want our student librarians to be able to update (or even view) some of the student record fields involving grades, fee payments, and personal health history. The DBA can guarantee such constraints with a set of *security* commands, using security in conjunction with the ability to create views on the data. Security commands act in the same way as integrity constraints, in that they are enforced automatically by the DBMS at a low level. They make it impossible for certain tables or fields within tables to be accessed or updated by any SQL statement performed on behalf of a user, *unless that user is explicitly given permission by the DBA*. Security is standardized in SQL with the Grant statement, available on almost all relational database products. The Grant statement has well-developed and flexible features. For example, it is possible to deny update access to a table by a certain group of users while permitting read access. An example of the syntax used to impose an integrity constraint in standard SQL is provided in Figure 1.9.

Grant permission to select, update, or insert, but not to delete rows on the `students` table to user poneil.

```
SQL: grant select, update, insert on students to poneil;
```

Figure 1.9   The Standard SQL Grant Statement

Database Views

A less obvious problem that arises from centralized control is the logical complexity associated with combining databases with related information. As a result of this, a simple application to validate insurance payments for university students may have to deal with dozens of tables to access needed column information; furthermore, many of these tables may have names and uses completely unrelated to health insurance. Thus it can become quite difficult to train new application programmers to navigate among the many tables of a combined database. It should also be clear that it is often impossible in a large organization to combine all related databases from the beginning—we must allow for phased implementation, where the benefits of centralization accrue in a number of steps as new databases are combined. This raises the specter of having to rewrite old applications as newer tables appear, with new columns that must be accessed in place of older columns, to eliminate data redundancy. Ideally we would like some way to assure that growing numbers of tables do not cause a training problem and also that old application code does not have to change as old tables are rearranged to eliminate redundant data.

Surprisingly, both of these problems are addressed by a single DBMS feature known as database views. A view command allows us to create an imaginary, or virtual, *view table*, which contains rows defined by an SQL Select statement in terms of other tables. Some of these other tables may also be views, but all rows in a view table are ultimately based on *base tables* that actually exist as files on disk. In Figure 1.10, we provide an example of the standard SQL syntax used to create a view table.

Create a view table, called `studentcourses`, that lists student names and `sid` values with course names and `cno` values for courses in which they are enrolled.

```
SQL: create view studentcourses (sname, sid, cname, cno)
        as select s.sname, s.sid, c.cname, c.cno
        from students s, courses c, enrollment e
        where e.cno = c.cno and e.sid = s.sid;
```

Figure 1.10 The Standard SQL Command to Create a View Table

The tremendous power of views comes from the fact that (theoretically) all SQL Select statements can access a view table as if it were real. Thus the DBA can combine the fields from several (new) tables into a virtual copy of an (old) table that is frequently accessed by existing application code. The view approach also allows the DBA to simplify the database environment for training purposes, creating a view with only that aspect of the total database that is relevant to a particular application mission. Views can also be used to make security seamless, so that the user is actually unaware of fields and tables that he or she is not authorized to access. Clearly the concept of a view extends the concept of program-data independence, in that not only is application logic immune to changes in *physical* storage structure, but even to *logical* changes in the structure of base tables.

Unfortunately, the view concept as currently implemented in the commercial SQL standard falls short of the sort of theoretical power we have been discussing. While it is possible to create a relatively general view table based on a number of base tables, there are limitations on the SQL statements that can access this view table. In particular, certain Select statements and most updates to a view are not permitted in many useful cases. It turns out there are theoretical limitations on certain update statements on views (that is, SQL Update statements, Insert statements, and Delete statements) where it is difficult to translate the view update into updates of the base tables that the user intends. We could do without statements of this theoretically intractable kind, but a number of other useful updates have also been excluded by the commercial standard in order to make system implementation simpler. We can expect to see less restrictive views in the future, but for now we must deal with numerous artificial limitations.

Physical Database Design and Performance

A major responsibility of a DBA is to decide how base tables are to be laid out on disk, and what indexes should be created to optimize access to the data required by the applications and ad hoc uses at the installation. This is known as physical database design. Chapter 7 explores design options, discussing data storage and indexing issues in relation to actual database systems.

Chapter 7, Indexing

Indexes and Table Layout

We start with some of the capabilities for physical design offered by the three RDBMS products under study, **ORACLE**, **DB2**, and **INGRES**, and we focus on indexing. When an index is placed on some column value of a table, for example, on the column sname of the students table in Figure 1.1, it is analogous to a card catalog being created in a library to locate book volumes on the shelves. As a result, the query

```
select sid, class from students where sname = 'Smith';
```

can be performed by the system through the sname index. The sname value "Smith" is located quickly in the index, and the index entry then gives the location of the students table row with sname = "Smith" (or rowsthere may be many different ones). Of course, with the extremely small number of students rows given in our example of Figure 1.1, query performance would not improve as a result of such an index. But with a more realistic table containing several thousand rows, the major alternative to looking up rows in an index is to examine each row individually to see if it should be retrieved by the query; thus an index offers important performance savings. It is also possible with some products to place the rows themselves in position by the values of some index, a practice known as *clustering*, comparable to ordering books on library shelves by author. Clustering can only be done with a single index, however, so additional indexes will still be necessary for efficient access.

The text details a number of different types of disk-based structures for row access, such as hashed and B-tree structures, together with a number of properties of such structures with which a DBA needs to be conversant, such as disk space utilization. There are also tradeoffs to consider in using a large number of indexes for large tables: as in a library catalog system, we get high performance for additional queries with more indexes, but there is also more effort involved in keeping the indexes up to date as new rows are inserted or old rows deleted.

Non-Procedurality and Query Optimization

Chapter 8,
Query
Processing

After the detailed introduction to indexing concepts provided in Chapter 7, we investigate in Chapter 8 the concept of *query optimization,* a process performed by the database system. For some of the more sophisticated SQL queries, it becomes a difficult problem to decide what step-by-step access strategy should be used to optimize performance, given that multiple indexes on different columns and different tables can be involved in the query, and that a range of different access techniques can be chosen at successive stages. SQL query syntax possesses an important property, known as *non-procedurality.* This means that the SQL query syntax allows the user to specify *what* is desired as an answer without specifying in any way *how* the answer is to be achieved, i.e., without specifying the step-by-step access plan to be performed. Because of the non-procedural nature of SQL queries, it is possible to leave the determination of the access strategy to the query optimization module of the DBMS. This is yet another aspect of program-data independence mentioned earlier as a feature of modern relational database management systems. The programmer writing an SQL query can be totally unaware of the physical layout of the data and table indexes.

The text provides rather complete coverage of most aspects of query optimization in **DB2**. We concentrate on a single database product to reduce confusion, since query optimization variations between products are quite difficult to present. In any event, **DB2** has excellent query optimization capabilities, subsuming most features of other products. After this, we provide an extended example of query performance by explaining the detailed results from the Set Query benchmark. A benchmark is an industry standard test to determine the relative cost-performance of different hardware-software (DBMS) product combinations for a particular type of use. The Set Query benchmark was created to measure cost-performance for common query applications arising in industry. The concept of *cost-performance* was developed to find some common measure of comparison across hardware-software platforms. It is often the case that the features of one kind of platform (**DB2** on an IBM mainframe) are difficult to compare with the features of a platform produced by different vendors (**ORACLE** on a PYRAMID UNIX machine). Each set of vendors claims that their own features are superior, and thus we are left with a problem in trying to compare the two. The concept of *cost-performance* deals with this problem by trying to codify a certain type of work that has common use in industrial applications. Units are invented for this work, such as a *query* unit (actually an average of a large number of different query types), and we measure on different platforms the *dollar cost* ($COST) to achieve a standard rate of work in terms of *queries per minute* (QPM). The final rating in $COST/QPM is claimed to be a fair measure of value for the hardware-software platforms measured.

Database Transactions

It turns out that the concepts and skills that go into understanding database query access are rather different from those that are needed to properly deal with database updates. When updates are performed on a database, we need some way to guarantee that a set of updates will succeed all at once or not at all—it is unacceptable, for example, that a transfer of money from one account to another should succeed in taking money out of the first account, but then, perhaps because of a system crash, fail in adding the transferred quantity into the second account. It is also important that a pure query retrieval application doesn't sum the balances in these two accounts while the transfer is "in flight," so that money has been taken out of one account but not yet added into a second. Such an event might lead to an invalid idea of the total assets of some individual, merely because he or she was in the act of transferring money. To guarantee that problems such as these don't arise, the concept of *database transaction* has been developed: a transaction draws a set of record reads and updates together into an indivisible package. We say that a transaction has the property of *atomicity,* meaning that other operations can only access any of the rows involved in transactional access either **before** the transaction occurs or **after** the transaction is complete, but never while the transaction is **partially** complete.

Understanding how a set of operations is packaged together in a transaction requires a number of other sophisticated concepts. Beginning with our discussion of Embedded SQL, we cover a preliminary set of SQL transactional commands available to application programmers on three different database products, including how to start and end (or *commit*) a transaction. While we put off the most detailed consideration of update transactions until Chapter 9, we need a certain amount of understanding of the transactional concept just to write query applications when updates might be taking place concurrently. Interactive update applications are an important area of concentration in database systems, often referred to as *transaction processing* or *OLTP* (for on-line transaction processing). A number of transactional concepts have important implications for an application writer—for example, the idea of *transactional abort*. It turns out that while trying to maintain atomicity of the transaction, the DBMS sometimes has no alternative but to give up trying to make forward progress, rollback all updates performed so far, and notify the application logic of this event. As a result, the application must be able to handle such an event by attempting to *retry* the transaction.

Chapter 9,
Update
Transactions

We explore the underlying theoretical concept of *concurrency* in transactional systems in Chapter 9. Concurrency deals with the need to make transactions atomic with respect to other, simultaneous user transactions that may attempt to access the same records—what is called *concurrent access*. The performance motivation for concurrent access is made clear. Then the problem arising from concurrency is expressed in the most general possible form, and a well-known theoretical approach to avoiding the problem is explained. This leads in practice to a scheme known as two-phase locking, whereby records accessed by a transaction are locked against access by concurrent users, generally speaking until the transaction is complete. This two-phase locking has a number of implications for later concepts of performance tuning.

After looking carefully into concurrency, the text considers the problem of what to do about a partial set of transactional record updates that have already been written to disk in the event that a system crash destroys the memory contents, so that the system loses the state of the transaction in the application logic. This is known as the problem of *database recovery*, and it is solved by a technique whereby the system writes notes to itself on disk so that it will remember after a crash how to reverse any record updates belonging to uncompleted transactions.

After these considerations have become clear, we deal with performance considerations in transactional processing. Some of the database administration commands for system tuning are explained, and we introduce the industry standard OLTP benchmark created by the Transaction Processing Performance Council, known as TPC-A. A number of cost-performance considerations of transaction processing are different from those we have already seen with query processing. These new concepts are explained in detail in Chapter 9.

Finally, in Chapter 10 we introduce the concepts of parallel and distributed database processing. The idea here is that a database can be partitioned so that one part of it sits on disks attached to one computer and another part sits on disks attached to a different computer. Any number of different computers can be involved. In spite of the partitioning, we wish to be able to perform queries and updates that require access to data on more than one computer at a time. Some of the concepts that motivate this approach to distributed databases are the following. First, we expect cost-performance to improve if we allow geographically distinct sites to store their data locally rather than having most sites access all information over long-distance communication lines. Centralized control of data, however, is still of crucial importance. For example, a large company depends on being able to place orders through company warehouses in a different city when it runs out of goods locally. *Reliability* is also an important consideration, especially since as the number of disks and computer processors involved in a database system increases, the expected *mean time to failure* (or *MTTF*) becomes worse—that is, smaller—with each new component added. The solution to the reliability problem is to replicate data on

Chapter 10, Parallel and Distributed Databases

24

different disks and make it available through independent computers of the system. Many of these considerations are relatively new, and only beginning to have their first expression in mission-critical applications.

1.4 Putting It All Together

We have now introduced the fundamental concepts and definitions discussed in this book. The coming chapters will provide a more in-depth understanding of how to create, maintain, and use a relational database. Our goal is an understanding of database theory along with a perception of practical details in existing database standards and products.

The Relational Model 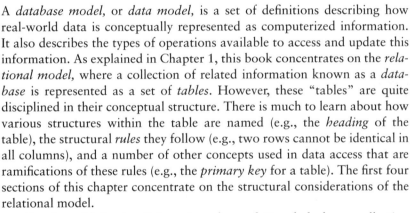 2

A *database model,* or *data model,* is a set of definitions describing how real-world data is conceptually represented as computerized information. It also describes the types of operations available to access and update this information. As explained in Chapter 1, this book concentrates on the *relational model,* where a collection of related information known as a *database* is represented as a set of *tables.* However, these "tables" are quite disciplined in their conceptual structure. There is much to learn about how various structures within the table are named (e.g., the *heading* of the table), the structural *rules* they follow (e.g., two rows cannot be identical in all columns), and a number of other concepts used in data access that are ramifications of these rules (e.g., the *primary key* for a table). The first four sections of this chapter concentrate on the structural considerations of the relational model.

Starting with Section 2.5, we introduce *relational algebra,* a collection of fundamental relational operations that can be used to create new tables from old ones, much as arithmetic calculation creates new numbers using operations such as addition and multiplication. Relational algebra is an abstract language, which means that it will not be possible to execute queries formulated in relational algebra on an actual computer. We introduce relational algebra in the current chapter in order to express, in the simplest form, the set of operations that any relational database query language must perform to answer English-language queries about the information in a database. All of these basic concepts will prove very useful in later chapters, where we explain the meaning of various constructs in SQL, the standard computerized query language for relational database systems.

Chapter 2 has a rather abstract approach (with mathematical definitions and theorems), compared with some of the later chapters that deal with computerized query languages. There are a number of reasons for this. Certainly, it is appropriate to be as precise as possible when introducing the fundamental concepts of a field of study. But even more important, the serious database practitioner will find a need to be able to move back and forth from one style of presentation to another. Most commercial database products, such as **DB2** and **ORACLE**, provide extremely well-written manuals that explain practical database concepts in the most approachable way. However, there are invariably a number of deeper concepts that such manuals do not attempt to cover in depth. To master these, the practitioner will often find it necessary to read reference books or even original research papers that take a much more abstract viewpoint. (For example, see Suggestions for Further Reading at the end of this chapter.) Here we try to prepare you for encounters with these more abstract references, without losing the simple presentation of the manuals in situations where this approach is appropriate.

2.1 The CAP Database

As we explained in Section 1.1, a *database* is a collection of computerized records maintained for a common purpose. In the following chapters we refer frequently to a specific example, which we call the CAP database (for the table names CUSTOMERS, AGENTS, and PRODUCTS). This database, illustrated in Figure 2.2, is used by a wholesale business to keep track of its *customers,* the *products* it sells to these customers, and the *agents* who place *orders* for products on behalf of these customers.

The tables and columns in the CAP database of Figure 2.2 are described in Figure 2.1. The customers listed are themselves retail businesses that order large quantities of various products from the wholesale company for resale. Distinct customers in the CUSTOMERS table are uniquely identified by values in the cid (customer identifier) column. Customers phone in orders to agents (uniquely identified by the aid value in the AGENTS table) based in cities nationwide to purchase products (identified by pid in the PRODUCTS table). Each time an order is placed, a new row is inserted in the ORDERS table, uniquely identified by ordno value. For example, the order identified in the ORDERS table by ordno 1011 was taken in the month of January (jan) from customer c001 by agent a01 for 1000 units of product p01 at a dollar cost of $450. Here are the meanings associated with all the tables and columns of the CAP database of Figure 2.2.

CUSTOMERS	A table containing information about customers
cid	Unique identifier for a customer/row—note 'c005' has ceased to exist
cname	Name of a customer
city	City where the customer (headquarters) is located
discnt	Each customer has a negotiated discount on prices
AGENTS	A table containing information about agent employees
aid	Unique identifier for an agent/row
aname	Last name of agent
city	City where agent is based
percent	Percentage commission each agent receives on each sale
PRODUCTS	A table containing information about products for sale
pid	Unique identifier for a product/row
pname	Descriptive name of product
city	City where this product is warehoused
quantity	Quantity on hand for sale, in standard units
price	Wholesale price of each unit product

Note that the same column name, city, appears in all three tables defined so far. This is not a coincidence.

ORDERS	A table containing information about orders
ordno	Unique identifier for this order
month	Month the order was placed; assume that orders started in January of this year
cid	This customer . . .
aid	. . . purchased through this agent . . .
pid	. . . this specific product . . .
qty	. . . in this total quantity. . .
dollars	. . . at this dollar cost

Figure 2.1 Table and Column Definitions for the CAP Database

CUSTOMERS

cid	cname	city	discnt
c001	TipTop	Duluth	10.00
c002	Basics	Dallas	12.00
c003	Allied	Dallas	8.00
c004	ACME	Duluth	8.00
c006	ACME	Kyoto	0.00

AGENTS

aid	aname	city	percent
a01	Smith	New York	6
a02	Jones	Newark	6
a03	Brown	Tokyo	7
a04	Gray	New York	6
a05	Otasi	Duluth	5
a06	Smith	Dallas	5

PRODUCTS

pid	pname	city	quantity	price
p01	comb	Dallas	111400	0.50
p02	brush	Newark	203000	0.50
p03	razor	Duluth	150600	1.00
p04	pen	Duluth	125300	1.00
p05	pencil	Dallas	221400	1.00
p06	folder	Dallas	123100	2.00
p07	case	Newark	100500	1.00

ORDERS

ordno	month	cid	aid	pid	qty	dollars
1011	jan	c001	a01	p01	1000	450.00
1012	jan	c001	a01	p01	1000	450.00
1019	feb	c001	a02	p02	400	180.00
1017	feb	c001	a06	p03	600	540.00
1018	feb	c001	a03	p04	600	540.00
1023	mar	c001	a04	p05	500	450.00
1022	mar	c001	a05	p06	400	720.00
1025	apr	c001	a05	p07	800	720.00
1013	jan	c002	a03	p03	1000	880.00
1026	may	c002	a05	p03	800	704.00
1015	jan	c003	a03	p05	1200	1104.00
1014	jan	c003	a03	p05	1200	1104.00
1021	feb	c004	a06	p01	1000	460.00
1016	jan	c006	a01	p01	1000	500.00
1020	feb	c006	a03	p07	600	600.00
1024	mar	c006	a06	p01	800	400.00

Figure 2.2 The CAP Database (Content at a Given Moment)

Note that the database administrator for the CAP database created the cid column to be a unique customer identifier (as described in Figure 2.1) because it was believed that no other single column properly filled this need. For example, the column cname can have duplicate values on different rows (and in fact the name "ACME" is duplicated). In a similar fashion, the aid, pid, and ordno columns have been created to act as unique identifiers of their respective tables. Note that the dollars value in any ORDERS row can be calculated separately by multiplying the qty value in that row by the corresponding price for that pid, and then taking a discount for the customer, as determined in the discnt column for the CUSTOMERS row with that cid. We do not also subtract the percent commission for the agent, since dollars is supposed to represent the total cost to the customer.

This example CAP database is quite artificial. It fits snugly on a page and is used here to illustrate our ideas. To be closer to reality we would need to consider more tables, and larger ones. To begin with, we would need more columns. There should be a first name to go with aname; each city column needs to have added columns for street address, state, and zip code; we would want to keep track of agents' total commissions for the most recent month, just as we keep track of quantity on hand for products; we need the name of a person to contact at each customer company, the name of a person in charge of each warehouse, and the person's address and telephone number, and so on. We need a more complete date and perhaps timestamp for each order (month alone is insufficient) and some way of keeping track of payments (wholesale customers have to be billed). There are probably additional employees not on agent commission (warehouse managers are one type), and we have to keep track of their salaries, tax withholdings, and so on. We would also expect to see a lot more rows in each of the tables.

2.2 Naming the Parts of a Database

Two different standard terminologies are (unfortunately) used in databases. One terminology refers to tables, columns, rows, etc., and the other refers to *relations* (the counterpart of tables), *tuples* (corresponding to rows), *attributes* (for columns), etc. We'll use both sets of terms so you can learn to recognize them easily. Thus we will frequently refer to the column names of a table as the *attributes* of that table (for instance, the attributes of the table CUSTOMERS are cid, cname, city, and discnt), or to rows as tuples.

A *database* is defined to be a set of named *tables*, or *relations*. For example, the CAP database consists of the set of tables:

    CAP = {CUSTOMERS, AGENTS, PRODUCTS, ORDERS}

We define the *heading* of a table to be the set of columns whose names appear at the top of the table, above the first row. We denote the heading of a table T by Head(T). For example, we have

    Head(CUSTOMERS) = {cid, cname, city, discnt}

In specifying the set of columns in a heading, there is a common convention to dispense with the standard set notation ({x, y, . . .}) and simply list the attributes, separated by spaces. Thus we will commonly write

    Head(CUSTOMERS) = cid cname city discnt

The heading of a table is also referred to as a *relational schema,* the set of attributes making up a relation; the set of all relational schemes for a database is known as a *database schema.*

The set of rows, or tuples, in a table is referred to as the *content* of the table. For example, the PRODUCTS table in Figure 2.2 contains seven rows. It is important to understand that the table name and heading are meant to be long-lived properties of a table, but the rows in the table are expected to change without warning in number and detailed values; this is why we refer to the content of a table "at a given moment" in Figure 2.2. The reader familiar with programming in languages such as Pascal or C should know that tables like the ones represented in Figure 2.2 can be thought of as (and are usually stored as) files of records, or structures. Each row of a table normally corresponds to a record in a file (or possibly several files), and the structure of fields within the record is determined by the heading of the table. However, in a relational database the application programmer is insulated from such details of storage by the principle of program-data independence, defined in Section 1.3, and the database can theoretically store the rows of a table in an entirely different type of disk structure.

Domains and Datatypes

A table must be declared in a computerized database system, just as a file and the records it contains must be declared in Pascal. In current database system products such as **INGRES** and **ORACLE**, each column in the table is declared to have a certain *type*. For example, we might define the CUS-TOMERS table so that the column discnt has type *float4* (a floating point number occupying 4 bytes), and the column city has type *char(13)* (a character string of length 13). In the more theoretical literature it has become common to say that an attribute A of a table T takes on values from a set D known as a *domain*. A domain is usually defined in such cases to contain the *exact* set of constants that can appear as values for the attribute, and thus a domain corresponds to the concept of enumerated type in Pascal. For instance, the domain of the attribute city, designated by CITY, might be the set of all character strings corresponding to cities in the United States (assuming that our firm does business only with U.S. customers). On the other hand, the domain of the discnt column, DISCNT, might be defined as consisting of all float numbers between 0.00 and 20.00, with at most two non-zero digits after the decimal point (assuming that this is the range of possible discounts offered by our wholesale company to its customers).

Most commercial database systems are currently unable to define types corresponding to enumerated sets (as with CITY), or with explicit accuracy after the decimal point (as with DISCNT). We usually have to be satisfied in such systems with saying that the values that may occur in the column named city belong to the type char(13), for example. However, we can think of the enumerated "domain" of an attribute as an ideal that is seldom realized in real systems, and we will often refer to a more generic type definition as a domain. The relatively recent computerized query language standard known as SQL-92 defines a syntactic object known as a domain that can be used to define values for a column. An SQL-92 domain is defined to represent a data type (such as float or char(13))—nothing new here—but it is also possible to associate with the domain a certain type of *integrity constraint*. With this constraint, we can be more specific about values that can occur—for example, a float number greater than or equal to 0.0, or an integer in the set {1, 3, 5, 7, 9}. An enumerated domain can therefore be specified in SQL-92, but there is a limit to the size that can be supported, and the capability to define a domain with all city names in the United States is out of reach. In any event, this new feature is not yet generally available in commercial database systems. A slightly different approach to an enumerated domain will be suggested in Chapter 6, when we introduce the constraint known as *referential integrity*.

The significance of declaring a column of a table to have a particular type (or domain) is that the ability to compare the values of two different columns rests on this declaration. For example, if the city column of the CUSTOMERS table were declared to be char(13), and the city column of the AGENTS table were declared to be char(14), we could not be confident in many computerized database systems of being able to answer the request to print out all agent-customer pairs in the same city, since the system might refuse to compare columns of different types.

Tables and Relations

The domain of an attribute A is denoted by Domain(A). Consider the sets CID, CNAME, CITY, and DISCNT, which denote the domains of the attributes in the CUSTOMERS table, cid, cname, city, and discnt, respectively. Thus, for example, Domain(cid) = CID, and if c is a value that occurs in the cid column, we must have c ∈ CID. Now consider the Cartesian product of the sets CID, CNAME, CITY, and DISCNT denoted by

```
CP = CID x CNAME x CITY x DISCNT
```

By the definition of Cartesian product, CP consists of the set of all possible 4-tuples, t = (c, n, t, d), where c is a customer identification number from CID, n is a customer name from CNAME (not necessarily corresponding to the customer whose identification number is c), t is some U.S. city in the set CITY, and d is some discount value in DISCNT. As an example, the Cartesian product CP contains such tuples as

t = (c003, Allied, Dallas, 8.00) and
t' = (c001, Basics, Oshkosh, 18.20).

Now a *relation* is a mathematical construct, defined as a subset of a Cartesian product. As an example, the table CUSTOMERS is a subset of CP = CID × CNAME × CITY × DISCNT. All rows (that is, all 4-tuples) of the table CUSTOMERS are contained in the set of tuples of the Cartesian product CP. On the other hand, not all tuples of the Cartesian product correspond to rows from the CUSTOMERS table. For instance, in the example above, t is contained in CUSTOMERS, while t' is not. The table CUSTOMERS is therefore a *proper subset*—that is, a subset that does not contain all elements—of the Cartesian product. Since not all component values sit with all other component values on a tuple of a relation, those that do are said to be *related*, and from this we get the term *relation*, which is used in mathematics. Note particularly that while each single row of a table relates the values of the different columns, it is the *set* of rows in a table that is called a relation.

As noted in Figure 2.1, each customer is supposed to have a distinct cid value, so it would not even make sense to have a CUSTOMERS table contain all the rows of the Cartesian product. If any of the domains CNAME, CITY, and DISCNT contained more than one value, at least two rows in the Cartesian product would have the same value from CID, but the CID value is supposed to be unique for each row.

EXAMPLE 2.2.1

Using the terminology just introduced, you should be able to see that if we define a table T that has a heading given by

Head(T) = $A_1 \ldots A_n$,

then T is a subset of the Cartesian product of the sets: Domain(A_1),. . ., Domain(A_n). ∎

As mentioned earlier, the heading of the table is a relatively stable part, which prescribes the structure of the rows of the table. It is not common to add or delete columns, and we would not expect to do so in the normal course of everyday business. In creating the column layout, we must plan ahead with a thorough analysis of the needs we will have for our database; as explained earlier in Chapter 1, this process is known as logical database design.

On the other hand, the *content* of the table changes frequently over time. New rows can be added or deleted easily: we expect to add new rows as we acquire new customers, and to delete rows as we lose them, for example, and it would be impossible to keep track mentally of these changes in a large wholesale company. Some tables might have millions of rows, but the number of columns is generally limited to the number of concepts a user can become familiar with. Query languages are created so that the user can retrieve information about the rows of one or more tables, with no advance knowledge except the names and characteristics of the columns. It would be a mistake, in most cases, to form a preconception of an answer based on the expected content of the tables before posing a query of the database. Small examples such as the CAP database are an exception: the reader can often use knowledge of the content of the CAP tables to validate query results as a check on whether the queries have been properly posed.

2.3 Relational RULES

A few well-known defining characteristics, or *rules,* of the relational model tell us what variations in table structure are permitted and limit possible retrieval operations. These relational rules serve the important purpose of pointing out areas to standardize in the various commercial product offerings, so that issues of database design are the same for all products. Unfortunately, there is a great deal of current disagreement between the school of thought that says that these rules are crucial and the school of thought that says that it is sometimes convenient to break them, or even that different rules should be the standard. As we will see in later chapters, a number of the relational rules are not obeyed by tables defined in commercial database products (or at least such compliance is not automatic). Because of this it is important that you become sensitive to the issues addressed, while remaining flexible to the variations you can expect to encounter in commercial systems.

RULE 1: First Normal Form RULE. In defining tables, the relational model insists that columns that look like multi-valued fields (sometimes called repeating fields) are *not* permitted! A table that has no multi-valued fields is said to be in *first normal form.* ∎

As an example, consider the table EMPLOYEES in Figure 2.3, which contains rows corresponding to the employees of a company. This table has a unique employee identification column eid, an ename column with the employee name, the position the employee holds in the company, and a multi-valued field listing the dependents for that employee. For example, John Smith, with employee ID e001, has two dependents, Michael J. and Susan R., listed on separate lines, whereas David Andrews has one dependent and Franklin Jones has three. (The capability to have repeating fields of this kind is present in certain languages such as COBOL.)

EMPLOYEES

eid	ename	position	dependents
e001	Smith, John	Agent	Michael J. Susan R.
e002	Andrews, David	Superintendent	David M. Jr.
e003	Jones, Franklin	Agent	Andrew K. Mark W. Louisa M.

Figure 2.3 An EMPLOYEES Table with a Multi-Valued "dependents" Attribute

Relational RULE 1 states that repeating fields of this kind are not permitted in relational tables. This is a real restriction in design, since if we now try to place the dependent names in a unique employee row of the EMPLOYEES table (as in Figure 2.4), we have to create separate column names for the maximum number of dependents that an employee might possibly have—for example, dependent1, dependent2,. . ., dependent20.

EMPLOYEES

eid	ename	position	dependent1	dependent2	. . .
e001	Smith, John	Agent	Michael J.	Susan R.	. . .
e002	Andrews, David	Superintendent	David M. Jr.	. . .	. . .
e003	Jones, Franklin	Agent	Andrew K.	Mark W.	. . .

Figure 2.4 An EMPLOYEES Table With All Dependent Names on Unique Employee Rows

This is usually not feasible because it wastes space and makes queries difficult, so the approach taken instead is to *factor* the EMPLOYEES table into two parts, creating a separate table called DEPENDENTS that consists of two columns, eid and dependent (Figure 2.5). We populate this table with one row for each dependent, giving the eid of each employee-dependent name pair. As we will see, all query languages allow us to connect an employee row to each of the dependent rows with the same eid.

Although other relational rules listed in this section are not universally honored in commercial systems, the first normal form rule is an exception; this rule is not broken by tables defined in any serious relational database system product. (There are some new database system products with a data model known as *extended relational* that permit *non-first normal form (NFNF)* tables. We will discuss this model in Chapter 3.)

EMPLOYEES

eid	ename	position
e001	Smith, John	Agent
e002	Andrews, David	Superintendent
e003	Jones, Franklin	Agent

DEPENDENTS

eid	dependent
e001	Michael J.
e001	Susan R.
e002	David M. Jr.
e003	Andrew K.
e003	Mark W.
e003	Louisa L.

Figure 2.5 EMPLOYEES and Associated DEPENDENTS Tables

RULE 2: Access Rows by Content Only RULE. A second rule of the relational model states that we can only retrieve rows by their *content,* the attribute values that exist in each row. So far as user queries are concerned, this implies that there is no order on the rows. Thus there is no way that a query in a (pure) relational language can ask, for example, to retrieve the third row of the ORDERS table. Instead, the query would need to refer to the row with the value 1019 in the ordno column, a unique row, as implied by the definition of ordno in Figure 2.1. In this sense the picture that is presented in Figure 2.2, with its physical layout on paper of the ORDERS table, is misleading. According to this rule, the ORDERS table does not have a first row, or a second row, or a third, etc. The set of rows making up the content of a table are unordered elements of a set. In the more abstract mathematical nomenclature, this simply says that a relation is a set of tuples, an incontrovertible fact. ■

Many commercial database systems break RULE 2, providing a method to retrieve a row of a table by its row identification number (RID), sometimes called the ROWID, or tuple identification number (TID). Usually the RID is easily calculable from the number of the row as it was loaded into the table. Commercial database systems seem to be saying that RULE 2 is sometimes an inappropriate rule, and that a new standard is called for. In justification of permitting access by RID value, it is important to realize that the rows of a database need to be stored on some nonvolatile medium, such as disk, in some real order. (Nonvolatile means that the medium retains the data when the power supply to the machine is interrupted.) The order of storage is predictable and, as we will see a bit later, retrieval by

RID is sometimes useful to a DBA in examining situations where it is suspected that the table data is not stored in the proper way. Current technology of disk storage usually means that rows stored close to each other are more quickly retrieved in sequence than they would be if they were stored far apart. We will use this fact in considerations of performance later in the book. All in all, the RID values are sometimes useful because we do not consider the order of row storage to be totally immaterial. At the same time, we would not advise most users to perform normal queries in terms of RID values, since this would undermine the program-data independence that is so valued.

It is worth mentioning here that the relational model also states that there should be no order to the *columns* of a relation, so once again our mental model of a table is slightly misleading. This rule is broken, however, by the standard SQL language, as we will see in Chapter 3.

RULE 3: The Unique Row RULE. A third rule of the relational model is that two tuples in a relation (rows in a table) cannot be identical in all column values at once. A relation can be thought of as a *set of tuples*, and of course a set never contains two identical elements; each tuple of the set must be unique. Furthermore, since a pure relational query language is able to distinguish rows only in terms of their column values (RULE 2), this is another way of saying that there must be a way of distinguishing any single row from all others in terms of these values, so that a query language statement can retrieve it uniquely.   ∎

In commercial database systems, a good deal of work is involved in ensuring that a newly inserted row in a table does not duplicate an existing row. Commercial systems regard this nonduplication as a reasonable aim in most cases, but they may provide some table formats that do not make such a guarantee in order to charge minimal overhead for inserts of new rows. In what follows, we assume that RULE 3 is obeyed by all our tables unless we specify otherwise.

What is the motivation for the relational rules? These rules (and others) were laid down in a series of journal articles by E. F. Codd, the inventor of the relational model. The rules reflect certain mathematical assumptions that have important implications for the good behavior of relational structures in various circumstances that will be covered in the following chapters. For example, RULE 3, which requires unique rows, simply reflects the mathematical idea that a relation is a set of tuples and a set never contains two identical elements. RULE 1, which requires first normal form, has certain important implications for the design of database tables. RULE 2, which requires that rows can be accessed by content only, simply guarantees that the methods provided a bit later in the chapter to retrieve rows will be the *only* methods permitted. Thus older products couldn't simply define tables, keep their original navigational access methods, and call the product relational. As mentioned in Chapter 1, relational rules serve the important purpose of standardizing the various product offerings so that issues of database design are the same in all cases. The reason that there is a certain amount of rule breaking by relational database products can usually be traced to the belief by many that these mathematically motivated rules can be somewhat compromised without harm, in order to better reflect some commercial concerns, especially in the area of performance. For the remainder of this chapter, we shall usually assume all relational rules hold, unless otherwise specified.

2.4 Keys, Superkeys, and Null Values

Relational RULE 3 states that two rows in a table cannot be identical in all their column values. This is the same as saying that any two distinct rows of a table can be distinguished by differences in some column value; or, looking at it a different way, that the set of all columns distinguish any two rows. Is it possible that some *subset* of the columns distinguishes any two rows? Yes. For example, in the CUSTOMERS table, the single cid column distinguishes between any two rows. (Recall that in Figure 2.1 we created the cid identifier to be a customer identifier, unique for each row.) We say that cid is a *superkey* for the CUSTOMERS table, meaning that any two rows in the table will always have distinct values in this (singleton) set of columns. The cid column is in fact a *key* for the CUSTOMERS table, which is a somewhat more restrictive thing, meaning that no subset of the set of columns making up the key is itself a superkey. Clearly the singleton column set cid contains only an empty subset, and an empty set of columns cannot distinguish two rows.

Now a very important question: Is pname a superkey for the PRODUCTS table? Even though every row has distinct pname values in the example table of Figure 2.2, the answer is no. This is because when we say that a superkey is a subset of columns that distinguishes between any two rows of the table, we mean this to be the *intention* of the database designer, the DBA. But we never intended in our design that pname be a unique identifier for rows of the PRODUCTS table. We created the pid column as a unique row identifier (as explained in Figure 2.1) to allow duplicates in other columns when adding future rows. The fact that there are no duplicate values for pname in Figure 2.2 is simply an accident, based on the content of the table at a given moment. This might change in the next moment. For example, we might want to create a new row with pid value 'p08', and pname 'folder'; the two rows named folders, identified by their pid values p06 and p08, might have different sizes.

We could build size into the name (half-inch folder), but this might not be sufficient. The two folders might then have the same size and different colors, or have different types of closing clasps or be made of different materials. All of these distinctions could be clearly spelled out in other columns of a more realistic table (color, size, material, etc.), but it is easy to imagine that after the table is defined, a new product is offered that is identical to some other product in all existing column values. To differentiate the rows for these two products, the pid column is needed. It is also efficient to have a single column identifier to distinguish rows in PRODUCTS, and for this reason we usually decide to define a unique identifier such as pid and then depend on the pid value alone.

A key or superkey for a table is required to *remain* a key or superkey as new rows are added—that is, a key reflects the *intention* of the designer under all future conditions, rather than simply being something we notice about the accidental contents of the current table. In what follows, we give some definitions to make the ideas of key and superkey more precise.

Given a table T with attributes represented by subscripted letters, $Head(T) = A_1, \ldots, A_n$, and a tuple t in T, we define the *restriction* of the tuple t to a subset $\{A_{i_1}, \ldots, A_{i_k}\}$ of $\{A_1, \ldots, A_n\}$, denoted $t[A_{i_1}, \ldots, A_{i_k}]$, as the k-tuple of values of t in the columns named. For instance, the restriction of the tuple

t = (c003, Allied, Dallas, 8.00)

from the table CUSTOMERS to the set that consists of the columns cid and cname is denoted t[cid, cname] = (c003, Allied).

Using this notation, we can formalize the notion of key.

DEFINITION 2.4.1 Keys and Superkeys of a Table. We are given a table T, with $\text{Head}(T) = A_1 \ldots A_n$. A *key* for the table T is a set of attributes, $K = A_{i_1} \ldots A_{i_k}$, with two properties:

[1] If u, v are distinct tuples of T, then by designer intention $u[K] \neq v[K]$; that is, there will always exist at least one column, A_{i_m}, in the set of columns K such that $u[A_{i_m}] \neq v[A_{i_m}]$.

[2] No proper subset H of K has property 1.

Property 1 is just a mathematical way of saying that the values any row u takes on for the set of attributes K are *unique*. Thus if two named rows, u and v, have the same value for K (i.e., $u[K] = v[K]$), they are really one row after all ($u = v$). We refer to a set of attributes that fulfills property 1 but not necessarily property 2 as a *superkey*. Property 2 assures us that a key is a *minimal* set of attributes with property 1. Thus a key is always a superkey, but a key has the additional property that no proper subset is a superkey. The fact that a singleton attribute with property 1 is always minimal follows from the fact that the empty set of attributes, φ, does not differentiate two rows: we say that $u[\varphi] = v[\varphi]$ for all rows u and v. ∎

A table can have more than one key, as we see in the following example.

EXAMPLE 2.4.2

Consider the table T given by

T

A	B	C	C
a1	b1	c1	d1
a1	b2	c2	d1
a2	b2	c1	d1
a2	b1	c2	d1

As we have explained, the content of a table at a given instant does not tell us what keys the table has, since these depend on the intentions of the table designer. However, for purposes of illustration we want to calculate the keys of T from a given content, so we impose an unusual condition: that *the content of this table is intended by the designer to remain constant for the life of the data-*

base. As a result of this, a situation on which we could not normally depend in real life, we can derive the keys of T by determining what combinations of columns make all rows unique.

To begin with, note that no single attribute in the table T can be a key, since in each column we have a least two equal entries. On the other hand, no set S of columns can be a key if it includes D, since D gives absolutely no help in distinguishing rows of T, and therefore S – D would also distinguish all rows of T. Therefore S would be a *superkey,* not a key. Next consider all pairs of attributes from T that do not contain D: AB, AC, and BC. All rows of T are distinguished by each of these pairs. Any other set of attributes either contains D or one of the sets AB, AC, or BC as a proper subset (just list all other sets to check this), and is therefore a superkey. Consequently, AB, AC, and BC is the complete set of keys for the table T. ∎

Since relational RULE 3 assures us that the set of all columns differentiates any two distinct rows, at least one key must exist for any relation. The proof of this gives a good illustration of how the definitions we have introduced are meant to be used.

THEOREM 2.4.3 Every table T has at least one key.

PROOF. Given a table T with $Head(T) = A_1 \ldots A_n$, we consider the attribute set S_1 with all these attributes. Now we know that the set S_1 is a "superkey," meaning that no two rows u and v of T have identical values in all the columns of S_1. For any u and v that are not the same row, there is an attribute (column) A_i in S_1 such that $u[A_i] \neq v[A_i]$. In what follows, we assume that we know the intentions of the table designer and can identify sets of attributes that will be superkeys. Now either the set S_1 is a key, or there is another set S_2, a proper subset of S_1, that is also a superkey. Given this, either S_2 is a key or there is another set S_3, a proper subset of S_2, that is also a superkey. Continuing in this fashion, we find a chain of sets: S_1, $S_2, \ldots, S_i, S_{i+1}, \ldots$, such that each set in the chain is a proper subset of the one preceding it, and all sets in the chain are superkeys. To show that a key exists, we merely keep going as long as possible, and then show that such a chain of sets comes to an end: there must be a final set S_k, which is contained in all the sets that have come before and has no smaller subset with the required property of being a superkey.

We can show that the chain comes to an end as follows. Represent by $\#S_i$ the number of attributes in the set S_i. Now S_1 has the n attributes in $Head(T) = A_1 \ldots A_n$, so $\#S_1 = n$. In addition, we see that $\#S_i > \#S_{i+1}$, since each successive set in the chain is a proper subset of the one preceding. Finally, each of the sets has a positive number of attributes, since a negative number is meaningless and the empty set is not a superkey. Therefore the chain given above is a descending sequence, given by: $n = \#S_1 > \#S_2 > \ldots > \#S_i > \#S_{i+1} > \ldots > 0$, and there must be a minimum number in this sequence that corresponds to the final set in the chain, S_k. Thus S_k has no proper subset that is a superkey and therefore must be a key for the table. Note that we have appealed to the fact that we can find a minimum element of a finite set of distinct integers bounded above and below. A pure mathematician might ask us to prove even this by mathematical induction.

■

Rigorous proofs will not usually be required in this text. However, you should be sure that you understand why *some* demonstration was necessary for the existence of S_k. It is as if we were proposing a program loop to eventually determine a key set of columns, and needed to be sure the loop would always terminate. This is a valid concern.

The various keys of a relation are often known as *candidate keys;* the name implies a selection process whereby one of the candidates will be designated as the *primary key.*

DEFINITION 2.4.4 Primary Key of a Table. A *primary key* of a table T is the candidate key chosen by the DBA to uniquely identify specific rows of T. Usually the primary key identifier is used in references from other tables.

■

For example, in the CAP database, the ORDERS table needs to identify the customer, agent, and product for the order on each row, and it does this by listing the cid, aid, and pid. An extended PRODUCTS table might have another candidate key (in addition to pid) consisting of the set of columns specifying the name, size, color, and material of each part. It would be rather clumsy to use all these columns as an identifier in rows of ORDERS, however, so we would probably continue to choose pid as the primary key.

Null Values

Suppose that a new stapler product is to be added to our PRODUCTS table, and we have not yet determined the quantity that has been stored at our warehouse, or even the warehouse city where it resides. We do know, however, that we have enough staplers on hand to start taking orders for the product, and we want to go ahead and start doing this. (Presumably the orders will be shipped at a later time, after we know the quantity on hand, so the inventory quantity can be kept up to date as we ship the product.) To record the information we have about staplers in the PRODUCTS table, we use a special value, known as a *null value*, in the city and quantity columns of the new PRODUCTS row:

pid	pname	city	quantity	price
p07	stapler	**null**	**null**	3.50

The null value used here should be interpreted as *unknown* or as *not yet defined,* meaning that when we know more we intend to fill in the value. A slightly different meaning for null occurs when a field value is *inapplicable,* as when we fill in the manager name column in an employee table for the president of the company (who has no manager), or the percent commission for an employee who does not receive a commission. It is important to realize that the null value has different properties than those of the number 0 (for a numeric attribute) or a blank or null-string (for a character attribute). As an example, if we were to query the average quantity on hand of all products in the PRODUCTS table, a zero value for the stapler product would bring down the average. However, the null value implies a more appropriate default behavior, in that the quantity for the stapler product is *left out* of the average.

Recall that a primary key for a table is used to identify individual rows of that table. We argue now for another relational rule requiring that a primary key cannot take on a null value. For example, we have placed a new product named "stapler" in the PRODUCTS table before knowing the warehouse city and quantity stored, so that we could start accepting orders for the product. But we wouldn't have such motivation for storing this row if it hadn't yet been assigned a pid value, since we need to be able to list in the ORDERS table the pid of any product ordered. Basically, we are arguing that since the pid value is the *designated identifier* for the row, until we have the identifier *value* settled we will not allow the row to be stored in the table.

Recall that a primary key is just a specially designated candidate key, which may contain more than one column. We generalize the null restriction above to state the Entity Integrity RULE.

RULE 4: Entity Integrity RULE. No column belonging to a primary key of a table T is allowed to take on null values for any row in T.

We will discuss more properties of null values and primary keys in later chapters.

2.5 Relational Algebra

Relational algebra was introduced by E. F. Codd in a series of journal articles that first appeared in 1970 and reached approximately the current form in 1972. The aim was to demonstrate the potential for a query language to retrieve information from a relational database system, although it was understood that several other languages were possible and perhaps even preferable for normal use. Information is stored in a relational system in the form of tables, so it seems natural to express the results of a query in table form. Relational algebra can be thought of as a collection of methods for building new tables that constitute answers to queries. The methods themselves are referred to as the *operations of relational algebra*.

Relational algebra is an abstract language, by which we mean that it is not possible to execute queries formulated in relational algebra on an actual computer. We introduce relational algebra here in order to express, in the simplest form, the set of operations that any relational database query language must perform. These basic operations are very useful in understanding the considerations of the next chapter, where we explain how to perform queries in SQL, the standard computerized query language for relational database systems.

For the remainder of the text, we will use the CUSTOMERS-AGENTS-PRODUCTS (or CAP) database introduced in Section 2.1 to illustrate various operations. We supplement tables in CAP with a few others.

Fundamental Operations of Relational Algebra

We distinguish two types of operations in relational algebra: set-theoretic operations that make use of the fact that tables are essentially sets of rows, and native relational operations that focus on the structure of the rows. Given two tables R and S where Head(R) = $A_1 \ldots A_n$ and in many cases

Head(S) is the same, we will define the following set of eight fundamental **45** operations building on R and S to provide new tables. The keyboard form given below is for use on keyboards that do not contain the indicated special symbols.

SET THEORETIC OPERATIONS			
NAME	SYMBOL	KEYBOARD FORM	EXAMPLE
UNION	$\cup$	UNION	R $\cup$ S, or R UNION S
INTERSECTION	$\cap$	INTERSECT	R $\cap$ S, or R INTERSECT S
DIFFERENCE	–	– or MINUS	R – S, or R MINUS S
PRODUCT	$\times$	TIMES	R $\times$ S, or R TIMES S

NATIVE RELATIONAL OPERATIONS			
NAME	SYMBOL	KEYBOARD FORM	EXAMPLE
PROJECT	R [ ]	R [ ]	R $[A_{i_1}...A_{i_k}]$
SELECT	R where C	R where C	R where $A_1 = 5$
JOIN	$\bowtie$	JOIN	R $\bowtie$ S, or R JOIN S
DIVISION	$\div$	DIVIDEBY	R $\div$ S, or R DIVIDEBY S

In addition to these operations, we will define a method of saving intermediate results, comparable to an assignment statement in a programming language such as Pascal or C.

2.6 Set-Theoretic Operations

We assume in this section that tables are defined as sets of rows, so relational RULES 2 and 3 apply: tables do not contain duplicate rows, and the order of the rows is immaterial.

The reader is expected to be familiar with such set operations as union, intersection, difference, and Cartesian product. These are the set-theoretic operations on which the first four relational algebra operations are based. For sets of rows to be involved in unions, intersections, or differences and to form new tables, the rows in different sets must have the same heading structure. A little reflection shows that we cannot, for example, create a new table consisting of the union of a table containing information about customers and a table containing information about products, since it would be impossible to accommodate in any meaningful way rows from CUSTOMERS and rows from PRODUCTS under the same table heading. Therefore, we introduce the following definition.

DEFINITION 2.6.1 Compatible Tables. Tables R and S are *compatible* if they have the same headings; that is, if Head(R) = Head(S). ∎

The Union, Intersection, and Difference Operations

Only tables that are compatible can be involved in unions, intersections, and differences.

DEFINITION 2.6.2 Union, Intersection, Difference. Let R and S be two compatible tables, where $Head(R) = Head(S) = A_1 \ldots A_n$. The *union* of R and S is the table $R \cup S$, with the same heading, consisting of all rows that are in R or in S or in both.

Similarly, the *intersection* of R and S is the table $R \cap S$, consisting of those rows that are in both R and S.

The *difference* of R and S is the table $R - S$, consisting of all rows that appear in R but do not appear in S. ∎

Note that all relational operations can be applied recursively, so that the tables R and S in Definition 2.6.2 can themselves be the results of other relational algebra expressions. We can also place parentheses around any of these expressions without changing the meaning; for instance, we can write (R − S) rather than R − S. This is useful to indicate order of evaluation. As in general mathematical expressions, sub-expressions inside the deepest nesting of parentheses are meant to be evaluated first. Thus the expression R − (S − R) means that we first evaluate S − R, and if we call the result T we then evaluate R − T to arrive at the final table indicated.

EXAMPLE 2.6.3

Consider the tables R and S:

R

A	B	C
a_1	b_1	c1
a_1	b_2	c3
a_2	b_1	c2

S

A	B	C
a1	b1	c_1
a_1	b1	c2
a1	b2	c3
a3	b2	c3

Then R ∪ S has five rows:

R ∪ S

A	B	C
a_1	b_1	c1
a_1	b1	c2
a_1	b_2	c3
a_2	b_1	c2
a3	b2	c3

Note that rows occurring in both R and S occur only once in the union, R ∪ S.
R ∩ S has two rows:

R ∩ S

A	B	C
a_1	b_1	c1
a_1	b_2	c3

R – S has only one:

R – S

A	B	C
a_2	b_1	c2

While S − R has two:

S − R

A	B	C
a_1	b1	c2
a3	b2	c3

∎

EXAMPLE 2.6.4

The operations of intersection, union, and difference are often pictured schematically using *Venn diagrams*, as illustrated below.

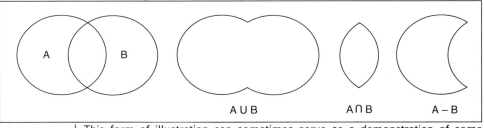

This form of illustration can sometimes serve as a demonstration of some principle of equivalence, as we will see below.   ∎

Assignment and Alias

During evaluation of relational algebra expressions, it is sometimes useful to be able to save certain intermediate results. We next introduce a notation meant to add this capability to relational algebra.

DEFINITION 2.6.5 Assignment, Alias. Let R be a table and let Head(R) = $A_1 . . . A_n$. Assume that $B_1, . . ., B_n$ are n attributes such that $Dom(B_i)$ = $Dom(A_i)$ for all i, $1 \leq i \leq n$. We define *a new table* S, whose heading is Head(S) = $B_1 . . . B_n$, by writing the assignment

$$S(B_1, . . ., B_n) := R(A_1, . . ., A_n).$$

The content of the new table S is exactly the same as the content of the old table R—that is, a row u is in S if and only if a row t exists in R such that $u[B_i] = t[A_i]$ for i, $1 \leq i \leq n$. The symbol := used in this assignment is called the *assignment operation*.

We've caused ourselves extra effort by requiring that the assignment operation allow a redefinition of all the attribute names in the heading of the original table. We will see the value of this shortly. For now, we note that a redefinition of attributes is not always necessary, and when all attributes are identical between the two tables, $B_i = A_i$ for all i, $1 \leq i \leq n$, we refer to S as an *alias* of the table R and simply write

$S := R$ ∎

Note that the table R on the right can result from an evaluation of a relational algebra expression, and thus gives us an opportunity to "save" intermediate results of evaluation, much as we do with assignment statements used in programming languages. The table S on the left of the assignment operation must always be a named table, however; it cannot be an expression.

EXAMPLE 2.6.6
Consider the tables R and S given in Example 2.6.3. Using the assignment operation, we can define a new table:

$T := (R \cup S) - (R \cap S)$

This has the form:

T

A	B	C
a_1	b1	c2
a_2	b_1	c2
a3	b2	c3

We could also have defined the table T by first defining two intermediate tables:

$T1 := (R \cup S)$
$T2 := (R \cap S)$
$T := T1 - T2$ ∎

Note that in Example 2.6.5, the two intermediate tables T1 and T2 are not mandatory, because expressions in relational algebra allow arbitrary nesting. If we are given an expression expr1 involving T1, and T1 is represented through an assignment as an expression expr2 involving other tables, then we can substitute expr2 for every occurrence of T1 in expr1 to achieve the same result. The major motivation for the assignment operation in the following sections will be to display intermediate results of a complex expression to improve human understanding.

The Product Operation

The *product* operation of relational algebra is based on the set theoretic operation of Cartesian product. In what follows, we will generally assume that R and S are two tables with Head(R) = A_1. . .A_n and Head(S) = B_1. . . B_m. Taking the product of R and S allows us to create a new table with rows containing all possible associations between the rows of the two tables. If r is a row in R consisting of the tuple of values ($r(A_1)$, . . ., $r(A_n)$), and s is a row in S with the tuple of values ($s(B_1)$, . . ., $s(B_m)$), then the usual definition of Cartesian product would imply that the product of R and S contains all *pairs* of tuples from R and S, with the form (($r(A_1)$, . . ., $r(A_n)$), ($s(B_1)$, . . ., $s(B_m)$)). This distinction between columns of R and columns of S, that their values fall in separate component tuples of a set of Cartesian pairs, doesn't jibe with our definition of a relational table, which makes all columns indistinguishable. Thus we need a more relationally oriented definition.

DEFINITION 2.6.7 Product. The *product* of the tables R and S is a table T whose heading is Head(T) = R.A_1. . .R.A_n S.B_1. . .S.B_m. We say that if r is a row of R and s is a row of S, then the concatenation of r with s, r ‖ s, is a row in the product table T. To define this idea of concatenation in a more basic fashion, we say that for every pair of rows u, v in R and S, respectively, there is a row t in T such that t(R.A_i) = u(A_i) for $1 \leq i \leq n$ and t(S.B_j) = v(B_j) for $1 \leq j \leq m$. The product T of R and S is denoted by R × S. ∎

We refer to attribute names of the form W.A (where W is a name of one of the tables involved in the product) as *qualified attribute names* or simply as *qualified attributes*. The heading of a product consists of qualified attributes, and we may use such attributes whenever we need to emphasize the table from which these attributes originated. Otherwise, if an attribute name appears in only one table, we can refer to it using its unqualified name.

EXAMPLE 2.6.8

Consider the tables R, S, and the product R × S given below:

R

A	B	C
a_1	b_1	c1
a_1	b_2	c3
a_2	b_1	c2

S

B	C	D
b1	c1	d_1
b1	c1	d3
b2	c2	d2
b1	c2	d4

R × S

R.A	R.B	R.C	S.B	S.C	S.D
a_1	b_1	c1	b1	c1	d_1
a_1	b_1	c1	b1	c1	d3
a_1	b_1	c1	b2	c2	d2
a_1	b_1	c1	b1	c2	d4
a_1	b_2	c3	b1	c1	d_1
a_1	b_2	c3	b1	c1	d3
a_1	b_2	c3	b2	c2	d2
a_1	b_2	c3	b1	c2	d4
a_2	b_1	c2	b1	c1	d_1
a_2	b_1	c2	b1	c1	d3
a_2	b_1	c2	b2	c2	d2
a_2	b_1	c2	b1	c2	d4

In the table R × S, the attributes A and D are unique and may be referred to without qualification, whereas the attributes R.B and S.B, for example, must be distinguished by their *qualifier names* (or simply *qualifiers*), R and S. ∎

This example shows that we can use the product operation to build large tables starting from tables that are relatively small. For instance, the product of two tables that have one thousand rows each is a table having one million rows!

A special situation arises if we intend to compute the product of a table with itself. Note that if we consider taking the product R × R, then

Definition 2.6.7 implies we would have a problem with the qualifier names, since $R \times R$ would have the heading $R.A_1 \ldots R.A_n \, R.A_1 \ldots R.A_n$. With these names it would not be possible to tell apart similarly named attributes of the two factors, and so this product, $R \times R$, is clearly unacceptable. Such a situation must be avoided by creating an *alias* of the table R, using the assignment S := R, and then performing the product between R and its alias: $R \times S$.

2.7 Native Relational Operations

We define four native operations that deal specifically with the relational structure of tables. The native operations of relational algebra are projection, selection, join, and division.

As in the definition of the product operation, we deal with tables R and S having headings $\text{Head}(R) = A_1 \ldots A_n$ and $\text{Head}(S) = B_1 \ldots B_n$.

The Projection Operation

The operation of *projection* acts on a table by deleting some of its columns, both in the heading and in the subordinate column values of the table content. Note that different rows of a table R, when projected onto a subset of columns, may become identical. If this is the case, duplicate rows will be deleted until only one copy of each duplicate set of rows is present in the result of the projection. Here is a somewhat more rigorous definition.

DEFINITION 2.7.1 Projection. The projection of R on attributes $A_{i_1}, \ldots,$ A_{i_k}, where $\{A_{i_1}, \ldots, A_{i_k}\} \subseteq \{A_1, \ldots, A_n\}$, is a table T whose heading is $\text{Head}(T) = A_{i_1} \ldots A_{i_k}$, with the following content. For every row r in the table R there will be a single row t in the table T such that $r[A_{i_j}] = t[A_{i_j}]$ for every A_{i_j} contained in $\{A_{i_1}, \ldots, A_{i_k}\}$. The projection of R on $A_{i_1}, \ldots, A_{i_k}$ is denoted by $R[A_{i_1}, \ldots, A_{i_k}]$. ■

The projection operation wipes out the columns of a table that are *not* named in the list of attributes enclosed in square brackets.

EXAMPLE 2.7.2

Suppose that we wish to post a list of customer names from the CUSTOMERS table of Figure 2.2 but not include their identification numbers, cities, and discounts. This can be accomplished in relational algebra by writing

    CN := CUSTOMERS[cname]

The resulting table CN shown below is a "vertical" section of the table CUSTOMERS consisting of the column cname.

CN

cname
Tiptop
Basics
Allied
ACME

Note that the two rows with duplicate ACME values in Figure 2.2 have resulted in a single row in the projection.   ■

This is the first time we have created a relational algebra expression to answer an English language request for data. We call such an expression a *relational algebra query,* or simply a *query.*

The Selection Operation

The next operation defined is *selection*, which creates a new table by limiting the set of rows of a given table according to a specified criterion. The general form of the condition that specifies this criterion is the subject of the following definition.

DEFINITION 2.7.3 Selection. Given a table S with $Head(S) = A_1 \ldots A_n$, the selection operation creates a new table, denoted by S where C, with the same set of attributes, and consisting of those tuples of S that obey the *selection condition,* or simply *condition* denoted by C. A condition of selection determines, for each given tuple of the table, whether that tuple is *qualified* to remain in the set of selected rows making up the answer. The form a condition C can take is defined recursively as follows.

[1] C can be any comparison of the form $A_i \propto A_j$, or $A_i \propto a$, where A_i and A_j are attributes of S having the same domain, a is a constant from $Dom(A_i)$, and $\propto$ is one of the comparison operators <, >, =, <=, >=, and <>. (Note that a comparison using the operator <> is true when the two values compared are unequal.) The table S where $A_i \propto A_j$ consists of all rows t of T with the property that $t[A_i] \propto t[A_j]$; the table S where $A_i \propto a$ contains all rows t of S with the property $t[A_i] \propto a$.

Examples in the case of the CUSTOMERS table of Figure 2.2 include city = 'Dallas', and discnt >= 8.00. Note that a character constant is placed between quotes when written in a condition. There are no pairs of attributes in CUSTOMERS that we would expect to have the same value, but an example of such a condition would be city > cname, where the operator > in the case of character constants means that the first operand comes later in alphabetical order than the second.

[2] If C and C' are conditions, then new conditions can be formed by writing C **and** C', C **or** C', and finally **not** C, possibly enclosing any such newly formed conditions in parentheses. If U := S where C_1, and V := S where C_2, then we have

- The **and** connector: S where C_1 and C_2 means the same as $U \cap V$.
- The **or** connector: S where C_1 or C_2 means the same as $U \cup V$.
- The **not** connector: S where not C_1 means the same as $S - U$.

The table denoted by S where C contains all rows of S that obey condition C. A condition is evaluated for a row by testing sub-expression comparisons of the form given in part 1 of Definition 2.7.3, and then checking whether the combined logical statement is true. ∎

EXAMPLE 2.7.4

In order to find all customers based in Kyoto, we need to apply the following selection:

```
CUSTOMERS where city = 'Kyoto'
```

The result of this query, assuming the content seen in Figure 2.2, is the table:

cid	cname	city	discnt
c006	ACME	Kyoto	0.00

As another example, suppose that we need to find the products stored in Dallas that cost more than $0.50. This can be accomplished by the selection:

```
PRODUCTS where city = 'Dallas' and price > 0.50
```

And the query gives the result:

pid	pname	city	quantity	price
p05	pencil	Dallas	221400	1.00
p06	folder	Dallas	123100	2.00

■

The operations introduced so far can be combined to solve more complicated queries.

EXAMPLE 2.7.5

It is simple to form a relational algebra expression to retrieve all agents who have a percentage commission of at least 6%. We use selection and define the table L:

```
L := AGENTS where percent >= 6
```

The table resulting from Figure 2.2 is given in Figure 2.6. Now assume that we want to retrieve all pairs of agents, both with a percentage commission of at least 6%, and both stationed in the same city. We can accomplish this by using the product operator, but we need to be careful not to specify the product L × L, which as we explained at the end of Section 2.6, is unacceptable. Therefore we start with another alias definition.

```
M := AGENTS where percent >= 6
```

L

aid	aname	city	percent
a01	Smith	New York	6
a02	Jones	Newark	6
a03	Brown	Tokyo	7
a04	Gray	New York	6

Figure 2.6 L := AGENTS where percent >= 6

And now we can create a solution expression.

```
PAIRS := (L x M) where L.city = M.city
```

With the table M, identical to L except in having a different name, we are able to specify a condition on the product L × M to qualify rows only if the two agent cities are identical. The result of the PAIRS expression based on Figure 2.2 is

PAIRS

L.aid	L.aname	L.city	L.percent	M.aid	M.aname	M.city	M.percent
a01	Smith	New York	6	a01	Smith	New York	6
a01	Smith	New York	6	a04	Gray	New York	6
a04	Gray	New York	6	a01	Smith	New York	6
a04	Gray	New York	6	a04	Gray	New York	6

This table contains a lot of redundant information. Actually only one distinct pair of aid values has the property we seek, (a01, a04), but the relational algebra expression for PAIRS also presents the pair in the opposite order, (a04, a01), and pairs of identical agents, such as (a01, a01). It is straightforward to create a more restrictive selection condition that will retrieve distinct pairs of agents only once.

```
PAIRS2 := (L X M) where L.city = M.city and L.aid < M.aid
```

The table resulting from this expression is given by

PAIRS2

L.aid	L.aname	L.city	L.percent	M.aid	M.aname	M.city	M.percent
a01	Smith	New York	6	a04	Gray	New York	6

■

EXAMPLE 2.7.6

We notice in the final answer, PAIRS2 of Example 2.7.5, that there is only a single row, and looking at Figure 2.2 we see why: only two agents are in the same city, and this city is New York. Now we ask the following question. Can we replace the query defined by PAIRS2 with a slightly different query, PAIRS3, where we specify the city of New York instead of specifying equal cities? That is, can we replace

```
PAIRS2 := (L X M) where L.city = M.city and L.aid < M.aid
```

with

```
PAIRS3 := (L X M) where L.city = 'New York' and M.city = 'New York'
          and L.aid < M.aid
```

If not, why not, since the two queries give the same answer?

This question illustrates a common misconception about relational algebra queries, and it is important to become sensitive to this issue. In fact the two queries are quite different, even though they seem to give the same answer. The two queries are guaranteed to give the same answer *only for the content at the given moment* of Figure 2.2. Recall that we made a point in the example of Figure 2.2 that the content of these tables might change quickly, and that our queries should give the right answer without any user knowledge of their contents. If we were suddenly to add to the AGENTS table of Figure 2.2 a new agent tuple, (a07, Green, Newark, 7), then the result of PAIRS2 would change because there is now another pair of agents, (a02, a07), with a percent commission of at least 6%, both in the same city (Newark). This is what we asked to retrieve, and it is appropriate for the answer to change. However, the result of the PAIRS3 query would not change, because we misguidedly substituted for a desired condition (L.city = M.city) a condition that depended on the accidental contents of AGENTS in Figure 2.2 (L.city = 'New York' and M.city = 'New York'). Be careful to avoid this kind of error, known as a *content dependency*, when creating your own relational algebra query expressions to answer questions in the exercises. The fact that two query formulations have the same result for a table of a given content is not sufficient to guarantee that the two formulations are equivalent; they must give the same result for *all possible* contents of the tables involved. ∎

Precedence of Relational Operations

Note that in the expressions of Example 2.7.6 defining PAIRS2 and PAIRS3, the product of L and M is enclosed in parentheses before the where clause is applied. This is because the expression $(L \times M)$ where C has the effect of taking the Cartesian product first and then performing the selection implied by the where clause on this product, whereas $L \times M$ where C has the implied effect of first creating the selection M where C and then taking the Cartesian product with L. Thus the form $L \times M$ where C has the same meaning as if we had written $L \times (M$ where C). In fact the example PAIRS2 would be undefined if we took the second form, since $L \times$ (M where L.city = M.city and L.cid < M.cid) has a where clause that refers to columns not in the table (M) that is the object of selection.

$L \times M$ where C has the same effect as $L \times (M$ where C) because relational algebra operations have an implicit *precedence*, or *binding strength*, that determines which operations are performed first in an expression with no parentheses. Parentheses in an expression override the implicit precedence, so that sub-expressions contained in parentheses are always evaluated first. An example of this in normal (numerical) algebra is the expression 5 * 3 + 4. It is probably obvious to you that the value of this expression is 19, because you recognize intuitively that multiplication (*) has a greater precedence than addition (+). Writing 5 * 3 + 4 is the same as writing (5 * 3) + 4. However, we can override the precedence by placing the parentheses differently: 5 * 3 + 4 is 19, but 5 * (3 + 4) is 35. In a similar manner, relational algebra operations have their own precedence, and now that we have seen most of the operations and are starting to combine them in more complex expressions, it's a good time to make this precedence clear.

DEFINITION 2.7.7 Precedence of Relational Operations. The order of precedence for the relational operators is given in Figure 2.7. The table includes the relational operators of join and divide, which will be covered shortly. ∎

Precedence	Operators	Symbols
Highest	project	R [ ]
	select	R where C
	times	×
	join, divideby	⋈, ÷
	difference	−
Lowest	union, intersection	∪, ∩

Figure 2.7 Precedence Rules for the Relational Operations

EXAMPLE 2.7.8
Suppose that we wish to determine those cities where we have either customers who have a discount of less than 10% or agents who make a commission of less than 6%. This is accomplished by the following relational algebra expression:

```
(CUSTOMERS where discnt < 10) [city]
    ∪ (AGENTS where percent < 6) [city]
```

Note that the union operator is absolutely required here. We cannot replace it by using an "or" connector of Definition 2.7.3 in a selection condition, because the cities in the result come from different tables entirely, with different criteria for inclusion in the final answer. ∎

The Join Operation

The purpose of the *join operation* is to create a table that relates the rows of two given tables that have equal values in identically named columns. For example, when we join the ORDERS table with the CUSTOMERS table, with common column name cid, the resulting table contains order information contained in ORDERS as well as additional information from CUS-TOMERS about the customer placing each order. Note that the join operation defined here is also known as *equijoin* or *natural join*.

DEFINITION 2.7.9 Join. Consider the tables R and S, with headings given by

$$\text{Head}(R) = A_1 \ldots A_n B_1 \ldots B_k \text{ and Head}(S) = B_1 \ldots B_k C_1 \ldots C_m$$

where $n, k, m \geq 0$. Note that $B_1 \ldots B_k$ is the complete subset of attributes shared by these two tables (and this subset may possibly be empty if $k=0$). The *join* of the tables R and S is the table represented as $R \bowtie S$, with a heading $\text{Head}(R \bowtie S) = A_1 \ldots A_n B_1 \ldots B_k C_1 \ldots C_m$. A row t is in the table $R \bowtie S$ if and only if there are two rows u in R and v in S, such that $u[B_v] = v[B_v]$ for all v, $1 \leq v \leq k$; then column values on the row t are defined as follows: $t[A_i]=u[A_i]$ for $1 \leq i \leq n$, $t[B_i] = u[B_i] = v[B_i]$ for $1 \leq i \leq k$, and $t[C_j] = v[C_j]$ for $1 \leq j \leq m$. When the rows u in R and v in S give rise to a row t in T, the two rows are said to be *joinable*.

We refer to $B_1 \ldots B_k$ as the attributes on which the tables R and S are joined. One of the rules of the relational model (which we merely mentioned in passing following RULE 2) states that the ordering of the columns of a table is not significant. In particular, it is not important that the attributes $B_1 \ldots B_k$ appear as a sequence at the end of table R and the beginning of table S, so long as they appear in some position in both tables. ∎

EXAMPLE 2.7.10

Consider the following tables R and S:

R

A	B_1	B_2
a_1	b_1	b_1'
a_1	b_2	b_1'
a_2	b_1	b_2'

S

B_1	B_2	C
b_1	b_1'	c_1
b_1	b_1'	c_2
b_1	b_2'	c_3
b_2	b_2'	c_4

As we see, the second row of table R has no row in S that matches it in the two columns B1 and B2 simultaneously; therefore, it gives rise to no row in R ⋈ S. On the other hand, the first row of the table R can be joined with two rows of S and, therefore, will generate two rows in R ⋈ S. The third row of the table R also matches a single row on the table S. We note that the fourth row in S matches no row in R in the two columns B1 and B2, therefore giving rise to no row in R ⋈ S. The new table T := R ⋈ S is the following:

T

A	B_1	B_2	C
a_1	b_1	b_1'	c_1
a_1	b_1	b_1'	c_2
a_2	b_1	b_2'	c_3

∎

If the two tables R and S being joined have no common attributes, then the content of the join coincides with the content of the (Cartesian) product of the two tables. That is, if $B_1 \ldots B_k$ is an empty set, k = 0, then R ⋈ S is the same as R × S. On the other hand, if R and S are compatible so that all attributes are in common, then the join of the two tables corresponds to the intersection of the two tables. Restated, if $A_1 \ldots A_n$ and $C_1 \ldots C_m$ are both empty sets, n = m = 0, then R ⋈ S is the same as R ∩ S. These equivalencies will be given as exercises at the end of the chapter, but you might give some thought to them now as an aid to understanding the definition.

Let us consider a few examples that involve the CAP database.

EXAMPLE 2.7.11

We wish to find the names of the customers who have ordered product p01. It
should be clear that we need to use information from two tables to answer this
question, since order information is in the ORDERS table, but the ORDERS table
does not contain the customer name; for that value (cname) we need to go to
the CUSTOMERS tables. It turns out that the natural way to pose this query in
relational algebra is to perform a join of the ORDERS and CUSTOMERS table, so let
us start by doing that and then look at the result. If we define CUSTORDS := CUS-
TOMERS ⋈ ORDERS, Figure 2.8 pictures the table result corresponding to the content of Figure 2.2.

CUSTORDS

cname	city	discnt	ordno	month	cid	aid	pid	qty	dollars
TipTop	Duluth	10.00	1011	jan	c001	a01	p01	1000	450.00
TipTop	Duluth	10.00	1012	jan	c001	a01	p01	1000	450.00
TipTop	Duluth	10.00	1019	feb	c001	a02	p02	400	180.00
TipTop	Duluth	10.00	1018	feb	c001	a03	p04	600	540.00
TipTop	Duluth	10.00	1023	mar	c001	a04	p05	500	450.00
TipTop	Duluth	10.00	1022	mar	c001	a05	p06	400	720.00
TipTop	Duluth	10.00	1025	apr	c001	a05	p07	800	720.00
Basics	Dallas	12.00	1013	jan	c002	a03	p03	1000	880.00
Basics	Dallas	12.00	1026	may	c002	a05	p03	800	704.00
Allied	Dallas	8.00	1015	jan	c003	a03	p05	1200	1104.00
Allied	Dallas	8.00	1014	jan	c003	a03	p05	1200	1104.00
ACME	Duluth	8.00	1021	feb	c004	a06	p01	1000	460.00
ACME	Kyoto	0.00	1016	jan	c006	a01	p01	1000	500.00
ACME	Kyoto	0.00	1020	feb	c006	a03	p07	600	600.00
ACME	Kyoto	0.00	1024	mar	c006	a06	p01	800	800.00

Figure 2.8 CUSTORDS := CUSTOMERS ⋈ ORDERS

The only column with a common name between the CUSTOMERS and ORDERS
tables is the cid column. Recall that the cid column is a key for the CUSTOMERS
table, meaning that the cid value is unique on each row. At the same time, the
ORDERS table has a specific cid value on each row listing the customer making
the order (duplicate cid values from one row of ORDERS to another is of course
possible). The effect of joining the two tables is to extend each row of the

ORDERS table with information on a unique row of the CUSTOMERS table with the given cid value. This is clearly an important operation, since we need to be able to relate information about the cid value in ORDERS with information in the CUSTOMERS table for that given cid. We can do the same thing with pid and aid, extending the information on ORDERS rows by providing information about the products and agents, by joining ORDERS with the PRODUCTS or AGENTS tables.

The solution to the problem, to find the names of the customers who have ordered product 'p01', is given by the relational algebra query:

    CNP01 := (CUSTOMERS ⋈ ORDERS where pid = 'p01') [cname]

Note that by the precedence rules of relational algebra, there is an implied parentheses around ORDERS where pid = 'p01'. This is fine, and it gives us the rows of ORDERS involving sales of product p01. Then the join with CUSTOMERS takes place, extending the information about ORDERS involving product p01 to include cname, and finally the projection on cname takes place so that only the cname column will appear in the answer, CNP01. The final answer is given by

CNP01

cname
TipTop
ACME

■

EXAMPLE 2.7.12
Now we wish to pose a query to get names of customers who order at least one product costing $0.50. This can be accomplished by first writing

    CHEAPS := (PRODUCTS where price = 0.50) [pid]

to extract the product numbers of products that cost 50 cents. Then, by computing

    ((ORDERS ⋈ CHEAPS) ⋈ CUSTOMERS) [cname]

we retrieve those ORDERS involving 50-cent products in ORDERS ⋈ CHEAPS, and we find the names of the customers who placed these ORDERS by joining this intermediate result with the CUSTOMERS table. We can, of course, avoid an assignment statement by combining the two steps above:

    ((ORDERS ⋈ (PRODUCTS where price = 0.50) [pid]) ⋈ CUSTOMERS) [cname]

A very important point is that it is *necessary* to project products costing 50 cents onto pid in creating CHEAPS. The expression:

    ((ORDERS ⋈ PRODUCTS where price = 0.50) ⋈ CUSTOMERS) [cname] does *not* properly solve the problem, since an extra unforeseen column in the second join is common to the two tables: this expression forces the `city` of the product to coincide with the `city` of the customer placing the order for that product. One of the exercises asks you to display the result of this latter query, together with the results obtained by the original relational algebra expression. The moral here is that projection must be performed at the proper time in the order of evaluation of a set of expressions to avoid undesired side effects in the join. ■

Both the product and join operations are *associative*. In other words, if R, S, T are any three tables, we have

$$(R \times S) \times T = R \times (S \times T)$$
$$(R \bowtie S) \bowtie T = R \bowtie (S \bowtie T).$$

Also, product and join are *commutative*; that is, $R \times S = S \times R$ and $R \bowtie S = S \bowtie R$ for all tables R, S. We discuss this and other properties of join in the exercises.

The Division Operation

To introduce division, the last of the native relational operations, consider two tables R and S, where the heading of S is a subset of the heading of R. Specifically, assume that

$$\text{Head}(R) = A_1 \ldots A_n B_1 \ldots B_m, \text{ and Head}(S) = B_1 \ldots B_m.$$

DEFINITION 2.7.13 Division. The table T is the result of the *division* $R \div S$ (which is read as "R DIVIDEBY S") if $\text{Head}(T) = A_1 \ldots A_n$ and T consists of exactly those rows t such that for *every* row s in S, the row resulting from concatenating t and s can be found in table R. ■

There are no columns in common between S ($\text{Head}(S) = B_1 \ldots B_m$) and T = $R \div S$ ($\text{Head}(T) = A_1 \ldots A_n$), but since $\text{Head}(R) = A_1 \ldots A_n B_1 \ldots B_m$, we see that S and T have the proper headings, so that it is possible that $T \times S = R$ (or $T \bowtie S = R$, the same thing when there are no columns in common between T and S). This is exactly the sort of division operation we want to define, the *inverse* of the product operation.

THEOREM 2.7.14 We are given two tables T and S, where $Head(T) = A_1 \ldots A_n$ and $Head(S) = B_1 \ldots B_m$. If the table R is defined by $R = T \times S$, then it is true that $T = R \div S$.

PROOF. Since $R = T \times S$, we have $Head(R) = A_1 \ldots A_n B_1 \ldots B_m$. If we denote by W the table resulting from $R \div S$, then by Definition 2.7.13, $Head(W) = A_1 \ldots A_n$, and W has the same heading as T. Now by the definition of product, if the row t exists in table T we see that for every row s in S, $t \parallel s$ (t concatenated with s) exists in $R = T \times S$. But that is exactly the condition specified in Definition 2.7.13 that will make the row t exist in $W = R \div S$. Thus $T \subseteq W$. By a similar argument we can demonstrate that $W \subseteq T$. ■

Unfortunately, the possibility exists that we might start with contents for a table R and a table S so that it is not possible that $R = T \times S$, for any possible choice of T. However, the definition of T implies that when $T = R \div S$, the table T contains the *largest possible set of rows* such that $T \times S \subseteq R$. We will see more about this in the exercises at the end of the chapter.

EXAMPLE 2.7.15

Suppose that we start with the table R given by

R

A	B	C
a1	b1	c1
a2	b1	c1
a1	b2	c1
a1	b2	c2
a2	b1	c2
a1	b2	c3
a1	b2	c4
a1	b1	c5

We list a number of possible tables S and the resulting table T := R ÷ S.

S

C
c1

T

A	B
a1	b1
a2	b1
a1	b2

In the case above, note that all of the rows in S × T are in R. There couldn't be any larger set of rows in T for which this is true, because only three rows in R have a c1 value in column C.

S

C
c1
c2

T

A	B
a1	b2
a2	b1

Note again that all of the rows in S × T are in R and that there couldn't be any larger set of rows in T for which this is true, as can be seen by looking at rows in R with C values c2.

S

C
c1
c2
c3
c4

T

A	B
a1	b2

Once again the rows in S × T are in R, and by looking at the rows in table R with C value c3 and c4, we see why T has the maximal content with this property.

S

B	C
b1	c1

T

A
a1
a2

Here we see an example of dividing R with three columns by a table S with two columns, resulting in a table T with a single column. Note that there are only two rows in R with B = b1 and C = c1, and these two rows have A = a1 and A = a2, respectively; thus T is maximal.

S

B	C
b1	c1
b2	c1

T

A
a1

You should be able to explain why T is maximal in this case. ∎

Next we give an example to see why we use division—what kind of question it answers about the data.

EXAMPLE 2.7.16

Suppose that we extract the list of product numbers for products ordered by customer c006. This list is stored in the table PC6

PC6

pid
p01
p07

and can be obtained using the query

```
PC6 := (ORDERS where cid = 'c006')[pid]
```

We are interested in finding the customers who have placed orders for *all* these products. We can extract from ORDERS the agent numbers, together with the products they order, by writing CP := ORDERS[cid, pid]. The query we wish to pose, to retrieve the customers (cid value will identify them) who have placed orders for all parts in PC6, can be solved by applying division. The resulting table T := CP ÷ PC6 is

T

cid
c001
c006

The reader should draw the lesson from this example that whenever the word "all" is used in a retrieval request, the query expression to use may very well include the division operation. ∎

Note that it is absolutely necessary in Example 2.7.16 to project ORDERS onto the two columns cid, pid before dividing by PC, rather than projecting on cid after division. Otherwise, we would be asking for additional column values in the ORDERS table to be constant in concatenation with the two pid values of PC6. To illustrate this point, consider the following tables R and S.

R

A	B	C
a1	b1	c1
a2	b1	c1
a3	b2	c1
a1	b1	c2
a2	b2	c2
a3	b3	c2

S

C
c1
c2

By the definition of division, $R \div S$ has a heading with columns A B and a single row with values (a1, b1). Thus $(R \div S)[A]$ has a single row with value a1. On the other hand, if we first project R on columns A C, R[A, C] has six distinct rows, and $R[A, C] \div S$ is a table with the single column A and three rows with values a1, a2, and a3. You should always ask yourself what columns of the table being divided need to be held constant in concatenation with all rows of the divisor.

EXAMPLE 2.7.17

We answer the request to get names of customers who order all products by writing

    T := ORDERS[cid, pid] ÷ PRODUCTS[pid].
    U := (T ⋈ CUSTOMERS)[cname].

Once again it is necessary to project ORDERS on the attributes [cid, pid] so that the resulting table T has only the attribute cid. There is a single customer, c001, corresponding to cname TipTop, who orders all products, so that will be the content of the solution table U. ∎

2.8 The Interdependence of Operations

Several of the relational operators defined in Section 2.7 are there simply for added convenience, in the sense that the full set of operations could be defined in terms of a smaller subset. We claim that a set of basic operations consists of union, difference, product, selection, and projection, together with the assignment operator, which allows us to redefine attribute names. To justify this claim we need to show how the remaining operations—intersection, join, and division—can be expressed using the operations mentioned above. The first two, difference and join, are easy to demonstrate.

THEOREM 2.8.1 Let R, S be two compatible tables, where $Head(R) = Head(S) = A_1 \ldots A_n$. The intersection operation can be defined in terms of subtraction alone:

$$A \cap B = A - (A - B)$$

PROOF. We demonstrate this by Venn diagrams.

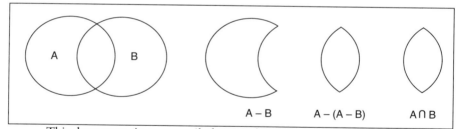

This demonstration can easily be translated into English, if desired.   ∎

THEOREM 2.8.2 The join of two tables R, S, where $Head(R) = A_1 \ldots A_n \ B_1 \ldots B_k$ and $Head(S) = B_1 \ldots B_k \ C_1 \ldots C_m$ and $n, k, m \geq 0$, can be expressed using product, selection, and projection.

PROOF. To show this, consider the table

$$T := (R \times S) \text{ where } R.B_1 = S.B_1 \text{ and } \ldots \text{ and } R.B_k = S.B_k$$

constructed by using product and selection. This has the appropriate association of rows in R and S to make a join. Now we simply cross out the undesired duplicate columns using projection and redefine the column names using assignment.

$$T1 := T[R.A_1, \ldots, R.A_n, R.B_1, \ldots, R.B_k, S.C_1, \ldots, S.C_m]$$
$$T2(A_1, \ldots, A_n, B_1, \ldots, B_k, C_1, \ldots, C_m) := T1$$

The table T2 is identical to R $\bowtie$ S. ∎

The demonstration that division can be expressed in terms of more basic operations is not as simple to grasp, and the proof is starred, meaning that the reader is not expected to follow it to have a good understanding of the course material. The proof is included for curious readers with a strong mathematics background.

THEOREM 2.8.3 Division can be expressed using projection, product, and difference.

PROOF*. Consider two tables R and S, where $Head(R) = A_1 \ldots A_n B_1 \ldots B_m$ and $Head(S) = B_1 \ldots B_m$. We can prove that

$$R \div S = R[A_1 \ldots A_n] - ((R[A_1 \ldots A_n] \times S) - R)[A_1 \ldots A_n].$$

To demonstrate this, suppose that u is a tuple from $R[A_1 \ldots A_n] - ((R[A_1 \ldots A_n] \times S) - R)[A_1 \ldots A_n]$. This means that u is in $R[A_1 \ldots A_n]$ and that u is not a member of the table $((R[A_1 \ldots A_n] \times S) - R)[A_1 \ldots A_n]$. Suppose that there is a tuple s in S such that u concatenated with s is not in R. Since u is in $R[A_1 \ldots A_n]$, this is another way of saying that u is a member of $((R[A_1 \ldots A_n] \times S) - R)[A_1 \ldots A_n]$, which is contradictory. Therefore, for every tuple s in S, u concatenated with s is in R and this means that u belongs to the table $R \div S$.

Conversely, if u is a tuple in the division $R \div S$, clearly u is in $R[A_1 \ldots A_n]$. On the other hand, u is not in the table $((R[A_1 \ldots A_n] \times S) - R)[A_1 \ldots A_n]$, for this would mean that there exists a tuple s in S such that u concatenated with s would be in $R[A_1 \ldots A_n] \times S$ but not in R. Therefore u belongs to the table $R[A_1 \ldots A_n] - ((R[A_1 \ldots A_n] \times S) - R)[A_1 \ldots A_n]$, which concludes our argument. You may want to work this out for specific tables, using the division example just given. ∎

Naturally, this leads us to wonder whether the set of basic relational operations (union, difference, product, selection, and projection) is in fact a minimal set. In other words, can we find an even smaller set of operations (among those five) such that we would be able to express all remaining operations with operations from the smaller set? It turns out that these five operations do indeed form a minimal set, and the mathematically inclined reader may wish to consider how this can be proven.

The *power*, or *expressive power*, of a relational query language such as relational algebra or SQL is the ability of that language to create new tables to answer queries from an existing set of tables. In a paper written in 1972, E. F. Codd compared the relational algebra with that of another language known as *tuple calculus*, which was based on symbolic logic, and showed that the two are equivalent in power. This became the test of a relational language, that it must have at least the expressive power of the relational algebra. A language that passes this test is said to be *complete*, or *relationally complete*, and all modern query languages (such as SQL) have this power. A certain school of thought maintains that the expressive power of relational algebra is insufficient, and we will encounter at the end of Chapter 3 an operation known as transitive closure that the relational algebra (and standard SQL) is unable to perform.

2.9 Illustrative Examples

Consider for a moment the power relational algebra gives us to pose queries on the data. We can retrieve any set of column values (projection) from any number of tables, where the rows of the different tables are concatenated into single rows (product) and then restricted by conditions on the different columns (selection). Even ignoring the operations of union and difference that add certain technical capabilities, this broad-brush outline seems to give us a good deal of power, when we consider how it matches with the English language requests we might make. The current section explores some of this capability.

In this section we will always derive a final query expression that does not depend on intermediate result tables created by the use of an alias. In general, it is always preferable to give a final answer in this form, a single self-contained expression, a form that will be required in the exercises in cases where an alias is not absolutely required. Note however that the following set of alias definitions can be used freely as shorthand for the CAP tables.

```
C := CUSTOMERS, A := AGENTS, P := PRODUCTS, O := ORDERS.
```

EXAMPLE 2.9.1

We want to get the names of customers who order at least one product priced at $0.50. The usual way to tackle a problem like this is to build the query inside-out. First, start with products priced at $0.50.

```
P where price = 0.50
```

Now how do we find the customers who order the products? Join with ORDERS!

```
(P where price = 0.50) ⋈ O
```

The result gives us a subset of the ORDERS table for the appropriate products, with extended columns containing product information. Unfortunately we do not yet have names of customers, only cid values. The natural idea is to join with the CUSTOMERS table, but first we have to get rid of the city column in the expression developed so far. The best way to do that is to go back to the first PRODUCTS selection and project out everything but pid. Then we join the result with CUSTOMERS and project the final expression on cname, for the final answer.

```
(((P where price = 0.50)[pid] ⋈ O) ⋈ C)[cname]
```

Note that (P where price = 0.50) is placed in parentheses before projecting on [pid] because otherwise, by the Precedence Table in Figure 2.7, projection would precede selection, so the selection condition on price would be meaningless. After being joined with O, the resulting expression, (P where price = 0.50)[pid] ⋈ O, is enclosed in parentheses again before joining with C. This is because we have only defined join as a binary operation; X ⋈ Y ⋈ Z is not defined, and we must write (X ⋈ Y) ⋈ Z. One of the exercises will ask you to show that join is associative: (X ⋈ Y) ⋈ Z = X ⋈ (Y ⋈ Z), so that we can define the expression X ⋈ Y ⋈ Z to stand for either one of these forms. Finally, the expression ((P where price = 0.50)[pid] ⋈ O) ⋈ C is placed in parentheses before projecting on cid; otherwise, the expression ((P where price = 0.50)[pid] ⋈ O) ⋈ C[cname] would project C onto cname before performing the join (precedence, Figure 2.7), and we would lose the join column cid.   ∎

EXAMPLE 2.9.2

We wish to find all names of customers who do not place any order through agent a03. We can begin by determining those customers who do place some orders through agent a03 by

```
(ORDERS where aid = 'a03') [cid]
```

Now the request originally posed can be solved either by writing

```
ORDERS[cid] - (ORDERS where aid = 'a03') [cid]
```

or

```
CUSTOMERS[cid] - (ORDERS where aid = 'a03') [cid].
```

depending on the nature of the answer we expect. In the first query we retrieve only cid values of customers who place at least *one* order but none through agent a03; in the second query, we also retrieve cid values of customers who do not place any orders at all. We should ask ourselves if we want to include such "inactive" customers in our solution. In the absence of any intuition about this (if we are posing an English query request that has been written down by somebody else, and we can't ask that person questions), the latter solution seems preferable, since it contains more information. ∎

EXAMPLE 2.9.3

Let us now retrieve customers who place orders *only through* agent a03. The query request can be solved by determining initially the customers who place an order through an agent other than a03, and then eliminating these customers from the list of customers who place some orders:

```
ORDERS[cid] - (ORDERS where aid <> 'a03')[cid].
```
∎

EXAMPLE 2.9.4

Suppose that we need to find products that have never been ordered by a customer based in New York through an agent based in Boston. It is obviously simpler to find initially those products that violate this condition—that is, products that *have* been ordered by a customer based in New York through an agent based in Boston:

```
(((C where city = 'New York')[cid] ⋈ ORDERS)
    ⋈ A where city = 'Boston')) [pid]
```

As before, it is important that C selection is projected on the cid column before the join with the A selection takes place, so that the join doesn't require matching city values between CUSTOMERS and AGENTS. All we need to do now is to remove this list of products from the list of all products:

```
PRODUCTS[pid] –
  (((C where city = 'New York')[cid] ⋈ ORDERS)
     ⋈ A where city = 'Boston')) [pid]
```

EXAMPLE 2.9.5

Get names of customers who order all products priced at $0.50. To get the cid values of these customers, we take our hint from the phrase, ". . .who order *all* parts . . .," and think of division to arrive at cid values of such customers:

```
O[cid, pid] ÷ (P where price = 0.50)[pid]
```

To get the names of these customers, we need to join with CUSTOMERS and project on cname.

```
((O[cid, pid] ÷ (P where price = 0.50)[pid]) ⋈ C)[cname]
```

EXAMPLE 2.9.6

Get names of customers who order all products that anybody orders. This is division again, and the divisor, the list of "all" products, must be projected from ORDERS rather than PRODUCTS.

```
O[cid, pid] ÷ O[pid]
```

If the divisor were P[pid] instead, we might include a few newly listed products that no one orders yet, and therefore the resulting cid list would certainly be empty.

EXAMPLE 2.9.7

Get aids of agents who take orders on at least that set of products ordered by c004 (and possibly more). Requests that seem difficult may only need to be rephrased. Try the request: Get aids of agents who take orders on all products ordered by c004.

```
O[aid, pid] ÷ (O where cid = 'c004')[pid]
```

EXAMPLE 2.9.8

Get cids of customers who order *both* product p01 *and* p07. Note that the following relational algebra expression does *not* answer this request.

```
O where pid = 'p01' and pid = 'p07'   **INVALID FORM **
```

The problem is that each row of ORDERS has only one value for pid, and that value may either be equal to 'p01' or to 'p07', but not to both at once. The proper query to pose is

```
(O where pid = 'p01')[cid] ∩ ( O where pid = 'p07')[cid]
```

using intersection to require that customers order both products in distinct ORDERS rows.

EXAMPLE 2.9.9

Get cids of customers who place an order through at least one agent who places an order for product p03. In Figure 2.9, the customers to be retrieved are represented in the rightmost circle, with connections only to the agents in the center circle. Note in particular that the cids retrieved might not place orders for product p03 themselves. In the ORDERS table of Figure 2.2, we see on the fourth row that c001 places an order through a06 for p03; also, on the fourth row from the bottom, c004 places an order through a06 for product p01; therefore, c004 should be included in our answer, since it places an order through at least one agent (a06) who places an order for p03. However, it is easy to check that c004 never places an order for p03.

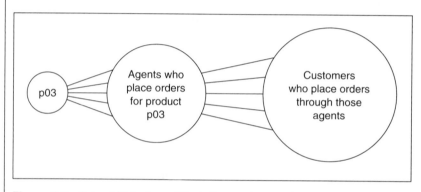

Figure 2.9   Sets of Objects and Their Connections to One Another in Example 2.9.9.

The correct way to pose this query is by proceeding from the inside out; starting with the middle circle of Figure 2.9, we retrieve the agents who place an order for product p03.

```
(O where pid = 'p03')[aid]
```

The answer we want to achieve is represented in the rightmost circle of Figure 2.9, and we need to retrieve cids of customers who place an order through one of these agents. This implies another use of the ORDERS table, and to be on the safe side we will use a different alias, X := ORDERS, so that there is no confusion of column names in an expression where the same table is used twice:

```
(X ⋈ (O where pid = 'p03')[aid])[cid]                    ∎
```

EXAMPLE 2.9.10

Get cids of all customers who have the same discount as any customer in Dallas or Boston. This is a counterexample to the idea that the division operation must be used whenever the word *all* is mentioned. In fact the use of the word *all* in this request is misleading. The request can be rephrased as follows to be analogous with other requests we have seen: "Get cids of customers who have the same discount as any customer in Dallas or Boston." The point is that when we ask for the cids of customers who have some property, naturally we want to retrieve all such customers; but this doesn't imply that division should be used. To answer this query, we start by finding all the discounts of customers in Dallas or Boston.

```
(C where city = 'Dallas' or city = 'Boston')[discnt]
```

Next, to find all cids of customers with this set of discnt values, we use join. First we create a new alias, D := CUSTOMERS, and then write

```
((C where city = 'Dallas' or city = 'Boston')[discnt] ⋈ D)[cid]
```

These cid values from the rows of table D that join with this set of discnt values give us the desired answer. ∎

EXAMPLE 2.9.11

Suppose that we have a rather complex query to pose. We wish to list pids of products that are ordered through agents who place orders for (possibly different) customers who order at least one product from an agent who has placed an order for customer c001. The secret of creating such a query is to work from the inside out—and not to lose our heads.

Working backward, we can determine immediately the agents who have placed some order for customer c001:

```
(O where cid = 'c001')[aid]
```

In turn, the customers who order products through these agents can be determined by

```
(X ⋈ (O where cid = 'c001')[aid])[cid],
```

where X := ORDERS. Given that Y := ORDERS, agents who place ORDERS for these customers can be listed by

```
(Y ⋈ (X ⋈ (O where cid = 'c001')[aid])[cid])[aid]
```

Finally, with Z := ORDERS, the products ordered through these agents are

```
(Z ⋈ (Y ⋈ (X ⋈ (O where cid = 'c001')[aid])[cid])[aid])[pid]
```

This is the answer to our original request. ∎

EXAMPLE 2.9.12

Get `pids` of products not ordered by any customer living in a `city` whose name begins with the letter D. How can we find customers in cities with names beginning with the letter D? Recall that inequalities for character strings reflect alphabetical order, and the following expression suggests itself.

```
C where city >= 'D' and city < 'E'
```

Now products that are not ordered by such customers can be discovered by starting with all products and subtracting the set of `ORDERS` that are ordered by them.

```
P[pid] - (O ⋈ (C where city >= 'D' and city < 'E'))[pid]
```
■

2.10 Other Relational Operations

The fundamental set of operations discussed so far is basically an attempt to provide a small collection of useful operations in order to make it possible to pose most English-language queries in relational algebra. There is a theoretical basis for claiming that a certain level of computational power is available to pose queries with the basic operations named. Additional operations can make the job much simpler, however, as we saw when we tried to express the division operation in terms of basic operations.

Next we discuss two additional useful relational operations that are not in the standard set, outer join and theta join (or θ-join). The usage of these operations appears in the following table.

NAME	SYMBOL	KEYBOARD FORM	EXAMPLE
OUTER JOIN	$\bowtie_0$	OUTERJ	R $\bowtie_0$ S, or R OUTERJ S
LEFT OUTER JOIN	$\bowtie_{LO}$	LOUTERJ	R $\bowtie_{LO}$ S, or R LOUTERJ S
RIGHT OUTER JOIN	$\bowtie_{RO}$	ROUTERJ	R $\bowtie_{RO}$ S, or R ROUTERJ S
THETA JOIN	$\bowtie_{A_i \theta B_j}$	JN($A_i \theta B_j$)	R $\bowtie_{A_1 > B_2}$ S, or R JN($A_2 > B_2$) S

The outer join in particular has significant ability to simplify queries in commercial database applications. The capability to perform such a join easily was originally left out of many computer-based query languages, but is now being added. Note that both of these operations can still be expressed in terms of the basic five operations.

Outer Join

To introduce the outer join we will use two tables, the AGENTS table we have dealt with up to now, and a new table known as SALES. SALES contains two columns, the agent aid that appear in the ORDERS table and a total column giving the dollar total of ORDERS taken by each such agent. If an agent has placed no ORDERS yet, we assume that the aid for that agent does not occur in SALES. Now we wish to print a table (as a report to a sales manager) that contains the name of all agents, their aid, and their total sales (the sales manager is familiar with all agent names and prefers that form, using aid only to distinguish duplicate names). One would think that we need simply write the relational algebra expression (AGENTS ⋈ SALES)[aname, aid, total]. However, this falls short of the aim described in one important case: if the agent has placed no ORDERS, then we have assumed that the agent's aid will not show up in the SALES table, and therefore it will not show up in the resulting report (no aid value is in SALES to join with the aid value in AGENTS). The sales manager who poses this query will certainly not want an agent's name to disappear from the resulting report when no sales have been made; indeed, this might be a good reason for personnel action. We might also conceivably encounter a situation where a new agent named 'Beowulf', with aid value 'a07', has been hired and has taken an order that shows up in the SALES table before the information on the agent appears in the AGENTS table. Then once again the expression (AGENTS ⋈ SALES)[aname, aid, total] would fail to provide needed information to the sales manager, since the aid column in SALES finds no match in AGENTS. The outer join operation, denoted by ⋈$_O$, is meant to solve problems of this kind. If we write instead:

    (AGENTS ⋈$_O$ SALES)[aname, aid, total]

we will get a table that has *all* values in both tables appearing. In the case of an agent who has made no sales, we would obviously not have a total value in SALES to correspond with this name; therefore, the corresponding total value would be filled in with a null value. The same holds for an agent who has made a sale but whose name is not known in AGENTS. For example, we might see the result:

OJRESULT

aname	aid	total
Smith, J	a01	850.00
Jones	a02	400.00
Brown	a03	3900.00
Gray	a04	**null**
Otasi	a05	2400.00
Smith, P.	a06	900.00
null	a07	650.00

Note that all unmatched column values show up in the outer join result.

To define outer join, consider the tables R and S, where $Head(R) = A_1 \ldots A_n B_1 \ldots B_k$ and $Head(S) = B_1 \ldots B_k C_1 \ldots C_m$, where n, k, m ≥ 0.

DEFINITION 2.10.1 Outer Join. The *outer join* of the tables R and S is the table $R \bowtie_o S$, where $Head(R \bowtie_o S) = A_1 \ldots A_n \ B_1 \ldots B_k C_1 \ldots C_m$. A row t is in the table $R \bowtie_o S$ if one of the following situations occurs:

[1] Two rows u and v are joinable in R and S, respectively, so that $u[B_i] = v[B_i]$ for all i, $1 \leq i \leq k$; in this case we define t by setting $t[A_l] = u[A_l]$ for $1 \leq l \leq n$, $t[B_i] = u[B_i] = v[B_i]$ for $1 \leq i \leq k$, and $t[C_j] = v[C_j]$ for $1 \leq j \leq m$.

[2] A row u is in R such that no v in S is joinable with u. In this case, $t[D] = u[D]$ for every D in Head(R) and t[D] is null for every D in $\{C_1, \ldots, C_k\}$.

[3] A row v is in S such that no u in R is joinable with v. In this case $t[D] = u[D]$ for every D in Head(S) and t[D] = null for every D in $\{A_1, \ldots, A_n\}$. ■

We say that the outer join preserves unmatched rows, in the sense that a row from a table on one side of the outer join, with unmatched join column values in the table on the other side, will still show up in the outer join result. The idea of the *left outer join* and *right outer join* operators is that we might wish to preserve unmatched rows on one side only. The left outer join operator preserves unmatched rows in the table on the left of the operator, filling in nulls for missing row values from the table on the right, and the right outer join does the opposite, preserving unmatched rows from the table on the right. For example, assume we have a table named SPECIAL_AGENTS, compatible with the AGENTS table but containing only rows for agents on a special list (say a01, a04, and a06). We want to see the same kind of report for these agents as was given in OJRESULT. Now if we use the expression

    (SPECIAL_AGENTS ⋈ SALES)[aname, aid, total],

we will not see the null sales total for agent a04, whereas if we use the expression

    (SPECIAL_AGENTS ⋈$_O$ SALES)[aname, aid, total],

we will see all agents, not just a01, a04, and a06 in the result, with nulls for the aname values not in SPECIAL_AGENTS, as follows:

OJRESULT2

aname	aid	total
Smith, J	a01	850.00
null	a02	400.00
null	a03	3900.00
Gray	a04	**null**
null	a05	2400.00
Smith, P.	a06	900.00
null	a07	650.00

But all we really want is a report for the agents in SPECIAL_AGENTS. In a company with thousands of agents, receiving all this unwanted extra information would be quite a serious problem. In order to get what we want, we would use the left outer join operator in the expression

    (SPECIAL_AGENTS ⋈$_{LO}$ SALES)[aname, aid, total],

with the resulting table:

LORESULT

aname	aid	total
Smith, J.	a01	850.00
Gray	a04	**null**
Smith, P.	a06	900.00

As an example of the use of right outer join, we would get the same result as this from the expression

```
(SALES ⋈RO SPECIAL_AGENTS)[aname, aid, total]
```

We leave it as an exercise for the reader to determine how Definition 2.10.1 of outer join must change in order to provide a valid definition of left outer join and right outer join.

Theta Join

The idea of a theta join, or θ-join, is that we might wish to join two tables where equality of attributes with the same name is not what is desired. The symbol θ stands for the comparison operator that will relate columns of different tables in the definition of the θ-join; it may be one of $>$, $<$, $>=$, $<=$, $=$, $<>$.

DEFINITION 2.10.2 Theta Join. Let R and S be two tables *having no column names in common* such that $Head(R) = A_1 \ldots A_n$ and $Head(S) = B_1 \ldots B_m$. Suppose that the attributes A_i and B_j have the same domain and the relational operation θ is one of the set $\{ >, <, >=, <=, <> \}$. The θ–*join* of the tables R and S is the table $T := R \bowtie_{A_i \theta B_j} S$, where

$$Head(R \bowtie_{A_i \theta B_j} S) = A_1 \ldots A_n B_1 \ldots B_m.$$

The rows of the new table have the form $t = (a_1, \ldots, a_n, b_1, \ldots, b_m)$, where

$$a_i \theta b_j, (a_1, \ldots, a_n) \text{ is in R, and } (b_1, \ldots, b_m) \text{ is in S.}$$

It is easy to see that θ-joins can be expressed using the basic operations of relational algebra. ∎

EXAMPLE 2.10.3

Find all `ordno` values for orders whose order quantity exceeds the current quantity on hand for the product. This is solved by the theta join:

```
(ORDERS ⋈ ORDERS.qty > PRODUCTS.quantity PRODUCTS)[ordno]
```

This is equivalent to the relational algebra expression:

```
((ORDERS x PRODUCTS) where ORDERS.qty > PRODUCTS.quantity)[ordno]   ∎
```

The condition `ORDERS.qty > PRODUCTS.quantity` is referred to as the *θ-condition*. A common way of referring to θ-join of this example is to say that it is a *greater-than-join*. You will recall that the standard join operator is referred to as an *equijoin* or, sometimes, a *natural join*.

Suggestions for Further Reading

The relational model has a large number of ramifications that we have not touched on in this short introduction. An excellent theoretical presentation is given by David Maier [2]. The founding paper on the relational model, by E. F. Codd, is contained in Section 1.2 of *Readings in Database Systems* [1]. A number of other papers in these *Readings* may also be of interest.

[1] E. F. Codd. "A Relational Model of Data for Large Shared Data Banks." In *Readings in Database Systems,* 2nd ed. Michael Stonebraker, ed. San Mateo, CA: Morgan Kaufmann, 1994.

[2] David Maier. *The Theory of Relational Databases.* New York: Computer Science Press, 1983.

Exercises

Some of the following exercises have solutions at the end of the book in "Solutions to Selected Exercises." These exercises are marked with the symbol •.

[2.1] Assume that the tables of this exercise are like Example 2.4.2, in that they have *all the rows they are ever going to have,* so that we can figure out the intentions of the designer regarding keys for table by merely looking at the contents of the rows.

T1

A	B	C	D
a1	b1	c1	d1
a2	b3	c1	d2
a3	b4	c2	d2
a4	b2	c2	d1

(a)• Consider the table T1, above. Find the three candidate keys for this table. One of the keys has two columns.

(b) Consider the table T2, following:

T2

A	B	C	D	E
a1	b1	c1	d1	e1
a2	b1	c1	d1	e2
a3	b1	c2	d1	e1
a4	b2	c1	d1	e1

Find the two candidate keys for this table.

(c)• Create an example of a table as in exercise (a) that has four columns and *only four rows,* but has only one candidate key, consisting of the first three columns. Be careful that *no pair* of the first three columns distinguishes all rows.

(d) Create an example of a table as in exercise (a) that has five columns, A B C D E, and only five rows, with only one candidate key consisting of the first four columns. Give an informal argument why no other set of columns forms a key.

[2.2]   Consider a database for the telephone company that contains a table SUBSCRIBERS, whose heading is

    name ssn address city zip information-no

Assume that "information-no" is the unique 10-digit telephone number, including area code, provided by information for each subscriber. Although subscribers may have multiple phone numbers, such alternate numbers are carried in a separate table; the current table has a unique row for each distinct subscriber. The DBA has set up the following rules about the table, reflecting design intentions for the data:

◆   No two subscribers have the same social security number.

◆   Two different subscribers can share the same information number (for example, husband and wife). They are listed separately in the SUBSCRIBERS table. However, two different subscribers with the *same name* cannot share the same address, city, and zip *and* they may not share the same information number. For example, if Diane and David Isaacs, who share the same information number, wish to both be listed as D. Isaacs, they will be asked to differentiate their two names, say by by spelling out at least one of them.

(a)• Identify all candidate keys for the SUBSCRIBERS table, based on the assumptions given above. Note that there are three such keys; one of them contains the information-no attribute and a different one contains the zip attribute.

(b)   Which of these candidate keys would you choose for a primary key? Explain why.

[2.3]   Recall that in Section 2.2, under the heading "Tables and Relations," we defined the Cartesian product: CP = CID X CNAME X CITY X DISCNT. In the paragraph just before Example 2.2.1, we pointed out that it would not make sense to have the CUSTOMERS table contain all the rows of this Cartesian product, because if any of the domains CNAME, CITY, and DISCNT contained more than one value, there would have to be at least two rows in the Cartesian product with the same CID value. Give an example to illustrate this, and explain why this implication is always true as long as any rows at all exist in CP.

[2.4] Solve in relational algebra the following queries involving the CAP database. These problems are basic and meant as a warm-up for the following exercise.

(a)• Find all (ordno, pid) pairs for orders of quantity equal to 1000 or more.

(b) Find all product names of products priced between $.50 and $1.00 inclusive.

(c)• Find all (ordno, cname) pairs for orders of dollar value less than $500. Use one join here.

(d) Find all (ordno, aname) pairs for orders in March. Use one join here.

(e)• Find all (ordno, cname, aname) triples for orders in March. Use two joins here.

(f) Find all the names of agents in New York who placed orders of individual dollar value less than $500.00.

(g)• Find all product names of products in Duluth ordered in March.

[2.5] Solve in relational algebra the following queries involving the CAP database. (These requests will be used again in the next chapter to demonstrate capabilities of the computer-based query language SQL.) NOTE: In all requests that follow, you should pose the query as a single, self-contained relational algebra expression that does not depend on any intermediate results created by means of an alias, except where absolutely necessary.

(a)• Find all (cid, aid, pid) triples for customer, agent, product combinations that are all in the same city. Nothing about orders is involved in this selection.

(b) Find all (cid, aid, pid) triples for customer, agent, product combinations that are *not* all in the same city (any two may be).

(c)• Find all (cid, aid, pid) triples for customer, agent, product combinations *no two of which* are in the same city.

(d) Get cities of agents booking an order from customer c002.

(e)• Get product names ordered by at least one customer based in Dallas through an agent based in Tokyo.

(f) Get pids of products ordered through any agent who makes at least one order for a customer in Kyoto. NOTE: The request posed here is not the same as asking for pids of products ordered by a customer in Kyoto.

(g)• Display all pairs of aids for agents who live in the same city.

(h) Find cids of customers who did not place an order through agent a03.

(i)• Find cnames of customers who have the largest discount; find those who have the smallest discount. NOTE: This is quite hard with the operations provided in relational algebra.

(j) Find cids of customers who order all products.

(k)• Find pids of products ordered through agent a03 but not through agent a06.

(l) Get pnames and pids of products that are stored in the same city as one of the agents who sold these products.

(m)•Get aids and anames of agents with aname beginning with the letter "N" who do not place orders for any product in Newark.

(n) Get cids of customers who order both product p01 and product p07.

(o)• Get names of agents who place orders for all products ordered by customer c002.

(p) Get names of agents who place orders for all products that are ordered by any customer at all. (Hint: The phrase, "any customer at all" means the same as "some customer.")

(q)• Get (cid, aid, pid) triples for customer, agent, product combinations so that *at most two* of them are in the same city.

(r) Get pids of products ordered by all customers who place any order through agent a03.

(s)• Get aids of agents who place individual orders in dollar value greater than $500.00 for customers living in Kyoto.

(t) Give all (cname, aname) pairs where the customer places an order through the agent.

[2.6] (a) Given the tables R and S in Example 2.6.3, display the table for R JOIN S.

(b)• Demonstrate why it is true (prove) that if Head(R) ∩ Head(S) = Ø (there are no columns in common), then the tables R × S and R ⋈ S are equal. Here and elsewhere in this book, two tables are said to be equal if they have the same column headings and content: the order of the rows does not change the content. Even if you do not give a mathematically perfect proof, you should be able to explain why R × S and R ⋈ S are equal here.

[2.7] • Let R and S be two relations with no attributes in common, as in 2.6. Show that

$$(R \bowtie S) \div S \text{ is equal to } R$$

[2.8] Recall that Theorem 2.8.2 shows how the expression R ⋈ S can be expressed in terms of product, selection, and projection (using assignment as well).

(a)• Show how outer join can be expressed in terms of other operations. You are allowed to use normal join, union, product, selection, and projection.

(b) Show how theta join can be expressed in terms of product, selection, and projection.

[2.9] Explain why, for any tables R, S, and T, the following formulas always hold.

(a)• $(R \bowtie S) \bowtie T = R \bowtie (S \bowtie T)$

(b) $R \bowtie S = S \bowtie R$

[2.10] Show that $R \bowtie S = R \cap S$ if and only if R and S are compatible.

NOTE: The following exercises require some mathematical training.

[2.11] •Show that for any conditions C_1, C_2 on the table R, the following queries are equivalent in meaning:

> (R where C_1) where C_2
> (R where C_2) where C_1
> (R where (C_1 and C_2))

[2.12] Prove that for any table R, attribute A of R, and value a in the domain of A, there always exists a table S_a such that the selection (R **where** A = a) can be expressed as $R \bowtie S_a$.

[2.13] •Let R, S be two compatible relations. If R and S are regarded as sets of tuples, then we can use the notation for set inclusion and write $R \subseteq S$ if every tuple of the relation R is also a tuple of the relation S. Prove that, if $R \subseteq S$, then $R \bowtie T \subseteq S \bowtie T$; also, if U and V are tables with appropriate headings, then $U \div R \supseteq U \div S$ and $R \div V \subseteq S \div V$. If C is a condition, then (R **where** C) $\subseteq$ (S **where** C).

[2.14] Let R, S be two relations, where Head(R) = H and Head(S) = K. Prove that the following equalities hold:

> $(R \bowtie S)[H] = R[H] \bowtie S[H \cap K] = R \bowtie S[H \cap K]$.

The common value of these relations is called the *semijoin* of R and S; it is denoted by $R \ltimes S$.

Note that in general $R \ltimes S$ is distinct from $S \ltimes R$. The semijoin $\ltimes$ plays an important role in distributed databases.

[2.15] Let R, S be two compatible relations and let H be a set of attributes that belongs to a common heading. Prove or disprove the following equalities:

(a) $(R \cap S)[H] = R[H] \cap S[H]$

(b)• $(R \cup S)[H] = R[H] \cup S[H]$

(c) $(R - S)[H] = R[H] - S[H]$

When you disprove one of these equalities, show that one side is included in the other.

Query Language SQL

This chapter introduces the database language known as SQL, a language that allows us to query and manipulate data on computerized relational database systems. SQL is the *lingua franca* for most database products currently available, and it is of fundamental importance for many of the concepts presented in this text.

3.1 Introduction

We begin with an overview of SQL capabilities, then we explain something about the multiple SQL standards and dialects and how we will deal with these in our presentation.

SQL Capabilities

In Chapter 2 we saw how relational algebra queries could be constructed to answer English-language requests for information about a database. In Chapter 3 we will learn how to pose comparable queries in SQL, using a form known as the *Select statement*. As we will see, the SQL Select statement offers more flexibility in a number of ways than relational algebra for posing queries. However, there is no fundamental improvement in power, nothing that couldn't be achieved in relational algebra, given a few well-considered extensions. For this reason, experience with relational algebra gives us a good idea of what can be accomplished in SQL. At the same time, SQL and relational algebra have quite different conceptual models in a number of respects, and it is hoped that the insight drawn from familiarity with the relational algebra approach will enhance your understanding of SQL capabilities.

The most important new feature you will encounter with SQL is the ability to pose queries interactively in a computerized environment. The SQL Select statement is more complicated and difficult to master than the relatively simple relational algebra, but you should never feel lost or uncertain as long as you have access to computer facilities where experimentation can clear up uncertainties about SQL use. The interactive SQL environment discussed in the current chapter allows you to type a query on a terminal screen and get an immediate answer. Such *interactive queries* are sometimes called *ad hoc queries*. (*Ad hoc* is a Latin phrase meaning "for this specific purpose.") This refers to the fact that an SQL Select statement is meant to be composed all at once on a few typewritten lines and not be dependent on any prior interaction in a user session. The feature of not being dependent on prior interaction is also known as *non-procedurality*. SQL differs in this way even from relational algebra, where a prior alias statement might be needed in order to represent a product of a table with itself. The difference between SQL and procedural languages such as Pascal or C is profound: you don't need to write a program to try out an SQL query, you just have to type the relatively short, self-contained text of the query and submit it.

Of course, an SQL query can be rather complex. In Section 3.8, after a good deal of introduction, we consider the full form of an SQL Select statement for the first time. A limited subset of this full form, known as a *Subselect,* is listed in Figure 3.1. You shouldn't feel too intimidated by the complexity of the Select statement, however. The fact that a Select statement is non-procedural means that it has a lot in common with a menu-driven application, where a user is expected to fill in some set of choices from a menu and then to press the Enter key to execute the menu choices all at once. The various clauses of the Select statement correspond to menu choices: you will occasionally need all these clauses, but you don't expect to use all of them every time you pose a query.

```
select [all|distinct] expression {, expression}
from tablename [corr_name] {, tablename [corr_name]}
[where search_condition]
[group by column {, column}]
[having search_condition]
```

Figure 3.1 General Form of a Subselect within a Select Statement

In addition to the ability to pose queries with an SQL Select statement, a relational database system must provide the means to perform a variety of other operational and housekeeping tasks. At the beginning of this chapter, we learn how to perform certain simple *data definition statements*, such as a limited version of the SQL Create Table statement that we need to create the tables in the CAP database. Housekeeping tasks of this kind are usually performed by a database administrator (DBA). We put off until Chapter 6 most other SQL statements used by a DBA for data definition purposes, such as creating views of the data, as well as more complex features of the Create Table statement required to impose integrity constraints on data updates. Investigation of the complex Select statement takes up most of the current chapter, and only in Section 3.9 do we present the other *data manipulation statements* of SQL. With these new statements we will be able to perform all needed update operations on database tables: inserting new rows into a table, deleting existing rows from the table, and changing column values in existing rows. All of Chapter 3 deals with SQL statements that can be posed by the user in the interactive environment we have described. In Chapter 4 we will consider how to write programs to execute these SQL statements and numerous others. The form of SQL that is used in programs is known as *Embedded SQL*, and is somewhat different from the interactive form.

SQL History—Standards and Dialects

The first SQL prototype was developed by IBM researchers during the 1970s. The prototype was named SEQUEL, an acronym for the words Structured English QUEry Language. The SQL language that grew out of this prototype is often thought to be an acronym for Structured Query Language and pronounced "sequel," although the acronym correspondence is denied and the pronunciation is officially "ess cue ell." Several relational database system products using SQL dialects were officially released in the early 1980s, and since that time SQL has become the international-standard database language. As SQL became the standard, a number of older languages fell into disuse when the commercial database system vendors that supported them rushed to introduce SQL dialects of their own. Notwithstanding the great similarity among most product dialects of SQL, the number of differences that do exist can be confusing to the beginner. For this reason, the current text concentrates on introducing a "standard" SQL (distilling a current target language out of a number of existing standards), and then tracks important differences from that standard in a few major database system products: **ORACLE** and **INGRES**, with a certain amount of consideration given to **DB2**. Occasional references are also made to other important products, such as **SYBASE** and **INFORMIX**. The reader who goes on to work with database systems will quite likely be using one of these.

Let us expand on the idea of an SQL standard. Several SQL "standards" are currently being referenced by database products and in course texts. The specification adopted by the American National Standards Institute (ANSI) in 1986, SQL-86, was also adopted by the International Organization for Standardization (ISO). A minor revision of SQL-86, adopted in 1989 to replace the 1986 standard, is known as SQL-89. Both of these were missing a number of important DBA capabilities, and Level 1 of SQL-86 in particular formed a sort of minimal standard—a common denominator that most relational database products were able to meet. This minimality amounted to a lack of guidance on incompatible product features, which detracted from interoperability. Because of this the X/OPEN "standard" was put forward by an open systems consortium, initially consisting of UNIX SQL vendors, to develop a common set of extensions to the ANSI/ISO standard and allow greater portability of SQL applications between products. The X/PEN standard is based on the ANSI/ISO SQL-89 standard, with differences that are well thought out and quite technical. There were a number of other standards attempts at this time, but we will ignore them for simplicity of presentation.

During the same period the ANSI and ISO committees were taking a new direction. The approach adopted was to leapfrog existing versions and provide an SQL standard to anticipate future needs, so that vendors could move forward with developing improved features without being plagued by the incompatibility problems that had arisen earlier. While this approach was under development, suggested future capabilities were assigned to two different revision lists, code-named SQL2 and SQL3. In 1992, the SQL2 version was released by ANSI/ISO, with the standard name SQL-92. There are a number of levels of compliance for SQL-92, from a level that is only a minor extension of SQL-89 to a level that most vendors will probably still be striving toward until near the end of the current decade. The SQL3 revision, with even more advanced features, is still being worked on by the standards committees. It will probably be approved sometime late in the decade.

As we can see, the SQL standard is a moving target. SQL-86 and SQL-89 are a bit limited, and the later compliance levels of SQL-92 contain a number of features that we probably won't see in commercial products for some time. Here we usually fix on the X/OPEN standard as being the most representative of current practice. In this chapter, presenting the basic interactive SQL data manipulation statements, very little difference exists among the standards in any event. However, there is a small amount of variation in syntax among the commercial database system products in areas where past standards have not defined a unique approach.

Now for a short history of the commercial products covered here. The **DB2** product is leased by IBM for use on mainframe IBM/3090 machines, and certainly the majority of development resources expended on database systems throughout the world go into applications using **DB2**. However, UNIX system database use is growing quickly. After **DB2**, the database product with the largest resource investment is probably **ORACLE**, a product famous for its portability between different platforms, but probably most prominent on IBM/PC and UNIX systems. Finally, the **INGRES** product was developed at the University of California at Berkeley on DEC VAX and UNIX systems, and because of its long university history was adopted by many computer science departments throughout the United States and elsewhere. There are many versions of each of these products, since a new released version is put out every year or so, and at present the difference from one version to the next is quite significant. We will be dealing with **DB2** release 2.3, **ORACLE** release 7 (and earlier PC-DOS release 6.3), and Commercial **INGRES** releases 6.3 and 6.4. We will not be dealing with the earlier University **INGRES**, a public-domain release that did not support SQL but instead an earlier database language known as QUEL. In general all database products are "upwards compatible," meaning that later releases may offer new features but should also support all features that were offered in earlier releases. Thus this text should be usable with later releases of all the products mentioned above.

The reader should be aware that there is still a great deal of debate on what many see as serious shortcomings in the SQL language. The "future standards" of SQL-92 and the as yet unreleased SQL3 propose to address some of these shortcomings by adding new constructs to the language. After the current state of SQL has been firmly established, we will explore some of the limits of SQL at the end of this chapter. A number of new products with an *extended relational data model,* such as Montage and UniSQL, are providing a more flexible approach that addresses some of these limits. From all this discussion of future standards and significant changes from one release to another in major commercial products, the reader will receive the impression that database systems are in a state of flux. This is very true. Although the database field has made a great deal of progress in the 40 or so years since its beginning, we are currently in a development stage that hasn't been seen in more mature scientific disciplines since the 17th century, shortly after the scientific method was first proposed. A number of important principles of current database systems will certainly remain valid, but we can also expect to see major changes in the coming years. In this text, we emphasize basic principles and point out limitations in current software practice where they exist.

3.2 Setting Up the Database

At the end of this section, Exercise 3.2.1 provides a computer assignment based on the SQL data definition statements introduced here and in Appendix A. You will be asked to create database tables to duplicate the `customers-agents-products` database (the CAP database) of Figure 2.2. Later computer assignments assume that this database exists and ask you to perform SQL data manipulation statements to retrieve and update data in these tables.

To begin, you will need to get an account on your computer system—a user ID and password to log in to the computer—and a separate account on the database system itself to enable you to enter the database system. Your instructor will tell you how to accomplish this. Once you have these accounts, the tutorials in Appendix A will instruct you in some of the fundamental product-specific skills you will need in the **ORACLE** and **INGRES** database systems. Skills include how to enter the database system from the operating system level, how to create tables or delete tables from the database, how to load data from an operating system file into an already defined table of the database, and how to deal with the database system terminal monitor. The terminal monitor is an interactive environment with a number of commands that allow you to compose SQL statements, edit them, save them to operating system files and then read them back, submit them to the database system for execution, and so on.

To create the CUSTOMERS table of the CAP database (using the lowercase table name customers we adopt to differentiate SQL from relational algebra), you would enter the terminal monitor and issue the SQL statement (in **ORACLE**):

[3.2.1] SQL > create table customers (cid char(4) not null,
          2 cname varchar(13), city varchar(20), discnt real);

Notice that after performing a carriage return on the first line, the system prints a prompt for the second line, "2". The prompt for the third line would be 3, and so on. There is no limit to the number of lines you can type. The system doesn't attempt to interpret what you have written until you end a line with a semicolon (;). A semicolon is used to terminate all SQL statements. The result of this *Create Table* statement is the creation of an empty customers table with column names cid, cname, city, and discnt. The *type* or *datatype* of each attribute (discussed as the *domain* of the attribute in Chapter 2) follows each attribute name specified. Thus cname is of type varchar(13) (a variable-length character string with a maximum of 13 characters), and discnt is of type real (the ANSI datatype for a 4-byte real number, equivalent to the C language type float). Appendix A, Section 3 contains a number of other possible datatypes that can be used in defining table columns. The *not null* clause coming after the cid column name and type means that a null value cannot occur in this column: any SQL data manipulation statement that would result in a null value in this column will fail and give a warning to the user. Recall from Section 2.4 that a null value represents an undefined or inapplicable value. But since the DBA has decided that the cid column should be a unique identifier for each row (a *key* for the table), a null value is not permitted. A number of other features of the Create Table statement can be used to guarantee additional integrity properties of the data, comparable to the **not null** clause. However, we do not need all the power of the Create Table statement until a later chapter. For the present purposes of defining the tables of the CAP database, a limited form of the Create Table command is given by

[3.2.2] ``create table`` ``tablename (colname datatype [not null]``
         ``{, colname datatype [not null]});``

    Bold terms in SQL statement forms are to be typed exactly as written; nonbold terms, such as ``tablename`` above, describe something that is named or chosen by the user. Thus every command of the form given in (3.2.2) begins with the words "create table . . . ," while the word "table-name" is not literally entered and should be filled in with a desired table name, such as "``customers``". A phrase in braces, { . . . }, may occur zero or more times. This implies that the syntax given in (3.2.2) requires a table to have one or more column names, since we see the phrase ``colname`` ``datatype [not null]`` once, and then it is repeated, with an initial separating comma, in braces. (There is actually an upper limit to the number of column names allowed, but this limit is not specified in the syntax and we can ignore it for now.) When a phrase occurs in brackets, [ ], it means that the phrase is optional. Thus we see that the phrase **not null** may or may not occur following any column name and datatype description. Look at (3.2.1) again as an example of the form specified in (3.2.2).

A Practical Exercise

If you are using the **ORACLE** or **INGRES** database products, you should at this point read Appendix A, which provides a tutorial on the skills you need to set up the CAP database. Even if you are using a different product, Appendix A will give you an idea of the skills required and the sequence of relatively standard Create Table commands you will need.

[3.2.1] Create a database, if this has not already been done for you, with *dbname* consisting of (up to) the first six characters of your login ID, suffixed by the string ". . . sql"—for example, "poneilsql". Next, create and load into your database the tables pictured in Figure 2.2—``customers``, ``agents``, ``products``, and ``orders``. You should create command procedure files with terminal monitor commands to do as much of the work as possible: for example, see the form given by "``makecusts``", in Appendix A.1 for **INGRES**, and try to replicate this for additional CAP tables, with the file names makeagents, makeprods, and makeords. You should then type in the data files to use in the copy commands—custs.in, agents.in, prods.in, and ords.in—and use these files in loading the tables. When the files have been created and loaded, use the appropriate database command to display the layout of the tables, as it is known to the database system, and then display the contents of each table with a Select statement.

3.3 Simple Select Statements

Queries are performed in SQL using the *Select* statement. The general form of the Select statement is quite complex, and we develop an explanation of the various features over the next several sections. In this section we introduce some of the most basic features of SQL queries, corresponding to the relational algebra operations of selection, projection, and product. As in the case of relational algebra, the result of a Select statement query is itself a table. We also give a brief idea of how a simple Select statement might be implemented in an *access plan,* a loop-oriented program to access the needed data of the query on a computerized database and to generate the desired solution.

EXAMPLE 3.3.1

Suppose that we wish to find the aid values and names of agents that are based in New York. In relational algebra this query can be expressed as

```
(AGENTS where city = 'New York')[aid, aname]
```

To solve the same problem in SQL, and to display the retrieved rows, we use the statement:

```
select aid, aname from agents where city = 'New York';
```

The reserved words of this statement, appearing literally in all SQL Select statements, are in **bold**. To execute this Select, the SQL interpreter starts with the table following the word **from**, performs the selection specified after the word **where**, and then extracts the projection defined by the field name(s) that follow the word **select** (we refer to this as the *target list*). Note that the table names are specified in lowercase (since they were defined that way in the Create Table command), and the constant 'New York' is enclosed in single quotes. (Double quotes can also be used in some database system products, but single quotes are always acceptable, and are part of the recommended standard.) ∎

EXAMPLE 3.3.2

In Appendix A, an example of a Select statement is given that displays all the values in every row of the `customers` table in order to check that the table load has taken place properly:

```
select * from customers;
```

The symbol "*" in the target list is a shorthand symbol meaning *retrieve all fields*. That is to say, there is no projection onto a limited set of fields in this case. Furthermore, all rows are printed in this case, since there is no selection restriction (the **where** clause is missing). ∎

The Select statement does not automatically cast out duplicate rows in the result; it is necessary to specifically request this service.

EXAMPLE 3.3.3

Retrieve all `pid` values of parts for which orders are placed. If we submit the query

```
select pid from orders;
```

the result will have a large number of duplicate `pid` values, one for each row where the corresponding `pid` appears in the `orders` table of Figure 2.2. For example, p01 will appear five times because of the appearances on rows of the `orders` table with `ordno` values 1011, 1012, 1021, 1016, 1024. In order to guarantee that each row in the result is unique, we need to give the query

```
select distinct pid from orders;
```

Note that the reserved word *distinct* actually guarantees that each *row* retrieved is unique (in comparison to other rows). Thus if we were to submit the query

```
select distinct aid, pid from orders;
```

we would only guarantee unique (`pid`, `aid`) pairs rather than unique `pid` values. Thus a01, p01 would appear only once in the result, although this pair appears on rows of the `orders` table with `ordno` values 1011, 1012, and 1016. ∎

The Select statement permits duplicate result rows when the **distinct** keyword is not used; this implies that relational RULE 3, the Unique Row RULE, is not obeyed by default. To cast out duplicate rows is extra effort, after all, and results in an actual loss of information: the fact that the `pid` value p01 occurs five times in the initial Select statement of Example 3.3.3 could conceivably be of great interest to the user.

If we intend to emphasize that all rows of a result are printed, that duplicates are *not* to be dropped, we can use the reserved word *all* before the target list to convey the opposite meaning from *distinct*:

```
select all pid from orders;
```

Since **all** is the default option, we don't need to type it except for better human understanding. Notice how this standard SQL behavior provides an alternative to relational RULE 3 of Section 2.3, since rows occurring in a result might not be unique.

Consider now a query that requires retrieval from several tables.

EXAMPLE 3.3.4

Let us specify a relational algebra expression to retrieve all customer-agent name pairs, (cname, aname), where the customer places an order through the agent. We need to involve tables CUSTOMERS, ORDERS, and AGENTS, since the cname column is in CUSTOMERS, the aname column is in AGENTS, and ORDERS keeps track of orders placed. In relational algebra we can solve this query by specifying the following expression:

```
((CUSTOMERS[cid, cname] ⋈ ORDERS) ⋈ AGENTS)[cname, aname]
```

Recall that it was important in relational algebra to project the CUSTOMERS table onto the columns [cid, cname] in order to get rid of the city column, since we didn't want to require joined rows between (CUSTOMERS ⋈ ORDERS) and AGENTS to have the same city value. Alternatively, we could use a relational algebra query involving the product operation rather than the join:

```
(((CUSTOMERS x ORDERS) x AGENTS) where CUSTOMERS.cid = ORDERS.cid
        and ORDERS.aid = AGENTS.aid)[cname, aname]
```

In this product form, we restrict rows by specifically naming the columns that must have equal values, which happens automatically in the join. Now the normal way to perform this query in SQL is

```
select distinct customers.cname, agents.aname
    from customers, orders, agents
    where customers.cid = orders.cid and orders.aid = agents.aid;
```

The syntax of the SQL Select statement is equivalent to the product form of the two relational algebra solutions above. The Select statement results in the following (conceptual) steps.

[1] Compute the product of the tables mentioned in the list that appears after the word **from** (this is known as the *from clause* of the Select statement).

[2] Apply the selection specified by the condition that follows **where** (the *where clause*).

[3] Project the resulting table on the attributes that appear in the *target list*. We see here that SQL also has the capability of using qualified attribute names, such as `customers.cid`, when more than one table is involved. However, the SQL standard says that it is not necessary that a column name be qualified in a Cartesian product retrieval such as this when the column name occurs in only one of the tables involved. Thus instead of writing

```
select distinct customers.cname, agents.aname . . .
```

in the first line above, we could have written instead

```
select distinct cname, aname . . .
```                                                                      ■

There is no natural equivalent to the join operation in the SQL Select statement.[1] It is always necessary to take the product (by naming the tables making up the product in the **from** clause) and include specific equate conditions to identify joinable column values in the **where** clause.

It is possible to write a Select statement query that performs calculations, and to print the resulting values in the target list.

EXAMPLE 3.3.5

Retrieve to the terminal screen a "table" form based on the `orders` table, with columns `ordno`, `cid`, `aid`, `pid`, and *profit*, where `profit` is calculated from `quantity` and `price` of the product sold by subtracting 60% for wholesale cost, the discount for the customer, and the percent commission for the agent.

```
select ordno, x.cid, x.aid, x.pid,
    .40*(x.qty*p.price) -.01*(c.discnt+a.percent)*(x.qty*p.price)
    from orders x, customers c, agents a, products p
    where c.cid = x.cid and a.aid = x.aid and p.pid = x.pid;
```

Note that the letters x, c, a, and p are associated with the `orders`, `customers`, `agents`, and `products` tables because they appear in the **from** clause as *correlation names*, analogous to the relational algebra aliases that would be created by writing x := `orders`, c := `customers`, a := `agents`, p := `products`. A corre-

---

[1] This is no longer true in the SQL-92 standard, in which join operations are defined. However, the join operation is still unusual in commercial products.

lation name is defined in a Select statement by following the table name with the desired correlation name, without an intervening comma. (A comma is used to indicate that a new table name follows.) A correlation name is associated with a table only within the context of the single Select statement where it is defined; therefore, the same correlation name can be defined for different purposes in different Select statements. Correlation names are used in this query to create a short form of qualification for column names. We have used qualified names in this Select statement for x.qty, p.price, c.discnt, and a.percent for ease of understanding, although qualification of these unique column names is not strictly necessary.

The target list of this query illustrates an important feature: we can calculate the value of an expression with terms that are either constants (such as .01) or values from the various columns of the current joined row (such as p.price). The standard arithmetic operators (+, −, *, /) are supported, and scalar functions can also be used, such as mod(n, b) (remainder of n when divided by b), as well as string functions such as lowercase(c). Additional details of such expressions are covered in Section 3.8; but note that there is implicit type conversion taking place, so that c.discnt (float type) adds to a.percent (integer type) to give a float type result. The value of the calculated expression does not have a well-defined column name, and different products handle the naming of the calculated column in different ways. This query results in the following answer in **INGRES**:

ordno	cid	aid	pid	COL5
1011	c001	a01	p01	120.00
1012	c001	a01	p01	120.00
1013	c002	a03	p03	210.00
1014	c003	a03	p05	300.00
1015	c003	a03	p05	300.00
1016	c006	a01	p01	170.00
1017	c001	a06	p03	150.00
1018	c001	a03	p04	138.00
1019	c001	a02	p02	48.00
1020	c006	a03	p07	198.00
1021	c004	a06	p01	135.00
1022	c001	a05	p06	200.00
1023	c001	a04	p05	120.00
1024	c006	a06	p01	140.00
1025	c001	a05	p07	200.00
1026	c002	a05	p03	184.00

Note that the correlation names x, c, a, and p, used in Example 3.3.5, are referred to by a number of names in different commercial products. The term *correlation name* is used in **DB2** as well as **INGRES**, and it appears in all help text in these products. **ORACLE** uses the term *alias* or *table alias*. The term *range variable* or *tuple variable* is also used occasionally, for reasons explained below. Nomenclature of this kind is important if the reader wants to be able to get around in the reference documentation provided by the various commercial database products. For example, in the *ORACLE SQL Language Reference Manual* [7], the terms *alias* and *table alias* are listed in the index, whereas the term *correlation name* is not to be found. The opposite is true in the *INGRES/SQL Reference Manual* [4]. The SQL-92 Standard SQL settles on the term *correlation name*, but the approved syntax for creating such correlation names has been changed. It is not clear if existing commercial products will adapt their nomenclature to comply with this.

A number of different approaches are taken by commercial database products regarding the column name used for the expression column of Example 3.3.5 representing profit, where there is no simple column name inheritance from a table. This variation among the commercial database system products results from the fact that earlier standards did not define a unique approach. The expression column in Example 3.3.4 has an automatically generated name, COL5, in **INGRES**. (The expression lies in column 5 of the target list.) In **ORACLE**, the full text of the symbolic expression would be copied and used as the column name. Furthermore, both **ORACLE** and **INGRES** allow the user to supply an ad hoc name for such a column in the Select statement. In **ORACLE** this is called a *column alias,* as differentiated from the table alias that we have already seen. In **ORACLE**, we could write

```
select . . . , expr [c_alias], . . .
```

to give a name, *c_alias*, to the column in a target list where an expression *expr* is displayed. In **INGRES**, the Select statement syntax allows the user to name an expression column with what is called a *result_column* name, using the following syntax:

```
select . . . , expr [as result_column], . . .
```

DB2 has no convention of this kind, so renaming such a calculated column is not possible. Thus in **ORACLE**, for example, we could write the query of Example 3.3.5 as

```
select distinct x.ordno, x.cid, x.aid, x.pid, .40*(x.qty*p.price)
    -.01*(c.discnt+a.percent)*(x.qty*p.price) profit /* col. alias */
    from orders x, customers c, agents a, products p
    where c.cid = x.cid and a.aid = x.aid and p.pid = x.pid;
```

to create a table with the heading

x.ordno	x.cid	x.aid	pid	profit

Note that comment text of the form /* . . . */ can be placed in any SQL statement of **INGRES** or **ORACLE** without having any effect on execution. In **DB2** (and in the SQL standard), by contrast, two consecutive hyphens (--) are used on a line to indicate that the text following the hyphens is a comment.

EXAMPLE 3.3.6

Suppose that we are asked to determine all pairs of customers based in the same city. To solve this query in relational algebra, we would start by computing the product of two copies of the CUSTOMERS table, then use an appropriate Select condition:

```
C1 := CUSTOMERS, C2 := CUSTOMERS
(C1 x C2) where C1.city = C2.city and C1.cid < C2.cid
```

We need two different names for CUSTOMERS, C1 and C2, so that columns in the product will be uniquely qualified. As we saw in Example 2.7.5, the restriction C1.cid < C2.cid allows us to drop redundant pairs of customers (two the same, or the same unequal pair twice). In SQL this query can be performed with the following Select phrase:

```
select c1.cid, c2.cid
from customers c1, customers c2
where c1.city = c2.city and c1.cid < c2.cid;
```

This is an example of an SQL query where correlation names are necessary in order to consider pairs of rows in the same table. Without such names, we would not be able to qualify the identically named columns of the product. Note that uppercase correlation names $C1$ and $C2$ are perfectly acceptable in SQL; however, we use lowercase names as a general rule. The name $C1$ is equivalent to $c1$ in the SQL standard (case is irrelevant). ∎

As mentioned in Example 3.3.4, the conceptual sequence of events to evaluate the Select statement in Example 3.3.6 is this: first the **from** clause equates tables $c1$ and $c2$ to the customers table and takes their product; then the **where** clause limits the rows of the product; and finally the values from this set of rows are projected on the target list. This gives us a correct *conceptual* view of the order of evaluation, but it would be surprising if this were the procedure actually followed by a database system in answering our query. To foreshadow an area of study known as *query optimization*, we explain a different algorithmic method, known as an *access plan*, that a database system might use to physically retrieve the data of the query. This method also illustrates a different conceptual point of view that has some value in helping us picture what is happening. We start by thinking of the correlation names $c1$ and $c2$ as they appear in the **from** clause as *range variables*; that is, variables that take on row position values in the customers table. The range variables $c1$ and $c2$ range *independently* over the rows of the customers table, as in a nested loop, and we can think of the results of the above query as being generated by the pseudo-code of Figure 3.2.

```
FOR c1 FROM ROW 1 TO LAST OF customers
    FOR c2 FROM ROW 1 TO LAST OF customers
        IF (c1.city = c2.city and c1.cid < c2.cid)
        THEN PRINT OUT TARGET-LIST VALUES: c1.cid, c2.cid
    END FOR c2
END FOR c1
```

Figure 3.2 Nested-Loop Access Plan Pseudo-Code for the Select Statement of Example 3.3.6

The values retrieved in Figure 3.2 will be identical to the ones we expect from the SQL Select statement of Example 3.3.6. This *nested-loop* algorithm generates the same pairs of rows from $c1 \times c2$ that would arise if we actually created the product of these two tables. Indeed a nested loop of this kind would be the only way we could go about generating the rows of a product table. But in the logic of Figure 3.2, instead of placing these rows in a temporary table, we short-circuit the process by performing the next conceptual phase of the Select statement and applying the selection condition of the **where** clause. As a result, the nested-loop approach is much more economical in terms of space utilization than the approach that would physically create the table product as a first step. This is an example of a principle of query optimization known as *deferred materialization,* where we put off actually materializing rows of an expression for as long as possible.

The nested-loop algorithm is only one of a number of algorithms that might be chosen as an access plan for a Select statement where a product of tables is involved. Other approaches exist—for example, to make use of *indexed lookup* efficiencies that can improve performance immensely. However, the nested-loop algorithm represents another useful conceptual viewpoint to help us understand the Select statement. We see why *range variable* is a common term for variables such as c1 and c2, representing looping variables for row positions in the nested loop; each pair of row positions corresponds to one row of the table product. Clearly, we can generalize this approach to any number of range variables defined on different or identical tables. Note that in cases where there is no alias for a named table, the table name itself may be thought of as a range variable that takes on specific row values. Consider again the query result of Example 3.3.4:

```
select distinct customers.cname, agents.aname
    from customers, orders, agents
    where customers.cid = orders.cid and orders.aid = agents.aid;
```

Here we can picture the Select statement as having three independent range variables, customers, agents, and orders. The values that arise as these three independent variables take up row positions in a triply nested loop in their respective tables are exactly the ones that would show up in a relational algebra product of the three tables. The restrictions in the **where** clause basically select the rows that would come out of a join of the three tables, except that equality in the city column between customers and agents is not requested.

EXAMPLE 3.3.7

Suppose that we need to find pid values of products that have been ordered by at least two customers. We can solve this problem using correlation names:

```
select distinct x1.pid
    from orders x1, orders x2
    where x1.pid = x2.pid and x1.cid < x2.cid;
```

The best way to think about this query is that x1 and x2 each range over the rows in the orders table (sometimes they represent the same row). The condition x1.cid < x2.cid assures us that these two rows represent orders by distinct customers, each pair once, while the condition x1.pid = x2.pid assures us that both customers are ordering the same product. We print out all products having the property that two different customers order them.   ∎

It is important in the above analysis that a product ordered by three customers, on different lines of the orders table, x, y, and z, not appear three times in the result: once for x and y, once for x and z, and once for y and z. To drop duplicate rows we need to use the reserved word **distinct** introduced in Example 3.3.3. Often the keyword **distinct** adds effort to the procedure that carries out the query. Usually the access plan requires the resulting rows to be placed in sorted order by the columns retrieved and successive rows to be tested for equivalence to avoid duplication. If the user knows that no duplication is possible, it may improve overall performance to avoid this extra effort. However, it is not always a simple matter to know when duplicates might exist in a join query and in some of the other forms that follow. We will return to this question in the exercises at the end of the chapter.

EXAMPLE 3.3.8

Get cid values of customers who order a product for which an order is also placed by agent a06. The important insight needed to frame this query is one we have encountered before in relational algebra (see Example 2.9.9). We must realize that this request is not asking for cid values of customers who place an order through a06—it is more indirect than that. See Figure 3.3, where the set of rows we wish to retrieve is contained in the circle on the far right.

3.3 Simple Select Statements

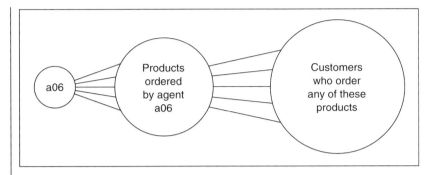

Figure 3.3 Sets of Objects and Their Connection to One Another in Example 3.3.8

First, consider the products for which an order is placed by agent a06, the set of rows contained in the middle circle of Figure 3.3.

```
select x.pid from orders x where x.aid = 'a06';
```

The set of product IDs retrieved by this query from the orders table of Figure 2.2 is {p03, p01}. Now we want to retrieve the customers who have placed an order for at least one of these products. We need to consider entirely different rows in the orders table to list such customers. For example, order number 1017 shows that 'p03' is ordered through agent 'a06', and at the same time this order row shows that customer 'c001' orders part 'p03'. However, order number 1013 shows that 'c002' also orders 'p03', although the order does not occur through agent 'a06'. We need to consider both order rows at once to show that 'c002' is in the target list for the request given above. We can put the whole thing together with the query:

```
select distinct y.cid
    from orders x, orders y
    where y.pid = x.pid and x.aid = 'a06';
```

Here we see that the customer cid 'c002' is retrieved when the range variable x corresponds to the orders row with ordno = 1017 (since x.aid = 'a06' and x.pid = 'p03') and the range variable y corresponds to the orders row with ordno = 1013 (since y.pid = x.pid and y.cid = 'c002'). This query returns the table:

cid
c001
c002
c004
c006

To review, this query form represents an extremely important concept, where two differently named range variables on the `orders` table are needed simultaneously to connect the `cid` values retrieved to the agent with `aid` a06.   ∎

In this section we have introduced a limited form of the Select statement, illustrated in Figure 3.4.

```
select [all | distinct] expression {, expression}
    from tablename [corr_name] {, tablename [corr_name]}
    [where search_condition]
```

Figure 3.4   Select Statement Syntax Introduced Through Section 3.3

The vertical line in the form [all | distinct] means that the user can choose one of the two literal terms all or distinct; the fact that this choice is contained in square brackets ([ ]) means that the entire phrase is optional, whereas the fact that all is underlined means that this is the default term that takes effect if the phrase is omitted. The search_condition object of the **where** clause turns out to be quite complex in itself, and will be the subject of discussion in a number of sections of this chapter.

3.4   Subselects

Each Select statement query results in a table, but Select statements cannot be arbitrarily nested in the way we were able to nest relational algebra expressions in Chapter 2. The most telling limitation is the requirement that a table listed in the **from** clause of a Select statement must have a tablename, as we see in the syntax of Figure 3.4, and therefore cannot itself

be the result of an ad hoc Select statement. This is an important point of
divergence from relational algebra, because it means that the Select statement, having lost some of the expressiveness of relational algebra, must
make up for it by adding power elsewhere. We find this added power in the
search_condition of the **where** clause. As we will see, Select statement nesting is permitted in a search_condition.

A Select statement appearing within another Select statement is known
as a *Subselect*. The general form of a Subselect is missing some syntax elements of a full Select statement, but it will be some time before we encounter these elements. For now we can think of the two forms as being
identical. A Subselect can appear in the search_condition of a **where** clause
for another Select statement in numerous ways. In the current section we
study a number of *predicates*, logical conditions with TRUE-FALSE values,
that allow us to perform meaningful tests on Subselects. To start with we
consider the *in predicate*, which tests membership in a set.

The In Predicate

Suppose that we wish to determine the `cid` values of customers who place
orders with agents in Duluth or Dallas. It is possible to do this in SQL
using a Cartesian product of tables, but we are concerned here with illustrating the use of the **in** predicate and the new Subselect syntax.

EXAMPLE 3.4.1
Get `cid` values of customers who place orders with agents in Duluth or Dallas.
We start by finding all agents based in Duluth or Dallas. We can do this with the
query

```
select aid from agents
    where city = 'Duluth' or city = 'Dallas';
```

This Select statement can be used to represent a *set of values* (a Subselect) in a
larger Select statement that solves the original problem:

```
select distinct cid from orders
    where aid in (select aid from agents
    where city = 'Duluth' or city = 'Dallas');
```

Conceptually, we regard the Subselect (the *inner* Select surrounded by parentheses) as returning a set of values to the *outer* Select **where** clause: "... where
`aid` in (set)". The outer Select **where** clause is considered true if the `aid` value
of the `orders` row under consideration in the outer Select is an element of the

set returned by the inner Select (the `aid` value is *in* the set). Specifically, for the database content of Figure 2.2, the set of `aid` values returned by the Subselect is a05 and a06. Then, in the outer Select, rows of the `orders` table are restricted to those whose `aid` values are members in this set, and the `cid` values for the resulting rows are printed. The solution of this query is

cid
c001
c002
c004
c006

■

Membership can be tested not only against the set provided by a Subselect but also against sets that are explicitly defined, as we see in the following example.

EXAMPLE 3.4.2

We wish to retrieve all information concerning agents based in Duluth or Dallas (very close to the Subselect in the previous example). This can be done by

```
select * from agents
    where city in ('Duluth', 'Dallas');
```

As we see, a set can be constructed from a comma-separated list of constant values enclosed in parentheses. This query returns the table

aid	aname	city	percent
a05	Otasi	Duluth	5
a06	Smith	Dallas	5

The query above has the same effect as one that uses logical "or":

```
select * from agents
    where city = 'Duluth' or city = 'Dallas';
```
■

As we see in the following example, multiple levels of Subselect nesting are allowed.

3.4 Subselects

EXAMPLE 3.4.3

Suppose we now wish to determine the names and discounts of all customers who place orders through agents in Duluth or Dallas. We use the following form:

```
select cname, discnt from customers
    where cid in (select cid from orders where aid in
        (select aid from agents where city in ('Duluth', 'Dallas')));
```

Note that the `city` column named in the innermost Subselect is unambiguously associated with the `agents` table, the most local "scope" for this column name, rather than with the `customers` table of the outermost Select. This query returns the table

cname	discnt
TipTop	10.000
Basics	12.000
ACME	8.000
ACME	0.000

∎

The Subselects considered in the examples so far deliver a set of rows to the outer Select phrase without receiving any input data. More generally, we can provide an inner Subselect with data that originates in the outer Select.

EXAMPLE 3.4.4

Suppose we need to find the names of customers who order product p05. Of course, we can solve this query using a straightforward Select statement:

```
select distinct cname from customers, orders
    where customers.cid = orders.cid and orders.pid = 'p05';
```

However, we are interested here in a solution involving a Subselect that receives data from the outer Select:

```
select cname from customers where 'p05' in
    (select pid from orders where cid = customers.cid);
```

This query returns the table

cname
TipTop
Allied

If the **distinct** keyword did not appear in the first Select statement, it would retrieve the cname value 'Allied' on two different rows. However, the second Select statement does not require a **distinct** keyword. In the exercises at the end of this chapter, you are asked to verify a number of rules that will help you to predict when a Select statement without the **distinct** keyword will produce duplicate rows.

Note that the unqualified cid reference inside the Subselect of the second Select statement above refers to the local orders table. When a Select or Subselect involves a single table, it does not require a qualified reference to a *local* column name. But since the Subselect reference to customers.cid is to a table in the outer Select, a qualifier is needed in that case. ∎

A Subselect using data from an outer Select is known as a *correlated Subselect*. Although variables from *outer* Selects can be used in *inner* Subselects, the reverse is not true. We can think of this as a kind of *scoping rule*, comparable to scope locality we see in a number of programming languages such as Pascal. In SQL, a local variable of a Subselect is undefined until the Subselect has been entered.

EXAMPLE 3.4.5

If we wanted to get the names of customers who order product p07 from agent a03, the following query form would not be legal:

```
select cname from customers
     where orders.aid = 'a03' and   ** ILLEGAL SQL SYNTAX **
     'p07' in (select pid from orders where cid = customers.cid);
```

The illegal syntax is due to the reference to orders.aid outside its proper *scope*. ∎

The general form of an **in** predicate expression so far has two alternate forms:

```
expr in (subselect) | expr in (val {, val})
```

The "expr" token stands for a character-string expression or numeric expression of the kind we saw in the target list of Example 3.3.5, most often a simple column name or constant; the "val" token stands for a constant value, such as 17 or 'Duluth'. It is important to understand that these expressions and values can only take on *simple values*. There is no way to retrieve a multi-column target list and test for inclusion.

EXAMPLE 3.4.6

Suppose we want to retrieve `ordno` values for all orders placed by customers in Duluth through agents in New York. The following subselect form will *not* work.

```
select ordno from orders
    where cid, aid in                ** ILLEGAL STANDARD SQL SYNTAX **
    (select cid, aid from customers c, agents a
    where c.city = 'Duluth' and a.city = 'New York');
```

The query fails because value pairs cannot be tested for inclusion. (Note that this form is perfectly acceptable in SQL-92, and presumably it will be acceptable in future database products.) An alternative standard SQL form that will work with current products is the following:

```
select ordno from orders where
    cid in (select cid from customers where city = 'Duluth')
    and aid in (select aid from agents where city = 'New York');   ■
```

The idea with the **in** predicate—a set of values is returned from the evaluation of the Subselect and then a test for membership is performed by the outer Select—is quite striking. It is important to realize that again this is only the *conceptual* course of events; it is frequently *not* the approach taken by the system in creating an access plan. As we will see later in this chapter, the SQL Select statement is *non-procedural*, meaning that the user stating the query is not dictating the algorithm to be used by the system in answering it. As we have already hinted, a part of the system known as the *query optimizer* performs transformations on a posed query to a number of different forms, and then it chooses the form that gives the result most efficiently. One of the exercises at the end of this chapter asks you to show that all queries so far introduced involving the use of the **in** predicate on Subselects can be transformed into an alternate form where the Subselects are replaced by a product of tables in the **from** clause. This is the sort of transformation form that may be executed.

In addition to an **in** predicate, there is also a **not in** predicate. For example, the clause

```
expr not in (Subselect)
```

is true if and only if the evaluated value of the expr is not found in the set returned by the Subselect. The **not in** predicate can also be used with the form that tests membership in a set of constant values, so the general form of this predicate now is seen in Figure 3.5, with an optional **not** preceding the **in** keyword.

```
expr [not] in (subselect) | expr [not] in (val [, val])
```

Figure 3.5 The General Form of an **in** Predicate Expression

The Quantified (Comparison) Predicate

A *quantified predicate* compares the simple value of an expression with the result of a Subselect. The general form is shown in Figure 3.6.

```
expr θ{any | all} (Subselect),
     where θ is some operator in the set {<, <=, =, <>, >, >=}
```

Figure 3.6 The General Form of a Quantified Predicate

Twelve predicates fit this general form. Given a comparison operator θ representing some operator in the set {<, <=, =, <>, >, >=}, the predicate expr θany (Subselect) is TRUE if and only if, for *at least one* element s returned by the Subselect, it is true that expr θ s; the predicate given by expr θall (Subselect) is TRUE if and only if expr θ s is true for *every one* of the elements s of the Subselect. Here are examples that illustrate two of these predicates.

EXAMPLE 3.4.7
We wish to find a i d values of agents with a minimum percent commission. This can be accomplished with the query

```
select aid from agents where percent <=all (select percent from agents);
```

The Subselect returns the set of all percent values from the agents table and
then the quantified comparison predicate **<=all** requires that the percent value
of a row selected be less than or equal to **all** rows returned by the Subselect;
therefore, the percent value for a row selected will be a minimum value of this
kind.   ∎

EXAMPLE 3.4.8
We wish to find all customers who have the same discount as that of any of the
customers in Dallas or Boston. (Note that while there are no customers in Boston in the example of Figure 2.2, the correct form of a query to answer a user
request is not dependent on the "accidental" table contents at a given
moment.) We use the query

```
select cname from customers
    where discnt =any (select discnt from customers
        where city = 'Dallas' or city = 'Boston');
```

The discnt value for a row selected must therefore be equal to at least one
discnt retrieved by the Subselect, and therefore have the same discnt as that
of some customer in Dallas or Boston. Note that the predicate **=any** *has exactly
the same effect* as the predicate **in**. This is a relatively startling fact, and we will
discuss it later in this section.   ∎

While the predicate expr **=any** (Subselect) means the same as expr **in**
(Subselect), the form expr **not in** (Subselect) is not the same as expr **<>any**
(Subselect). Instead, **not in** (Subselect) is identical to expr **<>all** (Subselect),
as the reader should verify.

All commercial products support this set of 12 quantified predicates.
The *ORACLE SQL Language Reference Manual* [7] refers to them separately as "ALL comparison operators" and "ANY comparison operators."
(There is no entry in the topic index of [7] for "quantified predicate," or
even "predicate.") *The INGRES/SQL Reference Manual* [4] refers only to
the "Any-or-All Predicate." Most other references use the term "quantified
predicate." The *DB2 SQL Reference Manual* [3] and the SQL-92 standard
[2] both permit an additional form, θsome, which has exactly the same
meaning as θany. The intention is to gradually replace use of the predicate
θany with the predicate θsome. This is done because the word "any" can
have an extremely misleading English use.

EXAMPLE 3.4.9

Get `cid` values of customers with `discnt` smaller than those of any customers who live in Duluth. If we were feeling a bit sleepy when we were given this request, we would be very likely to write the following Select statement, which does *not* have the desired effect:

```
select cid from customers
    where discnt <any    ** WRONG EFFECT **
        (select discnt from customers where city = 'Duluth');
```

Applied to the `customers` table of Figure 2.2, the Subselect above returns the set of `discnt` values {10.00, 8.00} for the two `customers` with `cid` values c001 and c004. Now by definition, a `discnt` value of 8.00 results in a TRUE value for the predicate `discnt` <any {10.00, 8.00}. This is because 8.00 < 10.00 (i.e., expr < s is true for at least one element s of the Subselect). Therefore the full Select statement will return the `cid` values {c003, c004, c006}. But this isn't what we really wanted. The request for `cid` values of customers with `discnt` less than those of **any** customers who live in Duluth could be rephrased to ask for the `cid` values of customers with `discnt` less than those of **all** customers who live in Duluth. The English meaning of the term **any** in the original phrasing was misleading. The proper Select statement to achieve our aim is

```
select cid from customers
    where discnt <all (select discnt from customers
        where city = 'Duluth');
```
∎

If we didn't have a predicate involving the word **any**, but only one using the word **some**, we would be much less likely to fall into this trap.

The Exists Predicate

The *exists predicate* tests whether the set of rows retrieved in a Subselect is non-empty. The general form is

```
[not] exists (Subselect)
```

Figure 3.7 The General Form of the Exists Predicate

The predicate **exists** (Subselect) is true if and only if the Subselect returns a non-empty set (if there *exists* an element in the set). The predicate **not exists** (Subselect) is true if and only if the returned set is empty.

EXAMPLE 3.4.10

Retrieve all customer names where the customer places an order through agent a05. The idea is to see whether an orders row exists that connects the cname with the agent

```
select c.cname from customers c
    where exists (select * from orders x
        where c.cid = x.cid and x.aid = 'a05');
```

Note that the subquery uses "*" rather than some single attribute; this is the simplest way of testing whether the result of the Subselect is empty. The customer names retrieved from the tables of Figure 2.2 are the ones associated with cid values c001 and c002, TipTop and Basics. Note that the correlation variable x in the query above is not needed, but it is included only for ease of comparison with the following alternate solution:

```
select c.cname from customers c, orders x
    where c.cid = x.cid and x.aid = 'a05';
```

This query also solves the problem posed. ■

We see that the second query form is very close to the first one, which uses the **exists** predicate. As a matter of fact, the first query form can be said to explicitly require a row x to exist in orders that connects row c in customers to the agent a05. The second query makes use of such a row, x, but doesn't say anything about it: it simply appears in the **where** clause with a reference in the search condition. A range variable that appears in the **where** clause without being used in the target list is analogous to what is called an *unbound variable* in mathematical logic. It is reasonable to ask: what circumstances must occur in such a case that will make the **where** clause TRUE? The answer, which we have been assuming intuitively all along, is that the **where** clause will be true if there *exists* a row for the unbound variable that makes the conditions true. In the case above, there must exist a row x such that c.cid = x.cid and x.aid = 'a05'. Thus the unbound variable x has the same meaning as if it were *bound* with the predicate exists(select * from orders x . . .). This whole discussion shows that the **exists** predicate, used in its positive sense, is not needed to pose queries; an unbound variable would do as well. In solutions to exercises you are urged to avoid complex forms in a Select statement, making unnecessary use of **exists**.

EXAMPLE 3.4.11

Recall Example 2.9.8, a request that required the relational algebra intersection operation to get c i d values of customers who order both products p01 and p07. The query used was

```
(O where pid = 'p01')[cid] ∩ (O where pid = 'p07')[cid]
```

It seems natural to use the **exists** predicate in the positive sense to achieve this in SQL:

```
select cid from orders x
    where pid = 'p01' and exists (select * from orders
        where cid = x.cid and pid = 'p07');
```

However, it is also possible to achieve this without a Subselect:

```
select x.cid from orders x, orders y
    where x.pid = 'p01' and x.cid = y.cid and y.pid = 'p07'    ■
```

The **not exists** predicate, on the other hand, *does* provide power that is not available without a Subselect.

EXAMPLE 3.4.12

Retrieve all customer names where the customer does *not* place an order through agent a05. This query should retrieve exactly those customer names that were not retrieved by the query resulting from Example 3.4.10. Note that simple negation of the search_condition in the second Select statement of Example 3.4.10 (implicit exists) will have the wrong effect.

```
select c.cname from customers c, orders x
    where not (c.cid = x.cid and x.aid = 'a05');   ** WRONG EFFECT **
```

What rows c in customers make the condition not (c.cid = x.cid and x.aid = 'a05') true? Consider customer c where c.cid = 'c001', and the first row x in orders where x.cid = 'c001' and x.aid = 'a01'. For these values of c and x, it is not true that x.aid = 'a05', and therefore the condition not (c.cid = x.cid and x.aid = 'a05') is true. As a result the cname value 'TipTop' will be returned, even though TipTop *does* place an order with agent a05. Because the implicit **exists** on the unbound variable x above sits outside the clause beginning with "not", the effect is to make the condition true because there **exists** an x such that "not (c.cid = x.cid and x.aid = 'a05')"; that is, there **exists** an x such that "c.cid <> x.cid OR x.aid <> 'a05' ". Both of these conditions are easy to fulfill (we found one where c.cid = x.cid but x.aid = 'a05'). What we really wanted was to return a cname when there *did not exist* an x such that (c.cid = x.cid and x.aid = 'a05'). For this, we have to be explicit about the **exists**.

```
select c.cname from customers c
    where not exists (select * from orders x
        where c.cid = x.cid and x.aid = 'a05');
```

This query solves the problem posed.   ∎

The **not exists** predicate as used in Example 3.4.12 seems to offer a new kind of power in phrasing queries. It turns out that we already had this power for many requests using the **not in** predicate and the equivalent **<>all** predicate.

EXAMPLE 3.4.13

We repeat the query of Example 3.4.12, retrieving all customer names where the customer does not place an order through agent a05, but using the two equivalent **not in** and **<>all** predicates in place of **not exists**. Here are the two queries:

```
select c.cname from customers c
    where c.cid not in (select cid from orders where aid = 'a05');
```

and

```
select c.cname from customers c
    where c.cid <>all (select cid from orders where aid = 'a05');
```

The question naturally arises whether the **not exists** predicate has any power that the **not in** and **<>all** predicates do not. This question is explored in the exercises at the end of this chapter.   ∎

The predicate **not exists** can be used to implement the difference operator from relational algebra.

EXAMPLE 3.4.14

In Example 2.9.3 we formulated a relational algebra expression for the request to find cid values of customers who do not place any order through agent a03. Recall that there were two possible solutions. The first solution only retrieved customers who had placed *some* order:

```
ORDERS[cid] − (ORDERS where aid = 'a03')[cid]
```

Corresponding to this we have the following SQL statement:

```
select distinct cid from orders x
    where not exists (select * from orders
        where cid = x.cid and aid = 'a03');
```

The table printed as a result of this query is

cid
c003

The alternative solution in Example 2.9.2 that would include customers who place *no* orders is

```
CUSTOMERS[cid] − (ORDERS where aid = 'a03')[cid]
```

We can parallel this in SQL with

```
select cid from customers c
    where not exists (select * from orders
        where cid = c.cid and aid = 'a03');
```

There is no difference between the two solutions in retrieving from the content of the database in Figure 2.2, because there are no customers who fail to place an order. ∎

In general, if R and S are two compatible tables (with $Head(R) = Head(S) = A_1 \ldots A_n$), then the difference $R - S$ can be computed by the following SQL statement:

```
select A1 . . . An from R
    where not exists (select * from S
        where S.A1 = R.A1 and . . . and S.An = R.An);
```

A Weakness of SQL: Too Many Equivalent Forms

We are now seeing one of the reasons that the SQL language is controversial: there are often a large number of different ways to pose the same query.

EXAMPLE 3.4.15

Consider the request to retrieve the city names containing customers who order product p01. There are four different major Select statement formulations:

```
select distinct city from customers where cid in
    (select cid from orders where pid = 'p01');

select distinct city from customers where cid =any
    (select cid from orders where pid = 'p01');

select distinct city from customers c where exists
    (select * from orders where cid = c.cid and pid = 'p01');

select distinct city from customers c, orders x
    where x.cid = c.cid and x.pid = 'p01';
```

In addition, there are a number of less obvious alternatives, such as

```
select distinct city from customers c where 'p01' in
    (select pid from orders where cid = c.cid)
```

■

Since the predicate **in** is identical to **=any**, it seems reasonable to ask why we need both. It might be a good idea to dispense with the predicate **in**, for example, since many people find a large number of alternate forms confusing. As a matter of fact, it is perfectly feasible to do without the **in** predicate and all the quantified (any-or-all) predicates, as long as we are left with the predicate **[not] exists**. In the early 1970s, an IBM group advocated the multiplicity of predicates as being more user-friendly than the **exists** predicate alone. This is certainly debatable. An important disadvantage of all these different forms is that it seems difficult on first encounter to mentally make an exhaustive search of the alternatives available in posing a query. A common mental trick in searching for a way to pose a new query is to say something like, "Well, I *know* I will have to join these three tables to get this answer." But now that we have Subselects, we have to worry what new power is available that we couldn't get out of a simple join. In fact some other part of the SQL language might be more powerful still: so many forms are available, a number of them yet to be discussed. To help with these problems, a complete general form for the Select statement is presented in a later section to allow you to do an exhaustive search of all the forms allowed in SQL. Furthermore, we indicate in the text and also in the exercises when a new SQL form adds additional descriptive power to the language and when it does not. Luckily, the set of concepts we need to learn is not limitless, although it might seem at first to be confusingly large.

| **3.5** | SQL Union and "FOR ALL . . ." Conditions |

In Section 3.3 we saw how the SQL Select statement is capable of implementing the relational algebra operations of projection, selection, and product. Join operations between any number of tables can also be achieved by listing the tables in the **from** clause and creating appropriate joining conditions in the **where** clause search_condition. In Section 3.4, we developed the power of the search_condition, providing a number of new predicate tests to create search_conditions involving Subselects, and adding the relational operations of difference and intersection to our bag of tricks for the Select statement. In the current section, we will see how to perform union and division. This completes the set of relational operations, so it would seem that we will be able to express any query of relational algebra in SQL form.

The Union Operator

To provide the ∪ (UNION operator) of relational algebra, SQL requires a new type of Select statement syntax. Any number of Subselects that produce compatible tables can be combined in a Select statement using a **union** operator. The general form of the Select statement now contains an operator that is not permitted in a Subselect:

```
Subselect {union [all] Subselect}
```

Figure 3.8 Select Statement General Form after Addition of the **union** Operator

The Subselect form is now limited to the former Select statement form of Figure 3.4. The keyword **all** that is optionally placed after **union** allows duplicate rows into the result if they exist in both Subselect results.

EXAMPLE 3.5.1

We wish to create a list of cities where **either** a customer **or** an agent is based. This can be accomplished by the following Select statement:

```
select city from customers
    union select city from agents;
```

It is conceivable that we would want to see the same city named twice if it fills both roles (more information is in such a result), and in that case we would use the statement

```
select city from customers
    union all select city from agents;
```
∎

The **all** keyword following **union** was not supported by **ORACLE** release 6.3, which is still the latest available version on DOS PCs, or by the X/OPEN standard. However, it is part of the Select syntax in **DB2**, **INGRES**, **ORACLE**7, and all ANSI standards, including SQL-92.

The Division Operator: SQL "FOR ALL . . ." Conditions

Suppose that we need to find the `cid` values of customers who place orders with all agents based in New York. In relational algebra this query is solved by the following expression involving division:

```
ORDERS[cid, aid] DIVIDEBY (AGENTS where city = 'New York')[aid]
```

Unfortunately, there is no equivalent DIVIDEBY operator in SQL, and we are not going to suddenly reveal a special new SQL syntax as in the case of **union**. Note too that this query cannot be posed using the quantified predicate forms <all, <=all, =all, etc., because no comparison operation is being performed involving attributes of `agents` based in New York. We are going to be forced to use an entirely new approach in SQL to perform this query, one that merits a slow and painstaking introduction because of its innate difficulty.

The approach we use is based on mathematical logic and the concept of mathematical proof. We start by asking: how would we go about proving or disproving that a specific customer row, represented by $c.cid$ for some range variable c, places orders with all agents based in New York? Clearly we could *disprove* this by finding a counterexample: an agent based in New York that does *not* take an order for $c.cid$. If we designate this agent by a.aid, we can represent this counterexample as an SQL search_condition (we label this cond1 for ease of reference, although this is not acceptable SQL syntax):

```
cond1:  a.city = 'New York' and
           not exists (select * from orders x
           where x.cid = c.cid and x.aid = a.aid)
```

This states that the agent represented by a.aid is in New York and that no row in orders connects c.cid to a.aid; that is, c.cid does not place an order with a.aid.

Now to prove that the specific customer represented by c.cid *does* place orders with all agents based in New York, we would have to come up with a condition guaranteeing that *no counterexample exists* of the kind we have just constructed. That is, we need to guarantee that there is no agent a.aid that makes cond1 TRUE. We can state this as a search_condition also, designated by cond2:

```
cond2:  not exists (select * from agents a where cond1)
```

Or writing it out in full:

```
cond2:  not exists (select * from agents a where a.city = 'New York'
           and not exists (select * from orders x
           where x.cid = c.cid and x.aid = a.aid))
```

This is a very difficult condition to grasp, so we need to think about cond2 for a moment. The logic says that there does *not* exist an agent a.aid in New York that fails to place an order for c.cid (the range variable in c.cid is still unspecified). Certainly this means that *all* agents in New York do place an order for c.cid. If you agree that cond2 has this meaning, then we are almost home, because all we need now is to retrieve all cid values that have the property of cond2. We bring this all together in the following example.

EXAMPLE 3.5.2

Get the cid values of customers who place orders with all agents based in New York. By the foregoing discussion, the answer to this request is given by

```
select cid from customers where cond2;
```

Or writing it out in full:

```
select c.cid from customers c where      /* select c.cid if...           */
    not exists (select * from agents a   /*...there is no agent a.aid     */
    where a.city = 'New York' and        /*...living in New York          */
    not exists (select * from orders x   /*...where no order row          */
    where x.cid = c.cid
        and x.aid = a.aid));             /*...connects c.cid and a.aid    */
```

This query returns the following table:

cid
c001

∎

We have nothing but sympathy for readers who are encountering this rather complex construct of symbolic logic for the first time. This is certainly the most difficult concept that exists in SQL queries. The proper way to approach it is to take an organized step-by-step approach, mastering the reason for each step until the concepts involved become second nature.

Whenever we are faced with an English-language query to retrieve some set of objects that obey a condition where the word "all" is fundamental, we proceed with the following steps.

[1] Give a name to the object considered for retrieval and consider how we would state a counterexample in English for an object considered for retrieval, where one of "all" the objects mentioned earlier fails to obey its required condition.

[2] Create a Select search_condition to reflect the logic of step 1. (Steps 1 and 2 will certainly refer to objects that are selected externally, so we need to be flexible in how we reference them, even to what tables they come from.)

[3] Create a containing search_condition, stating that no counterexample of the kind specified in step 2 exists. This will involve a **not exists** predicate.

[4] Create the final Select condition, retrieving the objects desired, with a condition reflecting step 3.

EXAMPLE 3.5.3

Get the aid values of agents in New York or Duluth who place orders for all products costing more than dollar. To proceed with step 1 above, we say that a.aid is an agent considered for retrieval (but we remain flexible about the range variable a to allow a containing table other than agents) and pose the counterexample:

"There is a product costing over a dollar that is not ordered by a.aid."

Now we state this as a search condition, step 2:

```
cond1:   p.price > 1.00 and not exists (select * from orders x
             where x.pid = p.pid and x.aid = a.aid)
```

Following step 3, we now create a condition stating that no such counterexample exists:

```
cond2:   not exists (select p.pid from products p where
             p.price > 1.00 and not exists (select * from orders x
             where x.pid = p.pid and x.aid = a.aid))
```

Finally, following step 4, we create the final Select condition. Note that, unlike Example 3.5.2, the condition reflecting step 3 is only *one* of the conditions needed for agents retrieved:

```
select a.aid from agents a
    where (a.city = 'New York' or a.city = 'Duluth')
    and not exists (select p.pid from products p
        where p.price > 1.00 and not exists (select * from orders x
            where x.pid = p.pid and x.aid = a.aid));
```

This Select statement results in the following table:

aid
a05

The condition occurring first in the above, (a.city = 'New York' or a.city = 'Duluth'), is placed in parentheses because the **and** connector has a higher precedence than the **or** connector, and natural precedence would lead to an unintended grouping: . . . where `a.city = 'New York' or (a.city = 'Duluth' and not exists . . .)`. The answer then would be

aid
a01
a04
a05

■

The sequence of steps listed typically leads to a pair of nested Subselects of the form:

```
select ... where not exists (select ... where not exists (select ... ));
```

It would have been a lot easier if the designers of SQL had included a **for all** predicate, similar to the **exists** predicate, but unfortunately they did not.[2] This means that we always need to create the equivalent predicate using other conditional operators that do exist. For readers who are familiar with mathematical logic, the approach we are taking, wherein we use the **not exists** predicate twice, is based on the following tautology:

[3.4.1] $\forall_z (\exists_y p(z, y)) \longleftrightarrow \neg\exists_z (\neg\exists_y p(z, y))$

To restate (3.4.1) in words, the following two statements are equivalent: (1) for all z, there exists a y such that the statement p(z, y) depending on z and y is true, and (2) it is false there exists a z such that no y exists with p(z, y) true. In Example 3.5.2, z is a row in the `agents` table, with `city` New York; y is a row in the `orders` table; and p(z, y) says the agent in row z is connected by the order in row y to the customer c (existing outside this Subselect part). The best way to think of the statement in (3.4.1) is that the form on the left is the **for all** predicate we wish to create and the form on the right is the nonexistence of a counterexample, as explained in Example 3.5.2. Note that there are two nested **not exists** predicates in the expression on the right of tautology (3.4.1).

---

[2] A **for all** quantifier is proposed for the far-future standard SQL3. Note that in mathematical logic, the for all operator, $\forall$, and the exists operator, $\exists$, are known as quantifiers rather than predicates. We use the term predicate to comply with current SQL conventions.

EXAMPLE 3.5.4

Find `aid` values of agents who place orders for product p01 as well as for all products costing more than a dollar. Note that the answer to this query is an empty table, given the CAP content of Figure 2.2, which was loaded into our Example database in Exercise 3.2.1. Of course we still have to create a Select statement that will act correctly if the content of the CAP database should change so that answer becomes non-empty. The query statement given is a minor variant of Example 3.5.3, where we asked for agents in New York or Duluth who place orders for all products costing more than a dollar. We can use the **for all** condition of this prior solution without change, by finding a way to specify the new first condition:

```
select a.aid from agents a where a.aid in
    (select aid from orders where pid = 'p01')
    and not exists (select p.pid from products
        where p.price > 1.00 and not exists (select * from orders x
            where x.pid = p.pid and x.aid = a.aid));
```

A somewhat more natural solution would arise from satisfying the first condition with the statement

```
select y.aid from orders y where y.pid = 'p01' and . . .
```

This simply means that the reference to the range variable "a" inside the **for all** condition needs to be altered:

```
select y.aid from orders y where y.pid = 'p01' and
    not exists (select p.pid from products p
        where p.price > 1.00 and not exists (select * from orders x
            where x.pid = p.pid and x.aid = y.aid));
```

Recall that in step 2 of our four-step procedure to create a **for all** condition, we said that the condition we create ". . . will certainly refer to objects that are selected externally, so we need to be flexible in how we reference them, even to what tables they come from." This is an example of a situation where `a.aid` must become `y.aid`.   ■

EXAMPLE 3.5.5

Suppose we are asked to find `cid` values for customers with the following property: if customer c006 orders a particular product, so does the customer under consideration. It is not immediately obvious how to create a Select statement to fill this request, and it would be even more puzzling if we were not in the middle of a section on how to pose **for all** conditions. Here we see the need to think in terms of rephrasing English-language statements. We rephrase this request to the following: find `cid` values for customers who order **all** products ordered by customer c006. We proceed as before in steps.

In step 1, above, we say that `c.cid` is a customer considered for retrieval and pose the English counterexample:

"There is a product ordered by customer c006 that is not ordered by `c.cid`."

Now we state this as a search condition, step 2. We will give the name `p.pid` to the product ordered by c006, but remain flexible:

```
cond1:  p.pid in (select pid from orders x where x.cid = 'c006')
             and not exists (select * from orders y
                 where y.pid = p.pid and y.cid = c.cid)
```

Following step 3, we now create a condition stating that no such counter-example exists:

```
cond2:  not exists (select p.pid from products p
             where p.pid in (select pid from orders x
                 where x.cid = 'c006') and
                 not exists (select * from orders y
                     where y.pid = p.pid and y.cid = c.cid))
```

Finally, following step 4, we create the final Select condition.

```
select cid from customers c
    where not exists (select p.pid from products p
        where p.pid in (select pid from orders x
        here x.cid = 'c006') and
        not exists (select * from orders y
        where y.pid = p.pid and y.cid = c.cid));
```

An obvious variant of this is

```
select cid from customers c
    where not exists (select z.pid from orders z
        where z.cid = 'c006' and
        not exists (select * from orders y
        where y.pid = z.pid and y.cid = c.cid));
```

As a result we obtain the table

cid
c001
c006

■

·After sufficient practice, it becomes possible in simple situations to write down the **for all** condition that no counterexample exists and from this immediately create the SQL statement required.

> **EXAMPLE 3.5.6**
>
> Find pid values of products supplied to all customers in Duluth. What we need to say is that there does *not* exist a customer in Duluth who fails to order the pid we want to retrieve.
>
> ```
> select pid from product p          /* Retrieve product p.pid if  */
>     where not exists
>     (select c.cid from customers c /* ... there is no customer   */
>         where c.city = 'Duluth'    /* ... in Duluth              */
>         and not exists
>         (select * from orders x    /* ... where no row in orders */
>             where x.pid = p.pid    /* ... connects p.pid         */
>             and x.cid = c.cid));   /* ... and c.cid              */
> ```

We can conclude at this point that SQL is capable of computing everything that can be computed by relational algebra. The accepted term for this is that SQL is *relationally complete*. As we will see in the next few sections, SQL goes beyond what relational algebra can do. But this is a good point to pause and work through the initial set of exercises at the end of the chapter (3.1–3.7), which reflects the Select statement features we have covered so far.

3.6 Set Functions in SQL

SQL provides five built-in functions that operate on sets of column values in tables: **count, max, min, sum,** and **avg.** With the exception of **count,** these *set functions* must operate on sets that consist of *simple values*—that is, sets of numbers or sets of character strings, rather than sets of rows with multiple column values.

EXAMPLE 3.6.1

Suppose that we wish to determine the total dollar amount of all orders. We can write

```
select sum(dollars) from orders;
```

The answer printed for our example database will be the one-entry table

sum(dollars)
9802.00

The column name used here is the one provided by **ORACLE; INGRES** and **DB2** would use the name COL1. We explained earlier (following Example 3.3.5) how a user-provided name might be possible in **ORACLE** and **INGRES**.   ■

Like many other terms in use in the database field, there is some variation in terminology concerning set functions. **INGRES** [4], the X/Open standard [11] and the SQL-92 standard [5] refer to the five *set functions;* C. J. Date, in his book on the SQL-89 ANSI standard [2], refers to *aggregate functions* (to *aggregate* means "to bring together a number of different elements into a single measure, or amount"); **ORACLE** [7] speaks of *group functions;* and the IBM product, **DB2** [3], uses the term *column functions.* You should have no difficulty being understood if you use the term *set function* in talking with people familiar with other products. Figure 3.9 describes the set functions.

Name	Argument type	Result type	Description
count	any (can be *)	numeric	count of occurrences
sum	numeric	numeric	sum of arguments
avg	numeric	numeric	average of arguments
max	char or numeric	same as arg	maximum value
min	char or numeric	same as arg	minimum value

Figure 3.9   The Set Functions in SQL

Note in particular that **max** and **min** when applied to character type arguments return the smallest and largest of the arguments in alphabetical order. Also, the **avg** of some numeric quantity over a set of values is the same as the **sum** divided by the **count** (as long as the quantities in both cases are well defined, without floating point overflow).

EXAMPLE 3.6.2

To determine the total quantity of product p03 that has been ordered, we can use the function **sum** and restrict its application to the set of rows satisfying the appropriate restriction. We give a name to the column in the table retrieved, using the **ORACLE** convention:

```
select sum(qty) TOTAL
      from orders where pid = 'p03';
```

In **INGRES**, we would change the first line above to select sum(qty) *as* TOTAL. The answer is the table consisting of a single row:

TOTAL
2400

. . . the sum of 600, 1000, and 800. ∎

The set functions should not be confused with the scalar functions, such as **abs**, **sqrt**, and **trim**, which can occur in expressions in the target list of a Select statement. These built-in scalar functions take single row values as arguments and return a single value associated with *each row*; set functions, on the other hand, combine values from a set of rows to return a value. Thus the Select statement

```
select sum(dollars) TOTAL from orders
    where pid = 'p03';
```

returns a single value, whereas the statement

```
select sqrt(dollars) ROOT from orders
    where pid = 'p03';
```

returns a column of values, *one value for each row* in the orders table, where pid = 'p03'. We provide a list of built-in functions in Section 3.8.

EXAMPLE 3.6.3

The query to find the total number of customers uses the **count** function and need not confine itself to a set of simple values. Either of the following forms is valid:

```
select count(cid)
    from customers;
```

or

```
select count(*)
    from customers;
```

The first Select statement counts the number of values that occur under the column cid: note carefully that null values in a column are not counted. The second statement counts the total number of rows of the table. The two statements give the same answer in our case, because the Create Table statement did not allow null values in the cid column of the customers table. ∎

The set functions can be required to act on *distinct* values fitting some description.

EXAMPLE 3.6.4

Get the number of cities in which customers are based. The Select statement

```
select count(distinct city)
    from customers;
```

produces the number of *distinct* cities where customers are based; once again, null values are not counted. Since two customers exist in Dallas as well as two in Duluth in the CAP database of Figure 2.2, the result of the query in this case will be three, quite different from the result of the same query without the **distinct** keyword:

```
select count(city)
    from customers;
```

The result in this second case is five. Note that the English-language request to get the number of cities in which customers are based would normally be interpreted as meaning the number of distinct cities, so the second form above is somewhat misleading. ∎

In ANSI SQL, the keyword **distinct** is required inside a **count** where a column argument is specified; if you simply want to count the number of rows, ANSI SQL says you should use the target count($\star$), and the option **distinct** is not allowed in the case of count($\star$). In X/OPEN SQL, the only form allowed for the aggregate function **count** is count($\star$), a rather severe limitation that we ignore in what follows.

Note that there is no value in using the **distinct** keyword with a **max** or **min** function, since a single value from the set is chosen without duplication in any event. Additionally, a query of the form

```
select sum(distinct dollars) from orders where . . .
```

would be an *unusual* request, insisting as it does that the dollar amounts to be added should be distinct; this is not normally a meaningful consideration in taking a **sum** or **avg**.

An important restriction is that set functions are not allowed to appear in comparisons of a **where** clause unless they are in the target list of a Subselect.

EXAMPLE 3.6.5

List the `cid` values of all customers who have a discount less than the maximum discount. The following approach is invalid:

```
select cid from customers
    where discnt < max(discnt);   ** INVALID SQL SYNTAX **
```

A rationale for this rule is that the Select statement given contains only a single range variable (with the name "`customers`") that ranges once over the rows of the table; in order for `max(discnt)` to have a meaningful value, there must have been a prior loop in which all `discnt` values of the `customers` table were considered. Providing a second disconnected loop is just not part of the Select philosophy. The user can request this information in a different way:

```
select cid from customers
    where discnt < (select max(discnt) from customers);
```

Note that two distinct range variables have the name "`customers`" here, and the Subselect is evaluated first to provide the needed value for the outer Select. The Subselect here returns only a one-element set, so we are able to use a comparison consisting of a single *less-than* (<). We could also have used the **<any** or **<all** comparison operators, since these mean the same thing for a Subselect that returns a set with one element. ■

EXAMPLE 3.6.6

Recall the query solved in Example 3.3.7 to find products ordered by at least two customers. We can now solve this problem in a way that generalizes easily to more than two customers.

```
select p.pid from products p
    where 2 <= (select count(distinct cid) from orders
        where pid = p.pid);
```

This query returns the table

pid
p01
p03
p05
p07

■

Handling Null Values

The concept of null values was introduced in Section 2.4, but we have waited for the definition of set functions before further detailing the ideas involved. A null value is a special scalar constant (meaningful in either a numeric or character string type column) that stands for a value that is undefined (inapplicable) or else one that is meaningful but unknown at the present time. As an example, when we are inserting a new row in an employees table, we might prefer to have a null value in the salary column because the salary is not yet determined; alternatively, a percent (commission) column for an employee may be null because the job category is 'librarian', and no sales commission is available for employees in this job category (thus the value is undefined, or inapplicable). The concept of null, as it is currently implemented on most commercial systems, does not differentiate between these two cases (although proposals have been made to do this).

NOTE: Some older database systems do not properly implement null values. Where a null occurs in what follows, we would expect to see in older systems a blank value for character types or a zero for numeric types; we will see that this has significant consequences.

Although we will not investigate the full syntax of SQL Insert statements for a while yet, it is appropriate to give a small foreshadowing here, to show how null values appear in a table.

EXAMPLE 3.6.7

Add a row with specified values for columns `cid`, `cname`, and `city` to the `customers` table. Recall from Figure 2.2 that a fourth column, `discnt`, is in the `customers` table, but we are assuming that this value is not known at the time that we wish to insert the new row—that is, it has not yet been negotiated.

```
insert into customers (cid, cname, city)
    values ('c007', 'Windix', 'Dallas');
```

Since the `discnt` column is not mentioned in the column names nor the values list of the Insert statement, it defaults to the null value for this row. Note that it is *not* usually possible to specify a null value literally in an Insert, although this becomes standard with SQL-92. The Select statement will always display such a null value in a row, however. ∎

A null value in a table has a number of important properties. First of all, note that the null value appearing in any normal comparison predicate makes that predicate evaluate to a special Boolean value, UNKNOWN, that is neither TRUE nor FALSE. For a row to be retrieved by a Select statement, the compound predicate in the **where** clause must evaluate to TRUE, so this UNKNOWN value has essentially the same effect as FALSE in most cases.

EXAMPLE 3.6.8

After adding the row (c007, Windix, Dallas, null) to the `customers` table in Example 3.6.7, the row will *not* be retrieved by the following Select statement.

```
select * from customers where discnt <= 10 or discnt > 10;
```

This is surprising! Although this **where** clause seems to cover all the bases, it has value UNKNOWN if the value null appears in a comparison to be less than 10, equal to 10, or greater than 10. The only way a row with null value in `discnt` can be retrieved by a predicate on `discnt` is by using the following special predicate:

```
select * from customers where discnt is null;
```

It is also possible to use the specially provided predicate, `discnt is not null`, but variants, such as `discnt = null`, are ** **ILLEGAL** ** . ∎

To reiterate this important point: if a null value appears in any normal comparison predicate, it will make that predicate evaluate to UN-KNOWN. (We will discuss more details of this special Boolean value in Section 3.8.) The only exception is the special predicate **is null.** This rule holds even in an equality predicate of the form col1 = col2, where both column values col1 and col2 in a row have null values; the predicate still evaluates to UNKNOWN. Note that no normal values, such as 0, or the empty string, represented by two single quotes in succession (''), have the property demonstrated in Example 3.6.8. A column value of the empty string will be less than 'a' (in alphabetical order), the value zero will be less than 10, and rows that are assigned genuine values will always be retrieved by some range predicate. But this is sometimes inappropriate. A new employee with a null value for salary is not necessarily a candidate for the poverty program, as would certainly be the case if the salary were 0. Another problem arises as well. If we are trying to calculate the average salary in a department, it is inappropriate to average in the new employee's salary as zero. Better to leave the employee out of consideration entirely, and this is exactly what is done with null values.

EXAMPLE 3.6.9
After inserting the row (c007, Windix, Dallas, null) to the customers table in Example 3.6.7, assume that we wish to find the average discount of all customers.

```
select avg(discnt) from customers;
```

In this SQL statement, the null value is discarded before the average is calculated. ∎

Similar considerations hold for the other set functions as well. As we mentioned in the discussion following Table 3.10, avg() = sum()/count(), so it is clear that the sum() and count() functions must also ignore null values. Here is another interesting question: what value is returned by a set function acting on an empty set of values (no relevant rows exist)? The answer depends on the function: count() returns zero for an empty set, but sum(), avg(), max(), and min() return the null value.

3.7 Groups of Rows in SQL

SQL allows Select statements to provide a kind of natural "report" function, grouping the rows of a table on the basis of commonality of values and performing set functions on the rows grouped. As an example, consider the Select statement

[3.7.1]
```
select pid, sum(qty) from orders
    group by pid;
```

The *group by* clause of the Select statement will result in a set of rows being generated as if the following loop-controlled query were being performed:

```
FOR EACH DISTINCT VALUE v OF pid IN orders;
    select pid, sum(qty) from orders where pid = v;
END FOR;
```

The result of the **group by** clause in the Select statement of (3.7.1) is the table (**INGRES** column label)

pid	COL2
p01	4800
p02	400
p03	2400
p04	600
p05	2900
p06	400
p07	1400

A set function occurring in the target list aggregates for the set of rows in each group and thus creates a single value for each group. It is important that all of the attributes named in the target list have a single atomic value, for each group of common **group by** values. For example, the following Select phrase is invalid:

```
select pid, cid, sum(qty) from orders
    group by pid;  ** INVALID SQL SYNTAX **
```

We cannot print multiple different cid values on a single line corresponding to a group of rows with the same pid value; for instance, the first group involving product p01 produces a set of cid values: {c001, c004, c006}. However, the **group by** clause of a Select statement *can* contain more than one column name. For example, we can group by two ID attributes from the $orders$ table and thus retrieve both in the target list.

EXAMPLE 3.7.1

Let us create a query to calculate the total product quantity ordered of each individual product by each individual agent. We group the table $orders$ on pid and aid, with the statement in the following **INGRES** Select statement:

```
select pid, aid, sum(qty) as TOTAL from orders
    group by pid, aid;
```

As a result of this query we obtain the following table:

pid	aid	TOTAL
p01	a01	3000
p01	a06	1800
p02	a02	400
p03	a03	1000
p03	a05	800
p03	a06	600
p04	a03	600
p05	a03	2400
p05	a04	500
p06	a05	400
p07	a03	600
p07	a05	800

■

We can select from a product of tables using the **where** clause together with the **group by** clause.

EXAMPLE 3.7.2

Print out the agent name and agent identification number, and the product name and product identification number, together with the total quantity each agent supplies of that product to customers c002 and c003.

```
select aname, a.aid, pname, p.pid, sum(qty)
    from orders x, products p, agents a
    where x.pid = p.pid and x.aid = a.aid and x.cid in
    ('c002', 'c003')
    group by a.aid, a.aname, p.pid, p.pname;
```

The default table returned by **ORACLE** for this query is

aname	aid	pname	pid	sum(qty)
Brown	a03	pencil	p05	2400
Brown	a03	razor	p03	1000
Otasi	a05	razor	p03	800

Note that since a.aname and p.pname are in the target list, it is necessary in the **group by** clause to include a.aname as well as a.aid, and p.pname as well as p.pid, in order to guarantee to the system that all columns in the target list will be single-values for each group. In fact, a.aid is a unique identifier for rows of agents and p.pid for rows of products, so including a.aname and p.pname in the group by list will not cause any further subdivision of the groups considered. However, most database systems remain unaware of this fact, and they will complain if the a.aname and p.pname columns are left out of the **group by** clause. ∎

Note that the **group by** clause is written following the **where** clause. You should conceive of the following *conceptual* order of events in evaluating a Subselect (with no **union** operation).

◆ First the Cartesian product of all tables in the **from** clause is formed.

◆ From this, rows not satisfying the **where** clause are eliminated.

◆ The remaining rows are grouped in accordance with the **group by** clause.

◆ Finally, expressions in the **target list** are evaluated.

As explained in the discussions following Examples 3.3.6 and 3.4.6, the reader is cautioned that the *conceptual* order of evaluation may be quite different from the *actual* order that a database product uses to execute a Select statement. Recall that null values are ignored in a set function and considered to fail all tests of equality and inequality, even a test that one null value is equal to another null value. However, null values in a column that is an object of a **group by** clause cause the corresponding rows to be grouped together. We will explore this further in the exercises at the end of the chapter.

If we wanted to eliminate rows from the result of a Select statement where a **group by** clause appears, for example eliminating result rows when an aggregate such as sum(qty) in the target list was too small, we could *not* do this by using a restriction in the **where** clause.

```
select pid, sum(qty) from orders    ** INVALID SQL SYNTAX **
    where sum(qty) > 1000
    group by pid;
```

For one thing, recall that a set function cannot occur in the **where** clause except in the target list of a Subselect (as illustrated in Example 3.6.5). Even more important, we have just finished saying that the **where** clause conceptually eliminates rows *before* the **group by** clause performs the grouping of the rows remaining; this means that the condition in the **where** clause cannot be aware of the aggregate quantities in the target list, since these quantities depend on the exact groups determined. To create a condition that depends on knowledge of this grouping, SQL Select statements are provided with a *new* restriction clause, known as the **having** clause, which is evaluated after the **group by**.

EXAMPLE 3.7.3
Print out all product ids and the total quantity ordered, when this quantity exceeds 1000.

```
select pid, aid, sum(qty) as TOTAL from orders
    group by pid, aid
    having sum(qty) > 1000;
```

Note that the action of the **having** clause follows the action of the **group by**, but it precedes evaluation of expressions for the target list. This query prints out the rows in the table resulting from query (3.7.1) that exceed 1000 in the right-hand column:

pid	aid	TOTAL
p01	a01	3000
p01	a06	1800
p05	a03	2400

∎

The **having** clause can only apply tests to values that are single-valued for groups in the Select statement (that is, values that could legally appear in the target list). The general form of a Subselect as it now stands is given in Figure 3.10. This is the final form; no new clauses will be defined for the Subselect, although a few new clauses are still to be specified for the full Select statement. As of now, the Select statement consists of any number of Subselects connected by **union [all]** operations, as shown in Figure 3.8.

```
select [all | distinct] expression {, expression}
from tablename [corr_name] {, tablename [corr_name]}
[where search_condition]
[group by column {, column}]
[having search_condition]
```

Figure 3.10 Subselect Statement Syntax

The **having** clause gives us yet another way of solving a problem already solved in two entirely different Select statements in Examples 3.3.7 and 3.6.6.

EXAMPLE 3.7.4
Provide pid values of all products purchased by at least two customers.

```
select pid from orders
    group by pid
    having count(distinct cid) >= 2;
```

It feels risky to even mention `cid` in the above Select statement since the `cid` column is not single-valued in grouping by `pid` value: the **having** clause needs to apply to values that could appear in the target list, and these values must therefore be single-valued in the group. However, the set function value **count**(`cid`) *is* single-valued by `pid` within the **group by**, and since it could appear in the target list it can also appear in the **having** clause. This results in the following table:

pid
p01
p03
p05
p07

∎

Note that we would normally not use the **having** clause unless a **group by** clause was present—if the **group by** clause is omitted then the **having** clause applies to the entire result as a single group. Thus in Example 3.7.4, if "`group by pid`" was missing but the **having** clause was still there, nothing would be printed unless there were at least two values for `cid` in the `orders` table.

3.8 | A Complete Description of SQL Select

The full general form of the Select statement is given in Figure 3.11, and we define new syntactic elements in the paragraphs that follow. At the end of this section, the reader should feel confident that no new SQL syntax remains to be introduced.

```
Subselect General Form
    select [all|distinct] expression {, expression}
    from tablename [corr_name] {, tablename [corr_name]}
    [where search_condition]
    [group by column {, column}]
    [having search_condition]
```

Full Select General Form
```
    Subselect
    {union [all] Subselect}
    [order by result_column [asc|desc]
        {, result_column [asc|desc]}]
```

Figure 3.11 Full Select Statement Syntax

As we see in this general form, the **union** and **order by** clauses are not allowed to appear in Subselect statements. The **order by** clause is new, and it allows us to place rows of the final answer in order by one or more result_column values appearing in the target list. When more than one result_column is specified, the rows are ordered first by the initial result_column, and a later result_column appearing in position j+1 of the **order by** sequence is taken into account only to order rows that are identical in the first j result_columns specified. Note that a result_column from the target list can be specified in the **order by** clause by one of the column numbers 1 through n, where n columns occur in the target list. This is because there are occasions when result columns have no valid names, as when an expression is evaluated. Another occasion occurs when Select is a union of a number of different Subselects, since we cannot assume that corresponding columns have the same qualified names in all cases. Note that in the [asc|desc] choice (ascending order or descending order), **asc** is the default and means that smaller values come earlier as rows of the answer table. Note that when null values appear in a column that is the object of an **order by** clause, the corresponding rows of output are placed in the same collating position, either larger ("high") or smaller ("low") than all non-null values in the column. The precise collating position for nulls is product dependent, since the various standards do not specify: in **ORACLE** and **DB2**, null values sort "high," in **INGRES** null values sort "low."

In the general form of Figure 3.11, **union** comes before **order by**, and the order of clauses in the Select statement is meant to carry over to the conceptual order of evaluation, as we see in Figure 3.12. The new steps in this conceptual order are perfectly reasonable, since evaluation of the **order by** clause to place resulting rows in sequence by column values is clearly a final step before display. The reader is once again reminded that the conceptual order of evaluation may be quite different from the actual order chosen by a query optimizer.

- ◆ First the Cartesian product of all tables in the **from** clause is formed.
- ◆ From this, rows not satisfying the **where** condition are eliminated.
- ◆ The remaining rows are grouped in accordance with the **group by** clause.
- ◆ Groups not satisfying the **having** clause are then eliminated.
- ◆ The expressions of the **select** clause target list are evaluated.
- ◆ If the key word **distinct** is present, duplicate rows are now eliminated.
- ◆ The **union** is taken after each Subselect is evaluated.
- ◆ Finally, the set of all selected rows is sorted if an **order by** is present.

Figure 3.12 Conceptual Order of Evaluation of a Select Statement

EXAMPLE 3.8.1

List all customers, agents, and the dollar sales for pairs of customers and agents, and order the result from largest to smallest sales totals. Retain only those pairs for which the dollar amount is at least equal to 900.00.

```
select c.cname, c.cid, a.aname, a.aid, sum(o.dollars)
    from customers c, orders o, agents a
    where c.cid = o.cid and o.aid = a.aid
    group by c.cname, c.cid, a.aname, a.aid
    having sum(o.dollars) >= 900.00
    order by 5 desc;
```

This query returns the following table:

cname	cid	aname	aid	sum(o.dollars)
Allied	c003	Brown	a03	2208.00
TipTop	c001	Otasi	a05	1440.00
TipTop	c001	Smith	a01	900.00

Note the syntax at the end: "... order by 5 desc". The **desc** keyword was used because we wished to order the results with the largest sales totals first, and the result column was given numerically because the fifth column of the target list has no name. Note that an **order by** form such as "... order by sum(o.dollars)" would not work in the Select statement above. The result_columns in the **order by** clause must be given in terms of the target list. ■

We have reached a good point to define more precisely the basic syntax objects that are combined to make up a search_condition. Much of what follows is a review of concepts we have already covered, but from a somewhat more rigorous standpoint.

Expressions, Predicates, and the search_condition

The search_condition is the condition used in the **where** clause to eliminate rows and in the **having** clause to eliminate groups: rows are retained in step 2 and groups in step 4 of Figure 3.12 exactly when the corresponding search_condition evaluates to TRUE.

We start by describing the syntax object known as an *expression (expr)*; that is, either an arithmetic or a character expression. **expr ::= aexpr | cexpr.** An expression occurs in a search_condition—for example, in comparing an attribute value (of a row) to a constant: x.dollars > 100: both x.dollars and 100 are simple expressions. Note that expressions defined below can also appear in the *target list* of a Select statement. An *aexpr* is an arithmetic expression, made up of constants, table attributes, arithmetic operators, built-in arithmetic functions, and set functions. A recursive definition is given in Figure 3.13.

aexpr	Examples
constant	6, 7.00
columname	dollars, price, percent
qualifier.columname	orders.dollars, p.price
aexpr arith_op aexpr	7.00 + p.price
(aexpr)	(7.00 + p.price)
function(aexpr)	sqrt(7.00 + p.price)
set_function(aexpr)	sum(p.price)

Figure 3.13a   Recursive Definition of an Arithmetic Expression (**aexpr**)

Next a character expression, *cexpr*, is defined in much the same way:

cexpr	Examples
constant	'Boston', 'TipTop'
columname	cid, aname
qualifier.columname	orders.cid, a.city
cexpr op cexpr	o.cid + 'Boston' (concatenate two strings with +)
(cexpr)	(o.cid + 'Boston')
function(cexpr)	right(o.cid+'Boston', 4) (= 'ston')
set_function(cexpr)	max(o.cid), count(distinct city)

Figure 3.13b   Recursive Definition of Character Expression (**cexpr**)

Functions that apply to arithmetic and character arguments, sometimes known as *scalar functions* to differentiate them from set functions, are not yet standardized: they are product specific. A list of functions that is common to **ORACLE** ([8], indexed under *Functions, number* and *Functions, character*) and **INGRES** ([4], indexed under *Functions, numeric* and *Functions, string*) is given in Figure 3.14.

Name	Description	Result datatype
abs(n)	Absolute value of n, n a numeric datatype	All numeric types
mod(n, b)	Remainder of n after division by b, n and b integers	Integer
sqrt(n)	Square root of n, n integer or float	Float

Figure 3.14   Arithmetic Functions in **ORACLE** and **INGRES**

In addition to these, **INGRES** has trigonometric functions, and **ORACLE** has ceil(n), and floor(n), as well as power(m, e). Character functions in **INGRES** and **ORACLE** have different names to accomplish most of the same functions. Figure 3.15 lists character functions in **ORACLE**.

Name	Description	Result datatype
instr(str1,str2[,n[,m]])	Position of m–th occurrence of string str2 in str1, search starts at position n; unspecified m, n are 1	Integer
length(str)	Length of string (number of characters) returned	Integer
lower(str)	Returns string with alphabetic chars in lowercase	Character
substr(str,m [,n])	Returns string from char m to end [or for length n]	Character
upper(str)	Returns string with alphabetic chars in uppercase	Character

Figure 3.15   Character Functions in **ORACLE**

INGRES implements **ORACLE's** character function upper( ) with uppercase( ); lower( ) with lowercase( ); substr(str,m,n) with left(right(str,m),n); instr(str1,str2,1,1) with locate(str1,str2); and length( ) by a function with the same name.

The SQL standard has seven kinds of *predicates*, the simplest forms of logical statements. These predicates take on values TRUE (T), FALSE (F), or UNKNOWN (U) when evaluated in the **where** or **having** clause. We will explain the motivation for the UNKNOWN value shortly.

Predicate	Form	Example
comparison predicate	expr1 θ (expr2|Subselect)	`p.price > (Subselect)`
between predicate	expr1 [**not**] **between** expr2 and expr3	`c.discnt between 10.0 and 12.0`
quantified predicate	expr θ[**all**|**any**] (Subselect)	`c.discnt >=all (Subselect)`
in predicate	expr [**not**] **in** (Subselect)	`pid in (select pid from orders)`
	expr [**not**] **in** (val {, val})	`city in ('New York', 'Duluth')`
exists predicate	[**not**] **exists** (Subselect)	`exists (select * . . .)`
is null predicate	columnname is [**not**] **null**	`c.discnt is null`
like predicate	columnname [**not**] **like** 'pattern'	`cname like 'A%'`

Figure 3.16 Predicates of Standard SQL (Valid for All Products)

We have encountered most of these predicates before; the new ones are explained below. Given these predicates, we can define a search_condition recursively as shown in Figure 3.17.

search_condition	Example
predicate	`o.pid='p01', exists (Subselect)`
(search condition)	`(o.pid='p01')`
not search_condition	`not exists (Subselect)`
search_condition **and** search_condition	`not (o.pid='p01') and o.cid='c001'`
search_condition **or** search_condition	`not (o.pid='p01') or o.cid='c001'`

Figure 3.17 Recursive Definition of search_condition

We have now described all the predicates in SQL and the logical search_condition that uses predicates as building blocks. When we have completely explained the meaning of these predicates, the reader should be able to create any possible search_condition.

A Discussion of the Predicates

Comparison Predicate

A comparison predicate takes the form

```
expr1 θ (expr2 | Subselect)
```

where θ is one of set {=, <>, >, >=, <, <=}. Note that in most database system products the q value for *not equal to* (<>) may also be indicated by (!=) or (^=). The Subselect on the right is only permitted provided that the resulting table is known to either contain a single value or be an empty set.

EXAMPLE 3.8.2

Recall Example 3.6.5, in which we listed the `cid` values of all customers with a discount less than the maximum discount. We were able to use the query

```
select cid from customers
    where discnt < (select max(discnt) from customers);
```

because we knew that the Subselect retrieved only a single value. We could just as easily have used the predicates **<any** or **<all**.   ∎

If the result of the Subselect on the right of a comparison predicate is an empty set, the comparison predicate of the form "expr1 θ (Subselect)" evaluates to UNKNOWN (U). An UNKNOWN result also occurs if either side of a comparison predicate has a null value, as we saw in the Select statement of Example 3.6.8:

```
select * from customers where discnt <= 10 or discnt > 10;
```

where a row in the customers table had a null value for `discnt`. The motivation for this UNKNOWN Boolean value is explained in the next section.

Truth Values: TRUE (T), FALSE (F), and UNKNOWN (U)

A predicate can evaluate to the truth value UNKNOWN for a specific row being qualified in a **where** clause (or a group in a **having** clause, but we will assume a **where** clause in what follows). What this basically means is that a null value or an empty Subselect has occurred in evaluating some row, so that if this predicate were the entire search_condition, the person posing

the query would probably *not* want this row retrieved. For example, if we
had a Select statement with the search condition

```
select * from customers where discnt < (Subselect);
```

and the Subselect retrieved an empty set, or only a single null value, we
probably wouldn't want to retrieve any rows. Since a search_condition
must evaluate to TRUE for a row to be retrieved, a new truth value called
UNKNOWN is equivalent to FALSE for this purpose.

However, UNKNOWN may not be equivalent to FALSE in all situations. Consider a search_condition that contains a predicate with
UNKNOWN value in logical combination. For example, consider what we
should do if we changed the Select just mentioned to

```
select * from customers where not (discnt < (Subselect));
```

and the predicate "discnt < (Subselect)" still had an UNKNOWN
result. We think of "not (discnt < (Subselect))" as having equivalent meaning to "discnt >= (Subselect)", which should certainly evaluate to UNKNOWN again if "discnt < (Subselect)" does. But this
explains why we need the UNKNOWN truth value, because if we had said
earlier that the predicate "discnt < (Subselect)" evaluated to FALSE
when the Subselect returned an empty set, then by normal rules of logic,
"not (discnt < (Subselect))" would evaluate to TRUE! This is not
the sort of behavior we want, so a new truth value UNKNOWN has been
invented with the property that not(UNKNOWN) = UNKNOWN. In Figure 3.18, we present the complete rules of operation for the three operators,
TRUE (T), FALSE (F), and UNKNOWN (U), under logical operations.

AND	T	F	U
T	T	F	U
F	F	F	F
U	U	F	U

OR	T	F	U
T	T	T	T
F	T	F	U
U	T	U	U

NOT	
T	F
F	T
U	U

Figure 3.18 The Behavior of UNKNOWN Truth Values under Logical
Operations

In the current section, we indicate the situations where UNKNOWN truth values arise during the evaluation of the various predicates. This has rather surprising effects in certain Select statements, and we explore these effects in the exercises at the end of the chapter.

The Between Predicate

A **between** predicate tests whether a value is within a range specified by two other values. It has the form

```
expr1 [not] between expr2 and expr3
```

The meaning (leaving out the **not**) is exactly as if we had written

```
expr2 <= expr1 and expr1 <= expr3
```

When the keyword **not** is included, the resulting predicate is true when the initial value is not in the range specified. The initial reason for providing this form was that an expression using the **between** predicate was more efficiently evaluated than the equivalent **and** of two comparison predicates. This is no longer true with all products, but it should be assumed for performance reasons whenever a restrictive range with two endpoints must be asserted and the question of portability from one product to another arises.

Quantified (Comparison) Predicate

The meaning of the quantified predicate, with form

```
expr θ[all|any] (Subselect)
```

was covered in Section 3.4.2, but we still have to define special UNKNOWN evaluations.

The result of "expr θ**all** (Subselect)" is FALSE if and only if the comparison is FALSE for at least one value returned by the subselect. Taking this definition to a logical conclusion, this means that the predicate evaluates to TRUE if and only if the comparison θ is TRUE for all values retrieved *or the Subselect results in an empty set*. However, if the expr value on the left or if one of the values returned by the Subselect is null, the result is UNKNOWN.

The result of "expr θ**any** (Subselect)" is TRUE if the comparison θ is TRUE for at least one value retrieved; the result is FALSE if the Subselect results in an empty set or the comparison is FALSE for every value returned. However, if the expr value on the left is null, or if one of the values returned by the Subselect is null with comparisons for all other returned values being FALSE, the result is UNKNOWN.

Let us illustrate, for example, why "expr θ**all** (Subselect)" should be TRUE if the Subselect results in an empty set.

EXAMPLE 3.8.3

Retrieve the maximum discount of all customers. Clearly we could answer this with the following query:

```
select max(discnt) from customers;
```

but we want to illustrate a point about the θ**all** predicate, and so use the query

```
select distinct discnt from customers c
    where discnt >=all (select discnt from customers d
        where d.cid <> c.cid);
```

In words, we are retrieving the `discnt` value for a row (on the left) that is greater than or equal to all `discnt` values for customer rows different from the original row (a correlated Subselect). If there is only a single customer row, the Subselect retrieves an empty set. Clearly we want to retrieve the single `discnt` value since it is maximum, but that means that the predicate of the search condition should be true for a Subselect retrieving an empty set.   ∎

The In Predicate

The **in** predicate has the form

```
expr [not] in {(Subselect)|(val {, val})}
```

Its use was covered in Section 3.4. The **in** predicate has identical behavior to that of the predicate **=any**.

The Exists Predicate

The **exists** predicate has the form

```
[not] exists (Subselect)
```

It evaluates to TRUE exactly when the Subselect does not result in an empty set. The use of this predicate was covered in Section 3.4.3, and there are no conditions under which this predicate evaluates to UNKNOWN.

The Is Null Predicate

The **is null** predicate, introduced in Example 3.6.8, has the form

```
columname is [not] null
```

There are no conditions under which this predicate evaluates to UNKNOWN.

The Like Predicate

The **like** predicate is new. The general form is given by

```
columname [not] like 'pattern'
```

The element represented by 'pattern' is a quoted string of normal and special characters that forms a template for character string values fitting a certain description. The special characters used in a 'pattern' are the following:

Character	Meaning
Underscore (_)	Wildcard for any single character
Percent (%)	Wildcard for any sequence of zero or more characters
Escape character	Precedes quoted literal character (explained below)
All other characters	Represent themselves

EXAMPLE 3.8.4

Retrieve all data about customers whose cname begins with the letter 'A'. We write

```
select * from customers where cname like 'A%';
```

This returns the table

cid	cname	city	discnt
c003	Allied	Dallas	8.00
c004	ACME	Duluth	8.00
c006	ACME	Kyoto	0.00

■

The convention by which the special pattern characters % and _ are quoted literally in a 'pattern' differs between different products. **DB2** and **INGRES** both use an escape character approach; preceding one of the pattern characters by an escape character means that the pattern character should be taken literally. Then the escape character itself needs an escape to be taken literally, so that two escape characters in a row have a literal value. **DB2** has the escape character plus (+) and **INGRES** has backslash (\). Thus in **DB2**

◆   '+%'   is a pattern consisting of a percent sign.
◆   '++%'   is a pattern starting with a plus, then zero or more characters.
◆   '+++%'   is a pattern consisting of a literal plus, then a literal percent sign.

We have the analogous case in **INGRES** with the patterns '\%', '\\%', '\\\%'. In **ORACLE**, it is necessary to use a special TRANSLATE function to create a pattern with a % or _ character.

EXAMPLE 3.8.5
Retrieve `cid` values of customers whose `cname` does *not* have a third letter equal to '%'. We use the **INGRES** option

```
select cid from customers where cname not like '_ _\%%';
```

Note that the final percent sign allows a trailing sequence of zero or more arbitrary characters.   ■

In the form of the **like** predicate, if the columname on the left takes on a null value, the result for the row in question is UNKNOWN.

3.9 Insert, Update, and Delete Statements

The three SQL statements—Insert, Update, and Delete—are used to perform data modifications to existing tables. The Insert statement acts to insert new rows into a table, the Update statement acts to change information in existing rows, and the Delete statement acts to delete rows that exist in a table. These three statements are often referred to collectively as *update statements*, since they all serve to update tables. There is some risk of confusion here, because the Update statement is the specific name of one of these three statements, and we need to take care to differentiate the two whenever confusion may result. For example, it should be clear that the *Update statement* is only one of the set of *update statements*. To perform an update statement on a given table, the current user must be the user who created the table or else have been granted *update privilege* on the table. We will cover the process of granting privileges in a later chapter.

The Insert Statement

The *Insert statement* in SQL acts to insert new rows into an existing table. It has the general form

```
insert into tablename [(column {, column})]
[values (expression {, expression})] | [Subselect]
```

The Insert statement inserts new rows into the specified table. One of two forms must be used (symbolized by the "or bar", "|"): either the **values** form, where a single row is inserted with specified values, or the Subselect form, where all rows that result from evaluating the Subselect (possibly involving a number of different tables) are inserted.

> **EXAMPLE 3.9.1**
> Add a row with specified values to the orders table.
>
> ```
> insert into orders (ordno, month, cid, aid, pid)
>     values (1107, 'aug', 'c006', 'a04', 'p01');
> ```
>
> The values for qty and dollars are not known at the time of insert, so they are not mentioned in the column names nor in the values list and will default to null. ∎

EXAMPLE 3.9.2

Create a new table called swcusts of southwestern customers, and insert into it
all customers from Dallas and Austin.

```
create table swcusts (cid char(4) not null, cname varchar(13),
    city varchar(20), discnt float4); /* same as customers */

insert into swcusts
    select * from customers
        where city in ('Dallas', 'Austin');                    ∎
```

This example shows how the specific columns to receive values need
not be named in the Insert statement. Omitting the column names is equivalent to specifying all the columns in the table in the same order as they
were defined in the Create Table statement. When the columns are named
specifically, as in Example 3.9.1, they need not appear in that order. Note
that in the Insert statement of Example 3.9.2, it is a *mistake* to surround
the Subselect following the tablename swcusts with parentheses.

The ability to use a Subselect to create input to an Insert statement
adds a great deal of power. Only one table receives new rows in an Insert
statement, but the Subselect can be on any number of tables, as long as it
produces the right number of columns of the right type to serve as new
rows to be inserted.

The Update Statement

The SQL Update statement acts to change information in existing rows of
a table. It has the general form

```
update tablename [corr_name]
    set column = {expression|null} {, column = {expression|null}}
        [where search_condition];
```

The Update statement replaces the values of the specified columns with the
values of the specified expressions for all rows of the table that satisfy the
search_condition. The expressions used above can reference only column
values on the specific row of the table currently being updated. Thus, for
example, set functions cannot be used.

EXAMPLE 3.9.3

Give all agents in New York a 10% raise in the percent commission they earn on an order.

```
update agents set percent = 1.1 * percent where city = 'New York'; ∎
```

The way to take values from other tables into account in deciding what columns are to be updated is to use a Subselect in the search_condition.

EXAMPLE 3.9.4

Give all customers who have total orders of more than $1000 a 10% increase in the discnt they receive.

```
update customers set discnt = 1.1 * discnt where cid in
    (select cid from orders group by cid having sum(dollars) > 1000);
```
∎

Note that only one table can be the object of the Update statement. Some database systems do not accept qualified attributes in the **set** clause:

```
update agents set agents.percent = 1.1 * ...    ** MAY BE INVALID **
```

The most serious limitation of the Update statement is that we cannot derive the values to put in place in the updated table by reference to other tables, as we could in the Insert statement. For example, we cannot update the discnt values in rows of the swcusts table created in Example 3.9.2 with more up-to-date discnt values by using the statement

```
update swcusts set discnt = c.discnt    ** INVALID SQL SYNTAX **
    where exists (select * from customers c
        where c.cid = swcusts.cid );
```

This isn't legal because the c.discnt qualification outside the Subselect is not in its proper scope. There is simply no way for a value from another table to be inserted into swcusts by a standard SQL Update statement. However, the **INGRES** product permits a somewhat extended syntax for the Update statement that addresses this problem.

INGRES SQL Update statement syntax

```
update tablename [corr_name]
    [from tablename [corr_name] {, tablename [corr_name]}]
     set column = (expression|null) {, column = (expression|null)}
    [where search_condition];
```

In this syntax the **from** clause allows more tables to enter the statement, so that the expressions in the **set** clause can contain references to column values in those tables (including set functions). The search_condition in the **where** clause can specify correspondences between the row of the table being updated and rows of tables named in the **from** clause.

The Delete Statement

The SQL Delete statement removes existing rows from a table. It has the general form

```
delete from tablename [corr_name]
    [where search_condition];
```

EXAMPLE 3.9.5
Delete all agents in New York.

```
delete from agents where city = 'New York';
```
■

Once again, the search condition can contain Subselects, allowing us to use data from other tables to decide what rows to delete.

EXAMPLE 3.9.6
Delete all agents who have total orders of less than $600.

```
delete from agents where aid in
    (select aid from orders group by aid having sum(dollars) < 600);
```
■

3.10   The Power of the Select Statement

A *procedural language* is one in which a program is written as an ordered sequence of instructions to accomplish some task. The order of statements is important because we can think of an earlier statement of a program having a long-term effect that is a precondition to the correct execution of a later statement. For example, if we wish to create a loop to sum a sequence of input variable values V, we might start by setting SUM = 0, then incrementally increase the sum with the statement SUM = SUM + V as the loop progresses. It is clearly important, for example, that we start with the statement SUM = 0, rather than executing this statement somewhere in the middle of the loop. The necessity to use a number of statements in a particular order to achieve a correct result can be thought of as demonstrating the *procedurality* of the language.

A *non-procedural language,* by contrast, is one where a desired end is described all at once! This means that we must specify *what* is desired rather than *how* it is to be achieved, with no implied ordering of effects for a programmer to keep track of. A perfect example of this kind of non-procedural language is an interface consisting of a terminal menu, where a user chooses a number of options to accomplish some task (with no order to the selection) and then presses the Execute key. Some of the early writers advocating the relational model held up non-procedurality as an extremely valuable goal. Database languages before that time usually required a kind of navigation to go from one piece of data to another. As a simple example, consider the program we just mentioned to sum a sequence of input values V. If we think of these values as existing in a file, then as we perform a loop to take the sum we are keeping a kind of cursor while we navigate through the data from beginning to end—we know which values have been summed so far and which have not—and so there is a preexisting context for each program statement. The advocates of the relational model pointed out that many potential database users (such as financial specialists, real estate agents, and lawyers) might find it beyond their abilities to write program loops to acquire information. If the information they required was not provided by some program that had been prewritten for their needs then they would be out of luck, and it seemed likely that many queries that they might want to perform could not be foreseen in advance. These were ad hoc queries, meaning that they arose from spur-of-the-moment needs, and could not be anticipated with a program written in advance.

The stated goal was to provide a query language to handle ad hoc needs, offering the user the capability of asking a single question about the data. This single question might be rather complex, but even so the language should avoid procedural complexities that would require a programmer. It was pointed out that the study of symbolic logic seemed relevant to this goal of designing a database language, and, as we mentioned in Chapter 2, it was shown by E. F. Codd that the relational algebra had all the power of a language based on a type of symbolic logic known as the *first-order predicate calculus*. From this result, a number of issues were raised in fixing on a standard database language. One issue is the question of just how non-procedural the language is—no complex language can be perfect in this regard, but some are better than others. A second issue is how much *power* the language has. Based on Codd's result, a language with the power of relational algebra was defined to be *complete* or *relationally complete*, and the implication was that this was an important milestone. However, we will describe a number of capabilities that are missing from the relationally complete language SQL, and there is an indication that a non-procedural approach may actually detract from the available power.

The Non-Procedural Select Statement

Let us start by examining the relative non-procedurality of two languages.

> **EXAMPLE 3.10.1**
> Recall the relational algebra query derived in Example 2.7.12, to retrieve the names of customers who order products costing $0.50:
>
>   ((ORDER ⋈ (PRODUCTS where price = 0.50)[pid])) ⋈ CUSTOMERS)[cname]
>
> ■

This query is accomplished in one statement, and thus it seems to have an important non-procedural advantage over using the assignment statement (:=) to hold intermediate results. However, this advantage is somewhat of an illusion. There *is* an important aspect of procedurality in this expression, since sub-expressions in parentheses must be evaluated first, and even in sub-expressions with no parentheses the precedence rules of Figure 2.7 place an order on the evaluation. Furthermore, the user clearly *intends* this order of evaluation. For example, it is necessary that (PRODUCTS where price = 0.50) should be projected on [pid] before the later join with CUSTOMERS, because we do not wish to require equal city values.

Now there are a number of equivalence rules in relational algebra, such as commutativity and associativity, that allow us to pass from one expression to another equivalent form. Thus the precise parenthetical form of a given relational algebra query will not necessarily keep a query optimizer from finding a more efficient variant form. However, there can be no question that the expression in Example 3.10.1 implies a precise order of evaluation, and the query optimizer will find it difficult to take a higher-level view of how to achieve its objective efficiently as long as the query is stated in parenthesized form. There is little difference between an expression with nested parentheses and a sequence of statements, with intermediate results created using the assignment statement. In other words, the relational algebra is quite procedural. Consider the difference between this and the SQL equivalent.

> **EXAMPLE 3.10.2**
>
> Here is the analogous SQL statement to retrieve the names of customers who order products costing $0.50:
>
> ```
> select cname from customers c, orders x, products p
>     where c.cid = x.cid and x.pid = p.pid and p.price = 0.50;
> ```
> ∎

If you recall the conceptual order of evaluation given in Figure 3.12 (at the beginning of Section 3.8), the Select statement of this example can be thought of as acting in the following way: first the relational product is formed of the `customers`, `orders`, and `products` tables named in the **from** clause, then rows not satisfying the **where** search_condition are eliminated, and finally expressions in the target list (simple `cname` values) are evaluated and output as the answer. Of course, this conceptual order is just a way of thinking of what will happen, and not necessarily the way a database query optimizer will actually decide to go about performing it. For example, as we mentioned earlier, it is almost certainly not appropriate for the computerized access strategy to start by creating a new table that is the product of the three tables listed in the **from** clause. Instead, the strategy might be to perform a triple loop through independent rows of the three tables, testing the **where** predicate as each new triple of rows is considered. Or an entirely different type of strategy might be used, where each `orders` row allows us to "look up" in some efficient index structure the unique row in `products` and the unique row in `customers` with matching `pid` and `cid` values, as required by the join condition.

The point of all this is that *we are not expressing any presumptions about the order of evaluation when we write an SQL Select statement!* A Select statement is simply a *prescription* for *what* data is to be retrieved, rather than a *procedure* describing *how* it is to be retrieved. The conceptual order of evaluation provided in Figure 3.12 is simply an order the user can imagine that will always work: a product of tables in the **from** clause comes before eliminating rows with the search_condition in the **where** clause because the search_condition often has no meaning before a product is taken (consider the predicates in Example 3.10.2); inappropriate rows must also be eliminated by the search condition before the target-list results are evaluated. But an important technique in the process of query optimization is to evaluate a Select statement in something other than the conceptual order, combining steps or even reversing them when this seems to offer added efficiency without changing the result. For example, in the triple-loop approach mentioned above, full materialization of the product is deferred while row elimination takes place with successive rows, so these two steps have been combined. It is an important consideration that the triple-loop procedure can pause once a sufficient number of rows have been generated for immediate needs—for example, when a screen full of rows has been displayed and further output awaits a user request to continue. This combines all three steps, and can result in important savings if the user decides to abort the display without going further. In the index approach, where we look up a row in customers (for example) based on the cid value in an orders row, we can even say that the **where** elimination precedes taking the product of the **from** clause and obviates the need to consider all rows in the customers table.

We have just seen an important advantage of the non-procedural Select statement. When we specify a prescription of *what* data is to be retrieved rather than a procedure describing *how* to do it, we leave the decision on the exact access strategy up to the database system. The database *query optimizer* theoretically has the resources to make a very sophisticated decision about exactly how to navigate through the data to retrieve the desired information. This decision can often be superior to one that a programmer could make, simply because a programmer writes a query at a given time and usually doesn't revisit it later (a programmer's time is quite valuable), so an access strategy determined by a programmer cannot be up-to-date about later developments of size and indexed access for tables. On the other hand, an unmodified Select statement can be recompiled at a later time and can result in a different access strategy if the query optimizer becomes aware of significantly changed conditions. We will talk more about query optimization in later chapters on indexing and performance.

The Select Statement

Readers who have studied *automata theory,* used in formal languages, may have encountered the concept known as *Turing's thesis.* The mathematician Turing investigated a type of conceptual machine, similar to a modern computer in capability except that it has an infinite tape (or memory) to store intermediate results. He demonstrated to almost everyone's satisfaction that such a machine, which could execute simple procedural programs of finite length, had all the power necessary to perform any computational procedure that it was possible to describe in specific (algorithmic) terms. Thus the Turing machine could compute how to play a perfect game of chess (it might take a long time) or create any kind of report on data to which it had access, just as long as the person requiring the report is able to describe exactly how to create it in a finite number of steps. The ability to perform such computations in a given language is called *computational completeness,* or sometimes *Turing power.* All modern programming languages, such as C, have Turing power if we just make the assumption that they have an arbitrarily large (infinite) addressing space to store intermediate results. This then is the benchmark against which the power of other languages is to be measured.

No non-procedural language can have Turing power. If we think of the model of choosing options from a menu, we see that we are limited to a relatively small number of possibilities: we can choose any subset of these options. Some of the options may have parameters we can use to enlarge this choice (such as naming columns in the **order by** clause), but unless we start encoding arbitrarily long sequential programs into the parameters (which would defeat our purpose) there is no possibility of Turing power coming out of this model.

This lack of Turing power is not necessarily a great disadvantage. The human mind, for example, doesn't really have Turing power, since it is presumably finite in its ability to store intermediate results. However, it is a starting point in thinking about what SQL is capable of in querying a database, and what we think we could do with a programming language such as C that had access to the same data. In the next chapter on Embedded SQL, when we learn how to perform SQL calls from within a program, we will find that we can write programs with this capability that cannot be performed using non-procedural SQL. It seems likely that few database practitioners today would disagree with this point. Although early advocates of the relational model justified it in terms of giving nonprogrammers the ability to do everything through an interactive interface, a number of difficulties arise in practice, and programmed database applications are used today for almost all access. The value of the SQL language is now thought to reside in the flexibility and generality it has to benefit the programmer, rather than the end user.

SQL and Non-Procedural Set Functions

For now, let us investigate the limits of power of SQL by listing some examples of queries that SQL is *not* able to perform. Recall that relational algebra was once shown to have all the power of first-order predicate logic. Perhaps this will seem less intimidating when we realize that none of the Set functions of SQL exist in relational algebra. (They could be included, but historically have not been.) Thus we cannot answer, in relational algebra, the question: how many orders have dollar values greater than $500? In SQL we have added the Set functions: sum, avg, max, min, and count. Can we think of any others?

EXAMPLE 3.10.3

The *median* is a type of statistical average, generally considered to be a more stable measure for certain statistics, such as monthly housing prices, than the mean average provided by the SQL set function avg( ). Given a sequence of n numbers, $a_1, a_2, \ldots, a_n$, with $a_i \leq a_{i+1}$, for i = 1, . . ., n − 1, the *median* is defined to be the value a_k in the sequence such that k = FLOOR((n+1)/2)). Because the median is not defined as an SQL set function, we are unable to write a Select statement of the following kind:

```
select median(dollars) from orders;   ** INVALID SQL SYNTAX **
```

To illustrate how such a median function would work, we place all dollars values of rows in the orders table of Figure 2.2 in nondecreasing sequence to get {180.00, 450.00, 450.00, 450.00, 460.00, 500.00, 540.00, 540.00, 600.00, 704.00, 720.00, 720.00, 800.00, 880.00, 1104.00, 1104.00}, with 16 entries. The median value is therefore entry number FLOOR((16 + 1)/2), entry 8, or 540.00. ■

Other set functions that might be valuable in various circumstances are *mode* and *variance*. The mode for a set of numbers is the most commonly occurring number in the set, while variance is an important statistical measure, the mean square of differences of individual observations from the mean average, the result of the avg( ) set function. As a matter of fact, the **ORACLE** product does have a variance( ) set function. Statisticians commonly think of the sum of squares of a set of observations as the *second moment*. We can express the variance in terms of the second moment and the mean average, known as the *first moment*. But there is no limit to the number of set functions that could be requested, since third moment (mean of third powers), fourth moment (mean of fourth powers), and higher moments are used for some purposes. Note that all of these set functions can easily be calculated by a program that has access to the data, simply by looping through the values and performing the appropriate aggregation, sum of squares, etc. However, in the non-procedural SQL model, if a set function isn't provided by the system then we won't be able to evaluate the functional result.

Another capability missing in SQL is the ability to *nest* set functions.

EXAMPLE 3.10.4

We would like to be able to pose a query to find the average, over all agents, of the total dollar sales by agent. The type of form that would seem a natural method of nesting set functions is something like the following:

```
select avg(select sum(dollars) from orders    ** INVALID SQL SYNTAX **
       group by aid);
```

However, this SQL statement is invalid because a Subselect is not allowed inside a set function in SQL. We are able to perform the Subselect in the above statement, with the following table resulting from the orders table of Figure 2.2:

sum(dollars)	.
1400.00
180.00
4228.00
450.00
2144.00
1400.00

The average of these values is 1633.67. ∎

It turns out that there does exist a way to find the average, over all agents, of the total dollar sales by agent. Since this average is the sum of the dollar totals by agent, divided by the number of agents, and since the sum of the dollar totals by agent is the sum of all dollar values, the desired result can be achieved with the statement:

```
select sum(dollars)/count(distinct aid) from orders;
```

However, the fact remains that it is not possible to nest set functions in SQL, and because of this we can list numerous requests that cannot be implemented by any Select statement. For example, there is no way to find the total of all average dollar sales by agent, or the maximum of all total dollar sales by agent. We will see in the next chapter how such queries can be answered, using programs that access SQL data in a procedural way.

Non-Procedural Reports

The **group by** clause, another concept missing from relational algebra, permits a kind of reporting function. But we don't have to look very far to find a report that SQL can't create.

EXAMPLE 3.10.5
We wish to create a report in which we break down total sales by category, according to the dollar size of the sale. Say the categories, which we will call **ranges**, are 0.01 to 500.00, 500.01 to 1000.00, . . . etc. We would like to be able to write something like

```
select range, sum(dollars) from orders    ** INVALID SQL SYNTAX **
       group by dollars in ranges from 0.01 in blocks of 500.00;
```

The idea here is to find the total contribution to sales by each category of dollar sales range. A sales manager might wish to do this to determine which sales amounts provide the bread-and-butter volume. The result for the orders table of Figure 2.2 would be

Range	COL2
0.01–500.00	1580.00
500.01–1000.00	5504.00
1000.01–1500.00	2208.00

For example, dollars values in the range 0.01–500.00 are 450.00, 450.00, 180.00, and 500.00, which sum to 1580.00. A report such as this cannot be generated with a legal SQL statement. ■

Clearly a report of this kind would be possible with a procedural programming language. Indeed, we can imagine an infinite number of report formats (literally) that SQL is incapable of creating non-procedurally, but that could be accomplished with a program.

Transitive Closure

A well-known weakness of first-order predicate calculus is its inability to perform something called *transitive closure*. Consider a directed graph G on a set of nodes {a, b, c, . . . }; we say that a -> b when an edge is directed from a to b. Then the graph is *transitive* if and only if the following property holds: whenever a -> b and b -> c, the edge a -> c also exists. If we start with a graph G that is not transitive, we can fill in edges to make transitivity hold for all triples of nodes (a, b, c): if a -> b and b -> c, fill in a -> c if it does not already exist. As we do this, we are basically saying that whenever c can be reached by a path of edges from a, there should be an edge from a to c. The result of this process of filling in edges is known as the *transitive closure* of the graph G. This kind of consideration comes up occasionally in real queries.

EXAMPLE 3.10.6

Let us create a table called employees, with the following Create Table command:

```
create table employees (eid char(4) not null, ename varchar(16),
    mgrid char(4));
```

The eid attribute stands for employee ID, a unique identifier for the employee represented on a row, and the mgrid attribute contains the employee ID of the manager of the represented employee. Assume we have loaded the following employees table:

employees

eid	ename	mgrid
e001	Jacqueline	null
e002	Frances	e001
e003	Jose	e001
e004	Deborah	e001
e005	Craig	e002
e006	Mark	e002
e007	Suzanne	e003
e008	Frank	e003
e009	Victor	e004
e010	Chumley	e007

Note here that employee e010, Chumley, reports to (has the manager) e007, Suzanne, and Suzanne reports to e003, Jose, who reports to e001, Jacqueline. Jacqueline has a null in the `mgrid` column because she is president and has no manager. We can easily write a Select statement to list all employees who report to any given employee (presumably a manager, or the list will be empty). For example, to retrieve all employees who report to Jacqueline, with employee id e001, we write:

```
select e.eid from employees e where e.mgrid = 'e001';
```

This would give us employees e002, e003, and e004. Now we can also retrieve all employees who report to employees who report to this manager:

```
select e.eid from employees e where e.mgrid in
    (select f.eid from employees f where f.mgrid = 'e001');
```

This would give us everyone who reports to one of the employees returned by the Subselect, the same as the Select we just did, and so we would get e005, e006, e007, e008, and e009. Employee e010 is not included, because e010 reports to e007, rather than to one of the managers returned by the Subselect. No single SQL expression is guaranteed to list all employees *at all different levels* who have e001 as a manager at some level above them. This would list all employee IDs other than e001.   ∎

If we say that the employees table represents a graph, with employee rows representing nodes and edges directed from `mgrid` to `eid`, then what we are pointing out in the above example is that we can list all employees with a Select statement that can be reached by a single edge from any specific `eid` such as e001; similarly, we can retrieve all employees that can be reached by paths of exactly two edges from any specific `eid`, such as e001. The query we are trying to pose will return all employees that can be reached from a specific `eid` by a path with an *arbitrary number* of edges. If the graph had the transitive closure property, then all employees reached by a path could be reached also by a single edge. The ability to pose such a query is commonly known as transitive closure in a query language.

The **ORACLE** product has the ability to pose this query, using non-standard Select clauses, the **connect by** and **start with** clauses. The query to retrieve all employees who have e001 as a manager at some level above them would have the following form in **ORACLE** SQL:

```
select e.eid from employees
    connect by prior eid = mgrid
    start with eid = 'e001';
```

There is also a proposed feature for SQL3 to support transitive queries.

Limited Power of Boolean Conditions

There is a general consensus in certain areas of information retrieval that the SQL language is seriously flawed, because the user is limited to Boolean conditions in posing queries. Gerald Salton, a preeminent author in the field of text retrieval, points out a number of examples where Boolean conditions do not provide the power needed to answer important questions (See [9], "Extended Boolean Retrieval Model, Fuzzy Set Extensions," Section 10.4).

EXAMPLE 3.10.7   171

Assume we are given a table named documents, with rows representing text documents (such as journal articles) with primary key docid, and where each document has up to a hundred keyword values that identify the subject matter (e.g., magnetic, resonance, superconductor, gallium arsenide, etc.). As we saw in explaining first normal form in Section 2.3, we need to implement this kind of relationship with a second table, keywords, having the two attributes keyword and docid. A simple example of this kind is

documents

docid	docname	docauthor
d12272	Intro Math	Thomas
d23753	Intro DB	Gray
. . .	. . .	. . .

keywords

keyword	docid
integer	d12272
integral	d12272
integrity	d23753
. . .	. . .
relation	d12272
relation	d23753
SQL	d23753
. . .	. . .

As we see, the keywords 'integer' and 'integral' occur in the 'Intro Math' document, the keyword 'SQL' appears in the 'Intro DB' document, and the keyword 'relation' occurs in both. We would normally expect to have hundreds of thousands of documents and many thousands of keywords, with a great deal of duplicate keyword use between documents. To retrieve all the keywords for a document, d12293 for example, we would use the query:

```
select k.keyword from keywords k where k.docid = 'd12293';
```

To retrieve all documents with the keyword 'Xyz1', we would use the query:

```
select * from documents d where d.docid in
    (select k.docid from keywords k where k.keyword = 'Xyz1');
```

A common approach to retrieving documents is to come up with a list of keywords we would like to see present. A query to retrieve all documents with ALL of a given set of six keywords (Xyz1, Xyz2, . . . , Xyz6) can be expressed, using the FOR ALL type of query we covered in Section 3.5, as follows:

```
select * from documents d                /* retrieve documents d */
    where not exists
    (select * from keywords k            /* ... where no keyword */
        where k.keyword in              /* ... in our list       */
        ('Xyz1','Xyz2','Xyz3',
        'Xyz4','Xyz5','Xyz6')
        and not exists
        (select * from keywords m        /* ... fails to equal    */
            where m.keywordd = k.keyword /* ... a keyword         */
            and m.docid = d.docid));     /* ... in the document d */
```

In words, we select any document d where there does not exist a keyword in our list that fails to be a keyword for our document. This is a relatively complex (and inefficient) query for such a simple idea, but this is not the worst of our problems. More important, what if there were no documents that had all six of these keywords? How could we pose a query to retrieve documents that had any five of the six keywords? Or any four? There is no such syntax in SQL. Indeed we would require six queries to retrieve documents with any five of the attributes, and (6·5)/2 = 15 queries to retrieve documents with any four of them.

∎

It should be noted that this *fuzzy set* concept of retrieving all rows with a large subset of the desired properties is only the beginning of what is expected in the field of document retrieval. The different keywords are often weighted as to importance, terms of the query might also be weighted, and different measures of k dimensional distance are used to retrieve the closest matching set of documents. The user is also empowered to ask for a specific number of documents in descending order of closeness of match. Interfaces have been proposed and prototyped that provide enormous ease of use, by posing the query for the user and using feedback to alter the weighting terms of the query, using statistical analysis of user-perceived closeness of fit to the desired retrieval for documents already returned. Most of these capabilities seem ruled out by the limitations of Boolean search conditions. We just consider one more of these capabilities in the familiar CAP database setting, the ability to ask for a specific number of documents in descending order of closeness of match.

EXAMPLE 3.10.8

In our standard CAP database, assume that we have an extremely large number of agents, and we want to print out a list of the twenty agents with the highest total sales so that we can reward them with a vacation in Hawaii. In SQL there is no way to ask for the twenty agents with the largest sales. Of course it is possible to list all agents in decreasing order by total sales:

```
select aid, sum(dollars) from orders x group by aid
    order by 2 desc;
```

From this output we can stop retrieving after the first 20 lines to limit to the agents we are concerned with. Of course this implies that a procedure is being performed. ∎

In the next chapter we will see how to create programs to answer any of the questions that have arisen in this section, indeed any questions for which we can imagine an algorithmic approach. The fuzzy set problem of Example 3.10.7 will still be extremely challenging, however, since the relational model is simply not well suited to retrieval by keywords.

3.11 Object-Orientation in Database Systems

By this time the reader will have gained a good deal of experience with the relational database model. In relational systems, all real-world data must be expressed as rows in tables obeying the first normal form RULE and various other rules and structural conventions from the first four sections of Chapter 2, amended in certain very limited ways by commercial practice. Users of such systems are empowered to query and update tables through languages that have relationally complete power—normally this boils down to using the SQL language. Since we have spent the previous section describing several limitations of the relational model in general and the SQL language in particular, it is probably no surprise to learn that a number of proposals have been made over the last 15 years or so to introduce new and (purportedly) improved data models.

In the current section we discuss two of these new models that have gained sufficient prominence to be adopted as new commercial database system products. Database systems in these two categories are generally referred to as *object-oriented database systems* (OODBS) and *extended relational systems*. An extended relational system is recognizable as a relational system with extensions (changes to structure rules, table structures, and permitted SQL syntax) in the direction of object-orientation. Because of our familiarity with the relational model, examples in extended relational systems are more easily appreciated in an introduction of limited length. In what follows we begin by giving an overview of the concepts that motivate the object-oriented model, and then illustrate some of these concepts with a particular extended relational product.

Object-Oriented Database Systems

One of the major motivations for the object-oriented data model was a desire to bring some of the concepts of object-oriented programming languages (such as Smalltalk and C⁺⁺) into database systems. In object-oriented languages, *objects* combine the concepts of data structures and program functions (which we shall refer to as *methods*) that can act on that data. An object is said to *encapsulate* data and methods, meaning that the programmer normally cannot access the data within the object except by use of the methods provided. Objects with a specific structure and set of methods are said to belong to an object *class* (objects belong to a class just as data variables in more traditional languages are declared to be of a given *type*). Finally, the model allows new classes to be created that extend the description of a previous class, and any such new class is said to *inherit* the data items and methods of the first class.

As an example, in an object-oriented language we might have a class named `employees` whose objects have data items for `employee_id`, `name`, `job_title`, `manager_id`, and `salary`, and associated methods to `promote()` (change the job title in an object), `change_name()` (because of marriage, for example), `reassign()` (change `manager_id`), and `change_salary()`. Now the standard object-oriented concept of *class inheritance* is illustrated by an example where a new class named `managers` is created as a *subclass* of `employees`, with all the same data items and methods (by inheritance), but also a new data item, `budget`, and a new method, `change_budget()`. The ability for a new class to inherit data items and methods from a parent class is sometimes known as *reuse*, and it is considered to be an important feature of object-oriented systems.

Over time, several different proposals for an object-oriented database system have been published, and a number of concepts added to the model that have little to do with object-orientation. One such proposed feature is known as *computational completeness,* the ability for the data manipulation language (DML) of the database system to perform any Turing computable function. As we learned in Section 3.10, SQL is not computationally complete. In Chapter 4, we will explain a method (known as Embedded SQL) of combining a programming language such as C or Fortran with SQL to achieve such power, but OODBS proponents feel that this approach exhibits an unfortunate property known as *impedance mismatch*, since normal programming language constructs (such as loops) are so out of accordance with the SQL model (where data is accessed non-procedurally as a *set* of rows). It is still the case in OODBS that computational completeness must be achieved through a connection between the DML and existing programming languages, but the connections used are considered to be more acceptable.

Some OODBS concepts were introduced with the objective of trying to find a marketing niche for this new type of database system. Since the relational model has been quite successful in the business-oriented, fill-in-the-form environment, proponents cast about for industry uses that would value the complex structured objects of OODBS. One major use identified was computer-aided design/computer-aided manufacturing (CAD/CAM) applications. A typical application of this kind keeps track of thousands of machine parts in structured assemblies and subassemblies. These structures must be stored on disk, accessed very efficiently, and then pictured on a terminal screen for modification. Such a modification (a new design for an assembly) doesn't wipe out the old design, but rather creates a new *version* of the assembly. To model these assemblies as made up of parts represented by rows in normalized relational tables is to lose the efficient access of complex structured objects (instead it is necessary to retrieve hundreds of rows related by joins). No CAD/CAM designer would consider such an inefficient database design, and instead a number of custom CAD/CAM database systems were developed by the companies using them. To support applications of this kind, OODBS added the concept of *object versioning* and a form of "pointers" between objects to reference subassemblies. These "pointers" are known as *object IDs*, or *OIDs* (comparable to RIDs in relational database systems except that OODBS objects typically contain data item OIDs pointing to other objects, while this is absolutely forbidden in the relational model). To increase performance even more, objects that are being worked on in a memory resident form will often have OID pointers to other memory-resident objects turned into actual memory pointers, a process known as *swizzling*, thus saving the CPU needed for an OID lookup with subsequent references. A database benchmark created by R.

G. G. Cattell demonstrates the performance advantage of such memory-resident optimization ([10], Chapter 6).

The large number of concepts that have been imported into object-oriented research means that there is really no common object-oriented data model. (There is relative unanimity in the field on this point.) Different OODBS products offer different capabilities from the possible set. This is detrimental to product sales, since commercial businesses prefer to deal with a standard interface. In 1989, a paper entitled, "The Object-Oriented Database System Manifesto," written by six highly respected practitioners in the field, attempted to prioritize features in the OODBS model ([1], Chapter 1). They listed 13 mandatory features, or "Golden Rules" for an OODBS. We present a selection of features from this list.

Types and Classes. The manifesto differentiates between types and classes. With types, the programmer is required to declare types for variables manipulated by the program, enabling the system to reason about the types involved and detect errors at compile or link time that might otherwise not be noticed until execution time. For example, a compiler knows that a character string cannot be divided by an integer and will notice if there is a mismatch in functional parameter types between a calling program and the function definition. A *class*, on the other hand, is an extension of the type concept that is not just used to check the correctness of a program, but to create and manipulate objects at runtime. In some implementations, classes themselves can be manipulated at runtime, new classes created or old classes changed, and then new objects generated from those classes. But the manifesto does not insist that an OODBS provide classes—providing only types is an acceptable alternative.

Extensibility of Types. A system comes with a number of predefined types, such as `integer` and `varchar`. *Extensibility* means that programmers must be able to define new types, together with operations that can act on those types: there should be no distinction in usage between user-defined and system-defined types. Normally, programmer-defined types are built out of simpler types in the same way as a C struct or Pascal record is defined, with a number of component parts (we call this a *composite type*). As an example, a user-defined type might consist of a pair of real number components, (a, b), and be named `complex`, with the first component corresponding to the real part and the second to the imaginary part of a complex number a + bi; then a multiplication operation on a pair of complex type objects could be defined to reflect the standard rules of complex multiplication: (a + bi) ⋆ (c + di) = a ⋆ c − b ⋆ d + (a ⋆d + b ⋆ c)i.

Complex Objects. This name seems to suggest that a complex object can have a composite structure like a C struct or a Pascal record, but of course this isn't right because that capability was already covered in the type extensibility feature above. Instead, the *Complex Objects* feature refers to the ability to apply *constructors* to objects, building *arrays* or *sets* of objects, and naming the resulting aggregate as a new object. Thus an array of char type objects (integers with 8-bit significance) could be defined as a char_string type. In the extended relational model of the next subsection, we can think of a user-defined composite type as being the "schema" for a "table" of objects: each object is like a row in a relational table, except that it can have a more complex composite structure with non-first normal form values, where components of the composite type are themselves composite types. Then a "table of objects" is a named *set* of objects, an object created by use of the *set constructor*.

Encapsulation. We gave an example of encapsulation earlier, with a class named employees containing objects with a number of data item values, and methods such as promote(), change_name(), and change_salary(). Strong encapsulation exists when the programmer cannot access data items in an object structure except through these methods, and results in a kind of *program-data independence*, where programs acting on objects will be unaware of changes in data structure as long as the methods the programs call are simultaneously changed to give a consistent answer. Thus an employees age data item can be replaced by an employees date_of_birth data item, and the method to return employee age can be altered to subtract the date of birth from the current date. However, Michael Stonebraker ([10], in the introduction to Chapter 10), argues that strong encapsulation is a bad idea—basically, because query optimization becomes difficult with loss of non-procedurality. The manifesto stops short of saying that encapsulated methods should be the sole means of access to the data of an object.

Class or Type Hierarchies. We gave an example of such a hierarchy earlier, where the managers type (or class) was given as a subtype of the employees type, inheriting many data items and methods and adding some of its own. In the next subsection on the extended relational model, we will give a specific example of this sort of inheritance.

Several other features are listed as mandatory in the manifesto. One of these is known as *object identity*, which states that two objects can be equivalent in all data item values while not being identical (they have distinct object identifiers). *Computational completeness* is also mentioned, along with a feature we do not discuss, listed as *overriding, overloading, and late binding*. Several standard database features are then added, with names such as *concurrency* and *recovery* (which will be considered in detail in Chapter 9), with the feature of an *ad hoc query facility* (such as interactive SQL) coming last. Unfortunately, this ordering seems to reflect the priorities of OODBS product developers, since most products have come to market without an SQL dialect by which queries could be performed, a problem that is only now being addressed in a partial and fragmentary fashion. The manifesto also suggests a number of other optional features, including *versioning*, which we mentioned earlier.

The current status of the object-oriented commercial market is not very encouraging. There are about a dozen OODBS products with gross revenues for 1993 variously estimated between $40 million and $80 million. The system vendors are certainly losing money as a group, although one or two companies may be making a small profit. Meanwhile the relational DBMS product market has gross revenues of at least $3 billion, so the OODBS vendors are competing in an extremely small niche market. It seems that the RDBMS products offer most of the capabilities needed by most commercial businesses and have more mature product offerings and fully accepted standards. Meanwhile, most of the CAD/CAM application users have stayed with their custom systems rather than take the leap to a new OODBS system. Clearly this situation can change as OODBS products mature and begin to compete more effectively. However, the relational camp is responding to the challenge of OODBS products by adding object-oriented features to their next version of SQL, SQL3. Object-oriented relational extensions are the topic of the next subsection.

Extended Relational Database Systems

It seems clear that a number of object-oriented features would be very nice to have in relational systems, if it were somehow possible to graft them carefully into the relational model to address known shortcomings. A few recently released commercial database products do just that, providing what we refer to as an *extended relational* data model. (This is sometimes called the *postrelational* data model, but since this term begs the question of whether the model will actually replace the older relational model, we avoid it.) Two products in this category are: *UniSQL* (founded by Won Kim, in Austin, Texas) and *Montage* (formerly Berkeley POSTGRES, commercialized under the name *Miró* for a short period until a trademark conflict in Europe led to the new name, Montage). A principal of the earlier POSTGRES work and more recent Montage is Michael Stonebraker of Berkeley, who was also responsible for developing and bringing **INGRES** to market: thus the name POSTGRES (in preference to other names Stonebraker jokingly mentioned, such as DIGRESS and REGRESS). Since Montage and UniSQL have slightly different assumptions for data modeling, it is appropriate to concentrate on one of them for a fully consistent presentation. The UniSQL user's manual is not yet freely available to parties who have not purchased the product, so we will concentrate on a description of the Montage product.

The reader should be aware that the early POSTGRES prototype has a number of points of difference from the commercialized Montage product (for one thing, the query language used in POSTGRES is based on an earlier language QUEL, rather than the extended SQL used in Montage). One early paper on POSTGRES is provided in Chapter 11 of reference [10], and another paper is in Chapter 7 of reference [12]. These papers are extremely clear and are recommended to readers interested in early motivation. For the most recent details of Montage syntax, however, the reader is referred to reference [6]. The presentation that follows of Montage usage is structured in terms of features we have listed from the Object-Oriented Database System Manifesto. Naturally, a large percentage of Montage syntax is not covered in this short introduction.

An Introduction to Montage Concepts

Types and Extensibility. Montage provides a rather large set of built-in *types* (rather than *classes*) and offers users the ability to define new types using what is called the *abstract data type (ADT)* facility. Types in Montage are broken into three categories:

- base types
- composite types
- constructed types

Base types. A base type is one that is *primitive* in terms of the Montage system—that is, the system has no concept of the internal structure of objects from this type but knows how to input and output type values (just as a text string "12345.6" is input or output as the value of a corresponding real type variable) and how to perform appropriate operations on objects of the type (such as '+' or '*' for real values). A few built-in types provided in Montage that we have not previously encountered include abstime, which has values representing an absolute date and time, and reltime, which has values representing a relative date and time (i.e., a time interval). A reltime value can be added to an abstime value, but two abstime values can't be added.

Extensibility of base types. A new base type can be added to the system by specifying the length in bytes that must be reserved for such an object, defining the internal structure of the type in the C language and creating input() and output() functions in C to convert between external text representations and internal format. It is also possible to create unary and binary operators on objects of new types, by creating a function (using the Create Function statement), either in C or Montage SQL (which has procedural capabilities), and then binding the operator symbol to the given function. A number of single symbols that are suitable as operators (such as '^') have been left unused by the system for this purpose.

Composite types. A composite type is one that is defined in the Montage system to have *component* data values, like a struct in C or a record in Pascal. Such a type can be defined with the Create Type statement, as follows:

```
create type person_t
    (
        fname       varchar(30),   /* component 1—first name    */
        lname       varchar(30),   /* component 2—last name     */
        age         int,           /* etc. ...                  */
        sex         char(1)
    );
```

One composite type can be used in the definition of a component in another type.

```
create type vehicle_reg
    (
        vehicle_id int,
        operator person_t
    );
```

However, composite types cannot be defined recursively: if T is a composite type, an object of type T cannot be a member of another object of type T. A table in Montage is a *set* (see constructed types, below) of composite objects of a given type. If the table T contains objects of type `vehicle_reg`, we can use *dot notation* to refer to members of nested types:

```
select vehicle_id from T
    where operator.age >= 65;
```

Constructed types. Constructed types are dealt with in the next manifesto topic.

Complex Objects. Recall that the Complex Objects feature refers to the ability to apply *constructors* to objects, building *arrays* or *sets* of objects, and naming the resulting construction as an object. In Montage, we can apply a constructor to an arbitrary type to get what is known as a *constructed type*. There are three constructors: **setof**, **arrayof**, and **ref**. Given an arbitrary type in Montage, x_t, we can create constructed types: setof(x_t), arrayof(x_t), and ref(x_t). We shall investigate these concepts in order.

Sets. A Montage set is an unordered collection of objects of the same type (sets of mixed types are not supported). Montage does not support uniqueness on set elements, so technically a Montage set is what is known as a *Multiset*, with duplicates allowed but no order to the elements.

A *table* is a special type of object that contains a set of elements of a given composite type. The type might be previously declared, as with `person_t`, which we saw earlier:

```
create table people of type person_t;
```

Alternatively, such a table could be created without a preexisting type:

```
create table people
    (
        fname    varchar(30)
        lname    varchar(30),
        age      int,
        sex      char(1)
    );
```

Finally, a table and type can be created at the same time:

```
create table people of new type person_t
    (
        fname    varchar(30),
        lname    varchar(30),
        age      int,
        sex      char(1)
    );
```

A single member of a table can also consist of a set, using the **setof** constructor:

```
create table employees
    (
        eid         empid_t,
        eperson     person_t,  /* characteristics of this employee*/
        salary      int,
        mgrid       empid_t,
        dependents  setof(person_t)    /* zero or more dependents*/
    )
```

Any expression that returns a set-type can appear in clauses of an SQL statement requiring a set-type, including target lists, search conditions, and **from** lists. To retrieve the eids of employees with more than six dependents, we could write the following SQL statement with a subselect returning a set of objects:

```
select eid from employees
    where (select count(*) from employees.dependents) > 6;
```

To retrieve eids of employees with no dependents, we could use the following statement, where a set-type component takes the place of the subselect statement from that component:

```
select eid from employees
    where not exists dependents;
```

To list names and eids of employees and with each the first name of the oldest dependent (if one exists), we could use a subselect statement in the target list of a Select statement:

```
select eid,(select fname from employees.dependents d1
        where d1.age = (select max(d2.age) from employees.
        dependents d2))
    from employees;
```

Arrays. An array is an ordered collection of objects of a base type only. The number of elements in the array might be fixed (in which case the common bracket [ ] notation is used in declaring it) or unknown and variable (like rows in a table), in which case the **arrayof** keyword is used. Here is a table T with two array components, group1 consisting of 100 int value elements, and group2 consisting of an unknown number of int value elements:

```
create table T
    (
        group1    integer[100],
        group2    arrayof(integer)
    );
```

It is possible in Montage SQL to reference individual elements of an array by subscript (subscripts start numbering from 1, rather than 0 as in C).

```
select group1[12] from T
    where group2[14] = 1234;
```

There are also a number of limitations on array type variables, which we do not cover here.

References. Given any composite type, Montage supports a reference (or pointer) to an object of that type. The object referenced must be a row in a table. For example,

```
ref(person_t)
```

represents a type containing a reference to a person_t object. For a use of this, recall that a composite type cannot recursively contain a component of the same type; however, it can contain a *reference* to another object of the same type. Consider the following definition of a police_patrolmen table, where every patrolman must have a partner:

```
create table police_patrolmen of new type police_patrolman_t
    (
        pol_person      person_t;
        badge_number    integer,
        partner         ref(police_patrolman_t)
    )
```

A **deref** operation on objects of reference types also exists to allow SQL syntax to refer to the components of the object referenced. Here is a query to retrieve the names of all patrolmen who have partners over sixty years of age:

```
select pol_person.fname, pol_person.lname from police_patrolmen
    where deref(partner).age > 60;
```

Encapsulation. Recall that strong encapsulation exists when a programmer cannot access data in an object except through methods associated with that object. In Montage, we have already mentioned that when the abstract data type (ADT) facility is used to create a user-defined base type, the internal structure of the type must be defined in the C language, and input() and output() functions in C must be defined and registered with Montage to perform conversion from external text representation to internal format.

In addition, a user-defined base type may also have optional associated C functions Assign() and Destroy() that function as methods on an object type. When a user stores the value of a user-defined base type in a row while executing a Montage SQL Insert, Update, or Copy statement,

Montage will look for an Assign() function that takes that type as its parameter before storing the value in the object. The Assign() function will return the value that should actually be stored in the table. For example, we might define a new cityname base type to look like a varchar(30) but always be in uppercase. Then the Assign() function could be used to transform the string to be stored to uppercase, or perhaps return an error if the string specified is in lowercase. The Destroy() function performs an analogous function to execute certain operations before a user-defined base type value is destroyed by an Update, Delete, or Drop statement. Finally, unary and binary operations can be defined as functions with parameter values of user-defined base types. Taken as a whole, programmer access to the various base types can be channeled through specially designed functions that serve as methods to whatever extent seems appropriate. On the other hand, access to composite and constructed types are not so constrained. Internal components of composite type objects can be accessed freely using dot notation in SQL statements such as Update. However this is a defining feature of SQL syntax, and it seems inappropriate to disallow such access. We can either define SQL statements to be valid object methods or else admit that the encapsulation in Montage is not particularly strong.

Functions. It seems appropriate at this point to say a bit more about Montage functions. A function can be defined either in the procedural SQL language of Montage or in C. If it is written in C it must be compiled and linked to run with Montage and declared in the Create Function statement (not covered here). The C function interface has extremely good parameter type checking, as might be expected. The C function interface is capable of supporting functions that

◆ Require type and bounds information for parameters and return types.

◆ Generate and return sets of objects to the caller from tables in the database.

◆ Accept NULL parameters and return NULL values.

◆ Maintain state between function invocations if desired.

Recall that operators on base types can be defined in terms of C functions. In addition, since a function can deal with sets of objects, it becomes possible to create new set predicates that can be used in search conditions of an SQL statement. This is an extremely impressive capability, and we will shortly give some examples of how it greatly improves the computational power of Montage SQL.

Class or Type Hierarchies. We explained the idea of a *hierarchy* earlier in terms of defining a new managers type (or class) as a subtype (subclass) of the employees type, where the subtype inherits the data items and methods of the supertype and adds some of its own. We illustrate how such inheritance through a hierarchy would take place in Montage. Recall the definition of the person_t type and table:

```
create type person_t
    (
        fname       varchar(30),    /* component 1-first name    */
        lname       varchar(30),    /* component 2-last name     */
        age         int,            /* etc. ...                  */
        sex         char(1)
    );
```

Assume that a function change_name() has been defined for objects of this type, accepting as parameters an object of type person_t and two values of type varchar(30) (either of which might be null) to represent new first and last names. Now we could define a subtype named employee_t as follows:

```
create type employee_t
    (
        eid         empid_t,
        salary      int,
        mgrid       empid_t,
    )
        under person_t;     /* says employee_t is subtype of person_t */
```

Now the top-level components of objects with the employee_t type consist of a *union* of components named in the two type definitions: eid, salary, mgrid, fname, lname, age, and sex. In addition, the change_name() function defined on the person_t type is inherited by objects of type employee_id. We can also define new functions

change_salary() and reassign() (to change the mgrid) for objects of **187**
type employee_id. Now a new type called manager_t can be defined as
a subtype of employee_t.

```
create type manager_t
    (
        budget      dollar_t,
        groupname   varchar(30)  /* name of group responsible for  */
    )
    under employee_t;
```

As before, objects of type manager_t inherit all components and
functions defined for employee_t. We can create a new function
change_budget() for objects of this type and also *override* the function
reassign() defined for the supertype, changing it to a new function that
modifies both the mgrid and the groupname for objects of manager_t
type. There are a number of considerations we don't discuss of overriding,
overloading, and late binding that are involved in defining functions on
typed parameters, especially where inheritance is concerned.

To create a table containing objects of a subtype such as manager_t,
it is NOT possible to declare the table directly to be of that type. The following will not work:

```
create table managers of type manager_t;
```

Instead it is necessary to use an alternate form of inheritance for tables,
starting with a table of the highest-level type and defining subtables:

```
create table people of type person_t;
create table employees
    (
        eid      empid_t,
        salary   int,
        mgrid    empid_t,
    )
    under people;   /* employees table is subtable of people   */
```

and finally:

```
create table managers
    (
        budget      dollar_t,
        groupname   varchar[30]
    )
    under employees;
```

Now a very important aspect of SQL behavior that makes table inheritance particularly valuable is that the query

```
select fname, lname, empid from employees
    where salary > $50,000;
```

will retrieve not only names and empid values of qualified employees from the employees table, *but also qualified employees in the* managers *table.* This is certainly the kind of behavior we normally want, and marks the difference between having the managers table defined so it contains a *component* of type employee_t and actually being declared as a subtable of the employees table. If we wanted to retrieve only non-managerial employees in this query, we would rewrite the select statement just given as

```
select fname, lname, empid from only (employees)
    where salary > $50,000;
```

We end this short introduction of the Montage system by simply mentioning a number of other important features such as *multiple inheritance, rules, alerters, versioning,* and *virtual columns* (whereby a table column can get its value from a Montage function of the same name).

The Power of the Montage Select Statement

Harking back to some of the examples of Section 10.3 that demonstrated a number of shortcomings in the SQL Select statement, we see that several of these problems are addressed in the extended relational model, as represented by Montage.

In Example 3.10.3, we noted that many set functions, such as median(), were not defined in the SQL set. In Montage there is a specific statement that defines new aggregates as well as various other functions to perform needed calculations. Furthermore there seems to be no obstacle to providing a set-type parameter with a subselect statement (called a subquery in Montage), so the nested aggregation of Example 3.10.4 becomes possible.

The problem of specifying all possible report formats in a non-procedural way is not addressed by the features of Montage, so certain problems of this nature remain out of reach. It is possible, however, to create a named function that will return various types of aggregation grouped on an arbitrary array of range intervals, so the functionality of Example 3.10.5 can be provided within the SQL framework by an appeal to a procedural function implementation. The only problem would be in limiting the total number of functions defined as the variations of report forms multiply.

The transitive closure problem of Example 3.10.6 can be solved in Montage. (Indeed it is possible to perform this query in the **ORACLE** database system, and a new Select form known as Recursive Union is specified in the future SQL3 standard.)

In Example 3.10.7, the problem of performing a query to retrieve all documents having a number of specified keywords is a nice illustration of Montage capabilities. First of all, instead of factoring documents into two tables, it is possible to define a single table named documents with a **setof** column named keywords.

```
create table documents
    (
            docid           docid_t,
            docname         docname_t,
            docauthor       person_name_t,
            keywords        setof(keyword_t)
    );
```

We don't have a Montage predicate to test whether a list of keywords is included in the set of keywords of a given document (such predicates are planned for a future release), but we can use extensibility to solve the problem now. We create a function subset() in C with two parameters of type setof(keyword_t), that tests whether the first set of keywords is included as a subset of the second set and returns a Boolean value. The syntax is something like this:

```
create function subset(setof(keywords), setof(keywords)) return bool
    as external name 'setlib.so(subset)' language C;
```

Then a particular query to retrieve documents with all keywords in a specified list can be written as follows:

```
select docid from documents
    where subset({Xyz1, Xyz2, Xyz3}::setof(keyword_t), document.
    keywords);
```

The syntax of the first parameter of the subset function above

```
{Xyz1, Xyz2, Xyz3}::setof(keyword_t)
```

denotes that the text string, {Xyz1, Xyz2, Xyz3}, is to be coerced by the system into a set of keywords.

It is also possible to create a function that will input a list of keywords and retrieve all documents that contain all these keywords or a subset from the list missing one or two elements. In the same way, by creating the appropriate funtion, it is possible to solve problem of Example 3.10.8 to retrieve the number of agents with the highest total sales.

Suggestions for Further Reading

A good guide to SQL-89 is C. J. Date, *A Guide to the SQL Standard,* second edition [2]. Note that the edition is important, since the third edition covers SQL-92. Many criticisms of the SQL language can be found in this guide, in Appendix F. An excellent presentation of the SQL-92 standard is given in a text by Jim Melton (who edited the SQL-92 standard) and Alan R. Simon [5]. The **ORACLE** SQL dialect for the version 6.0 PC release is taken from [7]; the **ORACLE**7 version from [8]. The **INGRES** SQL dialect from the UNIX release 6.3 is taken from [4]. The **DB2** SQL dialect is native to the MVS/XA and MVS/ESA Operating Systems and is taken from [3]. The X/Open standard is taken from [11]. An excellent reference work on text retrieval is by Gerald Salton [9]. Practitioners in the field of information retrieval, subsuming text retrieval, generally avoid use of the SQL language as being too limited and inefficient for their needs. A number of founding papers on data models and prototype systems to replace the relational systems is given in Stonebraker's "Readings" [10]. A more complete set of papers on object-oriented and extended relational (POSTGRES) data models is to be found in the "Readings" collection of Zdonik and Maier [12]. Reference [1] concentrates on the various aspects of a specific OODBMS, known as O$_2$. The "Object-Oriented Database System Manifesto" appears as the first chapter of reference [1] and the last paper of reference [10]. The details of the Montage DBMS are taken from [6].

[1] François Bancilhon, Claude Delobel, and Paris Kanellakis, editors. *Building an Object-Oriented Database System, The Story of O$_2$*. San Mateo, CA: Morgan Kaufmann, 1992.

[2] C. J. Date. *A Guide to the SQL Standard (SQL-89)*, 2nd ed. Reading, MA: Addison-Wesley, 1989. (Note that the second edition covers the SQL-89 standard; later editions do not.)

[3] *DB2 SQL Reference Manual*, version 2.3. IBM.

[4] *INGRES/SQL Reference Manual*, release 6.4, UNIX. Alameda, CA: ASK Group.

[5] Jim Melton and Alan R. Simon. *Understanding the New SQL: A Complete Guide*. San Francisco: Morgan Kaufmann, 1993. (This is a reference for SQL-92.)

[6] *MONTAGE DBMS User's Guide*, release 1.0. Oakland, CA: Montage Systems, Inc., 1993.

[7] *ORACLE SQL Language Reference Manual*, version 6.0. Redwood Shores, CA: Oracle.

[8] *ORACLE7 Server SQL Language Reference Manual*. Redwood Shores, CA: Oracle.

[9] Gerald Salton, *Automatic Text Processing*. Reading, MA: Addison-Wesley, 1988.

[10] Michael Stonebraker, editor. *Readings in Database Systems*, 2nd ed. San Francisco: Morgan Kaufmann, 1994. (See Chapter 10, "New Data Models," and Chapter 11, "Prototype Systems.")

[11] *Structured Query Language (SQL)*. Berkshire, UK: X/Open Company, Ltd., 1991. xospecs@xopen.co.uk

[12] Stanley B. Zdonik and David Maier, editors. *Readings in Object-Oriented Database Systems*. San Mateo, CA: Morgan Kaufmann, 1990.

Exercises

Exercises with solutions at the back of the book in "Solutions to Selected Exercises" are marked with the symbol •.

STUDENT HOMEWORK: We suggest the following method for student submission of the executable SQL statements. The student creates command files with names Q1A through Q1T, and so on, in an appropriate directory. These command files contain the correct (tested) queries. Then the student displays and runs these queries in a (script) mode that captures the results of the executions in a file that can be turned in. Note that a few of the early queries return an extremely large number of rows; in that case, the student should edit out most of those rows from the result file before turning it in.

NOTE: Exercises 3.1 through 3.7 deal only with SQL features covered through Section 3.5, features that offer the power provided by the relational algebra of Chapter 2.

[3.1] Create queries in SQL to answer the requests in Exercise 2.5, (a) through (t), at the end of Chapter 2.

[3.2] Use one of the All-or-Any predicates in (a) and (b) below.

(a)• Retrieve `aid` values of `agents` who receive more than the minimum commission (column name: `percent`).

(b) Retrieve `aid` values of `agents` who receive the maximum commission.

(c)• Explain why the following query fails to answer request (a) above, although it retrieves the right rows from the `agents` table of Figure 2.1: `select aid from agents where a.percent > 5;`

[3.3] Recall that the two predicates **in** and **=any** have the same effect (as explained in Example 3.4.8).

(a) • Given this, explain why the predicates **not in** and <>**any** (not equal any) do not have the same effect, but that <>**all** must be used to have the effect of **not in**.

(b) Execute the queries of Example 3.4.13 using **not in** and <>**all**. Execute an analogous query using the predicate <>**any**.

(c) • Execute the query of Example 3.4.7, which uses the predicate <=**all**. What predicate would you substitute in this query to retrieve exactly those rows that are *not* retrieved using <=**all**? Demonstrate by execution that this query returns the proper rows.

(d) Refer to the definitions of predicates <**any** and <**all**, and explain why these predicates have the same meaning as < in the condition expr < (Subselect), when the Subselect returns a single element.

[3.4] (a) • Compose an SQL statement that solves the problem of Example 3.4.1 without using a Subselect. (The **from** clause should reference all tables involved.)

(b) Is it always possible to avoid using a Subselect as we did in part (a)? Assume that we have a table S with attributes $A_1, \ldots, A_n$, a table T with attributes $B_1, \ldots, B_m$, and constants c and k, where A_i and B_i are from the same domain, for i = 1, 2, 3, and c and k are both from the same domain as A_2 and B_2. Consider the query:

```
select A1,..., An from S where A2 = k and
      A1 in (select B1 from T where B2 = c);
```

Rewrite this Select statement to get the same result but without using a Subselect. Don't forget to qualify attributes when needed.

(c) • Repeat part (b), rewriting without a Subselect, the query:

```
select A1,..., An from S where A2 = k and
      A1 in (select B1 from T where B2 = c and B3 = S.A3);
```

[3.5] Consider the problem to find all (cid, aid) pairs where the customer does not place an order through the agent. This can be accomplished with the Select statement:

```
select cid, aid from customers c, agents a
    where not exists (select * from orders x
        where x.cid = c.cid and x.aid = a.aid);
```

Is it possible to achieve this result using the **not in** predicate in place of the **not exists** predicate with a single Subselect? With more than one Subselect? Explain your answer, and demonstrate any equivalent form by execution.

[3.6] Look again at the pseudo-code in Figure 3.2.

(a)• Write comparable pseudo-code to show how the query of Exercise 3.4(b) can be evaluated *without* the use of nested loops. You should have two loops performed at distinct times (not one within another)—the first loop, corresponding to the Subselect, placing results (A, values) into a list of values L, and the second loop using a predicate to test if a value of A_1 is in L. We do not have a rigorous definition of what pseudo-code should look like, but try to make it clear what is happening, by analogy with the pseudo-code of Figure 3.2.

(b) Explain why we cannot avoid nested loops in pseudo-code for the query of Exercise 3.4(c). The reason is based on the fact that this query has what is known as a *correlated Subselect*.

[3.7] How would we show that SQL Select actually offers all the power of the relational algebra? Recall from Section 2.8 that all eight operations of relational algebra (listed at the end of Section 2.5) can be expressed in terms of the five basic operations: UNION, DIFFERENCE, PRODUCT, PROJECT, and SELECT. Consider any two tables R and S existing in an SQL database that have been created using the Create Table statement, which we will call *base tables*.

Explain how you would use SQL Select to retrieve any of the answer tables:

(a)• R UNION S

(b) R MINUS S, R TIMES S, R[subset of columns], R WHERE <condition> as in relational algebra. Use only the **not exists** predicate for Subselects. Assume that R and S have compatible headings where necessary.

(c)• (HARD) But we are not finished demonstrating the power of the SQL Select, because recursive expressions are possible in relational algebra where recursion is not possible in SQL Select. For example, if R, S, and T are all compatible base tables with headings $A_1 \ldots A_n$, then explain how we can express, using the SQL Select, the relational algebra expression (R UNION S) MINUS T.

(d) (VERY HARD; REQUIRES MATH BACKGROUND) Prove that if U and V represent any arbitrarily recursive relational algebra expressions achieved by SQL Subselect statements in terms of base tables, we can also achieve by SQL Select statements the deeper recursions:

U UNION V, U MINUS V, U TIMES V, U[subset of columns], U WHERE <condition>

(e)• (VERY HARD) Recall from Theorem 2.8.3 that R DIVIDEBY S can be expressed in terms of projection, difference, and product. Let R stand for the SQL statement "`select cid, aid from orders;`" and let S stand for "`select aid from agents where city = 'New York';`". Then R DIVIDEBY S gives the same answer as Example 3.5.2. Use the formula of 2.8.3 and express this in terms of an SQL Select, then execute the resulting statement and verify that it gives the right answer.

NOTE: Many of the exercises that follow require SQL features introduced after Section 3.5, features that expand on the power provided by the relational algebra of Chapter 2.

[3.8] Execute SQL statements to perform the following set of tasks.

(a)• For each agent taking an order, list the product `pid` and the total quantity ordered by all customers from that agent.

(b) We say that a customer x orders a product y in an average quantity A if A is avg(qty) for all orders rows with cid = x and pid = y. Is it possible in a single SQL statement to retrieve cid values of customers who order all the products that they receive in average quantities (by product) of at least 300?

(c)• Get aid values of agents not taking orders from any customer in Duluth for any product in Dallas.

(d) Get aid values of agents who order one common product for each customer who is based in Duluth or Kyoto.

(e)• Get cid values of customers who make orders only through agent a03 or a05.

(f) Get pid values of products that are ordered by all customers in Dallas.

(g)• Find agents with the highest percent (percent commission), using the max set function.

(h) In the agents table, delete the row with the agent named Gray, print out the resulting table in full, then put Gray back, using the Insert statement.

(i)• Use the Update statement to change Gray's percent to 11. Then change it back.

(j) Use a single Update statement to raise the prices of all products warehoused in Duluth or Dallas by 10%. Then restore the original values by rerunning the procedure that you originally used to create and load the products table.

(k)• Write an SQL query to get cid values for customers who place at least one order, but only through agent a04. On the same line with each cid, your query should list the total dollar amount of orders placed.

(l) Write an SQL query to get aid values of agents who take orders from all customers who live in Duluth. The aid values should be reported in order by decreasing percent (commission).

(m)•Write an SQL query to get `pid` values of products ordered by at least one customer who lives in the same city as the agent taking the order.

[3.9] In this problem, you are asked to write down the answers that you would expect SQL to give before checking your answer by executing the query. The point here is to understand how SQL arrives at the answer.

(a)• In the following query, show how the answer is built up; that is, show all Subselect sets of elements created, then write out the final answer you would expect.

```
select city from customers where discnt >=all
    (select discnt from customers where city = 'Duluth')
    union select city from agents where percent >any
        (select percent from agents where city like'N%');
```

(b) In the following query, explain in words how SQL arrives at the answer, then write out the final answer you would expect.

```
select cid, pid, sum(qty) from orders
    where dollars >= 500.00
    group by cid, pid having count(qty) > 1;
```

[3.10] Here is an exercise to investigate the question: What SQL queries are guaranteed to return answer tables with no duplicate rows without use of the **distinct** keyword? This can be important, because using the **distinct** keyword when it isn't necessary can cause unwanted resource use. We present a series of rules for queries that will not return duplicate rows and ask you to (i) explain why each rule works, and (ii) give an example of a query that returns duplicate rows when the rule fails. In parts (a) and (b), we consider only queries with no Subselects and no **group by** clauses.

(a)• In a query with only one table in the **from** clause, there will be no duplicate rows returned if the column names in the target list form a superkey for the table.

(b) In a query with multiple tables in the **from** clause, there will be no duplicate rows returned if the column names in the target list form superkeys for each of the tables involved.

(c)• Is it true that no query with a **group by** clause will have duplicate rows? Explain why or give a counterexample.

(d) In Select statements that contain Subselects in their **where** clause, queries should be guaranteed unique rows in at least the same situations as (a) and (b) above. The transformation of Exercise 3.4(b) from a Subselect form to a join form without a Subselect may result in duplicate rows, however, unless the **distinct** keyword is used before the target list. Give an example where a Select statement without duplicates gains duplicates during such a transformation.

[3.11] (a)•Rewrite the query of Example 3.8.4, using only comparison predicates, without any use of the partial Match Pattern form.

(b) Can you find another pattern that *cannot* be replaced with other predicate forms?

[3.12] Recall the definition of outer join from Section 2.10. Consider the (ordinary) join query:

```
select a.aname, x.aid, sum(x.dollars)
    from agents a,orders x
    where a.aid = x.aid group by a.aid, a.aname;
```

(a)• Rewrite this query in SQL to implement an outer join (this will require a union of three Select statements). An agent `aname` and `aid` should appear even if the agent takes no orders, and `orders` should appear (grouped by `aid`) even if there is no corresponding `aid` in `agents` listed. Supply constant values, blanks for `aname`, or (unfortunately) zeros for sum(`x.dollars`) when no proper value exists in a column. (We would like to use true null constants here, but these are not generally available until SQL-92.)

(b) To test your answer to part (a) add a new row to `orders`, (1027, 'jun', 'c001', 'a07', 'p01', 1000, 450.00), and a new row to `agents`, ('a08', 'Beowulf', 'London', 8), then execute the query. When you are satisfied, delete the two rows you just added.

[3.13] The following exercise illustrates some of the special properties of null values. To perform this exercise, we add a few new rows to the agents table with null values in the percent column (and delete them again at the end of the exercise). We execute two insert statements:

```
insert into agents (aid, aname, city)
      values ('a07', 'Green', 'Geneva')
insert into agents (aid, aname, city)
      values ('a08', 'White', 'Newark')
```

(a)• Predict the result of the following statement, then execute it and check your answer. The question is, how do nulls act in a **group by** clause?

```
select percent from agents group by percent;
```

(b) Predict the result of the following statement, then execute it. The question is, how do nulls act when placed in order with other values?

```
select aid, percent from agents order by percent;
```

(c)• Consider the following query.

```
select distinct aname from agents where percent >=all
      (select percent from agents where city = 'Geneva');
```

   (i)   Put into words the effect of this query: "get names of agents . . ."

   (ii)   Note that the Subselect here returns a single null value. Recall the explanation immediately preceding Example 3.8.3, which indicates that in this case the result of the **>all** predicate will be unknown for all percent values of any row in agents. What, therefore, do you expect will be the result of this query? Execute the query to test your understanding.

(d) Similarly consider the following query, and do parts (i) and (ii) as in (c).

```
select distinct aname from agents a where not exists
      (select * from agents b
          where b.city = 'Geneva'
          and a.percent <= b.percent);
```

Does it seem to you that the effect of this query is the same as the effect of the query of problem (c)? But there is a surprise here, because the only row for which `b.city` = 'Geneva' has `b.percent` = null, and all other `percent` values compare to null with an UNKNOWN result. Therefore the Subselect returns a null set of values and **not exists** is true for all agents `a`. This is *not* the result from part (c).

[3.14] More on "**all** means no counterexamples." Suppose we modify example 3.5.2 by changing New York to Los Angeles.

(a)• What is the answer now?

(b) Explain why.

Programs to Access a Database

One of the major motivations for developing the SQL language was that it could be employed directly by end users to pose ad hoc database queries, thus reducing the application programming backlog prevalent in most data processing centers. In the terminology of Chapter 1, an end user who accesses a database through Interactive SQL is known as a *casual user*. For a number of reasons, it turns out that the number of end users who now access data directly through SQL is not as great as originally conceived; instead, most users still work with data through an application program interface. The term *naive user* is commonly taken to refer to an end user who performs all database access through a menu application, offering fill-in-the-form choices on a terminal screen, and so avoids having to deal with the syntax of the SQL Select statement. A *menu application* or *form application* is a program written by an *application programmer* for this purpose. From the standpoint of the programmer, the application program logic interacts with the end user through a *form* interface to determine the user's desires and then executes SQL statements programmatically to carry out these desires. Most workers who deal with data, such as bank clerks and airline reservation agents, use form applications to perform their duties.

The dialect of SQL that can be executed from within a program is known as *Embedded SQL*, a name that signifies the SQL statements are "embedded" among the regular statements of a programming language, or *host language,* such as C, COBOL, Pascal, PL/I, or Fortran. Much of the early promise of the SQL language is achieved in this form, because application programmers find Embedded SQL a much easier platform from which to access data than those that existed before the relational model. In this chapter, and the ones that follow, we will concentrate on Embedded SQL programs written in the C language. If you are not completely familiar with the C language, this should not present an insurmountable obstacle, as long as you have good programming experience in some other language, since the programs we'll consider are rather simple. Copying program formats from the text (or from examples given on line), with only occasional original contributions in the form of different logical decisions, input names, or output formats, should suffice to get you through most assignments. At the same time, you may notice an acceleration in the pace of new concepts being introduced in the current chapter, especially if you lack a background in C, and you will probably need to make a special effort to grasp the details. A number of excellent C books are available for reference. Particularly recommended as an introductory text is *The C Programming Language,* by Kernighan and Ritchie [9].

Let us consider some of the reasons that customized form applications are preferred to interactive SQL for most common database tasks. To begin with, the mental effort required to keep track of all the tables and column names and to write appropriate SQL syntax detracts from a specialist's concentration on the real work to be performed. Imagine an airline reservation clerk trying to compose ad hoc SQL statements to make connecting reservations, book flights, make seat assignments, place customers on a waiting list, handle various modes of payment, and so on. Even the most knowledgeable database system programmers commonly use form applications to perform support work such as tracking bug reports; it is simply a less demanding interface to deal with than ad hoc SQL.

A second point in favor of application programs over ad hoc SQL is that many tasks we think of as single units of work cannot be performed non-procedurally with single SQL statements. Instead, some sort of programmatic looping is frequently required. We saw a number of tasks like this in Section 3.10, such as finding the median of a set of column values, which could not be performed with single Select statements. In the current chapter we will see how most of these tasks can be implemented by simple programs using Embedded SQL. In the same vein, certain tasks require sets of statements to read a number of different rows and then possibly update some of them on the basis of what has been read; a guarantee is needed that interfering updates from other users will not spoil the results. We need

to tie together sets of statements in special uninterruptible packages called
transactions, and the programmatic capabilities of Embedded SQL turn
out to be crucial in this area as well.

A third point in favor of programmatic usage is this: it should be clear
from some of the complex syntax we have encountered in SQL (such as the
forms used to implement FOR ALL conditions) that the process of phrasing queries can be quite error prone. In many business situations, an
incorrect query (or worse, an incorrect update statement) can have hor-
rendous results. It is therefore clearly preferable to leave such syntax to
professional programmers, who have both the time and the skill to provide
tested statements that accomplish exactly what is intended. Since these
statements are used over and over in the same situations, we also gain a
consistency that is extremely important in most business situations.

On the other hand, there are occasionally situations where interactive
SQL is preferred. Certain types of users need to perform unusual and complex queries, which no general purpose programming interface can foresee
and provide for. An example is a research librarian at the Library of Congress making custom searches for desired books, where mechanical search
methods have already proved ineffective. A somewhat less rarefied use for
interactive SQL is to provide tools for users in special situations where
form applications have not yet been written, because of the application
backlog mentioned earlier. However, the risk of erroneous results is always
a major concern in such situations, and application programs to handle
such special cases should always be a goal.

Before plunging into the detailed features of Embedded SQL, let us
pause for a moment to consider what we wish to achieve. The aim of this
chapter is to provide you with the skills you need to implement any conceivable algorithm in an Embedded SQL program. As we make progress
toward this goal, a number of considerations arise that require increasingly
sophisticated techniques. To avoid getting lost in a welter of detail, you
should keep in mind that these techniques are not ends in themselves: it is
important to identify the value of each new feature of Embedded SQL syntax in the context of what capability it offers to implement programs that
access a database. In Section 4.1 we introduce some of the basic syntax
needed to access data within a program using the Select statement; a slight
variation of the Select (retrieving rows through a declared *cursor*) is
required to allow a program to access multiple rows in a loop. In Section
4.2 we learn how to handle various error returns and also to recognize
other types of conditions, such as an end-of-loop condition, when retrieved

rows from a cursor run out, or conditions that say when null values appear in columns of a row retrieved. In Section 4.3 we specify the general form of a number of Embedded SQL statements, including new update statement forms that can be used within a program.

In Section 4.4 we consider a number of details of the transaction concept mentioned earlier, where a set of executed statements are tied together in a special uninterruptible package. Several examples from Section 3.10, of tasks that cannot be accomplished with non-procedural SQL, are implemented as programs in Section 4.5. Finally, in Section 4.6, we introduce a new type of SQL known as *Dynamic SQL*. Up to this point in *Static SQL*, all Embedded SQL statements needed to exist as textual statements in the program text before program compilation. In Section 4.6 we introduce much greater flexibility, permitting Embedded SQL statements to be built up in character string variables, so that statements that were not foreseen in detail at the time of program compilation can be executed dynamically in response to changing user needs.

In this chapter you will also encounter significant differences among the three database systems under study, **ORACLE**, **INGRES**, and **DB2**. We will try to make it clear when our descriptions apply to a specific system. If a description of an Embedded SQL capability contains no such warning, it is meant to be part of Standard SQL. The different SQL statement forms are also gathered together in alphabetical order in Appendix B, to serve as a reference that is not dependent on the narrative order of the next few chapters. You should take an occasional glance at Appendix B as you progress through the following introduction to Embedded SQL.

4.1 | Introduction to Embedded SQL in C

When a programmer writes an Embedded SQL statement in a host language source file, the SQL statement is preceded by the phrase `exec sql`, and may extend over several lines of the file. For example, here is an Embedded SQL statement in C:

[4.1.1] `exec sql select count(*) into :host_var`
            `from customers;`

Note that C language source files are normally written in lowercase, and we will follow this convention, although uppercase SQL statements are used in many texts. Free-form statements on multiple lines, ending with a semicolon, are the norm in the C language. In COBOL, where statements are not normally multiline free form as in C, the Embedded SQL statement would end with the phrase end-exec.

In what follows, we describe the features needed to implement a very simple Embedded SQL program, execute a single Select statement, and print the result. We have a number of occasions to provide parallel descriptions of two distinct forms for some of these features, one form native to the **INGRES** database system and one form native to **ORACLE**. The reader is encouraged to examine both of the parallel descriptions in what follows, no matter what database system product is being used in class. It is extremely valuable to understand the likely variations between Embedded SQL dialects, because it is a common desire to write programs that are portable between systems.

A Simple Program Using Embedded SQL

We start with descriptions of a number of general language features and lead up to the programs illustrated in Figures 4.1a (**INGRES** form) and 4.1b (**ORACLE** form). Note that C language compilers are not generally constructed to recognize exec sql . . . statements of Embedded SQL, so the source file is typically run first through a *precompiler* that converts such embedded statements into C function calls. We will explain the procedures needed to precompile and then compile programs in **ORACLE** and **INGRES** after the programs have been explained.

The Declare Section

In an Embedded SQL program, the program logic must be able to use normal program variables, sometimes known as *host variables,* to represent a number of syntax elements in SQL statements. For example, we might want to declare program variables to contain retrieved values for customer name, cname (using a variable cust_name, the structure of which is explained below), and discnt (using a variable cust_discnt), as well as one for a value normally provided by the user in the **where** clause for customer cid (using the variable cust_id). We can then perform a retrieval with the Embedded SQL statement:

[4.1.2] `exec sql select cname, discnt into :cust_name, :cust_discnt`
`from customers where cid = :cust_id;`

Note the new **into** clause of this Select statement, and also the colon (:) that always precedes host variables when they are used in Embedded SQL statements (but not in other program references, as we will see). As a result of this Select statement, if the character string in cust_id has been previously set to the string "c001" in the C program, the variables cust_name and cust_discnt will be filled in with values "TipTop" and "10.000," from the customers table of Figure 2.2.

In order to use these host variables in an Embedded SQL statement, they must first be declared to the precompiler. This is accomplished with a special Embedded SQL Declare section of the C program where all such declarations are performed. Here is an example, valid in **INGRES** but not **ORACLE**, that declares the variables needed in the Select statement of (4.1.2).

[4.1.3] `exec sql begin declare section;`
`    char cust_id[5] = "c001"; /* declare and initialize cust_id*/`
`    char cust_name[14];`
`    float cust_discnt;`
`exec sql end declare section;`

The declarations of these three variables are normal C declarations, occurring between the Begin Declare statement and the End Declare statement, and end up being understood in the same form by both the precompiler and the C compiler. It is important that host language variables used in Embedded SQL statements have data types that are known to the database system. A certain amount of type conversion is possible. For example, if we changed the declaration of cust_discnt in (4.1.3) so that it could only accept integer values:

`int cust_discnt;`

and then executed the Select statement of (4.1.2), the value retrieved into cust_discnt would be 10 instead of 10.00. However, any fractional accuracy would be lost, so that if customer c009 had discnt 11.3, and this discnt value was retrieved by the Select statement of (4.1.2), the resulting cust_discnt value would be 11. All of this is reasonably familiar, but the

forms of C variables that accept character strings used in Embedded SQL
statements require a good deal more explanation. We defer this explanation until we have had a chance to look at the first program example.

SQL Connect and Disconnect

At the beginning of an Embedded SQL program, the program logic is faced
with the same problem as any interactive user: how to connect with the
SQL database management system and the right database. This is accomplished with an SQL Connect statement that is not well standardized and
varies between products. In **INGRES**, it is common to write a Connect
statement of the form

```
exec sql connect poneilsql;
```

where the string `poneilsql` represents the database name directly (without quotes), and no password is required. This statement has the effect of
an interactive user typing the OS command, "`sql poneilsql`", although
of course there will be no terminal monitor maintaining an edit buffer in
the case of Embedded SQL.

In **ORACLE**, a constant character string cannot be used as an argument
for the Connect statement. We require the following declarations:

```
exec sql begin declare section;
    . . .                          /* unallied declarations    */
    VARCHAR user_name[10], user_pwd[10];/* ORACLE string declarations */
exec sql end declare section;
```

The **ORACLE** string types are explained in the subsection following Example 4.1.1. For now the user should simply accept the syntax provided here.
Assuming a password given by "XXXX", we would initialize the variables
above with the statements:

```
strcpy(user_name.arr, "poneilsql");  /* set user_name string    */
user_name.len = strlen("poneilsql"); /* set length of string    */
strcpy(user_pwd.arr, "XXXX");        /* set user password string */
user_pwd.len = strlen("XXXX");       /* set length of string    */
```

Then the Embedded SQL statement to connect with SQL in **ORACLE** is

```
exec sql connect :user_name identified by :user_pwd;
```

Note the colons used to identify the host variables as arguments for this SQL syntax. To disconnect from the database, the SQL Disconnect statement is standard for all database systems:

```
exec sql disconnect;
```

Program Example: ORACLE and INGRES Forms

Example 4.1.1 (following) illustrates the Embedded SQL features introduced up to now, together with a number of new concepts. For simplicity, here and in most examples of the text we will ignore possible errors in program execution resulting from program bugs, invalid database information, or inappropriate user entry. In the programs of Example 4.1.1, we deal with potential errors in executing Embedded SQL statements with two statements: `exec sql include sqlca;` at the beginning of a program allocates space for certain errors and statistics to be communicated by the database system monitor, a *communication area*; and `exec sql whenever sqlerror stop`; sets up an error trap condition to enforce simple default behavior in dealing with erroneous calls. The effect of these statements is to stop the program (and, in **INGRES**, print out an error message) if an error arises in any database runtime statement execution. Section 4.2 contains a more sophisticated treatment of SQL error handling.

4.1 Introduction to Embedded SQL in C

```c
#include <stdio.h>

exec sql include sqlca;                   /* communication area         */
int prompt1(char[ ], char[ ], int);       /* functional prototype       */

main( )
{
    exec sql whenever sqlerror stop;      /* error trap condition       */
    exec sql begin declare section;       /* declare SQL host variables  */
        char cust_id[5], cust_name[14];   /* INGRES character strings   */
        float cust_discnt;                /* host var for discnt value  */
    exec sql end declare section;
    char prompt[ ] = "PLEASE ENTER CUSTOMER CID: ";/* unknown to SQL     */

    exec sql connect poneilsql;           /* INGRES: connect to database */
    while((prompt1(prompt, cust_id, 4)) >= 0) {   /* main loop: get cid  */
        exec sql select cname, discnt
        into :cust_name, :cust_discnt     /* retrieve cname and discnt  */
            from customers where cid = :cust_id;
        exec sql commit work;             /* release read lock on row   */
                                          /* ... and print values       */
        printf("CUSTOMER'S NAME IS %s AND DISCNT IS %5.1f\n",
                cust_name, cust_discnt);  /* NOTE, (:) not used here     */
    }                                     /* end of main loop           */
    exec sql disconnect;                  /* disconnect from database    */
}
```

Figure 4.1a **INGRES** Embedded SQL Program (Illustrates Example 4.1.1)

EXAMPLE 4.1.1

Consider the Embedded SQL program illustrated in two parallel forms: Figures 4.1a (**INGRES** form) and 4.1b (**ORACLE** form). The program prompts a user repeatedly for a customer cid and replies by printing the customer name and discount, halting when the user inputs an empty string. There is a minor problem with this program, in that old values are printed even if a nonexistent cid is input. An exercise at the end of the chapter asks you to correct this problem.

Most of the syntax of these figures has already been covered. The character string variable formats used are explained in the next subsection; the prompt1( ) function that interacts with the user is explained in the second subsection following. Note that the statement at the end of the main loop of main( ), exec sql commit work, is used after a sequence of reads from a table, before any user interaction such as printing results. As explained later in this chapter, a lock is taken on any row when it is read to keep other users from performing updates and perhaps giving the reader an inconsistent view of the data. We need to find some point in the main loop to release read locks, so they don't accumulate indefinitely and make it impossible for other users to update rows that have been read in the distant past. One good time for this is just before user interaction. ∎

4.1 Introduction to Embedded SQL in C

```c
#include <stdio.h>
#include <ctype.h>                              /* header for ORACLE datatypes */

exec sql include sqlca;                         /* communication area          */
int prompt1(char[ ], char[ ], int);             /* functional prototype        */
char prompt[ ] = "PLEASE ENTER CUSTOMER ID: ";  /* unknown to SQL              */

main( )
{
    exec sql begin declare section;             /* declare SQL host variables  */
        VARCHAR cust_id[5], cust_name[14];      /* ORACLE character strings    */
        float cust_discnt;                      /* host var for discnt value   */
        VARCHAR user_name[20], user_pwd[10];
    exec sql end declare section;

    exec sql whenever sqlerror stop;            /* error trap condition        */
    strcpy(user_name.arr, "poneilsql");
    user_name.len = strlen("poneilsql");
    strcpy(user_pwd.arr, "XXXX"); user_pwd.len = strlen("XXXX");
    exec sql connect :user_name
        identified by :user_pwd;                /* ORACLE format: connect      */
    while((prompt1(prompt, cust_id.arr, 4)) >= 0) { /* main loop: cid          */
        cust_id.len = strlen(cust_id.arr);      /* set length of cust_id       */
        exec sql select cname,
            discnt into :cust_name, :cust_discnt   /* retrieve cname, discnt   */
                from customers where cid = :cust_id;
        cust_name.arr[cust_name.len] = '\0';    /* null terminated string      */
        exec sql commit work;                   /* release read lock on row    */
                                                /* ... and print values        */
        printf("CUSTOMER'S NAME IS %s AND DISCNT IS %5.1f\n",
            cust_name, cust_discnt);            /* NOTE, (:) not used here      */
    }               /* end of main loop                                        */
    exec sql disconnect;/* disconnects from database */
}
```

Figure 4.1b   ORACLE Embedded SQL Program (Illustrates Example 4.1.1)

The Character String Types

It is now time to provide an explanation of character string handling that we see in the programs of Figures 4.1a and 4.1b. This handling is complicated because character strings are treated differently in C than they are in certain database types, and because **INGRES** and **ORACLE** have different default behavior on reading a string into a host variable with a Select statement.

A character string in C is represented as an array of *char* type values, 8-bit integers—bytes—that represent individual character codes. Most character code values in C are represented by characters enclosed in single quotes (the character code 'c' in ASCII, for example, represents the integer value 99, while the character code '0' represents the integer value 48). By convention, all C functions expect the final char value in a character string to be a special "null" character represented by '\0' and having the integer value *zero*. (You should not confuse the "null" character, '\0', with the SQL **null** value.) The initialization statement in (4.1.3), which declares and initializes cust_id[5] to the character string "c001", creates the following array of char values:

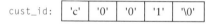

A constant string such as "c001", enclosed in double quotes, represents a *pointer* to a constant array of char values with terminal '\0', and the strcpy( ) function used in the program of Figure 4.1b

```
strcpy(user_name.arr, "poneilsql");
```

copies all characters in sequence from the right-hand array argument to the left-hand array argument, up to and including the terminal '\0'. A function call to copy or print out a character string that does not have a terminal null character will attempt to interpret all memory bytes starting at the string position pointed to, until it encounters some byte with 8 zero bits (a null, or '\0', character).

Database systems often use an entirely different format to represent character strings in columns declared in Create Table statements with type char(n) or varchar(n). The `cid` column in the `customers` table, with type char(4), takes up exactly four characters with no null terminator. If we were to place a string value "c9" in the char(4) type column `cid` for a new row of `customers`, then the actual characters stored would be 'c', '9', ' ', ' ', where the last two characters are filled in with blanks, and no terminal null character is needed to mark the end of the string because the string length is known by the database in advance. A *varchar* column type in a database column, such as `cname` in `customers`, does not have a constant string length; instead the varchar format begins with a 2-byte integer count of characters to follow. Since this count is provided, no terminal null character is needed to mark the end of string.

Now when an Embedded SQL statement retrieves a character column value into a C variable array, the program must be sure that the result is converted into a null terminated string, so that the C language will be able to deal with the string normally. This implies that the C variable arrays intended to hold character column values from SQL must always contain enough array entries to hold every character of the corresponding table column, together with a terminal '\0' character. Thus, where the Create Table statement (3.2.1) of Chapter 3 defines the table `customers` so that the column `cid` has type char(4), the declaration for cust_id in the Declare Section of (4.1.3) above allows an extra character, char cust_id[5].

*The **INGRES** database system automatically converts char and varchar columns into null-terminated strings in* C when it brings them into host variables through a Select statement. Thus the char array declarations for cust_name and cust_id in the Declare Section of (4.1.3) are appropriate, and dealing with character strings in **INGRES** is relatively simple. *However, the **ORACLE** database system does not perform this conversion.* Instead, a special VARCHAR type is generally used for C declarations of variables to contain character strings in **ORACLE**. The **ORACLE** version of the Declare Section in (4.1.3) is

[4.1.4]
```
      exec sql begin declare section;
          VARCHAR cust_id[5];    /* note we should not initialize    */
          VARCHAR cust_name[14];
          float cust_discnt;
      exec sql end declare section;
```

The **ORACLE** precompiler processes the VARCHAR declaration for cust_id (for example) and turns it into the following declaration for the C compiler:

[4.1.5]
```
struct {
        unsigned short len;
        unsigned char arr[5];
} cust_id;
```

The variable cust_id is a struct type, comparable to a record in Pascal, with two members (fields, in Pascal), cust_id.len and cust_id.arr[ ]. This is comparable to the varchar(n) form of a column type declaration in either **INGRES** or **ORACLE**, with an initial count of the characters to follow. The form is sometimes referred to as a *counted string*, as opposed to the *null-terminated string* form explained above. To initialize this variable from a constant string "c001", we would use two well-known C function assignments: strlen( ), which returns the number of characters in a null-terminated character string (not counting the null terminator), and strcpy( ), mentioned earlier, which copies the string in the second argument to the string position pointed to by the first argument:

```
cust_id.len = strlen("c001");   /* the value returned is 4        */
strcpy(cust_id.arr, "c001");    /* copies arg2 string to arg1     */
```

The result of these two assignment statements is the following C structure:

	cust_id.len	cust_id.arr				
cust_id:	4	'c'	'0'	'0'	'1'	'\0'

The null terminator for the character string in cust_id.arr is irrelevant to proper behavior of the Select statement in (4.1.2), but it is important for proper behavior of the printf( ) function in C. As a matter of fact, the string cust_name.arr retrieved by the Select statement has no null terminator. The cust_name variable has the format

	cust_name.len	cust_name.arr							
cust_id:	6	'T'	'i'	'p'	'T'	'0'	'p'	?	...	?

The array entries after the first six characters representing the `cname` Tip-Top are not set by the Select statement and are therefore denoted by question marks. If we want to print out this character string, cust_name.arr, using the C function printf( ), we have to first create a null terminator following the last character of the string. Since subscripts in C start with zero, the array entry following the first six characters of the array is subscripted by 6. More generally, we would write

```
cust_name.arr[cust_name.len] = '\0'; /* create null terminator   */
printf("%s", cust_name.arr);          /* print out string          */
```

The counted string form is the default supported by **ORACLE**. The form has a few advantages compared with the standard C form of null-terminated string, including the fact that binary types can be treated as strings, because embedded null values that may arise will not be incorrectly interpreted. For this reason, it is also possible to declare a special varchar struct form in **INGRES** (see *INGRES Embedded SQL Companion Guide for C* [5], indexed under "Varchar data type"). However, for the examples in this chapter, the null-terminated form is best because it saves C statements, so we will use it whenever possible in **INGRES**.

User Interaction

To explain the *prompt1( )* function used in Example 4.1.1, a *token* in an input string is a substring of characters with no embedded white spaces (blanks, tabs, etc.). The function prompt1( ) of Figure 4.2 prompts the user to type a line ending with a carriage return (CR), reads in that line as a string from the keyboard using the function *fgets,* and then extracts a single token from the string (the first token on the line) with the function *sscanf.*

```
#define LINELEN 1000
#include <stdio.h>

/* function prompts for one input token and places in array arg tk1    */
int prompt1(char prompt[ ], char tk1[ ], int max1)
{
    char line[LINELEN],                 /* char arrays for input line   */
         token1[LINELEN];               /* ... and token                */
    int count;                          /* count of tokens scanned      */

    printf("%s", prompt);               /* output prompt to user        */
    fgets(line, LINELEN, stdin);        /* get response from keyboard   */
                                        /* ... into array line[ ]       */
    count = sscanf(line, "%s", token1); /* scan one token               */
    if(count <=0)                       /* if only white space scanned  */
        return(-1);                     /* return -1: unsuccessful       */
    if(strlen(token1) > max1)           /* if token doesn't fit         */
        return(-1);                     /* ... in tk1, return -1        */
                                        /* otherwise, token fits        */
    strcpy(tk1, token1);                /* copy into return arg         */
    return(0);                          /* and return successfully      */
}
```

Figure 4.2 prompt1( ) Function

Note that the argument max1 gives the maximum length string that can be placed in the array of tk1. This is a common convention to ensure that the array whose pointer is passed as tk1 is not filled beyond its capacity. To read two or more tokens on a line of input, a different prompt function is required. Figure 4.3 contains a function, *prompt2*, to print out a supplied prompt and read in two tokens on a line.

It is possible to write a prompt9 function, for example, to return nine tokens, and then use this function in cases where fewer tokens are expected. But to guard against program error resulting from unexpected user input, we would always need to actually pass nine-character array arguments to prompt9. This is a lot of extra arguments for nothing in most cases, so we usually make a call to the appropriate prompt# function when needed. In the precompilation/compilation procedure of the next subsection, we assume that the different prompt# functions are all in a single source file (with the name prompt.c in UNIX).

Our programs have one unusual property that deserves mention. Notice that in Figures 4.1a and 4.1b, the function call to prompt1 contains a constant, 4, as an argument:

```
while((prompt1(prompt, cust_id, 4)) >= 0) { /* main loop, get cid */
```

```
/* function prompts for two input tokens, places in args tk1, tk2      */
int prompt2(char prompt[ ], char tk1[ ], int max1,
    char tk2[ ], int max2)
{
    char line[LINELEN],                    /* char arrays for input line */
        token1[LINELEN], token2[LINELEN];  /* ... and 2 tokens           */
    int count;                             /* count of tokens scanned    */

    printf("%s", prompt);                  /* output prompt to user      */
    fgets(line, LINELEN, stdin);           /* get response from keyboard */
                                           /* ... into array line[ ]     */
    count = sscanf(line, "%s %s", token1, token2); /* scan 2 tokens      */
    if (count <= 1)                        /* if less than 2 scanned     */
        return(-1);                        /* return - 1: unsuccessful   */
    if(strlen(token1) > max1
        || strlen(token2) > max2)          /* if either token doesn't fit */
            return(-1);                    /* ... return -1              */
    strcpy(tk1, token1);                   /* copy tokens                */
    strcpy(tk2, token2);                   /* ... to return args         */
    return(0);                             /* and return success         */
}
```

Figure 4.3 prompt2( ) Function

As we just explained, this constant represents the maximum length string that can be placed in the array cust_id. But the reader should understand that normal C conventions would require us to use a symbolic constant in this position, rather than the constant 4. This would entail a definition of the following form at the beginning of the source file:

```
#define CIDLEN 4
```

And then the call to prompt1( ) would be changed to look like this:

```
while((prompt1(prompt, cust_id, CIDLEN)) >= 0) { /* . . .          */
```

This is a very reasonable convention in normal programming. For applications with a large number of function calls of this kind, it is much better to have a single definition at the beginning of each source file that can be changed if the number of characters in the cid column changes, say from four to six, with a new table definition. We can thus make a single edit modification at the beginning of these files, and not have to perform a context search for the digit 4 in every application, making a logical decision from context whether to change that digit 4 to the digit 6. Having said this, we occasionally decide to break this convention in examples in this text, in order to make the value of a particular constant immediately obvious in context. Usage of this kind is not meant to controvert the standard convention.

As we mentioned earlier, a C language compiler won't recognize the syntax of an embedded exec sql . . . statement, so the source file is typically run first through a *precompiler*, which converts such embedded statements into appropriate statements in C. The precompilation/compilation procedure is different for the different systems; two examples follow.

Precompilation/Compilation Procedure on INGRES/UNIX

With the **INGRES** product on many UNIX sites, the programmer starts by creating a source file with a name such as "main.e", which contains all the C language statements and Embedded SQL (exec sql . . .) statements of the program. (The suffix ".e" denotes a source file with Embedded SQL constructs.) The **INGRES** programmer then invokes the precompiler by giving the UNIX command

```
esqlc main.e -f main.c
```

This command results in a new file, "main.c", with all `exec sql . . .` statements replaced by appropriate C statements. Consider the Select statement in Example 4.1.1:

```
exec sql select cname, discnt into :cust_name, :cust_discnt
    from customers where cid = :cust_id;
```

This would be replaced by a series of function calls to the **INGRES** monitor. After main.c is created, the normal compilation command is used to create an executable file, compiling and linking all related source files with a .c extension, such as prompt.c mentioned above. A number of libraries must be provided for the compilation-link step, and the directory specifications of these libraries are site specific. As an example, in a UNIX C Shell for **INGRES**, the compilation step might look something like this, using the Gnu C Compiler:

```
gcc -g main.c prompt.c -o runfile \   /* run-in with next line   */
    /nfs/rti/ingres/lib/libingres.a -lm
```

This compilation command, because of the -g option, allows you to use the UNIX debugger to debug the resulting executable file, runfile. Your instructor should provide you with the form to be used at your site. The resulting executable form may require a large quantity of disk space, because of all the library function code needed, and it is a good rule to try to limit the number of executable files in your directories.

Precompilation/Compilation Procedure on ORACLE/PC

With the **ORACLE** release 6 product on an IBM/PC under DOS, the programmer starts by creating a source file with a name such as "main.pc", which contains all the C language statements and Embedded SQL (`exec sql . . .`) statements of the program; the suffix ".pc" denotes a source file with Embedded SQL constructs. The **ORACLE** programmer then invokes the precompiler by giving the terminal command

```
proc include=\oracle6\pro\c iname=main.pc
```

This command results in a new file, "main.c", with all `exec sql . . .` statements replaced by appropriate pure C statements. Consider the Select statement in Example 4.1.1:

```
exec sql select cname, discnt into :cust_name, :cust_discnt
    from customers where cid = :cust_id;
```

This would be replaced by a series of function calls to the **ORACLE** monitor. After main.c is created, the following command is used to perform compilation:

```
cl -c -AL -FPc main.c
```

This creates a new object file called main.obj. A similar command would be used to compile the prompt.c file mentioned earlier, and to create a new file, prompt.obj. To link main.obj and prompt.obj into the same executable file runfile.exe, we need to create another file with a name such as linkit.mln, containing the following lines:

```
main.obj prompt.obj
runfile.exe
test.map /map /se:512 /nod /st:10000
\oracle6\pro\lib\sqllib.lib \oracle6\pro\lib\ora6dos.lib \ /*  run-in */
    \lib\libce.lib;
```

Given that this file exists, enter the following command:

```
link @linkit.mln
```

to create the executable file runfile.exe. Your instructor should provide you with any variations on this form to be used at your site. The resulting executable file may require a large quantity of disk space, and it is a good rule to try to limit the number of executable files in your directories.

Selecting Multiple Rows with a Cursor

The form of Embedded SQL Select statement dealt with in Example 4.1.1 can be used only when the Select is guaranteed to retrieve *at most one row* into a single set of column variables. How do we handle multiple row retrieval in a program? It is all very well with interactive queries to retrieve multiple rows in table form to a screen, but in a program we must specify exactly where each column of every row is to be placed, so we can refer to it by name. Conceivably we could declare arrays and then retrieve all rows of data "into" those arrays, but this is *not* a good idea—we can't generally know in advance how big the arrays should be, nor even that the data to be retrieved will all fit at once in a memory-based array. In fact, you should take this as a principle of Embedded SQL programming.

One-Row-at-a-Time Principle. Whenever an unknown number of rows is to be retrieved in an Embedded SQL program, the programmer should assume that these rows cannot all fit at one time in any conceivable array that can be declared, and the design of the program should reflect this assumption.

The problem of how to deal with an unknown number of rows reminds us of processing an unknown number of input values from a file, which we usually do one value at a time in a loop. It's clear that we're going to have to look at the rows from a Select statement one at a time anyway, since programs work in a sequential, one-step-at-a-time fashion. As we perform a Select on an unknown number of rows, retrieving the rows one at a time, we need a *cursor* to keep track of where we are.

Cursor Use

Given a specific customer, identified by the `cid` and provided interactively by the user, we want to retrieve rows listing `aids` of agents who placed orders for that customer, together with the dollar sum of orders placed for `cid` by each agent. We declare a cursor with the name agent_dollars to take the place of a simple Select statement as follows:

```
exec sql declare agent_dollars cursor for
    select aid, sum(dollars) from orders
    where cid = :cust_id group by aid;
```

A Declare Cursor statement is a declaration, and it is usually placed early in a program. After the cursor has been declared, it is still not in active use. Before the program can begin to retrieve information, an Embedded SQL statement must be executed to *open* the cursor. After the cursor is open, the program can then retrieve one row at a time from the cursor using a *fetch* operation; when the program is finished fetching, it must *close* the cursor once again. First, the statement to open the cursor

```
exec sql open agent_dollars;
```

When the Open Cursor statement is encountered during program execution, a call is made to the database system monitor, which prepares to execute the Select statement of the agent_dollars cursor. If the evaluation of the query is dependent on any host variables (cust_id in our case), *the values of these variables will be evaluated at this time.* It is important to realize that changing the value of cust_id at a later time will have no effect on successive rows retrieved. Once the cursor has been opened, we can begin to retrieve successive rows in the query, using the Fetch statement:

```
exec sql fetch agent_dollars into :agent_id, :dollar_sum;
```

The *into* clause appeared earlier in the Select statement, which retrieved a single row. In the case of multiple-row retrieval, the **into** clause is attached to the Fetch statement, rather than being declared as part of the cursor. This is to give us as much flexibility as possible, since it is conceivable that we might want to fetch row values from a single cursor into more than one set of variables in different circumstances. Clearly the **into** clause belongs with the Fetch statement, which actually retrieves values from the row.

A cursor can usually be thought of as pointing to the *prior* row, which has just been retrieved. When the cursor is first opened, it starts at a position *just before* the first row. In successive calls to fetch, the cursor position is first incremented, then values in that row are retrieved into the host variables specified. It is possible that a new fetch will increment the cursor to find that there are no rows left to retrieve; a condition indicating this event is returned to the program. This behavior is entirely analogous to many program situations where an arbitrary number of values are to be retrieved from a file. For example, in C the function getchar( ) retrieves characters from the standard input file, which acts like a disk file but reads input from the keyboard by default. If the standard input file has been redirected to input from a normal disk file, the getchar( ) function returns a special EOF value when it runs out of characters in the file it is reading. It is the responsibility of the programmer to test each value returned and proceed to new logic when EOF is encountered. In the case of the SQL fetch, the condition to indicate an end of file is returned, not in functional return values, but in a special structure known as the SQLCA.

The SQL Communication Area: SQLCA

The *SQL Communication Area*, or SQLCA, is a declared memory structure (a struct in C, a record in PASCAL) containing member variables used to communicate information between the database system monitor and the program. The SQLCA structure is being deprecated by the X/OPEN standard (i.e., phased out), but the SQLCA structure is still widely used in commercial database products (**INGRES**, **ORACLE**, and **DB2** all use the SQLCA), so this is the method we present. An alternative approach is discussed at the beginning of Section 4.2. The SQLCA is declared in C, usually before any other external declaration statements, by writing the Include statement:

```
exec sql include sqlca;
```

We have already seen this Include statement used in Example 4.1.1. The program can expect new values in the SQLCA after each Exec Sql statement that makes a runtime call to the database system monitor. Most commonly the information returned involves error or warning conditions, and we will continue to defer detailed consideration of error handling until Section 4.2. A number of different member variables are part of the SQLCA struct, but for now we mention only one, SQLCODE. This variable is referenced in C by its full name, sqlca.sqlcode, and takes on the value 100 in **INGRES** whenever *no rows* are processed by any of the SQL statements: Delete, Fetch, Insert, Select, or Update. In particular, following a Fetch statement an sqlca.sqlcode value of 100 indicates that no new row from the cursor was returned, and we have thus reached an end in our cursor retrieval. As we will see, the value 100 for sqlca.sqlcode is not used in **ORACLE**, so a more general approach is needed to make code portable from one database system to another.

```
#define TRUE 1
#include <stdio.h>

exec sql include sqlca;                          /* communication area      */
int prompt1(char[ ], char[ ], int);              /* functional prototype    */
exec sql begin declare section;
    char cust_id[5], agent_id[4];
    double dollar_sum;                           /* double float variable   */
exec sql end declare section;
main( )
{

    char prompt[ ] = "PLEASE ENTER CUSTOMER ID: ";

    exec sql declare agent_dollars cursor for
        select aid, sum(dollars) from orders /* cursor for select          */
        where cid = :cust_id group by aid;   /* note depends on cust_id    */

    exec sql whenever sqlerror stop;             /* error trap condition    */
    exec sql connect poneilsql;                  /* INGRES format: connect  */
    while(prompt1(prompt, cust_id, 4) >= 0) { /* main loop, get cid         */
                                                 /* cust_id must be set ... */
        exec sql open agent_dollars;             /* ... before open cursor  */
        while(TRUE)   {                          /* loop to fetch rows      */
            exec sql fetch agent_dollars     /* fetch next row and ...      */
                into :agent_id, :dollar_sum; /* ... set these variables     */
            if (sqlca.sqlcode == 100)            /* when no more rows ...    */
                break;                           /* ... exit fetch loop      */
            printf("%s %11.2f\n",                /* print out latest values  */
                agent_id, dollar_sum);

        }                                        /* end fetch loop          */
        exec sql close agent_dollars;            /* close cursor when done  */
        exec sql commit work;                    /* end locks on fetched rows */
    }                                            /* end of main loop        */
    exec sql disconnect;                         /* disconnect from database */
}
```

Figure 4.4 INGRES: Retrieve Multiple Rows (Illustrates Example 4.1.2)

EXAMPLE 4.1.2

Figure 4.4 shows a program to retrieve multiple rows, a **group by** Select statement listing agent id values and sum of dollar orders by these agents for any customer id provided by the user. This program is valid in **INGRES**, and the **ORACLE** form is easily constructed by using VARCHAR character string variables and the alternative Connect statement, as illustrated in Figure 4.1b, with one modification. Note that in the Fetch loop when condition sqlca.sqlcode == 100 arises in **INGRES**, we break out of the loop without printing the values of agent_id and dollar_sum. This is because each Fetch first increments the cursor and then reads the new row values. When no new row is found, no new values are actually fetched: the variables have the same values that were printed on the previous pass, so we must guard against printing them again. In **ORACLE** the test for sqlca.sqlcode == 100 is inappropriate, and the best solution is to use a more general condition-handling approach discussed at the beginning of Section 4.2, **whenever not found goto** <statement_label>. This approach works with **INGRES** as well.   ∎

4.2 Error Handling

When the esqlc preprocessor encounters the `exec sql include sqlca` statement, it reads in a header file (standard C practice with an Include statement) containing the definition for a C language struct, sqlca. Note that the sqlca declaration must lie in the scope of all functions in the program that reference it, so it is best to place the Include SQLCA statement at the beginning of a source file, outside of any function, as was done in Examples 4.1.1 and 4.1.2. The sqlca struct is rather long, with many elements that have no current use. As mentioned earlier, the X/OPEN SQL standard is attempting to deprecate the SQLCA approach, to move the standard to a new method of error reporting known as SQLSTATE. You will want to look up SQLSTATE and SQLCA in the index of the Embedded SQL reference guide for the database system product you are using to determine all major error conditions and how they are reported. However, SQLCA is still the most common usage, and we will concentrate here on a few useful variables: the long int variables sqlca.sqlcode and sqlca.sqlerrd[2].

The long int variable sqlca.sqlcode is set following an Exec Sql statement that performs a runtime call to a database system monitor routine. We have already seen a use in Figure 4.4, where we tested sqlca.sqlcode to see if it had a value of 100, meaning in **INGRES** that the latest Fetch from a cursor had failed to return values for a new row (no new rows were processed by the Fetch). For most database systems, the sqlca.sqlcode variable takes on values of three kinds:

value = 0   This indicates a successful call with no exceptional conditions.

value < 0   This indicates an error condition causing the call to fail, often because of a programming error. Error code significance is dependent on the specific DBMS. **ORACLE** error codes are found in the *ORACLE Error Messages and Codes Manual* [11]; for example, error return from `exec sql connect: -02019: database (link) does not exist`. **INGRES** error codes can be found in the *INGRES Error Message Directory* [7], listed without the minus sign; for example, error return from `exec sql connect: 16 database does not exist`.

value > 0   This indicates an exceptional (warning) condition. The call was successful, but the caller should be aware of some important condition. In **INGRES**, the value +100 means that no rows were processed by Fetch or other statement types. Other warnings may be identified by additional fields sqlca.sqlwarn#, where # is a digit, 1–8; for example, if sqlca.sqlwarn2 = 'W', at least one null value was eliminated in evaluating a set function. See the SQL reference manual of the relevant product for details.

The common programmatic use of sqlca.sqlcode is to test whether an error has occurred (if (sqlca.sqlcode < 0) . . .). A simple program usually aborts when it encounters an error, whereas a large commercial application program usually tries to find a way to recover. A test as to whether a Fetch from a cursor has run out of rows was demonstrated in Example 4.1.2, illustrating a situation where sqlca.sqlcode > 0.

The long int variable sqlca.sqlerrd[2] contains the number of rows affected following any Insert, Update, or Delete statements (as explained in Section 4.3). This information will be particularly valuable in cases we will encounter in Chapter 6, where integrity constraints might unexpectedly limit updates to a table.

Condition Handling with the Whenever Statement

To avoid testing the sqlca.sqlcode condition code following every Exec Sql statement, we can use the Whenever statement:

```
exec sql whenever condition action;
```

An example of such a statement is

[4.2.1]   `exec sql whenever sqlerror stop;`

The Whenever statement has a *stop* action that is valid in **ORACLE** and **INGRES** but not in all database systems, in particular not in **DB2**. We have already used the Whenever statement without explaining it in Examples 4.1.1 and 4.1.3. The effect is to set up a "condition trap" so that all subsequent runtime calls to the database system (resulting from Exec Sql statements) will be automatically tested for an error condition on return. If an error condition exists, the **stop** action is taken (see below).

Here is an explanation of conditions and actions that can occur in a Whenever statement.

CONDITIONS

◆ **sqlerror.** Tests if sqlca.sqlcode < 0 following an **exec sql . . .** call.

◆ **not found.** Tests when no rows are affected following some sql statement such as Fetch, Insert, Update, or Delete. Equivalent to the test sqlca.sqlcode == 100 in **INGRES**.

◆ **sqlwarning.** Tests if sqlca.sqlcode > 0, other than a **not found** condition. The case sqlca.sqlcode = 100 in **INGRES** is considered a warning, but that condition has been more precisely described by the **not found** condition. Note that the **sqlwarning** condition is not part of the X/Open SQL standard; however, it is widely implemented in various database products.

ACTIONS

◆ **continue.** This action is the default, meaning that no action should be taken on the basis of the associated condition—normal flow of control continues. The **continue** action cannot allow execution to continue after a *fatal error*, which prints an error message and aborts the program. A fatal error is one that the program could not have intended, such as

INGRES: "1330 Illegal context of (EXEC SQL statement) without preceding CONNECT statement. Exiting . . ." Fatal errors often end with the word "Exiting . . ."

◆ **goto** label. This has the same effect as a "goto label" statement in C. Note that the label named must be within the scope of all subsequent Exec SQL statements up to the point where another Whenever statement is encountered for the same condition. The preprocessor generates the statement:

```
if (condition) goto label;
```

after every Exec Sql statement. It is possible to use the *same* label in different functions to overcome this difficulty.

◆ **stop**. This action terminates execution of the program, and in the case of **INGRES** prints an error message. If a database is open at the time, it disconnects from it. The **stop** action cannot be specified for the **not found** condition. This action is defined in **ORACLE** and **INGRES**, but not in all database systems.

The **INGRES** database system has an additional useful action (not part of the standard)—the **call** function.

◆ **call** function. The condition causes a named C function to be called. On return from this function, flow of control continues from the statement after the Exec SQL statement that raised the condition.

Whenever Statement: Scope and Flow of Control

We can picture that the precompiler implements the condition trap of a Whenever statement by inserting tests after every subsequent runtime database system call. Given the Whenever statement of (4.2.1), the tests have the form "if(sqlca.sqlcode < 0) stopfn()", where a special database system function is called to perform the **stop** action. After a Whenever statement is encountered, the precompiler performs a simple statement-by-statement search and insertion as it passes through successive lines of code in the *source file,* changing its action only when a subsequent overriding Whenever statement is encountered. In particular, note that the action does not follow the flow of control if an intervening Whenever statement overrides the original prescription.

EXAMPLE 4.2.1

Consider the following sequence of statements in a program file.

```
main( )
{
    exec sql whenever sqlerror stop;    /* first whenever statement */
    . . .
    goto s1
    . . .
    exec sql whenever sqlerror continue; /* overrides first whenever*/
s1: exec sql update agents set percent = percent + 1;
    . . .
}
```

The action for an sqlerror condition in force at label S1 is always **continue** (the effect of the second Whenever statement), even though this update statement has been reached by a goto statement in the scope of the first Whenever statement. This is because the precompiler placed a test at label S1 under the influence of the second Whenever; the controlling factor is statement position in the file, not flow of control, of which the precompiler is unaware. ∎

Note that the default action when no Whenever statements have occurred is **continue**, meaning that no special action is taken and the normal flow of control continues. No test after a runtime call to the database is necessary to achieve this action. The default action can be specifically reestablished to override a Whenever statement with a different action, as in Example 4.2.1: exec sql whenever sqlerror continue.

We must be careful when using the Whenever statement to avoid infinite loops.

EXAMPLE 4.2.2 Avoiding Infinite Loops.

The following code fragment gives an example of an attempt to create a table in Embedded SQL:

```
exec sql whenever sqlerror goto handle_error;
exec sql create table customers
    (cid char(4) not null, cname varchar(13), . . .);
```

If the Create Table command fails because of some error (for example, in **INGRES** −18112, probably meaning insufficient disk space), the flow of control passes to the following labeled fragment:

```
handle_error:
    exec sql whenever sqlerror continue;
    exec sql drop customers;
    exec sql disconnect;
    exit(1);
```

The exec sql whenever sqlerror continue statement is important here, because an error might result from the call to drop the customers table—in fact, this is quite likely if we didn't succeed in creating the table. If the original Whenever statement were still in effect, the result would be to goto the handle_error label again, repeating the drop statement attempt and looping indefinitely. The new Whenever statement overrides the goto action, so a loop does not occur.

Note too that when an error occurs within a C program function, proper exit handling is important. After the disconnect statement above, the "exit(1)" statement aborts the program (in a UNIX system), rather than simply returning to the calling function as if the create had been successful. Of course appropriate behavior is up to the programmer. It is barely possible that there is some alternative action to take in the event that a Create Table statement is unsuccessful. In that case, a normal return with some warning value should take place, rather than a program abort. ∎

If there is a need to recognize explicit error conditions, this will normally not be possible if a Whenever statement is in force with any action other than **continue**. We see why this is so in Example 4.2.3.

EXAMPLE 4.2.3 Explicit Error Checking.
Consider the following code fragment:

```
exec sql whenever sqlerror goto handle_error;
/* this is in force below */
 . . .
exec sql create table custs
    (cid char(4) not null, cname varchar(13), . . .);
if (sqlca.sqlcode == -8112)                    /* out of disk space? */
    <call procedure to handle this condition>  /* NEVER REACH THIS*/
```

Recall that the preprocessor implements the Whenever statement by placing a test for sqlerror (if (sqlca.sqlcode < 0) goto handle_error) immediately after the Create Table statement. Therefore it should be obvious that the condition "sqlca.sqlcode == –8112" will never arise on the line following that tests for it. The **whenever** condition has gotten in first and short-circuited our intended test to recognize insufficient disk space. It turns out that if we want to recognize an explicit error condition, we need to drop our **goto** action for **sqlerror** beforehand, modifying the logic above as indicated below in italics.

```
exec sql whenever sqlerror goto handle_error;        /* this is in force below */
. . .
exec sql whenever sqlerror continue;                 /* but this overrides it */
exec sql create table custs
    (cid char(4) not null, cname varchar(13), . . .); /* as above             */
if (sqlca.sqlcode == -8112)                          /* out of disk space?    */
    <call procedure to handle this condition>        /* now this works        */
if (sqlca.sqlcode < 0) goto handle_error;            /* other error? handle it */
exec sql whenever sqlerror goto handle_error;        /* again in force below   */
. . .                                                                         ■
```

Advantages of the Whenever Statement

One major value of the Whenever statement lies in the fact that a condition trap can greatly reduce the number of lines of code written to handle error returns. Another advantage is that the Whenever syntax is extremely portable across different database systems. For example, the condition **not found** is commonly needed in Fetch loops and update statements whose effects are uncertain, but the condition has different sqlca.sqlcode values in **INGRES** and **ORACLE**. The Whenever statement will always be triggered in the appropriate situation.

On the other hand, for specific database products it is possible to detect any of the standard **Whenever** conditions by carefully inserting tests on the sqlca.sqlcode value after all database runtime calls. Indeed, such tests allow a greater flexibility in recognizing special conditions, and often in specifying an action to take (for example, on systems where a **call** function action is not legal in Whenever syntax, we can implement this useful action explicitly after testing the sqlcode).

Handling Error Messages

It is often valuable for debugging purposes for programs to access the system-generated error message associated with an error return. To exemplify this, we expand the handle_error code fragment of Example 4.2.2. The exact code sequence required to extract an error message is dependent on the database system in use: these methods are *completely nonstandard* and do not generalize, although some methods comparable to these are probably available in most database products.

EXAMPLE 4.2.4 Printing Error Messages in INGRES.

In **INGRES**, we begin by declaring a character array, errbuf, of length 256 in the SQL Declare Section.

```
#define ERRLEN 256

   . . .

exec sql begin declare section;
char errbuf[ERRLEN];

   . . .
```

Now we can expand the handle_error code fragment of 4.2.2 as follows:

```
handle_error:
    exec sql whenever sqlerror continue;
    exec sql copy sqlerror into :errbuf;  /* extra char at end   */
    printf("Aborting because of error:\n%s\n",
       errbuf);                           /* print out err msg   */
    exec sql drop customers;
    exec sql disconnect;
    exit(1);
```

Of course it might be inappropriate for the program to print out the error message in errbuf[ ] to the terminal screen if the end user is unable to interpret it. In this case it would be preferable to write the message to an error file for later interpretation by an application programmer. Here we are grateful for a flexible means of handling the message, rather than having to depend on the **stop** action of the Whenever statement that automatically prints it in **INGRES**. ∎

EXAMPLE 4.2.5 Printing Error Messages in ORACLE.

Recall that the **stop** action of the Whenever statement does not print an error message in **ORACLE**. It is therefore important that a special function call is provided to extract an error message and place it in errbuf. To start with, we need a few declarations (ERRLEN is as above):

```
int errlength = ERRLEN;  /* size of buffer             */
int errsize;             /* for actual message length  */
char errbuf[ERRLEN];     /* buffer to receive message  */
```

Now instead of writing

```
exec sql copy sqlerror into :errbuf with ERRLEN-1;
```

as in **INGRES** Example 4.2.4, **ORACLE** extracts the error message with the call

```
SQLGM(errbuf, &errlength, &errsize);
```

The "&" symbols in front of the two variables are used to create pointers to the variables as call arguments, so that the called routine will be able to modify the variable values. This is the method used in C to allow *call by reference* (also known as *call by name*) rather than *call by value,* so that a variable associated with a function argument can be used to return a value to the caller. A call to SQLGM can often be avoided, since the first 70 characters of all error messages will be passed in the SQLCA. The length of the message is contained in sqlca.sqlerrm.sqlerrml, and the array containing the message is sqlca.sqlerrm.sqlerrmc. Once again it is necessary to create a null terminator for any message handled by a C function. ∎

Indicator Variables

Recall from Chapter 3 that column values in a table can take on null values (unless they have been declared with the *not null* clause in the Create Table statement), and these null values are outside the range of normal values for the type declared. In Example 3.6.8 we pointed out that the statement

```
select * from customers where discnt <= 10 or discnt > 10;
```

would not retrieve a row from the customers table that has a null value in the discnt column. This is relatively surprising, since it would seem that all possible values are either less than, equal to, or greater than 10, but it is exactly the kind of behavior that null values are supposed to supply. Recall that the null value represents an unknown or undefined quantity. If a customer doesn't yet have a discnt value assigned, we don't want to count that customer as one who has discnt value <= 10, nor as a customer who has discnt value > 10. Now assume that we retrieved the discnt value of a row from CUSTOMERS into a host variable declared as "int cust_discnt" (and perhaps other column values into other variables), with the following Embedded SQL Select statement:

```
exec sql select discnt, . . . into :cust_discnt, . . .
    from customers where cid = :cust_id;
```

Consider what will happen if the discnt value is null in the row selected. Certainly cust_discnt has some pattern of bits as a C variable, and if we make the test

```
if (cust_discnt <= 10 || cust_discnt > 10) . . .
```

then the If statement will evaluate to TRUE, since any pattern of bits in cust_discnt obeys one of these two conditions (the '||' operator is the logical "or" in C). But this is the wrong behavior in many cases. We would like to mimic in our C decisions the logic of SQL as closely as possible, and this test fails in that regard. To better mimic SQL, what we need is some way to distinguish when a returned variable value is *null*, so we can write:

```
if ((cust_discnt <= 10 || cust_discnt >10)
    && not-null(cust_discnt))   /* INVALID */
```

(The "&&" operator is the logical "and" in C.) Our desire is that this test will *not* evaluate to TRUE when a null value is retrieved in cust_discnt. Unfortunately, there is not enough significance in the cust_discnt variable to tell us whether the retrieved value is null—all useful significance is taken up with the integer values retrieved from a non-null discnt attribute. Thus we need some other way to remember that cust_discnt has retrieved a null value, and the standard approach used in SQL is to declare an *indicator variable* to go with cust_discnt. We will name this indicator variable cd_ind. Here is the declaration we use:

```
exec sql begin declare section;
    float cust_discnt;
    short int cd_ind;
    . . .
exec sql end declare section;
```

Now in the Select statement, we would replace the :cust_discnt reference by the pair :cust_discnt :cd_ind, as follows:

```
exec sql select discnt into :cust_discnt :cd_ind
    from customers where cid = :cust_id;
```

Following this retrieval, a value of –1 (minus one) in the cd_ind variable means that the variable cust_discnt has a null value, whereas a value of 0 (zero) means that cust_discnt has a normal integer value. Now the logical test we suggested earlier, not-null(cust_discnt), can be implemented with a test of this indicator variable. We write

```
if ((cust_discnt <= 10 || cust_discnt >10) && cd_ind != -1). . .
```

This test will evaluate to TRUE only for non-null values retrieved from the attribute discnt into the pair :cust_discnt :cd_ind. Note that an indicator value of –1 means that the integer value that has been assigned to cust_discnt is actually meaningless and should be ignored: the value is null.

We can always represent a null value in this way, even when updating the database rather than retrieving from it. For example, to set the discnt value to null in a specific row of customers, we can write

```
cd_ind = -1;
exec sql update customers
    set discnt = :cust_discnt :cd_ind where cid = :cust_id;
```

There is one other standard use for the indicator variable. The database system will set the indicator variable to a positive value (ind > 0) if the associated host variable holds a character string (in one of the two formats explained earlier) and the SQL statement truncates the length of the string value it retrieves from the database to make it fit in the host variable. Typically, the value of the positive indicator variable after truncation is the length of the database string value that had to be truncated. Thus the possible values for indicator variables in standard use are

= 0   A database value, not null, was assigned to the host variable.

> 0   A truncated database character string was assigned to the host variable.

= –1   The database value is null, and the host variable value is not a meaningful value.

Clearly it is possible to expand on use of values retrieved in the indicator variable. The **DB2** product, for example, will assign a value of –2 if a null value is retrieved because of an error rather than as a stored value of the database. For example, an error may arise in calculating an expression in the target list of a Select statement if division by zero occurs. A future version of the SQL standard may use other negative values for null-related purposes.

4.3 Some Common Embedded SQL Statements

In this section we provide general forms of various Embedded SQL data manipulation statements, starting with a complete description of the Embedded SQL Select statement.

The Select Statement

Recall that a Select statement can be executed in a program without use of a cursor only when no more than one row is to be retrieved (zero or one rows are permitted). If more than one row is found by a Select, a runtime error will be returned. The syntax of the Select statement in Embedded SQL is given in Figure 4.5. See Chapter 3 for explanations of most of the syntax elements, including the definition of a valid search_condition. Note that the host-variable referred to in Figure 4.5 can contain an indicator delete variable as a part of it.

```
exec sql select [all | distinct] expression {, expression}
    into host-variable {, host-variable}
    from tablename [corr_name] {, tablename [corr_name]}
    [where search_condition]
    [group by column {column}]
    [having search_condition];
```

Figure 4.5 Embedded SQL Select Syntax

Since only a single row can be retrieved by an Embedded Select statement, the interactive SQL **union** and **order by** clauses are not included in this general form. This means that the Select statement of Figure 4.5 is

identical to the Subselect general form of Figure 3.12. The Embedded
Select statement will change in the future, since it has been noted that a
union of several Subselects can sometimes be known to contain only a single row (as when a product row is known to appear in exactly one of several regional tables), and so the **union** clause is permitted in the Embedded
Select of SQL-92. The variables named in the **into** clause must be in one-
to-one correspondence with the expressions retrieved, and need to have an
appropriate type. If the Select statement results in no row being retrieved,
the value of sqlca.sqlcode will be set to an appropriate warning value.

ORACLE type	**INGRES** type	**DB2** type	C data type
char(n)	char(n)	char(n)	char arr[n+1] or, in **ORACLE**, VARCHAR arr[n+1]
varchar(n)	varchar(n)	varchar(n)	char array[n+1] or, in **ORACLE**, VARCHAR arr[n+1]
number(6)	smallint	smallint	short int
number(10)	integer	integer	long int
real	float4	real	float
float	float	double precision	double

Figure 4.6 Type Correspondences: **INGRES**, **ORACLE**, **DB2**, and C

In the Select statement and other statements covered below, host variables that have been declared in an **exec sql declare . . .** section can be used
in the **into** clause to receive target list variables retrieved. Figure 4.6 gives a
partial list of normal type correspondences between column data types
specified in the Create Table command and C variable data types. Note
that a certain amount of automatic type conversion will also take place in
retrieval of various column types into a host variable. For example, in
ORACLE, a varchar string with the SQL value '1234' will be converted into
numeric form by the database system when it is retrieved into a C variable
of type short int. If you intend to depend on this, you should become familiar with the conversions supported by the database system you are using.

Host variables that have been declared in an **exec sql declare . . .** section can also be used in any search_condition syntax of an Embedded SQL
statement. However, host variables in the search_condition can only be

used to represent numerical or character string constants in an expression. In particular, host variables cannot hold character strings meant to represent more complex syntax elements, such as names of columns or tables or logical conditions in expressions, which would require compiler attention at runtime after the host variable value is set. The ability to use host variable character strings to represent entire statements is covered in Section 4.6.

The Declare Cursor Statement

The full syntax of the Declare Cursor statement is given in Figure 4.7. Most of this syntax is basically the same as the interactive Select syntax of Figure 3.12. The Subselect form permits **group by** and **having** clauses, for example, and can also contain host variable expressions. However, most database system products do not provide a column alias for an expression retrieved in the target list: such a feature is less valuable because there is no default table display in the embedded case (although it is sometimes used to provide a named column for use in the **order by** clause).

```
exec sql declare cursor_name cursor for
    Subselect
    {union subselect-form}
    [order by result_column [asc | desc] {, result_column
    [asc | desc]}
    | for update of columnname {, columnname}];
```

Figure 4.7 Embedded SQL Declare Cursor Syntax

In **DB2** it is necessary to choose only one of the two final clauses in this syntax, **order by** or **for update of**. However, both **INGRES** and **ORACLE** allow both forms to be used simultaneously. In the X/OPEN SQL specification, the **for update** clause must be included with the cursor declaration if the program logic attempts to update or delete a row through the cursor; more on this below.

Note that a cursor can only move forward through a set of rows. This limitation will disappear when SQL-92 features become generally available, because of the new scrollable cursor feature that is part of the SQL-92 standard. Until that time, however, you need to close and reopen a cursor in order to fetch a row a second time. The same cursor may be opened and closed successive times in a single program. It generally must be closed, however, before it can be reopened (**ORACLE** permits an exception to this rule, as explained below).

The Delete Statement

There are two forms of the Delete statement, the *Positioned Delete,* which deletes the current row (most recently fetched row) of a cursor, and the *Searched Delete,* which has the same sort of form we have already seen in interactive SQL in Section 3.9. Here is syntax that describes the two forms of delete:

```
exec sql delete from tablename [corr_name]
    [where search_condition | where current of cursor_name];
```

Figure 4.8   Embedded SQL Delete Syntax

The Positioned Delete uses a special "**current of** cursor_name" syntax. Only one of the two **where** forms can be used; if neither is used, all rows of the table will be deleted. The corr_name is for use in the search_condition and may cause a runtime error condition in some products if used with a Positioned Delete. Following a Searched Delete, the long int variable sqlca.sqlerrd[2] contains the number of rows affected. If no rows are affected, the **not found** condition of the Whenever statement arises.

In the Positioned Delete, after the delete is executed the cursor points to a new position, following the row deleted but just preceding the next row, if any. This is in the same sense that after an **open** of a cursor, the cursor points to a position just before the first row in the Select; this behavior is carefully chosen to work well with loops (as we see in Example 4.3.1). If the cursor is not pointing to a row when a delete is executed (that is, if it is pointing just before some row, or else Fetch has already returned a **not found** condition, so it is pointing to a position after all rows), a runtime error will be returned. For the Positioned Delete to work at all, the cursor stipulated in the delete must be already open and pointing to a real row, and the **from** clause of the delete must refer to the same table as the **from** clause of the cursor select. In addition, the cursor select must have been declared **for update** in order for the Delete statement to work (it suffices to specify any column names at all in the declare cursor **for update** clause).

EXAMPLE 4.3.1

Delete all customers from the customers table who live in Duluth and have made no orders (do not appear in the orders table). We can do this simply, with a Searched Delete, using the following statement:

```
exec sql delete from customers c where c.city = 'Duluth' and
    not exists (select * from orders o where o.cid = c.cid);
```

We could also use a cursor to perform this delete:

```
.  .  .
exec sql declare delcust cursor for
  select cid from customers c
  where c.city = 'Duluth'
  and not exists (select * from orders o where o.cid = c.cid)
  for update of cid;                        /* must declare cursor for update */
  whenever not found goto skip;             /* label "skip" lies later in code*/
  while (TRUE)                              /* TRUE has value 1: loop forever */
  {
     exec sql fetch delcust into :cust_id;  /* if notfound, goto skip         */
     exec sql delete from customers
       where current of delcust;            /* delete row under cursor        */
  }
  .  .  .
```

Note that after the Delete statement in the while(TRUE) loop, the cursor points to a position just before the following row. The Fetch statement at the beginning of the loop is needed to advance the cursor through each of the rows selected, whether or not a delete is performed. In cases where the delete may or may not be performed, depending on some complex logical condition, this is valuable default behavior because we can always depend on requiring a fetch at the top of the loop.   ∎

It would be possible to modify the program of Example 4.3.1, creating a cursor that retrieved city and cid for all customers who have made orders and then performing the test if(city == "Duluth") in the program logic to decide whether the row should be deleted. However, this approach would be a mistake for performance reasons. It is always best to provide as much of a selection criterion as possible for SQL to test, because that way SQL can perform a test without the extra overhead of having to extract the values from the table and send them back to the program, often a very time-consuming action. Indeed it is generally preferable to leave as much intended action as possible to SQL. The Searched Delete appearing at the top of Example 4.3.1 is more efficient than the loop below to perform equivalent positioned deletes through the cursor.

The Update Statement

As with Delete, there are two versions of the Update statement, a *Searched Update* analogous to the multi-row Interactive Update statement, and a *Positioned Update,* which acts through a cursor. The Searched Update is virtually identical to the interactive version presented in Section 3.9, and it contains no elements we haven't explained earlier:

```
exec sql update tablename [corr_name]
    set columnname = expression {, columnname = expression}
    [where search_condition];
```

Figure 4.9   Embedded SQL Searched Update Syntax

Following a Searched Update, the long int variable sqlca.sqlerrd[2] contains the number of rows affected. If no rows are affected, the **not found** condition of the Whenever statement arises.

```
exec sql update tablename
    set columnname = expression {, columnname = expression]
    where current of cursor_name;
```

Figure 4.10   Embedded SQL Positioned Update Syntax

As with Delete, for the Positioned Update statement to work properly the cursor must be open, the table named in the **from** clause of the Update and in the Declare Cursor statement must be identical, and the cursor must be pointing to a valid row, rather than to a position just before or after some row. In addition, the cursor must be declared **for update** on all the columns changed by the Update statement. If any of these conditions are not valid, a runtime error will be returned from the Positioned Update statement execution.

The Insert Statement

The Insert statement has only a single form, identical to the interactive version of the Insert statement presented in Section 3.9. The Insert statement syntax is given in Figure 4.11. Nevertheless, there are two Insert forms, one that inserts a single row with specified values and one that may possibly insert multiple rows, derived from a general Subselect statement as specified earlier in this section. Following an insert derived from a Subselect, the long int variable sqlca.sqlerrd[2] will contain the number of rows affected. If no rows are affected, the **not found** condition of the Whenever statement will arise.

```
exec sql insert into tablename [(columnname {, columnname})]
         {values (expression {, expression}) | subselect};
```

Figure 4.11 Embedded SQL Insert Syntax

Let us consider for a moment why there is no positioned insert, "**insert . . . where current of** cursor_name;". As we will learn in later chapters, a newly inserted row usually cannot be placed into a table at a designated position, but only at a position determined by the disk structure of the table. The phrase "**where current of** cursor_name" would thus overdetermine the problem to be solved by the database system in deciding where to place a newly inserted row.

Cursor Open, Fetch, and Close

The statement to open a previously defined cursor has the form shown in Figure 4.12.

```
exec sql open cursor_name;
```

Figure 4.12 Embedded SQL Open Cursor Syntax

When the Open statement is executed, the database system evaluates expressions in the **where** clause of the cursor specification for cursor_name and identifies a set of rows that become the active set for subsequent Fetch operations. Any host variables used in the cursor definition are evaluated *at the time the open statement is executed.* If these values later change, this does not affect the active set of rows. For many database products, the cursor cannot be opened again if it is already open. **ORACLE** allows an exception to this rule, since an already open cursor can be reopened, redefining the active set of rows.

The statement to fetch a row from an active set of an opened cursor has the form illustrated in Figure 4.13.

```
exec sql fetch cursor_name
    into host-variable {, host-variable};
```

Figure 4.13 Embedded SQL Fetch Syntax

Executing the Open statement positions the cursor, cursor_name, to a position just before the first row of an active set of rows. Each successive Fetch statement repositions cursor_name to the next row of its active set and assigns column values from that row (named in the Declare Cursor statement) to the host variables named in the Fetch statement. In order for a Fetch statement to work, cursor_name must already be open and the number of host variables must match the number of columns in the target list of the Define Cursor. The **not found** condition of the Whenever statement arises when a Fetch statement is executed on an active set of rows that is empty, or when the cursor is positioned after the last active row.

The statement to close a cursor has the form shown in Figure 4.14.

```
exec sql close cursor-name;
```

Figure 4.14 Embedded SQL Close Cursor Syntax

This statement closes the cursor so that the active set of rows is no longer accessible. It is an error to close a cursor that is not open.

Other Embedded SQL Operations

A number of other Embedded SQL statements will be explained in the following sections. Here is a list of ones we have already seen:

```
exec sql create table
exec sql drop table
exec sql connect
exec sql disconnect
```

The syntax for these and other statements can be found in Appendix B. While most of these statements have quite simple syntax, the Create Table statement has numerous syntax elements that have not yet been introduced and that require careful explanation. These elements will be covered in Chapter 6.

4.4 Programming for Transactions

So far we have dealt mainly with non-procedural SQL statements. It is not surprising that a number of new considerations arise with the ability to create procedures that use several SQL statements in sequence to accomplish a single task. In this section we introduce the concept of *database transactions*. We show that there is sometimes a need to group several SQL statements together into a single uninterruptible, all-or-nothing transactional package, and that this concept has important ramifications for the way we write our programs.

The Concept of a Transaction

Most database systems allow multiple users to execute simultaneously and to access tables in a common database. You have probably seen situations where a large number of users on different terminals interacted with a single computer (students in a terminal room connected to a time-shared computer, bank clerks at their terminals, airline reservation agents, etc.). A major task of a computer operating system is to keep track of these users, all running different work streams known as *user processes*. The database system cooperates with this user process concept by permitting multiple processes to access data at the same time. This is known as *concurrent access*, or *concurrency*.

It turns out that without adequate controls on concurrent access, it is possible for a user process to view a collection of data elements that would never exist simultaneously.

EXAMPLE 4.4.1 Inconsistent View of Data.

Assume that a depositor has two bank accounts in a table A, represented as distinct rows with unique account id values, aid, equal to A1 and A2. We represent A.balance where A.aid = An by An.balance, for short (note that this is not standard SQL notation), and assume that we start with A1.balance containing $900.00 and A2.balance containing $100.00. Now assume that process P1 attempts to move $400.00 from account A1 to A2, to even out the balances. In order to do this, it must perform two row updates, first subtracting $400.00 from A1.balance, then adding $400.00 to A2.balance. Thus we have three "states" in which we can find the two row balances.

S1   A1.balance == $900.00, A2.balance == $100.00
        Values before any change has taken place.

S2   A1.balance == $500.00, A2.balance == $100.00
        Values after subtracting $400.00 from the balance of account A1.

S3   A1.balance == $500.00, A2.balance == $500.00
        Values after adding $400.00 to the balance of account A2.

Now let's say that another process, P2, is running simultaneously to perform a credit check on this depositor, requiring a total of at least $900.00 before the depositor will be allowed to take out a credit card. To do this, process P2 must read the two rows with aid values A1 and A2 and add the account balances. If it does this while the two balances are in state S2, then the sum will be $600.00, and the depositor will fail the credit check; it would have passed the credit check if there had been $1000.00 in the two accounts. Here is a schedule of operations that could lead to this view of the balance total by P2:

Process P1	Process P2
	int bal, sum = 0.00;
Update A set balance = balance - $400.00 where A.aid = 'A1'; (Now balance = $500.00.)	
	select A.balance into :bal where A.aid = 'A1'; sum = sum + bal; (Now sum = $500.00.)
	select A.balance into :bal where A = 'A2'; sum = sum + bal; (Now sum = $600.00.)
	(Credit card issuance refused.)
Update A set balance = balance + $400.00 where A.aid = 'A2'; (Now balance = $500.00. Transfer complete.)	

But the $600.00 total `balance` in state S2 seen by process P2 is actually an illusion. The depositor started with $1000.00 and process P1 was not trying to withdraw money, only to transfer it. The fact that state S2 exposes a `balance` of $600.00 is known as an "inconsistent view." We say there are certain consistency rules that are being observed (money is neither created nor destroyed by process P1, so the total of account values should not change), but in order to achieve the correct final state, the logic of process P1 must go through possibly inconsistent states along the way (e.g., state S2). We would like to keep other processes (such as P2) from viewing these temporary inconsistent states. ∎

To avoid inconsistent views and a number of other difficulties that can arise with concurrent access, database systems provide a feature called *transactions*. Each process is able to package together a series of database operations that make up a consistent change in state (such as the two updates of process P1) or an attempt at a consistent view (such as the two reads of process P2); such a package of database operations is called a *transaction*. Note that many transactions require a consistent view of the data as a basis for updates; for example, each of the two updates of process P1 can be thought of as a read followed by a write, and the two reads must be consistent or we may make an error in the final amounts stored in these balances. We will have more to say about this later.

A database system that supports transactions provides guarantees to programmers of a number of transactional properties that make the programming job easier. The most important guarantee for the current discussion is known as *isolation*. Isolation guarantees that even though transaction T1 (which might be the one that packages the two reads of process P1) and T2 (which might package the two updates of P2) execute concurrently, it appears to each that it has operated on the database in isolation from the effects of the other. When we say *in isolation*, we mean that it appears that either T2 executes *before* T1 has begun making any changes, or that T2 executes *after* T1 has completed; T2 sees state S1 or state S3 of Example 4.4.1, but never state S2, and thus cannot take an inconsistent view.

How Transactions Occur in Programs

Immediately after connecting to a database, a program has no active transaction in progress. A program that has no active transaction can begin one by executing any SQL statement that operates on rows of the database (such as Select, Open Cursor, Update, Insert, or Delete). The transaction remains active during a number of such executed statements, and the program ends the transaction by executing one of the following two Embedded SQL statements:

◆ `exec sql commit work`; This statement causes the transaction to end successfully; all row updates made during the transaction become permanent in the database and visible to concurrent users. All rows read during the transaction once again become available to concurrent users for update.

◆ `exec sql rollback work`; This statement causes the transaction to end unsuccessfully (to *abort*); all row updates made during the transaction are reversed and the prior versions of these rows are put in place and become visible again to concurrent users. All rows read during the transaction become once again available to concurrent users for update.

If neither a Commit nor a Rollback statement is executed for a transaction in progress before a program terminates, a product-dependent default action (Commit or Rollback) is performed. We saw the Commit Work statement used in the two examples at the beginning of this chapter, Examples 4.1.1 and 4.1.3, to release locks taken on the rows that had been read during the transaction. These locks are used to implement the transaction isolation guarantee, as we will see shortly. A transaction usually consists of the set of database operations (Select statements or Update statements or both) that take place between one Commit Work statement and the next—a Rollback is less common. A typical way for an application program to behave is for each concurrent user process to loop around through a large number of statements, alternately requesting input from the user and then performing a set of database operations on the user's behalf. As we will see, it is a bad idea to keep a transaction active across user interactions, so a Commit Work statement is usually performed before requesting input. However, there might be more than one transaction for each user interaction, so it isn't safe to assume that transactions extend from one user input to the next, although that is the most typical case.

It should be clear in the situation just outlined that it is up to the programmer to specify to the system when a transaction begins and ends—the system cannot guess. A transaction involving database updates is a set of updates that should either all succeed or all fail as a unit. The situation of Example 4.4.1 can be extended to a transfer of money between a large number of account balances, coming out even at the end, so that money is neither created nor destroyed. But the system is unable to tell when such a balance has been achieved (it doesn't follow the math performed) unless the programmer says so with a Commit Work statement. After the Commit Work, all row updates performed during the transaction become permanent and visible to concurrent users. After Rollback, all updates are reversed, and the (old) values likewise become visible. A transaction T2 involving only database reads (a read-only transaction) must never see a temporary inconsistent state in a sequence of updates performed by transaction T1—the kind of problem that might arise in Example 4.4.1, where transaction T2 (representing process P2) reads some account values *before* they have been updated by T1 (representing process P1) and other account values *after* they have been updated by T1. It turns out that a read-only transaction T2 must freeze all the data it touches as of a given instant, and this sets up a tension with update transactions that want to perform updates. Therefore we need to end a read-only transaction when we have completed our task, and once again the system is unable to guess when this should happen. The programmer needs to indicate the transaction end with a Rollback or Commit Work statement. In the case of read-only transactions, there is no difference in effect between Rollback and Commit Work, since no updates were attempted.

The Rollback statement is extremely convenient for an application programmer writing an *update transaction*. Consider the example of the last paragraph, where money is transferred between a large number of account balances. Assume that withdrawals will be made from the first N-1 account balances, and the sum of these withdrawals will be added to the final account balance. The simplest method of programming this is to read each new account row, check that the balance is sufficient to cover whatever withdrawal is needed and, assuming that the answer is yes, make the withdrawal from this row balance, then pass on to the next account row, finally committing after updating the last row to receive the sum of the prior withdrawals. No other transaction is able to view these intermediate updates until the transaction commits, so there is no danger that other users will see updates while we are still uncertain of success. But assume now that some account balance in the series has insufficient funds, so that we cannot complete the transaction. Rather than read backward through the series of rows already updated and reverse the withdrawals (an error-prone programming task), the program can simply execute the Rollback statement. A common synonym for rolling back is that the transaction *aborts*. All updates made so far are reversed automatically by the system, and it is as if the updates we were trying to form into a transaction had never occurred.

This ability of the database system to rollback (abort, reverse, undo) all updates performed by a partial transaction illustrates another guarantee (like isolation) that is made by the system, a guarantee called *atomicity*. Atomicity guarantees the programmer that the set of row updates performed in a transaction is "atomic," that is, indivisible: either all updates occur or none of them occur. In order to support atomicity, to know what row updates in the database must be reversed when a transaction aborts, the database system must have some way of noting row updates and storing these notes for later access. This all-or-nothing update guarantee holds even in the presence of a system crash, where memory is lost and it becomes impossible to remember what the program was doing, what updates it had made, or why it had made them.

The fact that a transaction that has successfully committed is resilient to system crash is called *durability*, a third guarantee of the database system to the programmer, along with isolation and atomicity. To support durability, the database system must make additional notes to remind itself of its intentions and see that they are placed on disk, so it can recover from memory loss. We see that the transactional guarantees have a number of implications, but we won't discuss many of the complexities until we deal with update transactions in a later chapter. In the current section we discuss updates only in the depth necessary to shed light on consistent views in a sequence of reads; we concentrate in the remainder of this section on read-only transactions and the isolation guarantee.

The Transaction Isolation Guarantee and Locking

The Isolation property guarantees that when transactions T1 and T2 execute concurrently, it appears to each that it has operated on the database in isolation from the effects of the other. More precisely, it seems that all database operations belonging to T2 occur before T1 starts or else after T1 has completed. A different way of saying this is that any set of concurrently executing transactions acts as if they are executing in some *serial* order; that is, for any two transactions in the set, one of them must complete all its operations before the other begins. This property of transactions, that they act as if they were occurring in serial order, is also called *serializability*, a property we will study in depth in a later chapter. Serializability is equivalent to isolation for our purposes.

If we think of T1 as a read-only transaction executing concurrently with a *set* of update transactions, the definition of the last paragraph means that T1 sees only consistent states of a database, after some number (possibly zero) of these concurrently executing update transactions have completed. The most common approach taken by database systems to implement the isolation guarantee is known as *database row locking*. The following, somewhat simplified, set of locking rules helps to support transaction isolation:

[1] When a transaction accesses a row R, it must begin by locking that row in an exclusive mode.

[2] All locks taken by a transaction are held until that transaction ends (commits or aborts).

[3] If T1 has locked a row R and a different transaction, T2, attempts to access the row, then T2 also attempts to lock R exclusively before accessing it and is refused, because a lock by T2 of R conflicts with the lock already held by T1.

[4] The usual approach with such a conflict is for the system to make T2 WAIT until T1 commits or aborts and releases its lock on R, after which T2 can be granted its lock request and proceed with further execution.

Figure 4.5 Simplified Rules of Database Row Locking to Guarantee Isolation

The more general locking approach, covered in a later chapter, differentiates between read access locks (R locks) and update, or write access, locks (W locks); but for now the simplified approach of exclusive locks in all cases gives a reasonable picture.

EXAMPLE 4.4.2 Locking and Inconsistent Views.
Consider the following sequence of events, a restatement of Example 4.4.1, where the balance for account A1 starts at $900.00 and for A2 at $100.00:

Transaction T1 (update transaction)	Transaction T2 (read-only transaction)
	`int bal, sum = 0.00;`

`Update A set balance`
`= balance - $400.00`
`    where A.aid = 'A1';`
(Now `balance` = $500.00.)	

	`select A.balance into :bal`
	`    where A.aid = 'A1';`
	`sum = sum + bal;` (Now `sum` = $500.00.)

	`select A.balance into :bal`
	`    where A = 'A2';`
	`sum = sum + bal;` (Now `sum` = $600.00.)

`Update A set balance`
`= balance + $400.00`
`    where A.aid = 'A2';`
(Now `balance` = $500.00.)	

	`commit work;`
`commit work;`	

This sequence of events corresponds to Example 4.4.1, which allowed process P2 to get an inconsistent view of the two `balances` of accounts A1 and A2. In this schedule, transaction T1 represents process P1 and transaction T2 represents process P2; row accesses on later lines come later in time, so the accesses of the two transactions are interleaved. To start, there is a `balance` of $900.00 in account A1 (`A.aid` = 'A1') and a `balance` of $100.00 in A2.

Transaction T2 has seen an inconsistent view of the two rows A1 and A2, the view associated with state S2 in Example 4.4.1. But now consider how these rows would be locked in the approach outlined above. We see that T1 would start by locking row A1 before updating it. Thereafter, when transaction T2 attempts to lock row A1 before reading it through a Select statement, it would not be granted the lock and would have to wait until transaction T1 completed its work and committed. This would have the effect that all operations of transaction T2 would be delayed until both updates of T1 are complete, and T2 would proceed with its reads and see the consistent state S3. This sequence of events is pictured next.

Transaction T1 (update transaction)	Transaction T2 (read-only transaction)
	`int bal, sum = 0.00;`

`Update A set balance = balance - $400.00`
`   where A.aid = 'A1';`
(Now `balance` = $500.00.)	

	`select A.balance into :bal`
	`   where A.aid = 'A1';`
	(Same row as T1 just locked; must WAIT.)

`Update A set balance = balance + $400.00`
`   where A.aid = 'A2';`
(Now `balance` = $500.00; transfer complete.)
 	
`commit work;`	

	(Prior select can now achieve needed lock.)
	`select A.balance into :bal`
	`   where A = 'A1';`
	`sum = sum + bal;` (Now `sum` = $500.00.)

	`select A.balance into :bal`
	`   where A = 'A2';`
	`sum = sum + bal;` (Now `sum` = $1000.00.)

	`commit work;`

■

This is only an example, naturally, and does not constitute a proof that the isolation property is guaranteed in all situations by row locking. There are in fact a few other details that must be addressed to achieve such a guarantee (in particular, there is a problem associated with a set of rows activated by an Open Cursor statement), but row locking is the basic approach used by most database systems that guarantee isolation, and we assume in what follows that such locking takes place in all data accesses.

Special Considerations in Transactions

With the guarantee of isolation there is a potential problem: what to do when the accesses of two transactions deadlock against each other. We also explain in what follows why it is usually necessary to avoid user interaction during a transaction.

Deadlock

A somewhat surprising concomitant of database row locking to guarantee Isolation is the potential that arises for deadlock.

EXAMPLE 4.4.3 Transaction Deadlock.

Let us recapitulate Example 4.4.2 but reverse the order of data access attempted by transaction T2.

Transaction T1	Transaction T2
	`int bal, sum; sum = 0.00;`

`Update A set balance = balance - $400.00`
`    where A = 'A1';`
(Lock achieved.)	

	`select A.balance into :bal`
	`    where A = 'A2';`
	`sum = sum + bal;` (Lock achieved.)

	`select A.balance into :bal`
	`    where A = 'A1';`
	(Conflict with T1: WAIT.)

	. . .

`Update A set balance = balance + $400.00`
`    where A = 'A2';`
(Conflict with T2: WAIT).
	. . .

. . .	. . .
. . .	. . .

In this example, T1 starts by locking row `A1` before updating it. Then transaction T2 successfully locks row `A2` before reading it through a Select statement. But now transaction T2 tries to lock row `A1`, which is already locked by T1, and it fails. As a result the system causes transaction T2 to WAIT until T1 commits and releases its locks. Following this, transaction T1 tries to lock `A2`, which is already locked by T2, and fails. Now the system would normally cause T1 to WAIT until T2 commits and releases its locks, but in this case the system needs to recognize a deadlock situation. T1 cannot proceed until T2 commits and releases its locks, but that's never going to happen because T2 is waiting for T1 to complete and release its own locks. Neither can proceed until the other releases its locks. In this situation, the system has only one course available if it doesn't want to leave these transactions hanging forever. It chooses one of the two transactions to *abort* (rollback). This is called a *deadlock abort*. All updates that have been made by the aborted transaction are undone, the process running the transaction receives an error message return from the latest data access statement, and the process logic continues from that point. One avenue open to the process with the aborted transaction is to *retry* the transaction (that is, to attempt to run it again). Note that not only are all row updates by the aborted transaction undone, but also any row values that were read are untrustworthy (some of them might have been changed by a different update transaction after the locks were released), so the only safe approach is to run the transaction over again from scratch. ∎

The deadlock abort condition has important implications for application programming in Embedded SQL. If the system aborts a partially completed chain of logic in a transaction to resolve a deadlock situation, the program needs to detect this situation and attempt to execute the transaction again, to *retry*. The retry approach was mentioned in Example 4.4.3, but it is often up to the program logic to actually implement it, and this may entail a good deal of complexity. Attempting a retry is appropriate because the earlier failure to complete was not a logical problem—rather it was merely a matter of bad timing—so we have a good hope that the transaction will complete if it is run again.

After beginning a transaction, the program must be on the lookout for the "deadlock abort" error return in sqlca.sqlcode from certain SQL statements entailing data access. The error numbers corresponding to this condition for the **ORACLE** and **INGRES** database systems are shown in Figure 4.16.

```
ORACLE    INGRES
-00060    -4700
```

Figure 4.16 Deadlock Abort Error Conditions: **ORACLE** and **INGRES**

The deadlock abort error return can occur nearly any time an Exec SQL statement attempts to read or update data in the database. A program should react to a deadlock abort return by repeating the transaction a certain number of times. If a deadlock continues to occur, some serious problem might be implied and the program should advise the user to speak with the system manager (the end user generally lacks understanding of any details of transactions). Note that if you were to set up a condition handler such as "whenever sqlerror stop" in advance of the statement where you want to detect the deadlock abort error, the error would never be detected. As we saw in Section 4.2, the Whenever statement reacts to the error before explicit tests for an error (unfortunately, there is no Whenever condition associated with deadlock abort). Therefore it is important to have the default **continue** action in place for error returns before attempting to trap deadlock abort errors.

EXAMPLE 4.4.4 Deadlock Abort Detection.
In the following program fragment, we write a transaction to contain the multiple row changes of a Searched Update statement. The symbolic constant for a deadlock abort error return is the one used by **ORACLE**.

```
    . . .
    #define DEADABORT -00060
    whenever sqlerror continue;
    . . .
    count = 0;
again: exec sql update customers
    set discnt = 1.1*discnt where city = 'New York';
    if (sqlca.sqlcode == DEADABORT) {
        count = count + 1;/* count up deadlock aborts*/
        if (count < 4) goto again;/* retry up to four times*/
    }                              /* otherwise fall through      */
    if (sqlca.sqlcode < 0)  {/* abort program if other errors*/
        call sqlprint;
        exit(1)
    }
```

Note that other transactional errors—such as time-out on a lock request—can occur, but deadlock abort is the one where it seems most reasonable to retry the transaction.   ∎

One other important consideration is associated with performing transaction retry. It is possible that the program has reset local program variables in memory during the course of the transaction, before the deadlock abort. These local variables might represent flags for products to be ordered, for example, which are turned off as the appropriate products are taken from the database; another possibility is that a local variable represents the dollar total ordered by the user. After the deadlock abort occurs, all *database* information is rolled back to the point that the program logic first found it. However, local program variables in memory are not under the control of the database, so the programmer should take care that these variables return to their original values as well. If the original state is difficult to reestablish, the programmer should go as far as copying, before starting the transaction logic, all status variables that might change in the course of the transaction, and then copying the original values back again if a deadlock abort occurs.

No User Interaction During Transactions

One of the more important points of database row locking is that any locks that have been taken by a transaction continue to be held while the transaction remains active—that is, until a Commit Work or Rollback statement has been executed in the program. This places a limit on the appropriate duration of a transaction. Every second that goes by could be holding up other users who wish to access the same row. One cardinal rule is to never initiate a user interaction while a transaction is in progress (the user might get involved in a conversation or wander off to get a cup of coffee while crucial data remains inaccessible). However, there seem to be numerous situations where a program would like to confer with the user in the midst of a transaction.

EXAMPLE 4.4.5 User Interaction During a Transaction.
Consider the **INGRES** program fragment of Figure 4.17, where we are taking orders from an agent and updating the quantity column in the products table, which represents the number of product units still available at the warehouse. The fragment interacts with an agent to test that an order can be filled, and it is not bulletproofed against all possible errors.

```
        /*   Interaction with agent taking product order—no bulletproofing      */
        . . .
        prompt1("Give pid for product your customer desires:\n",
            req_pid, REQPIDLEN);
        exec sql select price, quantity into :price, :qoh
            from products where pid = :req_pid; /* get info for later use    */


ask:    printf("We have %d units on hand at a price of %d each\n", qoh, price);
        prompt1("How many does your customer desire?\n",
            quantord, QUANTORDLEN);
        if (quantord > qoh) goto ask;          /* loop until fits in qoh      */
        exec sql update products                /* reflect new order          */
            set quantity = quantity - :qoh      /* now know this fits         */
            where pid = :req_pid;
    /* now insert new order in orders table                                   */
        . . .
        exec sql commit work;                   /* transaction complete       */
        . . .
```

Figure 4.17 INGRES Program Fragment (Illustrates Example 4.4.5)

Note that when the user interaction starting at the label "ask:" is initiated, a read of the products row has already been performed by the Select statement: a transaction has begun and a row in products is locked. No other agent can order this product while the agent confers with the customer about the size of the order desired. Performing user interaction while rows are locked is not a database system runtime error—the database system has no knowledge of user interaction in the example above—but it is a practice that should be avoided in any program where the row locked is likely to be accessed by another user.   ∎

However, a surprising problem can arise when transactions don't span user interactions.

EXAMPLE 4.4.6 User Interactions without Enclosing Transaction.
Consider the **INGRES** program fragment of Figure 4.18, a rewrite of the fragment in Figure 4.17, to avoid user interaction during a transaction.

This seems a straightforward modification of the logic in Example 4.4.4 to avoid having a lock held across a user request. However, if we look carefully, we note that something strange can happen. After retrieving the price and quantity of the product selected, we now commit the transaction before asking the agent what quantity is desired. We no longer hold a lock on the row while the agent responds (this was our aim), but this means that the quantity value for the row with this given pid value might be changed by some other transaction between the time we first read it and the time we try to update the row with the agent response. Therefore we cannot trust the qoh value we print out to the agent to remain valid. We must test the quantity ordered (quantord) *in the Update statement itself,* to be certain that the update of products.quantity will take place only if subtracting quantord does not bring quantity below zero. If no rows are affected by the update (**not found** condition) the order is rejected because the quantity ordered is excessive. The surprising thing is that we might reject the order *even though the quantity ordered is less than the quantity we printed out as being on hand just a moment before.* For example, we might have printed out that there were 500 on hand, asked for an order, then rejected an order for 400, saying, "Sorry, there are not enough units on hand to fill your order." What is worse, if we return to the label agn, select the new quantity value into qoh, print this, saying that (for example) 300 product units are on hand, and the customer now tries to order 300, we may reject the order again! ∎

```
        /* Interaction with agent—no bulletproofing—Version 2        */
          . . .
          prompt1("Give pid for product your customer desires:\n",
              req_pid, REQPIDLEN);
agn: exec sql select price, quantity into :price, :qoh
              from products where pid = :req_pid;    /* get info for later use */
        /* shouldn't hold lock during user interaction, so need to commit    */
          exec sql commit work;
          printf("We have %d units on hand at a price of %d each\n",
              qoh, price);
          prompt1("How many does your customer desire?\n",
              quantord, QUANTORDLEN);
          exec sql update product                    /* new type of update    */
              set quantity = quantity - :quantord
              where pid = :req_pid
              and quantity - :quantord >= 0;        /* test quantord fits here*/
          if (sqlca.sqlcode == 100){                /* if no row selected     */
                                                    /* ... quantord didn't fit */
              printf("There are not enough units to fill your order.\n");
              exec sql rollback;                    /* unneeded: no lock held  */
              go to agn;                            /* go query user again     */
          }
          else                                      /* order successful       */
        /* insert new order in orders table                                   */
            . . .
              exec sql commit work;                 /* transaction complete   */
          . . .
```

Figure 4.18   INGRES Program Fragment (Illustrates Example 4.4.6)

This type of inconsistency is rare, and is one we usually need to accept in writing transactional systems. You may even have encountered events like this in booking seats on an airplane flight, where the agent starts by saying, "There's a window seat; I'll try to get it for you," and then a little later, "Oh, I'm sorry, someone else got it!"

4.5   The Power of Procedural SQL Programs

In this section we show how a number of tasks that could not be performed with non-procedural SQL statements, as shown in Section 3.10, can now be achieved with a procedural approach.

```
#include <stdio.h>
exec sql include sqlca;                              /* communication area    */
char prompt[] = "Please enter a customer ID: ";

main()
{
    exec sql begin declare section;
        VARCHAR cid[5],user_name[20], user_pwd[10];
        double dollars;
        int cnt;
    exec sql end declare section;
    exec sql declare dollars_cursor cursor for    /* to calculate median    */
        select dollars from orders
        where cid = :cid order by dollars desc; /* ... order important    */
    exec sql whenever sqlerror stop;
    strcpy(user_name.arr, "poneilsql");
    user_name.len = strlen("poneilsql");
    strcpy(user_pwd.arr, "XXXX");
    user_pwd.len = strlen("XXXX");
    exec sql connect :user_name
        identified by :user_pwd;                     /* ORACLE: connect       */

    while (promptl(prompt, cid.arr, 4) > 0) {   /* main loop: get cid    */
        cid.len = strlen(cid.arr)                    /* set cid length        */
        exec sql select count(cid) into :cnt    /* count orders by cid   */
            from orders where cid = :cid;
        if (cnt == 0)      {
            printf("No orders retrieved for cid value %s\n",cid);
            continue;      }                     /* go loop again         */
        exec sql open dollars_cursor;
/*  open cursor and loop until midpoint of ordered list                      */
        do                              ╱ .        /* loop at least once    */
            exec sql fetch dollars_cursor into :dollars;
        while ((cnt -=2 ) > 0);                      /* fetch thru midpoint   */
        exec sql close dollars_cursor;              /* loop completed        */
        exec sql commit work;                       /* release locks         *
        printf ("Median dollar amount = %f\n", dollars);
    }                                                /* end main loop         */
    exec sql disconnect;
}
```

Figure 4.19 Program in **ORACLE** to Retrieve Median (Illustrates Example 4.5.1)

Customized Set Functions

In Example 3.10.3, it was pointed out that SQL lacks the median set function. We can now overcome this limitation programmatically.

EXAMPLE 4.5.1 Simulating a Median Set Function.

The program in Figure 4.19 repeatedly requests the user to input a `cid` value, then prints out the value that would be retrieved if we could write the SQL statement:

```
select median(dollars) from orders where cid = :cid;
```

The approach used in Figure 4.19 to find the median value is to count the number of `dollars` values in `orders` rows selected, then to fetch halfway through this count of rows, ordered descending by `dollars` value, to find the median. The way the **do . . . while** statement works in C, if the count retrieved is represented by n, and n is odd, then the final row retrieved above will be row number (n+1)/2—for example, row number 1 for n = 1, 2 for n = 3, 3 for n = 5, etc., the perfect median position. If n is even, the row retrieved will be numbered n/2, 1 for n = 2, 2 for n = 4, 3 for n = 6, etc., one of two equally valid median positions in the even case. Note that it is important that the count( ) function is performed in the same transaction as the Open Cursor and Fetch loop, to guarantee that no changes by concurrent transaction inserts will invalidate the median calculation. The treatment of null values is significant, since we don't want to count null values in making our median determination. The set function count(dollars) does not count null values, and the **order by . . . desc** clause also ignores null values, since all null values come earlier in order than all non-null values in **ORACLE**. We could retrieve the full count of n rows and all `dollars` would have non-null values. Note that with **INGRES**, null values sort to the opposite end of collation order as a result of an **order by** clause. A better way to ignore null values in the retrieval is to include "and dollars is not null" in the **where** clause of the cursor definition, since this approach will be portable from one database system to another.

   Note that the variable name to hold the interactively returned `cid` value is itself `cid`, so we see a search condition: . . . where `cid` = :cid. There is nothing wrong with this, since the colon (:) clearly differentiates the host variable from the column name.   ∎

Other Capabilities: Transitive Closure

Most other examples from Section 3.10, of tasks that cannot be achieved with non-procedural SQL, are easily implemented as Embedded SQL programs. A request to nest set functions in any predetermined order is straightforward in a program. Any imaginable report, such as the generalization of **group by** in Example 3.10.5, can be built up in a procedural manner by printing out one line at a time. Exercises at the end of the chapter ask you to write programs of these kinds. The transitive closure limitation of Example 3.10.6, however, is not so easily overcome.

EXAMPLE 4.5.2 Transitive Closure.

Given the `employees` table of Example 3.10.6, we wish to prompt the user for an `eid` and then retrieve all employees who eventually report to an employee with the `eid` specified (through any number of intermediate managers). The hard part about doing this in Embedded SQL is rather surprising. We can create a cursor listing all the employees who report directly to the given `eid`, then for any direct report create a cursor for all second-level reports, and so on. But we don't know the total number of reporting levels, and since we need to declare all simultaneously used cursors in the beginning, this is a serious problem if we need one cursor for each level. We get around this limitation by performing a rather tricky doubly recursive breadth-first search of the employee tree.

```
#include <stdio.h>
#define EIDLEN 5
exec sql include sqlca;
void breadth_srch(char *start_eid,            /* functional prototype      */
    int cursor_open);
main()
{
char prompt[ ] = "Enter Employee ID to see all lower level reports: ";
char start_eid[EIDLEN];

exec sql whenever sqlerror stop;
exec sql connect poneilsql;
while(prompt1(prompt, start_eid) >= 0) { /* loop for eids */
   breadth_srch(start_eid, 0);                    /* recurse: retrieve subtree */
   exec sql commit work;                       /* release read locks       */
}                                              /* end of prompt loop       */
exec sql disconnect;
}                                              /* end of main              */
exec sql begin declare section;
    static char eid[EIDLEN], ename[17];        /* INGRES character strings */
exec sql end declare section;
```

Figure 4.20 INGRES Program (Illustrates Transitive Closure, Example 4.5.2)

(continued next page)

```
exec sql declare dirrept cursor for          /* cursor to retrieve ...     */
    select eid, ename                        /* ... direct reports ...      */
    from employees where mgrid = :eid;       /* ... of given employee eid  */


void breadth_srch(char *start_eid, int cursor_open)
{
    char save_eid[EIDLEN];                   /* remember eid for recursion */

    if (!cursor_open) {                       /* reached new report subtree */
        strcpy(eid, start_eid);               /* eid is at head of subtree  */
        exec sql open dirrept;                /* get direct reports of eid  */
    }
    exec sql fetch dirrept into :eid, :ename; /* next direct report         */
    if (sqlca.sqlcode == 100) return;         /* if none left, return       */
    printf ("%s %s\n", eid, ename);           /* print current ename, eid   */
    strcpy(save_eid, eid);                    /* save this eid*/
    breadth_srch(eid, 1);                     /* get other emps, this level */
    exec sql close dirrept;                   /* this level is exhausted     */
    breadth_srch(save_eid, 0);                /* recurse: retrieve subtree   */
}
```

FIGURE 4.20 Continued

In the program of Figure 4.20, each time the function breadth_srch is entered with argument cursor_open == 1, it means we are moving from left to right on an already existing cursor level of employee reports. Thus breadth_srch fetches the next employee on this level, prints out the eid and ename, then saves the eid value in a local value and nests to a deeper level by calling itself for the next employee (to the right) on the same cursor. On return from the nested call, the implication is that all subtrees of eids to the right have been explored; now breadth_srch reestablishes the local eid value and opens a cursor once more to look at the *next level down*, and recursively explore subtrees of those eids. When all lower-level employees of the current subtree have been visited, the nested breadth_srch returns, either to explore subtrees of remaining eids on this level or, if eids on this level are exhausted, to the function that initiated the breadth_srch on this level. Eventually we return to main, which commits all work and disconnects from the database.   ■

Note that, although it is possible to overcome the limited power of Boolean conditions explained in Example 3.10.7 by a programmatic approach, efficiency is terrible. The query to retrieve all documents with four out of six keywords (or ten out of twenty) will always be extremely complex in SQL. We can try to hide the complexity in a program, but we cannot simplify the SQL statement or make the complex SQL approach efficient in operation.

4.6 Dynamic SQL

Recall that in Section 4.3.1 we said that the host variables named in a Declare section could be used only as *constant* values in a search condition; the variables could not contain character strings meant to represent more complex expressions—parts of statements requiring compiler parsing. In the current section, we learn a new approach, known as *Dynamic SQL*, that allows us to parse a character string in a host variable as an SQL statement. All the Embedded SQL statements we have seen up to now are known as *Static SQL*. Dynamic SQL allows us to create new SQL statements that were not foreseen in detail at the time of program compilation, and to execute them dynamically in response to changing user needs.

Execute Immediate

There are a number of advantages to being able to parse new statements dynamically in a program; but before going into the advantages, we need an example.

EXAMPLE 4.6.1 Execute Immediate.
The program of Figure 4.21 illustrates an **INGRES** program where a character array, sqltext[ ], is filled in with a character string representing an SQL statement, and then parsed and executed, using a new Embedded SQL statement, Execute Immediate. The current example sets the contents of sqltext[ ] from a constant string, but it is more normal to build up such string in response to expressed user wishes in a menu interaction. The example given here illustrates an immediate execution of a Delete statement, but other statements, such as Update and Insert, are also possible. However, a Select statement cannot be executed using this syntax; Select statements require another approach, to be explained shortly. ∎

```
#include <stdio.h>
exec sql include sqlca;

exec sql begin declare section;
char sqltext[ ] = "delete from customers where cid = 'c006'";
exec sql end declare section;

main()
{
    exec sql whenever sqlerror stop;
    exec sql connect poneilsql;
    exec sql execute immediate :sqltext;     /* execute immediate */
    exec sql disconnect;
}
```

Figure 4.21 INGRES Program with Execute Immediate SQL Statement (Illustrates Example 4.6.1)

The general form of the Execute Immediate statement is very simple:

```
exec sql execute immediate :host_variable;
```

The character string contents of the host_variable array must represent a valid SQL statement of the following types that we have so far encountered: Create Table, Delete (either Searched or Positioned), Drop Table, Insert, and Update (either Searched or Positioned). A few other permitted statement forms, explained later in the text, are listed in the Appendix B coverage of Execute Immediate.

Consider a menu interaction that allows a user to delete rows from the customers table of the CAP database, when the rows obey some set of user-specified conditions. The conditions can be identified in plain English through the menu interface, as shown in Figure 4.22.

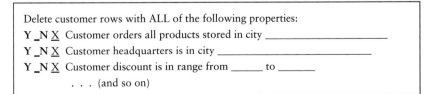

Delete customer rows with ALL of the following properties:
Y _N X Customer orders all products stored in city _____
Y _N X Customer headquarters is in city _____
Y _N X Customer discount is in range from _____ to _____
          . . . (and so on)

Figure 4.22 Example Menu to Delete Rows from the Customer Table

The menu user can fill in an "X" following the "Y" choice (meaning "yes," overriding the default "no" choice), and then provide related parameters on the right. The program should accept these choices, create the appropriate sqltext[ ] to perform the desired Delete statement, and then immediately execute that statement. For example, consider the case where only a single line in the menu of Figure 4.22 was designated "Y", as follows:

> Y X N _   Customer headquarters is in city _Duluth_____

The "Y" alternative has been chosen and the city name filled in with the name "Duluth." Assume the program has read this city name into an array cname2[ ] (still assuming **INGRES** character array string types); the program must also initialize the sqltext[ ] array to contain the beginning of the Delete statement, with plenty of space left over, and an int posn variable:

```
char sqltext[256] = "delete from customers where ";
int posn = 28;                      /* length of sqltext so far   */
```

The program now fills in the rest of the sqltext[ ] Select statement:

```
strcpy(&sqltext[posn], "city = \'");/* catenate string: city = '  */
posn += strlen("city = \'");        /* increment to next position */
strcpy(&sqltext[posn], cname2)      /* catenate cityname: (Duluth) */
posn += strlen(cname2)              /* increment to next position */
strcpy(&sqltext[posn], "\'");       /* catenate quote character: ' */
```

Note that the single quote character (') must be preceded by an escape character (\) within a C character string. The result of all this is as if we had written

```
char sqltext[256] = "delete from customers where city = 'Duluth'";
```

Clearly an Execute Immediate with this string will now accomplish what the user requested. Of course we might want to perform some preliminary processing and user interaction to confirm that we are doing the desired thing, especially where updates are concerned. For example, we could start by counting the number of rows to be deleted and ask the user if it seems appropriate to delete this number of rows. For simplicity we ignore such confirmations in what follows.

But why do we need an Execute Immediate statement at all? We already have the ability to perform a delete with the Searched Delete statement, which we could embed in the program as

```
exec sql delete from customers where city = :cname2;
```

How does the Execute Immediate statement add to our flexibility? To see the answer, look again at Figure 4.22, where three different options are listed for the user and more are suggested by the last line," . . . (and so on)". Clearly we would need an entirely different Delete form if the user were to fill in line 3; for example:

```
exec sql delete from customers
    where discnt between :lowval3 and :hival3;
```

where the values for lowval3 and hival3 have been input from the two fill-ins of line 3. This seems OK: we could declare a different Delete statement for each line of the menu in our Embedded SQL program. But that is not enough! What if both line 2 and line 3 were selected? It would be necessary to create still another Embedded Delete statement in our Embedded program. Since there might be (say) 15 options in such a menu, and we have to allow for any possible subset of options being selected (2^{15} options), clearly it is impossible to foresee all conceivable user desires by providing statements in Static SQL. We simply refuse to place 2^{15} different Select statements in a source program. Instead, we need to be able to build statements "on the fly" with Dynamic SQL, to react flexibly to user requests.

Prepare, Execute, and Using

But sometimes we need to build a statement on the fly that will be used repeatedly after it is built.

EXAMPLE 4.6.2 Prepare, Execute, and Using.
Instead of using the Execute Immediate statement, it is possible to use two distinct Dynamic SQL statements to accomplish the same task. Figure 4.23 illustrates an **ORACLE** program, where the Prepare statement on the third line of the main program has the effect of parsing the character string in sqltext[ ] into a compiled form with the name "delcust". Following this the Execute statement causes delcust to execute. Note that the sqltext variable has been initialized with a text SQL statement containing a *dynamic parameter* (represented by "?"). Successive dynamic parameters in the prepared statement can be filled in by host variable values specified in the **using** clause of the Execute statement. ∎

```
#include <stdio.h>
exec sql include sqlca;

exec sql begin declare section;
    VARCHAR cust_id[5], sqltext[256], user_name[20], user_pwd[10];
exec sql end declare section;
char prompt[ ] = "Name customer cid to be deleted: ";

main()
{
    strcpy(sqltext.arr,
        "delete from customers where cid = ?");   /* note arg: "?"       */
    sqltext.len = strlen("delete from customers where cid = ?");
    exec sql whenever sqlerror stop;
    strcpy(user_name.arr, "poneilsql");
    user_name.len = strlen("poneilsql");
    strcpy(user_pwd.arr, "XXXX"); user_pwd.len = strlen("XXXX");
    exec sql connect :user_name identified by :user_pwd;
    exec sql prepare delcust from :sqltext;        /* prepare for loop    */
    while((prompt1(prompt, cust_id.arr, 4)) >= 0) {/* loop for cid        */
        cust_id.len = strlen(cust_id.arr);         /* string length       */
        exec sql execute delcust using :cust_id;   /* using clause ...    */
                                                   /*.. replaces "?" above */
        exec sql commit;                           /* commit delete       */
    }                                              /* prompt again        */
    exec sql disconnect;
}
```

Figure 4.23 ORACLE Program Using Prepare and Execute Statements (Illustrates Example 4.6.2)

The Execute Immediate approach provides much of the functionality of the approach where we prepare-execute. The SQL statements that are accepted by Prepare are the same as those that can be used by Execute Immediate, so we gain no flexibility there. The **using** clause is not available with Execute Immediate, but this is not a serious defect since the variable values can usually be converted to text and concatenated into the text statement for immediate execution. The Prepare-Execute approach is probably simpler if several nontext variable values exist; it is easier to place these variables in a **using** clause than to convert and concatenate them into the text. A more common reason for preferring the Prepare-Execute approach is performance, in the case that a statement must be created dynamically but will be executed repeatedly. The Prepare phase of compilation can consume significant resources, and it is good to get it out of the way before repeated execution of the compiled form. The Execute Immediate form must recompile a new statement each time.

Dynamic Select: The Describe Statement and the SQLDA

We have still not introduced a way to dynamically create and execute a Select statement. The problem with a dynamically created Select statement is that the number of *column* values to be retrieved may be unknown in advance of compilation. Therefore the rather simple-minded **into** clause syntax used in static SQL won't work in general. Consider the statement:

```
exec sql select cname, city into :cust_name, :cust_city
    from customers where cid = :cust_id;
```

It works perfectly well in this case to declare two host variables cust_name and cust_discnt of known type to receive the values from the two columns retrieved. But to provide dynamic flexibility, we have to allow for *any* set of columns being retrieved, four columns, or perhaps twelve, and of arbitrary type. In order to handle such arbitrary retrieval sets, we need to consider a new type of structure, known as the SQL Descriptor Area, or SQLDA. To begin with, we illustrate a Dynamic Select in the **INGRES** database product, and later consider differences in the **ORACLE** case.

EXAMPLE 4.6.3

Consider the **INGRES** program of Figure 4.24. We will present a parallel **ORA-CLE** program in the next subsection. The `exec sql include sqlda` statement in the fourth line of Figure 4.24 includes a header file that defines some type-defs for C structs, one of which is a new type IISQLDA, together with a few symbolic constants. (The header file is presented in Figure 4.26.) This Include statement does not actually define an SQLDA structure, however. The fifth line of Figure 4.24 defines a memory resident struct of this type, named sqlda_var, and a pointer sqlda that points to it.

At the beginning of the main program, a constant text string sqltext[ ] with an SQL Select statement is defined. A constant string such as this would not normally be dynamically executed: we know the full syntax in advance, and it would be much easier to use an Embedded Select statement. However, we consider this simple case to provide a concrete example. Immediately after the Declare Section, a cursor named crs is declared. Although in this case we know that only one row will be retrieved, a cursor must *always* be used for a dynamic select. The first runtime statement in main sets the value of the sqln variable in the SQLDA, the number of columns that can be handled by this SQLDA, to the symbolic constant IISQ_MAX_COLS, the maximum permitted. See Figure 4.26 for the SQLDA layout.

When the Prepare statement is called to prepare the sqltext[ ] Select statement, the compilation process calculates the number and types of the column values to be retrieved (two, `cname` and `city`, are defined in the Create Table statement (3.2.1) as varchar(13) and varchar(20), respectively). For the program to learn this information, it must now call a new Dynamic SQL Describe statement, which places the information for all columns retrieved into the SQLDA variable struct. The program pointer sqlda points to this struct.

4.6 Dynamic SQL

```
#include <stdio.h>
#include <malloc.h>

exec sql include sqlca;                /* communication area         */
exec sql include sqlda;                /* SQL descriptor definition   */
IISQLDA sqlda_var, *sqlda = &sqlda_var; /* SQL descr var and ptr      */


main()
{
    exec sql begin declare section;
        char sqltext[] = "select cname, city "  /* array holds sql        */
        "from customers where cid = \'c003\'";   /* ... statement          */
    exec sql end declare section;
    exec sql declare crs cursor for stmt;  /* cursor used below         */
    int i;                                 /* index used in loops       */

    sqlda->sqln = IISQ_MAX_COLS;           /* max # of columns          */
    exec sql whenever sqlerror stop;       /* trap SQL runtime errors   */
    exec sql connect poneilsql;            /* connect to database       */
    exec sql prepare stmt from :sqltext;   /* compile select statement  */
    exec sql describe stmt into sqlda;     /* describe statement        */
                                           /* ... returns select desc   */
    for (i = 0; i < sqlda->sqld; i++) {    /* loop on cols: sqld == 2   */
        sqlda->sqlvar[i].sqldata =         /* place col data here       */
            malloc(sqlda->sqlvar[i].sqllen + 3);/* alloc space for data */
        sqlda->sqlvar[i].sqlind =
            malloc(sizeof(short));         /* alloc space for indicator */
    }
    exec sql open crs;                     /* opens cursor for select   */
    exec sql fetch crs
        using descriptor sqlda;            /* only 1 row to retrieve    */
    printrow();                            /* printrow(), Fig 4.25      */
    for (i = 0; i < sqlda->sqld; i++) {    /* loop on columns in sqlda  */
        free(sqlda->sqlvar[i].sqlind);     /* free col indicator space  */
        free(sqlda->sqlvar[i].sqldata);    /* free col data space       */
    }
    exec sql commit;                       /* commit session            */
    exec sql disconnect;                   /* and disconnect            */
}
```

Figure 4.24 INGRES Program, Dynamic Select (Illustrates Examp

The loop following passes through each of the columns described and allocates space for each column and space for the column indicator variable. This is necessary because the sqlda variable itself does not contain a memory area for retrieval of these column values, but only pointers to these areas. Many of the variables returned will need to start a byte boundary that is a multiple of two, or even eight on some machines, so the malloc function, which guarantees such starting boundaries, is used to allocate these areas. Now the cursor crs is opened and the row fetched into the sqlda. At this point the printrow function is called to print out the results. This function is explained in Figure 4.25. The purpose is to print out the values of the two columns to the users. Finally areas acquired with malloc are freed, and the transaction is committed.   ∎

The printrow function in Figure 4.25 provides a general purpose function to print any number of column variables of character string type. Note that even in **INGRES**, columns of char or varchar type are retrieved into VARCHAR format strings. It is simple enough to extend the printrow function to print out multiple different column types. To do this we need to read the datatype of each column, from sqlda->sqlvar[i].sqltype, and perform a SWITCH statement to handle each of the types named at the end of Figure 4.26. There are additional types not mentioned that would be handled by any generic printrow function.

```
#include <stdio.h>
exec sql include sqlda;              /* SQL descriptor def and constants */
extern IISQLDA *sqlda;               /* references var in main file      */

printrow()                           /* print two varchar cols in sqlda  */
{
    int i, type;
    struct vchar {                   /* definition of varchar struct     */
        short len;                   /* contains length of varchar       */
        char buf[1];                 /* var length buffer                */
    } *v;                            /* ptr to varchar structure         */
    for (i = 0; i < sqlda->sqld; i++) {  /* loop through columns         */
        if (*(sqlda->sqlvar[i].sqlind)) {/* if actually null . . .       */
            printf("null");          /* . . . display null               */
            continue;                /* done with this column            */
        }
/*  now point to varchar column value                                    */
        v = (struct vchar *)sqlda->sqlvar[i].sqldata;
        v->buf[v->len] = '\0';       /* null-terminate string            */
        printf("%s ", v->buf);       /* print string in array posn       */
    }                                /* finished printing columns        */
printf ("\n");                       /* go to new line                   */
}
```

Figure 4.25   An **INGRES** Printrow Function to Handle Multiple Varchar

The printrow function of Figure 4.25 is declared to lie in a separate source file; there is an extern declaration for sqlda_var to reference the struct variable in the source file of the main function. The printrow function handles the possibility of a null value by checking the value of global variable sqlda->sqlvar[i].ind, printing out the "null" character string if the indicator variable indicates a null. As mentioned above, each column string retrieved by the Select is in VARCHAR form, although this datatype is not available in **INGRES**. Instead, we use the struct varchar definition, which provides a struct definition for such a string, assuming an array of only one char (but the length is actually indeterminate). Note carefully how in the program of Figure 4.24 we performed a malloc for the maximum length of the varchar string plus 3. This was to allow room in the varchar struct for the len and the terminal '\0' in buf.

```
#define IISQ_MAX_COLS 128                  /* maximum number of columns handled */
typedef struct sqlvar_ {                   /* SQLDA variables, 1 per column      */
    short        sqltype;                  /* type of column                     */
    short        sqllen;                   /* length of column values            */
    char         *sqldata;                 /* pointer to column value read in    */
    short        *sqlind;                  /* indicator value: 1 means null      */
    struct{
        short    sqlnamel;
        char     sqlnamec[34];
    } sqlname;
} IISQLVAR;                                 /* this is the SQLDA variable type    */

typedef struct sqlda_ {                     /* SQLDA structure                    */
    char         sqldaid[8];
    long         sqlabc;
    short        sqln;                      /* number of cols in this SQLDA       */
    short        sqld;                      /* number of columns retrieved        */
    IISQLVAR sqlvar[IISQ_MAX_COLS];         /* handle max # cols by default       */
} IISQLDA;                                  /* type to declare SQLDA variable     */
/* symbolic constants, codes for column types appearing in sqltype               */
#defineIISQ_CHA_TYPE20                      /* char(n) column in Declare Table    */
#defineIISQ_VCH_TYPE21                      /* varchar(n) column                  */
#defineIISQ_INT_TYPE30                      /* smallint or integer column         */
#defineIISQ_FLT_TYPE31                      /* float or float4 column             */
. . . (and so on)
```

Figure 4.26 Contents of the **INGRES** Definitions Read in by `exec sql include sqlda`

```
struct sqlda
{
    long      N;      /* maximum # of columns handled by this SQLDA        */
    char      **V;    /* pointer to array of pointers to col values        */
    long      *L;     /* pointer to array of lengths of column values      */
    short     *T;     /* pointer to array of types of columns              */
    short     **I;    /* pointer to array of ptrs to ind variables         */
    long      F;      /* actual number of columns in this SQLDA            */
    char      **S;    /* pointer to array of pointers to column names      */
    short     *M;     /* pointer to array of max lengths of col names      */
    short     *C;     /* pointer to array of actual lengths of col names   */
    char      **X;    /* pointer to array of addresses of ind var names    */
    short     *Y;     /* pointer to array of max lengths of ind var names  */
    short     *Z;     /* pointer to array actual lengths of ind var names  */
};
```

Figure 4.27 ORACLE Definition Read in by exec sql include sqlda

Dynamic Select in ORACLE

The SQLDA struct in **ORACLE** is different from the one in **INGRES**. Figure 4.27 provides the contents of the header file read in by the **ORACLE** statement:

```
exec sql include sqlda;
```

```
#define MAX_COLS 100                       /* number of cols in sqlda variable */
#define MAX_NAME 20
#include <stdio.h>
#include <malloc.h>
#include <ctype.h>
exec sql include sqlca;                    /* communication area              */
exec sql include sqlda;                    /* descriptor area                 */
SQLDA *sqlald(int, int, int);              /* prototype fn, allocate sqlda var */

exec sql begin declare section;            /* global declaration              */
    VARCHAR sqltext[256];
    VARCHAR user_name[20], user_pwd[10];   /* for connect statement           */
exec sql end declare section;
SQLDA *sqlda;                              /* pointer to sqlda struct         */

main()
{
    int i;                                 /* index used in loops             */

    sqlda = sqlald(MAX_COLS, MAX_NAME, 0)/* alloc, point to sqlda var         */
    strcpy(sqltext.arr,
    "select cname, city from customers where cid = \'c003\'";
    sqltext.len = strlen(sqltext.arr);    /* sqltext statement now set        */

    exec sql whenever sqlerror stop;      /* trap SQL runtime errors          */
    strcpy(user_name.arr, "poneilsql");
    user_name.len = strlen("poneilsql");
    strcpy(user_pwd.arr, "XXXX");
    user_pwd.len = strlen("XXXX");
    exec sql connect :user_name
        identified by :user_pwd;          /* ORACLE format: connect           */
    exec sql prepare stmt from :sqltext;  /* compile select statement         */
    exec sql describe stmt into sqlda;    /* describe this statement          */
    for (i = 0; i < sqlda->N; i++) {      /* loop through cols, N = 2         */
        sqlda->L[i]++;                    /* add space for null at end        */
        sqlda->V[i] = malloc(sqlda->L[i])/* alloc space for col data          */
        sqlda->I[i] = malloc(sizeof(short));  /* alloc space for ind val      */
    }
    exec sql open crs;                            /* open cursor              */
    exec sql fetch crs using descriptor sqlda;/* only 1 row: no loop          */
    printrow();                                   /* print out row (Fig 4.29) */
    for (i = 0; i < sqlda->N; i++) {          /* loop through cols in sqlda   */
        free(sqlda->V[i]);                    /* free col data space          */
        free(sqlda->I[i]);                    /* free indicator space         */
    }
    exec sql commit;                              /* commit session           */
    exec sql disconnect;                          /* and disconnect           */
}
```

Figure 4.28   ORACLE Program to Perform Dynamic Select (Analog to Figure 4.24)

Note that the **ORACLE** SQLDA keeps multiple types of column information in corresponding array entries of multiple arrays, including V[ ], L[ ], T[ ], I[ ], instead of in an array of structs of type IISQLVAR as in **INGRES**. Note too that the various datatypes are not defined in this header file, and they must be defined instead in the source file using them.

The **ORACLE** program in Figure 4.28 accomplishes exactly the same task as the **INGRES** program in Figure 4.24. The **ORACLE** printrow function for character column datatypes only is in Figure 4.29.

```
exec sql include sqlda;              /* SQL descriptor def and constants */
extern SQLDA *sqlda;                 /* references var in main file       */

printrow()                           /* print two varchar cols in sqlda   */
{
    char *s;                         /* pointer to a char                 */
    int i, type;

    for (i = 0; i < sqlda->N; i++) { /* loop through columns              */
        if (*(sqlda->I[i])) {        /* if actually null ...              */
            printf("null");          /* ... display null                  */
            continue;                /* we're done with this column       */
        }
        s = (char *)sqlda->V[i];                 /* point to col value     */
        s[sqlda->L[i]] = '\0';              /* null-terminate string       */
        printf("%s ", s);            /* print string in column            */
    }                                /* finished printing columns         */
    printf ("\n");                                  /* go to new line      */
}
```

Figure 4.29 An **ORACLE** Printrow Function to Handle Multiple varchar Columns

Clearly **INGRES** and **ORACLE** have quite different definitions of the SQLDA. In the SQL-92, this has been standardized by describing a dynamic descriptor area that must be system resident.

4.7 Some Advanced Programming Concepts

This section contains a short introduction to the concepts of scrollable cursors, cursor sensitivity, and fourth-generation languages (4GLs).

Scrollable Cursors

A limitation of the Fetch statement on a standard cursor, mentioned in the discussion following Figure 4.7, is that a cursor can only move forward through a set of rows. This means that it is necessary to close and reopen a cursor in order to fetch a row for a second time. In SQL-92, important generalizations of the Declare Cursor and Fetch statements are provided. The new Declare Cursor statement is given in Figure 4.30.

```
exec sql declare cursor_name [insensitive] [scroll] cursor for
    Subselect
    {union subselect-form}
    [order by result_column [asc | desc]
        {, result_column [asc |desc]}
    [for read only | for update of columnname {, of columnname}];
```

Figure 4.30 The SQL-92 Declare Cursor Statement

Basically the two new syntax elements are the keywords *insensitive* and *scroll*. We will talk about cursor sensitivity in a moment. When the scroll keyword is used in a cursor definition, the cursor is said to be *scrollable*, and the new capabilities of the SQL-92 Fetch statement can be exercised. This Fetch statement is given in Figure 4.31.

```
exec sql fetch
    [{next | prior | first | last
    |{absolute | relative} value_spec} from ]
    cursor_name into host-variable {, host-variable};
```

Figure 4.31 The SQL-92 Fetch Statement

The specification of position movement (*next, prior, . . .*) is known as *orientation*. The current standard behavior is the default, *next*, meaning "Retrieve the next row in sequence following the current position in the cursor." The *prior* orientation means "Retrieve the row in sequence prior to the current position." The orientations *first* and *last* retrieve the first or last row within the cursor sequence. The *absolute* orientation, with value_spec given by an integer from 1 to the number n of rows in the cursor, retrieves that numbered row in the cursor sequence; *absolute 1* is equivalent to first. Negative numbers can also be used, from −1 down to −n; *absolute −1* is equivalent to last. The *relative* orientation means to retrieve the row, an integer number of rows away from the current position. Thus *relative −1* is the same as prior, *relative 1* is the same as next, and *relative 0* retrieves the row just retrieved a second time. Note that a scrollable cursor of this general capability is already available in the SQL Server product from Microsoft Corporation, and it is part of the ODBC standard promulgated by Microsoft and affiliated database system vendors.

Cursor Sensitivity

Recall that the concept of transaction was invented to isolate a stream of logic being performed by one user from the effects of concurrent updates by others on the data being accessed. We will learn more about transactions in Chapter 9, but certainly one implication of such isolation is that once a cursor is opened in a transaction, no rows in that cursor can be updated by any other concurrent user. Fine, but what can we say about updates to rows of the cursor that are side effects of updates made in the same transaction?

EXAMPLE 4.7.1

Assume that we are writing an application known as *ord_ship*, to actually ship products that were ordered earlier. Orders in the orders table have not yet been shipped, and ord_ship logic finds all orders in the orders table placed in the month of this_mo, calls the routine that ships this product to this customer, then deletes the current row from the orders table and places it in a table with identical columns known as shipped_ords. The cursor to access all the relevant rows in orders is the following.

```
declare cursor ship_em cursor for
    select * from orders for update of ordno
    where month = :this_mo:
```

Occasionally the routine to ship an order gives a return value that indicates the order can't be shipped because the product is out of stock. The normal thing to do under these circumstances is to create a back order, meaning that the order will be shipped when it comes back into stock. Let us say that the simple-minded way we have to do this is to simply back date the order, calculating next_mo as the next month after this_mo, and replacing the month column value for relevant orders. Assume that we do this with the following statement:

```
update orders set month = :next_mo
    where pid = :ord_rec.pid;
```

where `ord_rec.pid` is the `pid` value of the product we have just found to be out of stock. Now assume that numerous other rows in the ship_em cursor are orders for the same `pid` value that we have just encountered. Are these rows still in existence in the cursor? The defining property for the orders rows of the ship_em cursor was that the `month` column had the value :this_mo, and now this is no longer true. Will they be encountered in the fetch loop or not? Perhaps the user remembers that if we changed the value of this_mo after opening the cursor, that would not affect the rows selected; but this is a different thing, since we are actually varying the data that qualifies the rows for occupancy. If this answer seems straightforward, consider the following. What if instead of just updating the `month` of `orders` rows for the out-of-stock product, the proper approach was to put these `orders` rows in a different table and delete rows ordering that product from `orders`?

```
delete orders where pid = :ord_rec.pid;
```

Now what happens when we fetch one of these rows in the ship_em cursor? The row doesn't even exist anymore, so it doesn't seem that we can retrieve it. And there is no way for a Fetch statement to retrieve a nonexistent row, so we can't just point to where it used to be; presumably we will have to jump over the hole left by the former row. Of course it is possible that the system took a "snapshot" of the data when the cursor was originally opened, so that we have copies of the rows that have been deleted and can provide them for Fetch requests. ∎

The answer to the question of Example 4.7.1 is that there was no standard prior to SQL-92, and different products do different things. The answer might depend on whether the cursor in question was read-only, or on something else entirely. With SQL-92, however, this option becomes determined by the Declare Cursor syntax. Look again at the general form of Figure 4.30, and note the **insensitive** keyword. When that keyword is present the cursor is said to be *insensitive*, and this means that the rows contained in the cursor will *not* change as a result of a Searched Update or Searched Delete outside the cursor itself. The effect is as if the system took a snapshot of rows under the cursor when the cursor is opened. (This would be an inefficient way to implement it, however.) Now the program logic can look at rows that are no longer there; but if an attempt is made to perform a Positioned Update or Positioned Delete (using **where current of cursor** syntax), an error to show that the row no longer exits is returned. If the **insensitive** keyword is left out of a Select statement that complies with this SQL-92 feature, then updates and deletes outside the cursor are immediately reflected in the rows retrieved in the cursor. In the case of scrollable cursors, this means that a fetch with **absolute** 23 might refer to different rows when called twice in a row.

Fourth-Generation Languages

A number of products, such as **INGRES, ORACLE**, and **SYBASE**, have procedural languages to extend SQL capabilities. These product-specific languages generally have local memory variables, if-then-else type statements, and the ability to create and call functions. In most cases there is also a method for constructing a friendly visual user interface, with quickly constructed forms, menus, the ability to scroll on retrieved cursors with point-and-click controls, and a myriad other features that make developing applications easier. These languages are generally known as *forms languages* or *fourth-generation languages* (4GLs). Indeed, the only difficulty with these language interfaces is that they vary so much in detail; each product has its own dialect, and there is not yet any beginning of a standard to draw them together. As a matter of fact, it is probably too early for a standard, since new graphical interface languages, such as Microsoft's Visual Basic, continue to arrive on the scene and promise continuing evolutionary change. As a result, a section on 4GL interfaces is beyond the scope of this text. But the reader is encouraged to try a 4GL on a convenient database product. The best way to learn is to take one of the simple program exercises at the end of the current chapter and implement it, using as many features as possible of the 4GL (for example, scrollable selection with point and click).

282

Suggestions for Further Reading

A good guide to the C language is Kernighan and Ritchie's *The C Programming Language,* second edition [9]. The various SQL standards and individual product SQL reference manuals referenced in Chapter 3 continue to be useful. New reference manuals of use for Embedded SQL include manuals on general Embedded SQL constructs as well as special companion guides for SQL in the C language. The practitioner will also want to have access to the error code reference manuals for individual products.

[1] C. J. Date. *A Guide to the SQL Standard (SQL/89),* 2nd ed. Reading, MA: Addison-Wesley, 1989. (The second edition covers the SQL/89 standard; later editions do not.)

[2] *DB2 Application Programming Guide,* version 2.3. IBM. (Details of Embedded SQL, with C language specifics.)

[3] *DB2 SQL Reference Manual,* version 2.3. IBM.

[4] Jim Gray and Andreas Reuter. *Transaction Processing: Concepts and Techniques.* San Mateo, CA: Morgan Kaufmann, 1993.

[5] *INGRES/Embedded SQL Companion Guide for C,* release 6.4, UNIX. Alameda CA: ASK Group.

[6] *INGRES/Embedded SQL User's Guide and Reference Manual,* release 6.4, UNIX. Alameda CA: ASK Group.

[7] *INGRES/Error Message Directory,* release 6, VAX/VMS, UNIX. Alameda CA: ASK Group.

[8] *INGRES/SQL Reference Manual,* release 6.4, UNIX. Alameda CA: ASK Group.

[9] Brian W. Kernighan and Dennis M. Ritchie. *The C Programming Language,* 2nd ed. Englewood Cliffs, NJ: Prentice-Hall, 1988.

[10] Jim Melton and Alan R. Simon. *Understanding the New SQL: A Complete Guide.* San Francisco: Morgan Kaufmann, 1993. (This is a reference for SQL-92.)

[11] *ORACLE Error Messages and Codes Manual,* version 6.0 (PC DOS version). Redwood Shores, CA: Oracle.

[12] *ORACLE Programmer's Guide to the ORACLE Precompilers,* version 1.3. Redwood Shores, CA: Oracle. (General Embedded SQL for the PC.)

[13] *ORACLE SQL Language Reference Manual,* version 6.0 (PC DOS version). Redwood Shores, CA: Oracle.

[14] *ORACLE7 SQL Language Reference Manual.* Redwood Shores, CA: Oracle.

[15] *Pro*C Supplement to the ORACLE Precompilers Guide,* version 1.3.

[16] *Structured Query Language (SQL).* Berkshire, UK: X/Open Company, Ltd., 1991. xospecs@xopen.co.uk.

Exercises

Exercises with solutions at the back of the book in "Solutions to Selected Exercises" are marked with the symbol •.

In writing the programs of these exercises, you should be aware that the executable files may be quite large because database code libraries are large and in some cases (**INGRES** 6.4, for example) are bound into the individual application programs. Be careful to limit the number of executable files in your directories to save disk space.

NOTE: Exercises [4.1] and [4.2] deal only with Embedded SQL features covered through Section 4.1, and do not require bulletproofing except as specified.

[4.1]   Type the program of Example 4.1.3, making necessary modifications for the database product at your site, and run it.

[4.2] • Write a program to prompt a user in a loop to input a customer id (cid) and product id (pid), both on a single line. (Use the function prompt2( ) of Figure 4.3.) The program should then print out lines listing aids of agents who provide pid to cid, and the total of qty supplied by each agent. If a cid or pid value provided does not exist in the customers or products table, the program should simply return no lines. The program should terminate when the user types a blank line.

[4.3] There is a minor problem with Example 4.1.1: if the user inputs a cust_id value that doesn't exist, the program prints out the left-over values from the previous retrieval or the initial values. Create and execute a modified version of Example 4.1.1 to solve this problem.

[4.4] Modify the program assigned in Exercise 4.2 to notify the user and ask for a new input if a cid or pid input does not exist in the customers or products table, respectively. Specifically request reentry of a bad cid, keeping a validly input pid, or reentry of a bad pid keeping a valid cid—that is, save user keystrokes as much as possible.

[4.5] Here is a good-sized application program to write.

(a) Write a main program that calls a menu( ) function, presenting three options to the user: (1) City Agent and Products List, (2) Agent Performance, and (3) Exit This Program. The menu( ) function should return a value to the main program, which then calls a function city( ), or perform( ), or exit, according to user option. After option (1) or (2) the main program should loop for more menu( ) input. At all times in these programs you should create decently formatted I/O statements, so the user knows what is happening.

The function city( ) should request for input the name of some city (such as "Duluth"), and then return a list of customer cids and a list of agent aids who live in that city, and obey the following properties. (1) We want both lists clearly labeled and differentiated. (2) We do *not* want to return a cid from the given city unless the cid places at least one order through some aid in the same city. Similarly, we do not want to return an aid unless the aid places an order for some cid in the same city. (3) We do *not* want any aid to appear twice in its list or any cid to appear twice in its list. Test this by inserting a few rows to the orders table that might cause duplicates if we're not careful. In a large orders table, a huge number of duplicates might appear if this guarantee does not hold. Note that you will have to create *two* cursors in your program to guarantee this property—a single SQL statement probably cannot do it. Think of the city( ) function as being used by traveling executives of our wholesale company to invite customers and their agent contacts to dinner to meet each other when the executive is in town.

The function perform( ) should ask the user to input an agent aname and ensure uniqueness, *only* in case a duplicate aname exists in the agents table, by listing the city and aid values for two or more agents rows with that aname, asking the user to choose one by input of the aid. The function perform( ) should then calculate the total sales by that agent, the maximum of total sales for all agents, and finally the ratio of this agent's sales to that maximum.

(b) Here is another way of handling the task of discriminating which agent of the same name is wanted. Fetch rows and output a list of agents and their cities numbered 1, 2, 3, etc., and ask the user to choose a number, performing a commit before asking for user input. Then refetch the rows using the same cursor declaration (but a new open of that cursor), count through the number of rows specified, and bingo—there's the desired agent. Explain why this is not guaranteed to work in a nonstatic database. Is the method of part (a) safe in this sense? Explain.

NOTE: Many of the following program assignments deal explicitly or implicitly with transactions. In what follows, you should assume that there is no need to write error handling routines to deal with transactional dead-lock, unless the potential for deadlock is explicitly mentioned.

[4.6] (a) Write a program to input an order from an agent and enter it into the database. The main program should (repeatedly, in a loop) prompt for cid, the customer making the order; aid, the agent taking the order; pid, the product ordered; quantord, the quantity of the product being ordered; and the month of the order. Then it calls the function do_transaction to perform a transaction to place the order, with the user-input values passed as arguments of do_transaction. Note that the user-input values (cid, pid, etc.) are just ordinary program variables in main, so they will need to be copied into an SQL-declared area in do_transaction. To begin with, the transaction checks that pid exists in products, aid in agents, and cid in customers, and that subtracting quantord from products.quantity will not reduce products.quantity below zero. Given this, the transaction subtracts quantord units of this product and calculates the cost for these quantord units using products.price. Next the transaction adjusts cost by subtracting the customer discount. If any of the pid, cid, or aid do not exist (are **null**), or any other condition fails, the program should abort the transaction, then output an appropriate message and return from do_transaction. If all conditions are successful, the transaction inserts a new row into the orders table, placing the calculated cost value in the dollars column. The ordno value should be supplied by a special call that guarantees a new value to all executions of this program. For this exercise, write a function int fake_get_ordno() that uses a static var with initial value 1027 and increments and returns it on each call. Finally, the transaction should commit. The program *should* be on guard against transactional deadlock abort, and retry the transaction up to four times if such an abort occurs.

(b) Consider how to implement get_ordno(), a function that returns a new ordno to each caller even if several programs are using it at the same time. Clearly we need to use the database itself to ensure consistent behavior. Set up a table ordno with just one row and column curordno containing the current ordno, and write short int get_ordno(char *errmsg) to access and update this table. It returns a new ordno or -1 on failure, in which case errmsg has an appropriate error string. Assume that get_ordno will be called from within the order-entry transaction; because of this, it must not have its own commits or rollbacks. Explain why.

(c) Note that the ordno table of (b) will become a "hot spot" of a multiuser database, because every order-entry transaction accesses its one row. Explain why all concurrent transactions must wait for the commit or rollback of the one transaction that has the current ordno before they can get ordnos for their own work. One way to improve performance is to break out the ordno acquisition into a separate transaction done before the order-entry transaction. In this case, get_ordno can and should have commits, rollbacks, and deadlock-retry logic. Explain why the resulting ordnos in the orders table will have skipped numbers—ordnos 1100, 1101, 1102, 1104, ..., for example. Will this happen with the solution in (b)?

(d) • Explain why you should not have a Commit Work statement after the cid, aid, pid entry tests, and the test that there is enough quantity on hand to satisfy the request (the reading part of the transaction), and before the Update and Insert statements (the writing part). Are there any places before the last read/write action (the insert) where a Commit Work would be a good idea?

[4.7] In Example 4.5.1, the approach we used in Figure 4.19 to find the median value of dollars for a selection of rows from orders was to count the number of dollars values, n, in the rows selected, then to fetch halfway through this count of rows to median position (n+1)/2. We did not count null values in n (using the set function **count(dollars)**), and used an **order by . . . desc** clause to count to the valid median position, assuming that null values came earlier than non-null values, as is the case in **ORACLE**. With **INGRES**, we would need to proceed in the opposite direction, since null values come later than non-null values, but it would not simply be a case of changing to an **order by . . . asc** clause. *We would also need to change the median position formula to match the answer in* **ORACLE** when the number of non-null dollars values has an even number of terms. This is the sort of complex consideration we sometimes need to take into account in order to make an application truly portable. It is your job to indicate precisely how you would change the code for Example 4.5.1 to deal with the situation in **INGRES** where null values come later than non-null values in order. Note that there is a simple approach, suggested in the text.

[4.8] Write a program to repeatedly prompt the user for a customer id and then print out the agent name, agent id, and dollar orders placed by the different agents for that customer in their *median* dollar amount, as if we were performing the statement:

```
select aname, aid, median(dollars) /* INVALID SYNTAX */
    from orders
    where cid = :cid group by aname, aid;
```

[4.9] Write a program to print out the total of average dollar sales for all agents. Give a simple example to show that this is not the same as the average of total dollar sales for all agents (mentioned in Example 3.10.4).

[4.10] •Write a program to print out the report explained in Example 3.10.5.

[4.11] Create an `employees` table as given in Example 3.10.6, and write a program to repeatedly prompt for `eid`. Write out the sequence of managers to which `eid` ultimately reports, in ascending hierarchy position. Be careful to terminate properly.

NOTE: Treat the following problems as short-answer questions of the kind that might appear on an exam.

[4.12] (a)• Write a code fragment in C beginning `exec sql begin declare section`, to declare an array called "city" that will hold a `city` name from the `agents` table declared varchar(20).

(b)• Now declare cc as a cursor for an SQL query that retrieves exactly once all city names that contain agents who place orders for some part costing less than a dollar.

(c)• Now write a loop to retrieve successive cities into the array city, and print out each one. The loop should fall through as soon as there are no more cities to retrieve.

[4.13] Write the equivalent test (of an sqlcode) that you would place after executable SQL statements to take the place of the Whenever statement listed.

(a)• `exec sql whenever not found go to handle_error;`

(b)• `exec sql whenever sqlerror go to handle_error;`

[4.14] Consider the following SQL statement:

[4.E.1]
```
select c.city, cid, aid, pid
    from customers c, agents a, products p
    where c.city = a.city and a.city = p.city;
```

To begin with, we would like to make sure that all (cid, aid, pid) triples are grouped together (rows occur one after another) when they are from the same city (i.e., `c.city`).

(a)• How would you change the SQL statement in (4.E.1) to guarantee that all triples with the same `c.city` occur one after another? (HINT: Use a non-procedural Select statement.)

(b)• If there are 30 rows in `customers` with `c.cid` = 'New York', 10 rows in `agents` with `a.city` = 'New York', and 20 rows in `products` with `p.city` = 'New York', how many rows in (4.E.1) will have `c.city` = 'New York'?

(c)• To restrict the amount of information to look at in situations such as part (b), we would like to write a report where *each* relevant `city` occurs once (in a header), followed by three labeled lists of `cid`, `aid`, and `pid` values that have that `city` value. Give pseudo-code to show how you would do this in Embedded SQL (declare the cursors carefully).

[4.15] Assume that we have 500 distinct `pid` values in the `products` table and that all these rows show up in the `orders` table. We want to list the *ten best sellers*—that is, the `pid` values of products with the biggest total dollar sales from the `orders` table, together with the `pname` values and the total dollar sales.

(a)• It is not possible to do what we want in non-procedural SQL, because there is no way of stopping at the ten biggest. We need to write an Embedded SQL program where we pick off the ten highest dollar sales from a cursor. Show how the cursor would be declared with a non-procedural SQL statement, so that all desired information appears as early as possible in the rows fetched.

(b)• In performing the loop to fetch rows from the cursor in (a), note that a problem might arise if we begin to fetch rows with a total of null dollars (nulls occur larger than other numbers when listed in order in **INGRES** but otherwise in **ORACLE**). Show how you would write a fetch loop from the cursor of part (a) to skip over the early null values for totals in rows fetched.

[4.16] •Consider the following code fragment, where the two statements are meant to represent a single transaction:

```
    exec sql whenever sqlerror stop;
begintx:
    exec sql update orders
        set dollars = dollars - :delta
        where aid = :agent1 and pid = :prod1 and cid = cust1;
    exec sql update orders
        set dollars = dollars + :delta
        where aid = :agent2 and pid = :prod1 and cid = cust1;
```

Rewrite this fragment, *modifying and adding statemen*ts, to test for a "Deadlock Abort ERROR" (sqlca.sqlcode == -4700 for **INGRES**, or sqlca.sqlcode == -00060 for **ORACLE**) that might occur during the transaction, then *retrying these two statements if a deadlock occurs.* Be careful that your tests actually work! Your rewrite should also commit the transaction after both statements above are complete; if a different error occurs instead, your logic should goto handle_err.

[4.17] In Dynamic SQL, assume a declaration of an **INGRES** SQLDA of the kind given at the top of the program in Example 4.6.3. the variable sqlda is a pointer to a struct of type IISQLDA.

(a)• After the Prepare statement, show how you would test if the number of column values to be retrieved is greater than or equal to 2, and go to the label "ge2" if this is the case.

(b)• After a fetch from the dynamic cursor, show what C test you would use to see if the second column retrieved has a null value, and go to the label "null_back" if this is the case.

(c)• After the Prepare of another statement, explain how you would test if the statement prepared was not a Select statement, but rather some other statement such as Insert or Delete, and go to the label "not_select" if this is the case.

Database Design   5

Until now we have dealt with databases made up of a number of distinct tables, without concerning ourselves very much with how the tables and their constituent columns were originally generated. *Logical database design,* also known simply as *database design* or *database modeling,* studies basic properties and interrelationships between data items, with the aim of providing faithful representations of such items in the basic data structures of a database. Databases with different data models have different structures for representing data; with relational databases the fundamental data structures to provide such representations are what we have been calling *relational tables.* It is the responsibility of the database administrator (DBA) to perform this design, assigning the related data items of the database to columns of tables in a manner that preserves desirable properties. The most important test of logical design is that the tables and attributes faithfully reflect interrelationships between objects in the real world, and that this remains true after all likely database updates in the future.

The DBA starts by studying some real-world enterprise, such as a wholesale order business, a company personnel office, or a college registration department, whose operation needs to be supported on a computerized database system. Often working with someone who has great expertise about the details of the enterprise, the DBA comes up with a list of data items and underlying data objects that must be kept track of (in college student registration, this list might include `student_names`, `courses`, `course_sections`, `class_rooms`, `class_periods`, etc.), together with a number of rules, or *constraints,* concerning the interrelatedness of these data items. Typical rules for student registration are the following:

◆ Every registered student has a *unique* student ID number (which we name "sid").

◆ A student can be registered for *at most one* course section for a given class period.

◆ A classroom can house *at most one* course section for a given class period.

And so on. From these data items and constraints, the DBA is expected to perform the logical design of the database. Two common techniques covered in this chapter are used to perform the task of database design. The first is known as known as the *entity-relationship* approach (or *E-R* approach), and the second as the *normalization* approach. The E-R approach attempts to provide a taxonomy of data items to allow a DBA to intuitively recognize different types of data classification objects (entities, weak entities, attributes, relationships, etc.) to classify the listed data items and their relationships. After creating an E-R diagram that illustrates these objects, a relatively straightforward procedure allows the DBA to translate the design into relational tables and integrity constraints in the database system. The normalization approach seems entirely different, and perhaps less dependent on intuition: all the data items are listed, and then all interrelatedness rules (of a recognized kind, known as *dependencies)* are identified. Design starts with the assumption that all data items are placed in a single huge table, and then proceeds to break down the table into smaller tables. In the resulting set of tables, joins are needed to retrieve the original relationships. Both the E-R modeling approach and the normalization approach are best applied by a DBA with a developed intuition about data relationships in the real world and about the way those relationships are ultimately modeled as relational tables. The two approaches tend to lead to identical relational table designs, and in fact reinforce one another in providing the needed intuition. We will not attempt to discriminate between the two in terms of which is more applicable.

One of the major features of logical database design is the emphasis it places on rules of interrelationships between data items. The naive user often sees a relational table as made up of a set of descriptive columns, one column much like another. But this is far from accurate, because there are rules that limit possible relationships between values in the columns. Recall that in Section 2.2 we pointed out that the customers table, conceived as a relation, was a subset of the Cartesian product of four domains, CP = CID × CNAME × CITY × DISCNT. However, we also pointed out that in any legal customers table, two rows with the same cid value could not exist; this was because of the definitions in Figure 2.1 that described cid as a unique identifier for a customers row. Here is a perfect example of the kind of rule we wish to take into account in our logical database design. A faithful table representation enforces such a requirement by specifying that the cid column is a *candidate key* or the *primary key* for the customers table. Recall that a candidate key is a designated set of columns in a table such that two table rows can never be alike in all these column values, and where no smaller subset of the key columns has this property. A primary key is a candidate key that has been chosen by the DBA for external reference from other tables to unique rows in the table.

A faithful representation in a computerized database table of a candidate key or primary key is provided when the table is created with the SQL Create Table statement. We will present a more complete syntax for this statement in Chapter 6, but a foreshadowing of the syntax is given in the two declarations of Figure 5.1.

```
create table customers (cid char(4) not null unique, cname
    varchar(13), city varchar(20), discnt real);

create table customers (cid char(4) not null, cname varchar(13),
    city varchar(20), discnt real, primary key (cid));
```

Figure 5.1 SQL Declarations of customers Table with Candidate or Primary Key cid

When the cid column is designated as *not null unique* in a Create Table statement, it simply means that in any possible customers content, two rows cannot have the same cid value, and thus it is a candidate key. When cid is designated as a primary key in the Create Table statement, this is a more far-reaching statement making cid the identifier of customers rows that might be used by other tables. Following either of the table definitions of 5.1, a later SQL Insert or Update statement that would duplicate a cid value on two rows of the customers table is *illegal* and *has no effect*. The faithful representation of the table key is maintained by the database system. Also a number of other clauses of the Create Table statement serve a comparable purpose of limiting possible table content, and we refer to these as *integrity constraints* for a table. The interrelationships between columns in relational tables must be understood at a reasonably deep level in order to properly appreciate some constraints. Although not all concepts of logical design can be faithfully represented in the SQL of today, SQL is moving in the direction of modeling more and more such concepts. In any event, many of the ideas of logical design can be useful as an aid to systematic database definition even in the absence of direct system support.

In the following sections, we first introduce a number of definitions of the E-R model. The process of normalization is introduced after some E-R intuition has been developed.

5.1 Introduction to E-R Concepts

The entity-relationship approach attempts to define a number of data classification objects; the database designer is then expected to classify data items by intuitive recognition as belonging in some known classification. Three fundamental data classification objects introduced in this section are *entities*, *attributes*, and *relationships*.

Entities, Attributes, and Simple E-R Diagrams

We begin with a definition of the concept of entity.

DEFINITION 5.1.1 Entity. An *entity* is a collection of distinguishable real-world objects with common properties. (A somewhat older nomenclature referred to an entity as an *entity set*, in the sense that it contains a collection of real-world objects, but we will use the more modern terminology.)■

For example, in a college registration database we might have the following entities: Students, Instructors, Class_rooms, Courses, Course_sections, Class_periods, etc. (Entity names are capitalized, while the real-world objects contained in the entity are not.) Clearly, the set of classrooms in a college fits our definition of an entity: individual classrooms in the entity `Class_rooms` are distinguishable (by location—i.e., room number), and have other common properties such as seating capacity (not common values, but a common property). `Class_periods` is a somewhat surprising entity—is an interval of time a real-world object?—but the test here is that the registration process deals with these class periods as if they were objects, assigning class periods in student schedules in the same sense that rooms are assigned. To give an example of entities that we have worked with a good deal in the CAP database, we have `Customers`, `Agents`, and `Products`. There is a foreshadowing here of entities being mapped to relational tables. An entity such as `Customers` is usually mapped to an actual table, and each row of the table corresponds to one of the distinguishable real-world objects that make up the entity, called an *entity occurrence*, or sometimes an *entity instance*. Note that we do not yet have a name for the properties by which we tell one entity occurrence from another, the analog to column values to distinguish rows in a relational table. For now we simply refer to entity instances as being distinguishable, in the same sense that we would think of the classrooms in a college as being distinguishable, without needing to understand the room-labeling scheme used.

In what follows we always write an entity name with an initial capital letter, but the name becomes all lowercase when the entity is mapped to a relational table in SQL. Note that we have chosen an unusual notation by assigning plural entity names: `Students`, `Instructors`, `Class_rooms`, etc. More standard would be entities named `Student`, `Instructor`, `Class_room`, etc. Our plural usage is chosen to emphasize the fact that each entity is a *set* of real-world objects, usually containing multiple elements, and carries over to our plural table names, also somewhat unusual, which normally contain multiple rows. Entities are represented by rectangles in E-R diagrams, as we see in Figure 5.2.

In mathematical discussion, for purposes of definition, we usually represent an entity by a single capital letter, possibly subscripted where several exist: E, or E_1, E_2, ... An entity E is made up of a set of real-world objects, which we represent by subscripted lowercase letters: E = $\{e_1, e_2, . . ., e_n\}$. As mentioned above, each distinct representative e_i of an entity E is called an entity occurrence, or sometimes an entity instance.

DEFINITION 5.1.2 Attribute. An *attribute* is a data item that describes a property of an entity or a relationship (defined below). ∎

Recall from the definition of entity that all entity occurrences belonging to a given entity have common properties. In the E-R model, these properties are known as attributes. As we will see, there is no confusion in terminology between an attribute in the E-R model and an attribute or column name in the relational model, because when the E-R design is translated into relational terms the two correspond. A particular instance of an entity is said to have attribute values for all attributes describing the entity (a null value is possible). The reader should keep in mind that while we list distinct entity occurrences $\{e_1, e_2, \ldots, e_n\}$ of the entity E, we can't actually tell the occurrences apart without reference to attribute values.

Each entity has an *identifier,* an attribute or a set of attributes, that takes on unique values for each entity instance; this is the analog of the relational concept of *candidate key*. For example, we define an identifier for the Customers entity to be the customer identifier, cid. There might be more than one identifier for a given entity, and when the DBA identifies a single key attribute to be the universal method of identification for entity occurrences throughout the database, this is called a *primary identifier* for the entity. Other attributes, such as city for Customers, are not identifiers but *descriptive attributes*, known as *descriptors*. Most attributes take on simple values from a domain, as we have seen in the relational model, but a *composite attribute* is a group of simple attributes that together describe a property. For example, the attribute student_name for the Students entity might be composed of the simple attributes lname, fname, and midinitial. Note that an identifier for an entity might contain an attribute of composite type. Finally, we define a *multi-valued attribute* to be one that can take on multiple values for a single entity instance. For example, the Employees entity might have an attached multi-valued attribute named hobbies, which takes on multiple values provided by the employee asked to list any hobbies or interests. One employee might have several hobbies, so this is a multi-valued attribute.

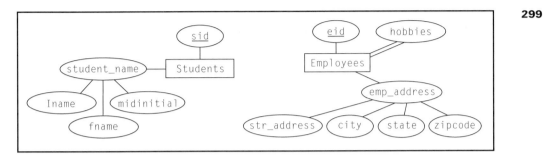

Figure 5.2   Example of E-R Diagrams with Entities and Attributes (Simple and Composite, Single- and Multi-Valued)

As mentioned earlier, E-R diagrams represent entities as rectangles. Figure 5.2 shows two simple E-R diagrams. Simple, single-valued attributes are represented by ovals, attached by a straight line to the entity. A composite attribute is also in an oval attached directly to the entity, while the simple attributes that make up the composite are attached to the composite oval. A multi-valued attribute is attached by a double line, rather than a single line, to the entity it describes. The primary identifier attribute is underlined.

Transforming Entities and Attributes to Relations

Our ultimate aim is to transform the E-R design into a set of definitions for relational tables in a computerized database, which we do through a set of transformation rules.

Transformation RULE 1. Each entity in an E-R diagram is mapped to a single table in a relational database; the table is named after the entity. The columns of the table represent all the single-valued simple attributes that are attached to the entity (possibly through a composite attribute, although a composite attribute itself does not become a column of the table). An identifier for an entity is mapped to a candidate key for the table, as illustrated in Figure 5.1, and a primary identifier is mapped to a primary key. Note that the primary identifier of an entity might be a composite key, which therefore translates to a set of attributes in the relational table mapping. Entity occurrences are mapped to rows of the table.   ■

EXAMPLE 5.1.1

Here are the two tables, with one example row filled in, mapped from the Students and Employees entities in the E-R diagrams of Figure 5.2. The primary key is underlined.

students

sid	lname	fname	midinitial
1134	Smith	John	L.
...	...	...	...

employees

eid	staddress	city	state	zipcode
197	7 Beacon St	Boston	MA	02122
...	...	...	...	...

■

Transformation RULE 2. Given an entity E with primary identifier p, a multi-valued attribute a attached to E in an E-R diagram is mapped to a table of its own; the table is named after the plural multi-valued attribute. The columns of this new table are named after p and a (either p or a might consist of several attributes), and rows of the table correspond to (p, a) value pairs, representing all pairings of attribute values of a associated with entity occurrences in E. The primary key attribute for this table is the set of columns in p and a. ■

EXAMPLE 5.1.2

Here is an example database of two tables reflecting the E-R diagram for the Employees entity and the attached multi-valued attribute, hobbies, of Figure 5.2.

employees

eid	staddress	city	state	zipcode
197	7 Beacon St	Boston	MA	02102
221	19 Brighton St	Boston	MA	02103
303	153 Mass Ave	Cambridge	MA	02123
...	...	...	...	...

hobbies

eid	hobby
197	chess
197	painting
197	science fiction
221	reading
303	bicycling
303	mysteries
...	...

■

Relationships among Entities

DEFINITION 5.1.3 Relationship. Given an ordered list of m entities, E_1, E_2, . . ., E_m, (where the same entity may occur more than once in the list), a *relationship* R defines a rule of correspondence between the instances of these entities. Specifically, R represents a set of m-tuples, a subset of the Cartesian product of entity instances $E_1 \times E_2 \times . . . \times E_m$. ∎

A particular occurrence of a relationship, corresponding to a tuple of entity occurrences $(e_1, e_2, . . . , e_n)$, where e_i is an instance of E_i in the ordered list of the definition, is called a *relationship occurrence* or *relationship instance*. The number of entities m in the defining list is called the *degree* of the relationship. A relationship between two entity sets is known as a *binary relationship*. For example, we define "teaches" to be a binary relationship between Instructors and Course_sections. We indicate that a relationship instance exists by saying that a particular instructor teaches a specific course section. Another example of a relationship is works_on, defined to relate the two entities Employees and Projects in a large company: Employees works_on Projects. A relationship can also have attached attributes. The relationship works_on might have the attribute percent, indicating the percent of work time during each week that the employee is assigned to work on each specific project (see Figure 5.3). Note that this percent attribute attached to the works_on relationship would be multi-valued if attached to either entity Employees or Projects; the percent attribute is only meaningful in describing a specific employee-project pair, and it is therefore a natural attribute of the binary relationship works_on.

A binary relationship that relates an entity to itself (a subset of $E_1 \times E_1$) is called a *ring*, or sometimes a *recursive relationship*. For example, the Employees entity is related to itself through the relationship "manages", where we say that one employee manages another. Relationships are represented by diamonds in an E-R diagram, with connecting lines to the entities they relate. In the case of a ring, the connecting lines are often labeled with the names of the roles played by the entity instances involved (see Figure 5.3).

Note that we often leave out attributes in an E-R diagram to concentrate on relationships between entities without losing our concentration in excessive detail.

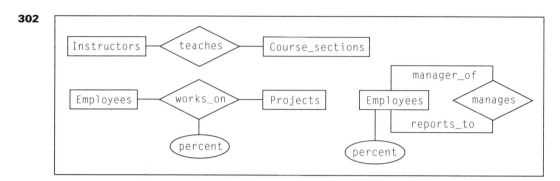

Figure 5.3 Examples of E-R Diagrams with Relationships

EXAMPLE 5.1.3 The orders table in CAP does not represent a relationship. By Definition 5.1.3, the `orders` table in the CAP database is not a relationship between `Customers`, `Agents`, and `Products`. This is because (`cid`, `aid`, `pid`) triples in the rows of the `orders` table do not identify a subset of the Cartesian product, `Customers × Agents × Products`, as required. Instead, some triples of (`cid`, `aid`, `pid`) values occur more than once in the example of Figure 2.2, and this is clearly the designer's intention, since the same customer can order the same product from the same agent on two different occasions. Instead of a relationship, the `orders` table represents an entity in its own right, with identifier attribute `ordno`. This makes a good deal of sense, since we might commonly have reason to look up a row in the `orders` table for reasons unconnected to relating entity occurrences in `Customers`, `Agents`, and `Products`. For example, on request we might need to check that a past order has been properly billed and shipped (we are assuming attributes that are not present in the simple `orders` table of Figure 2.2). Thus the `Orders` occurrences are dealt with individually as objects in their own right. Of course the entity `Orders` is related to each of the entities `Customers`, `Agents`, and `Products`, as we will explore in the exercises at the end of the chapter. ∎

Although the `orders` table doesn't correspond directly to a relationship, it is clear that there are any number of possible relationships we could define in terms of the `orders` table between the `Customers`, `Agents`, and `Products` entities.

EXAMPLE 5.1.4

Assume that we are performing a study in which we commonly need to know total sales aggregated (summed) from the orders table by customers, agents, and products for the current year. We might do this, for example, to study sales volume relationships between agents and customers as well as between customers and products, and how those relationships are affected by geographic factors (city values). However, as we begin to plan this application, we decide that it is too inefficient to always perform sums on the orders table to access the basic measures of our study, so we decide to create a new table called *yearlies*. We define this new table with the SQL commands:

```
create table yearlies (cid char(4), aid char(3), pid char(3),
    totqty integer, totdoll float);
insert into yearlies
    select cid, aid, pid, sum(qty), sum(dollars) from orders
    group by cid, aid, pid;
```

Once we have the new yearlies table, the totals can be kept up to date by order application logic: as each new order is entered, the relevant yearlies row should be updated as well. Now the yearlies table is a relationship, since the (cid, aid, pid) triples in the rows of the table identify a *subset* of the Cartesian product, Customers × Agents × Products; that is to say, there are now no repeated triples in the yearlies table. Since these triples are unique, (cid, aid, pid) forms the primary key for the yearlies table. ∎

A relationship on more than two entities is called an *N-ary relationship*. The yearlies relationship on three distinct entities is also known as a *ternary relationship*. An N-ary relationship with N > 2 can often be replaced by a number of distinct binary relationships in an E-R diagram, and some practitioners recommend this practice. Most current thinking, however, maintains that there is sometimes a loss of expressiveness in this replacement, and then the N-ary relationship should be retained. In converting an E-R design to a relational one, a relationship is sometimes translated into a relational table, and sometimes not. (We will have more to say about this in the next section.) For example, the yearlies relationship is translated into a relational table named yearlies. However, the manages relationship between Employees and Employees, shown in Figure 5.4, does not translate into a table of its own. Instead, this relationship is usually translated into a column in employees identifying the mgrid to whom the employee reports, as we saw in Example 3.10.6.

Note the surprising fact that `mgrid` is *not* considered to be an attribute of the `Employees` entity, although it exists as a column in the `employees` table. The `mgrid` column is what is known as a *foreign key* in the relational model, and it corresponds to the actual `manages` relationship in the E-R diagram of Figure 5.4. We deal more with this in the next section, after we have had an opportunity to consider some of the properties of relationships.

employees

eid	ename	mgrid
e001	Jacqueline	null
e002	Frances	e001
e003	Jose	e001
e004	Deborah	e001
e005	Craig	e002
e006	Mark	e002
e007	Suzanne	e003
e008	Frank	e003
e009	Victor	e004
e010	Chumley	e007

Figure 5.4 Example of an `Employees` Table Representing an Entity, `Employees`, and a Ring (Recursive Relationship), `manages`

To summarize this section, Figure 5.5 contains a table listing the concepts introduced up to now.

Classification	Description	Example
Entity	A collection of distinguishable real-world objects with common properties	`Customers`, `Agents`, `Products`, `Employees`
Attribute	A data item that describes a property of an entity or relationship	See below
Identifier (set of attributes)	Uniquely identifies an entity or relationship occurrence	customer identifier: `cid`, employee identifier: `eid`
Descriptor	Non-key attribute, describing an entity or relationship	`city` (for `Customers`), `capacity` (for `Class_rooms`)
Composite attribute	A group of simple attributes that together describe a property of an object	`emp_address` (see Figure 5.2)
Multi-valued attribute	An entity attribute that takes on multiple values for a single entity instance	`hobbies` (see Figure 5.2)
Relationship	Named set of m-tuples, identifies subset of the Cartesian product $E_1 \times E_2 \times \ldots \times E_m$	
Binary relationship	A relationship on two distinct entities	`teaches`, `works_on` (see Figure 5.3)
Ring, recursive relationship	A relationship relating an entity to itself	`manages` (see Figure 5.4)

Figure 5.5   Basic E-R Concepts

5.2   Further Details of E-R Modeling

Now that we've defined some fundamental means of classification, let's discuss properties of relationships in the E-R method of database design.

Cardinality of Entity Participation in a Relationship

Figure 5.6 illustrates the concepts of minimum and maximum cardinality with which an entity participates in a relationship. Diagrams (a), (b), and (c) of that figure represent entities E and F on the left and right, respectively, by two sets; elements of the two sets are connected by a line exactly when a relationship R relates the two entity occurrences represented. Thus the connecting lines themselves represent instances of the relation R. Note that the diagrams of Figure 5.6 are *not* what we refer to as E-R diagrams.

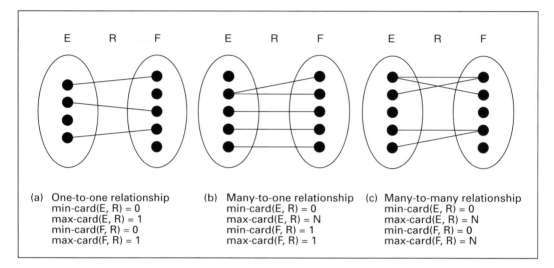

(a) One-to-one relationship
    min-card(E, R) = 0
    max-card(E, R) = 1
    min-card(F, R) = 0
    max-card(F, R) = 1

(b) Many-to-one relationship
    min-card(E, R) = 0
    max-card(E, R) = N
    min-card(F, R) = 1
    max-card(F, R) = 1

(c) Many-to-many relationship
    min-card(E, R) = 0
    max-card(E, R) = N
    min-card(F, R) = 0
    max-card(F, R) = N

Figure 5.6   Relationships R between Two Entities E and F

The minimum cardinality with which an entity takes part in a relationship is the minimum number of lines that the DBA allows to be connected to each entity instance. Note that the diagrams of Figure 5.6 would normally only give examples of relationships at a given moment, and the line connections might change, just as the row content of a table can change, until some entity instances have different numbers of lines connected. On the other hand, the minimum and maximum cardinality properties of an entity are meant to represent rules laid down by the DBA for all time, rules than cannot be broken by normal database changes affecting the relationship. In diagram (a), the DBA clearly permits both entity set E and F to take part in relationship R with minimum cardinality zero; that is to say, the DBA does not *require* a connecting line for each entity instance, since some elements of both sets have no lines connected to them. We symbolize this by writing min-card(E, R) = 0 and min-card(F, R) = 0. The maximum cardinality with which E and F take part in R is not obvious from diagram (a), however. No entity instances have more than one line connected to them, but from an example as of a given moment we have no guarantee that the line connections won't change in the future until some entity instances have more than one line connected. However, we will assume for purposes of simple explanation that the diagrams of this figure are meant to represent exactly the cardinalities intended by the DBA. Thus, since no entity instances of E and F in diagram (a) have more than one incident connecting line, we record this fact using the notation max-card(E, R) = 1 and max-card(F, R) = 1.

In diagram (b), assuming once again that this set of lines is representative of the designer's intention, we can write min-card(E, R) = 0, since not every element of E is connected to a line, but min-card(F, R) = 1, since at least one line is connected to every element of F, and our assumption implies that this won't change. We also write max-card(E, R) = N, where "N" means "more than one," and this means that the designer does not intend to limit to one the number of lines connected to each entity instance of E. However, we write max-card(F, R) = 1, since every element of F has exactly one line leaving it. Note that the two meaningful values for min-card are zero and one (where "zero" is not really a limitation at all, but "one" stands for the constraint, "at least one"), and the two meaningful values for max-card are one and N ("N" is not really a limitation, but "one" represents the constraint "no more than one"). We don't try to differentiate numbers other than zero, one, and many. In diagram (c) we have min-card(E, R) = 0, min-card(F, R) = 0, max-card(E, R) = N, and max-card(F, R) = N. Starting with Definition 5.2.2, we explain the meaning of the terms used for the three diagrams: one-to-one relationship, many-to-one relationship, and many-to-many relationship.

EXAMPLE 5.2.1

In the relationship *teaches* of Figure 5.3, Instructors teaches Course_sections, the DBA would probably want to make a rule that each course section needs to have at least one instructor assigned to teach it by writing: min-card(Course_sections, teaches) = 1. However, we need to be careful in making such a rule, since it means that we will not be able to create a new course section, enter it in the database, assign it a room and a class period, and allow students to register for it, while putting off the decision of who is going to teach it. The DBA might also make the rule that at most one instructor can be assigned to teach a course section by writing max-card(Course_sections, teaches) = 1. On the other hand, if more than one instructor were allowed to share the teaching of a course section, the DBA would write max-card(Course_sections, teaches) = N. This is clearly a significant difference.

We probably don't want to make the rule that every instructor teaches some course section (written as min-card(Instructors, teaches) = 1), because an instructor might be on leave, so we settle on min-card(Instructors, teaches) = 0. And in most universities the course load per instructor is greater than one in any given term, so we would set max-card(Instructors, teaches) = N. ■

DEFINITION 5.2.1 When an entity E takes part in a relationship R with min-card(E, R) = x (x is either 0 or 1) and max-card(E, R) = y (y is either 1 or N), then in the E-R diagram the connecting line between E and R can be labeled with the ordered cardinality pair (x,y). We use a new notation to represent this minimum-maximum pair (x,y), writing simply card(E, R) = (x,y). ■

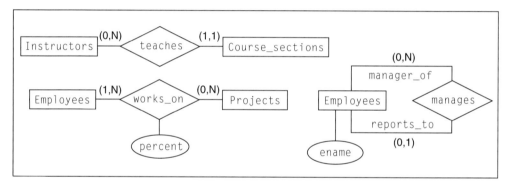

Figure 5.7 An E-R Diagram with Labels (x,y) on Entity Relationship Connections

According to Definition 5.2.1 and the assignments of Example 5.2.1, the edge connecting the entity Course_sections to the relationship teaches should be labeled with the pair (1,1). In Figure 5.7 we repeat the E-R diagrams of Figure 5.3, with the addition of ordered pairs (x,y) labeling line connections, to show the minimum and maximum cardinalities for all entity-relationship pairs. The cardinality pair for the Instructors teaches Course_sections diagram follows the discussion of Example 5.2.1, and other diagrams are filled in with reasonable pair values. We make a number of decisions to arrive at the following rules: every employee must work on at least one project (but may work on many); a project might have no employees assigned during some periods (waiting for staffing), and of course some projects will have a large number of employees working on them; an employee who acts in the manager_of role may be managing no other employees at a given time and still be called a manager; and an employee reports to at most one manager, but may report to none (this possibility exists because there must always be a highest-level employee in a hierarchy who has no manager—if it weren't for that single person, we could give the label (1,1) to the reports_to branch of the Employees-manages edge). Note that the notation card(Employees, manages) is ambiguous in Figure 5.7, since there are two different *roles* played by the Employees entity in that relationship. To correct for this ambiguity, we write

```
card(Employees(reports_to), manages)= (0,1)
```

and

```
card(Employees(manager_of), manages) = (1,N).
```

One-to-One, Many-to-Many, and Many-to-One Relationships

DEFINITION 5.2.2 When an entity E takes part in a relationship R with max-card(E, R) = 1, then E is said to have *single-valued* participation in the relationship R. If max-card(E, R) = N, then E is said to be *multi-valued* in this relationship. A binary relationship R between entities E and F is said to be *many-to-many*, or N-N, if both entities E and F are multi-valued in the relationship. If both E and F are single-valued, the relationship is said to be *one-to-one*, or 1-1. If E is single-valued and F is multi-valued, or the reverse, the relationship is said to be many-to-one, N-1. (See the note following: we do not normally speak of a 1-N relationship as distinct from an N-1 relationship.)   ■

Note particularly that the "many" side in a many-to-one relationship is the side that has single-valued participation! In Figure 5.6(b), the entity F corresponds to the "many" side of the many-to-one relationship, even though it has card(F, R) = (1,1). The "many" side of a many-to-one relationship is the side where a *large* number of instances are connected to a *single* instance from the other entity. This is perhaps better understood by considering the relationship given in Figure 5.7, Instructors teaches Course_sections, where card(Course_sections, teaches) = (1,1), and the Course_sections entity represents the "many" side of the relationship. This is because one instructor teaches "many" course sections, while the reverse is not true.

In Definition 5.2.2, we see that the values max-card(E, R) and max-card(F, R) determine whether a binary relationship is many-to-many, many-to-one, or one-to-one. On the other hand, the values min-card(E, R) and min-card(F, R) are not mentioned, and they are said to be independent of these characterizations. In particular, the fact that min-card(F, R) = 1 in Figure 5.6(b) is independent of the fact that diagram (b) represents a many-to-one relationship. If there were additional elements in entity F that were not connected by any lines to elements in E (but all current connections remained the same), this would mean that min-card(F, R) = 0, but the change would not affect the fact that R is a many-to-one relationship. We would still see one element of E (the second from the top) related to two elements of F; in this case, the entity set F is the "many" side of the relationship.

Although min-card(E, R) and min-card(F, R) have no bearing on whether a binary relationship R is many-to-many, many-to-one, or one-to-one, a different characterization of entity participation in a relationship is determined by these quantities.

DEFINITION 5.2.3 When an entity E that participates in a relationship R has min-card(E, R) = 1, E is said to have *mandatory participation* in R, or is simply called *mandatory* in R. An entity E that is not mandatory in R is said to be *optional*, or to have *optional participation*. ∎

Transforming Binary Relationships to Relations

We are now prepared to give the transformation rule for a binary many-to-many relationship.

Transformation RULE 3. N-N Relationships. When two entities E and F take part in a many-to-many binary relationship R, the relationship is mapped to a representative table T in the related relational database design. The table contains columns for all attributes in the primary keys of both tables transformed from entities E and F, and this set of columns forms the primary key for the table T. T also contains columns for all attributes attached to the relationship. Relationship occurrences are represented by rows of the table, with the related entity instances uniquely identified by their primary key values as rows. ∎

EXAMPLE 5.2.2

In Figure 5.7, the relationship works_on is many-to-many between the entities Employees and Projects. The relational design in Figure 5.8 follows Transformation RULE 1 to provide a table for the entity Employees (as specified in Example 5.1.2) and a table for the entity Projects; it also follows Transformation RULE 3 to provide a table for the relationship works_on.

employees

eid	st_address	city	state	zipcode
197	7 Beacon St	Boston	MA	02102
221	19 Brighton St	Boston	MA	02103
303	153 Mass Ave	Cambridge	MA	02123
. . .	. . .	. . .	. . .	. . .

works_on

eid	prid	percent
197	p11	50
197	p13	25
197	p21	25
221	p21	100
303	p13	40
303	p21	60
. . .	. . .	. . .

projects

prid	proj_name	due_date
p11	Phoenix	3/31/95
p13	Excelsior	9/31/96
p21	White Mouse	6/30/95
. . .	. . .	. . .

Figure 5.8 Relational Design for Employees works_on Projects of Figure 5.7

We generally assume that the eid column in the employees table and prid column for the projects table cannot take on null values, since they are the primary keys for their tables, and must differentiate all rows by unique values. Similarly, the (eid, prid) pair of columns in the works_on table cannot take on null values in either component, since each row must uniquely designate the employee-project pair related. This general observation was summed up in Relational RULE 4, at the end of Section 2.4, the Entity Integrity RULE, that no primary key column of a relational table can take on null values. Note that although we refer to this as the *Entity Integrity RULE,* it applies as well to tables arising out of the relationships in the E-R model. Recall that the SQL Create Table command, introduced in Section 3.2, provides syntax to impose an integrity constraint on a table that guarantees this rule will not be broken, that no nulls will be assigned. For example, the SQL statement

```
create table products (prid char(3) not null . . .);
```

guarantees that the `prid` column of the `projects` table cannot take on null values as a result of later Insert, Delete, or Update statements. There are other constraints as well that have this effect. ∎

Transformation RULE 4. N-1 Relationships. When two entities E and F take part in a many-to-one binary relationship R, the relationship will not be mapped to a table of its own in a relational database design. Instead, if we assume that the entity F has max-card(F, R) = 1 and thus represents the "many" side of the relationship, the relational table T transformed from the entity F should include columns constituting the primary key for the table transformed from the entity E; this is known as a *foreign key* in T. Since max-card(F, R) = 1, each row of T is related by a foreign key value to at most one instance of the entity E. If F has mandatory participation in R, then it must be related to exactly one instance of E, and this means that the foreign key in T cannot take on null values. If F has optional participation in R, then each row of T that is not related can have null values in all columns of the foreign key. ∎

EXAMPLE 5.2.3
Figure 5.9 shows a relational transformation of the `Instructors teaches Course_sections` E-R diagram of Figure 5.7. Recall that we made the rule that one instructor can teach multiple course sections, but each course section can have only one instructor. The `insid` column in the `course_sections` table is a foreign key, relating a `course_sections` instance (row) to a unique `instructors` instance (row).

instructors

insid	lname	office_no	ext
309	O'Neil	S-3-223	78543
123	Bergen	S-3-547	78413
113	Smith	S-3-115	78455
...	...	...	...

course_sections

secid	insid	course	room	period
120	309	CS240	M-1-213	MW6
940	309	CS630	M-1-214	MW7:30
453	123	CS632	M-2-614	TTH6
...	...	...	...	...

Figure 5.9 Relational Design for `Instructors teaches Course_Sections` of Figure 5.7

The Create Table command in SQL can guarantee that a column does not take on null values; therefore it is possible to guarantee a faithful representation for mandatory participation by the "many" side entity in a many-to-one relationship. Here we can create the `course_sections` table so no nulls are allowed in the `insid` column. What we mean by "faithful" is that it becomes impossible for a user to corrupt the data by a thoughtless update, because SQL does not allow a `course_sections` row with a null value for `insid`. As we will see in the next chapter, SQL can also impose a constraint that the foreign key `insid` value in a row of the `course_sections` table actually exists as a value in the `insid` primary key column in the `instructors` table. This constraint is known as *referential integrity*. ∎

Unfortunately, it is not possible in standard SQL to guarantee a mandatory participation by the "one" side of a many-to-one relationship, or by either side of a many-to-many relationship. Thus in Example 5.2.3 there would be no way to provide a faithful representation in an SQL table definition that would guarantee that every instructor teaches at least one course.

Note that there are differences of opinion among texts on some of these E-R transformation rules for relationships. Reference [4] gives the equivalent to Transformation RULE 4 for N-1 relationships, but reference [1] provides an alternate transformation where the relationship is mapped onto a table of its own if the entity at the "many" side of the relationship has an optional participation. The reason for this is to avoid possibly heavy use of null values in the foreign key (`insid` in Example 5.2.3); but since there seems to be nothing wrong with using null values, we follow the transformation of reference [4].

Transformation RULE 5. 1-1 Relationships, Optional Participation. Given two entities E and F that take part in a one-to-one binary situation R, where participation is optional on either side, we wish to translate this situation into a relational design. To do this, we create a table S to represent the entity E, following the prescription of Transformation RULE 1, and similarly a table T to represent the entity F. Then we adjoin to the table T a set of columns (as a foreign key) constituting the primary key for table S. If we wish we may also adjoin to table S a foreign key set of columns referring to the primary key of table T. For any relationship instance in R, a unique entity instance in E is related to a unique instance in F—in the corresponding rows of S and T, the foreign key column values filled in to reference the row in the other table arising from the instances related by R. ∎

Transformation RULE 6. 1-1 Relationships, Mandatory Participation on Both Sides. In the case of a one-to-one relationship with mandatory participation on both sides, it seems most appropriate to combine the tables for the two entities into one, and in this way avoid any foreign keys. ■

We do not present transformation rules for all possible N-ary relationships with N > 2. Usually such an N-ary relationship is transformed into a table of its own, but if all but one of the entities of the relationship participate with max-card = 1, then it is possible to represent the relationship with foreign key in the one table that participates with greater cardinality.

5.3 Additional E-R Concepts

In this section we introduce a number of additional concepts useful for E-R modeling.

Cardinality of Attributes

To begin with, we note that the min-card/max-card notation can be used to describe the cardinality of attributes attached to entities.

DEFINITION 5.3.1 Given an entity E and an attached attribute A, we write min-card(A, E) = 0 to indicate that the attribute A is optional, and min-card(A, E) = 1 to indicate that the attribute A is mandatory. An attribute that is mandatory should correspond to a column declared in the table representing the entity E with no nulls allowed. We write max-card(A, E) = 1 to indicate that the attribute is single-valued, and max-card(A, E) = N to indicate that the attribute is multi-valued. An attribute A is said to have card(A, E) = (x,y) when min-card(A, E) = x and max-card(A, E) = y. The (x,y) pair can be used to label an attribute-entity connection in an E-R diagram to indicate the cardinality of the attribute. ■

Attributes that have unlabeled connectors in an E-R diagram can be assumed to have cardinality (0,1) if they are descriptor attributes, and cardinality (1,1) if they are identifier attributes. Figure 5.10 recapitulates Figure 5.2 with labeled attribute-entity connectors. (Note that these are not the default cardinalities we would have expected from Figure 5.2, which was left with unlabeled cardinalities only because of lack of notation.)

In Figure 5.10 we note that the attribute midinitial is optional (some people don't have middle names). The composite attribute student_name is mandatory for Students, but emp_address is optional for Employees. However, given that emp_address exists, all four simple attributes making up the address are mandatory. Both sid and eid have cardinality (1,1); this is always the case for entity identifiers. The multi-valued hobbies attribute has max-card N, as we can also tell from the fact that it is connected to its entity by a double line. The fact that min-card(hobbies, Employees) = 1 is somewhat surprising, and indicates that the employee *must* name at least one hobby for inclusion in the database.

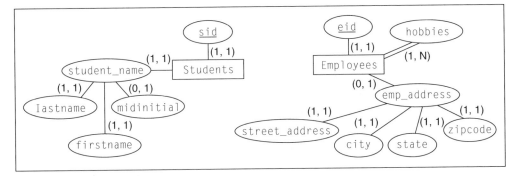

Figure 5.10 E-R Diagrams with Labeled Attribute-Entity Connectors

Weak Entities

DEFINITION 5.3.2 A weak entity is an entity whose occurrences are dependent for their existence through a relationship R on the occurrence of another (strong) entity. ■

As an example, we have been assuming in our CAP design that an order specifies a customer, agent, product, quantity, and dollar cost. A common design variant that allows multiple products to be ordered at once will create an orders table that relates to customers and agents rows, as well as a line_items table containing individual product purchases; a number of rows in the line_items table relate to one master orders occurrence. The design of this in the E-R model is given in Figure 5.11.

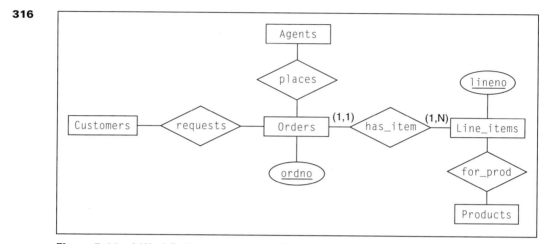

Figure 5.11 A Weak Entity, Line_items, Dependent on the Entity Orders

As we see, the entity Orders is mandatory in its relationship to Line_items, since some line-item must exist for every order. Line_items is also mandatory in the relationship, because an order for a product cannot exist without a master order containing it to specify the customer and agent for the order. If the Orders occurrence goes away (the customer cancels it), all occurrences of the weak entity Line_items will likewise disappear. A dead giveaway for a weak entity is the fact that the primary identifier for Line_items (lineno) is only meaningful within some order. In fact, what this implies is that the primary identifier for the weak entity Line_items must include the attributes in the primary identifier for the Orders entity. These are what are known as *external identifier* attributes.

When the Line_items weak entity is mapped to a relational table line_items, an ordno column is included by Transformation RULE 4 to represent the N-1 has_item relationship; thus the primary key for the line_items table is constructed from the external attribute ordno and the weak entity identifier lineno. Note that there is sometimes no distinction between a weak entity and a multi-valued attribute. For example, hobbies in example 5.1.2 could be identified as a weak entity Hobbies, with an identifier hobby_name.

Generalization Hierarchies

Finally, we introduce the concept of a *generalization hierarchy* or *generalization relationship*. The idea here is that several types of entities with common attributes can be generalized into a higher-level entity type. In the other direction, an entity can be decomposed into lower-level entities. The purpose is to attach attributes to the proper level of the entity, and thus avoid having a large number of null values. For example, assume that we distinguish between Managers and Non_managers as *subtype* entities of the *supertype* Employees. Then all attributes having to do with expense accounts and other management concerns can be attached only to the Managers entity, while non-manager concerns such as union status can be attached to Non_managers. At this point, we might also note that Consultants forms another entity type that shares many properties with Employees, and create a new supertype entity named Persons to contain them both. Clearly the generalization hierarchy concept can be implemented with the object-oriented concepts of subtypes, subtables, and inheritance that we encountered in the Montage extended relational database system of Section 3.11. An E-R diagram showing a generalization hierarchy normally has arrows (unnamed) directed from the subtype to the supertype entities (see Figure 5.12).

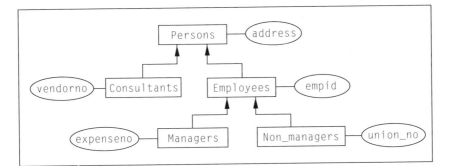

Figure 5.12 A Generalization Hierarchy with Examples of Attributes Attached

A subtype entity such as Managers in Figure 5.12 is said to be a *subset entity* to the supertype entity Employees, which is the *superset entity*, since managers form a subset of employees in a company. The arrow relationship between the subset entity and the superset entity is often referred to as an *ISA relationship,* since a consultant *is a* person, a manager *is an* employee, etc.

The relational model provides no support for the concept of generalization hierarchy, so it is necessary to support it in a computerized database by reconfiguration into simpler concepts. As with some other aspects that have been mentioned, this can happen either prior to transformation into relational tables or as part of the transformation. Here we give an idea of how to perform such a reconfiguration while remaining in the E-R model, before transformation into a relational representation. We consider one level of generalization hierarchy at a time, and give two alternatives.

[1] We can collapse a one-level generalization hierarchy of subtype and supertype entities into a single entity, by adding all attributes of the subtype entities to the supertype entity. An additional attribute must be added to this single entity that will discriminate among the various types. As an example, the Employee entity of Figure 5.12 could be augmented to represent managers and non-managers as well, by affixing the attributes union_no, expenseno, and emptype to the Employee entity. Now the union_no attribute will be null when emptype has value 'Manager', and similarly expenseno will be null when emptype is 'Non-Manager'. The emptype attribute might also designate the supertype case, an important alternative when some entity instances in the supertype fall in none of the named subtypes.

[2] We can retain the supertype entity and all subtype entities as full entities and create explicit named relationships to represent the ISA relationships.

Alternative 2 is particularly useful when the various subtypes and supertype are quite different in attributes and often handled differently by application logic.

We do not investigate all concepts of the entity-relationship model in full depth here. See the references at the end of this chapter for a list of texts devoted to complete coverage of the E-R model and logical database design.

5.4 Case Study

Let us try to perform an E-R design from the beginning, ending up with a set of relational tables.

Consider a simple airline reservation database, in which we need to keep track of passengers, flights, departure gates, and seat assignments. We could get almost arbitrarily complex in a real design, since a "flight" actually brings together a flight crew and an airplane, serviced by a ground crew, slotted into a regularly scheduled departure time with an assigned flight number on a specific date. But for simplicity, we will assume that we can represent flights with an entity *Flights*, having primary identifier flightno (unique identifier values, not repeated on successive days) and descriptive attribute depart_time (actually made up of date and time), and that other details are hidden from us. Passengers are represented by another entity, *Passengers*, with primary identifier attribute ticketno; a passenger has no other attribute that we care about. We also need to keep track of seats for each flight. We assume that each seat is an entity instance in its own right, an entity *Seats*, identified by a seat number, seatno, valid only for a specific flight (different flights might have different airplane seat layouts, and therefore different sets of seat numbers). We see therefore that seat assignment is a relationship between Passengers and Seats, which we name *seat_assign*.

Now think about this specification for a moment. The Passengers entity is easy to picture, and so is the Flights entity. The depart_time attribute for Flights is composite, consisting of simple attributes dtime, and ddate. We can add another entity *Gates*, with primary identifier gateno. We have already defined a Seats entity, but the entity seems to be a little strange: the seatno primary identifier for Seats is only meaningful when related to a Flights instance. This is what is referred to in the previous section as a weak entity, and thus there must be a relationship between Flights and Seats, which we name *has_seat*. The identifier for Seats is partially external, encompassing the identifier of the containing flight.

What other relationships do we have? If we draw the E-R diagram for what we have named up to now, we notice that the Gates entity is off by itself. But clearly passengers go to a gate to meet a flight. We model this as two binary relationships rather than as a ternary relationship: each passenger is related to a specific flight through the relationship Passengers *travels_on* Flights, and gates normally act as marshaling points for multiple flights (at different times) through the relationship Gates *marshals* Flights. Figure 5.13 shows the E-R diagram so far. The arrow from seatno to flightno symbolizes the fact that the primary identifier for Seats includes the identifier for the master entity Flights.

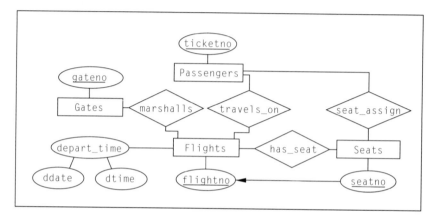

Figure 5.13 Early E-R Design for a Simple Airline Reservation Database

Now we need to work out the cardinalities with which the various entities participate in their relationships. Considering the marshals relationship first, clearly there is exactly one gate for each flight, so card(Flights, marshals) = (1, 1). A single gate might be used for multiple flights at different times, but there is no rule that a gate must be used at all, so card(Gates, marshals) = (0, N). Now each passenger must travel on exactly one flight, so card(Passengers, travels_on) = (1, 1). At the same time, a flight must have multiple passengers (the flight will be canceled and the gate reassigned if there are too few), but the best we can do is set a minimum of 1, and card(Flights, travels_on) = (1, N). A flight must have numerous seats for passengers, so card(Flights, has_seat) = (1, N), and each seat is on a unique flight, so card(Seats, has_seat) = (1, 1). Each passenger must have a seat, and only one, so card(Passengers, seat_assign) = (1, 1), and seats can be used by at most one passenger and may go empty, so card(Seats, seat_assign) = (0, 1). The E-R diagram with these cardinality pairs added is pictured in Figure 5.14.

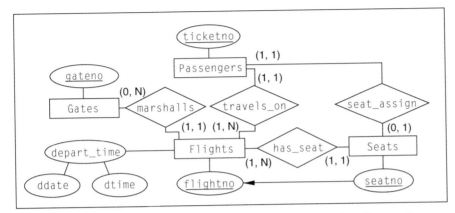

Figure 5.14 E-R Design with Cardinalities for a Simple Airline Reservation Database

Now the E-R design is complete, and we need to transform the design into relational tables. We can begin by creating tables to map entities, even though this means that we might overlook some attributes that will be needed to represent foreign keys for relationships. We will simply have to return later when we consider the relationships and add attributes to these tables. To begin with, we notice with the Flights entity that we don't have "multi-valued attributes" in relational tables, so following the hint of Transformation RULE 1, we create columns for ddate and dtime in the flights table. All other tables are easily mapped, except for the seats table, where we take the easy way out and use the single column seatno, even though this is not a complete key for the table. Here are the tables so far:

Now consider the relationship has_seat, which is N-1 in Figure 5.14, with Seats on the "many" side. By Transformation RULE 4, a foreign key in the seats table will connect each seats row to the appropriate flights row. This completes the primary key for the seats table, which represents a weak entity and therefore needs a foreign key to identify each row.

passengers		gates	flights			seats	
ticketno		gateno	flightno	ddate	dtime	seatno	flightno
. . .							

The `seat_assign` relationship is 1-1, with optional participation by Seats, so by Transformation RULE 5 we can represent this by adjoining to the `passengers` table a foreign key for `seats` (this requires two additional columns). We don't expect that we will ever need to look up the passenger for a given seat, so we place no additional foreign key on the `seats` table. The resulting table definitions are as follows:

passengers			gates
ticketno	seatno	flightno	gateno
. . .			

flights			seats	
flightno	ddate	dtime	seatno	flightno

Now consider the `marshals` relationship. This is N-1, with Flights on the "many" side, so by Transformation RULE 4 a foreign key in the `flights` table, `gateno`, will connect each `flights` row to the appropriate `gates` row:

passengers			gates
ticketno	seatno	flightno	gateno
. . .			

flights				seats	
flightno	gateno	ddate	dtime	seatno	flightno

Similarly the `travels_on` relationship is N-1, with `Passengers` on the "many" side, so by Transformation RULE 4 a foreign key, `flightno`, in the `passengers` table will connect each `passengers` row to the appropriate `flights` row. This column already exists in the `passengers` table, however, so the relational table design is complete.

5.5 Normalization: Preliminaries

Normalization is another approach to logical design of a relational database that seems to share little with the E-R model. However, it will turn out that a relational design based on normalization and a careful E-R design transformed into relational form have nearly identical results, and in fact the two approaches reinforce one another. In the normalization approach, the designer starts with a real-world situation to be modeled and lists the data items that are candidates to become column names in relational tables, together with a list of rules about the relatedness of these data items. The aim is to represents all these data items as attributes of tables that obey restrictive conditions associated with what we call *normal forms*. These normal form definitions limit the acceptable form of a table so that it has certain desirable properties, thus avoiding various kinds of anomalous behavior. There is a series of normal form definitions, each more restrictive than the one before; the forms covered in the current chapter are first normal form (1NF), second normal form (2NF), third normal form (3NF), and Boyce-Codd normal form (BCNF). Other types of normalization, 4NF and 5NF, are less commonly considered, and are not covered in detail in this text.

To begin with, a table in first normal form (1NF) is simply one that has no multi-valued (repeating) fields; that is, a table that obeys Relational RULE 1 from Section 2.3, the first normal form rule. As a matter of fact, the relational database products and SQL standards we have been studying make it impossible to break this rule in a table definition, although a few new extended relational products, such as Montage, provide facilities for non-first normal form tables. In what follows we assume that tables are in 1NF unless otherwise specified. Second normal form (2NF) also turns out to be of mainly historical interest, since no sensible designer would leave a database in 2NF form, but would always continue normalization until the more restrictive 3NF was reached. From an initial database containing data items that are all in the same table (sometimes referred to as a *universal table*) and relatedness rules on these data items, there is a procedure to create an equivalent database with multiple tables, all of which are in third normal form. (This is what we mean by having a database in 3NF—that all of its tables have 3NF form.) As we proceed through this chapter we will find that any table that does not obey third normal form can be factored into distinct tables in such a way that (1) each of the factored tables is in a valid third normal form, and (2) the join of all these factored tables contains exactly the information in the table from which they were factored. The set of 3NF tables resulting from the initial universal table is known as a 3NF *lossless decomposition* of the database.

There is a third desirable property that we can always provide with a 3NF decomposition. Note that when a new row is added to one of the tables in the 3NF decomposition (or an old row is updated), it is possible that an erroneous change might break one of the rules of data item relatedness, mentioned earlier as part of the design input. We wish to impose a constraint on Insert and Update operations so that such errors will not corrupt the data. The third property that we consider important in a decomposition, then, is (3) when a table Insert or Update occurs, the possible relatedness rules that might be broken can be tested by validating data items in the single table affected; there is no need to perform table joins in order to validate these rules. A 3NF decomposition having the three desirable properties just mentioned is generally considered an acceptable database design. It turns out that a further decomposition of tables in 3NF to the more restrictive BCNF is often unnecessary (many real-world databases in 3NF are also in BCNF), but in cases where further decomposition results, property (3) no longer holds in the result. Many database designers therefore settle on 3NF design.

We will need a good deal of insight into the details of the normalization approach before we are able to properly deal with some of these ideas. Let us begin to illustrate them with an example.

A Running Example: Employee Information

We need an example to clarify some of the definitions of database design that follow. Consider the data items listed in Figure 5.15, representing the employee information that must be modeled by the personnel department of a very large company.

```
emp_id
emp_name
emp_phone
dept_name
dept_phone
dept_mgrname
skill_id
skill_name          From one up to a large number
skill_date          of skills useful to the company
skill_lvl
```

Figure 5.15 Unnormalized Data Items for Employee Information

The data items beginning with "emp_" all represent attributes of what we would refer to in the E-R approach as the entity Employee. Other entities underlying the data items of Figure 5.15 include Departments where employees in the company work and Skills that the various employees need in order to perform their jobs. In the normalization approach, we leave the entity concept unnamed, but reflect it in the data item interrelatedness rules that will be explained shortly, rules known as *functional dependencies*. The data item emp_id has been created to uniquely identify employees. Each employee works for some single department in the company, and the data items beginning with "dept_" describe the different departments; the data item dept_name uniquely identifies departments, and each department normally has a unique manager (also an employee) with a name given in dept_mgrname. Finally, we assume that the various employees each possess some number of "skills," such as typing or filing, and that data items beginning with "skill_" describe the skills that are tested and used for job assignment and salary determination by the company. The data item skill_id uniquely identifies the skill, which also has a name, skill_name. For each employee who possesses a particular skill, the skill_date describes the date when the skill was last tested, and skill_lvl describes the level of skill the employee displayed at that test.

Figure 5.16 provides a universal table, emp_info, containing all the data items of employee information from Figure 5.15. Because of first normal form, there can only be atomic values in each row and column position of a table. This poses a difficulty, because each individual employee might have any number of skills. As we argued in Section 2.3, it is inappropriate to design a table with unique rows for each emp_id and a distinct column for each piece of skill information—we don't even know the maximum number of skills for an employee, so we don't know how many columns we should use for "skill_id-1, . . ., skill_id-n". The only solution that will work in a single (universal) table is to give up on having a unique row for each employee, and replicate information about the employee, pairing the employee with different skills on different rows.

emp_info

emp_id	emp_name	...	skill_id	skill_name	skill_date	skill_lvl
09112	Jones	...	44	librarian	03-15-90	12
09112	Jones	...	26	typing	06-30-92	10
09112	Jones	...	89	word-proc	01-15-93	12
12231	Smith	...	26	typing	04-15-92	5
12231	Smith	...	39	filing	07-30-92	7
13597	Brown	...	26	typing	09-15-92	6
14131	Blake	...	26	typing	05-30-92	9
14131	Blake	...	89	word-proc	09-30-92	10
...	...	...	...	...	...	...

Figure 5.16 Single Employee Information Table, emp_info, in First Normal Form

The intention of the database designer in the emp_info table of Figure 5.16 is that there is a row for every employee-skill pair existing in the company. From this, it should be clear that there cannot be two rows with the same values for the pair of attributes emp_id and skill_id. We have already introduced terminology to describe this state of affairs when we defined a table key in Definition 2.4.1. We claim that the table emp_info has a (candidate) key consisting of the set (pair) of attributes emp_id skill_id. Recall the shorthand notation of presenting a set of attributes by writing a list of attributes separated by spaces. We confirm that these attributes form a key by noting that the values they take on distinguish any pair of rows in any permissible content of the table (i.e., for any rows u and v, either $u(emp\_id) \neq v(emp\_id)$ or $u(skill\_id) \neq c(skill\_id)$), and that no subset of this set of attributes does the same (there can be two rows u and v such that u(emp_id) = v(emp_id), and there can be two rows r and s such that r(skill_id) = s(skill_id)). We assume in what follows that emp_id skill_id is the primary key for the emp_info table.

It turns out that the database design of Figure 5.16 is a bad one, because it is subject to certain anomalies that can corrupt the data when data manipulation statements are used to update the table.

Anomalies of a Bad Database Design

It appears that there might be a problem with the emp_info table of Figure 5.16 because there is replication of employee data on different rows. It seems more natural, with the experience we have had up to now, to have a unique row for each distinct employee. Do we have a good reason for our feeling? Let us look at the behavior of this table as SQL updates are applied.

If some employee were to get a new phone number, we would have to update multiple rows (all rows with different skills for that employee) in order to change the emp_phone value in a uniform way. If we were to update the phone number of only one row, we might *corrupt* the data, leaving some rows for that employee with different phone numbers than others. This is commonly known as an *update anomaly,* and it arises because of *data redundancy,* duplication of employee phone numbers and other employee attributes on multiple rows of emp_info. Calling this an "anomaly," with the implication of irregular behavior under update, may seem a bit extreme, since the SQL language is perfectly capable of updating several rows at once with a Searched Update statement such as

```
update emp_info set emp_phone = :newphone where emp_id = :eidval;
```

In fact, the consideration that several rows will be updated is not even apparent from this syntax—the same Searched Update statement would be used if the table had a unique row for each emp_id value. However, with this replication of phone numbers on different rows a problem can still arise in performing an update with a Positioned Update statement. If we encountered a row of the emp_info table in fetching rows from a cursor created for an entirely different purpose, the program might execute the following statement to allow the user to correct an invalid phone number:

```
update emp_info set emp_phone = :newphone
    where current of cursor_name;
```

This would be a *programming error,* since an experienced programmer would realize that multiple rows need to be updated in order to change an employee phone number. Still, it is the kind of error that could easily occur in practice, and we would like to be able to create a *constraint* on the table that makes such an erroneous update impossible. It turns out that the best way to provide such a constraint is to reconfigure the data items into different tables so as to eliminate the redundant copies of information. This is exactly what is achieved during the process of normalization. We sum up the idea of an update anomaly in a definition that makes reference to our intuitive understanding of the E-R model.

DEFINITION 5.5.1 Update Anomaly. A table T is subject to an *update anomaly* when changing a single attribute value for an entity instance or relationship instance represented in the table may require that several rows of T be updated. ∎

A different sort of problem, known as the *delete anomaly,* is reflected by the following definition.

DEFINITION 5.5.2 Delete Anomaly, Insert Anomaly. A table T is subject to a *delete anomaly* when deleting some row of the table to reflect the disappearance of some instance of an entity or relationship can cause us to lose information about some instance of a different entity or relationship that we do not wish to forget. The *insert anomaly* is the other face of this problem for inserts, where we cannot represent information about some entity or instance without including information about some other instance of an entity or relationship that does not exist. ∎

For example, assume that a skill possessed by an employee must be retested after five years to remain current for that employee. If the employee fails to have the skill retested (and the skill_date column updated), the skill will drop off the emp_info list (an automatic process deletes the row with this emp_id and skill_id). Now consider what happens if the number of skills for some employee goes to zero in the emp_info table with columns of Figure 5.16: *No row of any kind will remain for the employee!* We have lost the phone number and the department the employee works in because of this delete! This is clearly inappropriate design. The other anomaly of Definition 5.5.2, known as the insert anomaly, exists in the emp_info table because we cannot enter a new employee into the table until the employee has acquired some skill; thus it becomes impossible to hire an employee trainee. Clearly this is just the other face of the delete anomaly, that information about an employee is lost when the employee loses his or her last skill.

Let us jump ahead to a solution for some of the problems mentioned up to now. We simply factor the emp_info table and form two tables, the emps table and the skills table, whose column names are listed in Figure 5.17. Notice that the emps table has a unique row for each emp_id (and emp_id is the key for this table), while the skills table has a unique row for each emp_id skill_id pair, and this pair forms a key for the table. Since there are multiple skills associated with each employee, the emp_id column that we have included in the skills table acts as a *foreign key*, relating skills back to employees. When we form the natural join of these two tables, the result is exactly the emp_info table we started with. (We will need to demonstrate this fact in what follows, but for now you should take it on faith.) However, the delete anomaly is no longer a problem, since if we delete all rows corresponding to skills for any individual employee, this merely deletes rows in the skills table; the emps table still contains the information we don't want to lose about the employee, such as emp_phone, dept_name, etc.

emps tbl
emp_id
emp_name
emp_phone
dept_name
dept_phone
dept_mgrname

skills tbl
emp_id
skill_id
skill_name
skill_date
skill_lvl

Figure 5.17   The emp_info Database with Two Tables

In the sections that follow we will learn how to perform normalization, to factor tables so that all anomalies are removed from our representation. Note that we haven't yet achieved this with the tables of Figure 5.17, since we will see shortly that a number of anomalies still exist. We will need a good deal of insight into the details of the normalization approach before we are able to properly deal with fundamental normalization concepts. In the following sections we present some needed mathematical preliminaries to database normalization. Because it is not always possible to show a real-life application for all these concepts as they are introduced, we ask the reader to be patient. The value of the concepts will become clear in the end.

5.6 Functional Dependencies

A *functional dependency* (FD) defines the most commonly encountered type of relatedness property between data items of a database. We usually only need to consider relatedness between column attributes of a single relational table, and our definition reflects this. We represent rows of a table T by the notation $r_1, r_2, \ldots$, and for technical reasons refer in what follows to attributes, rather than columns, of the table T. We represent individual attributes of a table by letters such as A, B, $\ldots$, and X, Y, $\ldots$ refer to subsets of attributes. We follow the notation of Chapter 2, that $r_i(A)$ represents the value of row r_i at attribute A.

DEFINITION 5.6.1 Given a table T containing at least two attributes designated by A and B, we say that $A \rightarrow B$ (read "A functionally determines B" or "B is functionally dependent on A"), if and only if it is the intent of the designer, for any set of rows that might exist in the table, that two rows in T cannot agree in value for A and disagree in value for B. A more formal way of saying this is: given two rows r_1 and r_2 in T, if $r_1(A) = r_2(A)$ then $r_1(B) = r_2(B)$. We will usually try to use the less formal statement in what follows. ∎

Definition 5.6.1 is comparable to the definition of a *function* in mathematics: for every element in the attribute A (which appears on some row), there is a unique corresponding element (on the same row) in the attribute B. See Figure 5.18 for a graphical representation of the functional dependency concept.

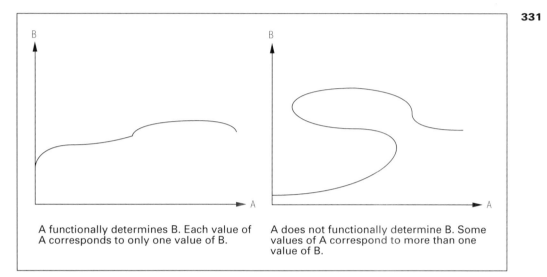

B

B

A functionally determines B. Each value of A corresponds to only one value of B.

A does not functionally determine B. Some values of A correspond to more than one value of B.

Figure 5.18 Graphical Presentation of Functional Dependency

EXAMPLE 5.6.1

In the emp_info table of Figure 5.16, the following functional dependencies hold:

```
emp_id → emp_name
emp_id → emp_phone
emp_id → dept_name
```

In E-R terms, we know this is true because emp_id is an identifier for the Employee entity, and the other data items simply represent other attributes of the entity; once the entity is identified, all the other attributes follow. But we also recognize these facts intuitively. If we saw two rows in the single table emp_info design of Figure 5.16 with the same emp_id value and different emp_phone values, we would believe that the data is corrupted (assuming that every employee has a unique phone), but if we saw two rows with the same emp_phone value and different emp_id values, our first thought would be that they represented different employees who shared a phone. But the two situations are symmetric; it is simply our understanding of the data that makes the first one seem to imply corrupted data. We look to emp_id to break ties and uniquely identify employees. Note that what we are saying implies that, while emp_id functionally determines emp_phone, emp_phone does *not* functionally determine emp_id. We sometimes express this second fact with the notation:

```
emp_phone ↛ emp_id
```
∎

EXAMPLE 5.6.2
Here are three tables to investigate for functional dependencies between attributes (note that some of the tables break Relational RULE 3, the Unique Row RULE, but we accept them as valid tables for purposes of illustration). In these tables we assume that it is the intent of the designer that *exactly* this set of rows should lie in each table—no changes will ever occur in the tables. Thus we can determine what functional dependencies exist by examining the data. This is *a very unusual situation.* Normally we determine functional dependencies from understanding the data items and rules of the enterprise (for example, each employee has a single phone number, employees can share a phone . . .), as in Example 5.6.1. These rules exist before any data has been placed in the table.

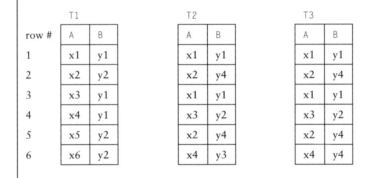

row #	T1 A	T1 B		T2 A	T2 B		T3 A	T3 B
1	x1	y1		x1	y1		x1	y1
2	x2	y2		x2	y4		x2	y4
3	x3	y1		x1	y1		x1	y1
4	x4	y1		x3	y2		x3	y2
5	x5	y2		x2	y4		x2	y4
6	x6	y2		x4	y3		x4	y4

In table T1 we can easily see that A → B; we merely need to check that for every pair of rows r_1 and r_2, if $r_1(A) = r_2(A)$ then $r_1(B) = r_2(B)$. However, there is no pair of rows in T1 with equal values for column A, so the condition is trivially satisfied. At the same time, in T1, B ↛ A (read: column B does *not* functionally determine column A), since, for example, if r_1 is row 1 and r_2 is row 3, then $r_1(B) = r_2(B) = y1$, but $r_1(A) = x1 \neq r_2(A) = x3$. In table T2, we have A → B (we just need to check that rows 1 and 3, which have matching pairs of A values, also have matching B values, and similarly check rows 2 and 5), and B → A. Finally, in table T3, A → B but B ↛ A (note that if r_1 is row 2 and r_2 is row 6, then $r_1(B) = r_2(B) = y4$, but $r_1(A) = x2 \neq r_2(A) = x4$). ∎

It is obvious how to extend the definition for functional dependency to its full generality, dealing with *sets* of attributes.

DEFINITION 5.6.2 We are given a table T with two sets of attributes, designated by $X = A_1 A_2 \ldots A_k$ and $Y = B_1 B_2 \ldots B_m$, where some of the attributes from X may overlap with some of the attributes from Y. We say that X → Y (read "X functionally determines Y" or "Y is functionally dependent on X"), if and only if it is the intent of the designer, for any set of rows that might exist in the table, that two rows in T cannot agree in value on the attributes of X and simultaneously disagree in value on the attributes of Y. Note that two rows agree in value on the attributes of X if they agree on *all of* the attributes of X, and they disagree in value on the attributes of Y if they disagree on *any of* the attributes of Y. More formally, given any two rows r_1 and r_2 in T, if $r_1(A_i) = r_2(A_i)$ for every A_i in X, then $r_1(B_j) = r_2(B_j)$ for every B_j in Y. ∎

In what follows, we often use the abbreviation FD for "functional dependency."

EXAMPLE 5.6.3
We list here what we claim are all the functional dependencies for the `emp_info` table of Figure 5.16 (with missing attributes in Figure 5.15). With this FD list, all the information needed for the normalization procedure has been provided.

(1) `emp_id` → `emp_name emp_phone dept_name`

(2) `dept_name` → `dept_phone dept_mgrname`

(3) `skill_id` → `skill_name`

(4) `emp_id skill_id` → `skill_date skill_lvl`

You should be able to interpret each of these functional dependencies and see if you agree with them. For example, FD (1) states that if we know the `emp_id`, then the `emp_name`, `emp_phone`, and `dept_name` are determined. Note that FD (1) is just another way of stating the FDs of Example 5.6.1. That is, if we know the FDs given there:

`emp_id` → `emp_name`, `emp_id` → `emp_phone`, and `emp_id` → `dept_name`,

we can conclude that FD (1) holds:

(1) `emp_id` → `emp_name emp_phone dept_name`

To say this in yet another way, the three FDs of Example 5.6.1 together imply FD (1). Similarly, from FD (1) we can conclude that the three FDs of Example 5.6.1 hold. A simple rule of FD implication is used to arrive at these conclusions, based on the FD definition. We will learn more about such rules shortly.

Because the FDs given in (1) through (4) are *all* the FDs for the `emp_info` table, we can conclude, for example, that the designer does *not* intend that `skill_name` be unique for a specific skill. Since `skill_id` is a unique identifier for the skill, to have a unique `skill_name` would presumably mean that `skill_name → skill_id`, the reverse of FD (3). However, this FD does not exist in the set, nor is it implied. (A quick test to see that it isn't implied is to note that `skill_name` does not occur on the left side of any FD in the set.) We also note that we do not have the FD `dept_mgrname → dept_name`, which presumably means that although each department has a unique manager, one manager might simultaneously manage more than one department. Finally, note that `skill_lvl` and `skill_date` are only meaningful as attributes of the *relationship* between an `Employee` entity and a `Skill` entity. If we said that a given employee had a skill level of 9, it would be necessary to ask, "For what skill?"; and if we said that we know there is a skill level of 9 for 'typing', we would wonder, "What employee?" Thus we need to name both the `emp_id` and the `skill_id` to determine these attributes. ∎

Logical Implications among Functional Dependencies

In Example 5.6.3 a number of conclusions were drawn that depended on understanding implications among functional dependencies. In what follows, we will derive certain rules of implication among FDs that follow directly from Definition 5.6.2. The reader needs to understand many such rules at both a rigorous and an intuitive level to properly appreciate some of the techniques of normalization that are presented in later sections. We begin with a very basic rule.

THEOREM 5.6.3 Inclusion Rule. We are given a table T with a specified heading (set of attributes, as defined in Section 2.2), Head(T). If X and Y are sets of attributes contained in Head(T), and Y $\subseteq$ X, then X → Y.

PROOF. We appeal to Definition 5.6.2. In order to show that X → Y, we need only demonstrate that there is no pair of rows u and v that agree in value on the attributes of X and simultaneously disagree in value on the attributes of Y. But this is obvious, since two rows can never agree in value on the attributes of X and simultaneously disagree on a subset of those attributes. ∎

The inclusion rule provides us with a large number of FDs that are true for any table of attributes, irrespective of the intended content.

DEFINITION 5.6.4 Trivial Dependency. A *trivial dependency* is an FD of the form X → Y that holds for any table T where X, Y $\subseteq$ Head(T). ∎

We can prove that trivial dependencies always arise as a result of the inclusion rule.

THEOREM 5.6.5 Given a trivial dependency $X \rightarrow Y$, it must be the case that $Y \subseteq X$.

PROOF. Create a table T with a heading consisting of the attributes in $X \cup Y$, and consider the set of attributes $Y - X$ (attributes in Y that are not in X). Since $X \rightarrow Y$ is a trivial dependency, it must hold for any possible content of the table T. We will assume $Y - X$ is non-empty, and reach a contradiction. If the set $Y - X$ is non-empty, let A be an attribute contained in $Y - X$. Since $A \notin X$, it is possible to construct two rows, u and v in the table T, alike in values for all attributes in X, but having different values for A. But with these two rows in T, the dependency $X \rightarrow Y$ does not hold, since rows u and v agree in value on attributes of X and disagree on attributes of Y (because $A \in Y$). Since a trivial dependency is supposed to hold for any possible content of the table T, we have created a contradiction, and from this we conclude that the set $Y - X$ cannot contain an attribute A, and therefore $Y \subseteq X$. ■

Armstrong's Axioms

The inclusion rule is one rule of implication by which FDs can be generated that are guaranteed to hold for all possible tables. It turns out that from a small set of basic rules of implication, we can derive all others. We list here three basic rules that we call Armstrong's Axioms (although other sets of rules could be given just as easily—see the exercises at the end of the chapter).

DEFINITION 5.6.6 Armstrong's Axioms. Assume in what follows that we are given a table T, and that all sets of attributes X, Y, Z are contained in Head(T). Then we have the following rules of implication.

    [1] Inclusion rule: If $Y \subseteq X$, then $X \rightarrow Y$

    [2] Transitivity rule: If $X \rightarrow Y$ and $Y \rightarrow Z$, then $X \rightarrow Y$

    [3] Augmentation rule: If $X \rightarrow Y$, then $X\,Z \rightarrow Y\,Z$

Just as we list attributes with spaces between them in a functional dependency to represent a set containing those attributes, two sets of attributes in sequence imply a union operation. Thus the augmentation rule could be rewritten: if $X \rightarrow Y$, then $X \cup Z \rightarrow Y \cup Z$. ∎

We have already proved the inclusion rule in Theorem 5.6.3. Let us prove the augmentation rule and leave transitivity for the exercises at the end of the chapter.

THEOREM 5.6.7 Augmentation. We wish to show that if $X \rightarrow Y$, then $X Z \rightarrow Y Z$. Assume that $X \rightarrow Y$, and consider any two rows u and v in T that agree on the attributes of X Z (i.e., $X \cup Z$). We need merely show that u and v cannot disagree on the attributes of Y Z. But since u and v agree on all attributes of X Z, they certainly agree on all attributes of X; and since we are assuming that $X \rightarrow Y$, then u and v must agree on all attributes of Y. Similarly, since u and v agree on all attributes of X Z, they certainly agree on all attributes of Z. Therefore u and v agree on all attributes of Y and all attributes of Z, and the proof is complete. ∎

From Armstrong's Axioms we can prove a number of other rules of implication among FDs. Furthermore, we can do this without any further recourse to the FD definition, using only the axioms themselves.

THEOREM 5.6.8 Some Implications of Armstrong's Axioms. Again we assume that all sets of attributes below, W, X, Y, and Z, and the single attribute B are contained in the heading of a table T.

[1] Union rule: If $X \rightarrow Y$ and $X \rightarrow Z$, then $X \rightarrow Y Z$

[2] Decomposition rule: If $X \rightarrow Y Z$, then $X \rightarrow Y$ and $X \rightarrow Z$

[3] Pseudotransitivity rule: If $X \rightarrow Y$ and $W Y \rightarrow Z$, then $X W \rightarrow Z$

[4] Accumulation rule: If $X \rightarrow Y Z$ and $Z \rightarrow B W$, then $X \rightarrow Y Z B$

PROOF. We prove only the accumulation rule, leaving the rest for the exercises. We are given (a) $X \rightarrow Y Z$ and (b) $Z \rightarrow B W$. By (b) and the augmentation rule, we can derive (c) $Z Y \rightarrow B W Y$. (We are substituting in the augmentation rule form Z for X, B W; that is, $B \cup W$ for Y, and Y for Z.) Now by (a) and (c) and transitivity, we derive (d) $X \rightarrow B Y Z$, but since B Y

Z is the same as B ∪ Y ∪ Z and union is commutative, this is the same as (d) X → Y Z B, and the accumulation rule has been demonstrated. ∎

We state without proof the rather startling result that *all* valid rules of implication among FDs can be derived from Armstrong's Axioms. In fact, if F is any set of FDs, and X → Y is an FD that cannot be shown by Armstrong's Axioms to be implied by F, then there must be a table T in which all of the FDs in F hold but X → Y is false. Because of this result, Armstrong's Axioms are often referred to as being *complete*, meaning that no other rule of implication can be added to increase their effectiveness.

Recall that in Example 5.6.3 we pointed out that the three FDs from Example 5.6.1:

```
emp_id → emp_name, emp_id → emp_phone, and emp_id → dept_name
```

allowed us to conclude that FD (1) holds:

```
(1) emp_id → emp_name emp_phone dept_name
```

This fact follows from two applications of the union rule of Theorem 5.6.8. The inverse implication, that FD (1) implies the first three, follows from two applications of the decomposition rule in the same theorem. Whenever we have some set of attributes X on the left of a set of FDs, we can take a union of all sets of attributes on the right of these FDs and combine the FDs into one. For example, if we have the attributes A B C D E F G in the heading of a table T, and we know that the following FDs hold:

B D → A, B D → C, B D → E, B D → F, and B D → G

Then we can combine these FDs into one by successive applications of the union rule:

[5.6.1]   B D → A C E F G

As a matter of fact, we can add the trivial dependency B D → B D and conclude:

B D → A B C D E F G

However, we normally try to avoid including information in a set of dependencies that can be derived using Armstrong's Axioms from a more fundamental set. Thus we might want to return to the FD form of (5.6.1). Given another attribute H, we might determine that in addition to the FD given in (5.6.1), the following FD holds:

$$B D H \rightarrow A C E F G H$$

But since this FD can be derived from FD (5.6.1) by using the augmentation rule, we would once again prefer the shorter FD (5.6.1).

EXAMPLE 5.6.4

List a minimal set of functional dependencies satisfied by the table T, below, where we assume that it is the intent of the designer that *exactly* this set of rows lies in the table. Once again, we point out that it is unusual to derive FDs from the content of a table. Normally we determine functional dependencies from understanding the data items and rules of the enterprise. Note that we do not yet have a rigorous definition of a minimal set of FDs, so we simply try to arrive at a minimal set in an intuitive way.

T

row #	A	B	C	D
1	a1	b1	c1	d1
2	a1	b1	c2	d2
3	a2	b1	c1	d3
4	a2	b1	c3	d4

Analysis. Let us start by considering FDs with a single attribute on the left. Clearly we always have the trivial FDs, $A \rightarrow A$, $B \rightarrow B$, $C \rightarrow C$, and $D \rightarrow D$, but we are asking for a minimal set of dependencies, so we won't list them. From the specific content of the table we are able to derive the following. (a) All values of the B attribute are the same, so it can never happen for any other attribute P (i.e., where P represents A, C, or D) that $r_1(P) = r_2(P)$ while $r_1(B) \neq r_2(B)$; thus we see that $A \rightarrow B$, $C \rightarrow B$, and $D \rightarrow B$. At the same time no other attributes P is functionally dependent on B since they all have at least two distinct values, and so there are always two rows r_1 and r_2 such that $r_1(P) \neq r_2(P)$ while $r_1(B) = r_2(B)$; thus $B \nrightarrow A$, $B \nrightarrow C$, and $B \nrightarrow D$. (b) Because the D values are all different, in addition to $D \rightarrow B$ of part (a), we also have $D \rightarrow A$ and $D \rightarrow C$; at the same time D is not functionally dependent on anything else since all other attributes have at least two duplicate values. So in addition to $B \not\to D$ of part (a), we have $A \not\to D$, and $C \not\to D$. (c) We have $A \not\to C$ (because of rows 1 and 2) and $C \not\to A$ (because of rows 1 and 3). Therefore we can list all FDs (and failed FDs) with a single attribute on the left. (Letters in parentheses are keyed to the paragraphs above that give us each fact.)

(a) $A \to B$	(a) $B \not\to A$	(c) $C \not\to A$	(b) $D \to A$
(c) $A \not\to C$	(a) $B \not\to C$	(a) $C \to B$	(a) $D \to B$
(b) $A \not\to D$	(a) $B \not\to D$	(b) $C \not\to D$	(b) $D \to C$

By the union rule, whenever a single attribute on the left functionally determines several other attributes, as with D above, we can combine the attributes on the right: $D \to A\,B\,C$. From the analysis so far, we have the following set of FDs (which we believe to be minimal):

(1) $A \to B$, (2) $C \to B$, (3) $D \to A\,B\,C$

Now consider FDs with *pairs* of attributes on the left. (d) Any pair containing D determines all other attributes, by FD (3) above and the augmentation rule, so there is no new FD with D on the left that is not already implied. (e) The attribute B, combined with any other attribute P on the left, still functionally determines only those attributes already determined by P, as we see by the following argument. If $P \not\to Q$ this means there are rows r_1 and r_2 such that $r_1(Q) \neq r_2(Q)$ while $r_1(P) = r_2(P)$. But because B has equal values on all rows, we know that $r_1(B\,P) = r_2(B\,P)$ as well, so $B\,P \not\to Q$. Thus we get no new FDs with B on the left.

(f) Now the only pair of attributes that does not contain B or D is A C, and since A C has distinct values on each row (examine table T again!), we know that $A\,C \to A\,B\,C\,D$. This is new. It is trivial that $A\,C \to A$, and $AC \to C$, and we already knew that $A \to B$, so it is easy to show that $A\,C \to B$ ($A\,C \to B\,C$ by augmentation, $B\,C \to B$ by inclusion, so $A\,C \to B$ by transitivity). Thus the only new fact we get from seeing that $A\,C \to A\,B\,C\,D$ is that $A\,C \to D$, and we are searching for a minimal set of FDs, so that is all we include as FD (4) in the following list. If we now consider looking for FDs with triples of attributes on the left, it is clear that we can derive from the FDs we already have that any triple that does not contain D (which would assure that it functionally determines all other attributes) must contain A B C (and A C alone functionally determines all other attributes). Clearly the same holds for any set of four attributes on the left.

The complete set of FDs implicit in the table T is therefore the following:

(1) $A \to B$, (2) $C \to B$, (3) $D \to A\,B\,C$, (4) $A\,C \to D$

The first three FDs come from the earlier list of FDs with single attributes on the left, while the last FD, $A\,C \to D$, is the new one generated with two attributes listed on the left. It will turn out that this set of FDs is not quite minimal, despite all our efforts to derive a minimal set. We will see this after we have had a chance to define what we mean by a minimal set of FDs. ∎

Closure, Cover, and Minimal Cover

The implication rules for FDs derived from Armstrong's Axioms mean that whenever a set F of functional dependencies is given, a much larger set may be implied.

DEFINITION 5.6.9 Closure of a Set of FDs. Given a set F of FDs on attributes of a table T, we define the *closure* of F, symbolized by F⁺, to be the set of all FDs implied by F.   ∎

EXAMPLE 5.6.5
Consider the set F of FDs given by

$$F = \{ A \rightarrow B, B \rightarrow C, C \rightarrow D, D \rightarrow E, E \rightarrow F, F \rightarrow G, G \rightarrow H\}$$

By the transitivity rule, A → B and B → C together imply A → C, which must be included in F⁺. Also, B → C and C → D imply B → D. Indeed, every single attribute appearing prior to the terminal one in the sequence A B C D E F G H can be shown by transitivity to functionally determine every single attribute on its right in the sequence. We also have trivial FDs such as A → A. Next, using the union rule, we can generate other FDs, such as A → A B C D E F G H. In fact, by using the union rule in different combinations, we can show A → (any non-empty subset of A B C D E F G H). There are $2^8 - 1 = 255$ such non-empty subsets. All FDs we have just derived are contained in F⁺.   ∎

Functional dependencies usually arise in creating a database out of common-sense rules. In terms of E-R concepts, it is clear that data items corresponding to identifiers of entities functionally determine all other attributes of that entity. Similarly, attributes of relationships are uniquely determined by the identifiers of entities that take part in the relationship. We would normally expect to start with a manageable set F of FDs in our design, but as Example 5.6.5 shows, the set of FDs that is implied by the F could conceivably grow exponentially. In what follows, we try to find a way to speak of what is implied by a set F of FDs without this kind of exponential explosion. What we are leading up to is a way to determine a *minimal set* of FDs that is equivalent to a given set F. We will also provide an algorithm to derive such a minimal set in a reasonable length of time.

DEFINITION 5.6.10 FD Set Cover. A set F of FDs on a table T is said to *cover* another set G of FDs on T, if the set G of FDs can be derived by implication rules from the set F, or in other words, if G ⊆ F⁺. If F covers G and G covers F, then the two sets of FDs are said to be equivalent, and we write F ≡ G.   ∎

EXAMPLE 5.6.6

Consider the two sets of FDs on the set of attributes A B C D E:

$$F = \{B \rightarrow C\ D,\ A\ D \rightarrow E,\ B \rightarrow A\}$$

and

$$G = \{B \rightarrow C\ D\ E,\ B \rightarrow A\ B\ C,\ A\ D \rightarrow E\}$$

We will demonstrate that F covers G, by showing how all FDs in G are implied by FDs in F. In what follows we derive implications of FDs in F using the various inference rules from Definition 5.6.6 and Theorem 5.6.8. Since in F we have (a) B → C D and (b) B → A, by the union rule we see that (c) B → A C D. The trivial FD B → B clearly holds, and in union with (c), we get (d) B → A B C D. By the decomposition rule, B → A B C D implies (e) B → A D, and since (f) A D → E is in F, by transitivity we conclude (g) B → E. This, in union with (d), gives us B → A B C D E. From this, by decomposition we can derive the initial two FDs of the set G, and the third one also exists in F. This demonstrates that F covers G. ■

In Example 5.6.6 a technique was used to find *all* the attributes functionally determined by the attribute B under the set F of FDs. (This turned out to be all the attributes there were.) In general we can do this for any set X of attributes on the left, finding all attributes functionally determined by the set X.

DEFINITION 5.6.11 Closure of a Set of Attributes. Given a set F of FDs on a table T and a set X of attributes contained in T, we define the *closure* of the set X, denoted by X^+, as the largest set Y of attributes such that X → Y is in F^+. Note that the set Y contains all the attributes of X, by the inclusion rule, but might not contain any other attributes. ■

Here is an algorithm for determining the closure of any set of attributes X.

ALGORITHM 5.6.12 Set Closure. This algorithm determines X^+, the closure of a given set of attributes X, under a given set F of FDs.

```
I = 0; X[0] = X;                         /* integer I, attr. set X[0]    */
REPEAT                                   /* loop to find larger X[I]      */
    I = I + 1;                           /* new I                         */
    X[I] = X[I-1];                       /* initialize new X[I]           */
    FOR ALL Z → W in F                   /* loop on all FDs Z → W in F    */
        IF Z ⊆ X[I]                      /* if Z contained in X[I]        */
            THEN X[I] = X[I] ∪ W;        /* add attributes in W to X[I]   */
    END FOR                              /* end loop on FDs               */
UNTIL X[I] = X[I-1];                     /* loop until no new attributes  */
RETURN X⁺ = X[I];                        /* return closure of X           */
```

■

Note that the step in Algorithm 5.6.12 that adds attributes to X[I] is based on a simple inference rule, the *set accumulation rule*, stated thus: if $X \rightarrow Y\,Z$ and $Z \rightarrow W$, then $X \rightarrow Y\,Z\,W$.

PROOF. Since (a) $X \rightarrow Y\,Z$ is assumed, by the decomposition rule we have (b) $X \rightarrow Z$. Since (c) $Z \rightarrow W$ is assumed, by (b) and (c) and transitivity, (d) $X \rightarrow W$. By (a) and (d) and the union rule, $X \rightarrow Y\,Z\,W$.

In our algorithm we are saying that since $X \rightarrow X[I]$ (our inductive assumption) and X[I] can be represented as Y Z (because $Z \subseteq X[I]$), we can write $X \rightarrow X[I]$ as $X \rightarrow Y\,Z$; and since F contains the FD $Z \rightarrow W$, we conclude by the set accumulation rule that $X \rightarrow Y\,Z\,W$. Or in other words, $X \rightarrow X[I] \cup Z$. ■

EXAMPLE 5.6.7

In Example 5.6.6 we were given the set F of FDs:

$$F = \{B \rightarrow C\,D,\ A\,D \rightarrow E,\ B \rightarrow A\}$$

Given X = B, we determined that X⁺ = A B C D E. In terms of Algorithm 5.6.12, we started with X[0] = B. Then X[1] = B, and we begin to loop through the FDs. Because of B → C D, X[1] = B C D. The next FD, A D → E, does not apply at this time, since A D is not a subset of X[1]. Next, because of B → A, we get X[1] → A B C D. Now X[0] is strictly contained in X[1] (i.e., X[I-1] ⊂ X[I]) so X[I-1] ≠ X[I]. Thus we have made progress in this last pass of the loop and go on to a new pass, setting X[2] = X[1] = A B C D. Looping through the FDs again, we see that all of them can be applied (we could skip the ones that have been applied before since they will have no new effect), with the only new FD, A D → E, giving us X[2] = A B C D E. At the end of this loop, the algorithm notes that X[1] ⊂ X[2]. Progress has been made, so we go on to create X[3] and loop though the

FDs again, ending up this pass with X[3] = X[2]. Since all of the FDs had been applied already, we could omit this pass by noting this fact. Note that a different *ordering* of the FDs in F can change the details of execution for this algorithm. ∎

Given a set F of functional dependencies on a table T, we use the following algorithm to determine a minimal set of dependencies M that covers F.

ALGORITHM 5.6.13 Minimal Cover. This algorithm constructs a minimal set M of FDs that covers a given set F of FDs. M is known as the *minimal cover* of F—or, in some texts, as the *canonical cover* of F.

Step 1. From the set F of FDs, we create an equivalent set H of FDs, with only single attributes on the right side.

```
H = ∅;                          /* initialize H to null set          */
FOR ALL X → Y in F              /* loop on FDs in F                  */
    FOR ALL A IN Y              /* loop on attributes in Y           */
        H = H ∪ {X → A};        /* add FD to H                       */
    END FOR                     /* end loop on attributes in Y       */
END FOR                         /* end loop on FDs in F              */
```

Since step 1 derives H by successive applications of the decomposition rule, and F can be reconstructed from H by successive applications of the union rule, it is obvious that $F \equiv H$.

Step 2. From the set H of FDs, successively remove individual FDs that are *inessential* in H. An FD X → Y is considered inessential in the set H of FDs, if X → Y can be removed from H, resulting in the set J, where $H \equiv J$. That is, removal of the FD from H has no effect on H^+.

```
FOR ALL X → A in H           /* loop on FDs in H                  */
    J = H - {X → A};         /* try removing this FD             */
    DETERMINE X⁺ UNDER J;    /* set closure algorithm 5.6.12     */
    IF A ∈ X⁺                /* X → A is still implied by J      */
        H = H - {X → A};     /* ...so it is inessential in H     */
END FOR                      /* end loop on FDs in H             */
```

Since each time an FD is removed from H in step 2 the resulting set is equivalent to the previous, larger H, it is clear that the final resulting H is equivalent to the original. However, a number of FDs might have been removed.

Step 3. From the set H of FDs, successively replace individual FDs with FDs that have a smaller number of attributes on the left-hand side, as long as the result does not change H+.

```
FOR ALL X → A in H                      /* loop on FDs in H            */
   FOR ALL B ∈ X                        /* loop on attributes in X     */
      Y = X - {B}                       /* try removing this attribute */
      J = (H - {X → A}) ∪ {Y → A};      /* left-reduced FD             */
      GENERATE Y+ UNDER J, Y+ UNDER H;/* set closure algorithm 5.6.12*/
      IF Y+ UNDER H = Y+ UNDER J        /* Y+ is unchanged             */
         UPDATE CURRENT X → A in H      /* this is X → A in outer loop */
            SET X = Y;                  /* change X, continue outer loop*/
   END FOR                              /* end loop of attributes in X */
END FOR                                 /* end loop on FDs in H        */
```

Step 4. From the remaining set of FDs, gather all FDs with equal left-hand sides and use the union rule to create an equivalent set of FDs M where all left-hand sides are unique.

```
M = ∅;                                  /* initialize M to null set    */
FOR ALL X → A in H                      /* loop on FDs in H            */
   IF THIS FD IS FLAGGED, CONTINUE;     /* if already dealt with, loop */
   FLAG CURRENT FD;                     /* deal with FDs with X on left */
   Y = {A};                             /* start with right-hand side A */
   FOR ALL SUCCESSIVE X → B in H        /* nested loop                 */
      FLAG CURRENT FD;                  /* deal with all FDs, X on left */
      Y = Y ∪ {B};                      /* gather attributes on right  */
   END FOR                              /* gathering complete          */
   M = M ∪ {X → Y};                     /* combine right sides of X → ? */
END FOR                                 /* end outer loop on FDs in H  */
```

We state without proof that this algorithm grows in execution time only as a polynomial in n, the number of attributes in the listed FDs of F (counting repetitions). Step 3 is the most costly, since we need to perform the set closure algorithm once for each attribute on the left-hand side of some FD in H. ∎

EXAMPLE 5.6.8
Construct the minimal cover M for the set F of FDs given by

$$F = \{A \rightarrow A\,C, B \rightarrow A\,B\,C, D \rightarrow A\,B\,C\}$$

Step 1. We output H = {A $\rightarrow$ A, A $\rightarrow$ C, B $\rightarrow$ A, B $\rightarrow$ B, B $\rightarrow$ C, D $\rightarrow$ A, D $\rightarrow$ B, D $\rightarrow$ C}.

Step 2. We consider cases corresponding to the sequence of eight FDs in H. (1) A $\rightarrow$ A is trivial and thus clearly inessential (since A^+ contains A), so it can be removed. (2) A $\rightarrow$ C cannot be derived from the other FDs in H by the set closure algorithm, Algorithm 5.6.12, because there is no other FD with A on the left-hand side. (A^+ contains only A.)

(3) Is B $\rightarrow$ A inessential under the set of other FDs that remains: {A $\rightarrow$ C, B $\rightarrow$ B, B $\rightarrow$ C, D $\rightarrow$ A, D $\rightarrow$ B, D $\rightarrow$ C}? To see if B $\rightarrow$ A is inessential, we generate B^+ under the given dependencies. (Using the set closure algorithm, 5.6.12, to generate X^+ in what follows, we avoid reference to internal algorithm variables X[I], and refer to new attributes being added to the final result X^+ in each pass.) Starting with B^+ = B, B $\rightarrow$ B doesn't help. Since B $\rightarrow$ C, we have B^+ contains B C. But B^+ does not grow further and thus never contains A, so B $\rightarrow$ A remains in H. (4) Clearly B $\rightarrow$ B is inessential, so it is removed. (5) Is B $\rightarrow$ C inessential under the set of FDs that remains: {A $\rightarrow$ C, B $\rightarrow$ A, D $\rightarrow$ A, D $\rightarrow$ B, D $\rightarrow$ C}? The set closure algorithm notes that B $\rightarrow$ A, so B^+ contains A B. Then, since A $\rightarrow$ C, B^+ contains A B C. Therefore B $\rightarrow$ C, so that FD is inessential and can be removed.

(6) Is D $\rightarrow$ A inessential under the set of other FDs that remains: {A $\rightarrow$ C, B $\rightarrow$ A, D $\rightarrow$ B, D $\rightarrow$ C}? Clearly with this set we derive D^+ to successively contain D, then D B, then D B A. So we can derive D $\rightarrow$ A, and it should be removed.

(7) Is D $\rightarrow$ B inessential under the set of other FDs that remains: {A $\rightarrow$ C, B $\rightarrow$ A, D $\rightarrow$ C}? The answer is no, since deriving D^+ with this set of FDs, we get only D C. (8) Finally, is D $\rightarrow$ C inessential under the set of other FDs that remains: {A $\rightarrow$ C, B $\rightarrow$ A, D $\rightarrow$ B}? The answer is yes, because deriving D^+, we start with D, then get D B, then D B A, then D B A C, so this FD can be removed.

We end up with the set H = {A $\rightarrow$ C, B $\rightarrow$ A, D $\rightarrow$ B}. Clearly all inessential FDs have been removed, since all left-hand sides are single unique attributes. Thus if any FD is removed, its initial attribute no longer occurs on the left-hand side of any FD and the closure of that attribute is now trivial (with A $\rightarrow$ C gone, A^+ cannot progress beyond A). The fact that left-hand sides in H are unique single attributes also implies that the left-hand sides cannot be left-reduced in step 3, and step 4 will have no effect. The output set M is therefore:

$$M = \{A \rightarrow C, B \rightarrow A, D \rightarrow C\}.$$ ∎

EXAMPLE 5.6.9

The functional dependencies derived in Example 5.6.4 turn out *not* to be minimal, despite our attempt to derive a minimal set in the example. The demonstration of this is left as an exercise. ∎

EXAMPLE 5.6.10

The set of functional dependencies stated in Example 5.6.3 for the `emp_info` database:

(1) `emp_id → emp_name emp_phone dept_name`

(2) `dept_name → dept_phone dept_mgrname`

(3) `skill_id → skill_name`

(4) `emp_id skill_id → skill_date skill_lvl`

already forms a minimal set; that is, the minimal cover algorithm will not reduce it further. We leave this derivation as an exercise. ∎

The algorithm for finding a minimal cover of a set F of FDs will be useful in later sections.

5.7 Lossless Decompositions

The process of normalization depends on being able to *factor* or *decompose* a table into two or more smaller tables, in such a way that we can recapture the precise content of the original table by joining the decomposed parts.

DEFINITION 5.7.1 Given a table T, a *decomposition* of T into k tables is a set of tables $\{T_1, T_2, \ldots, T_k\}$ such that $\text{Head}(T) = \text{Head}(T_1) \cup \text{Head}(T_2) \cup \ldots \cup \text{Head}(T_k)$. Given any specific content of T, the rows of T are projected onto the columns of each T_j during the decomposition. A decomposition of a table T with a set F of FDs is said to be a *lossless decomposition*, or sometimes a *lossless-join decomposition* if, for any possible future content of T, the FDs F guarantee that the following relationship will hold:

$$T = T_1 \bowtie T_2 \bowtie \ldots \bowtie T_k$$ ∎

When a table T is decomposed, it is sometimes not possible to recover with a join all the information that was originally present in some specific content of table T, not because we don't get back all the rows we had before, but because we get back other rows that were not originally present.

EXAMPLE 5.7.1 A Lossy Decomposition.
Consider the following table ABC:

ABC

A	B	C
a1	100	c1
a2	200	c2
a3	300	c3
a4	200	c4

If we factor this table into two parts, AB and BC, we get the following table contents:

AB

A	B
a1	100
a2	200
a3	300
a4	200

BC

B	C
100	c1
200	c2
300	c3
200	c4

However, the result of joining these two tables is

AB JOIN BC

A	B	C
a1	100	c1
a2	200	c2
a2	200	c4
a3	300	c3
a4	200	c2
a4	200	c4

This is *not* the original table content for ABC! Note that the same decomposed tables AB and BC would have resulted if the table we had started with was ABCX, with content equal to AB JOIN BC above, or either of two other tables, ABCY or ABCZ:

ABCY

A	B	C
a1	100	c1
a2	200	c2
a2	200	c4
a3	300	c3
a4	200	c4

ABCZ

A	B	C
a1	100	c1
a2	200	c2
a3	300	c3
a4	200	c2
a4	200	c4

Since we can't tell what table content we started from, information has been lost by this decomposition and the subsequent join. This is known as a *lossy decomposition,* or sometimes a *lossy-join decomposition.* ∎

The reason we lost information in the decomposition of Example 5.7.1 is that the attribute B has duplicate values (200) on distinct rows of the factored tables (with a2 and a4 in table AB and with c2 and c4 in table BC). When these factored tables are joined again we get cross product rows that did not (or might not) exist in the original:

a2	200	c4

and

a4	200	c2

EXAMPLE 5.7.2 A Different Content for Table ABC.

Now let's say that table ABC started with a different content, one that had no duplicate values in column B:

ABC

A	B	C
a1	100	c1
a2	200	c2
a3	300	c3

The question is this: If we decompose this table ABC into the two tables AB and BC as we did in Example 5.7.1, is the resulting decomposition lossless? And the answer is no, because the definition of a lossless decomposition requires that the join of the factored tables recapture the original information for *any possible future content* of the original table. But the table ABC content we have just shown could change with the insert of a single row to give the content of Example 5.7.1. There doesn't seem to be any rule that would keep this from happening.   ■

What sort of rule would we need to limit all possible future content for table ABC so that the decomposition into tables AB and BC would be lossless? Of course functional dependencies spring to mind, because they represent rules that govern future content of a table. Notice that in Definition 5.7.1 of a lossless decomposition, a set F of FDs is considered to be part of the table T definition. We extend the database schema definition of Chapter 2.

DEFINITION 5.7.2 A database schema is the set of headings of all tables in a database, together with the set of all FDs that the designer wishes to hold on the join of those tables.   ■

EXAMPLE 5.7.3 Table ABC with a Functional Dependency.

Assume that table ABC is defined with the following functional dependency: $B \rightarrow C$. Now the table content of Example 5.7.2 is perfectly legal:

ABC

A	B	C
a1	100	c1
a2	200	c2
a3	300	c3

But if we tried to insert a fourth row to achieve the content of Example 5.7.1,

a4	200	c4

this insert would fail because it would break the FD $B \rightarrow C$. A new row with a duplicate value for B must also have a duplicate value for C in order for $B \rightarrow C$ to remain true:

a4	200	c2

Is it true then that this new content for ABC can be decomposed and then rejoined losslessly? The answer is yes. Starting with

ABC

A	B	C
a1	100	c1
a2	200	c2
a3	300	c3
a4	200	c2

if we factor this table into two parts, AB and BC, we get the following table contents:

AB

A	B
a1	100
a2	200
a3	300
a4	200

BC

B	C
100	c1
200	c2
300	c3

Note that four rows are projected onto three in table BC because of duplicate values. Now when these two tables are joined again, the original table ABC with the FD B → C results. ■

Because of the functional dependency B → C in table ABC of Example 5.7.3, the projection of ABC on BC will always have *unique values* for attribute B. Recall from Definition 2.4.1 that this means attribute B is a *key* for table BC. The reason that the decomposition of ABC into AB and BC is lossless is that no cross terms can ever arise in joining them: although duplicate values for column B can occur in table AB, every row in table AB joins with a *unique* row in table BC (assuming that this B value exists in table BC, as it always would in an initial decomposition that projects rows from ABC). This is reminiscent of what happened with our CAP database when we joined ORDERS with CUSTOMERS. We simply extended rows of ORDERS with more information about individual customers. While duplicate values can exist in the cid column of the ORDERS table, the cid values are unique in the CUSTOMERS table, so every row in ORDERS joins to exactly one row in CUSTOMERS.

We generalize the above discussion somewhat to deal with sets of attributes.

THEOREM 5.7.3 Given a table T and a set of attributes X ⊆ Head(T), then the following two statements are equivalent: (1) X is a superkey of T; (2) X → Head(T), that is, the set of attributes X functionally determines *all* attributes in T.

PROOF. (1) Implies (2). If X is a superkey of the table T, then by Definition 2.4.1, for any content of the table T, two distinct rows of T must always disagree on X; that is, distinct rows cannot agree in value on all attributes of X. But from this it is clear that two rows u and v cannot agree on X and disagree on some other column in Head(T) (since if two rows agree in X then they both represent the same row), and this means that X → Head(T). **(2) Implies (1).** Similarly, if X → Head(T), then for any possible content of T, two rows in T cannot agree in value on X and simultaneously disagree on Head(T). But if the two rows u and v don't disagree on any attributes of Head(T), then by Relational RULE 3, they must be the same row. Therefore this argument has shown that two distinct rows cannot agree in value on X, and therefore X is a superkey for T. ∎

We have reached a point where we can give a general rule for the kind of lossless decomposition we will need in performing normalization.

THEOREM 5.7.4 Given a table T with a set F of functional dependencies valid on T, then a decomposition of T into two tables $\{T_1, T_2\}$ is a lossless decomposition if one of the following functional dependencies is implied by F:

(1) Head(T_1) ∩ Head(T_2) → Head(T_1)

or

(2) Head(T_1) ∩ Head(T_2) → Head(T_2).

NOTE: In Example 5.7.3, we can show that we have a lossless decomposition by substituting ABC for T, AB for T_1, BC for T_2, and B → C, equivalent to B → B C, for Head(T_1) ∩ Head(T_2) → Head(T_2). Note that a different FD, B → A, would also guarantee a lossless decomposition.

PROOF OF THEOREM 5.7.4. We take as given the table T, its decomposition into T_1 and T_2, and FD (1), Head(T_1) ∩ Head(T_2) → Head(T_2). (The case with FD (2) is proven similarly.) In what follows, we denote by X the set of attributes Head(T_1) ∩ Head(T_2), Y is the set of attributes in Head(T_1) − Head(T_2), and Z is the set of attributes in Head(T_2) − Head(T_1). To begin, we note by the definition of decomposition (Definition 5.7.1) that T_1 and T_2 are projections of T, and Head(T_1) ∪ Head(T_2) = Head(T). From this we can demonstrate that T ⊆ T_1 ⋈ T_2. Every column of T appears in T_1 ⋈ T_2, and if u is a row in T, we say that the projection of u on Head(T_1) is given by y_1x_1, a concatenation of attribute values, where y_1 represents values for attributes in Y and x_1 represents values for attributes in X; similarly x_1z_1 is the projection of u on $\text{Head}(T_2)$. Clearly the projection of u on $\text{Head}(T_1)$ has the same values as the projection of u on $\text{Head}(T_2)$ on all attributes in $X = \text{Head}(T_1) \cap \text{Head}(T_2)$, and by the definition of join (Definition 2.7.9) the row u, a concatenation $y_1x_1z_1$, will appear in $T_1 \bowtie T_2$.

Now we show under the given assumptions that $T_1 \bowtie T_2 \subseteq T$. Assume that from the row u in T, we get by projection a row y_1x_1 in T_1, as above. Similarly, assume that from the row v in T, we get by projection the row x_2z_2 in T_2, with x_2 representing values for attributes in X. Now assume that the two rows y_1x_1 and x_2z_2 in T_1 and T_2 are joinable, so that x_1 is identical in all attribute values to x_2, and $y_1x_1z_2$ is in $T_1 \bowtie T_2$. This is the most general possible form for a row in $T_1 \bowtie T_2$, and we have only to show that the row is also in T. We denote the additional attribute values of u that project on y_1x_1 in T by z_1, so that $u = y_1x_1z_1$, and claim that $z_1 = z_2$. This is because the row u is identical to v in the attributes of X, and $X \rightarrow \text{Head}(T_2)$, so in particular $X \rightarrow \text{Head}(T_2) - \text{Head}(T_1) = Z$, and since u and v are alike on X, they must be alike on attributes of Z. Thus $z_1 = z_2$, and the row $y_1x_1z_2$ that is in $T_1 \bowtie T_2$ is identical to the row $y_1x_1z_1$ in T. ∎

5.8 Normal Forms

Let us return now to the example of bad database design from Section 5.5 that motivated the long mathematical digression of the last two sections. Recall that we wish to create a database on a set of data items given in Figure 5.15, with rules of interrelatedness stated in the set of functional dependencies in Example 5.6.3. We repeat these here as Figure 5.19.

```
    emp_id        dept_name        skill_id
    emp_name      dept_phone       skill_name
    emp_phone     dept_mgrname     skill_date
                                   skill_lvl


    (1) emp_id → emp_name emp_phone dept_name
    (2) dept_name → dept_phone dept_mgrname
    (3) skill_id → skill_name
    (4) emp_id skill_id → skill_date skill_lvl
```

Figure 5.19 Data Items and FDs for the Employee Information Database

We started with a first normal form table, `emp_info`, that combined all these data items (repeated in Figure 5.20), and noted that there were a number of design problems, referred to as *anomalies*. In the following section, we perform a sequence of table factorizations, which are in fact lossless decompositions, to eliminate redundancies from the employee information database.

As explained in Definition 5.7.2, a database schema is the set of headings of all tables in a database together with a set of all FDs intended by the designer. The emp_info table in Figure 5.20, together with the FDs given, make up such a database schema.

emp_info

emp_id	emp_name	...	skill_id	skill_name	skill_date	skill_lvl
09112	Jones	...	44	librarian	03-15-90	12
09112	Jones	...	26	typing	06-30-92	10
09112	Jones	...	89	word-proc	01-15-93	12
12231	Smith	...	26	typing	04-15-92	5
12231	Smith	...	39	filing	07-30-92	7
13597	Brown	...	26	typing	09-15-92	6
14131	Blake	...	26	typing	05-30-92	9
14131	Blake	...	89	word-proc	09-30-92	10
...	...	...	...	...	...	...

(1) `emp_id → emp_name emp_phone dept_name`
(2) `dept_name → dept_phone dept_mgrname`
(3) `skill_id → skill_name`
(4) `emp_id skill_id → skill_date skill_lvl`

Figure 5.20 Employee Information Schema with a Single Table: `emp_info`

A Succession of Decompositions to Eliminate Anomalies

One anomaly of the database represented in Figure 5.20 is that if the number of skills for some employee goes to zero in the emp_info table, no row of any kind will remain for the employee! We have lost the phone number and the department the employee works in because of this deletion of a skill! At the end of Section 5.5, we proposed a solution for this anomaly by factoring the emp_info table into two tables, the emps table and the skills table, whose column names were given in Figure 5.17 and are repeated in Figure 5.21.

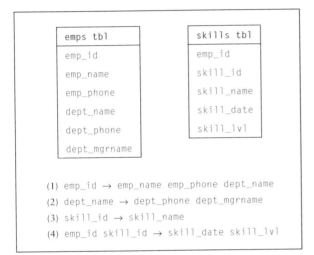

Figure 5.21 Employee Information Schema with Two Tables, emps and skills

When the emps table and the skills table were originally proposed, a number of features of this factorization were mentioned without justification. We are now in a position to demonstrate these points.

PROPOSITION 5.8.1 The key for the emp_info table is the attribute set emp_id skill_id. This is also the key for the skills table, but the emps table has a key consisting of the single attribute emp_id.

PROOF. By Theorem 5.7.3 we can determine a superkey for a table T by finding a set of attributes X ⊆ Head(T) such that X → Head(T). Then, to show the set X is a key, we need merely show that no properly contained subset Y of X has this property. We start our search by finding the set closure of X for all attribute sets X found on the left-hand side of any of the FDs in Figure 5.19, repeated here.

```
(1) emp_id → emp_name emp_phone dept_name
(2) dept_name → dept_phone dept_mgrname
(3) skill_id → skill_name
(4) emp_id skill_id → skill_date skill_lvl
```

Starting with X = emp_id skill_id (the left side of FD (4) above), we use Algorithm 5.6.12 and the FD set F given to determine X^+. Starting from X^+ = emp_id skill_id and applying FD (4), we get X^+ = emp_id skill_id skill_date skill_lvl. Next, applying FD (3), since skill_id is in X^+, we add skill_name to X^+. Applying FD (1), since emp_id is in X^+, we add the right-hand side of FD (1) to get X^+ = emp_id skill_id skill_date skill_lvl skill_name emp_name emp_phone dept_name. Finally we apply FD (2), and since dept_name is now in X^+, we add the right-hand side of FD (2) to get X^+ = emp_id skill_id skill_date skill_lvl skill_name emp_name emp_phone dept_name dept_phone dept_mgrname. This final list contains all the attributes in emp_info, that is, Head(emp_info). By the definition of X^+, this means that

[5.8.1]   emp_id skill_id → Head(emp_info)

By Theorem 5.7.3, then, emp_id skill_id is a superkey for emp_info.

To show that emp_id skill_id is in fact a key for emp_info, we need only show that no subset (either emp_id or skill_id alone) functionally determines all these attributes. Let us take the closure of the set emp_id to find what attributes are functionally determined. We can immediately apply FD (1) to get emp_id → emp_id emp_name emp_phone dept_name. Next we can apply FD (2), and derive

[5.8.2]   emp_id → emp_id emp_name emp_phone dept_name dept_phone
                    dept_mgrname

Since `skill_id` is not in the right-hand set of (5.8.2), no other FDs can be applied, so this is the maximum right-hand set that is functionally determined by `emp_id`.

Finally, starting with `skill_id` alone in the set X to be closed, FD (3) is the only one that can be applied, and we see that the maximum right-hand set functionally determined by `skill_id` is given as

[5.8.3]   `skill_id → skill_id skill_name`

Neither (5.8.2) nor (5.8.3) contains all attributes of `emp_info`, and thus we can conclude from (5.8.1) that

[5.8.4]   `emp_id skill_id` is a key for the `emp_info` table

In addition, we note from (5.8.2) that `emp_id` functionally determines all attributes in the `emps` table of Figure 5.20, and since no subset of a singleton set can be on the left side of an FD:

[5.8.5]   `emp_id` is a key for the `emps` table

Finally we note that the `skills` table has attributes that are not functionally determined by either `emp_id` or `skill_id` individually, `skill_lvl` is not on the right-hand side in either (5.8.2) or (5.8.3), and therefore the only possible key for the `skills` table is `emp_id skill_id`:

[5.8.6]   `emp_id skill_id` is a key for the `skills` table.   ∎

PROPOSITION 5.8.2 The factorization of the `emp_info` table into the `emps` table and `skills` table is a true lossless decomposition.

PROOF. To see that this is a valid decomposition, we note that Head(`emps`) ∪ Head(`skills`) = Head(`emp_info`). Furthermore, Head(`emps`) ∩ Head(`skills`) = `emp_id`, and since functional dependency (5.8.2) shows that `emp_id` → Head(`emps`), by Theorem 5.7.4 the decomposition is lossless.   ∎

From Proposition 5.8.2, we see that the decomposition that brings us from the `emp_info` table of Figure 5.20 to the `emps` table and `skills` tables of Figure 5.21 will always allow us to recapture any content of emp_info by a join of the two factored tables. But the real motivation for this decomposition was to deal with the various anomalies mentioned earlier.

How did the delete anomaly mentioned in Section 5.5 arise in the emp_info table of Figure 5.20? The basic reason is that the pair of attributes emp_id skill_id form the key for that table, but there are attributes that we wish to keep track of that are functionally determined by a single one of those two attributes, emp_id. If we delete the last skill_id value for some specific emp_id, we no longer have any (emp_id skill_id) pairs with that specific emp_id, *but we still have information that is dependent only on emp_id, which we don't want to lose!* Putting this in terms of the E-R model, employees are real entities whose attributes we want to keep track of (and so the employee identifier, emp_id, shows up on the left of a functional dependency). In the decomposition of Figure 5.21, we factored the emps table out of the emp_info table so that we wouldn't lose information in this way. With this new schema, we can keep a row for a given employee in the emps table even if the employee has no skills. Recall that the insert anomaly is the inverse face of the delete anomaly, making it impossible to insert a new employee without skills—a trainee—into the emp_info table. As before, this problem is solved by factoring out the emps table, since a new row can be inserted into emps that doesn't have any join to a row of the skills table. As far as the update anomaly is concerned, this problem arises in the emp_info table once again because attributes dependent only on emp_id are in a table with key emp_id skill_id; we can therefore have multiple rows with the same employee phone number in this table that must all be updated at once. Once again, factoring out the emps table solves this problem, because each employee is now represented by a single row.

The question now is this: Are there any more anomalies remaining in the database schema of Figure 5.21? The answer, perhaps unsurprisingly, is yes. There is another anomaly of the kind we have just analyzed in the skills table. This table has the primary key (skill_id emp_id), and we recall FD (3) of Figure 5.19:

[5.8.7] skill_id → skill_name

What this FD seems to be saying is that skills is an entity in its own right, that skill_id is an identifier for the entity, and that skill_name is a descriptor. (There might be two distinct skills with different skill_id values but the same skill_name, since skill_name → skill_id is not an FD that is implied by the list we presented.) But recall that the key we have discovered for the skills table is emp_id skill_id. This situation seems to be symmetric with the one that caused us to factor out the table emps from emp_info. Can we construct (for example) a delete anomaly of the kind that led to this step? The answer is yes, for if we assume that some skill is rare and difficult to master, and we suddenly lost the last employee who had it, we would no longer have any information about the skill at all, neither the skill_id nor the skill_name. We therefore need to factor out another table to solve this anomaly, and we see the result in Figure 5.22.

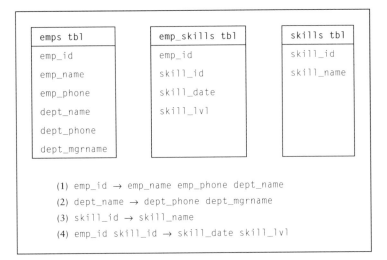

Figure 5.22 Employee Information Schema with Three Tables

From examination of the new emp_skills table and skills table of Figure 5.22, it should be clear that these two tables form a lossless decomposition of the skills table of Figure 5.21. Indeed, the three tables of Figure 5.22 (by transitivity) form a lossless decomposition of the single emp_info table we started with in Figure 5.20. Most importantly, we have dealt with the anomalies that arise from keeping attributes of skills entities in a table with a key of two attributes. In terms of the E-R model, what we have just done is to factor out the relationship emp_skills from the two entities Emps and Skills.

Consider now the three tables of Figure 5.22. Everything in the emps table, as we showed earlier in Proposition 5.8.1, is functionally determined by the singleton attribute emp_id; a similar situation holds with the skills table, as we see from the FD in (5.8.7); in the emp_skills table, a glance at (5.8.2) and (5.8.3) makes it clear that no remaining attributes in this table are dependent on a subset of the (emp_id skill_id) key. We ask then if any further anomalies can remain in these tables. Once more, the answer is yes! To see how this is possible, consider what would happen if we had a large reorganization in the company, so that every employee in one department is to be transferred to other departments (even the manager will be transferred—presumably, at some later time, different employees will take their place in the department that has just been emptied). Now notice that when the last employee is removed, there remains no row in the emps table containing information about the department: we have lost even the phone number of the department, and the name it goes under! The solution to this problem is obvious: we must factor out a separate table for departments. This will result in the emp_info database of Figure 5.23; this database is in third normal form (3NF), or equivalently in this case, a Boyce-Codd normal form (BCNF). We will give definitions for these normal forms shortly.

With the factorization of the depts table of Figure 5.23, the update anomaly relating to department information will no longer trouble us. In terms of the E-R model, what we have done is to differentiate between the two entities Emps and Depts, between which there is a many-to-one relationship (represented by the foreign key dept_name in the emps table).

emps tbl	depts tbl	emp_skills tbl	skills tbl
emp_id	dept_name	emp_id	skill_id
emp_name	dept_phone	skill_id	skill_name
emp_phone	dept_mgrname	skill_date	
dept_name		skill_lvl	

(1) emp_id → emp_name emp_phone dept_name
(2) dept_name → dept_phone dept_mgrname
(3) skill_id → skill_name
(4) emp_id skill_id → skill_date skill_lvl

Figure 5.23 Employee Information Database Schema in 3NF (Also BCNF)

At this point, we claim that the database schema of Figure 5.23 is in some sense a final result—no anomalies remain in the representation to trouble us. For the rationale to justify this statement, we look to the four FDs listed that must be maintained in the database, which we refer to in what follows as the set F of FDs. In every case where we have noted an anomaly in earlier schemas, the underlying reason for the anomaly has turned out to hinge on the fact that some attribute (it could have been a set of attributes in a different schema) on the left-hand side of an FD in F might have multiple duplicate occurrences (or possibly zero occurrences) in the table where it appeared. The solution was to create a separate table, placing the attributes on the left-hand side of this FD, together with all attributes on the right-hand side in that table, while the attributes on the right-hand side were removed from the table where they previously appeared. Look carefully at the successive decompositions presented in Figures 5.20 through 5.23 to see that this is an accurate description of what was done. Since the attributes on the left-hand side of the FD are in both the old and the new table and determine all other attributes in the new table, the decomposition is lossless. Thus FD (1) generates the `emps` table, FD (2) the `depts` table, FD (3) the `skills` table, and FD (4) the `emp_skills` table. Since no more FDs exist in F, we maintain that no more anomalies will arise, and therefore no further decomposition is necessary. Thus we have reached a final form.

Normal Forms: BCNF, 3NF, and 2NF

The tables in the final schema of Figure 5.23 each have unique candidate keys, which we may think of as a primary keys for the tables. One way to characterize why no further decomposition is needed to address anomalies in these tables is to say that all functional dependencies involving attributes of any single table in this schema arise from the table keys alone. We provide definitions to make this idea precise.

DEFINITION 5.8.3 Given a database schema with a universal table T and a set of functional dependencies F, let $\{T_1, T_2, \ldots, T_k\}$ be a decomposition of T. Then an FD $X \rightarrow Y$ of F is said to be *preserved* in one of the tables T_i of the decomposition if and only if $X \cup Y \subseteq \text{Head}(T_i)$. When this is the case, we also say that the FD $X \rightarrow Y$ *lies in* T_i or *is in* T_i. ∎

EXAMPLE 5.8.1

We have derived a number of successive decompositions of the Employee Information schema of Figure 5.20 with a universal table: a decomposition with two tables (Figure 5.21), three tables (Figure 5.22), and four tables (Figure 5.23). Each of these decompositions preserves all given dependencies in F. For example, in the four-table decomposition of Figure 5.23, FD (1) lies in the emps table, FD (2) lies in the depts table, FD (3) lies in the skills table, and FD (4) lies in the emp_skills table. ■

Because every FD in F is preserved in one of the four tables of Figure 5.23, whenever any table in the schema is updated, it is possible to verify that any FD affected by the update is still valid by testing the validity of that FD in a single table, without any need for a join. This is the motivation for seeking to preserve functional dependencies in a decomposition.

DEFINITION 5.8.4 Boyce-Codd Normal Form. A table T in a database schema with FD set F is said to be in *Boyce-Codd normal form* (BCNF) when the following property holds. For any functional dependency $X \rightarrow A$ implied by F that lies in T, where A is a single attribute that is not in X, then X must be a superkey for T. A database schema is in BCNF when all the tables it contains are in BCNF. ■

Consider a table T, and let $X \rightarrow A$ be a functional dependency in T. If the BCNF property holds for this case, then X is a superkey, so for some set K of attributes representing a key for T, $K \subseteq X$. (Note that there might be a number of different sets K that are keys for T, but for easiest intuition, you can assume there is only one.) If the BCNF property fails, then X does not contain a key set K, and $K - X$ is non-empty for all K. Then two cases are possible: either (1) $X - K$ is empty; that is, $X \subset K$ for some K, and we say that some attributes of T are functionally determined by a *proper subset* X of a key K; or else (2) $X - K$ is non-empty, so X and K overlap for all keys K (in fact, now both $K - X$ and $X - K$ are non-empty), and we say that some attributes of T are functionally determined by a *different* set of attributes that does not contain and is not contained in any key set.

EXAMPLE 5.8.2

In the emp_skills table of Figure 5.23, a unique key consists of the set emp_id skill_id. We claim that this table is in BCNF and will demonstrate this in the next example. As we just pointed out, the BCNF property of Definition 5.8.4

implies that attributes of this table are not functionally determined by any *subset* of this key set, or any *different* set of attributes that does not contain this key set.

In the skills table of Figure 5.21, the unique key for this table consists of the two attributes emp_id skill_id, while the FD skill_id → skill_name lies in this table. Clearly the left-hand side of this FD is a *subset* of the key emp_id skill_id. Because of this the BCNF property failed for this table (and an anomaly arose that required us to perform further decomposition).

In the emps table of Figure 5.21 (identical to the emps table in Figure 5.22), the unique key for this table consists of the attribute emp_id, while the FD dept_name → dept_phone is implied by FD (2) of F and lies in the table. Since the left side of this FD is *different* from the key set (neither a subset nor a super-set), the BCNF property fails, and further decomposition is necessary. Note, by the way, that a table emps2 containing all the attributes of emps except the attribute dept_phone would still not obey the BCNF property. Although the FD dept_name → dept_phone does not lie in the table emps2, the FD dept_name → dept_mgrname, which is also implied by FD (2), does lie in emps2. ∎

EXAMPLE 5.8.3
We claim that the database schema of Figure 5.23 is in BCNF. We need to show that for any FD X → A implied by F that lies in one of the tables of Figure 5.23, where A is an attribute not in X, then X contains a key for that table. We have shown in Example 5.8.1 that for the set of tables in Figure 5.23 one FD of F lies in each table, and this FD has as its left side the key for the table. This does not quite conclude the issue, however, because we also need to consider all FDs that are implied by F, that is, all FDs that are true in the schema. In Proposition 5.8.1, FDs (5.8.1), (5.8.2), and (5.8.3), we determined the closure of all sets X of attributes that fall on the left side of three FDs of F, and showed that these three sets form keys for three of the tables. For the fourth FD, we need merely take the closure of skill_id, which is easily seen to consist simply of the set skill_id skill_name, or Head(skills):

[5.8.8] skill_id → Head(skills)

Now we claim that all attribute sets Z that do not contain one of these sets X, the left side of an FD in F and therefore a key for one of the tables of Figure 5.23, must have trivial closure $Z^+ = Z$. This follows from the fact that no FDs of the form X → Y exist with $X \subseteq Z$, and by Algorithm 5.6.12, no attributes will ever be added to the set closure of Z.

From this we can easily see that all of the tables in Figure 5.23 are BCNF, because if X → A holds and A is an attribute not contained in the attribute set X, then X → A X, and therefore X^+ is not identical to X. But we have just shown that any attribute set that does not contain a table key has a trivial closure, and this must mean that X contains some table key K. In that table, we have also included all attributes functionally determined by K, and therefore A is in that table as well. ∎

EXAMPLE 5.8.4

Suppose we changed the rules in the employee information database so that dept_mgrname was a second identifier of the Departments entity, duplicating the effect of dept_name. This would add a new FD to the set F: dept_mgrname → dept_name; by transitivity, since dept_name is a key for the depts table in Figure 5.23, dept_mgrname would also be a key. The question now is whether the depts table is still in BCNF. And the answer is yes, because the BCNF property was specially constructed not to require a unique key for the table. The only thing that has changed in the depts table is that there are now two keys, but any FD of the form X → Y in this table has the necessary property that X contains dept_mgrname or X contains dept_name. ∎

Recall that every FD in F is *preserved* in one of the four tables of Figure 5.23, so that whenever any table in the schema is updated, it is possible to verify that an affected FD still holds by testing data items in that table alone. We would like to be able to guarantee that this property, preservation of FDs, can always be achieved starting from a universal table and proceeding to a lossless decomposition into BCNF. Unfortunately this is not true, because the BCNF for a table is too strict.

EXAMPLE 5.8.5

Assume that we added a number of attributes to the employee information database of Figure 5.19 to keep track of the full addresses of all employees. We assume that employees live in the United States, and add the following attributes:

    emp_cityst, emp_straddr, emp_zip

where emp_cityst reflects the city and state and emp_straddr the street name, number, and apartment, if any. We can assume that when we reach the decomposition of Figure 5.23, the emps table contains all of these attributes in addition to the ones that are already there, as we see in Figure 5.24.

Each employee is required to provide a single address, so it is clear that
the emp_id value functionally determines all these new attributes, and FD (1) is
modified accordingly:

> (1) emp_id → emp_name emp_phone dept_name emp_straddr emp_cityst
>   emp_zip

No keys for any of the tables of Figure 5.23 are affected. In particular, the key for
the emps table is still emp_id. Now it turns out that the way the post office has
assigned zip codes, we have the following new FDs to add to the set F:

> (5) emp_cityst emp_straddr → emp_zip
> (6) emp_zip → emp_cityst

emps tbl
emp_id
emp_name
emp_phone
dept_name
emp_cityst
emp_straddr
emp_zip

Figure 5.24   The emps Table Extended to Contain Employee Addresses

Because of FD (5), since the set of attributes emp_cityst emp_straddr is not a
superkey of the emps table, we need to perform a further decomposition to
achieve the BCNF property. Following the prescription explained in the discussion following Figure 5.23, we place the attributes on the left-hand side of FD
(5), together with all attributes on the right-hand side of this FD in a separate
table (empadds), while the attributes on the right-hand side are removed from
the table where they previously appeared (emps). The result is given in Figure
5.25.

emps tbl
emp_id
emp_name
emp_phone
dept_name
emp_cityst
emp_straddr

empadds tbl
emp_cityst
emp_straddr
emp_zip

Figure 5.25   A 3NF Decomposition of Figure 5.24

This is a perfectly reasonable lossless decomposition of the previous table (lossless because of Theorem 5.7.4, since emp_cityst emp_straddr is the key for empadds, and this is also the intersection of the headings of the two tables). Furthermore, the emps table is now in BCNF, since neither FD (5) nor (6) lies in emps, and so the BCNF property holds. Finally, this decomposition preserves FDs (5) and (6), which both lie in the empadds table. However, at this point FD (6) forces us to perform a further decomposition to achieve BCNF, since emp_zip does not contain a key of emp_adds. The result is given in Figure 5.26.

emps tbl
emp_id
emp_name
emp_phone
dept_name
emp_cityst
emp_straddr

empadds tbl
emp_zip
emp_straddr

zip tbl
emp_zip
emp_cityst

Figure 5.26 A BCNF Decomposition of Figure 5.25

Once again this is a lossless decomposition, since emp_zip is the key for the zip table, the intersection of Head(empadds) and Head(zip) is emp_zip, and the union of these table headings contains all the attributes of the previous empadds table. Furthermore, both these new tables are in BCNF form. The only FD in the zip table is FD (6) and emp_zip is the key for the zip table. The new empadds table has *no* FD in it, and so emp_zip emp_straddr is the key, since two rows cannot be alike in all attributes. (Realistically, the key is not emp_straddr alone because there might be several identical street addresses in different cities that have different zip code values.) The decomposition in Figure 5.26 does *not* preserve dependencies of the extended set F, since FD (5) does not lie in either table. In order to test this FD in a single table, the decomposition from Figures 5.25 to 5.26 must be reversed. ∎

It seems as though we have gone too far in decomposition if we really want to preserve dependencies. What we would like is a definition for normal form that allows us to stop at Figure 5.25 and not press on to Figure 5.26. In order to do this, we have to come up with a new definition for normal form (3NF, as it turns out) so that the extra FD (7) in the empadds table of Figure 5.25 is acceptable. We achieve this with the following definitions.

DEFINITION 5.8.5 Prime Attribute. In a table T, an attribute A is said to be *prime* if and only if the attribute A exists in some key K for the table.

■

DEFINITION 5.8.6 Third Normal Form. A table T in a database schema with FD set F is said to be in *third normal form* (3NF) under the following condition. For any functional dependency X → A implied by F that lies in T, where A is a single attribute that is not in X, one of the two following properties must hold: either (1) X is a superkey for T; or (2) A is a prime attribute in T. A database schema is in 3NF when all the tables it contains are in 3NF. ■

EXAMPLE 5.8.6
Consider the database schema of Figure 5.23. Each of the tables in this schema is in BCNF, and therefore in 3NF. The BCNF prescription for a table requires that the table has property (1) of the 3NF definition, and it doesn't permit the "escape clause" of property (2). Therefore any table in BCNF is also in 3NF, but the reverse doesn't hold. ■

EXAMPLE 5.8.7
Consider the empadds table of Figure 5.25. This table is in 3NF but not in BCNF. The reason we required a further decomposition of this table was that the empadds table of Figure 5.25 had as a key the attributes emp_cityst emp_straddr and at the same time FD (6), emp_zip → emp_cityst lies in the table. This is an FD whose left-hand side does not contain a key of emp_adds; so the FD does not fulfill the BCNF property. However, we note that the attribute on the right of this FD does lie in the unique key and is therefore prime. Thus the FD does fulfill property (2) of the 3NF definition. ■

In performing a decomposition of a database to achieve a final normal form, the BCNF and 3NF forms are often identical, as we saw in Example 5.8.6. They differ exactly when further decomposition to achieve BCNF will cause dependencies to not be preserved, as we saw in Example 5.8.7. Many database designers aim for a 3NF design that preserves dependencies.

Another definition for a table property, known as second normal form, or 2NF, is weaker than 3NF and of mainly historical interest since no advantage arises from stopping short of 3NF. From Definition 5.8.6 we see that when a table fails to be 3NF it must contain a valid nontrivial functional dependency X → A, where A is non-prime and X is not a superkey for T. Recall from the discussion of BCNF following Definition 5.8.4, that if X is not a superkey for T then two cases are possible: either $X \subset K$ for some K and we say that some attributes of T are functionally determined by a **proper subset** X of a key K, or else $X - K$ is non-empty for all keys K in T, and we say that some attributes of T are functionally determined by a **different** set of attributes that does not contain and is not contained in any key set. This latter case is also known as a *transitive dependency*, since we have $K \rightarrow X$ for any key K; since we also have $X \rightarrow A$, the functional dependency $K \rightarrow A$ is implied by transitivity. A table in 2NF is not allowed to have attributes that are functionally determined by a subset of a key K, but it may still have transitive dependencies.

DEFINITION 5.8.7 Second Normal Form. A table T in a database schema with FD set F is said to be in *second normal form* (2NF) under the following condition. For any functional dependency $X \rightarrow A$ implied by F that lies in T, where A is a single attribute that is not in X and is non-prime, X is not contained in any key of T. A database schema is in 2NF when all the tables it contains are in 2NF. ∎

> **EXAMPLE 5.8.8**
> The database schema of Figure 5.22 is in 2NF. A demonstration of this is left for the exercises at the end of the chapter. ∎

An Algorithm to Achieve Well-Behaved 3NF Decomposition

For a number of technical reasons it turns out that the approach of successive decompositions to achieve a 3NF lossless join decomposition preserving functional dependencies is distrusted by many practitioners. This is the only approach we have seen, used in Figures 5.20 through 5.24. Certain technical problems arise because the set F of functional dependencies used in the successive decompositions has not been carefully defined, and as we saw in Section 5.6 numerous equivalent sets F are possible. Algorithm 5.8.8 provides a straightforward method to create the desired decomposition.

ALGORITHM 5.8.8 This algorithm, given a universal table T and set of FDs F, generates a lossless join decomposition of T that is in third normal form and preserves all FDs of F. The output is a set S of headings (sets of attributes) for tables in the final database schema.

```
REPLACE F WITH MINIMAL COVER OF F;    /* use algorithm 5.6.13      */
S = ∅;                                /* initialize S to null set  */
FOR ALL X → Y in F                    /* loop on FDs found in F     */
    IF, FOR ALL Z ∈ S, X ∪ Y ⊄ Z      /* no table contains X → Y    */
        THEN S = S ∪ Heading(X ∪ Y);  /* add new table Heading to S*/
END FOR                               /* end loop on FDs            */
FOR ALL CANDIDATE KEYS K FOR T        /* loop on Keys found in F    */
    IF, FOR ALL Z ∈ S, K ⊄ Z          /* no table contains Key      */
        THEN S = S ∪ Heading(K);      /* add new table Heading to S*/
END FOR                               /* end loop on FDs            */
```

Note that the function Heading(K) generates a singleton set containing the set K of attributes, which can then be added to the set S which is a set of sets of attributes.   ∎

EXAMPLE 5.8.9

To see why the loop on candidate keys of Algorithm 5.8.8 is necessary, consider the following small school database. We are given a universal table T with heading

```
Head(T) = instructor class_no class_room text
```

and FD set F given by

```
F = {class_no → class_room text}
```

In E-R terms, there is an entity Classes, identified by class_no, and the actual class holds all its meetings in the same classroom with a unique text. Whether or not there is an entity Class_rooms with identifier class_room is a matter of opinion. Since there is no FD with class_room on the left, such an entity would have no descriptor attributes and so no table exists for it in the relational model; thus we can think of class_room as a descriptor attribute for Classes if we like. The same argument can be applied to the text attribute in Head(T). But the instructor attribute in Head(T) is a different situation. Since the instructor attribute is not functionally determined by class_no, there can be several instructors for the same class, and since instructor does not determine class_no, this means that one instructor might teach several classes. From this it is clear that instructors have independent existence from classes, and in fact represent an entity, Instructors. Indeed, the table T contains a relationship between Instructors and Classes.

By standard BCNF/3NF normalization, since the attributes class_room and text are dependent on class_no alone in the table T, we need to factor T into two tables, T_1 and T_2, with

```
Head(T₁) = class_no class_room text

Head(T₂) = instructor class_no
```

But in Algorithm 5.8.8, only table T_1 will be created in the initial loop on FDs, since the `instructor` attribute does not figure in any FDs of F. However, it is clear from the standard set closure approach that the unique candidate key for T is `class_room instructor`. Therefore the loop on candidate keys in Algorithm 5.8.8 is necessary to create the table T_2 for the set S. ∎

It is commonly said that the normalization approach and the E-R approach reinforce one another. Example 5.8.9 gives an example of this. Without considering functional dependencies, it is not clear why the `instructor` data item must represent an entity but the `class_room` data item might not. On the other hand, the E-R approach gives the motivation for why the loop on candidate keys in Algorithm 5.8.8 is appropriate to create table T_2. We need table T_2 to represent the relationship between the `Instructors` and `Classes` entities.

A Review of Normalization

In the normalization approach to database design, we start out with a set of data items and a set F of functional dependencies that the designer wishes to see maintained by the database system for any future content of the database. The data items are all placed in a single universal table T, and the set F is replaced by an equivalent minimal cover, then the designer determines a decomposition of this table into a set of smaller tables $\{T_1, T_2, \ldots, T_k\}$, with a number of good properties, as follows.

[1] The decomposition is lossless, so that $T = T_1 \bowtie T_2 \bowtie \ldots \bowtie T_n$.

[2] To the greatest extent possible, the only FDs $X \rightarrow Y$ in tables T_i arise because X contains some key K in T_i; this is the thrust of the BCNF/3NF definitions.

[3] All FDs in F of the form $X \rightarrow Y$ are preserved in tables of the decomposition.

The value of property (2) is that we can avoid the various anomalies defined in Section 5.5. It is also important that with these normal forms we can guarantee functional dependency will not be broken, so long as we guarantee the uniqueness of all keys for a table. In the beginning of the next chapter we will see that the Create Table statement of SQL gives us a way to define such keys K for a table, and the uniqueness of these keys will then be guaranteed by the system for all SQL table update statements that follow (an update that breaks such a uniqueness constraint will result in an error). As we will see a bit later, such a uniqueness condition is a particularly easy condition to check with an index on the key columns involved, whereas a general functional dependency $X \rightarrow Y$ in a table T_i, where multiple rows with the same value for X can exist, is more difficult. Standard SQL does not provide a constraint to guarantee such general dependencies against update errors.

The value of property (3) should also be clear, since we want to guarantee that all functional dependencies provided by the designer hold for any possible content of the database. Property (3) means that FDs won't cross tables in the final database schema, so that if an update of one table occurs, only FDs in that table need to be tested by the system. On the other hand, the very decomposition we are providing does result in a certain amount of join testing, since the standard lossless join decomposition into tables T_1 and T_2 leads to a key for one table with attributes in both—that is, a key consisting of (Head(T_1) $\cap$ Head(T_2)). Standard SQL provides a constraint, known as *referential integrity*, that can be imposed with the Create Table statement to guarantee that these attribute values continue to make sense between the two tables they join, a constraint also known as a *foreign key condition*.

To sum up, the standard 3NF decomposition eliminates most anomalies and makes it possible to verify efficiently that desired functional dependencies remain valid when the database is updated.

Additional normal forms exist that are not covered here, 4NF and 5NF. In particular, fourth normal form, or 4NF, is based on an entirely new type of dependency, known as a *multi-valued dependency*. The reader is referred to reference [4] or [5] for good descriptions of these.

We should mention at this point that *overnormalization*, factoring a database into more tables than are required in order to reach 3NF when this is the goal, is considered a bad practice. For example, if we factored the depts table into two tables, one with dept_name and dept_phone and a second with dept_name and dept_mgrname, we would certainly still have a 3NF database, but we would have gone further than we need to in decomposition. Unnecessary inefficiencies would arise in retrieving all department information together, because of the join that would now be required.

5.9 Additional Design Considerations

The E-R and normalization approaches both have weaknesses. The E-R approach, as it is usually presented, is extremely dependent on intuition, but if intuition fails there is little fallback. As we saw in Example 5.8.9, it can be difficult on the basis of intuition alone to determine whether a data item represents an entity or not. It helps to have the concept of functional dependency from normalization. Normalization is more mathematically based and mechanical in its application, but the idea that one can write down a complete set of FDs as a first step of logical database design is often a delusion; it may be found later that some have been missed. The intuitive exercise of trying to discover entities and relationships and weak entities and so on aids the designer in discovering FDs that might otherwise be overlooked.

Another factor affecting the normalization approach is that a certain amount of judgment might be needed to decide whether a particular functional dependency should be reflected in a final design. Consider the CAP database schema with tables listed in Figure 2.2. It might seem that all functional dependencies that hold for the database are reflections of the table key dependencies, so that all the tables are in BCNF. However, there is a rather unexpected FD of the following form:

[5.9.1] `qty price discnt → dollars`

That is, for each order, from the order quantity, product price, and customer discount we can calculate the dollars charge for the order—this relationship is mentioned in the second to last paragraph of Section 2.1 and expressed in the following SQL Insert statement (5.9.2). Now the question is, does this FD make the set of tables in Figure 2.2 a bad design? Clearly the FD as it stands crosses tables, and therefore the decomposition does not preserve dependencies. Note that we can create another table, `ddollars`, that contains all the attributes on both sides of FD (5.9.1), `qty price discnt dollars`, and simultaneously remove the `dollars` attribute from `orders`. The result, a five-table schema for CAP including the `ddollars` table, is a 3NF design that would be arrived at by Algorithm 5.8.8. The unique key for the `ddollars` table is `qty price discnt` and the only FD is given in (5.9.1). There is a problem with this design, however. Whenever we want to retrieve the dollar cost for an order, we have to perform a join with `products` to get `price`, `customers` to get `discnt`, and `ddollars` to read off the `dollars` value for the given `qty`, `price`, and `discnt`. Is all this really necessary? The original design of Figure 2.2 seems preferable from this standpoint.

If we consider the original motivations for a decomposition such as this, we have two: to remove anomalies and to validate all FDs whenever changes are made in the data. But do we really want to validate this FD by a unique key constraint in normal form? Presumably, when a new order is inserted, the program logic does a calculation of the dollars amount to store, something like this:

[5.9.2]
```
exec sql insert into orders
        values (:ordno, :month, :cid, :aid, :pid, :qty,
        :qty*:price - .01*:discnt*:qty*:price;
```

With this Insert statement we guarantee the FD (5.9.1); and more than that, we guarantee an exact numerical relationship that an FD is incapable of representing. The only validation that the `ddollars` table is capable of providing is this: if a previous row exists with a given `qty`, `price`, and `discnt`, then the calculated `dollars` value will be identical. This seems like a rather strange validation, since if there are a lot of products and customers, with real variation in order sizes and some limit on the number of orders tracked, we can expect to be adding many (`qty`, `price`, `discnt`) triples for the first time. Thus the unique key constraint offers no real value in verification: there is no old row with the same key to compare with it. One would much rather depend on the Insert statement (5.9.2) to perform the correct calculation. In this regard, it certainly makes sense to provide this insert in a tested function that must be used by all logic-performing inserts of new orders.

Now the delete and insert anomalies amount to saying that we don't want to lose track of any (`qty`, `price`, `discnt`) triples, but this is a questionable proposition given that we don't really value this method of validation. As for the update anomaly, we consider the case of needing to update all dollars values at once for a given (`qty`, `price`, `discnt`). Presumably this might happen if the `price` or `discnt` value needed to be changed for orders that were previously entered, perhaps because that value was originally entered erroneously and now has to be corrected. But this change would be so unusual and have such major ramifications for a wholesale business that it is unreasonable to assume that an inexperienced programmer might write code to correct a single row in orders by mistake. Indeed many designers would model the dollars column as an insert-only quantity that should not be updated at all (except to correct input errors). We are therefore willing to forego the protection from the update anomaly.

We have gone into detail here to exemplify a type of situation that arises with some frequency in commercial applications, a need for *denormalization* to improve performance. Most design practitioners will agree that there is frequently a need for this.

Database Design Tools

A number of commercial products are aimed at providing environments to support the DBA in performing database design. These environments are provided by *database design tools,* or sometimes as part of a more general class of products known as computer-aided software engineering (CASE) tools. Such tools usually have a number of components, chosen from the following kinds. It would be rare for a single product to offer all these capabilities.

E-R Design Editor. A common component is an interface in which a designer can construct E-R diagrams, editing and making changes to the diagrams using the graphical drag-and-drop methods common to products such as the Apple Macintosh and Microsoft Windows.

E-R to Relational Design Transformer. Another common component of such tools is a transformer that automatically performs a transformation of an E-R design to a set of relational table definitions, following the steps outlined in Section 5.5.

With database design tools, the flow of development usually starts with E-R design and proceeds to a relational table definition. However, a number of products deal with functional dependencies. One tool advises loading a small universal table, and abstracts from this data the possible functional dependencies that might hold for the data. A transformation to BCNF/3NF for this set of FDs can then be automatically generated.

FD to E-R Design Transformer. Another type of component that is sometimes offered takes a set of FDs for the database and generates a valid E-R diagram to reflect the rules of the data.

As indicated in the previous section, a design that is theoretically perfect may also be inefficient in terms of performance. Thus a good design tool tries to analyze the performance implications of a design and accepts designer decisions to perform certain kinds of denormalization to improve performance. In addition, a tool must be forgiving of errors and omissions in FDs and entity classifications, in order to produce some kind of best guess at a design that the designer can picture while making corrections. This brings up another kind of standard tool component.

Design Analyzers. These components analyze design in the current stage and produce reports that might help the DBA to correct errors of various kinds.

For an excellent overview of database design tools, the reader is referred to the last chapter of reference [1].

Suggestions for Further Reading

Many variations in terminology are prevalent in the field of logical database design. The E-R approach is sometimes referred to as *semantic modeling*. The real-world objects known as entity occurrences in our notation are often referred to in the literature as entities, and the entity in our notation that makes up a category of entity occurrences then becomes an entity type. Attributes are also sometimes called *properties*.

Let us try to give an idea of what is meant by semantic modeling. In a programming language, the *syntax* of the language specifies how the statements are formed out of basic textual elements. The syntax does not associate any meaning with the statements, however. A specification of how programming language statements act under all possible conditions, what the statements mean in terms of their effect, is known as the *semantics* of the language. The term *semantic modeling* implies that in the E-R approach we are getting into the topic of what data items *really mean* in order to model their behavior in terms of database structures such as relational tables.

References [1], [2], and [4] have excellent coverage of the topic of logical database design. Reference [1] also contains as its final section an article by David Reiner on commercial products used for database design, known as database design tools. References [3] and [5] contain excellent coverage of many normalization concepts that are not covered in the current chapter. Reference [3] is extremely complete, while reference [5] is more approachable. However, both texts assume a very strong understanding of rigorous mathematical proofs.

[1] C. Batini, S. Ceri, and S. B. Navathe. *Conceptual Database Design.* Redwood, CA: Benjamin-Cummings, 1992.

[2] I. T. Hawryszkiewycz. *Database Analysis and Design*, 2nd ed. New York: Macmillan, 1991.

[3] David Maier. *The Theory of Relational Databases.* New York: Computer Science Press, 1983.

[4] Toby J. Teorey. *Database Modeling and Design: The Fundamental Principles*, 2nd ed. San Francisco: Morgan Kaufmann, 1994.

[5] Jeffrey D. Ullman. *Principles of Database Systems*, 2nd ed. New York: Computer Science Press, 1982.

Exercises

Exercises with solutions at the back of the book in "Solutions to Selected Exercises" are marked with the symbol •.

[5.1] • In Figure 5.6, if we do not assume that the number of connectors of R in the three diagrams *precisely* represents the designer's intention, but instead that the number is accidental but falls within the limits of the designer's intention, we can still conclude in some cases the min-card and max-card values for E and F relative to R. List all such values for the three diagrams of Figure 5.6.

[5.2] • As pointed out in Example 5.1.4, the orders table does not represent a relationship, but rather an entity, Orders. The Orders entity is itself related by a binary relationship to each of the three entities Customers, Agents, and Products. The relationships are the following: Customers *requests* Orders, Agents *places* Orders, and Orders *ships* Products. Draw the E-R diagram for all these entities and relationships, and attach all relevant attributes, designating primary keys and labeling cardinalities. Note that the diagram of Figure 5.11 is quite different, with an `Orders` entity made up of multiple `Line_items`.

[5.3] As in the case study of Section 5.4, create an E-R design, and from this generate a relational table design for a database to represent a banking business. In the database, we need to keep track of **customers** who have **accounts** at **branches** (of the bank). Each account is held at a specific branch, but a customer may have more than one account and an account may have more than one associated customer. We identify account by `acctid`, with additional attributes `acct_type` (savings, checking, etc.) and `acct_bal` (the dollar balance of the account). Each branch has an identifier `bno` and attribute `bcity`. Customers are identified by `ssn` (social security number) and have attribute `cname`, made up of `clname`, `cfname`, and `cmidinit`.

In this E-R design, you should think about how to represent the customers-accounts-branches combination. Perhaps all three of these are entities and there is a ternary relationship between them. Or perhaps there are two binary relationships, for example one between `Customers` and `Accounts` and one between `Accounts` and `Branches`. Or perhaps there are only two entities, `Customers` and `Branches`, and `has_account` is a relationship between them with its own attributes, where the relationship instance represents an account. More than one solution might be correct, but you should be able to rule out at least one of these alternatives. You should explore these three designs, decide which one you prefer, and *justify ruling out at least one of them*. Think about the following question in justifying your decision: Do all of these designs allow several customers to hold the same account jointly?

[5.4] In Example 5.6.4, assume that the functional dependencies (FDs) derived from the content are true, but now new rows can be added (that must still obey these FDs). Which of the following rows can be legally added to the rows that already exist? If it cannot be added, specify the FD number in the example that makes it illegal to add it.

(a)•

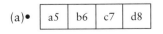

| a5 | b6 | c7 | d8 |

(b) | a2 | b2 | c1 | d8 |

(c)● | a3 | b1 | c4 | d3 |

(d) | a1 | b1 | c2 | d5 |

[5.5] ● As in Example 5.6.4, list all functional dependencies satisfied by the following table T, where we assume that it is the intent of the designer that exactly this set of rows should lie in the table.

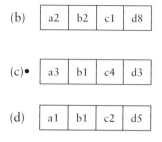

row #	A	B	C	D
1	a1	b1	c1	d1
2	a1	b1	c2	d2
3	a1	b2	c3	d1
4	a1	b2	c4	d4

T

[5.6] Repeat the previous exercise with the following table T:

row #	A	B	C	D
1	a1	b2	c1	d1
2	a1	b1	c2	d2
3	a2	b2	c1	d3
4	a2	b1	c2	d4
5	a2	b3	c4	d5

T

[5.7] (HARD) We expand on the idea of Example 5.6.4, of tables with fixed content where it is the intent of the designer that *exactly* that set of rows should lie in each table, so that the functional dependencies can be determined by examination. Notice that if we are presented with a table T having a given heading (set of attributes), but containing either zero rows or one row, examination seems to allow all possible FDs to hold. In order for Definition 5.6.2 of an FD to fail, there must be at least two rows in the table that match in some column values but not in others. An *Armstrong table* is one that contains a set of rows so that from its content a specific set of FDs F will be true (and of course all FDs in F+ as well), but all FDs not in F+ will be false.

(a)• Is the table in Example 5.6.4 an Armstrong table? Explain. Can you give a table with fewer rows that determines the same set of FDs? (Maybe not.)

(b) Is the table given in Exercise 5.6 an Armstrong table? Support your answer as in part (a).

(c) Create an Armstrong table to represent the following set of FDs on the attributes A, B, C, D, and *no others*. If other FDs exist as well, the answer fails. Try to create a table with the smallest set of rows you can find that has this property.

(1) $AB \to D$, (2) $BC \to A$

(d) (VERY HARD) Specify an algorithm to generate an Armstrong table from a given set of FDs on a list of attributes. This algorithm shows that such an Armstrong table will always exist.

[5.8] Give a proof of the transitivity rule of Armstrong's Axioms in Definition 5.6.6, following the form of proof used for the inclusion rule in Theorem 5.6.3 and the augmentation rule in Theorem 5.6.7.

[5.9] • Use Armstrong's Axioms from Definition 5.6.6 to derive the rules listed in Theorem 5.6.8 for which no proof was given.

[5.10] Consider the following set of rules of inference for FDs, where X, Y, X, and W are sets of attributes and B is an individual attribute.

1. **Reflexivity rule:**   It is always true that $X \to X$.
2. **Projectivity rule:**   If $X \to Y Z$, then $X \to Y$.
3. **Accumulation rule:**   If $X \to Y Z$ and $Z \to B W$, then $X \to Y Z B$.

Show how to derive the three rules of inference in Definition 5.6.6, Armstrong's Axioms, from these rules, and how these rules can be derived from Armstrong's Axioms. Since all rules can be derived using Armstrong's Axioms (because of completeness), these three rules form an alternate complete set of rules.

[5.11] (HARD) Given a set of attributes S and a set F of FDs, we say that a set X of attributes contained in S has a nontrivial set closure under F whenever $X^+ - X$ is non-null. Let F be a minimal set of dependencies, that is, where the minimal cover for F is F. We create a *nontrivial FD basis* B by forming set closures of all sets X_i on the left side of some FD in F, then creating the FD_i in B: $X_i \rightarrow (X_i^+ - X_i)$.

(a)• Show that if X is a set of attributes that does not contain the left-hand side X_i of some FD in F, then $X^+ = X$ under closure by FDs in F.

(b) It seems like a reasonable hypothesis that all FDs $W \rightarrow Z$ in F^+, where W and Z have no attributes in common, arise directly from the nontrivial FD basis B, so that if the attribute $A \in Z$, then $A \in (X_i^+ - X_i)$ for some FD_i in B of the form $X_i \rightarrow (X_i^+ - X_i)$, with $X_i \subseteq W$. However, this simplistic hypothesis is invalid. Construct a set S of attributes and a set F of FDs that constitutes a counterexample. Only two FDs are needed in F.

[5.12] Use Armstrong's Axioms and the results of Theorem 5.6.8, together with the following set of FDs from Example 5.6.2

(1) A $\rightarrow$ B, (2) C $\rightarrow$ B, (3) D $\rightarrow$ A B C, (4) A C $\rightarrow$ D

to derive the FDs labeled (a) through (c) below. Perform your derivation in a step-by-step manner, labeling each step with the rule from the above axioms.

(a)• D $\rightarrow$ A B C D

(b) A C $\rightarrow$ B D

(c) A C $\rightarrow$ A B C D

[5.13] As in Example 5.6.6 in the text, where it is shown that the set F of FDs covers the set G, show the reverse, that the set G covers the set F.

[5.14] (a)•Demonstrate the statement of Example 5.6.9, that the functional dependencies derived in Example 5.6.4 are *not* minimal, by going through the steps of finding a minimal cover.

(b) In part (a), only one FD derived in Example 5.6.4 needed to change to make a minimal cover. Explain the need for this change with a simple application of reasoning about FD implications.

[5.15] •In Algorithm 5.6.13, step 3, show that the test performed to determine that Y^+ is unchanged passing from the set of FDs H to the set J, as defined in the algorithm, also implies that H^+ is the same as J^+.

[5.16] Demonstrate the statement of Example 5.6.10, that the FDs given in Example 5.6.3 for the emp_info database (the set F) form a minimal set. Demonstrate this by going through the steps of finding a minimal cover.

[5.17] Assume that we wish to construct a database from a set of data items, {A, B, C, D, E, F, G} (which will become attributes in tables), and a set F of FDs given by

$$F = (1)\ B\ C\ D\ \rightarrow\ A,\ (2)\ B\ C\ \rightarrow E,\ (3)\ A\ \rightarrow\ F,\ (4)\ F \rightarrow\ G,$$
$$(5)\ C\ \rightarrow\ D,\ (6)\ A \rightarrow\ G.$$

(a) Find the minimal cover for this set of FDs, and name this set G.

(b)• Start with the table T containing all these attributes, and perform a lossless decomposition into two tables, T_1 and T_2, that make up a 2NF decomposition. List carefully the keys for each table (T, T_1, and T_2) and the FDs that lie in each table.

(c) Continue decomposition to bring this database to 3NF. Is this decomposition also BCNF?

(d)• Use Algorithm 5.8.8 and the set G of FDs to achieve a lossless 3NF decomposition that preserves FDs of G. Is this the same as the decomposition in part (c)?

[5.18] Assume that we wish to construct a database from a set of data items, {A, B, C, D, E, F, G, H} (which will become attributes in tables), and a set F of FDs given by

(1) A → B C , (2) A B E → C D G H, (3) C → G D, (4) D → G,
(5) E → F

(a) Find the minimal cover for this set of FDs, and name this set G.

(b) Start with the table T containing all these attributes, and perform a lossless decomposition into a 2NF but not a 3NF schema. List carefully the keys for each table (T, T_1, and T_2) and the FDs that lie in each table. Justify the fact that the decomposition is lossless. Explain why it is 2NF but not 3NF.

(c) Continue decomposition to bring this database to 3NF. Is this decomposition also BCNF?

(d) Use Algorithm 5.8.8 and the set G of FDs to achieve a lossless 3NF decomposition that preserves FDs of G. Is this the same as the decomposition in part (c)?

[5.19] •Repeat the relational design of the banking database of Exercise 5.3, but this time use a normalization approach. This will require you to come up with the proper set of FDs, and you should make sure that your answer makes sense. Compare your output to the E-R solution.

[5.20] Consider again the airline reservation database from the case study of Section 5.4. Note that passengers come together at gates to depart on flights; it might seem that we could replace the two binary relationships marshals and travels_on of Figure 5.14 with a ternary relationship, departs, that relates Passengers, Gates, and Flights. See below.

We note that the relationship is 1-1-N; that is, two entities have max-card = 1 in the relationship. As mentioned at the end of Section 5.2, this means that we can represent the relationship by foreign keys in one of the entity tables. Specifically, since the Passengers entity participates with max-card = N, we adjoin foreign keys for gates and flights to identify the unique gate and flight for a passenger.

(a) Translate the E-R design with the ternary relationship departs into relational tables.

(b) How does this relational table design differ from the design at the end of Section 5.4? Say which is preferable and justify your answer. (You might try to come up with a question like the ones at the end of Exercise 5.3.)

(c) Create the proper set of FDs for the airline reservation database, and then perform normalization to arrive at a relational table design. Does this shed any light on the question of part (b)?

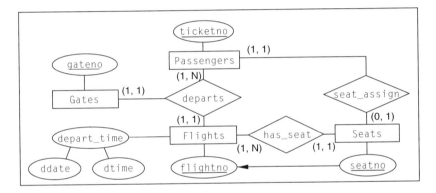

(d) If you created the right FDs, you should find that there is no distinct table for gates. One problem with having gate as the attribute of another table is the delete anomaly: if the last flight leaves from some gate, we no longer have any record that the gate exists. But what the normalization process is saying is that there doesn't seem to be any *reason* to remember that the gate exists. We can imagine adding a new attribute to the design, gatecap, which represents the seat capacity for passengers waiting at a gate. Now a new attempt at normalization will come up with a separate table for gates. Explain why.

(e) Note that with the design of part (d) for gates and capacity, we can easily imagine program logic that assigns a gate for a flight that is not already assigned to a flight during the hour before departure, and that has seating capacity to hold passengers for the seats of the flight. But suppose that all gates have the same seating capacity. We might still want to assign gates to flights, and now the delete anomaly mentioned in part (d) is a real problem. What does this imply about the normalization approach?

Integrity, Views, Security, and Catalogs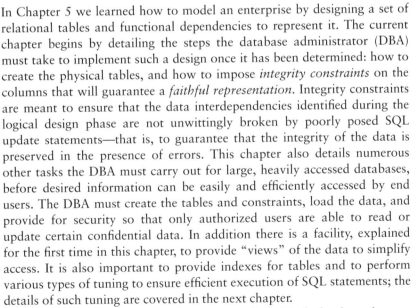

6

In Chapter 5 we learned how to model an enterprise by designing a set of relational tables and functional dependencies to represent it. The current chapter begins by detailing the steps the database administrator (DBA) must take to implement such a design once it has been determined: how to create the physical tables, and how to impose *integrity constraints* on the columns that will guarantee a *faithful representation*. Integrity constraints are meant to ensure that the data interdependencies identified during the logical design phase are not unwittingly broken by poorly posed SQL update statements—that is, to guarantee that the integrity of the data is preserved in the presence of errors. This chapter also details numerous other tasks the DBA must carry out for large, heavily accessed databases, before desired information can be easily and efficiently accessed by end users. The DBA must create the tables and constraints, load the data, and provide for security so that only authorized users are able to read or update certain confidential data. In addition there is a facility, explained for the first time in this chapter, to provide "views" of the data to simplify access. It is also important to provide indexes for tables and to perform various types of tuning to ensure efficient execution of SQL statements; the details of such tuning are covered in the next chapter.

The DBA who deals with an enterprise-critical database has an extremely responsible position and must be aware of the needs of all database users supported by the system—end users as well as application programmers. One aim of this text is to provide a basic grounding in the concepts needed by a DBA. The current chapter introduces many of the commands and features a DBA needs to do his or her work. Throughout the text we concentrate on database concepts from an "operational" standpoint. This means that the emphasis is on material required to make intelligent tradeoff decisions as a DBA, rather than on the details needed by a systems programmer to design and implement a database system software product. An operational approach does not imply a less rigorous coverage of concepts, but it does mean that we will concentrate on effects, say of a B-tree data indexing structure, rather than on the details of programming a B-tree. It is probably fair to say that an operational understanding must precede most system programming considerations: a programmer writing database system code who doesn't have a clear understanding of the considerations important to a DBA is operating under a serious handicap.

We have already seen some of the commands that a database administrator uses to create and load a database. In Chapter 3 we introduced the SQL statement:

```
create table customers (cid char(4) not null, cname varchar(13),
    city varchar(20), discnt real);
```

As we will see, this example illustrates only a small part of the full syntax.

6.1 Integrity Constraints

An *integrity constraint* is a *rule,* usually formulated by the creator of a database (the database administrator for important tables), that must be obeyed by all SQL update statements. As an example, if we make the rule that the cid value in the customers table of our CAP database must be unique (i.e., a *candidate* or *primary key*), then it should be impossible in a future insert to the customers table to create a row that duplicates an existing value in its cid column. This is what is known as a *faithful representation.* Indeed, for the integrity constraints we will be introducing, an update action—Insert, Update, or Delete—that breaks the integrity constraint will fail to execute. As we saw in Chapter 5, a number of integrity constraints come out of the design process—for example, columns that are part of a key in a table cannot be null and must have unique values. Before discussing some of the virtues and limitations of integrity constraints, we need to explain how they are implemented on commercial database systems. This is not a simple task, since various database products differ with regard to what statements they provide to impose integrity constraints. We will begin by explaining the current SQL standard, which dictates that integrity constraints are specified in the Create Table command.

Integrity Constraints in the Create Table Statement

The X/OPEN standard for the SQL Create Table statement has the general form given in Figure 6.1.

```
create table tablename
    (columnname data-type [default {defaultvalue|null|user}] [col_constr]
    {, columnname data-type [default {defaultvalue|null|user}] [col_constr]}
    {, table_constr})
```

The col_constr form that constrains a single column value follows:

```
[not null [unique]]
[references tablename [(columnname)] ]
[check (search_condition)]
```

The table_constr form that constrains multiple columns at once follows:

```
unique (columnname {, columnname}
| check (search_condition)
| primary key (columnname {, columnname})
| foreign key (columnname {, columnname})
| references tablename [(columnname {, columnname})]
```

Figure 6.1   Full X/OPEN Standard Create Table Syntax

The ANSI/89 and ISO standards for Create Table syntax are basically identical to the X/OPEN standard. This syntax is accepted by **ORACLE**, largely supported by **DB2** version 2.3 (with some minor variations), and not at all closely supported by **INGRES** as of version 6.3. We define some of the clauses of Figure 6.1, and then give an example for our CAP database. Following that, we explain special syntax variations in **ORACLE**, **DB2**, and **INGRES**. The SQL-92 constraints are discussed in a later subsection.

DEFINITION 6.1.1 Clauses of the Create Table Command. The Create Table command of Figure 6.1 begins by naming the table being created and then lists in parentheses a comma-separated sequence of columnname definitions. Each columnname definition contains columnname and datatype, and an optional **default** clause. This clause specifies the default value that the database system will supply for the column if the SQL Insert statement does not furnish a value. (Note that bulk-load commands such as Load or Copy are not covered by the SQL standard and are therefore not constrained to provide this value.) The default value supplied can be a constant of appropriate datatype supplied as "defaultvalue", or **null**, or **user**. The keyword **user** represents a character string whose value is the current user name.

Each columnname definition is optionally followed by a list of *column constraints*, symbolized in Figure 6.1 by col_constr, which consists of a sequence of optional clauses. At the end of the list of columnname definitions, a comma-separated list of *table constraints*, symbolized by table_constr, is appended before the defining parentheses are closed. ∎

We explain the column constraint clauses before passing on to the table constraints.

DEFINITION 6.1.2 Column Constraints. The col_constr clauses appearing in the Create Table statement of Figure 6.1 each consist of one of the following optional clauses.

The **not null** condition has already been explained; it means that null values cannot occur in this column. Only if **not null** is specified can **unique** be added, and the column is then constrained to contain a different value on every row inserted in the table. Basically this means that the table creator wants this single column to function as a *candidate key*.

If **not null** appears in a col_constr, then the **default** clause cannot specify **null**; if neither the **default** clause nor the **not null** clause appears in a column definition, then **default null** is assumed.

For a column defined with a **references** clause, each row is constrained to contain in this column one of the values that appears in the tablename referenced, either in the columnname specified or, if no columnname is specified, in the single column primary key of that table. This constraint is a means of defining a column to be a *foreign key* referencing the primary key, or possibly a candidate key, of a different table. In the case of a multi-column foreign key, we need a somewhat more general definition (see Definition 6.1.3, Table Constraints).

If the **check** clause appears, then each row is constrained to contain a value in this column that satisfies the specified search_condition. In the X/OPEN standard, this search_condition is only permitted to contain references to constant values; no other column references or set functions are permitted.   ∎

EXAMPLE 6.1.1

Here is a possible Create Table statement for the customers table.

```
create table customers (cid char(4) not null unique, cname
    varchar(13), city varchar(20), discnt real check(discnt <= 15.0));
```

Note that the cid column is defined here to be a *candidate key* for the customers table because of the **unique** clause; while cid must have unique values on each row, it is not understood as a result of this statement to be a *primary key;* we will see what this means shortly. The Create Table statement above also constrains any row of the customers table to have a discnt value that does not exceed 15.0.   ∎

DEFINITION 6.1.3 Table Constraints. The table_constr clauses appearing in the Create Table statement of Figure 6.1 each consist of one of the following optional clauses.

The **unique** clause has the same meaning as **unique** in the case of a col_constr, except that it is possible to specify a set of columns that must be unique in combination (the col_constr form is merely a special case of the table_constr from). Therefore this is a way to specify a multi-column candidate key for a table. Every column that participates in a **unique** clause must be defined to be **not null**.

The **check** clause as a table constraint is similar to the column **check** clause and limits acceptable values for a set of columns; the search_condition can refer to any column values in the same table, on the same row for which an Update or Insert statement is in process. As in the column analog, no Subselects or set functions are allowed in the X/OPEN standard. This limitation is removed in SQL-92, and the expanded power is extremely significant, but most database products currently maintain the limitation of an X/OPEN search_condition.

The **primary key** clause specifies a non-empty set of columns to be a primary key—that is, a candidate key referred to by default in another table in a **references** clause (see below). Every column that participates in a **primary key** clause must be defined to be **not null**. There can be at most one **primary key** clause in any Create Table statement.

The **foreign key** and **references** clauses always occur together (although because they are independent optional clauses in the Create Table syntax, they can occur in any order). The **foreign key** columnname list specifies a set of columns in the table being created whose values on each row are constrained to be equal to the values of a set of columns on some row of another table, as specified by the associated **references** clause. When the columns in the other table being referenced form the primary key, the **references** clause does not specify a list of columns. A detailed discussion of the concepts of primary key, foreign key, and referential integrity is deferred until a later part of this section.

Note that the **primary key** clause has much the same effect as the **unique** clause; the only added factor is that a **references** clause from another table will reference the primary key by default if no columns are specified. This means that a **unique** specification for a column is considered redundant with the **primary key** specification: only one of the two clauses will be accepted by many products. ∎

Here is an example to illustrate some of these concepts.

EXAMPLE 6.1.2

We provide appropriate Create Table statements for the `customers` and `orders` tables in the CAP database. See Figure 6.2 for the E-R diagram on which these Create Table definitions are based, a solution to Exercise 5.2 at the end of Chapter 5. Recall that the (x, y) pair labeling a connection between an attribute A and an entity E means that x = min-card(A, E) and y = max-card(A, E). In particular, a value x = 0 means that nulls are allowed in this column, and a value x = 1 implies *mandatory participation* and means that the column should be defined with a **not null** clause in the Create Table statement. The identifier attribute for each entity in the E-R diagram is underlined, and this generally translates to a **primary key** clause in the Create Table statement. We add a few **check** clauses in the Create Table statement that have no counterpart in the E-R diagram. Discussion of the **foreign key** . . . **references** clauses in the `orders` table is deferred until we discuss referential integrity a bit later in this section.

```
create table customers (cid char(4) not null, cname varchar(13),
    city varchar(20), discnt real check(discnt <= 15.0),
```

```
      primary key (cid) );

  create table orders ( ordno integer not null, month char(3),
         cid char(4) not null, aid char(3) not null, pid char(3) not null,
         qty integer not null check(qty >= 0),
         dollars float default 0.0 check(dollars >= 0.0),
         primary key ( ordno ),
         foreign key (cid) references customers,
         foreign key (aid) references agents,
         foreign key (pid) references products);
```

Constraints for the orders table are examined further in Example 6.1.5, when we discuss how the motivation for referential integrity arises from E-R transformations. ■

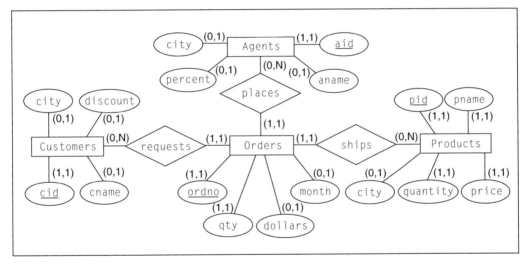

Figure 6.2 E-R Diagram for CAP Database

In the following subsections, we discuss variations from the standard of how constraints are imposed in the database products **ORACLE**, **DB2**, and **INGRES**.

Create Table in ORACLE

The **ORACLE** Create Table statement accepts all of the integrity constraint clauses (col_constr and table_constr clauses) of the X/OPEN standard syntax in Figure 6.1. However, if you are using an **ORACLE** release prior to version 7.0, most of these clauses are merely accepted syntactically by the Create Table statement, with no power to actually enforce constraints on later update statements.

The **ORACLE** Create Table statement is given in Figure 6.3 (there are two forms). Note that this statement contains a number of clauses that define how rows of the table will be stored on disk and set limits on concurrent update transactions. We defer consideration of these clauses until the next chapter. For further details of the **ORACLE** Create Table statement, refer to the *ORACLE SQL Language Reference Manual* [13] and the *ORACLE RDBMS Database Administrator's Guide* [12].

The **ORACLE** product provides an optional constr_name for every specified constraint for later reference. The second Create Table form of Figure 6.3, with the **as** Subselect clause, allows the user to create a table containing the result of a Subselect from existing tables. The columnnames of the table created and the elements of the target list of the Subselect must be in one-to-one correspondence, and column names of the new table can be inherited from the target list as long as they are unique in the new table. Note that the column definition elements following the columnnames are left out of the Create Table syntax when the **as** Subselect clause is used, since the column datatypes are determined from the Subselect. Furthermore, column and table constraints are not included in this syntax; such constraints can be added to the table at a later time using the Alter Table statement, covered later in this section.

```
create table tablename
    (columnname data-type [default {defaultvalue|null|user}] [col_constr]
    {, columnname data-type [default {defaultvalue|null|user}] [col_constr]}
    {, table_constr})
    [disk storage and update transaction clauses (not covered, or deferred)]
| create table tablename (columnname {, columnname})
        [as subselect]
```

Figure 6.3 ORACLE Create Table Syntax

Create Table in DB2

We start by outlining the **DB2** variations from the standard. The **DB2** format is somewhat complex, and we avoid consideration of a number of features as we did with **ORACLE**, above. For further details, see the *DB2 SQL Reference Manual* [4] and the *DB2 Administrator's Guide* [2].

The **DB2** Create Table statement has fewer constraints that are specific to a column. The **DB2** Create Table format that we cover is given by

```
create table tablename
    (columnname data-type [col_constr] {, columnname data-type
    [col_constr]}
    {, table_constr)]]
```

The col_constr form for **DB2** is

```
[not null [unique | with default
| fieldproc program-name (const {,const})]]]
```

The **not null unique** phrase means what the same phrase would mean in the X/OPEN standard. If **not null with default** is chosen, a null will never appear in this column; but if an Insert statement leaves this column unspecified, it will be replaced with a default value determined in advance for each specific type; for example, 0 (zero) for numeric type and a string of length zero for varchar.

A **fieldproc** option names a program containing a set of functions, one of which is called to examine a char or varchar datatype value that is about to be placed in this column (for example, by an SQL Update statement) and encode it before it is stored. Similarly, any values read from this column (for example, by a search_condition) are first passed to a function in this program and decoded. The *const* arguments are passed to a function of the program at the time of the Create Table statement. Clearly the **fieldproc** option offers a great deal of power to deal with inserted char or varchar values, allowing the DBA to create a flexible analog to the **check** clause, for example, or to perform sophisticated types of data compression and decompression.

The table_constr form for **DB2** is given in Figure 6.4.

```
unique (columnname {, columnname})
| primary key (columnname {, columnname})
| foreign key [constr_name] (columnname {, columnname})
    references tablename
[on delete {restrict | cascade | set null}];
```

Figure 6.4   table_constr Form in **DB2**

DB2 supports the **primary key** and **foreign key** table_constr clauses of the X/OPEN standard. The columns making up a foreign key must always match in value the primary key columns, left to right, in the referenced tablename. The optional constr_name attached to the foreign key definition is used in any error messages associated with this constraint, and also in the Alter Table statement to drop such a foreign key constraint.

The optional **on delete** clause specifies an "action" that should take place when some update would break the foreign key integrity constraint. For example, consider the foreign key, cid, in the orders table that references the primary key of the customers table. What action should be taken in response to a Delete statement that removes a row from the customers table whose cid value is referenced as a foreign key from rows of the orders table? The three actions permitted are **restrict, cascade,** and **set null.** With the **restrict** effect, the delete of the customers row would be rejected. With the **cascade** effect, when the customers row with a given cid value was deleted, all orders rows referring to that customer cid would also be deleted, and deletes would continue recursively for other rows with a cascaded foreign key dependency on other rows deleted. With the **set null** effect, the customers row would be deleted and cid values in the orders table that refer to that row would be set to null. (The column cid in orders must therefore not be created with the **not null** specification.) If the **on delete** clause is missing from this **foreign key** specification, then the **on delete restrict** option is assumed. The **on delete restrict** action is also the default action assumed by the SQL standards, where no **on delete** clause is provided.

We will see in the next section how the capability of the **check** clause that we saw in the X/OPEN Create Table syntax and not in **DB2** can be provided by careful use of the View facility.

Integrity in INGRES

The **INGRES** Create Table statement has only one column constraint clause and no table constraint clauses. The Create Table syntax is

```
create table tablename
    (columnname datatype [not null [with default | not default]
        | with null]
    {, columnname datatype [not null [with default | not default]
        | with null]})
    [with_clause]
| create table tablename (columnname {, columnname})
        as subselect
        [with_clause]
```

The optional **with null** clause means that nulls are supplied for updates that do not supply a value for this column; **not null with default** means that **INGRES** supplies a default value instead; **not null not default** means that the Update statement must supply a value for this column or encounter a runtime error. If no clause at all is provided, **with null** is assumed. If only **not null** is provided, **not null with default** is assumed.

The optional with_clause specifies details of disk placement and transactional conventions (not covered in this text; see the *INGRES/SQL Reference Manual* [8]). The with_clause also allows for an **INGRES** guarantee of Relational RULE 3, which states that duplicate rows cannot exist in the table. The form, used after all columns have been defined in parentheses, is the following:

```
with noduplicates
```

Even when this clause is used, the guarantee that rows will not be duplicated does not hold unless a primary index structure is imposed on the table, to provide efficient reference through some column values. (This is known in **INGRES** as an indexed *storage structure,* imposed through the Modify command. Indexes are explained in Chapter 7.)

INGRES has no **unique** keyword. Unique values for columns and combinations of columns are supported separately by creating a unique table storage structure on these columns with the Modify command (see Chapter 7 for details). **INGRES** has no **check** clause to constrain columns or combinations of columns, but it provides this function with a Create Integrity statement, explained below. As of release 6.4, **INGRES** does not support any **primary key** clause, **foreign key** clause, or **references** clause, for either a single column or a set of columns. However, **INGRES** does support a form of procedural constraint known as *database rules,* similar to the **SYBASE** triggers capability described a bit later in this section. By creating appropriate database rules (not covered here), it is possible to simulate the referential integrity constraint imposed by the X/OPEN Create Table statement.

Here is an example of the Create Integrity command in **INGRES**, which creates an integrity constraint comparable to a **check** clause in the standard Create Table command.

EXAMPLE 6.1.3
Create an integrity constraint to require that any row in the customers table have a discnt value of at least 4.0 and no more than 12.0.

```
create integrity on customers is discnt >= 4.0 and discnt <= 12.0;
```

After this integrity constraint is successfully executed, any Insert or Update statement that would create a row in the customers table with a discnt outside the required range will fail. A full explanation of how this failure occurs is given below. ∎

If the Create Integrity command of Example 6.1.3 is issued for the already loaded CAP database of Figure 2.2 that we have been using, the following error message is returned:

```
16492: INTEGRITY on customers constraint does not initially hold
```

and the integrity rule does not "take." This is because we have tried to initiate the rule when the customers table contains a row (with cid value c006) that breaks the rule with the value 0.0 for discnt. In order to successfully issue this integrity command, we must first correct all offending rows of the table, deleting unqualified rows or else updating the discnt values so that the constraint is initially valid. The most natural time to use the Create Integrity command is right after creating the table and before adding any rows. Having seen how to add such a constraint in **INGRES**, we now need to know how to list all constraints and then how to delete them.

EXAMPLE 6.1.4

To get a list of all constraints in the `customers` table resulting from the Create Integrity statement, give the **INGRES** command:

```
help integrity customers;
```

This prints out a list of all the constraints placed on the table, with an integer identifier for each, numbered 0, 1, ... To remove integrity constraint 0 (zero) on the employee table, give the command:

```
drop integrity on customers 0;                                    ■
```

The general form of the Create Integrity statement in **INGRES** is

```
create integrity on tablename [corr_name] is search_condition;
```

The search_condition here can refer only to column values in the same table, on the same row for which an update statement is in process. No subselect or aggregate set functions can be used. The general form of the Help Integrity command is

```
help integrity tablename;
```

This command provides a list of integers. The general form for the Drop Integrity command is

```
drop integrity on tablename integer {, integer};
```

Integrity constraints are implemented on **INGRES** by an application of an approach known as *query modification*. For example, given the statement

[6.1.1]   `update customers set discnt = discnt + 0.5 where cid = :cust_id;`

which might be automatically executed on the anniversary of becoming a customer in good standing, the system looks up the integrity constraints present on the `customers` table. Given the integrity constraint of Example 6.1.3, the next step is to alter statement (6.1.1) to become

[6.1.2]   `update customers set discnt = discnt + 0.5 where cid = :cust_id`
`             and discnt + 0.5 >= 4.0 and discnt + 0.5 <= 12.0;`

We see that the search condition reflecting the integrity constraint has been *added to* the search condition of the update—this is the sense in which the update is *modified*, why we call this process *query modification*. The modified update will now not "take" if the host variable cust_id has the value 'c002', since c002 has already reached a discnt value of 12.00, and the addition of 0.5 would bring the discnt outside the admissible range. We see now why no error message results from the failure of the modified statement (6.1.2); it merely seems as if the set of rows being updated is overconstrained, so that no rows are selected to change. No error message is issued in **INGRES**; this is a variation from behavior with the X/OPEN standard **check** clause. To test if a constraint has kept an update statement from succeeding, it is always necessary in Embedded SQL to test the number of rows affected. The number of rows affected by an interactive update statement is stated in the system response.

Primary Keys, Foreign Keys, and Referential Integrity

We assume in what follows that the **primary key** and **foreign key** clauses exist in the Create Table statement and are enforced as integrity constraints for ensuing update statements. (This is currently not true for the **INGRES** and **SYBASE** products, which depend on triggered rules for constraints of this kind, but it will probably be true for all database products eventually.) We begin with an example from our CAP database to motivate the definition of referential integrity in Definition 6.1.4.

> **EXAMPLE 6.1.5 Referential Integrity.**
> In the E-R diagram of the CAP database pictured in Figure 6.2, we note that all relationships, requests, places, and ships, are many-to-one, with the Orders entity representing the "many" side of the relationship. Each single customer requests many orders, each agent places many orders, each product is shipped in many orders, but each order has only one defining customer, agent, and product. Thus, by Transformation RULE 4 in Section 5.2, the orders table needs to contain a *foreign key* column to represent each of the entity instances for Customers, Agents, and Products to which the Orders instance is related. For example, the orders table in the Create Table statement of Example 6.1.2 contains a foreign key cid to represent the Customers instance that requests the particular order represented by this row. Note in particular that the cid column in the orders table does not represent an *attribute* of the Orders entity, but actually represents an *instance* of the requests relationship.

This is such an important concept that we repeat it again in a slightly different way: each specific `cid` value in a row of `orders` actually corresponds to a relationship instance connecting an `Orders` entity and `Customers` entity. The *referential integrity* constraint simply insists that we avoid "dangling" references in foreign keys to nonexistent primary keys in another table, so the relationship instance being specified will always make sense for each row in the `orders` table. Thus a cid value in `orders` must exist also in `customers`. This constraint is guaranteed in Example 6.1.2 by the `foreign key (cid)` references `customers` clause in the Create Table statements for `orders`.

There is also a different constraint on `cid`, arising in Figure 6.2 from the fact that the `Orders` entity has mandatory participation in the `requests` relationship (because the label on the connecting link between `Orders` and `requests` has a min-card of 1). Given this, it is necessary that there is a non-null `cid` value for in each row in `orders` (clearly different from referential integrity, which states that every non-null `cid` value in `orders` must reference a real `cid` value in `customers`). This mandatory participation constraint is imposed in Example 6.1.2 by the **not null** clause following the `cid` definition in the Create Table statement for orders. ∎

To repeat: referential integrity implies a rule for the CAP database that no row in the `orders` table can contain a `cid`, `aid`, or `pid` value unless it refers to an existing value in the corresponding `customers`, `agents`, or `products` tables. This rule basically says that as we place rows in `orders`, we want to avoid an implicit statement of the form: "Trust me. Although I'm referring to a nonexistent agent (or product or customer) in this order, it will all make sense eventually when I have a chance to define a new row in the `agents` table." We are insisting that the `agents` row be inserted *first*, before the `orders` row that refers to it. The reason we are imposing the referential integrity rule comes from fundamental considerations of logical design, but it also works well in practice. We can now say that if an attempt is made to insert such a "nonreferential" value in `orders`, it probably means that an error has been made by someone typing data for the `orders` table. For example, consider a row such as the following to be added to the `orders` table with the content of Figure 2.2.

ordno	month	cid	aid	pid	qty	dollars
1011	jan	c001	a0@	p01	1000	450.00

There is no `aid` value "a0@" in the primary key for `agents`; this attempted row insert probably means that there was a slip in typing the digit "2" after the letters "a0" in the `orders` column `aid` ("@" is the shift value of 2). It seems there is no good argument that a new `cid`, `aid`, or `pid` value should validly appear in `orders` for the first time; we are making a reasonable rule that a new customer, agent, or product must appear in the appropriate "home" table first, to give us a chance to catch important errors. Of course a referential integrity constraint comes at a certain cost in performance: the resources used to perform an insert to the `orders` table may be quite badly affected when three referential integrity rules such as this are imposed, since each insert of an order will require a lookup in three separate tables.

Now let us clarify our thinking to create a definition: a *referential integrity* constraint insists that values appearing in the foreign key of some table in a database must be matched by values in a primary key of another table (possibly the same one, as when rows in an `employees` table, with primary key `eid`, reference through the `mgrid` column the `eid` of some other employee). But what are we to do about null values? We know that a null value cannot exist in a primary key (see RULE 4, the Entity Integrity RULE, at the end of Section 2.4, and the explanation of the **primary key** clause near the end of Definition 6.1.1). But what rule do we wish to adopt about nulls existing in a foreign key? Recall that one of the actions of the **on delete** clause of Create Table in **DB2** (Figure 6.4) is to set nulls in the foreign key when a row with that primary key value is deleted. So database products allow nulls to exist in a foreign key, and we need to give a careful definition.

DEFINITION 6.1.4 Foreign Key, Referential Integrity. A set of columns F in table T1 is defined as a *foreign key* of T1 if the combination of values of F in any row is required to either contain null values or else to match the value combination of a set of columns P representing a candidate or primary key of some table T2. More precisely, we say that a referential integrity constraint is in force if the columns of F in any row of T1 must either (1) have null values in at least one column that allows null values, or (2) have no null values and be equal to the value combination of P on some row of T2. ∎

This definition is a bit futuristic, since null values for some columns of a foreign key were not supported in any standard until SQL-92, and some textbooks and database products do not allow them. In particular, such a concept is not supported in the X/OPEN standard that we have generally adopted in this text. However, it is the coming standard and seems to be the proper solution in a more fundamental sense. Note that some of the columns of a foreign key for a table might figure in a candidate key or even a primary key for that same table, and therefore not be *nullable*; that is, they must be defined as **not null** in the Create Table statement. However, Definition 6.1.4 implies that if *optional participation* in a relationship is to be supported by the foreign key, that at least one column of a foreign key must be nullable and thus be able to represent the *existence* of a relationship instance; if the relationship instance is no longer valid, possibly because of a delete of a primary key row with a **set null** action on the candidate key, then a null value in such a nullable column means that the entire foreign key is invalid, i.e., null.

EXAMPLE 6.1.6
Recall that in Section 2.2 we said that the *domain of an attribute* is usually considered to be an *enumerated* set of possible values from which column values can be drawn. Most commercial databases do not currently support such enumerated datatypes. Thus, for example, the city columns of customers, agents, and products are simply constrained to be character strings. However, it is possible to provide the functionality of an enumerated type if we are willing to create a new table known as cities, containing all acceptable city names. (The same city name might appear numerous times in distinct states, and even in distinct countries, but assume that we don't care about that; we ignored states and countries for simplicity in our original example tables, and it is clear how to generalize, for example, to unique city-state pairs.)

```
create table cities (city varchar(20) not null,
    primary key ( city) );
create table customers (cid char(4) not null, cname varchar(13),
    city varchar(20), discnt real check(discnt <= 15.0),
    primary key (cid),
    foreign key (city) references cities);
```

The city values in the cities table are unique, and make an appropriate primary key, whereas the city value in customers is a secondary key that must match some (primary key) value in the cities table. This constraint ensures that no city values will occur in customers that are not listed in the cities table, and therefore has the effect of an enumerated domain. ∎

The SQL-92 standard provides a new type of object known specifically as a *domain* to be used in column definitions, but the concept of an enumerated type is explicitly *not* supported; rather, the SQL-92 domain is merely an alias for a datatype definition. The approach illustrated in Example 6.1.6 to support an enumerated type using the referential integrity constraint will therefore be the only solution for the foreseeable future.

What restrictions on row updates are actually implied by foreign key constraints? What tests must be performed to guarantee conformance? Recall that in the **on delete** clause of Figure 6.4, three different actions, **delete, cascade,** and **set null**, were defined in the event that a row of the primary key table was deleted, affecting rows in a foreign key table that referenced that row. However, this is not the only situation that can arise. Consider the three SQL statements, Insert, Delete, and Update, that might be used to perform row updates, and the two columns that might be affected, the primary key of one table and the referencing foreign key of a different table. We have the following matrix of necessary tests to detect broken integrity constraints:

	Insert	Delete	Update
Primary key	no test	test-1	test-2
Foreign key	test-3	no test	test-4

Figure 6.5 Matrix of Tests for Referential Integrity

It should be clear that the two cells in the matrix that specify "no test" represent cases that cannot conceivably cause the referential integrity constraint to fail. For example, given that all value combinations in a foreign key correspond to value combinations in the primary key, it is impossible that inserting a new row with new primary key values will invalidate this property. The cells in the matrix labeled test-1 through test-4, on the other hand, correspond to situations where the system needs to perform a test to ensure that an update of this kind does not invalidate referential integrity. For example, in deleting a row from a primary key (test-1), we might remove a primary key value that is referenced by some set of rows in the foreign key column. An update of a primary key column (test-2) could also have this effect, and the **on delete** actions of **DB2** are extended to include this case. Clearly we must also test any new insert of a row in the foreign key table (test-3) to assure ourselves that it references a valid primary key,

and an update of a foreign key column (test-4) to a new value also requires
such a test. The default action if this test fails is to **restrict**; that is, to disallow the insert or update that would affect the foreign key. From the types
of tests being performed, efficiency must clearly be a primary consideration. For example, when inserting a new row in the customers table of
Example 6.1.6, the system will need to look up the city value in a cities table that may contain many thousands of rows, a nontrivial additional responsibility. The functionality provided might be exactly what the
DBA desires, but it is important to be aware of the cost in terms of
diminished capacity of updates on any given hardware configuration.

The Alter Table Statement

The Alter Table statement allows the DBA to alter the structure of a table
originally specified in a Create Table statement, adding or deleting columns
of the table, and with many products adding or deleting various constraints as well. The Alter Table statement is intended to apply to tables
that have existing columns, which brings up a number of new considerations of disk storage. The Alter Table statement is not specified in the
ANSI/89 SQL or ISO standard. The X/OPEN standard, shown in Figure
6.6, provides only the capability to add new columns, not to delete old columns or to add or drop constraints.

```
alter table tablename
    add columnname data-type
    | add (columnname data-type [,columnname data-type])
```

Figure 6.6 X/OPEN Standard for Alter Table Syntax

The **ORACLE** product, on the other hand, provides many other features. The only action not permitted is to *drop* an existing column from the
table. The **DB2** product offers approximately the same capabilities as the
DB2 Create Table form, except that a new column cannot be specified as
unique and the constraints that can be added or dropped are limited to **primary key** (which is, of course, unique for the table) and **foreign key . . . references**, which is the only named constraint in the **DB2** syntax. The
ORACLE standard for Alter Table syntax is illustrated in Figure 6.7.

```
alter table tablename
    [add (columnname data-type [col_constr]
        {, columnname data-type [col_constr]}
        {, table_constr} ) ]
    [modify (columnname data-type [col_constr]
        {, columnname data-type [col_constr]})]
    [drop constraint constr_name]
    [disk storage and update transaction clauses (not covered, or deferred)]
```

Figure 6.7   ORACLE Standard for Alter Table Syntax

INGRES does not provide the Alter Table statement as of release 6.3. See the SQL reference manual for the specific product you are working with to determine the exact form of Alter Table statement available. The SQL-92 standard provides a very large set of features. All constraints are given names, and all columns and constraints can be added or dropped. See Melton and Simon, *Understanding the New SQL (SQL-92)* [9].

If a new column is added by an Alter Table statement, it must be created as all nulls or all default values, and therefore cannot be specified as **not null**, unless, in **DB2**, it is **not null with default**. An added constraint that does not originally hold, such as **not null** for a column containing nulls, normally results in a restrict action—that is, the statement will not succeed. In SQL-92, when a column is to be dropped a [cascade | restrict] action defines whether constraints in other tables that depend on this column are to be dropped or the action to drop the column is to be restricted.

Adding new columns to a table definition has important implications for the physical storage of the rows, which may now be expanded in size to a point where they will not fit in their current disk area. Most products allow the DBA to alter the table and to assume null values in new columns without moving all rows of the table to a new disk area at that time, a task that can require tremendous computer resources for very large tables. There is a good deal of variation among the different database products in treating physical storage considerations, and we defer these considerations to a later point.

SQL-92 Integrity Constraints

The SQL-92 standard has a number of new integrity features, most of which are not yet available on commercial database products. One important modification is in the optional **check** clause of the Create Table statement:

```
check (search_condition)
```

In SQL-92 this form accepts any valid search_condition form. In the X/OPEN clause of Definition 6.1.1, and in most current database products, the search_condition of the **check** clause can refer only to column values in the same table, on the same row for which an Update or Insert statement is in process, with no Subselects or set functions allowed. This is quite a strong limitation, a form known technically as a *restriction predicate,* and it should be obvious that there are many business rules we might wish to impose that cannot be provided without more powerful search_conditions.

EXAMPLE 6.1.7

We want to ensure that any customers with discnt of 0.0 (new customers who have not yet had a credit check) cannot place total orders in excess of $2000.00. In SQL-92 we can impose this requirement by placing the following check on the orders table:

```
create table orders( . . .
    constraint newcustlimit check
        (orders.cid not in (select cid from customers c
            where c.discnt = 0.0)
        or (select sum(x.dollars) from orders x
            where x.cid = orders.cid) <= 2000.00
            . . .)
```

The search_condition of Example 6.1.7 is stated as a condition that should always hold, and has a qualifier, orders, by which we refer to column value on the row(s) being inserted or updated in the orders table on which the **check** clause is defined. This is a natural result of the following definition of the **check** constraint. Given a table t with a **check** clause, if we represent the associated search_condition by y, then a row modification to the table t will fail if and only if, after modification, the following statement is false:

```
not exists t.* where not y
```

In the specific example just given, an update to the `orders` table will fail if, after modification, the given search_condition is false for some `orders` row. Using the rule of logic that not(p or q) means the same as (not p and not q), this means that there *is* an `orders` row whose `cid` has `discnt = 0.0` *and* that the sum of orders by that customer exceeds 2000.00.

There is a rather surprising situation that can result from this definition.

EXAMPLE 6.1.8

Suppose that we wanted to create a **check** constraint in SQL-92 to guarantee that the `agents` table always has at least one row. Presumably we would want to impose such a constraint with an Alter Table statement, after we've had a chance to insert some rows into the table; but leaving that question aside, we ask whether the following constraint would accomplish our aim.

```
constraint agents_never_empty
    check( (select count(*) from agents) > 0);
```

Surprisingly, this **check** clause would *not* impose the desired constraint. In the definition of a check constraint given above, if we replace the table t with the `orders` table and the search_condition y with "`(select count(*) from agents) > 0`", then a modification of the `agents` table will fail only if, after modification, the following statement is false:

```
not exists agents.* where not((select count(*) from agents) > 0)
```

But this statement cannot be false! If there is no row in the `agents` table, then there does not exist a row in `agents` that makes y false (never mind that y does not depend on the row `agents.*` chosen). And clearly if the `orders` table contains at least one row, then the condition on count of rows from `agents` being greater than zero is satisfied. Therefore an empty table, or indeed any table, is acceptable under this constraint. ∎

This rather strange side effect of a **check** constraint from a Create Table statement always being true for an empty table gives a motivation for another new feature of the SQL-92 standard, the *Create Assertion* statement. This statement has the syntax:

```
create assertion constraint constr_name check (search_condition);
```

The way an assertion search_condition differs from the search_condition in the **check** clause of a Create Table statement is that the assertion is not associated with any specific table (it is meant to span multiple tables), and therefore the constraint test is not automatically true if the associated table is empty.

EXAMPLE 6.1.9

In our attempt to centralize data, we incorporate a newly acquired wholesale company in our CAP database, with its own equivalents to our products, agents, customers, and orders tables. We rename the tables products1, products2,..., orders1, orders2, to keep everything straight. Note that the products1 table might have a number of attributes that are different from those of products2, so we cannot simply merge the two tables; however, we would like to create a rule, imposed by our insurers, that total inventory of all products housed in our Dallas warehouse has a total worth of less than $1 million (we assume that we are warehousing products from the products1 and products2 tables together). There was no way to do this with constraints before SQL-92. But in this standard we can write:

```
create assertion constraint dallasvalue check

    ( (select sum(quantity*price) from products1
        where city = 'Dallas'
   + select sum(quantity*price) from products2
        where city = 'Dallas')
    < 1000000.00);
```

Note that if this search_condition were specified as a constraint affiliated with the products1 table through a Create Table **check** clause, then the constraint would cease to operate if the products1 table became empty (as might happen with further consolidation). ∎

Non-Procedural and Procedural Integrity Constraints

The designers of SQL integrity clauses seem to have had the goal of trying to foresee all important rules that could arise from logical database design and implementing these rules as non-procedural constraints. The constraints would then be impossible to break, since they would be validated during all SQL update statement executions, and would guard against loss of data integrity resulting from erroneous ad hoc updates, or even update errors in application logic. In the rest of this section we examine various aspects of these integrity constraints, and contrast a different method of imposing active rules, known as *triggers,* that provides a facility for imposing procedural constraints. As with the discussion of non-procedural SQL Select statements in Section 3.10, we claim that non-procedural constraints will miss a good deal of power that would be available if constraints were instead procedurally specified. We start with a discussion of triggers so that we have an idea of alternatives before considering pros and cons.

Procedural Constraints and Triggers

Relatively powerful triggered procedures are currently available in the **SYBASE** commercial database product, and somewhat less powerful forms in a number of other products, such as Interbase and the Microsoft SQL server. SQL-92 offers no standard for triggers, and Melton and Simon [9] state that ". . . the standards committees simply guessed wrong: they didn't realize how rapidly the demand for triggers and the implementations of triggers would come along . . . However, most vendors have simply gone beyond SQL-92 and used the SQL3 trigger specification as the basis for their implementation." The authors go on to make the point that the SQL3 trigger specification is not final, since the standard has not been released. However, we will attempt to postulate the capability of the current proposed Create Trigger syntax, shown in Figure 6.8.

```
create trigger trigger_name before | after
    insert | delete | update [of columnname [, columnname]]
    on tablename [referencing_clause] [when (search_condition)]
    (statement [, statement]) [for each row | for each statement]
```

Figure 6.8 SQL3 Create Trigger Syntax

The Create Trigger syntax creates an object named trigger_name. The name is used in error messages and in a later request to drop this trigger from currency: **drop** trigger_name. The trigger is *fired* (executed) either **before** or **after** one of the events listed (**insert, delete,** or **update** optionally limited to a set of named columns) takes place to the table given by tablename. If the trigger is fired, the optional search_condition, if present, is executed to determine if the current row or set of rows affected should cause further execution, and if so the triggered *action,* a program given by the comma-separated list of statements in parentheses, is executed. The *granularity* of the action is either **for each row** or **for each statement** (the default), and this determines how frequently the action is executed—once for each row affected or else at the end of the statement. (Clearly we might have a multi-row update, delete, or insert, so there can be an important distinction here.) In the case of a triggered **update** event, the sequence of statements in the action program may wish to distinguish between values in each row affected *before* the update and values *after* the update occurs. To achieve this we have an optional referencing_clause in the Create Trigger syntax of the form:

```
referencing [old [as] old_corr_name]
       [new [as] new_corr_name]
```

The two correlation names used to qualify a column name identify whether the column value comes from the old table (before update) or the new table (after update). Either the old or the new correlation name specification clause may be left out, but not both.

Because a trigger causes a series of statements (the comma-separated list we call the *action*) to be executed, a trigger is said to implement a *procedural constraint*. The DBA can specify the sequence of statements to perform the constraint-implementing program action (although a relatively simple program is most common). The exact forms of statements permitted in the action program of the trigger will probably be the subject of a good deal of further discussion before a final syntax is determined. Certainly all standard SQL statements will be included among the statements provided, but in addition most current database products (**SYBASE**, **ORACLE**, **INGRES**) have a number of procedural extensions to the SQL language that provide local memory-resident variables, permit if-then-else logic, and offer a means to return errors to the caller. In what follows we will assume that statements with these capabilities are available, and provide an imaginary syntax for purposes of discussion. We begin the illustration of triggers by duplicating a few integrity constraints we have seen provided by the Create Table statement. To begin with, here is how a **check** clause might be implemented.

EXAMPLE 6.1.10
Use a trigger to restrict the discnt value of a new customers row to not exceed 15.0.

```
create trigger discntmax after insert on customers
       when (discnt > 15.0) (unwind_statement, return_error(-11101));
```

After each insert to the `customers` table, this trigger tests the search_condition of the **when** clause, "`discnt` > 15.0". to see if it is satisfied for any rows. If any are found, the trigger performs two statements, the first to unwind the statement that is being performed, backing out all newly inserted rows, and the second to return a site-specific error code that application programmers will know how to handle. (Note that the statements used here are not in a supported language standard, but are merely pseudo-code.) A minor variant of this trigger can be used to restrict `discnt` values of greater than 15.0 from arising in the `customers` table as a result of an *update* statement; a change in future syntax will probably allow us to handle both events in one Create Trigger statement. ∎

EXAMPLE 6.1.11

A **unique** value constraint from the Create Table statement can be implemented on the `cid` column of the `customers` table using a slightly more general search condition, one that would not have been permitted by a **check** clause before SQL-92.

```
create trigger uniquecid after update on customers
    referencing new as ncust old as ocust
    when (ncust.cid in (select cid from ocust))
    (unwind_statement, return_error(-11102));
```

Each time a new `cid` value arises in the `customers` table as a result of an Update statement, we test whether the `cid` value existed previously, and if so return a site-specific error code. ∎

To implement a **primary key**, a **foreign key**, and a **references** clause, for the first time we need to reference a second table in our search_condition.

EXAMPLE 6.1.12

Here is how we would implement the policy known as **on delete restrict** in the **DB2** product, where we refuse to perform a delete of a `customers` row that would make `cid` references in the `orders` table invalid.

```
create trigger foreigncid after delete on customers
    when (customers.cid in (select cid from orders))
    (unwind_statement, return_error (-11103));
```
∎

The **set null** policy can also be implemented as a procedure, but the **cascade** policy turns out to be exceptionally difficult to implement procedurally. For this reason, the current thinking on the SQL/3 committee is that the non-procedural actions of SQL-92 will be retained as preferred behavior even after a procedural capability is added.

Pros and Cons of Procedural and Non-Procedural Constraints

All the constraints we have been considering make it important to guard against accidental loss of data integrity due to erroneous SQL update statements. This suggests a preoccupation with errors that might arise from ad hoc SQL updates by casual users, and historically the concept of integrity constraints did arise during a time when casual users were seen to be an important group. Today, most practitioners agree that casual users should not be permitted to perform interactive updates on important tables. It is too easy for a casual user to erroneously change column values in some set of rows to reasonable-seeming values (thus obeying any conceivable constraints) that are, however, *totally wrong!* It is much more appropriate to allow table updates by users to take place only through a program interface, using programs that have been carefully designed so that erroneous changes in the data are unlikely to occur. This being the case, why don't we just rule out ad hoc SQL updates, and leave constraints up to the program logic? Such logic is totally flexible, and would seem to be ideally suited to guarantee whatever integrity rules the DBA might desire.

The danger of course lies in *too much* flexibility. A new programmer who is not aware of all the rules, or even an experienced programmer who allows a subtle bug to slip through, is perfectly capable of subverting the very rules the programs are supposed to maintain. To avoid this, it is possible to develop a programmatic layer through which all database updates must be performed, that will reduce or even eliminate the possibility of such errors; that is, to update a table the application programmer cannot perform an Embedded SQL statement directly, but must call a function layer call, update( ). But providing a strong guarantee of integrity with a flexible and efficient programmatic layer is not a simple design task. The triggers feature was originally meant to provide this same capability in a slightly different but still procedural form.

Clearly, non-procedural constraints that we see in the Create Table statements are of a limited number of types (**check** constraint, **unique** value constraint, **foreign key—references** constraint, etc.). This limits their power, but also guarantees that they are more easily understood than some possibly infinitely variable and complex set of procedural constraints. As we will see, such a limited set of non-procedural constraints can be listed in the same way as data values in system tables (covered later in this chapter), and can be extracted and even updated by a program in response to the needs expressed by someone with DBA privileges. This is an important consideration. All the rules for the system are automatically gathered in a single place and can be examined by the DBA as a whole in an easily understood data-like form.

Another common argument in favor of non-procedural integrity constraints over procedural triggers is that the non-procedural constraints, since they are known directly by the system, can be checked much more efficiently than is possible with procedural logic. This is probably true in many cases, but may be overblown. Often the system needs to do approximately the same work as the procedural logic to implement a comparable constraint, and having the system in charge does not necessarily mean a great deal of performance saving.

Arguing against non-procedural system constraints are examples of the greater power available with procedural constraints. Here are two major areas where non-procedural constraints currently appear deficient.

Specifying Constraint Failure Alternatives. A major weakness of non-procedural constraints as they are currently implemented is that they do not aid in specifying what course the program is to take if the constraint fails. In a database that keeps track of employees, we might wish to create an integrity constraint to ensure that all employee ages are between 18 and 70. But if an automatic routine updates an employees age to 71 on his or her birthday, we would certainly want to take some action other than simply making sure the update fails—we don't want the employee to continue working at the company, simply keeping the recorded age at 70 when the true age has increased. While the constraint makes the update refusal automatic, the alternative action to be performed must be supplied by the application programmer. As another example, we might have a rule to accept only valid name and address data from order entry clerks—for example, to guarantee that the zip code is correct for the state named. (Zip codes do not cross state borders—this constraint could be implemented using referential integrity.) If such a check fails, however, we wouldn't want to simply refuse to accept the data. We would presumably want to call a routine that asked the clerk to re-enter the information, and if the error is repeated, accept it provisionally, possibly in a separate table. After all, data that is not totally accurate may still be of some value to an enterprise, and it might be possible for later analysis to correct the entry. In both of these examples, specifying the test for the non-procedural constraint is the simplest part of the job. The hard part is specifying the course to take if the test fails; clearly a procedural approach is needed for this.

Guaranteeing Transactional Consistency. Another common example of
an important constraint is that of *consistency,* one of the guarantees made
to the programmer in update transactions. For example, in moving money
between different account records in a commercial transaction, a consistency rule might be that money should be neither created nor destroyed.
Application programming managers who are responsible for such update
transactions would be extremely happy about a constraint capability to
catch subtle consistency-breaking program bugs at runtime. However, no
major commercial product provides constraints that apply to interactive
effects between two or more updates at the end of a transaction. While
SQL-92 assertions that are triggered by table updates can be deferred until
a transaction is committed, it is not clear how a consistency rule of this
kind could be guaranteed: there seems to be no way to add up the balance
increments without adding error-prone responsibility to the programs. The
triggers of SQL/3 could conceivably be extended to perform consistency
checks if a final procedure triggered by the Commit Transaction statement
were permitted, but at present it is unclear if a new standard will offer this
capability.

Without a constraint capability to specify alternative actions and test
consistency rules, it is natural to ask the following question: if we leave it
up to the programmers to guarantee the complex rules and handle the difficult alternatives in program logic, why create a separate mechanism for
the simple cases?

A major value of procedurality has to do with convenience in implementing new ideas. While new constraints with any given functionality can
be provided eventually at the system level in any commercial product, the
delay in waiting for a system implementation in a future release is very dis-
heartening. Referential integrity was not provided by **DB2** for several years
after it was raised as an important benefit, and **INGRES** still doesn't have it
as of release 6.3. This area of constraint specification is still in a state of
rapid development, and a complete answer to the questions raised in this
section will probably not be possible until a more unified system is developed. Probably some of the constraints offered to the DBA in the database
system of the future will be extremely common non-procedural ones, and
some constraints to handle more complex situations will be procedural.

6.2 Creating Views

A table defined by the Create Table statement is often referred to as a *base table* in what follows. A base table contains rows that are actually stored on disk, often in the form of physical records with contiguous fields of different types, as specified in the Create Table statement. Now an important property of the relational model is that data retrieved by any SQL Select statement is also in the form of a table, and from here it is a short step to defining the concept of a view table: A *view table* is a table that results from a Select statement, but which can be treated in most ways as if it were a base table. Thus a view table is a logical window on selected data from the base tables of a database that can be named in the **from** clause of other Select statements, and even updated in certain carefully limited cases.

EXAMPLE 6.2.1
Create a view table, called "agentorders," that extends the rows of the orders table to include all information about the agent taking the order. This is done with the SQL Create View statement:

```
create view agentorders (ordno, month, cid, aid, pid, qty, charge,
    aname, acity, percent)
  as select o.ordno, o.month, o.cid, o.aid, o.pid, o.qty, o.dollars,
    a.aname, a.city, a.percent
  from orders o, agents a where o.aid = a.aid;
```

Note that we have given a new name, charge, to the retrieved o.dollars column. All column names in the Select target list except o.aid are unique to their containing table and therefore do not actually require the qualification used in the target list: o.ordno, a.city, etc.   ∎

When the Create View statement is executed, no data is retrieved or stored. Instead, the definition of the view is placed in the system catalogs as a distinct object of the database, to be retrieved later whenever a query or update statement is issued with this view name used in the **from** clause. The database system often simply modifies such a query or update statement—the definition of the view table is taken into account along with the intent of the statement—so that the modified query or update actually performs accesses on base tables. This approach is known as *query modification*.

EXAMPLE 6.2.2

Find the dollar sum of all orders taken by agents in Toledo, using the `agentorders` view table of Example 6.2.1. Here is the query the user would pose:

```
select sum(price) from agentorders where city = 'Toledo';
```

The database (at least conceptually) modifies this query to take account of the definition of the `agentorders` view table in Example 6.2.1, and the resulting modified query is the following (view definition elements substituted are underlined):

```
select sum(o.dollars) from orders o, agents a
    where o.aid = a.aid and city = 'Toledo';                    ■
```

It is extremely important to realize that a view is a *window* on the data of the base tables. We are not taking a snapshot of the data at the time a view is created, but only storing definitions that must be interpreted with each new query; thus queries on views are immediately responsive to changes in the underlying base table data.

The complete description of the Create View statement used in this text is shown in Figure 6.9.

```
create view viewname [(columnname [, columnname])]
    as subselect [with check option];
```

Figure 6.9   Full Create View Syntax

Recall that a Subselect, first defined in Figure 3.11, is missing the **union** and **order by** clauses of the full Select statement, which imposes a limitation on view tables we can define. (SQL-92 adds the ability to use a **union** clause.) The Create View command is legal within a program as an Embedded SQL statement; however, the Subselect statement of the view must not contain any host variables or contain any dynamic parameters. The user creating the view becomes the *owner* of the view and is given update privileges on the view, assuming that the view is updatable (explained below) and that the user has the needed update privileges on the base table on which the view is defined (there will be only one such table).

The optional **with check option** clause specifies that Inserts and Updates performed through the view to result in base table changes should not be permitted if they result in rows that would be invisible to the view Subselect; see Example 6.2.4 for an explanation. Note that the **with check option** clause is not a part of the X/OPEN standard and may not currently exist in all database products; however, it is offered by **ORACLE**, **DB2**, and **INGRES**, and is part of the SQL-89 standard. If the optional *columnname* list in Figure 6.9 is not specified, then the columns of the new view table will inherit names of single columns in the target list of the Subselect statement. However, names must be provided when any view columns represent expressions in the target list. Also, qualifiers that result in unique columnnames in the target list are absent in the inherited view, so we need to create specific column names for a view if the original column names of a target list would become identical without qualifiers.

EXAMPLE 6.2.3

Create a view table, called `cacities`, that lists all pairs of cities from the `customers` and `agents` tables, where the agent places an order for the customer. The following does not work, because it allows the two `city` columns in the resulting view to take on identical names.

```
create view cacities as      /* ILLEGAL VIEW DEFINITION */
    select c.city, a.city
    from customers c, orders o, agents a
    where c.cid=o.cid and o.aid=a.aid;
```

This statement results in a runtime error. We need to specify distinct view `city` names:

```
create view cacities (ccity, acity) as
    select c.city, a.city
    from customers c, orders o, agents a
    where c.cid=o.cid and o.aid=a.aid;
```

∎

As we saw in Figure 6.4, **DB2** has no **check** clause to constrain columns. We can overcome this limitation using views.

EXAMPLE 6.2.4

We show how the functionality of the **check** clause of the Create Table statement can be supplied by a **with check option** clause in a view, as long as all updates are then made through the view. We assume that the table customers has been created as in Example 6.1.2, but with no **check** clause to ensure that discnt <= 15.0. We create the following view:

```
create view custs as select * from customers
    where discnt <= 15.0 with check option;
```

Now any update of custs that would result in a row in customers with discnt > 15.0 fails, because the resulting row would be invisible to the view. Consider the update:

```
update custs set discnt = discnt + 4.0;
```

This update fails for customer c002 on the basis of the values of Figure 2.2, because the resulting discnt value would be 16.0, and therefore invisible to the view. If the **check option** fails for any row of an update statement, an error occurs and no changes are made to the table.   ∎

As we will explain shortly, not all views can accept updates and translate them into updates on the base tables. Views that permit this are called *updatable views*. Note that it is entirely possible to create a view based on other views—that is, to create nested view definitions.

EXAMPLE 6.2.5

Create a view table, called acorders, that gives all order information and names of agent and customer involved in the order:

```
create view acorders (ordno, month, cid, aid, pid, qty,
        dollars, aname, cname)
as select ao.ordno, ao.month, ao.cid, ao.aid, ao.pid, ao.qty,
        ao.dollars, ao.aname, c.cname
from agentorders ao, customers c where ao.cid = c.cid;
```

As we see, the view agentorders of Example 6.2.1 is used in the **from** list of the acorders view definition.   ∎

Listing Defined Views

The standard method of listing all accessible views in a database is to use a Select statement to retrieve view names from the system catalogs, a set of system-maintained tables listing defined objects that is explained later in this chapter. For example, the X/OPEN standard would use the following statement to list views:

```
select tablename from tables where table_type = 'VIEW';
```

The different database products have different names and structures for their system catalog tables. In **ORACLE**, we might write (alternatives exist):

```
select viewname from user_views;
```

In **INGRES**, we could write:

```
select tablename from iitables where table_type = 'V';
```

In general the definition of various named views can also be retrieved from system catalog tables. In some products a help facility also exists to provide information about defined objects. In **INGRES**, for example, to get a list of all view tables in existence in a database, you would give the monitor command:

```
help\g
```

INGRES prints out a list of tables and views, naming the owner and whether each is a table or view. To list the definition of a view in **INGRES**, you would give the command:

```
help view viewname\g
```

Deleting Views

The standard SQL statement used to delete a view definition from the system catalogs is basically the same Drop statement form that is used to drop a table. The complete description of the Drop statement is

```
drop [table tablename | view viewname | index indexname]
```

Only the owner of a table, view, or index (usually the original creator) is authorized to drop it. We will explain the meaning of an index, the third type of object that can be dropped, in Chapter 7. Most products use the

Drop statement to delete other types of objects from the system catalogs as well (tablespaces, aliases, etc.), but these three objects are all part of the X/OPEN standard.

When a view or table is dropped, there is some question of what happens to other objects whose definitions depend on it. The X/OPEN standard actually adds an optional choice after the tablename and viewname, [cascade | restrict]. If **cascade** is included, then other objects depending on the object to be dropped are also dropped; and if **restrict** is used, then the object cannot be dropped while other dependencies exist. None of the products we are tracking—**ORACLE**, **INGRES**, or **DB2**—currently offer this option. Rather unexpectedly compared to referential integrity constraints, **cascade** behavior is presumed with the Drop statement.

Restrictions on Querying and Updating a View

Views are not as flexible as base tables in every respect. Some queries do not work on certain kinds of views. As for updates, some views cannot be updated at all, while others do not accept all possible update statements that a base table with the same columns and row content would accept. The best reason for not accepting update statements is if it is not clear how to translate an update statement on a view into unique updates of the underlying base tables in a way that will reflect the intention of the view creator and the user posing the update statement. The most stringent restrictions on view access appear in standards such as X/OPEN and ANSI SQL. This is because the earlier SQL standards were intended to describe SQL capabilities that *all* database systems are capable of supporting. Surprisingly, even the SQL-92 standard does not extend the power of view updates to any appreciable extent, and this is certainly one of the greatest current weaknesses in database standards. Some of the more sophisticated commercial systems do allow additional view update capabilities, thus weakening the restrictions given in the standards.

Select Statements from Grouped Views

We start by describing restrictions on Select statements from the X/OPEN standard. A *grouped view* is a view whose defining Subselect contains a **group by** clause. The grouped view restriction rules of Figure 6.10 apply in valid Select statements from a grouped view.

If a Select statement references a grouped view in its **from** clause:

[1] The **from** clause should mention only that single view table.

[2] The Select statement cannot contain a **where**, **group by**, or **having** clause.

[3] The target list cannot contain a set function.

Figure 6.10 X/OPEN Restrictions on Select Statements from a Grouped View

The following example illustrates some of the problems these grouped view rules are intended to address.

EXAMPLE 6.2.6

Let us define a view table, called `agentsales`, whose rows contain `aid` values of `agents` who have taken orders, together with their total dollar sales:

```
create view agentsales (aid, totsales) as select aid, sum(dollars)
    from orders group by aid;
```

Now the grouped view rule 3 of Figure 6.10 disallows the use of set functions retrieval from such a view, so we are unable to write:

```
select avg(totsales) from agentsales; /* ILLEGAL SYNTAX */
```

A possible reason for this restriction is that this query would translate through query modification to a nesting of set functions on the base table:

```
select avg(select sum(dollars) from orders
    group by aid);                      /* ILLEGAL SYNTAX */
```

As we mentioned in Example 3.10.4, when we were investigating the power of the Select statement, such nesting is not possible in SQL. Of course, this is not a very good reason for such a restriction—there is nothing conceptually difficult about the average of totsales over the view table created—as mentioned earlier, standard SQL view restrictions have been designed for the lowest common denominator of database product, based on rather simple-minded query modification algorithms. Because of this, a number of restrictions on view access are unnecessarily strict.

A second restriction of X/OPEN SQL disallows a **where** clause in selecting from `agentsales`. For example, the following query is illegal:

```
select * from agentsales
    where totsales > 1000.00;        /* ILLEGAL SYNTAX */
```

Since `totsales` is actually a set function reference on the `orders` table, this statement would result in the following query against the base table, assuming rather simple-minded query modification.

```
select aid, sum(dollars) as totsales from orders
    where sum(dollars) > 1000.00 group by aid;/* ILLEGAL SYNTAX */
```

However, set functions are not permitted in the **where** clause, so this query is illegal. It is perfectly possible to achieve the aim of this query in a different way, by writing:

```
select aid, sum(dollars) as totsales from orders
    group by aid having sum(dollars) > 1000.;
```

so the restriction is unnecessarily strict in this case as well.   ∎

We leave possible explanations of other illegal Selects from a grouped view as an exercise for the reader. Why should there be no other table or view mentioned in the **from** clause, for example?   The reader should beware of one possible misapprehension in interpreting the rules of Figure 6.10. These rules do *not* apply to Select statements that use a **group by** clause in retrieving from a nongrouped view. It is only when the view definition itself contains a **group by** clause that these rules come into play.

Updatable and Read-Only Views

In X/OPEN SQL, a view table is either updatable or read-only. Insert, Update, and Delete operations are permitted for updatable views and not permitted for read-only views (note that all base tables are considered updatable). Figure 6.11 gives the rules that must be followed for a view table to be updatable.

A view table is said to be *updatable* when the following conditions hold for its Sub-select clause:

[1] The **from** clause of the Subselect must contain only a single table, and if that table is a view table it must also be an updatable view table.

[2] Neither the **group by** nor the **having** clause is present.

[3] The **distinct** keyword is not specified.

[4] The **where** clause does not contain a Subselect.

[5] All result columns of the Subselect are simple column names (that is, there are no arithmetic expressions such as `avg(qty)` or `qty+100`), and no column name appears more than once in distinct result columns.

Figure 6.11 Restrictions on the Subselect Clause for an Updatable View

Let us illustrate the reason for some of these restrictions with examples.

EXAMPLE 6.2.7

Consider following the view definition, called `colocated`:

```
create view colocated as select cid, cname, aid, aname, a.city
    from customers c, agents a where c.city = a.city;
```

This view lists customers and agents who are located in the same city, so they can be invited out and introduced by visiting executives. Assuming the CAP database content of Figure 2.2, two rows that exist in this view are

```
c002    Basics    a06    Smith    Dallas
```

and

```
c003    Allied    a06    Smith    Dallas
```

However, the view definition breaks rule 1 above, in that there are more than two tables in the **from** clause, and therefore the view table is restricted to being read-only, not updatable. Let us try to understand this restriction by investigating some update statements as they would apply to the view. We start by asking the question, What update should occur on the base tables if we give the command to update the `aname` in the second row listed above (specified as the row with `cid = 'c003'` and `aid = 'a06'`), changing it from Smith to Franklin? Clearly if agent a06 changes its name to Franklin, the first row above will also change, so a row update on such a view can have unexpected side effects on other rows. This is not the sort of behavior we expect from a base table.

A slightly different consideration applies to performing a delete of the second row. Exactly what update needs to be applied to the base tables to achieve this? Do we need to delete the whole `customers` row for c003, or the whole `agents` row for a06, or change the `city` value of one of them (to what?), or something else entirely? Similarly, if we try to insert a new row:

```
c003    Allied    a12    Watanabe    Dallas
```

this insert seems to create a new row in the `agents` table, a12 Watanabe Dallas, with the `percent` field left null. Fine, but doesn't this have unexpected side effects in that we now also have to insert a row to pair customer c002 with agent a12 in our view?

To avoid complications of this kind, the standards restrict the **from** clauses to a single table. More sophisticated approaches are taken in some database system products that allow some updates on join views, but do not discuss them in this text. ∎

Here is another example to illustrate the reason for rule 2 in Figure 6.11.

EXAMPLE 6.2.8

Recall the `agentsales` view of Example 6.2.6, defined as

```
create view agentsales (aid, totsales) as select aid, sum(dollars)
    from orders group by aid;
```

Rule 2 above implies that this view is not updatable since the **group by** clause is present. The reason for this restriction is that once again it is impossible to perform an update on this view that would be straightforward for a base table. For example, assume that we want to increment the total sales of agent a01 by $1000.00 through the `agentsales` table.

```
update agentsales
    set totsales = totsales + 1000.00; /* ILLEGAL SYNTAX */
```

The problem with this update is that we can't figure out how to add needed information to make the change "take" on the base table, `orders`. What are the `cid` and `pid` values for the order that was added to the `orders` table for agent a01? Is there indeed only a single order, or are there several? Or perhaps one or more of the dollars rows in `orders` was updated to larger values? We don't know. ∎

To reiterate, we cannot make updates "take" on a view if we can't figure out exactly what changes the update should create for some underlying base table. Thus rule 3, which restricts updatable tables to have no distinct keyword, is easily understood. If the resulting table view contains a single row where two or more existed in the base table, how are we to decide what to do with a request that updates one of the attributes of that specific row? Should we update one of the rows of the underlying base table, or all such rows?

The Value of Views

Chapter 1 mentioned some problems that arise out of centralized control of data. The first was logical complexity. For example, an application to validate insurance payments for university students may have to deal with dozens of tables to access needed column information, and many of these tables may have names and uses completely unrelated to health insurance. As a result, it can be quite difficult to train new application programmers to navigate among the many tables involved. A second aim of centralized control is a desire for phased implementation, where the benefits of centralization accrue in a number of steps as new databases are combined. We don't want to have to rewrite old applications as newer tables appear to eliminate data redundancy, with new column names that must be accessed in place of older columns. Ideally we would like some way to ensure that growing numbers of tables do not cause a training problem, and also that old application code does not have to change as old tables are rearranged to eliminate redundant data and new table columns appear to take their place. Views are generally used to handle both of these problems, and others as well.

[1]   Views provide a way to make complex, commonly issued queries easier to compose. We saw this in Example 6.2.2, where we were able to pose the query:

```
select sum(price) from agentorders where city = 'Toledo';
```

instead of

```
select sum(o.dollars) from orders o, agents a
    where o.aid = a.aid and a.city = 'Toledo';
```

Rather than specify a join of tables and a complex search_condition in nearly every query, it is possible to hide this complexity in a view and depend on subsequent query modifications performed invisibly by the system. (In real applications, much greater complexity is frequently hidden in views.)

[2] Views allow obsolete tables, and programs that reference them, to survive reorganization. Imagine reorganizing the orders table as a new table, ords:

```
create table ords ( ordno integer not null, month char(3),
    custid char(4) not null, agentid char(3) not null,
    prodid char(3) not null,
    quantity integer default null check(quantity >= 0),
    primary key ( ordno ),
    foreign key (cid) references customers,
    foreign key (aid) references agents,
    foreign key (pid) references products);
```

We have performed a few minor renamings of the cid, aid, and pid columns and done away with the dollars column from orders; we now intend to derive the dollars total for each orders row by multiplying the quantity value by the cost of the product ordered. If a large number of programs are accessing the old-style orders table, we can create a view for use by these programs defined in terms of the newly reorganized ords table and the products table.

```
create view orders (ordno, month, cid, aid, pid, qty,
dollars) as
    select ordno, month, custid, agentid prodid, quantity,
    quantity*cost
    from products p, ords m where m.prodid = p.pid;
```

In this way we make the program's view of the data independent of changes in the physical structure, a feature mentioned earlier as program-data independence (Definition 1.4.1). Note that the independence is not complete: since the Subselect of the orders view contains two tables, updates through the orders view are not possible, so the program logic that enters new orders must be rewritten.

[3] Views add a security aspect to allow different users to see the same data in different ways. Centralized control of data provides support for an important principle of data management: there should be only one copy of any piece of information crucial to the enterprise. The risk is that with more than one copy, versions might get out of synchronization (the same stock might be listed with two different prices by a brokerage), and bad decisions might result. However, it is also the case that not everyone should have access to every piece of information. An employee row might have an office number and location, facts that should be available to fellow employees; salary data, which should be available only to managers, the human resources department, and accounting; and performance review ratings, which should be available only to managers and human resources.

We can create different views of the same employees table and associate security for different user classes to access these views: see the Grant statement for granting security authorization, discussed in the next section. In granting access to a view for a user class and restricting access to the underlying base tables, we automatically provide security for fields not named in the view.

6.3 Security: The Grant Statement in SQL

The Grant statement is an SQL command issued by the owner of a table (base table or view table) to authorize various kinds of access (select, update, delete, or insert) to the table by another user or class of users. It is a form of table access security, but column access can also be implemented through views. The other user must already be able to enter the database containing the table, an authorization provided by the database administrator.

EXAMPLE 6.3.1
The owner of the customers table wishes to give select-only access to the user with logon ID "eoneil".

```
grant select on customers to eoneil;
```
■

The general form of the Grant command in the SQL-89 standard
(slightly more general than the X/OPEN standard) is

```
grant {all privileges | privilege {, privilege}}
    on tablename | viewname
    to {public | user-name {, user-name} } [with grant option]
```

The Grant command either grants all types of access privileges, or else a
comma-separated list of privileges from the following set:

```
select
delete
insert
update [columnname {, columnname . . . }]
references [columnname {, columnname . . . }]
```

The privileges named (select, delete, . . .) give authorization to all
present and future users (in the case of **public**) or else to the list of user-
names specified, to use the corresponding SQL statement with this table-
name/viewname as an object; the references privilege (supported in **ORA-
CLE** but not in **INGRES**, **DB2**, or **SYBASE**) gives a user authorization to
create a foreign key constraint in another table that refers to this table. If
the columnname list is not specified with the update privilege, then authorization is given to update *all* present or future columns in the table. The
optional **with grant option** clause provides the user(s) receiving these privileges the additional authority to grant other users these same privileges.
Note that the **grant option** clause is not included in the X/OPEN SQL standard, and in particular it is not supported by **INGRES**, although **DB2** and
ORACLE allow it. A Grant statement can be issued in Embedded SQL.
The owner of a table automatically has all privileges, and they cannot
be revoked. To grant privileges on a viewed table to other users, the
granter must own the viewed table (and have necessary privileges on all
tables from which the view is derived), or else must have been granted
these privileges with a **with grant option** clause. To grant the insert, delete,
or update privilege on a viewed table, the table must be updatable.

EXAMPLE 6.3.2
Grant permission to select, update, or insert, but not to delete to eoneil, on the table orders. Then give eoneil authorization for all operations on the products table.

```
grant select, update, insert on orders to eoneil;
grant all on products to eoneil;
```
∎

We can combine the idea of creating views with the Grant statement to provide field security. A Grant statement to provide privileges on a view will have the desired effect without granting privileges on the underlying view or base table.

EXAMPLE 6.3.3
Grant permission to user eoneil on the customers table to insert or delete any row, update only the cname and city columns, and select all columns other than the discnt column. Since there is no field specification associated with the select privilege, the owner first creates a view, named custview:

```
create view custview as select cid, cname, city from customers;
```

Now the owner provides the necessary authorization on custview:

```
grant select, delete, insert, update (cname, city) on custview
    to eoneil;
```

Since eoneil has not been granted any privileges on the base table customers, the discnt column values cannot be selected by eoneil.
∎

It is also possible, using a view, to grant authorization on a selected subset of rows from a table.

EXAMPLE 6.3.4
Grant permission to user eoneil to perform all accesses on agents with percent greater than 5.

```
create view agentview as select * from agents where percent > 5;
grant all on agentview to eoneil;
```
∎

The SQL statement to revoke privileges on a table has the following general form in X/OPEN standard SQL:

```
revoke {all privileges | privilege {, privilege . . .} }
    on tablename | viewname
    from {public | user-name {, user-name . . .} }
    [cascade | restrict];
```

The Revoke statement can revoke a subset of privileges earlier granted to a user. Unlike the Grant statement, the Revoke statement cannot specify specific columnnames in revoking update privileges. The owner of a table automatically has all privileges, and they cannot be revoked. The Revoke statement can be issued in Embedded SQL, and an attempt to revoke privileges that were not previously granted results in an sqlwarning condition, not an sqlerror.

Note that neither **ORACLE** nor **DB2** implements the optional [cascade | restrict] clause, while **INGRES** doesn't support the syntax of the Revoke command, as explained below. The effect of the **cascade** option is to revoke privileges or drop views that depended on the privilege currently being dropped (to create a view, one must have a **select** privilege on an underlying table), while the **restrict** option retains those objects, created in the past, that are dependent in this way. If neither **cascade** nor **restrict** is specified, effects of this kind differ among different commercial database system products.

INGRES does not have the Revoke statement. In **INGRES** one can list all privileges that have been granted on a table with the command:

```
help permit tablename\g
```

A list of privileges (permits) on this table is printed, numbered by integers on the left. A privilege can then be revoked by typing

```
drop permit on tablename integer {, integer};
```

where the command lists all integers numbering permits retrieved through the List Permit command.

Variations in Database Products

The **INGRES** product has approximately the capabilities supported in the X/OPEN SQL standard for the Grant and Revoke statements (the **with grant option** clause and the *references* privilege are not supported). However, **DB2** and **ORACLE** have a large number of additional privileges. For example, **ORACLE** has something called a *DBA* privilege that is needed to run most of the SQL commands in this chapter. In addition, a *connect* privilege in a database in **ORACLE** allows a user to enter a database, and the *resource* privilege permits the user to create database objects such as tables and indexes that take up disk resources. For details of such **ORACLE** capabilities, the user is referred to the *ORACLE SQL Language Reference Manual* [13] and the *ORACLE RDBMS Database Administrator's Guide* [12].

 DB2 has an even wider selection of privileges that are allocated through the Grant statement. There are five general classes: database privileges, plan privileges, system privileges, table privileges, and use privileges. *Database* privileges usually grant authority to perform specific commands on named databases. For example, the *load* privilege gives the user authority to use the LOAD utility to load tables. There is also a *dbadm* privilege, somewhat weaker than the **ORACLE** DBA authority. *Plan* privileges grant authority to perform operations on objects known as plans. These are procedural plans for physical data access that are created by the query optimizer on the basis of SQL access statements and underlying indexes on the database tables accessed. *System* privileges are authorizations that are not limited to an individual database, such as the authority to create new databases and take on DBADM authority. In addition, the *sysadm* privilege gives the user *all* privileges and the ability to grant them. *Table* privileges are the kind of we have presented in this section. *Use* privileges allow the user to use disk space in creating database objects such as indexes. For operational details of such **DB2** capabilities, the user is referred to the *DB2 SQL Reference Manual* [4].

6.4   System Catalogs

All relational database systems maintain system catalogs, tables maintained by the system that contain information about objects defined in the database. Such objects include tables defined with the Create Table statement, columns, indexes, views, privileges, constraints, and so on. For example, the TABLES catalog table contains one row with information about each table defined. A DBA visiting from another site could conceivably reference catalog tables to learn about the local table layout. The DBA would use normal SQL Select statements to retrieve this information—for example, select TABLENAME from TABLES. An application program executing Dynamic SQL might need to access catalog tables to make certain decisions—for example, to learn the number and names of columns defined in a specific table. The database system itself uses these catalog tables as a basis for translating queries on views and imposing constraints on runtime update statements. (We need to be careful in saying this, however, since the system may use a more efficient method for such purposes than access through a Select statement to character columns of the catalog tables. A catalog table can be thought of as an analog to program source code, and some type of compilation may be required for efficient execution—for example, to allow the system to respond to submitted dynamic update statements by retrieving all constraints that can apply.)

Every commercial database system has a different set of catalog table names with different structures and refers to them with different terminology. **DB2** refers to *catalog tables;* **INGRES** to *system catalogs* (which are tables); **ORACLE** to the *data dictionary* (which is a set of system-maintained views); and the X/OPEN standard to *system views*. The catalog tables are created at the time that a database is created, and the underlying base tables of the catalog are meant to be updated only by the system in response to data definition statements and a few other statement types. The user is not supposed to update catalog tables directly, as this may compromise data integrity (for example, if a user were to delete a row in TABLES with a table object that has not been dropped). Some systems give the user access to the catalogs only through read-only views (with only **select** privilege for **public**) in order to guarantee that no updates can occur.

The information contained in catalog tables is sometimes called *metadata*, meaning that it is "data about data." The metadata is even self-descriptive, in that the TABLES catalog table contains a row for the table TABLES (possibly a view type of table if that is how TABLES is defined). In what follows, we give catalog table names in uppercase, and note that all object identifiers are carried in the catalogs in uppercase as well. Thus if a user were to define the orders table with Create Table, the name would be entered into TABLES as ORDERS. The same rule holds if the user were to define the table name in mixed case—Orders or OrdErs; the object catalogued would be ORDERS.

Catalog Variations in Database Products

Since each database product has different conventions for its catalog tables, the standards are only able to give an idea of what tables and columns *must* exist. The following section contains short descriptions of the catalog tables in **ORACLE**, **DB2**, and **INGRES**. These descriptions are not by any means complete, and the reader is referred to the appropriate product manual for details.

The ORACLE Data Dictionary

The **ORACLE** data dictionary consists of views, many of which have three different forms distinguished by their prefixes:

Prefix	Purpose
USER_	User's view (objects owned by the user)
ALL_	Expanded user's view (objects that the user can access)
DBA_	DBA's view (all user and system objects)

For example, the dictionary has the views USER_TABLES, ALL_TABLES, and DBA_TABLES. The ALL_TABLES and DBA_TABLES views contain over a dozen columns, many of which have to do with disk storage and update transaction clauses of the Create Table statement that we have deferred. Columns of interest are these:)

ALL_TABLES (or DBA_TABLES

Column name	Description
OWNER	Owner of the table
TABLENAME	Name of the table
(other columns)	Disk storage and update transaction information

The USER_TABLES view would differ from the ALL_TABLES view by not having the OWNER column, since the owner is the current user by definition. (In fact, the USER_TABLES view could be defined in terms of the

ALL_TABLES view, with OWNER = current_user selected and the
OWNER column left out of the result.)

Information about columns of all tables and views (and clusters, **ORA-CLE**-specific structures) accessible to the user is kept in the ACCESSIBLE_COLUMNS view, a standard ANSI catalog name, and in the identical synonym view ALL_TAB_COLUMNS. The DBA_TAB_-COLUMNS has the same structure, and USER_TAB_COLUMNS is the same except for a missing OWNER column.

ALL_TAB_COLUMNS (or ACCESSIBLE_COLUMNS)

Column name	Description
OWNER	Owner of the table, view, or cluster
TABLENAME	Name of the table, view, or cluster containing the column
COLUMN_NAME	Column name
DATA_TYPE	Datatype of the column
DATA_LENGTH	Length of the column in bytes
(other columns)	Other properties: nullable? default value? etc.

The primary key for ALL_TAB_COLUMNS clearly includes TABLE-NAME and COLUMN_NAME, since it is possible to have identical column names for different tables. It is also possible to duplicate table names with different users; to distinguish such names in SQL, the tables may be qualified by user names: username.tablename. Thus to access all column-names in the orders table created by poneil (where you are not the user poneil, but have access to that orders table), we could use the Select statement:

```
select COLUMN_NAME from ALL_TAB_COLUMNS
    where OWNER = 'PONEIL' and TABLENAME = 'ORDERS';
```

ORACLE also has catalog views known as ALL_TAB_COMMENTS and ALL_COL_COMMENTS (and associated USER_ and DBA_ variants) to contain descriptions of the tables and columns that expand on their purpose and use for a hypothetical visiting DBA. The **ORACLE** language has a nonstandard SQL statement, **comment on** tablename | tablename.column-name **is** 'text', by which a text comment can be associated with such tables or columns.

In addition, **ORACLE** has the relatively standard catalog views; TABLE_PRIVILEGES (or ALL_TAB_GRANTS) and COLUMN_PRIV-ILEGES (or ALL_COL_GRANTS), listing privileges granted on accessible tables, as well as CONSTRAINT_DEFS (or ALL_CONSTRAINTS), listing constraints on accessible tables. The DICTIONARY view lists all data dictionary table and view names (TABLE_NAMES) and descriptive comments (COMMENTS), and DICT_COLUMNS view lists all columns in such dictionary columns and views (TABLENAME, COLUMN_NAME as primary key), along with descriptive comments (COMMENTS column). A number of other objects that we have not yet covered, such as indexes, are also listed in the catalog. They will be explained as needed. Information about users and performance statistics are also contained in the data dictionary.

For detailed information about the **ORACLE** data dictionary, see the *ORACLE RDBMS Database Administrator's Guide* [12].

The DB2 Catalog Tables

The **DB2** product contains an almost overwhelming set of catalog tables and defined columns within those tables. The user can access these tables with a SYSIBM qualifier. For example, to list all columns in the orders table created by poneil, we would write:

```
select NAME from SYSIBM.SYSCOLUMNS
     where TBCREATOR = 'PONEIL' and TBNAME = 'ORDERS';
```

DB2 has catalog tables for tables (SYSTABLES), columns within tables (SYSCOLUMNS), views (SYSVIEWS), and privileges held on tables and views (SYSTABAUTH). Various types of constraints are held in distinct tables—for example, SYSFOREIGNKEYS contains one row for each column of every foreign key. **DB2** also uses catalog tables to contain access plans created for static Embedded SQL statements. We will discuss such access plans later in the text.

For detailed information about the **DB2** catalog, see the *DB2 SQL Reference Manual* [4] and the *DB2 Administrator's Guide* [2].

The INGRES System Catalogs

INGRES system catalogs depart from the standard in that they use lower-case names. All catalog tables begin with the letters "ii. . .". Important tables include iitables, iicolumns, and iiviews. The iitables catalog, for example, actually contains information about views and indexes.

iitables

Column name	Description
tablename	The object's name
table_owner	User name for owner of the object
create_date	Creation data for object, blank if not known
alter_date	Last alteration date for object
table_type	Type of object: T for table, V for view, I for index
(other columns)	Other properties

For detailed information about the **INGRES** system catalogs, see the *INGRES SQL Reference Manual* [8].

Suggestions for Further Reading

The various SQL standards and individual product SQL manuals referenced in Chapters 3 and 4 continue to be useful. New reference manuals for the DBA are cited in bold type in the following list. You will also need to have access to the error code reference manuals for the specific products you work with.

[1] C. J. Date. *A Guide to the SQL Standard (SQL-89)*, 2nd ed. Reading, MA: Addison-Wesley, 1989. (The second edition covers the SQL-89 standard; later editions do not.)

[2] *DB2 Administrator's Guide.* (See Chapter 4, "Designing a Database.")

[3] *DB2 Application Programming Guide*, version 2.3. (Details of Embedded SQL, with C language specifics.)

[4] *DB2 SQL Reference Manual*, version 2.3.

[5] *INGRES/Embedded SQL Companion Guide for C*, release 6.4, UNIX. Alameda, CA: ASK Group.

436

[6] *INGRES/Embedded SQL User's Guide and Reference Manual,* release 6.4, UNIX. Alameda, CA: ASK Group.

[7] *INGRES/Error Message Directory,* release 6, VAX/VMS, UNIX. Alameda, CA: ASK Group.

[8] *INGRES/SQL Reference Manual,* release 6.4, UNIX. Alameda, CA: ASK Group. (Contains many INGRES DBA details.)

[9] Jim Melton and Alan R. Simon. *Understanding the New SQL (SQL-92).* San Francisco: Morgan Kaufmann, 1993.

[10] *ORACLE Error Messages and Codes Manual,* version 6.0. Redwood Shores, CA: Oracle.

[11] *ORACLE Programmer's Guide to the ORACLE Precompilers,* version 1.3. Redwood Shores, CA: Oracle. (General Embedded SQL.)

[12] *ORACLE RDBMS Database Administrator's Guide.* Redwood Shores, CA: Oracle.

[13] *ORACLE SQL Language Reference Manual,* version 6.0. Redwood Shores, CA: Oracle.

[14] *Pro*C Supplement to the ORACLE Precompilers Guide,* version 1.3.

[15] *Structured Query Language (SQL).* X/Open Company, Ltd.

Exercises

Exercises with solutions at the back of the book in "Solutions to Selected Exercises" are marked with the symbol •.

In the following exercises, unless otherwise specified, you should always assume that the X/OPEN standard syntax is to be used for all SQL statements.

[6.1] (a)• Provide a reasonable Create Table statement with integrity constraints for the `agents` table and `products` table to go with the `customers` and `orders` definitions of Example 6.1.2. You should make sure that `percent` remains between 0 and 10, and that `quantity` and `price` are always greater than zero (give zero values of the proper datatype form).

(b) Assume that the DBA wants the possible discnt values for customers to be between 0.00 and 10.00, with values that differ only by 0.02, so that acceptable values are 0.00, 0.02, 0.04, . . . , 9.96, 9.98, 10.00. Show how you would be able to achieve a constraint of this kind using appropriate Create Table statements. Note that it is *not* appropriate to try to use a **check** clause for such a large number of possible values; you need to define and load another table to impose this constraint.

[6.2] Provide Create Table statements to define the tables passengers, gates, flights, and seats at the end of Section 5.4. Try to create tables that faithfully represent the cardinalities of entity-relationship participation in Figure 5.14.

[6.3] • Fill in missing cardinalities of entity-relationship participation in Figure 5.11, then perform a relational table design, and finally give the Create Table statements you would use to faithfully represent this design.

[6.4] In which of the following cases (a), (b), and (c) is it possible to faithfully represent mandatory participation of an entity in a relationship, using constraints provided in the Create Table statement?

(a)• When the entity is on the "one" side of an N-1 relationship.

(b) When the entity is on the "many" side of an N-1 relationship.

(c)• When the entity is on either side of an N-N relationship.

(d) With referential integrity, we can guarantee that a foreign key of a table (which might represent a relationship instance) refers to a real primary key in another table (which might represent an entity participating in that relationship). Unfortunately, referential integrity cannot be used to guarantee mandatory participation of the entity in the relationship. Can you describe a new (imaginary) type of integrity that you would invent to achieve this type of constraint?

[6.5] (a) Which of the following SQL statements are legal, given current restrictions for querying and updating a view? (The example where the view is created is specified in parentheses.)

    (i) `update agentorders set month = 'jun';` (Example 6.2.1.)

    (ii) `select sum(dollars) from acorders group by aid;` (Example 6.2.5)

    (iii) `select aid, totsales from agentsales where aid = 'a03' or aid = 'a04';` (Example 6.2.6.)

(b)• Assume that we have failed to include an integrity constraint in the Create Table statement of Exercise 6.1(a), to limit the value of the `percent` column. Create a view, `agentview` on the table `agents`, that is updatable and will keep any user who updates `agentview` from changing the `percent` column to a value less than zero or greater than ten.

(c) Under the same assumption that we have a missing integrity constraint on the `percent` column for `agents`, there is a way in **ORACLE** to *add* this integrity constraint to the table without re-creating the table. Give the necessary **ORACLE** command.

(d)• We would like to issue a sequence of two statements to grant privileges to a user named Beowulf to be able to look at the `products` table columns `pid`, `pname`, `city`, and `quantity` (but not `price`), and update either of the columns `city` and `quantity` (but no others). Give the statements you would use to accomplish this.

[6.6] Answer the following true/false questions, and explain your answers. Try to cite a section of the text (definition, example, figure, or any discussion on a specified page) that supports your answer.

(a)• A row of a table is allowed to have a null value in one of the columns making up the primary key for the table. True or false?

(b) A row of a table is allowed to have a null value in one of the columns making up a foreign key defined for the table. True or false?

(c)• In the X/OPEN standard Create Table syntax, it is possible to impose a **foreign key . . . references** constraint with a special Select statement constraint under a **check** clause. True or false?

(d) Although there is a way in X/OPEN to impose a constraint that defines a primary key, there is no way to define other "candidate" keys in a table. True or false?

Questions (e) through (g) refer to details covered in "Restrictions on Querying and Updating a View," specific to the X/OPEN standard.

(e)• The following query is legal: `select count(*) from colocated group by aid`; True or false? (The view `colocated` is defined in Example 6.2.7.)

(f) The following query is legal: `update acorders set qty = qty + 1 where ordno = 1124`; True or false? (The view `acorders` is defined in Example 6.2.5.)

(g)• The following query is legal: `select totsales from agentsales where aid = 'a04'`; True or false? (The view `agentsales` is defined in Example 6.2.6.)

[6.7] One of the database products allows the DBA to specify in its integrity constraints the action to take when a row is deleted from one table whose primary key value might be referenced by foreign key values of rows in another table.

(a)• Name the actions that are possible.

(b) Name the action that is performed by default in other SQL products.

(c) Referring to the CAP database content in Figure 2.2, state in words what would happen if there were an attempt to delete customer c001 and the action named in (b) were in effect.

[6.8] • Give **INGRES** statements you would use to create the table `customers` and impose the constraints analogous to the X/OPEN constraints of Example 6.1.2. Hint: You will need at least two statements — how do you guarantee that `cid` is unique?

[6.9] Assume that we have a table `employees`, with columns `eid`, `ename`, and `mgrid`, and the float columns `salary1` and `salary2`, where there are two different kinds of salary (perhaps for different work projects). Now assume a Create View statement that creates a view `emps`:

```
create view emps (eid, ename, mgrid, totsal) as
    select eid, ename, mgrid, salary1 + salary2;
```

This is not an updatable view. What is the rule that is broken? Explain why this rule is a good idea by giving an example of an update on the `emps` view that is difficult to translate into changes on the base table `employees` (that is, the changes that should be made to the underlying `employees` table are not clear).

[6.10] (HARD) Example 6.2.7 shows us a view, `colocated`, where a join of two tables `customers` and `agents` by the `city` columns leads to unexpected results when we try to delete a row or update a column. But what if we defined a view, `agentords`, based on a join on the column `aid` between `agents` and `orders` (the natural foreign key to primary key join). We want to justify permitting updates on a natural view of this kind, by considering updates, deletes, and inserts on the resulting View table. Come up with a reasonable interpretation of what *should* happen to the base tables as a result of each operation on the view. Note that some difference of opinion is possible.

(a)• In the case of inserts, consider what happens if a new `aid` value is inserted or an old `aid` value is inserted, possibly with a different `aname`. (What do you think should happen, based on functional dependencies?)

(b) What should you do about deletes?

(c) In the case of updates, consider separately non-key columns that are part of `agents` and non-key columns that are part of `orders` key columns `aid`, `cid`, and `pid`.

Machine Assignments. Create procedures or programs for the following exercises.

[6.11] In the interactive monitor for your class database system connected to the CAP database, give a command to list all views. You may need to query the system catalog. Now create a view, `custview`, based on the `customers` table that selects rows with `discnt < 12.0`, and add the "with check option" clause to the view definition. List views again to see that `custview` has been added. Perform the Select statement `select * from custview`. Next, try to update `custview` so that the `customers` row with `cid` equal to c001 gets a `discnt` equal to 13.0. Does the update "take"? Show that it doesn't by typing "`select * from customers`". Now re-create the `custview` without the check option (you'll have to drop the old one first) and try the update again. Show that it works this time. Leave the `customers` table in this modified state for the time being.

[6.12] •In your terminal monitor, issue a command to list all integrity constraints. You may need to query the system catalog. Now create an integrity constraint on the `customers` table to require that `discnt <= 12.0`. Does this work? What happens? Now update `customers` so that the `customers` row with `cid` equal to c001 has value 10.0, and try again to create the integrity constraint. Next, try to update `customers` so that the `customers` row with `cid` equal to c001 has `discnt` equal to 16.0. Does the update "take"? Show that it doesn't by typing "`select * from customers`". Now remove the constraint and try the update again, showing that it is successful this time. Finally, perform the `customers` table load to bring all `customers` table values back to their original value.

[6.13] (a)• Insert a new row in the `orders` table: 1031, jul, c001, a01, p01, 1000, 450.00. Now create a view called `returns` based on `orders` that shows columns `ordno`, `month`, `cid`, `aid`, `pid`, `qty`, `dollars` and, in addition, `discnt` (from the `customers` table), `percent` (from `agents`), and `price` (from `products`). Show that `returns` exists as a view, using a terminal command. Also use a command to see what the column names are.

(b) Execute the statement `select ordno, qty, dollars, discnt, percent, price from returns where cid = 'c001'`. Then update the underlying base table `customers` by changing the discnt for c001 to 13.0. Now repeat the previous Select statement from returns again. Notice that updates in the base tables are reflected in the view. Change the discnt for c001 back to 10.0 at the end (or just reload customers).

(c)• Note that the dollars column in returns should be equal to qty times price minus the discnt percentage for this amount. Test your ability to write expressions in terms of the returns view by selecting columns ordno, qty, dollars, discnt, percent, and price of all rows, with an extra column in the select calculating this expression. The extra expression column should give the same value as dollars.

(d) Now create a new view, profits, based on the returns view, with columns ordno, cid, aid, pid, and profit, where the profit column has been calculated in the Create View statement to equal qty times the price for that pid, minus 60% of this for wholesale cost, minus the percent royalty for the particular agent and the discnt for the customer in question. Be sure that the expression makes sense. Demonstrate the effectiveness of this by typing "select * from profits".

[6.14] Given an assigned partner in the class, trade "privileges" with your partner. Grant privilege to your partner's database account to perform selects (only) on customers where discnt < 10. You will need a view to do this. Show that the view and privilege exist, using appropriate commands. Leave this permit in force and demonstrate your access to your partner's database. (You need to access that database account and type the statement "select * from customers".)

[6.15] Show how to retrieve all view names, then all base table names in your database from the system catalog tables. Then retrieve all column names from the returns view. Can you also use the catalog to retrieve the *definition* of the returns view?

[6.16] Write an Embedded SQL program to update customers, setting discnt in the row with cid c001 to the old value plus 1. Include a test to check if no rows are updated, and print out a user warning. Then place a constraint on customers that keeps discnt <= 15.0, and execute your program until the warning is printed.

[6.17] In the last subsection of Section 6.1, the text suggests developing a programmatic function layer to perform all database updates. The layer itself would guarantee any necessary constraints, and possibly do other things such as implementing alternative actions when constraints are broken. For this problem you should create a new table, ords, with all the columns of the orders table with the same datatypes, *but no constraints*, not even **not null** for ordno. The ords table should have one other column, named "constrok", of type integer. Then you are to write a C function called insertords( ), declared

```
int insertords(int *ordnop, char *monthp, char *cidp,
    char *aidp, char *pidp, int *qtyp, double * dollarsp);
```

A program that wishes to insert a row in the ords table must call insertords, with pointers to each of the values to be inserted in the relevant columns. A null pointer indicates that no value is specified and that a null should therefore be placed. The insertords function should *test all eleven constraints* of the orders table given in Example 6.1.2. If the row to be inserted passes the test, the function should insert the row in ords, with a constrok column value of 1, and return the value 0. If the row fails any of the constraints, the function should print an indicative message to the terminal user (for example, "Error: null ordno, continue? Enter Y or N"). If the row user answers anything but Y or N, a "Y or N, Please" message is printed and we take another input. If an N is input, then insertords returns without inserting a row, with value –1. If a Y is input, then insertords inserts the row as it stands (broken constraints and all) and sets the constrok flag to 0. It then returns the value 1.

Your instructor will provide you with a driver, driveord.c, to test this function, and sample input for the driver program. Note that this method is not proposed to replace constraints, but rather to show their convenience compared to programming, and to show how to proceed if the database product does not support all the contraints you need.

Indexing  7

When an SQL query is submitted to a database system, a software module of the system known as the *query optimizer* analyzes the non-procedural prescription of the query to determine an efficient step-by-step method to retrieve the desired data. The resulting procedural sequence of steps to carry out the query is known as the *access plan*. We will go into detail in the next chapter about how a query optimizer arrives at an access plan; in the current chapter we lay a foundation by learning how query efficiency depends on the existence of *database indexes* that channel accesses to data in a table.

7.1 The Concept of Indexing

A *database index*, or simply *index*, is much like many memory-resident data structures you have probably encountered in earlier studies. It is meant to improve the efficiency of data lookup to rows of a table by a *keyed access* retrieval method. This chapter assumes that you have some familiarity with memory-resident structures that support lookup of this type, such as the *binary tree*, *(2-3)-tree*, and *hash tables*. If not, numerous textbooks can introduce you to these concepts. The difference in our case is that database indexes are meant to reside on disk, being made partially memory resident only when they are accessed. Thus a database index can contain more data than can be held in memory at one time and the structure *persists*, like the rows of a table, when the computer is turned off and memory-resident data is lost.

A database index consists of a set of *index entries* that are stored on disk, one index entry for each row existing in a table specified, and responsive to future row updates. Index entries look like rows of a table with two columns: the *index key*, consisting of the concatenation of values from certain column values in the row, and a "row pointer" to the disk position of the row from which this specific entry was constructed. The index entries are placed on disk, usually in sorted order by index key (although hashed access is also possible), and are then used by the system to speed up certain Select statements. Standard lookup through an index locates one or more index entries with a given key value or range of key values, and follows the entry pointers to the associated rows. The fact that a database index normally resides on disk has far-reaching ramifications, because it turns out that access to disk is extremely slow compared with memory access speeds. This fact has an important effect on the database index structures we will study, such as the B-tree. The most important feature of an index is to minimize the number of disk accesses to read desired data.

You can best picture an index to a database table by analogy to a card catalog in a library, indexing the books on the shelves in various categories. One set of cards in the catalog might be placed in alphabetical order by book author, another in order by title, and a third in order by subject name (several subjects are possible). Each card in the catalog contains a call number to locate the book indexed, so that once we find a catalog entry for a book with the title *The Three Laws of Robotics*, we can immediately locate the book on the shelves. Now, returning to the discussion of indexes on a table, consider what should happen when a database system receives the following SQL query.

[7.1.1]   `select * from customers where city = 'Boston'`
`and discnt between 12 and 14;`

The query optimizer would now have to decide how to access the rows requested by this query from the `customers` table. One alternative that always exists is to perform a *table scan*, in which the system successively accesses all rows of the table and discards rows that don't satisfy the two ANDed predicates in the **where** clause of query (7.1.1). (In doing this, we say that we *qualify* the rows by direct inspection of the row data.) In the case where there are fewer than ten rows in the `customers` table, as in Figure 2.2, a table scan is probably the appropriate strategy; direct examination of all the rows is quick when the table isn't extensive. In an analogous sense, looking up a book through a card catalog isn't as efficient as direct scan when there are fewer than ten books on the shelves. In a table with 1 million rows, however, access by lookup through some index directory structures can represent a very substantial performance advantage.

What is the proper course to take with such a large `customers` table, in performing query (7.1.1), assuming that there is no index associated with the column `discnt` but there is one on the column `city`? In this case, the system would probably decide to "look up" customers in Boston and then access all the `customers` rows in Boston through the index-supplied *row pointers*, a special form of identifier for rows on disk, analogous to the call-number of a library book. The total number of rows accessed would presumably be greatly reduced by limiting the query to customers in Boston, and we would only have to qualify the single remaining predicate, `discnt between 12 and 14`, by looking at the rows retrieved.

An end user or application programmer posing a query is often not aware of the underlying indexes that speed up access. When an application program executes an SQL request like the query in (7.1.1), the query optimizer determines how to fill the request, basing its judgment on factors (such as existing indexes) that may have been significantly different at the time the program was originally written. As a matter of fact, it is considered an important feature of the relational model that a programmer is insulated from this issue and can therefore write programs that don't depend on the existence of particular indexes (because the method of table scan is always available). This is another aspect of *program-data independence*, which we have seen before. The database administrator thus gains flexibility in being able to create and destroy indexes in response to the disk space needs of the moment. This, at any rate, is the theory. In practice, we sometimes see a difference between a query performed in 2 seconds with appropriate indexes and the same query taking 2 minutes without them. Removing existing indexes ceases to be an option when increased resource use significantly degrades the total performance of the system.

In considering the various aspects of indexing, we enter an area where the SQL standards have very little to say. To give an idea of what is to come, Figure 7.1 presents the X/OPEN standard specification of the Create Index statement.

```
create [unique] index indexname
      on tablename (columnname [asc | desc] {, columnname [asc |desc]});
```

Figure 7.1 X/OPEN Syntax for the SQL Create Index Statement

The table specified by tablename in the Create Index syntax must be a base table that already exists at the time that the statement is issued. The statement of Figure 7.1 creates a set of *index entries* that are then stored on disk, one index entry for each row existing in the table specified by tablename. As mentioned earlier, index entries look like rows of a table with two columns: the *index key*, consisting of the concatenation of values from the columns named in the Create Index statement, and a pointer to the disk position of the row from which this specific entry was constructed. The index entries are placed on disk in sorted order by index key (hashed access is not supported in the standard), with **asc** or **desc** order for each component column, as in the **sort by** clause of the Select statement. Lookup through an index locates a sequence of index entries with a given key value or range of key values and follows the entry pointers to the associated rows. Note that entries of the index automatically respond to changes in the table after the Create Index statement has been performed. When a row is inserted in the table, a new index entry is created in the index and placed in the appropriate index structure position for efficient lookup. Similarly, row updates that change the index key value are reflected by a change in the associated index entry.

EXAMPLE 7.1.1

Create an index on the city column of the customers table.

```
create index citiesx on customers (city);
```

Note that each index key value (i.e., city name) in the citiesx index can correspond to a large number of different customers rows. ∎

Note carefully that the term *index key* has a significantly different meaning from the relational concept of a *table key*, that is, a *primary key* or *candidate key* for a table. An index key is made up by concatenating a set of columns in a specific order, whereas a relational key has unordered columns. More basically, an index key is constructed with the aim of supporting efficient lookup, and it is perfectly possible to have multiple identical index key values for different rows of a table when the **unique** keyword of the Create Index statement is missing. We saw such duplicate index key values for `citiesx` in Example 7.1.1. On the other hand, the definition of a relational key says nothing about efficiency of lookup, and keys are created in the Create Table statement with the **unique** or **primary key** clause only to reflect the designer's intention that unique key values should exist on each row. We will carefully differentiate between these two concepts in what follows by always referring to an *index key* in distinction to a *table key* (or other specific terms for table key such as *primary key* or *candidate key*) when there can be any chance of confusion.

Of course, in real life efficiency is usually an important consideration, and it is perfectly possible to guarantee the uniqueness of a primary or candidate key for a table by specifying a unique index on a set of columns making up a primary or candidate key. This approach is used in some products such as **INGRES** to take the place of a **primary key** or **unique** constraint missing from the Create Table statement.

EXAMPLE 7.1.2

Create an index on the `cid` column of the `customers` table to guarantee that each `customers` row has a unique `cid` value.

```
create unique index cidx on customers (cid);
```

When the `cidx` index is first created, the system tests whether duplicate `cid` values already exist in the `customers` table; if duplicates are found, the index will not be created. After the index is created, any update to the table is immediately reflected in the index, and Insert or Update statements that would duplicate the unique index key will fail to execute. ∎

Before the **unique** and **primary key** constraints were part of the standard for the Create Table statement, a unique index was the accepted way to guarantee a uniqueness constraint for a candidate or primary table key. Now that Create Table constraints exist, it is usually preferable to use them for this purpose. Such table constraints are usually supported by a system-created unique index in any event, since quick lookup is needed to guarantee a unique value if new row inserts or updates affect the index key value.

The X/OPEN standard Create Index statement of Figure 7.1 is relatively simple, but even this limited form is absent from the SQL-92 standard. The reason no standard has been attempted is that an indexing strategy deals with considerations of the internal architecture of the database system, including the explicit design for row access on disk, and there is no agreed-upon optimal approach to this design. There are actually a number of different types of indexes, and it is impossible to understand the advantages of some of these types without understanding some detailed properties of disk access, covered in the next section. For example, we will learn that a binary search algorithm, which we can show provides nearly optimal efficiency to find a key value in a sorted list of memory-resident key values, is *not* optimal for a disk-based structure. All of the commercial database system products have taken quite different, one might say almost idiosyncratically different, approaches to the exact structures used to place rows on disk, assign pointers of custom type to the rows for outside reference by indexes, and accomplish a myriad other details covered in the following sections. At the same time, although there are many differences between the products, the product architectures have a lot in common, and we will present indexing details of three commercial database products, **DB2**, **ORACLE**, and **INGRES**, with an emphasis on these common aspects.

7.2 Disk Storage

Up until now we have been content to say that the rows of base tables (as well as any indexes that are created) are stored on disk and read into memory when they are accessed. As mentioned in Chapter 1, the fact that the database must be persistent over time means that disk storage is the most practical storage medium available. We say that computer memory is *volatile storage,* meaning that although it can be accessed very efficiently, the data contents of memory do not persist when electrical power is turned off, or when certain kinds of system failures occur. Disk storage is referred to as *nonvolatile storage,* or sometimes *stable or persistent storage,* meaning that it retains data through loss of electrical power—as everyone knows who has moved data on a diskette from one computer to another. Various software methods covered later in the text can also make disk storage resistant to other types of errors that arise from system failures. Disk storage is extremely cheap and therefore plentiful in most systems, but it is also very slow to access. As we will see, the extremely slow speed of access to disk storage dictates many details of database index structures.

Disk Access Is Excruciatingly Slow

As nearly everyone knows, computers have been getting faster and cheaper for decades. It has been said that if the auto industry had kept up with the computer industry since 1950, you would now be able to buy a car for $9 that would take you to the moon in an hour on a gallon of gas. Furthermore, this rate of progress seems to be continuing. A relatively inexpensive computer today can execute program logic with its central processing unit (CPU) at a rate of (say) 25 million instructions per second (25 MIPS). Of course different instructions take different lengths of time, but this rate is a rough measure of the average speed for a "standard" instruction mix.

Disk access speed, an extremely important aspect of database system performance, has not kept pace with the enormous improvements in CPU execution speed. A *disk* is a rotating magnetic recording medium, typically several platters stacked one above another, with a current industry-standard rotation speed of 60 rotations per second (rps), and a disk arm that moves in and out like an old-style record player arm. (A new rotation speed of 90 rps is becoming the standard, but we assume 60 rps in what follows.) The disk arm terminates in a set of *read-write heads* that sit on the surfaces of the various platters. As the arm moves through its range of positions, the heads all move together to address successive concentric *cylinders* of data, made up of circles or *tracks* on the stacked set of surfaces. A track is broken up into a sequence of angular pieces, called *sectors*. A typical disk unit today contains a gigabyte of data. Each track might contain 40,000 bytes, with ten surfaces (thus 400,000 bytes per cylinder), and 2500 cylinders on the disk unit. In order to read or write data on a disk, the disk arm must first move in or out to the appropriate cylinder position, then wait for the disk to rotate until the appropriate sector on one of the disk surfaces is just about to pass under the disk arm head. At this point the disk head reads the data from a sequence of sectors on one surface of the rotating medium. A disk access is usually modeled as having three phases, based on this physical analysis:

Seek time	The disk arm moves in or out to the proper cylinder position.
Rotational latency	The disk platter rotates to the proper angular position.
Transfer time	The disk arm reads/writes the data on the appropriate disk surface.

Because a disk access requires physical action, the time needed to read in a random piece of data from disk is enormous, about .025 seconds or 1/40 of a second. This is usually thought of as being amortized over the three phases as follows:

Seek time	.016 seconds
Rotational latency	.008 seconds
Transfer time	.001 seconds (for a few thousand bytes of transfer)

The seek time is actually highly variable, depending on the starting position of the disk arm and how far the arm has to move before it arrives at the proper cylinder. If two successive reads from disk are close to one another on the disk medium, the seek time can be very small, zero for two reads from the same cylinder. The average seek time of .016 seconds is based on a model where successively accessed pieces of data occur with equal likelihood at any cylinder position between the two extreme disk arm extents. The rotational latency is equal to half a disk rotation at 60 rps, an average value assuming that the start sector can be anywhere on the track after the disk arm seek is completed.

Once the data has been brought into memory, it can be accessed by an instruction in .00000004 seconds (one 25-millionth of a second), or .04 μs (.04 microseconds or millionths of a second) by a machine with a speed of 25 MIPS. The disparity between time for memory access and disk access is enormous: we can perform 625,000 instructions in the time it takes to read or write a disk page. For an analogy, imagine yourself as Voltaire's secretary around the time of the American Revolution, with the duty of making copies of Voltaire's many letters to correspondents. If we assume that it takes you about a second to copy each word, you can picture writing a letter as analogous to executing a computer program of several hundred instructions, each taking .04 μs. Now say that you come to a word with which you are not familiar, and Voltaire's handwriting is difficult to read. Unfortunately, Voltaire is in St. Petersburg, so you need to take time out to write a letter to him, asking for the exact spelling of the word. (In the analogy, there is information on disk needed by the database system, and it executes a series of instructions to start a disk read.) You post the letter to him, go back to your office, and wait three weeks doing nothing until the letter reaches him and you receive his reply. This is analogous to the system waiting .025 seconds for the disk read to bring the needed data into memory where it can be accessed directly by the system. Clearly we want to avoid performing more disk reads than are absolutely necessary.

It's important to realize that once the disk arm reaches the appropriate spot on disk, you don't want to ask for just a byte or so. It takes very little time for each additional byte returned—most of the disk access time was spent getting the disk arm into the right position on the rotating disk medium. Once the arm is in position, the transfer rate is millions of bytes per second. As a result, we see that all disk access is "page-oriented," a page being a long contiguous sequence of bytes: 2048 bytes, or 2 KB, is the standard page size for database systems running on UNIX, while 4096 bytes, or 4 KB, is standard on IBM mainframes. Retrieving a 2- or 4-KB page from disk in the analogy we have been using is like getting back a long letter from Voltaire that answers your question as well as a few others you might have later: the cost for such an extensive letter is only a few additional hours of waiting. Similarly, it's clearly worthwhile, after bringing back a page from disk and placing it in memory, to keep a popular page around so we won't have to access it from disk again later. The database system reads disk pages through an interface where it provide a *disk page address,* symbolized by *dp,* bringing the pages into memory *buffers* contained in memory space that was set aside when the database system was initiated. The dp values might be a logical succession of integers or they might be constructed from the device number, cylinder, surface, and starting sector position of the page on disk. Each page that is read in has its disk page address hashed (h(dp)) into a small entry of a *hash lookaside table,* which points to the buffer slot where the page will reside (see Figure 7.2). From that point on, every time a new page is to be read from disk we start by hashing the disk page address and looking in the hash lookaside table to see if the desired page is already in a memory buffer. If it is, we can skip the disk access step. Otherwise we will have to find a disk page to drop from memory buffers so we can read in this new page. We try to drop a page that hasn't been referenced for a long time, so that we keep popular pages buffer resident.

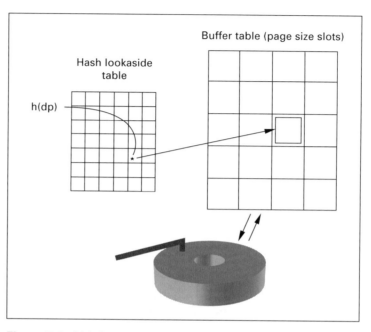

Hash lookaside table

Buffer table (page size slots)

h(dp)

Figure 7.2 Disk Page Buffering and Lookaside

Since we know we're going to be reading entire pages from disk, we try to structure all our access so that all useful information for any particular task tends to occur on the same page. As we will see, this has an important effect on the index structures. The most important feature of an index is to minimize the number of disk accesses to read desired data.

Since disk is so much slower than memory, it is natural to ask why we bother with it: Why don't we just use memory? Historically, of course, memory was volatile, so that data would be lost if there was a power interruption. However, in the last several years a type of memory with an uninterruptible power supply (battery backup) has become commercially available, so that even an electrical outage does not cause loss of data. Still, there has not been a wholesale stampede to memory storage. Of course disk media can be extremely convenient for backing up data and transferring it from one computer to another, but this doesn't explain why a busy database would be stored on disk in preference to being kept in memory while it is being accessed. The overriding fact that determines this usage pattern is that disk storage is extremely *cheap* compared with memory storage. There is a wide spectrum of costs among PC machines, UNIX servers, and IBM mainframes, and the speed of price reductions in the industry is ferocious. Still, a rough idea of the difference in costs can be gleaned from these very approximate rules of thumb from the PC industry:

> Memory storage costs about $50 per megabyte.
> Disk storage (disk arms attached) costs about $1000 per gigabyte.

That is, we can purchase a thousand times as much disk storage for only twenty times the cost. Considering that it is not at all uncommon for a medium-sized university to use several gigabytes of storage in a database, it is clear that the difference between a $50,000 charge and a $1000 charge per gigabtye is of overriding importance. Still, many designers are looking forward to a time when memory costs will drop so low that most database systems can maintain all their active data in memory. Before that can happen, computer designers will have to extend the memory address size, which is currently limited to 32 bits, or about 4 billion bytes of addressing on most processors. Some of the new massively parallel machine architectures have already started using 64-bit architecture, and IBM mainframes now provide a means of switching between different 32-bit addressing spaces. Reasonably soon we will be driving to Mars in a few minutes in a car that costs 15 cents.

The DBA and Disk Resource Allocation in ORACLE

In dealing with DBA responsibilities in Chapter 6, we avoided consideration of disk resource allocation. Although this is one of the most important tasks of the DBA, the many different data architectures of commercial database systems defeat any standard SQL approach. Most commercial systems deal with data allocation in the same *general* way, however, even though the details can be quite different. To give an idea of the considerations that arise, we provide the following rough description of the commands used in the **ORACLE** product to allocate disk storage resources. For additional details, see the *ORACLE SQL Language Reference Manual* [7] and the *ORACLE RDBMS Database Administrator's Guide* [5].

Before creating a database, the DBA might start by allocating a large number of operating system files on disk, with names such as fname1, fname2, . . . , etc. These are the same kind of files that a user would encounter when editing text or compiling C source files into executable program files. Various operating systems give the DBA the ability to specify the size of the file in bytes and the disk device on which the file is to be allocated. We say that disk storage is *contiguous* if it consists of sectors on disk as close together as possible—successive sectors on successive surfaces of a cylinder within a succession of adjoining cylinders. Keeping disk space contiguous minimizes seek time, as we have explained, and most systems try to allocate space to a file in long contiguous chunks. At the same time, most operating system files do not have the flexibility to span disk devices. Given these operating system files, the DBA might issue an **ORACLE** command of the following kind:

```
create tablespace tspace1 datafile 'fname1', 'fname2';
```

A *tablespace* is the basic allocation medium of an **ORACLE** database, out of which tables and indexes as well as other objects requiring disk space receive their allocations. A tablespace corresponds to one or more operating system files and can span disks. On most operating systems, **ORACLE** is perfectly capable of creating operating system files from the SQL level, although the administrator does lose some precision. Here is an example of a Create Tablespace statement in which it is left to **ORACLE** to create the files fname3 and fname4.

```
create tablespace tspace2 datafile 'fname3' size 200M,
    datafile 'fname4' size 300M;
```

The integer following the **size** keyword can be given in bytes, in kilobytes (an integer followed by the letter K), or in megabytes (with the letter M). Many **ORACLE** databases contain several tablespaces, including a special tablespace named SYSTEM, which is automatically brought into being when the Create Database command is issued (not covered here). The SYSTEM tablespace contains the *data dictionary* for the database (what we have been calling the system catalog tables) and may also be used to provide disk space for user-defined tables and indexes, as well as other objects. It is up to the DBA to decide whether to create multiple named tablespaces. The advantages of having multiple tablespaces on large systems are better control over which disk devices are used for what purposes (load balancing), and the ability to take some disk space offline without bringing down the whole database.

When a table or index is created by a DBA (or any user with the RESOURCE privilege), an optional clause of the Create Table or Create Index statement, known as the **tablespace** clause, allows the creator to name the tablespace from which disk space will be allocated (see Figure 7.5 for an example in the Create Table syntax). If no tablespace is named, then the table is created in the user's default tablespace, set when the user is first granted a tablespace resource. When a table is created, its tablespace allocation is identified with an object known as a *data segment;* when an index is created, it is identified with an *index segment.* There are other types of segments as well, with common properties of allocation, the next logical unit of storage subdividing a tablespace. When a data or index segment is first created, it is given an initial allocation of disk space from the tablespace, known as an *initial extent.* By default, an initial extent contains 10 KB (10,240 bytes) of disk storage. Each time a data segment comes close to running out of space, it is given additional allocations of space, known as a *next extent,* and numbered by an integer starting from 1. Figure 7.3 is a schematic diagram of the logical structures just named.

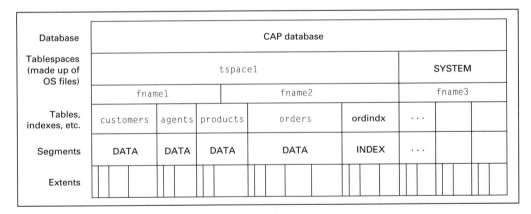

Figure 7.3 Database Storage Structures

An extent must consist of contiguous disk space, and is therefore usually within a single file making up a tablespace. It is possible to specify a number of parameters in a tablespace definition to define how disk space allocation is to be handled. All segments that are defined within a tablespace inherit these parameters, but definitions of objects such as tables and indexes can also override these default values with their own parameters. Figure 7.4 contains the complete syntax form for the Create Tablespace statement.

```
create tablespace tblspacename
    datafile 'filename' [size n [K|M]] [REUSE]
        {, 'filename' [size n [K|M]] [REUSE]}
    [default storage ([initial n] [next n] [minextents n]
        [maxextents n] [pctincrease n] ) ]
    [online | offline];
```

Figure 7.4 ORACLE Create Tablespace Statement Syntax

As already explained, the tablespace is constructed from a set of operation system files named in the **datafile** clause. The **reuse** keyword specifies that existing filenames should be reused, thereby destroying any information contained. If the **size** keyword is omitted, the file must already exist. A tablespace is created **online** by default, meaning that it is immediately available for use by the database system. The tablespace can be brought **offline** and online again by the DBA for various purposes with the Alter Tablespace statement (not covered here). The **default storage** clause of Create Tablespace allows the tablespace creator to specify default parameters governing how allocation of disk extents is to be handled in contained segments. Here are explanations of these parameters.

initial n	The integer n specifies the size in bytes of the initial extent to be assigned. The default is 10,240.
next n	The integer n specifies the size in bytes of the next extent numbered 1; the size of subsequent next extents may increase (but not decrease) if a positive **pctincrease** value is specified. The default is 10,240.
maxextents n	The integer n specifies the maximum number of extents, including the initial extent, that can ever be allocated. The default is 99.
minextents n	The number of extents to be allocated initially when the segment is created. Since extents must be contiguous, this allows for a large initial space allocation, even when the space available is not contiguous. The default is 1.

pctincrease n   The percentage by which each successive next extent grows over the previous one. If the integer is zero, there is no increase. The default of 50 causes successive next extents to grow by a factor of one and a half times over the prior next extent.

All extent sizes are rounded to an integral multiple of a block (page) size. The minimum size for an extent is 4096 bytes, the maximum is 4095 MB.

We have seen an earlier form of the **ORACLE** Create Table statement in Figure 6.3. A more complete syntax that takes storage allocation options into account is provided in Figure 7.5. Note that the optional storage clauses of this Create Table syntax allow the creator of a table to override the parameters for extent allocation associated with the tablespace in which the table is defined.

```
create table tablename
    (columnname datatype [col_constr] {, columnname datatype [col_constr]}
    {, table_constr} )
    [tablespace tblspacename]
    [storage ([initial n] [next n] [minextents n] [maxextents n]
        [pctincrease n] ) ]
    [pctfree n] [pctused n]
    [other disk storage and transactional clauses not covered or deferred]
    [as subselect]
```

Figure 7.5 ORACLE Create Table Statement Syntax

The **pctfree** and **pctused** clauses together determine how much space on each disk page can be used for inserts of new rows (see Figure 7.6 for a schematic of row layout on a disk page), as opposed to how much space must be set aside for future expansion in the size of existing rows. The **pctfree** value must be an integer n from 0 to 99, where a value of 0 means that all page space can be used for new row inserts. The default is 10, meaning that new inserts to the page will stop when the page is 90% full. The **pctused** value specifies where new inserts to the page will start again if the amount of space used by stored rows falls below a certain percentage of the total. The value must be an integer n from 1 to 99. The default value is

40. The sum of the **pctfree** and **pctused** values must be less than 100, and together determine a range in which the behavior with respect to inserts on the disk page remains stable, depending on the last percentage value encountered.

Data Storage Pages and Row Pointers: ORACLE, DB2, and INGRES

Once a table has been created and the initial extents of disk storage allocated, we are ready to load or insert rows into the table. In a typical data architecture for row placement, rows are simply inserted one after another on the first page of the first extent until the space on the first page is exhausted, after which the next page is used. When the initial allocation of pages runs out with repeated row inserts, the database allocates a new extent for the table and continues this process with additional extensions up to the maximum number of extents or pages that can be allocated. Each row placed on a disk page consists of a contiguous sequence of bytes containing column values of various types, and each row begins at a known offset in bytes from the beginning of the page. It is possible in some architectures for long rows to exceed the size that can be accommodated on a single disk page, but we defer consideration of this issue until later.

A typical data storage page layout is given in Figure 7.6, where we show N rows on a disk page (called a *block* in **ORACLE**). The header info section might contain fields to show what type of disk page this is, the number of the page within the database file, and so on. Each row is a contiguous sequence of bytes, starting at a specific byte offset within the page (recall that because of varchar(n) datatypes, the rows might have different lengths). Entries in the row directory number the rows within a page and give the page byte offset to where each row begins. In the following sections, we usually refer to a row number within a page as a *slot* number. In the architecture shown in Figure 7.6, it is assumed that newly inserted rows are placed right to left in the disk page, and directory entries from left to right, leaving free space for future inserts in the space between. This implies that if a row is deleted from a disk page and its space reclaimed, then the remaining rows are shifted flush right in the page and the directory entries flush left, so that all free space remains in the middle. **ORACLE** can defer shifts of this sort, however. Other forms of free space are possible, and this is only a simplified schematic structure. Other types of information can also occur in the row directory area. For example, both **DB2**

and **ORACLE** allow rows from multiple tables to appear on the same disk
page, and in that case additional identifying information is needed in the
row headers or directory to distinguish rows from the different tables.

Figure 7.6 Row Layout on a Disk Page

A row in a database table can be uniquely identified by specifying the
disk page on which the row appears and the slot number of the row within
the page. This is the form of row pointer we referred to earlier, used in
indexes to point to rows that correspond to a given index key value. It
turns out that we gain flexibility by pointing to a row using a logical slot
number within a disk page, because of the *information hiding* that takes
place. If instead we used the byte offset of the row within the page, then
external row pointers would need to change when rows had to be moved
in a page reorganization, for example to allow for a larger value in a varchar column. By using logical slot numbers in row pointers instead, external index references to the rows remain stable when the disk page row
layout is reorganized. A row pointer has somewhat different names in different systems. In **ORACLE** it is called a ROWID, in **DB2** an RID (for row
identifier), and in **INGRES** a TID (for tuple identifier). Remember that the
concept of row pointer is not part of any standard, but the general form
explained here is very common.

In **INGRES**, successive disk pages allocated to a database table are
assigned an integer disk page number P, ranging from 0 to $2^{23} - 1$, requiring 23 bit positions, a maximum of 8,388,608 pages. We allow at most
512 rows on a page, so that a slot number S ranges from 0 to 511 and can
be expressed in 9 bits. A row pointer, or TID, in **INGRES** is calculated from
the disk page number P and the slot number S for the particular row using
the following formula:

$$TID = 512 \cdot P + S$$

For example, the TID value for a row with slot number S = 4 on page P = 2
has a TID value calculated as $2 \cdot 512 + 4 = 1028$. The slot number within a

page is not permitted to exceed the value 511, so the formula for a TID is always unique for rows on different pages. The slot number fits in 9 bits and the page number in 23, so the TID value is guaranteed to fit in 32 bits, a 4-byte unsigned integer. In addition to serving as a pointer to a row associated with a given index key value, an **INGRES** TID can also be retrieved by normal SQL queries as a "virtual" column value, as we see in the following examples.

EXAMPLE 7.2.1

Assume that an **INGRES** DBA has just loaded a table named employees with 10,000 rows and believes each row of the employees table to be 200 bytes long, with little variation in size. This means that a UNIX database system disk page of 2048 bytes should contain about ten such rows. (The header info section and row directory represent overhead space common to most systems, and there is also a certain amount of overhead for various columns, which we assume has already been included in the 200-byte row length. Without descending into detailed calculations of overhead usage, ten rows of length 200 on a 2048-byte page should be about right, although we may only be able to fit nine rows.) To test that the rows have been loaded ten to a page, the DBA can pose the following SQL query to retrieve the TID values for an initial sequence of rows:

```
select tid from employees where tid <= 1024;
```

The DBA expects to see a sequence of TIDs with values 0, 1, 2, 3, 4, 5, 6, 7, 8, 9, 512, 513, 514, 516, 517, 518, 519, 520, 521, 1024,..., and so on. Any other displayed sequence means that there are not ten rows on each page. ∎

A **DB2** record pointer RID also encodes the table page number and slot number into a 4-byte integer. However, a **DB2** RID is *not* available through a Select statement as a virtual column value in an arbitrary table.

In **ORACLE**, a record pointer ROWID specifies the block (disk page) number on which the row falls, the slot number within the block, and the number of the operating system file within which the block exists. Multiple blocks can have the same block number within different files making up the tablespace. A ROWID requires 6 bytes of storage in a unique index, and can be retrieved as a virtual column by an SQL Select statement on any table. The ROWID is displayed as a string of three hexadecimal numbers, with component parts having the following layout:

BBBBBBBB.SSSS.FFFF

Here BBBBBBBB represents the block number within the file, SSSS the slot number, and FFFF the file number. For example, 0000000F.0003.0002 represents the row in slot 3 of block 15 within file number 2.

We use the **ORACLE** ROWID nomenclature generically in what follows to refer to record pointers in arbitrary database systems; we often use a lowercase form, rowid.

EXAMPLE 7.2.2
Consider the following Embedded SQL code to retrieve a row from a relation and, depending on a complex decision procedure, perform an update on the row to set a taxcode flag column to 1.

```
exec sql select * into :emprec
    from employee where eid = :empidval;  /* unique row          */
decisionproc(&emprec, &yesno);           /* perform decision proc */
if (yesno)                               /* if flag was set to yes */
   exec sql update employee set taxcode = 1   /* perform update   */
      where eid = :empidval;
exec sql commit;
```

Note that the Update statement setting taxcode to 1 will need to perform a second lookup, probably through a unique empid index, in order to update the desired employee row. This lookup could be avoided and performance improved by remembering the rowid of the row from the initial Select statement. The original Select would have to be modified to read as follows (e.rowid names the virtual column in **ORACLE**; use e.tid in **INGRES**):

```
exec sql select e.*, e.rowid into :emprec, :emprid
    from employee e where eid = :empidval;
```

The emprid variable would be declared as a long integer in C for **INGRES** and as an 18-character string for **ORACLE**. Now the final update statement can be rewritten:

```
exec sql update employee set taxcode = 1
    where rowid = :emprid;  /* perform update */            ■
```

Recall that RULE 2 of the relational model in Section 2.3 states that rows can only be retrieved by their content. The existence of a rowid value in SQL to retrieve a row by pointer value is a definite contravention of this rule, but many commercial database systems support such a feature. The reason is the very pragmatic one that the rowid value is useful for certain purposes. As we have seen, rowids in a table are useful for at least two reasons:

◆ They can be used to see how the rows of a table are stored on disk.

◆ They can be used as the fastest way to access a particular row.

Nevertheless, Relational RULE 2 is valid in the following sense: a rowid should not take the place of a primary key for a table. The rowid should not be stored over an extended period for use in retrieval, because it might become invalid. For example, various types of database reorganization utilities exist where rows are moved to new disk pages for a variety of reasons, and thus change their rowid values. When this happens, an outmoded rowid value points to a new row, and an error in retrieving the wrong row associated with an outmoded rowid value can be fatal. A DBA should be able to advise application programmers on safe intervals for using rowid values, during which such values will not go out of date. A rowid held for the space of a single transaction is usually safe, because a lock is kept on the row accessed to keep it from being deleted or reorganized.

Another point that might make us wish to avoid heavy rowid use is that the rowid format is not portable from one system to another; nor is it necessarily supported by the database system in the same way as some other aspects of SQL. **INGRES** warns that the format of the TID might change in the future; therefore, any logic that depends on calculating the page number from the rowid (for example) might have to be rewritten at some new **INGRES** release.

Can Rows Extend Over Several Pages? Product Variations

Different products have different rules about whether rows can extend over several pages. The maximum row size in **DB2** is limited to the largest disk page, and each row lies entirely in a single disk page of this size. Disk pages and buffer sizes of 4 KB and 32 KB are possible, although the 4-KB size is much more common. **INGRES** allows a row size up to 2000 bytes, and each row lies on a single 2-KB page. **ORACLE**, however, allows rows to split between pages. If a row on some page grows to a point where no free space remains, then the row splits. Its rowid remains the same and it leaves a row fragment in the original slot position on its original page, but a pointer at the end of that row fragment points to the rowid of a continuation fragment. The continuation fragment is placed, just as a row is placed, on a new disk page with a slot position and a rowid. However, the rowid of the continuation fragment is not made available to any external access method; it is an internal property of row access.

Clearly we would like to avoid fragmented records whenever possible. A fragmented record is analogous to sending a letter off to Voltaire without listing all your questions, saying that you will send another letter with more of the questions you have in mind after you receive a response. We try to minimize fragmentation in **ORACLE** by leaving extra free space on each page with the **pctfree** clause of the Create Table statement to handle most row enlargements. However, since **ORACLE** permits rows that cannot fit on a single page, extra free space on a page is not a general solution. When a row in **DB2** or **INGRES** grows to a point that it cannot fit in its original slot together with neighboring rows on the same page, it is moved entirely to a new page. A certain kind of fragmentation exists in this case. A ROWID or TID forwarding pointer must be left on the original page, because we don't want to change all index entry pointers to the original row position. Reducing fragmentation arising from forwarding pointers of this kind is one of the reasons that the database reorganization utilities mentioned earlier are valuable.

7.3   The B-Tree Index

A *B-tree* is a keyed index structure, comparable to a number of memory-resident keyed lookup structures you have probably encountered in earlier reading, such as the *balanced binary tree*, the *AVL-tree*, and the *(2-3)-tree*. The difference is that a B-tree is meant to reside on disk, being made partially memory-resident only when entries in the structure are accessed. A number of other disk-based index structures, based on alternate access methods such as hashing, also offer performance advantages in certain applications; we cover some of these later in the chapter. However, the B-tree structure is the most commonly used index type in databases today.[1] It

---

[1] What we call a "B-tree" in this text is more precisely known as a "B⁺-tree" in many other references, and represents a more recent variation on the original published B-tree structure. Almost all commercial products have adopted the B⁺-tree variations, however, and the resulting structure is often referred to by the simpler name "B-tree."

is the only index structure available on **DB2**, and it was the only one provided by **ORACLE** until release 7, when a facility known as *hash cluster* was added. **INGRES**, on the other hand, has offered a wide set of different index structures for some time. In defense of **DB2**, which offers only the B-tree index, it should be said that the B-tree provides a good deal of flexibility for different types of indexed access, and the **DB2** implementation has special features (such as sequential prefetch I/O, covered in the next chapter) that make it extremely competitive in performance for many applications.

The following subsections provide an extended introduction to the structure of a B-tree. The discussion is summarized in Definition 7.3.1, where the important properties of the B-tree are listed. To begin, Figure 7.7 provides the **ORACLE** syntax for a Create Index statement, which assumes a B-tree index (hashed access is provided by **ORACLE** with the Create Cluster statement, not covered here). This **ORACLE** syntax is more specific about disk resource use than the X/OPEN Create Index statement of Figure 7.1.

```
create [unique] index indexname on tablename
    (columnname [asc | desc] {, columnname [asc | desc]})
    [tablespace tblspacename]
    [storage ([initial n] [next n] [minextents n] [maxextents n]
        [pctincrease n] ) ]
    pctfree n
    [other disk storage and transactional clauses not covered or deferred]
    [nosort]
```

Figure 7.7   ORACLE Create Index Statement Syntax

Recall that the list of columnnames in parentheses on the second line specifies a concatenation of column values that make up an *index key* on the table specified. When the Create Index statement is issued, an initial set of extents is created in the named tablespace. Then an *index entry* of the form (`keyval`, `rowid`) is extracted for each of the N rows of the table.

This sequence of index entries is then placed on disk and sorted in order by key value:

```
(keyval1, rowid1), (keyval2, rowid2), . . . , (keyvalN, rowidN),
```

so that after the sort, $keyval1 \leq keyval2 \leq \ldots \leq keyvalN$. We will consider algorithms for sorting sequences of index entries (or rows) on disk in the next chapter; a good deal of disk space and memory space as well as CPU and disk arm use can be required for this sort step. We defer consideration of the **pctfree** option until we have had a chance to investigate the B-tree index node layout. The **nosort** option of Figure 7.7 indicates that the rows already lie on disk in sorted order by the key values for this index. Thus index entries are extracted in that order, and the effort of the sort step can be saved. **ORACLE** checks that the key values extracted are actually in increasing order and returns an error if the order is not as promised.

EXAMPLE 7.3.1 Special Binary Search in a Memory Array.
The reader is expected to have encountered a binary search in an earlier text on data structures, but the special algorithm given here is constructed to handle the case where multiple duplicate values exist in the sorted list. In what follows, assume that we are given a table with seven rows (generalizable to N), and create a special index-like sorted list in a memory-resident array of structs, arr[7], so that the ($keyvalK$, $rowidK$) pair of values in the Kth entry is given by arr[K-1].keyval and arr[K-1].rowid. (Recall that subscripts range from 0 to N-1 with N entries.) If the structs in arr[ ] are ordered by the keyval component, so that arr[0].keyval $\leq$ arr[1].keyval $\leq \ldots \leq$ arr[6].keyval, the C function binsearch of Figure 7.8 implements a binary search to locate the *leftmost* key value x in this array.

```
int binsearch(int x)/* return K so that arr[K].keyval == x, or else -1
    if no match;arr assumed to be external, dimension 7 is wired in*/
{
    int probe = 3,                    /* start subscript K = 3        */
        diff = 2;                     /* difference to 2nd probe      */

    while (diff > 0) {                /* loop until K to return       */
        if (probe <= 6 && x > arr[probe].keyval)/* if probe too low*/
            probe = probe + diff; /* raise the probe position     */
        else                          /* otherwise                    */
            probe = probe - diff; /* lower the probe position     */
        diff = diff/2;                /* home in on answer, K         */
    }                                 /* we have reached K            */
    if (probe <= 6 && x == arr[probe].keyval) /* have we found x?   */
        return probe;                 /* if so, return K              */
    else if (probe + 1 <= 6
        && x == arr[probe+1].keyval)/* might have undershot          */
            return probe + 1;     /* then return this K           */
    else return - 1                   /* else, return failure         */
}
```

Figure 7.8 Function binsearch, with Seven Entries Wired In

Consider the sequence of keyval values {1, 7, 7, 8, 9, 9, 10} at subscript positions 0–6. Then if x = 1, binsearch probes successive subscripts 3, 1, and 0 and returns 0. If x = 7, the successive subscript probes are 3, 1, 0, and then since 7 is not equal to arr[0].keyval, we test arr[1].keyval that has the value 7, and return 1. If x = 8, the successive probes are to 3, 1, 2, and then 3 is returned. With x = 9, we probe 3, 5, 4 and return 4. With x = 10, we probe 3, 5, 6 and return 6. Given duplicate values in the array, the binsearch logic of Figure 7.8 always returns the smallest subscript K such that x == arr[K].keyval. (One of the exercises at the end of the chapter asks you to demonstrate this fact.) The binsearch function generalizes easily: given N entries instead of 7, choose m so that $2^{m-1} \leq N < 2^m$; then initialize probe to $2^{m-1}-1$ and diff to 2^{m-2}. Tests that probe <= 6 or probe + 1 <= 6 become probe <= N − 1 or probe + 1 <= N − 1. ∎

The number of passes through the binsearch loop to locate x in a sequence of N entries is m − 1, where 2^m is the smallest power of 2 that exceeds N (one for each value of diff, counting down in powers of 2 from

2^{m-2} to 2^0). Then there is a test with the final probe value and possibly with probe + 1. Another way to put this is that the number of probe tests is between m and m + 1, where we can calculate m as CEIL($\log_2$(N)). (Recall that the CEIL function rounds up to the next larger integer.) Although we can show that this is nearly the most efficient possible search in terms of the total number of comparisons performed, it is not optimal for disk-based lookup. If we performed a binary search on a large sorted list placed in disk storage, we would probably perform more I/Os than necessary.

EXAMPLE 7.3.2 Binary Search of a Million Index Entries.
Assume that we have a million rows in our table, and therefore a million entries in our sorted list arr[ ]. A rather minimal assumption for entry size is 4 bytes for the rowid and 4 bytes for the key value (appropriate for an integer key value; it could be much more for a character string index key). With 8 bytes for each entry, the number of entries we can fit on a 2-KB disk page is at most 2048/8 = 256, ignoring overhead. The pattern of binary search is to make a first probe to compare the value x sought to the `keyval` at entry number $2^{19}-1 = 524,287$ of the sorted list. After this, the next pass moves left or right in the list by $2^{18} = 262,144$ entries, depending on how the comparison comes out. Each successive probe is a "distance" half as far from the previous one. Here is the pattern of successive probes, and the distance moved in each case from the previous probe.

Probe number	Distance from previous probe
1	(no previous probe)
2	262,144 entries away
3	131,072 entries away
4	65,536 entries away
6	32,768 entries away
7	16,384 entries away
8	8192 entries away
9	4096 entries away
10	2048 entries away
11	1024 entries away
12	512 entries away
13	256 entries away
14	128 entries away
. . .	. . .

The point of all this is that on probe 14, for the first time there is a *chance* that the previously probed entry and the current entry lie on the same page! Recall that there are only 256 entries on a page, and for the first 13 probes binary search is jumping over numerous pages of entries between successive probes. If we assume that the pages accessed are not already resident in memory buffers from some prior reference, this means we need at least 13 I/Os to locate the desired entry. ∎

We can improve on binary search from a standpoint of disk I/O with a B-tree structure.

EXAMPLE 7.3.3 B-Tree Structure for a Million Index Entries.

If we assume that 256 index entries will fit on a page, then the number of pages containing entries is CEIL(1,000,000/256) = 3907. These pages, containing index entries of the form (`keyval, rowid`), are known as *leaf nodes* in a B-tree structure. Now let us create the most efficient possible *directory* entries to direct us to the right leaf node, given that we wish to locate an entry with arbitrary key value x. All we need is a pointer to each leaf node (a page number, which we refer to as a node pointer, np) and what we call a *separator* key value between pairs of such pointers. Figure 7.9 gives an example of such a structure with specific key values. Note that rowid values of leaf-level entries are not shown.

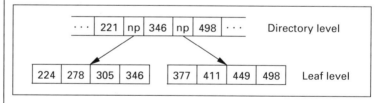

Figure 7.9 Directory Structure to Leaf-Level Nodes

In searching for an entry with key value x, say 305, at the leaf level, we need merely find the leftmost directory separator value S_1 such that $x \le S_1$. The separator value 346 has this property in the example given, and we can then follow the node pointer on the left of this separator down to the leaf level. At the leaf level, we perform a separate search for the precise key value we are seeking. Since there are 3907 pages at the leaf level, we only need 3907 node pointers at the directory level, with 3906 separator values to distinguish between all the leaf-level entry pages. We assume that a directory entry, analogous to a leaf-level index entry, contains a node pointer and a separator key value, (`np,sepkeyval`). Because the space needed for directory entries is about the same as that for the leaf entries, we see that these 3907 entries will fit on CEIL(3907/256)

= 16 pages, which we call *directory nodes* of the B-tree. The next step is to create a new *higher* directory level to guide us to the proper index node of the first directory we have just created! We can use the same approach in this higher-level directory, with key value separators and pointers down to nodes of the subsidiary directory level, and the number of entries we need at this new level is only 16! Certainly this small number of entries will fit on a single page, and this is called the *root* of the B-tree. Figure 7.10 shows a schematic picture of a three-level B-tree, such as we have just created. ∎

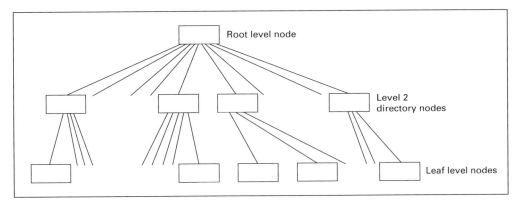

Figure 7.10 A Three-Level B-Tree

Note that a B-tree is built upside down, with the root at the top and the leaves at the bottom. We refer to all nodes above the leaf level, including the root, as *directory nodes,* or sometimes *index nodes.* Directory nodes below the root are sometimes called *internal* nodes of the tree. The root node is also known as level 1 of the B-tree, and successively lower levels are given successively larger level numbers, with the leaf nodes at the lowest level, level 3 in Figure 7.10. The total number of levels is called the *depth* of the B-tree. Now we can find our way down to any leaf-level entry by first reading in the root page, then finding our way to successive level directory pages, which ultimately direct us to the appropriate leaf page. We then examine the leaf page to find the leaf-level entry we want, assuming that it exists. In Figure 7.10, this means that we require a maximum of three I/Os to access the desired index entry, much fewer than binary search for 1 million entries, which required 13 I/Os.

The relative I/O efficiency of a B-tree over binary search results from the fact that the B-tree is structured to get the most out of every disk page (B-tree node) read. All entries on a directory node page have real value in determining which lower-level node to access, and something like 256 lower-level nodes can be pointed to. In the binary search, only a binary decision is made, and only two nodes are accessed as a result. If we look at the tree of page accesses resulting from a binary search, we notice that the B-tree is *bushy*, whereas the binary search tree is *sparse*. The B-tree is flatter as a result, because we can reach as many as 256^3 leaf level entries in a three-level tree. The B-tree is said to have *fanout* of 256, compared to the fanout of 2 for the binary search. The leaf-level nodes of the tree also have their own large fanout, with 256 entry rowid values pointing down to rows indexed. The rows of the table can be pictured as another level lying below the leaf level of a B-tree.

If we assume a B-tree with a fanout of f, we can access N entries at the leaf level in CEIL($\log_f(N)$) probes. Thus with the fanout of 256 we have been assuming, we can access 1 million leaf-level entries in CEIL($\log_{256}(1,000,000)$) = 3 probes. This compares to CEIL($\log_2(1,000,000)$) = 20 probes in the case of the binary search of Figure 7.8. Of course probes past a certain point in the binary search don't cause page I/Os. Furthermore, in the case of a B-tree, multiple probes are made on each index node to locate the appropriate separator value to channel access down to the subordinate level. But the I/Os are what we are trying to minimize, so the multiple probes within a node page don't count. In fact, because of the relatively frequent access to the upper-level index nodes of an actively used B-tree, it is likely that *these pages will remain in memory buffers!* There is only a total of 17 such pages in the top two levels of Example 7.3.3, after all, not a lot of space when compared with the 3907 nodes at the leaf level. This would reduce the number of I/Os for an index entry lookup to only *one!* In the case of binary search, we could cut out only the first 5 out of 13 probes by keeping as many as 31 pages memory resident (31 = 1 + 2 + 4 + 8 + 16 counts the number of pages commonly branched to on the first five probe levels).

Dynamic Changes in the B-Tree

What we have been talking about so far is how to access entries at the leaf level through a multi-level B-tree directory. We also need to consider inserts to the tree quite closely, since we want to claim that a B-tree is an efficient

self-modifying structure when new entries are inserted, pointing to new
rows inserted in the indexed table. Note that a normal sorted list of entries
on disk can always be reconstructed when a new entry is added, but only
by moving all successive entries one position to the right to create the hole
for the insert, implying an I/O for about half the pages holding entries in
the list. But in any application with frequent inserts such a course is much
too inefficient for a large index.

473

   The means by which a B-tree is kept ordered (and balanced) as new
entries are added at the leaf level is explained based on the example in Figure 7.11. The nodes of the B-tree at every level are generally assumed not
to be "full" (we assumed full nodes earlier when calculating 256 entries per
page). Instead, space is left so that inserts are often possible to a node at
any level without new disk space being required. When a new entry is to be
inserted, we follow the directory structure down to the leaf page where it
would exist if we were simply looking it up, so that after the insert the
directory structure channels us to the new entry key value. An insert of a
new entry always occurs at the leaf level, but occasionally the leaf node is
too full to simply accept the new entry. In this case, for additional space
the leaf-level node is *split* into two leaf pages (the entries are kept in order,
lower key values to the left split page, higher ones to the right). This means
that the higher-level index node must be modified so that a new separator
exists, along with a new pointer to the new page resulting from the split
(the other page has simply been reused). Occasionally the modification of
adding a new separator and pointer to the next higher level of index will
exceed the space available on that index node. In that case the index node
is split, as at the leaf level, with resulting changes at the next higher level of
the index. Eventually an additional entry may be placed at the root level,
and if the root splits, then a new root node is created at a higher level, having as its children the split nodes resulting from the former root.

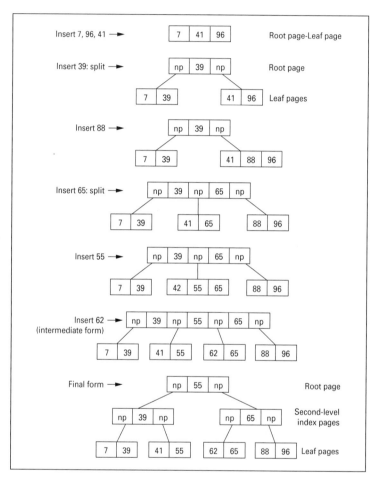

Figure 7.11 Growth of a B-Tree (rowids in Leaf Entries Not Shown)

Now look again at Figure 7.11. We are assuming that a B-tree leaf page will accept up to three entries, but not four. (This is much smaller than is realistic for disk pages, but keeping it small simplifies our explanation.) We also assume that higher-level index nodes have room for as many as three subordinate node pointers, designated by "np", but not four (there are only two separator values associated with three pointers, but we equate index entries with the number of node pointers). Such a structure is basically the same as a (2-3)-tree, a balanced memory-resident tree that is introduced in many data structures courses.

The B-tree starts out empty. As the first three entries are inserted into the B-tree, we have a simple structure, a leaf page that is also a root—that is, no higher-level directory entries are needed, since all entries fit on a single page, the initial page brought in from disk. Note that we dispense with showing rowid values in leaf entries—it is assumed that each of the key values being inserted at the leaf level has a corresponding rowid value. Higher-level node entries have visible pointers np to lower-level nodes. Now when the value 39 is added to the one-level B-tree in the figure, the root splits and a new root is created, with pointers to the two lower leaf-level pages. After this, the values 88 and then 65 are added, a new split occurs, and the new upper-level entry is accepted in the root node. Finally, the insert of 62 causes a double split. First the leaf node splits, sending a new separator entry to the higher level node. This causes the next node up to split and create a new root.

Note in particular that the only way in which the depth of a B-tree can increase is when the root node splits. Immediately after a root-node split, all leaf nodes increase their depth by one from the root node, and it is clear that there is no way in which two leaf nodes can ever come to be at different depths down from the root in a growing B-tree—the B-tree remains totally balanced.

Now what happens when entries are deleted from a B-tree in response to rows being deleted or column values updated in the indexed table? If we consider the final form of the B-tree of Figure 7.11, and imagine deleting the entry with key value 62 at the leaf level, it is clear that this would result in a leaf node with only a single entry, having key value 65. Looking to the right at the leaf level, we see that two leaf nodes now contain only three entries, and they could therefore be *merged* (the opposite of splitting) into a single node with three entries, 65, 88, and 96. At the directory-level node above, we no longer need two node pointers after these leaf nodes are merged, but only one. We also no longer need the separator 65; the separator 55 at the root serves perfectly well. Now, with a little bit of thought, we can see how to merge this directory-level node (which has only one node pointer and no separators) with the directory node to its left; the separator from the root must move down to that merged node to distinguish the two node pointers in the standard way. This does away with the need for the root node, and the tree collapses one level to be comparable in structure (although not quite identical) to the B-tree of Figure 7.11 just prior to the insertion of the entry with key value 62.

An algorithm that performs the actions just outlined when entries are deleted from a B-tree could be used to keep a shrinking B-tree balanced and all nodes below the root at least half full. However, very few commercial database systems implement this algorithm. The logic to merge nodes is somewhat complicated, and it requires extra disk I/O to keep nodes well populated. Since disk space is cheap, most systems architects have decided to allow nodes to become depopulated without automatic reorganization. Usually nodes of the tree are released if they become completely empty, so that an index that grows on the right and gets deleted on the left (such as an index by calendar date/time for a schedule table) releases old nodes as it uses new ones. The major reason for concern with a sparsely populated index is not the disk space (which is cheap, as we have said), but the extra disk I/Os entailed in a range search for some number of entries that are spread on an unusually large number of leaf nodes. To respond to such inefficiencies, the various database systems provide utilities to *reorganize* the B-tree. Such utilities duplicate the work of the original index creation and result in a clean new copy, with efficient disk utilization. We introduce a number of other disk storage considerations in the following sections.

Properties of the B-Tree

Definition 7.3.1 describes a B-tree structure that we have discussed. The definition assumes that entry key values can have variable length because of variable-length column values appearing in the index key; many definitions in the literature assume fixed-size entries. The definition also assumes that when a node split occurs, equal lengths of entry information are placed in the left and right split node; some products allow the nodes to split in an uneven fashion, for example, to optimize for a situation where rows are being inserted in increasing order by key value. Finally, the definition assumes that rebalancing actions in the B-tree occur when entries are deleted, as explained in the previous paragraph, or else that delete operations are overwhelmed by insert operations, so that the B-tree structure stays totally balanced.

DEFINITION 7.3.1 Properties of the B-Tree (B$^+$-Tree) Structure. A B-tree has a tree-like structure with multi-way fanout from the root down to the leaves, so that the following properties hold.

[1] Every node is disk-page sized and resides in a well-defined location on the disk.

477

[2] Nodes above the leaf level contain directory entries, with n − 1 separator keys and n disk pointers to lower-level B-tree nodes.

[3] Nodes at the leaf level contain entries with (`keyval`,`rowid`) pairs pointing to individual rows indexed.

[4] All nodes below the root are at least half full with entry information.

[5] The root node contains at least two entries (except in the case where only one row is indexed and the root is a leaf node containing a single (`keyval`, `rowid`) pair). ■

Index Node Layout and Free Space

An index node page has a relatively simple structure. Figure 7.12 shows the schematic layout of a normal leaf-level index node with unique key values. Because of the splits that occur in a growing B-tree, the nodes of a tree that results from random insert activity will vary randomly from half full to full (except for the root, which may have as few as two subsidiary node pointer entries). The average node below the root level will be about 71% full in an extremely active growing B-tree, *not* three-quarters full, as might seem more intuitive. This fullness percentage can be derived by mathematical analysis, and matches well with empirical observations. The percentage holds for all nodes except the root, and it means that the earlier analysis of the number of leaf pages required for a million-row table is not likely to be correct if the B-tree results from a large number of randomly inserted rows.

Figure 7.12 Layout of a Leaf-Level Index Node with Unique Key Values

EXAMPLE 7.3.4 Corrected B-Tree Structure for a Million Index Entries.
As in Example 7.3.3, we assume once again an index entry size of 8 bytes and a node page size of 2048 bytes. But now we allow 48 bytes for the header and assume that the average node below the root level is only 70% full (close to 71%). This implies 1400 bytes of entries per node, and 1400/8 = 175 entries per node. With 1,000,000 entries at the leaf level, this means we will require CEIL(1,000,000/175) = 5715 leaf node pages. With 5715 entries at the next-higher directory level, we will have CEIL(5715/175) = 33 page nodes on that level. Thus we have 33 directory entries at the root level, and we still have a B-tree of depth three. In general, we encourage rather rough calculations in sizings of this kind; a header size of 48 bytes is probably incorrect for any particular product, but (with a fullness of 70%) this gives us a round number for our calculations. ■

Recall that the purpose of a B-tree index is to minimize the number of disk I/Os needed to locate a row with a given index key value. The depth of a B-tree bears a close relationship to the number of disk I/Os used to reach the leaf-level entry where the rowid is kept. It is common to estimate the fanout at each level to have the value n, where n is the expected number of entries that appear in each node. Assuming that there are n directory entries at the root node and every node below that, the number of entries at the second level is n^2, the number at the third level n^3, and so on. For a tree of depth K, the number of leaf-level entries is n^K just before a root split occurs in the tree to make it a tree of depth K+1. Putting this a different way, if we want to build a B-tree with entries for M rows, then we need to have K levels, where

$$K = CEIL(\log_n(M))$$

Thus the depth of the tree bears a logarithmic relationship to the number of rows to be indexed. The depth K is then taken to be the number of I/Os that must be performed to look up a key value entry at the leaf level. However, it turns out that both of these statements are misleading. Because of buffering, the upper levels of the B-tree are almost certain to be buffer resident for any B-tree that is commonly used (and we don't really care very much about performance of B-trees that are infrequently used). Generally an active B-tree of depth three has all nodes buffer resident above the leaf level, but very few leaf-level nodes resident, so the effective number of real I/Os that must be performed to look up a leaf entry is one, rather than three. At the same time, the logarithmic relationship of tree depth to number of entries indexed is misleading because the fanout n is so large as to be unintuitive. With the assumptions of Example 7.3.4, the average number of entries in each node is 175, and this is also the fanout n. Ignoring the fact the number of entries in the root will be somewhat greater, this means that when a B-tree of depth two is about to have a root split it contains $175^2 = 30,625$ entries at the leaf level. We then have a B-tree of depth three, and there will not be another root split until we have $175^3 = 5,359,375$ entries! This provides enough entries to index a 5-million-row table, and it is fairly unusual to have B-trees with more than three levels.

It is usually most efficient, when creating indexes on a table with many database products, to first load the table with the initial set of rows and then to create the indexes. This is advantageous because the process used by Create Index to first extract the index entries, then sort the entries by key value, and finally load the sorted entries into the leaf level of the B-tree is extremely efficient. (In **DB2**, the REORG utility has the equivalent effect for the Index load.) The nodes of the B-tree are all loaded in a left-to-right fashion, so that successive inserts normally occur to the same leaf node, held consistently in memory buffer. When the leaf node splits, the successive leaf node is allocated from the next disk page of the allocated extent. Node splits at every level occur in a controlled way and allow us to leave just the right amount of free space on each page. On the other hand, as rows are inserted after the initial Create Index statement, this normally results in B-tree entries that are inserted to random leaf-level nodes, requiring much more I/O (because the B-tree leaf page affected is often not in buffer) and random node splits.

Create Index Statement in ORACLE and DB2

It is possible of course that a B-tree index will remain unchanged after being created. This would occur if the table indexed is guaranteed to have no new row inserts or updates that affect the columns indexed. If no changes are envisioned, we should start with all B-tree nodes packed full. However, if new entry inserts are likely, it is a bad idea to have fully packed nodes in a newly created index. A small number of new inserts will cause a very large number of initial node splits (costly in I/O and CPU), with the result that the number of nodes quickly doubles and ends up only half full, an unfortunate waste of resources. In most database systems we can control how full the index B-tree gets packed during its initial creation. In

Figure 7.13, which repeats the syntax presented in Figure 7.7, we illustrate this with a clause provided with the **ORACLE** Create Index statement, known as the **pctfree** clause.

```
create [unique] index indexname on tablename
    (columnname [asc | desc] {, columnname [asc | desc]})
    [tablespace tblspacename]
    [storage ([initial n] [next n] [minextents n]
        [maxextents n] [pctincrease n] ) ]
    [pctfree n]
    [other disk storage and transaction clauses not covered or deferred]
    [nosort];
```

Figure 7.13 **ORACLE** Create Index Statement Syntax, with **pctfree** Clause

The value of n in the **pctfree** clause can range from 0 to 99, and this number determines the percentage of each B-tree node page (recall that a page is known as a *block* in **ORACLE**) that will be left unfilled when the index is originally created. This space is then available for new index entry inserts when rows are inserted to the underlying table. The default value for pctfree is 10, and larger values permit more row insertions before node splits occur. A comparable parameter for leaving free space in index nodes is provided by **DB2**. Indeed, **ORACLE** makes an effort to remain compatible with **DB2** syntax, so we can expect identical naming conventions when differences in disk storage architecture don't require variations. A simple version of the **DB2** Create Index statement syntax is given in Figure 7.14.

```
create [unique] index indexname on tablename
    (columnname [asc | desc] {, columnname [asc | desc]})
    [using . . .]
    [freepage n]
    [pctfree n]
    [additional clauses not covered or deferred];
```

Figure 7.14 Simple Version of **DB2** Create Index Statement Syntax

The **using** clause of the **DB2** Create Index statement specifies how the index is to be constructed from disk files (called *data sets* in IBM nomenclature) and takes the place of the **tablespace** and **storage** clauses of the **ORACLE** Create Index statement. The **pctfree** clause in **DB2** is identical in meaning to the **ORACLE** form, but **DB2** adds another free storage specification with the **freepage** clause. The integer n of the **freepage** clause specifies how frequently an empty free page should be left in the sequence of pages assigned to the index when it is loaded with entries by a **DB2** utility. One free page is left for every n index pages, where n varies from 0 to 255. The default value for n is 0, meaning that no free pages are left. A value of n =1, however, means that alternate disk pages are left empty. The intention here is to leave some free pages for node splits in the B-tree, so that newly split nodes can remain as close as possible on disk to the immediate sibling nodes from which they split. As we will see in the next chapter, **DB2** makes extremely efficient use of contiguous disk storage when doing index range retrievals, so it is especially important to keep leaf nodes as contiguous as possible on disk.

Create Index Statement in INGRES

The Create Index statement in **INGRES** has the syntax given in Figure 7.15.

```
create [unique] index indexname on tablename
       (columnname {, columnname})
     [with                   /* commas separate clauses following */
        [location = . . . ]
        [structure = btree | isam | hash | . . . ]
        [key = (columnname {, columnname})]
        [fillfactor = n]
        [nonleaffill = n]
        [additional clauses not covered or deferred] ];
```

Figure 7.15 INGRES Create Index Statement Syntax

Note that the **asc | desc** descriptor for columnnames of the index is missing. However, this is not visible to the SQL user, who can still specify ascending or descending columns in the **order by** clause of a Select statement. The **with** keyword must be present if any of the later comma-separated clauses appear. The **location** clause specifies how the index is to be constructed from disk files and takes the place of the **tablespace** and **storage** clauses of the **ORACLE** Create Index statement. The **structure** clause is unique to **INGRES** and names the access structure that the index will be assigned when it is created. The structure with which we are familiar is known as *btree,* and we will explore the other structures shortly.

The **key** clause indicates that the index key value will be constructed from the columnnames listed, a subset of the columnnames on the second row of the syntax, listed in the same order. Columns appearing on the second row that are not part of the **key** clause are available to the **INGRES** Query Optimizer to perform an efficient type of index-only retrieval, as explained more fully in Chapter 8.

The **fillfactor** and **nonleaffill** parameters of the **INGRES** Create Index statement compare to the **pctfree** parameters of the **DB2** and **ORACLE** statements, except that where **pctfree** gives the percentage of node space that should remain *unfilled* during the initial creation of the index, **fillfactor** and **nonleaffill** give the percentage of the node space that should be *filled*. Fillfactor gives the percentage for what we can think of as leaf nodes of the index, and **nonleaffill** the percentage for non-leaf nodes.

INGRES pictures indexes rather differently than other products do, and this difference is somewhat subtle. Recall that a B-tree index entry consists of a pair of values (keyval, tid). **INGRES** pictures the index as a *table in its own right,* containing two-column rows of the form (keyval, tid), but a special form of table because the system uses it for lookup and users are not allowed to update the table (that is, index) directly. **INGRES** always defines something called a *structure* for all its tables; a structure determines the way in which rows are stored on disk and often determines too a *primary index* lookup directory for keyed access to the table. For example, one of the structure types possible for a table is the *heap* structure, where new rows are simply placed in entry order and there is no lookup directory. Another type of structure is known as btree. In this case a B-tree type directory is created for the table, and **INGRES** attempts to store rows of the table on disk in the same key value order as the entries at leaf level of the B-tree directory. We will have more to say about such structures in Section 7.4, when we deal with clustered indexes. The disk pages that contain the "rows" of an **INGRES** index can be thought of as the leaf nodes of a classical B-tree. If we now impose a btree structure on these rows, it seems from the descriptions of the structures involved that there will be an extra layer of entries in what we have been calling our B-tree index, as depicted in Figure 7.16—a btree structure imposed on the rows of an index. However, **INGRES** detects the inefficiency and removes one of the redundant layers.

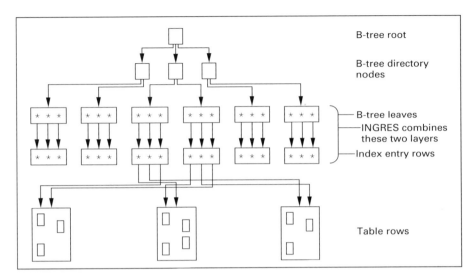

Figure 7.16 Extra Layer Removed by **INGRES** from an Index with a btree Structure

To enlarge on the potential problem arising in Figure 7.16, it would seem from the description of index rows given in the **INGRES** manuals [4, 5] that the index entries have been created to correspond one-to-one with the rows of the table. Meanwhile, the btree structure on the index also normally has a leaf level, whose entries correspond one-to-one with the index entry "rows." The resulting structure would have two leaf levels in the directory, corresponding to both the B-tree leaf level and the index entry level. With such an extra leaf level, assuming a large index that cannot fit in memory buffers, we would be increasing the number of I/Os by about one for every row access through this index. It is therefore important to realize that **INGRES** detects this special case and omits storing the index entry rows on separate data pages. Instead the (keyval, tid) entries on the leaf level of the btree structure point directly to the corresponding table rows, and the extra layer is removed. Thus the btree structure on an **INGRES** index defined on a table is completely analogous to the B-tree index on a table we have been studying.

Another structure available in **INGRES** is known as the *isam* structure, shown in Figure 7.17.

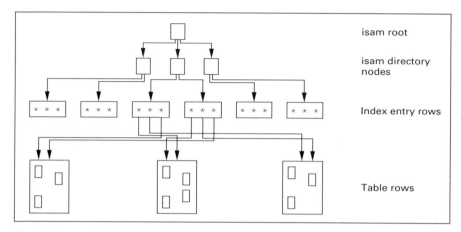

Figure 7.17 An **INGRES** Index with an isam Structure

In an **INGRES** isam structure, the "rows" of the index lie on pages in order by key value, and an isam directory sits above these rows and channels access to the index page where the desired entry can be found. There is no leaf level to the isam directory, and the "rows" at the index level act like B-tree leaf level entries. The isam structure is the default structure imposed on the index created by the Create Index statement in **INGRES**. The result is very much like the types of B-tree indexes we have been studying up to now. However, an important weakness with the isam structure is that the directory nodes are *static:* they do not create new separators in the way that we are used to with upper nodes of a B-tree index when a page of leaf-level entries splits. Thus, as new entries are added to the index "table," new pages are sometimes created to contain entries between a pair of static separators, and the isam structure always channels a keyed search to the same page of entries it pointed to originally. Multiple pages split from that original page are chain-linked on disk, and a search for a particular entry key value often leads to reading in all entry pages that have been linked together. Needless to say, this can be extremely costly in terms of I/O when the chain of index entry pages grows long, and we need to think of defensive tactics in certain situations. For tables that might expect a great deal of growth at one end of a key value range, for example, we would probably prefer a btree structure on the index so that we achieve more flexibility in accessing newly created entries without having to follow a chain of disk pointers.

On the other hand, an isam structure on a table has a number of
advantages over a btree structure, as we will explain in Section 7.4.

Duplicate Key Values in an Index

In our discussion of B-tree structure so far, we have not assumed a unique
restriction on the entry key values. Indeed, in Example 7.3.1, when discussing binary search, we considered the possibility of duplicate key values and
provided an algorithm to find the leftmost key value in a set of duplicates.
The succession of key values inserted into the B-tree index of Figure 7.11 is
7, 96, 41, 39, 88, 65, 55, 62. These values have no duplicates, but looking
at the final B-tree form at the bottom of this figure, we can easily imagine
how we would handle a new row insert with a duplicate key value of 88. A
new index entry with key value 88 would be placed in the rightmost leaf-
level node, next to the existing entry with key value 88; the rowid of the
latest 88 entry (not pictured in Figure 7.11) would point to the newly
inserted row, while the rowid of the former 88 entry would continue to
point to the earlier row with that key value. Thus the two index entries are
actually different—although they have the same key values, they have different rowid pointers—and both pieces of information are needed for a
proper B-tree directory to reflect key values of all rows of the table.

But what would happen now if we inserted two more rows with key
value 88? In the example pictured, where no leaf-level node can contain
more than three entries, this would mean that the entries with key value 88
would have to continue from one leaf node to another. This in turn means
that the separator entry in the directory above the leaf needs to distinguish
these two leaf-level nodes by using the separator value 88. See Figure 7.18,
where we also assume that there are nodes at the leaf level with entry key
values above 96, so that a separator of 96 is appropriate.

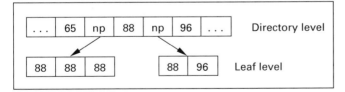

Figure 7.18 B-Tree Structure with Multiple Duplicate Key Values

Using a separator value of 88 seems a bit strange, since this value does not really distinguish key values in the two nodes below (there are key values of 88 in both cases). Therefore the system has to take this fact into account in answering queries. Specifically, when the system processes a query to retrieve all rows that have this key value equal to 88, it passes down the directory level to find the leftmost entry with value 88. This is in the leaf node with directory pointer between the separator values 65 and 88 in Figure 7.18. After reaching the leaf level, the system reads through all leaf-level entries that have key value 88, jumping from one leaf node to the next if the possibility of another match exists on the successive leaf node. Note that this approach to retrieving successive duplicate entries on successive leaf pages for an exact match condition (key value = 88) generalizes naturally to range retrieval (for example, key value between 88 and 120). To make this kind of successive retrieval easy, leaf nodes usually have *sibling pointers* in their header info segment that point to successive leaf nodes. (There should also be sibling pointers to the *prior* leaf node in sequence, in case a Select request in descending order requires retrieval in that direction.)

Now consider the case where the number of key value entries of 88 increases to a point that we must have two duplicate separator values in the directory level above. Nothing is wrong with this as long as our directory search algorithm is reasonably intelligent about always finding the way to the leftmost entries at the leaf level, thus always following the leftmost directory pointer to a desired value. We will still be able to retrieve all entries with key value = 88 by starting at the left and proceeding through all successive entries with the same key value. An interesting situation arises, however, when we wish to delete a row that has key value 88. To properly complete the row delete, the associated entry from the B-tree leaf level must be removed as well; otherwise we are left with an index entry pointing to a nonexistent row. Since the entry is not uniquely identified by its key value, the system may have to read through a succession of entries, possibly on multiple leaf node pages, to retrieve the entry with key value equal to 88 *that has the rowid value of the row being deleted*. It is possible to keep the leaf-level lookup entries in order by rowid within key value and to allow directory separator values to carry this rowid information as well. Then successive separators are unique, since they contain a unique rowid suffix value, and a fast lookup of any particular rowid with key value 88 can be performed through the B-tree directory. However, such an approach is currently not implemented on most commercial database systems. A delete of a row that corresponds to a heavily duplicated key value usually entails a long search through the leaf-level of the B-tree.

Although duplicate separators are theoretically acceptable in a B-tree structure with careful search algorithms, they are not permitted in all commercial database systems. **INGRES**, for example, does not allow duplicate separator values at the level above the leaves, while **DB2** does permit such duplicates.

Index Compression with Multiple Duplicates

There is an opportunity when multiple duplicate key values are present to save a good deal of space in the leaf nodes. Because the same key value is repeated for a large number of rows, it is possible to list the key value only once for a long list of rowid values. Because the key value is often a relatively lengthy character string and the rowid value is usually quite short, this represents a large saving. In **DB2**, where the ROWID is referred to as RID, the leaf nodes of a B-tree index have somewhat different forms, depending on whether the key value is unique or has a number of duplicates. We have already seen, in Figure 7.12, what the **DB2** leaf-node layout with unique key values would look like. Figure 7.19 shows the layout where multiple duplicate key values are present.

Figure 7.19   Layout of a **DB2** Leaf Node with Non-Unique Key Values

We see that where non-unique key values are the rule, **DB2** is able to represent the key value once, followed by a string of RID values. There is a prefix of 6 bytes for each distinct RID list block, represented by Prx in the figure. This block prefix contains a 2-byte offset to the next and prior blocks, together with a 1-byte count of the number of RID values contained in the current block and 1 byte of unused space. The number of RID values in a block has an upper limit of 255, but clearly it is possible to create a successive block with the same key value. If we assume a character string key value of length 10 bytes, then each unique key takes up 14 bytes (length of keyval + RID), and 100 such entries take up 1400 bytes. On the other hand, 100 duplicate entries take up 6 + 10 + 100 • 4 = 416 bytes (length of prefix + `keyval` + 100 RID values), a significant saving. Clearly, as the number of duplicates grows, the space needed for leaf-level indexes becomes quite close to the space needed for RID values alone.

7.4 | Clustered and Non-Clustered Indexes

We saw in the discussion of Figure 7.6, and in the heap structure we mentioned for **INGRES**, how rows of a table are typically inserted on successive data storage pages on disk, one after another. In a library, this would correspond to placing volumes on shelves in order by acquisition—an unusual procedure, admittedly, but one that would be feasible as long as various card catalog indexes allowed us to locate all books by any useful category, including Dewey decimal classification for nonfiction texts. It is more common to place books on the shelves in order by Dewey decimal number for nonfiction and author's name for fiction. (Actually, the order for fiction books is usually determined by the concatenated index key: authlname ‖ authfname ‖ authmidinitial ‖ title.) The advantage of such ordering on the shelves is convenience. If we want to locate all the novels by Charles Dickens, we can look up any Dickens novel in the card catalog and proceed to the shelves, where all novels by Dickens are grouped together. This saves us quite a few steps. Similarly, if we want to find books on building bridges, we will probably find them all clustered together under the appropriate Dewey classification (the classification is by the major topic of a nonfiction work).

Placing books on shelves—or rows on disk—in order by some common index key value is called *clustering*. An index with referenced rows in the same order as its key values is known as a *clustered index*, or sometimes a *clustering index*. A slightly more general concept is a *primary index* for a table, which determines the placement of the rows (not necessarily the ordering, since there is no ordering in a hash index, for example). The advantage of a clustered index in a database is that certain queries are more efficiently answered when the desired rows are close to one another. The average row takes up only a small fraction of a page, so that when rows with common index key values are clustered together and we read in the data page from disk containing one of the rows with a given key value, other rows with the same key value are likely to lie on the same page.

Thus, in accessing those other rows, we don't have to repeat the disk I/O required to access the first row. Even if our database access method is relatively naive and accesses the rows only one at a time on the basis of their rowid values, we find that second and successive rows in a clustered index lie on a page that is already in memory buffers (Figure 7.2), which were constructed to save I/O for accesses to popular pages. On the other hand, a non-clustered index does not have this advantage. Successive index entries of a non-clustered index reference rows on disk pages that are likely to be far apart, so there is no saving from one row to another. It is as if we placed books on library shelves in order by acquisition, and then had to walk all over the library to retrieve all the Dickens novels. See Figure 7.20 for a schematic idea of a clustered versus a non-clustered index.

EXAMPLE 7.4.1

A large department store with hundreds of branch stores has records of 10 million customers in 200 cities. Occasionally it wants to perform a mailing to announce a sale in a specific metropolitan area, and it generates mailing labels with a query such as the following:

```
select name, address, city, state, zip from customers
    where city = 'Boston';
```

Of course the fields would be formatted for mailing labels through an application program and the query would be performed in Embedded SQL through a cursor, but the I/O performance considerations are the same in both cases. Now let us assume that the department store uses a database system with 2-KB pages, and each customer row requires 100 bytes. We can therefore calculate that each page contains 20 rows. We can also calculate that the average city contains 50,000 customer rows (dividing 10 million by 200). Of course some cities contain more than others, but let us use this figure as an average.

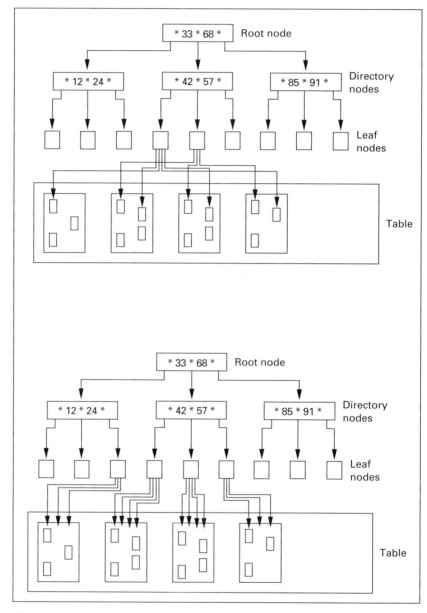

Figure 7.20 A Comparison of Non-Clustered (Top) and Clustered (Bottom) Indexes

Now if the `customers` table is clustered by the `city` column (or some concatenated index key such as state ‖ city ‖ address that implies clustering by `city`
value), then these 50,000 rows occur on a succession of 50,000/20 = 2500 disk
pages. If we ignore I/O for index pages (relatively small in comparison), and use
the approximation of Section 7.2 that a disk arm can perform 40 I/Os per second, this query requires 2500/40 = 62.5 seconds to perform.

On the other hand, if the rows of the `customers` table are *not* clustered by
city, successive entries from the index point to rows on randomly scattered
pages of the table. Since there are 10 million rows of 100 bytes each, this is a
gigabyte of storage, and it is quite likely that most of the table pages are not
memory-buffer resident. Therefore we require essentially one I/O for each row
retrieved and 50,000 I/Os for the query. The time required for the query is
50,000/40 = 1250 seconds, about 20 minutes. ■

We made a large number of assumptions in arriving at the time estimates of Example 7.4.1, but we will defer detailed considerations of such
performance assumptions until the next chapter. For now, we simply say
that the estimates we have just made are probably in the ballpark for most
commercial applications, and the enormous variation in performance
between clustered and non-clustered conditions makes the value of clustering obvious. We should add that we do not require a large number of
duplicate key values in a table to see large differences between clustered
and non-clustered performance. A query that uses a **between** predicate,
"`between keyval1 and keyval2`" (sometimes called a range predicate), can also benefit enormously from clustered indexes even when key
values are unique. Unfortunately, we can only cluster a table by one index
at a time. Clearly we can't place nonfiction books on library shelves in
order by Dewey decimal classification and by author name simultaneously—we must choose one or the other. The index we use to cluster the
underlying data rows depends a great deal on the most common query
types in use at a database site. The DBA usually makes this clustering decision in consultation with application managers and programmers who are
aware of the most common query needs.

Clustered Index in DB2

The next question, of course, is, How do we create a clustered index? The
Create Index statement forms we have seen up to now don't give any special syntax for ensuring that the rows are ordered in the same way as the
index entries. In fact, the approach to creating a clustered index differs

from one product to another. In **DB2** the Create Index statement has a special **cluster** clause.

```
create [unique] index indexname on tablename
    (columnname [asc | desc] [, columnname [asc | desc]])
    <numerous clauses omitted>
    [cluster . . . ];
```

Figure 7.21   DB2 cluster Clause for Create Index

The **DB2 cluster** clause has no arguments, except in the case that the index being created is a partitioned index, a variation we do not cover here. Only one index for a table can be identified as a **cluster** index. When an index is identified as a clustered index in an empty table that is about to be loaded with new rows, the **DB2** LOAD utility causes rows to be sorted into the appropriate order when they are placed on disk. Existing rows of a table are not rearranged immediately into a clustered sequence after a clustered index is defined, however. A special utility, known as the REORG utility, must be run to cause the reordering of the rows to match this clustered index. The result in **DB2** looks like the tree structure at the bottom of Figure 7.20, a B-tree index conceptually lying above a sequence of table rows placed in data pages in the same order. Indeed the entire structure looks a bit like a B-tree with an extra level, with the data rows in order by key value at the new leaf level and the former leaf level of the index acting as a higher-level directory to the rows (not just the data pages, as it would be for a true directory to the leaf level of a B-tree).

Unfortunately, the analogy is somewhat inaccurate because of the behavior of the structure as new rows are inserted. **DB2** advises the table creator to leave free space on the data pages for the table, and successive row inserts are directed by **DB2** to the free slots on the appropriate data page to maintain the clustering order whenever this is feasible. However, when a data page runs out of slots and new rows are inserted that would normally be placed on such a page, the B-tree approach of *splitting* the leaf node does not take place on the data pages. Instead a new data page is allocated in the current extent, probably far removed from the clustered page position, and newly inserted rows are placed on this data page in rather arbitrary order as the original clustered data pages fill up. The longer we proceed with new inserts, the less clustered the index becomes because of latecomer rows that are entirely out of clustered sequence. Eventually the index can lose much of its clustering property, and the user is advised to run the REORG utility again in order to cause the rows to be resorted in appropriate order.

Clustered Index in INGRES

The **INGRES** database system provides a new statement, the Modify statement, to create a clustered index that places the rows of the table in order by index key value. The general form of the Modify command in **INGRES** is shown in Figure 7.22.

```
modify tablename | indexname
     to [btree | isam | hash | heap | . . . ]
         | [merge | relocate | reorganize | truncated ]
     [unique] [on columnname [, columnname]]
     [with                  /* commas separate clauses following    */
         [location = ...] [, newlocation = ...] [, oldlocation = ...]
         [minpages = n] [, maxpages = n]
         [fillfactor = n]
         [leaffill = n]
         [nonleaffill = n] ];
```

Figure 7.22   INGRES Modify Statement to Create a Clustered Index Structure

Recall from the discussion following Figure 7.15 that **INGRES** pictures an index as a table with rows of two columns, (keyval, tid), and a default isam-type directory. More generally, **INGRES** creates such a directory on an arbitrary table when the Modify statement is applied to the table with structure-type btree or isam. Refer again to Figures 7.15 and 7.16 for the directory structures btree and isam on an arbitrary table, except that after the Modify statement used above, the table rows at the bottom layers are also in clustered order, as in the bottom tree of Figure 7.20. Clearly these structures are what we have been referring to as clustered indexes. (Structure-type *heap* is simply a structure with no directory where new inserts are placed left to right on new pages of new extents; heap is the normal default structure for newly created tables. We defer consideration of hash structured tables until the next section.)

When the Modify statement is issued to create btree or isam structures, all rows of the named table are immediately sorted in order by key value and placed on data pages. The clustering index is created with no name—it is simply the primary means of access to the rows of the table. Note too that an index name can be given as the object of a Modify command in order to provide the index with a new structure. For example, an existing index with structure isam can be given a new btree structure. If instead of a structure name in the Modify command, one of the verbs **merge, relocate, reorganize,** or **truncated** is specified, the action specified is relative to an already existing structure type for the table. The **merge** action, for example, performs a minor reorganization of a btree directory structure (only this structure is affected), spreading the information evenly on the nodes at all levels. The **truncated** action deletes all the rows of the table, releases the disk space used, and converts the resulting empty table to the heap structure.

We have seen the **location** clause before with the Create Index statement of Figure 7.15. It specifies how the modified table is to be constructed from disk files. The **oldlocation** and **newlocation** clauses are appropriate only when the **relocate** verb is used, which specifies how the table is to be moved to a new location on disk. The **minpages** and **maxpages** clauses are relevant only for hash structures, and we therefore defer consideration. The **fillfactor** parameter determines how full of rows each data page will be during the initial reorganization to this structure, with a value n varying from 1 to 100. The **leaffill** and **nonleaffill** parameters determine how full of index entries the leaf-level nodes of a B-tree (immediately above the data-page level) and higher-level directory nodes (nonleaf nodes of a btree or isam structure) will be during the initial reorganization. In considering the Create Index statement, we referred to the **fillfactor** parameter as controlling how full leaf nodes of the index will be, identifying data pages of an index with leaf nodes of other btree indexes we had been discussing, and left out consideration of the **leaffill** parameter under the assumption that the index would have an isam structure.

EXAMPLE 7.4.2

Consider again the `customers` table of Example 7.4.1, with 10 million customers in 200 cities, each row requiring 100 bytes. Consider the following Modify statement in **INGRES**:

```
modify customers to btree on state, city, street
    with fillfactor = 80, leaffill = 70, nonleaffill = 75;
```

7.4 Clustered and Non-Clustered Indexes

We assume pages of 2 KB, with roughly 2000 bytes available after leaving space for the header. With a fillfactor of 80, this means that 1600 bytes are available for rows, which implies that we ought to be able to fit 16 rows of 100 bytes (we might have only 15 rows after leaving space for the row directory of Figure 7.6, 16 2-byte offsets, but we left too much for the header, so it may even out—these are rough calculations, and a difference up to 10% doesn't matter much). Now with 10 million rows and 16 rows per page, we see that we will have about CEIL(10,000,000/16) = **625,000 data pages**. Next we assume that the state column is declared char(2), city as varchar(16), and street as varchar(16), where the average length of city and state values together amounts to 16 bytes, so that the key value in the index is (on the average) 18 bytes. The tid is 4 bytes; therefore, each leaf-level entry in the btree structure requires about 22 bytes. Since **leaffill** is 70, we have available 1400 bytes at the leaf level, and we can calculate the number of entries that will fit on a page as FLOOR(1400/22) = 63 (leftover space, less than entry size, is wasted of course).

Now we can calculate the number of pages needed for the leaf level of the B-tree, one entry for each row of the table, as CEIL(10,000,000/63) = **158,730 leaf node pages**. At all higher levels of the btree, the **nonleaffill** parameter of 75 is determining, with 1500 bytes available. We still have an entry size of 22 bytes and therefore can calculate the number of entries per page as FLOOR(1500/22) = 68. We need 158,729 separators to distinguish between the leaf-level nodes, a total of 158,730 directory entries, and therefore the number of nodes needed at this level is CEIL(158,730/68) = **2334 directory node pages**. At the next level up, we need CEIL(2482/68) = **34 directory node pages**. And at the level above, we can fit the 34 entries required in a single node: **1 root page**. We have arrived at a four-level btree assuming a 10-million-row table, so clearly a five-level btree is very rare indeed.

We might instead have used the isam structure:

```
modify customers to isam on state, city
    with fillfactor 80, nonleaffill = 75;
```

No **leaffill** parameter is required because there is no leaf level for an isam structure. With 625,000 data pages (as calculated above), the next level of isam directory has 625,000 entries, 68 entries to a page as we calculated for nonleaffill = 75, and the number of nodes can be calculated as CEIL(625,000/68) = **9192 directory node pages**. At the next higher level, we require CEIL(9192/68) = **136 directory node pages**. The next higher level requires CEIL(136/68) = **2 directory node pages**, and there is one further level with **1 root page** (only two entries). This is still a four-level tree, but the first three levels will probably remain in buffer relatively consistently (1 + 2 + 136), assuming several hundred buffer pages, so a random row lookup will often require only two disk accesses (the lowest-level directory and data page). The B-tree mentioned above will probably only be able to fit two levels in buffer (1 + 37—the 2482-node level three is too large), and therefore most random row lookups will require three disk accesses. Recall the inflexibility of the isam structure, however, in that newly inserted rows do not cause new separators to be created in the directory. We may wish to avoid an isam structure for this reason. ∎

New rows inserted in a table with a btree or isam structure are placed on available slots of the appropriate data page, containing nearby rows in key value sequence, as long as space remains on the page. This is important in cases where a range retrieval is performed, as in Example 7.4.1, to minimize the number of data pages that must be accessed to answer the query. After space on the data pages runs out, successive row inserts are placed on a faraway page, and we begin to lose the clustered index property, just as we did with **DB2**. We can perform a complete reorganization of the table, creating a fresh btree or isam structure, by issuing the original Modify statement again. Performing a Modify on a large table can be very time consuming, of course. In addition, when the Modify statement is performed the rows all move to new positions, and as a result all existing indexes on the table become invalid and must be recreated, adding more overhead.

7.5 A Hash Primary Index

As background for this section, the reader is assumed to have encountered the concept of a memory-resident hash table in an earlier data structures text. As with tree structures, the difference between a memory-resident hash structure and a database index structure using hashed access is that the database index is meant to reside on disk, being made partially memory resident only when entries in the structure are accessed. We start with the definition of what is meant by a *primary index*.

DEFINITION 7.5.1 Primary Index. A primary index is an index in which the row placement in the table is determined by the index value. ∎

We saw examples of a primary index when we considered clustered B-tree and isam indexes, but the connotation associated with a clustered index is that rows with nearby key values are close to one another on disk. The idea of a primary index is slightly more general and encompasses the hash primary index situation. Note that an **INGRES** table structure created by the Modify command always imposes a primary index unless no index key is specified (that is, a primary index is created with all structures except heap).

A *hash primary index* for a table provides keyed lookup by a method that is entirely different from the btree and isam directory structures just studied. With a hash primary index, rows inserted in a table are placed in a pseudo-random data page determined by a hash function applied to the key value, and retrieved in the same way, usually with a single I/O operation. There is no key value *directory*: lookup depends on proceeding directly to the appropriate pseudo-random data page slot by hashing on key value. There is no *order by key value* possible in such a structure. Normally in hashing, we can only ask for a specific key value, not for "the next key value in sequence after this one," as we could in a B-tree directory. We would expect two rows with successive key values to be located on entirely uncorrelated data pages, depending on the caprice of the hash function. As a result, SQL retrievals using the **between** predicate on some column value will not be aided by a hash primary index on that column; unless the possible values in the range of the **between** predicate can be shown to consist of only a small number of possible values, a scan of the entire table is needed to determine all rows that satisfy the given predicate. This is a serious limitation, but the compensating value of hash primary indexes lies in speedy access to rows in large tables by specific key value. The ability to access a desired row with a single I/O is a great advantage when compared with btree or isam directory structures, which often require extra I/O for directory search in large tables, as we saw in Example 7.4.2.

It is perfectly possible in **INGRES** to create an index for a table using the Create Index statement and then to modify the structure of the index to hash. Now the entries of the index rather than the table rows themselves are directly accessed on disk by a hash function. The index entry is then retrieved in a single I/O and points to the row indexed with its contained tid, entailing a second I/O. We say that this type of hash index is no longer a *primary index*, but rather a *secondary index*. Most indexes we have seen are secondary, in the sense that they do *not* determine the placement of the rows they index, and we therefore have an intervening layer of access through the tid pointer.

Hash primary indexes exist in **INGRES**, and an alternative hash feature exists in **ORACLE** version 7, but hashing is not possible in **DB2** at this time. We illustrate the discussion that follows with **INGRES** hash-structured tables. The general form of the Modify command to give a table a hash structure is shown in Figure 7.23.

```
modify tablename | indexname
    to hash [unique] [on columnname {, columnname}]
    [with
        [location = . . . ]
        [minpages = n] [, maxpages = n]
        [fillfactor = n] ];
```

Figure 7.23 INGRES Modify Statement to Create a Hash Index

As with isam and btree, we do not insist on unique key values unless the keyword **unique** is present. If no column names are specified in the Modify command, the index key defaults to the first column mentioned in the Create command for the table. To see how the hash structure is built, we provide the following explanation.

In Figure 7.24 we see a picture of a hash-structured table with 7 stored rows sparsely filling 96 slots on 8 data pages (12 rows can fit on each page, and a page is pictured as a sequence of 12 slots on each level of the figure). A hash function h is being applied to the same key values that were inserted into the B-tree of Figure 7.11, and we see only the key values of the rows stored in the slots of the current figure. Slots for a given row key value might be determined in a number of different ways. One way is to hash on a given key value to a given disk page and then find an empty slot somewhere on the page where the row can be stored. However, we assume in what follows that the precise slot among all slots on any page of the table is being determined by the hash function; if this slot is already in use (a situation known as a *hash collision*), then *rehashing* is performed in some deterministic way to locate successive slots to place the row. Rehashing might simply consist of looking at all other slots on the same page in some predetermined order until an empty one is found. In rehashing, *every attempt is made to find a new slot on the same page* as the one where the initial slot appeared, to minimize the number of I/Os needed to search through a chain of collisions. Only if we run out of slots on a page is a slot on a succeeding page used.

In Figure 7.24 we watch the final insertion of the row with the given key value 55 in the slot that has been determined by the hash function h

and then rehashed. In the figure we see that the row with key value 55 has
collided in slot 66 with the row already stored there (having key value 39)
and has been rehashed to slot 69.

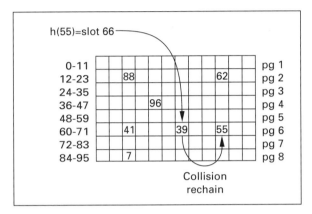

Figure 7.24 Hash-Structured Table, Inserting a New Row with Key Value 55
(Table pages correspond to single levels of 12 slots.)

How does **INGRES** arrive at the number of slots and data pages for a
table? At the time that the Modify command of Figure 7.23 is issued, a
certain number, S, of data page slots on a known sequence of pages is set
aside for occupancy by rows of the table. If we assume that there are N
rows in the table, and the Modify statement specifies a **fillfactor** of f (an
integer from 1 to 100), then the number of slots set aside is expressed as
S = CEIL((100/f)$\ast$N). For example, if we had N = 100,000 rows in the
table and a **fillfactor** of 40, we would set S to (100/40)$\ast$100,000, or
250,000 slots. As a result of this calculation, if we place 100,000 rows into
250,000 row slots in pseudo-random locations, we find that the slots are
40% full, which gives us the motivation for our **fillfactor** calculation. Next
we calculate the number of pages P required for this number of slots,
and—assuming that we can guarantee placing at least R rows per page
(with maximum row sizes)—we get P = CEIL(S/R). In the above example
with 250,000 slots, if we could fit 20 rows per page, the number of pages P
required is 250,000/20 = 12,500 pages. If the optional parameters
minpages and **maxpages** are specified in the Modify statement, then
INGRES now overrides the calculated number of pages P. If P is greater
than **maxpages**, then P will be replaced by **maxpages**; if P is less than

minpages, then P will be replaced by **minpages**. The Modify command insists that the specified **minpages** parameter be smaller than **maxpages** and will not accept input where this relationship does not hold.

With this final number of pages P, we recalculate the number of slots, $S = P \cdot R$. If S is now too small to contain the number N of rows in the table (which might occur if too small a value for **maxpages** was specified), the Modify statement increases the number of pages available, using a type of overflow page chaining similar to the form of chaining used in the isam structure. Then an attempt is made to place the rows of the table into the slots 0 through $S - 1$. First each of the rows in the table modified would have its key value extracted. Then the database system uses a hash function, h, to generate a number between 0 and $S - 1$ based on the key value of each row; this is the slot value where we will attempt to store this row. The rows are then sorted by slot value, and later row collisions are rehashed to new slot numbers and then stored on the appropriate slots of successive data pages.

When all the rows have been inserted and we wish to look up a row by key value x, we apply the hash function h(x) to derive a slot number S_x and proceed directly to read in the known page containing that slot. We test the key of the row in the given slot and check that the key we are seeking is the one we've accessed—that is, that the row with key value x is in that slot. If not, then a collision has occurred, and we rehash our key value to find the rehash successor slot on the same page. We check this row key value for a match as well, and we rehash if it fails again. Eventually, if we do not find a row with matching key value, we will come to the end of the chain of collisions (the end of the chain is the first time we encounter an empty slot), usually while we remain on the same page that we originally read in from disk. We then know that there is no match on key value. Note that when duplicate keys are allowed, we must always continue to rehash while successive values of the collision chain remain, since finding a matching value does not guarantee there are no others to follow.

No Incremental Changes in the Number of Slots Used

It is important to realize that once the number of slots S in the hash data table has been specified, it cannot be incrementally enlarged (as we could with B-tree node splitting) when the slots fill up. The reason for this limitation in a hash index is as follows. The hash function can be thought of as having two phases in its calculation. In the first of these phases it generates a pseudo-random number based on the key value, x = r(keyvalue), where x is a floating point number uniformly distributed in the range 0 < x < 1. Next, the slot number h(keyvalue) resulting from the hash function can be generated with the following formula:

h(keyvalue) = INTEGER_PART_OF(S * r(keyvalue))

The formula results in a random slot number from the sequence 0, 1, . . . , S – 1. We take this two-phase approach because in this way the generic function r can easily lead to a uniform distribution of integers from 0 to S – 1, *for any given value of S*. However, if the total number of slots were now to change, say to S', we would find that the hash function

h'(keyvalue) = INTEGER_PART_OF(S' * r(keyvalue))

would not give the same slot number for all slot placements previously calculated. For example, if r(keyvalue) is 0.33334, and S is 2, then

h(keyvalue) = INTEGER_PART_OF(2 * 0.33334) = 0

since 2 * 0.33334 is 0.66668, which is between 0 and 1. However, if S is 3, we would have

h'(keyvalue) = INTEGER_PART_OF(3 * 0.33334) = 1

since 3 * 0.33334 is 1.00002. This is the reason that we cannot incrementally enlarge the number of pages used for data in a hash-organized table. Instead, it is necessary to give the Modify command again to reorganize the table completely when the slots start to fill up. We will notice this happening when the average length of collision chains begins to get large. Most database systems offer statistics on the length of collision chains to aid the DBA in tuning.

A few database systems, such as Amdahl's Huron, offer a more modern hash feature, based on an algorithm known as *linear hashing,* where the size of the disk-based hash table can increase incrementally with the number of rows or index entries that need to be stored. This form of hashing is outside the scope of this text. For more information, see the paper that introduced linear hashing in Stonebraker, chapter 2 [11].

In composing a Modify command, the usual approach is to use the **fillfactor** to specify the average number of filled slots per page. The **fillfactor** doesn't guarantee that all pages will have this ratio of filled slots, since random variations will cause some pages to have more and some to have fewer, but this is the simplest approach to take. The **minpages** parameter might be used if the DBA knew that the number of rows in the table was going to grow to a greater size and knew the likely number of pages that would ultimately be required. Then the DBA would want to start with a very sparsely filled table, but wouldn't want to have to calculate an exact fillfactor value, since minpages is going to increase the number of pages used in any event. The **maxpages** parameter is used if disk space is tight and the DBA wants to limit the number of pages used. However, there is a risk that the number of long collision chains will grow unacceptably if the resulting number of slots comes too close to the number of rows.

Collision Chain Length and Page Overflow

The major advantage of the hash structure is that it is usually possible to go directly to the page where we can find the record we seek. This is especially likely if we can use a lot of disk space to specify a very low fillfactor. In this case we use a lot of pages. The occupancy of the pages tends to be low, and the collision chains short, and it is extremely likely that we will find each particular row on the page we originally hash to.

It turns out to be possible to estimate the average collision chain length in a hash structure, given the **fillfactor** that is valid at a given moment. In what follows, we use mathematical reasoning requiring understanding of elementary probability and polynomial differentiation. If you do not have this knowledge, you should skip forward to the graph of the result, Figure 7.25. We start by assuming that all the key values are unique and that their hashed values are random and independent of one another. We want to estimate the probability P that the *last* hashed record, as it is added, encounters an already filled slot on its first probe. If the **fillfactor** is f, the likelihood that any given hash slot is occupied is $P = (f/100)$. This means that the probability that the slot is empty is $(1 - P)$, and this is also the probability that we will be able to place the final record in the first position we come to. We call this a collision chain of length 1 (only one probe is necessary) and write

$$\Pr(\text{collision chain of length 1}) = (1 - P)$$

On the other hand, in order to have a collision chain of length 2, the first position hashed to must be full (with probability P) and the second position that we reach in the rehash sequence must be empty (with probability $(1 - P)$). Using the principle of multiplication by which we calculate the probability of two or more independent events happening together:

Pr(collision chain of length 2) = $(1 - P)P$

Now for a collision chain of length 3, we must start with full slots in the first two positions we reach (with probability $P \cdot P = P^2$) and then an empty slot in the third with probability P. Simple extension of this argument gives

Pr(collision chain of length 3) = $(1 - P)P^2$
Pr(collision chain of length 4) = $(1 - P)P^3$
. . .
Pr(collision chain of length K) = $(1 - P)P^{K-1}$

Now the *expected* length of the collision chain, E(L), is given by the sum of all these probabilities times the associated lengths:

E(L) = $(1 - P) + 2(1 - P)P + 3(1 - P)P^2 + 4(1 - P)P^3 + \ldots$

or, factoring:

[7.5.1]   E(L) = $(1 - P)(1 + 2P + 3P^2 + 4P^3 + \ldots)$

where the sum extends to some large number of terms, proportional to the maximum number of possible collisions in the table. Now we would like to be able to give a simple formula for this sum. To see how to do this, start by considering the function f(x) given by the infinite series:

f(x) = $x + x^2 + x^3 + x^4 + \ldots$

This is the well-known infinite geometric progression, $a + ar + ar^2 + ar^3 + \ldots$, where a and r are both x. The formula for the sum is known from algebra, $a/(1 - r)$, so we can give a closed-form solution for the infinite series f(x):

[7.5.2]   f(x) = $x + x^2 + x^3 + x^4 + \ldots = x/(1 - x)$

504

Now, taking the derivative of all terms in the equations of (6.1.2), we get

[7.5.3] $f'(x) = 1 + 2x + 3x^2 + 4x^3 + \ldots = 1/(1 - x)^2$

Rewriting the formula of (6.1.1) for the expected length E(L) of a collision chain, we see that we can represent the infinite sum on the right with f'(P), replacing x with P in the left-hand equality of equation (6.1.3):

[7.5.4] $E(L) = (1 - P)(1 + 2P + 3P^2 + 4P^3 + \ldots) = (1 - P)(f'(P))$

Now, using the right-hand equality of equation (6.1.3), we can replace f'(P) with $1/(1 - P)^2$, to get

[7.5.5] $E(L) = (1 - P)(f'(P)) = (1 - P)(1/(1 - P))^2 = 1/(1 - P)$

Thus we see that the expected length of the collision chain is the reciprocal of $(1 - P)$. Recall that P=(f/100) and consider a few examples. If the hash structure is 50% full (fillfactor = 50) then P = 0.5, and E(L) = 1/0.5 = 2. If the table is 90% full, then fillfactor = 90, P = .9, and E(L) = 1/0.1 = 10. The graph of this relationship is given in Figure 7.25.

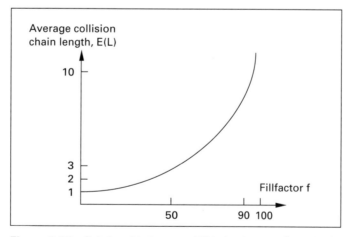

Figure 7.25   Relationship between E(L), the Average Length of a Hash Collision Chain in a Hashed Table, and the **fillfactor** f, E(L) = 1/(1 − (f/100))

As we would expect, the more full we set the table, the longer the average collision chain. What might be surprising, however, is how quickly the average chain increases in length once the fillfactor comes close to 100. If we can fit 20 rows on a page and set and load a table half full, a fillfactor of 50, it seems quite unlikely that a collision chain of average length 2 will grow long enough (L = 21) to continue to a successive page. However, if the fillfactor is 0.95, the average length of a chain is 20, so about half the collision chains will continue to a new page. The point of all this is to show how important it is to keep the fillfactor small relative to 100. On the average, we will be able to find a row associated with a unique key value halfway through a collision chain, so significant overhead starts to occur when a significant number of entries start to hash to position 21 or later of the chain. A hashed table containing duplicate key values tends to have longer collision chains, since equal value rows are certain to collide. In our derivation, we assumed independent random positions for separate hash entries, which is obviously not the case when duplicate entries exist.

Readers who have studied statistics can follow the rough argument that follows. Assume a million-row table, where 20 rows will fit on each page. If we have a fillfactor of 50, we try to load each page half full, with 10 rows per page; therefore we use 100,000 data pages. However, the occupancy is random, and we need to use the normal distribution function to estimate the number of rows that occupy an arbitrary page. For any page of the table, we calculate the probability that a particular row in the table hashes to this page as 1/100,000, p = 0.00001. We denote by q = (1 − p) = 0.99999 the probability that the slot is empty (a number so close to 1 that the difference in the calculations that follow is not significant). Then the expected number of rows hashed to the current page, E(r), is N • p, where N is the total number of rows hashed:

E(r) = 0.00001*1,000,000 = 10

This is what we would expect, that the average page rows in 10 out of the 20 slots used. Now the standard deviation for this probability distribution, σ, is given by the formula:

$$\sigma = \sqrt{N \cdot p \cdot q} = \sqrt{1.000,000 \cdot 0.00001 \cdot 0.99999} \approx \sqrt{10} = 3.162 \; .$$

Then the likelihood that there are more than E(r) + σ = 13.162 rows on a page is a 1-sigma event, with a probability of $\Phi(1) = 0.158$, as determined by the normal Φ function. To get $10 + 2 \times 3.162 = 16.324$ rows is a 2-sigma event, with a probability of $\Phi(2.0) = .0228$. In particular, the probability that more than 20 rows hash to this page is $\Phi(10/3.162) = .000831$. Since there are 100,000 pages in the table, we can expect overflows for about 83 of them.

Readers with a bit of statistics and access to a normal distribution table will be able to apply these estimates to the table of their choice.

Disadvantages of a Hash Primary Index

To begin with, it should be very clear that a hash primary index is of use only with exact match predicates, such as pname = 'comb'. A range predicate, such as city between 'Ch' and 'Cy', cannot be resolved by reference to a hash index. If a hash index is the only one present for a given column, and a range predicate on that column is the only one used in a Select statement, then a direct search (table scan) of all rows in the table is necessary. Since the slots of a hash table are rather sparsely filled to restrain collision chain length, a table scan entails even more I/Os than usual in a heap structure. Another disadvantage of the hash primary index is that we have to leave room for expansion in the initial layout of the table, rather than depending on incremental expansion for later inserts. Given normal uncertainty about growth of a table, we usually tend to overestimate the extra space needed.

A third point is that if we don't have unique key values, the retrieval routine will need to go through the entire rehash chain for a given value, not stopping when a single row for the value sought is located. It should also be clear that if we sometimes have a large number of duplicate values, as we might with a key of dname (department name) for the employees table, there could be a very long rehashing chain, which will detract seriously from the efficiency of the structure. Note that "null" values count as duplicate values. While more sophisticated hashing techniques can be used to partially overcome such problems, it is certainly the case that key values with multiple duplicates are not handled well by primary hashing methods.

There are other interesting details in choosing between a hash primary index and a B-tree index. A large number of database texts analyze the advantage of a hash primary index over a B-tree index, in the case of an exact match predicate, as being one of reduced I/O. This seems obvious, in that access through a B-tree structure requires passing through a number of higher-level directory nodes before the desired row is retrieved. For large tables where efficient keyed access becomes most important, usually three levels of B-tree directory nodes are involved. We should note, however, that these three levels of access are normally not real—the existence of memory buffers usually guarantees that some fraction of those levels is resident in memory, and often only one real directory page I/O is required for each random row access. Still, the advantage of one I/O directly to the data rows in the hash case over two I/Os in the B-tree case would seem to be very important.

But another factor sometimes enters. Consider the following two tables.

autodeposit

eid
...

employees

eid	bank	acctid	weeksal	...
...	...	...	...	...

The first table, called `autodeposit`, is a single-column list of employee ids (`eid`) for individuals who have asked that their weekly checks be automatically deposited. The second table, `employees`, has the column `eid`, the bank and account number, and the weekly salary for each employee.

A common type of application program, performed once a week, would read the `eid` values from the `autodeposit` table one after another, then use these `eid` values to access the rows of the `employees` table and make the desired automatic deposit in the appropriate account. This appears to be a long sequence of indexed accesses to the `employees` table by an `eid` index, and we might decide to use a primary hash index on `eid` for the `employees` table, since this will give us the most efficient I/O access to these rows. However, this approach would be a mistake. If we were instead to give the employee table a B-tree or isam index on `eid`, the resulting table would be clustered by `eid` value. Now if we also clustered the rows of the `autodeposit` table by `eid` sequence, we would find that the application, looping through the `autodeposit` rows, makes all accesses to the `employees` table in order by the clustered key. In general, successive accesses to the `employees` table pass down through a directory through nodes that almost always remain in memory buffers from the prior access, and then to a row on a page that is also already in buffer.

The total number of employee pages involved in I/O is equal to the total number in the table. (We are assuming that a large proportion of employees receive autodeposit, so most employee table data pages will be involved.) On the other hand, in the hash case, as each new row is accessed it lies on a random page, unrelated to the previous one even if it was accessed by a contiguous key. If there are (say) an average of 10 rows on each hash data page that desire direct deposit, there will be 20 times as many I/Os in the hash primary index case as in the B-tree or isam clustered index case. We are assuming that there are too many data pages to remain in memory buffers between accesses, and that the B-tree or isam index pages are few in number compared with the data pages, both common assumptions.

Thus we see an example where the hash structure is not as I/O efficient for row access as other ordered structures. Of course we stacked the deck, since the eid references are not actually random. On the other hand, this is a common sort of situation, and you should be aware how the order of the rows in a table can imply a big resource saving in access to the table.

7.6 Throwing Darts at Random Slots

In deriving the collision chain length for a hash table in Section 7.5, we solved a probabilistic problem of a kind we will meet a good deal in the following chapters. We refer to the general problem as *throwing N darts at M random slots*. We picture ourselves with some number N of darts and imagine that we are throwing them at a dart board from a great distance, so that, although we always manage to hit the board, each cross-hatched slot on the dart board is equally likely to be hit by any dart we throw. We might vary the problem a bit with further restrictions, and then ask some question about the eventual likely configuration of darts on the board. For example, we might ask:

How many slots on the board have a dart in them?

Since some of the slots might contain multiple darts, this question doesn't usually have the simple answer N. The problem of the collision chain mentioned earlier is one of the more complicated ones to pose in this format. We can describe it with the following shorthand:

N darts in M slots. Slot occupancy 1. Retries until all darts in board

What we mean by "Slot occupancy 1" is that each slot in the board is assumed to have room for only a single dart. If a second thrown dart tries to enter that slot, it bounces off. The phrase "Retries until all darts in board" means that each time a dart bounces off, we retrieve it and try again until it sticks in the target. Eventually all darts are in slots, so we must have N ≤ M, because of the slot-occupancy limit and the fact that each of the darts lies in only one slot. In this case, the question of how many slots have a dart in them does have the simple answer N. But we now ask a different question:

In throwing dart N, what is the expected number of retries to get it in some slot?

It should be obvious that this problem with darts and slots is identical to the problem of collision chain length we solved in the previous section. The answer we derived was that the expected number of retries with dart N, represented by R, is given by

$$R = 1/(1 - (N - 1)/M) = M/(M - N + 1)$$

This depends on the fact that the probability P—that a random slot is occupied when dart N is thrown—is (N −1)/M. This is calculated from the number of darts (1 through N − 1) occupying slots, divided by the total number of slots.

Unlimited Slot Occupancy: How Many Slots Are Occupied?

Let us solve the most standard problem for N darts in M slots, when there is no limit to the number of darts that will fit in each slot. After throwing the N darts, what is the expected number of slots that contain darts? We denote by S the number of slots containing darts in any particular configuration resulting from this experiment, and the expected number of such slots for a given N and M by E(S).

Probably the best way to picture this problem is to break it down into three cases: case 1, there are only a very few darts in comparison to the number of slots, signified by N << M; case 2, the number of darts is comparable to the number of slots, written N ≈ M; and case 3, the number of darts is somewhat greater than the number of slots, or N > M. We expect in case 1, where the number of darts is quite small compared to the number of slots, that it is rare for many slots to be doubly occupied. Therefore the number of occupied slots will be close to the number of darts, $S \approx N$. (S will be just slightly less than N in most cases.) We expect in case 3, where the number of darts is somewhat greater than the number of slots, say three times as great, that most slots will contain several darts (three, on the average). However, if there are a lot of slots, we expect some slots to still be empty. Therefore in this case we assume $M - S << M$, but probably $M - S \neq 0$. In case 2, where the number of darts is about the same as the number of slots, to be precise let us say $N = M$, we certainly expect a reasonable number of slots with two darts and some with three. This means that a decent fraction of the slots will have no darts ($M - S$ is some reasonable fraction of M, since there are just enough darts to go around once), but intuition fails us in trying to estimate the number of empty slots. As we will see in a moment, with $N = M$ we can estimate that $E(S) = M (1 - e^{-1})$, where e is the base of the natural logarithms, $2.71828. \ldots$

To begin our derivation of $E(S)$ given N and M, consider the probability P that a particular slot s does *not* get hit by a specific thrown dart d. Since there are M slots and the dart will hit any particular slot with equal likelihood, the probability that it hits s is $1/M$ and the probability that the slot s does *not* get hit is given by

$$\Pr(\text{slot } s \text{ does not get hit by dart } d) = (1 - 1/M)$$

This is a fairly large probability if we have a large number M of slots. But now let's say that we throw some number N of darts in succession, and ask the probability that the slot s does not get hit by any of these darts. Each dart throw is an independent event, and the probability that the slot never gets hit is given by the following conjunction of events: slot s does not get hit by dart 1 *and* slot s does not get hit by dart 2 *and* . . . *and* slot s does not get hit by dart N. The probability for this conjunction of events is the product of the probabilities for each of the individual events, so

$$\Pr(\text{slot } s \text{ does not get hit by } N \text{ darts thrown in succession}) = (1 - 1/M)^N$$

Since there are M slots, each with the same probability, the expected number of slots that do not get hit is the number of slots times the probability that a specific slot will not be hit:

[7.6.1] $E(\text{Number of slots that do not get hit}) = M (1 - 1/M)^N$

Thus the number of slots that *do* get hit, E(S), is M minus the quantity just calculated:

[7.6.2] $E(S) = M (1 - (1 - 1/M)^N)$

From calculus, we know that the number represented by e is defined in a limit form as

$$e = \lim_{x \to 0} (1 + x)^{1/x}$$

If we assume that M is quite large, we can substitute x for $- 1/M$ and derive the approximation for e:

$$e \approx (1 - 1/M)^{-M}$$

or

[7.6.3] $e^{-1} \approx (1 - 1/M)^M$

From (7.6.2), we see that

$$E(S) = M (1 - ((1 - 1/M)^N)) = M (1 - ((1 - 1/M)^M)^{N/M})$$

and substituting (7.6.3), we get

[7.6.4] $E(S) \approx M (1 - e^{-N/M})$

Thus the expected number of slots hit by darts is approximated by $M (1 - e^{-N/M})$ and the expected number of slots not hit is

[7.6.5] $E(\text{Slots not hit}) \approx M\, e^{-N/M}$

In the exercises we provide some examples using these formulas.

Suggestions for Further Reading

The various product SQL reference manuals referred to in earlier chapters continue to be useful in understanding how to index tables. The standard SQL reference manuals give little guidance. New reference manuals are listed in bold type below.

[1] *DB2 Administration Guide.* (See Chapter 4, "Designing a Database," and Chapter 7, "Performance Monitoring and Tuning.")

[2] *DB2 SQL Reference Manual.*

[3] M. Folk and B. Zoellick. *File Structures,* 2nd ed. Reading, MA: Addison-Wesley, 1992.

[4] *INGRES/SQL Reference Manual.* Alameda, CA: ASK Group.

[5] **INGRES Technical Notes.** Alameda, CA: ASK Group.

[6] *ORACLE RDBMS Database Administrator's Guide* (version 6.0 through ORACLE7). Redwood Shores, CA: Oracle.

[7] **ORACLE RDBMS Performance Tuning Guide** (version 6.0 through ORACLE7). Redwood Shores, CA: Oracle.

[8] *ORACLE SQL Language Reference Manual* (version 6.0 for PC DOS). Redwood Shores, CA: Oracle.

[9] *ORACLE7 Server SQL Language Reference Manual.* Redwood Shores, CA: Oracle.

[10] B. Salyberg. *File Structures.* Englewood Cliffs, NJ: Prentice-Hall, 1988.

[11] Gio Wiederhold. **File Organization for Database Design.** New York: McGraw-Hill, 1987.

[12] Michael Stonebraker, ed. *Readings in Database Systems,* 2nd ed. San Mateo, CA: Morgan Kaufmann, 1994. (See pages 96–107, "Linear Hashing: A New Tool for File and Table Addressing," by W. Litwin.)

Exercises with solutions at the back of the book in "Solutions to Selected Exercises" are marked with the symbol •.

Assume disk pages of 2048 bytes in all questions that follow unless otherwise stated.

[7.1] Assume that a DBA issued the following Create Table statement in **ORACLE:**

```
create table customers (cid . . .)
    storage (initial 20480, next 20480,
    maxextents 8, minextents 3, pctincrease 0);
```

(a)• How many bytes of disk space will be allocated to this file when it is first created?

(b)• What is the maximum space capacity (in bytes) of this table?

(c) How would the answer to (b) change if we changed from pct-increase 0 to pctincrease 100? Show calculations.

[7.2] Consider the definition of the **INGRES** TID given just before Example 7.2.1. A TID must fit in an unsigned 4-byte integer, with values from 0 to $2^{32} - 1$. The TID allows for 512 slots on each 2048-byte disk page, although there will usually be fewer rows than this actually placed. For each row on a page, a 2-byte offset to the row is held in the row directory.

(a)• If we actually had 512 fixed-length rows on a 2048-byte page, what would be the maximum length of the row? (Don't forget about the row directory offsets.)

(b) How many rows of length 50 can be stored on a 2048-byte page?

(c)• What is the precise maximum number of disk pages that can be represented in a TID?

(d) How many rows of length 50 can be stored in an **INGRES** table?

(e) Provide a different definition for a TID that would increase the maximum number of rows (of most sizes) that could be stored in an **INGRES** table. The TID definition for each table would depend on the minimum length m in bytes of a row in the table (calculated from the Create Table statement), and use a more realistic estimate of the maximum number of rows that can be placed on a page.

[7.3] Consider the function binsearch of Example 7.3.1. Generalize it to handle any size N sorted array and allow it to find nearest matches above x, if any, as follows:

```
int binsearch(int x, int N)
```

so that for a given x and N the K that is returned is the smallest K such that arr[K].keyval >= x, or −1 if x is larger than any keyval value.

[7.4] Consider a table emp (for employees) with 200,000 rows of 100 bytes each, created with the statement:

```
create table emp (eid integer not null, . . . ) pctfree 25;
```

where the **pctfree n** clause refers to the amount of free space that must be left on each data page in placing the rows on the page.

(a)• Assuming a very small header and only 2-byte offsets in the row directory, make a *rough* calculation of the number of data pages needed to hold the rows of the table emp.

Now assume that the following command has been issued in **ORACLE** to create a unique index on emp (eid is the primary key for emp, but we forgot to mention this in the Create Table statement).

```
create unique index eidx on emp (eid) pctfree 20;
```

(b) The **ORACLE** rowid takes up 6 bytes (it would be 7 bytes for a non-unique key) and there is a 1-byte overhead per column of the key; the int eid column value takes 4 bytes, of course. Make a rough calculation of the number of index entries per leaf page and the total number of leaf-level pages there will be in the eidx B-tree. Notice the **pctfree** clause of Create Index.

(c) Make a rough calculation of the number of node pages this B-tree will have at *each* higher directory level. Show all work. Assume that the byte length of an entry in the B-tree (Sepkey-val, np) is the same as an entry at the leaf level. The **pctfree** clause above still affects calculations in the directory.

(d)• How many I/Os are needed to perform the query `select * from emp where eid between 10,000 and 20,000`? Assume that the `eid` values have no gaps and range from 1 to 200,000. Do NOT assume that the rows of `emp` are clustered by `eid`. Assume that data pages are not buffered, so that each data page reference requires a disk read. Assuming 40 I/Os per second (ignore CPU time), how long will this query take to execute?

(e) Repeat the calculation of (d) where you do assume that the rows of `emp` are clustered by `eid`. How long will this query take to execute in terms of I/O?

(f)• How many I/Os are needed to perform the query `select count(*) from emp where eid is between 10,000 and 20,000`? Hint: The query optimizer doesn't pick up rows from the table unless it needs to. How long will this query take to execute?

[7.5] Rework Example 7.3.4, assuming nodes 70% full, but with 4096-byte pages for an IBM machine and assuming the **DB2** index compression of Figure 7.3.8. There are 1 million entries in the index, the index key is "city" declared char(16), and there are 200 different cities evenly distributed among the rows of the table. As always, *rough calculations* are acceptable. Assume that **DB2** does not use compression in the directory-level B-tree nodes.

[7.6] (a) Are the following statements true or false? Please justify your answer.

(i) • **DB2** allows rows to split over several data pages.

(ii) **ORACLE** ROWIDs are slightly longer than **DB2** RIDs.

(iii)• The binary search algorithm on a sorted list is inefficient in terms of disk I/O compared with that of a B-tree algorithm.

(iv) A binary search will take ten probes to find one key value among a list of 1 million distinct key values.

(v)• If we have a disk page memory buffer with 1000 pages and we are retrieving rows at random from 1 million pages, after some time we will have one chance in a thousand with each retrieval that we do *not* have to perform a disk I/O.

(b) Write an **ORACLE** storage clause (just the clause) for a Create Table statement to start the table with 10 KB of disk storage, and let the size increase in incremental jumps that double after the first two and stop with at least 5120 KB total. (10 + 10 + 20 + 40 + . . . + 2560.) Show calculations.

[7.7] In **ORACLE**, consider a table named students of 400,000 rows with 200 bytes each, and assume that the following command has been issued to load the students table.

```
create table students (stid char(7) not null unique primary
    key, . . . <other columns>)
    pctfree 20;
```

(a) How many pages will the rows of students sit on? Assume 2000 bytes per page, and ignore row directory offsets and page header. Show calculations in all parts that follow.

(b)• Assume an index on stid with pctfree = 25. Calculate the entry size assuming rowid of 6 bytes, and 1 byte overhead for the single column key. Then calculate how many leaf-level pages there will be in the B-tree.

(c) Calculate how many pages exist on various upper levels of the B-tree.

(d) How many I/Os are needed to perform this query?

```
select stid from students
    where stid between 'e000001' and 'e020000';
```

Assume that 1/20th of all students have `eid` values in this range, that the `stid` index is *not* a clustering index for students, and that we do not save any I/Os because of buffering.

(e)• Recalculate part (d) with the assumption that the `stid` index *is* a clustering index for the `students` table.

(f) Under the assumptions of part (e), calculate how many I/Os are required for the following query:

```
select count(*) from students
    where stid between 'e000001' and 'e020000';
```

[7.8] Assume that we are given a hash organized table with slots for 20 rows on a page.

(a) Given 100,000 pages in the hash table, how many slots exist? Show calculations.

(b)• Given 100,000 pages, assuming that 1 million rows are hashed into this table, calculate the probability on a single page that a hash chain of length 21 exists. Show calculations.

(c) We say that a page "overflows" when a row is hashed to the page, but there is no room for it on that page and it must be placed on a different page.

  (i)   Does the fact that a hash chain of length 21 exists on a page imply that the page overflows?

  (ii) Does a page overflow imply that a hash chain of length 21 or more exists on the page?

[7.9] Assume as in Section 7.6 that we are throwing N darts at M slots. We want to examine some of the formulas derived.

(a)• Use your calculator to determine the number of slots that get hit throwing 128 darts at 10,000 slots. Use both formulas (7.6.2) and (7.6.4). Note that 128 is a power of 2, so formula (7.6.2) can be evaluated by successive squaring of $(1 - 1/M)$, and you should do it this way. Is the number of slots that do get hit close to 128 in both cases?

(b) Repeat problem (a), throwing 16,384 darts at 16,384 slots. Note that the number is a power of 2, so you can calculate by successive squaring again. Are the two numbers close? Is the fraction of slots that get hit close to $(1 - e^{-1})$?

(c) Use formula (7.6.5) to calculate the number of slots that do *not* get hit when there are 10,000 slots and 30,000 darts.

[7.10] (a)• When we throw one dart at a board, there is no chance that two darts will go in the same slot, and the probability remains low as the number of darts remains very small relative to the number of darts. However, for a given number of slots M, there is a first point in throwing darts (a number N) where the probability is greater than 1/2 that two darts will fall in the same slot. Calculate this point for 365 slots. (This is called the "birthday surprise point" because the number of people you need in a room for it to become likely that two people have the same birthday is surprisingly small.)

(b) (HARD) Calculate the "birthday surprise point" as a formula in terms of M.

Query Processing  8

Recall query (7.1.1) from the beginning of Chapter 7:

```
select cid from customers
    where city = 'Boston' and discnt between 12 and 14;
```

When a database system receives a query such as this, it goes through a series of *query compilation steps* before it begins execution. In the first phase, the *syntax-checking phase,* the system parses the query and checks that it obeys the syntax rules, then matches objects in the query syntax with views, tables, and columns listed in system tables, and performs appropriate query modification. During this phase the system validates that the user has appropriate privileges and that the query does not disobey any relevant integrity constraints. At this point the *query optimization phase* begins. Existing statistics for the tables and columns are located, such as how many rows exist in the tables, and relevant indexes are found with their own applicable statistics. A complex procedure now takes place, which we can think of as "figuring out what to do," and the result is a procedural *access plan* to perform the query. The access plan is then put into effect with the *execution phase,* wherein the indexes and tables are accessed and the answer to the query is derived from the data.

The goal of this chapter is to explain some of the basic principles of query processing, with particular emphasis on the ideas underlying query optimization. There are normally a large number of competing access plans that will work to perform a given query, just as there are a large number of ways to play a chess game with the object of winning (or at least not losing). The system query optimizer tries to choose an access plan that will minimize run time as well as various other types of resource use, such as CPU time, number of disk I/Os, and so on. The query optimizer will probably not choose the best possible plan for a complex query, any more than a chess player plays the perfect game, but the objective is to spend enough effort in the optimization process to ensure a reasonably good choice. Basic issues in query optimization include how to use available indexes, how to use memory to accumulate information and perform intermediate steps such as sorting, how to determine the order in which joins should be performed, and so on. At the end of this chapter you should be able to display and analyze an access plan chosen by the database system for a specific query. You should also understand what constitutes a "good" or "bad" access plan. As a result, you will have a much better grasp of what "tuning" steps a DBA can take to improve query performance: indexes to be added, different clustering of rows by index, denormalization of tables, and so on.

This current chapter also explains many of the considerations that go into choosing an access plan for a given SQL query, but it is limited to explaining *why* a specific access plan should be chosen, based on the details of the possible alternatives, rather than *how* it is chosen by the query optimizer. In general, a query optimizer generates a number of alternative strategies from which it must select a plan, and choosing among these alternatives can become quite a complex problem. Because a computer program has no "intuition," the programmers responsible for writing the query optimizer have the difficult job of creating an efficient algorithmic decision procedure that will choose between competing access plans. Algorithmic procedures of this kind (such as *dynamic programming* techniques) are outside the scope of the current text. We will depend a great deal on the reader's intuition to follow arguments as to why one access plan is better than another, and simply assume that the query optimizer comes to the same conclusion by using some algorithmic search. Such an approach is commonly used in texts that explain the effect of programming language statements, without detailing how the compiler achieves the effects.

Up until now we have presented features from a number of different database products in parallel, but in this chapter we concentrate on IBM's **DB2**. We have found architectural differences to be too pervasive to allow a presentation that moves between examples of query optimization in different products—the chance of confusion is simply too great. **DB2** has an extremely sophisticated approach to query optimization, and it provides a number of advanced execution features that support high performance for queries. It is probable that many of these features will be offered by most other database products in the near future. Query optimization is a young field, dating from about the mid '70s, and no single product has a monopoly on good ideas. Indeed a number of research ideas suggest new performance capabilities that have not yet been implemented in any commercial products. The current chapter concentrates on commercial features, but a few research references are given at the end of the chapter. The final three sections of the chapter present a query *benchmark,* an industry-standard test of query performance, that has been performed on the **DB2** product. You should find that the benchmark measurement results and accompanying discussions of concrete query access plans are an enormous aid in cementing your understanding of the query performance principles presented in earlier sections.

8.1 Introductory Concepts

We start by introducing some fundamental concepts as a preliminary to our discussion of query optimization. To begin with, we consider exactly what resource use the system is trying to minimize in optimizing a query. Ultimately this reduces to the question of saving money on computer equipment and the time of users (also a money issue for the employer). We also consider special commands the DBA needs to tune the database system and to understand the plans output by the query optimizer.

Query Resource Utilization

The query optimizer attempts to minimize the use of certain resources by choosing the best of a set of alternative query access plans. The resources considered are CPU time and the number of I/Os required. Computer memory is also an important resource, but memory capacity for various purposes is normally determined at system initialization time. For example, the number of buffers used to keep popular disk pages in memory is set in advance by the DBA. Since the query optimizer can have no effect on this, it usually reacts in a relatively simple way by choosing different types of behavior in query plans at various thresholds of memory availability. We will see examples later in the chapter.

	$COST_{CPU}(PLAN)$	$COST_{I/O}(PLAN)$
$PLAN_1$	9.2 CPU seconds	103 reads
$PLAN_2$	1.7 CPU seconds	890 reads

Figure 8.1 Two Query Plans with Incomparable I/O and CPU Cost Pairs

By contrast, the CPU and I/O resources that can be used in a query are under the control of the query optimizer—whatever is necessary to perform the query. For each alternative access PLAN there is an associated *CPU cost*, with notation $COST_{CPU}(PLAN)$, and *I/O cost,* or $COST_{I/O}(PLAN)$. Whenever there are two incomparable costs it is possible that two query plans, $PLAN_1$ and $PLAN_2$, will be incomparable in resource use. See Figure 8.1.

Clearly $PLAN_2$ is superior to $PLAN_1$ in terms of having smaller CPU cost, but $PLAN_1$ is superior in terms of smaller I/O cost. To provide a single measure that can be minimized unambiguously, the **DB2** query optimizer defines the *total cost* of an access PLAN, COST(PLAN), as the weighted sum of the I/O cost and the CPU cost.

[8.1.1] $COST(PLAN) = W_1 \cdot COST_{I/O}(PLAN) + W_2 \cdot COST_{CPU}(PLAN)$

Here W_1 and W_2 are both positive numbers, weighting the relative importance of the two measures in the total cost. The job of the optimizer is to choose the lowest value COST(PLAN) ranging over all alternative plans that answer a given query. In the following sections we discuss how to analyze alternative access plans to derive, relatively accurately, the associated I/O cost. It is not so easy from theoretical considerations alone to derive the associated CPU usage, since this depends on the details of the CPU instruction set and the efficiency of the database system implementation. (Of course, the query optimizer for a specific database system release is able to estimate CPU cost for a plan, using a tabulation of measured CPU times for internal functions required, but there is a great deal of uninteresting detail here that we don't want to have to address in the current chapter.) As a general rule, the CPU cost to perform a query does not vary as much from one access plan to another as does the I/O cost, except that often the CPU cost overhead associated with each I/O is an important contribution, so that minimizing the I/O minimizes the CPU as well. This implies that the incomparable CPU and I/O cost pairs of Figure 8.1 are unusual. The following sections concentrate on quantitative estimates of the I/O cost and discuss CPU differences in a qualitative way only in circumstances where major variations are likely to arise.

The Workload of a System

We define the *workload* of a system as a mix of queries and the frequencies with which these queries are posed by the users of the system. For example, we might have a query system built to help a group of 5000 insurance adjusters perform their everyday work. It may be that the adjusters pose two types of queries, Q1 and Q2, in their work.

> Q1 retrieves information from an accident claim form using the claim number.
> Q2 retrieves all claim numbers, indexed by (`lastname`, `firstname`) of the insured.

When they are submitted, queries of these types have different specific values for claim numbers and insured names, but the CPU and I/O resource needed to answer such queries are approximately the same for any specific values of these parameters. From observing the adjusters during their peak work period we note that, on the average, some member of the group poses a query of type Q1 40 times each second and a query of type Q2 20 times each second. These frequencies are reflected in Figure 8.2. Of course this is a simplified example of a workload; in real life there would be more types of queries and fewer round numbers for submission rates.

Query type	RATE(query) in submissions/second
Q1	40.0
Q2	20.0

Figure 8.2   Simple Workload with Two Queries

For a given workload on a system, and the query execution plans generated by the query optimizer for the queries that make up the workload, the required CPU and I/O resource needs per second can be calculated.

From this and a list of equipment costs we can translate the requirements into a measure that may seem more immediate: the dollar cost of the system to support the workload. For example, consider a workload with a large frequency of queries that performs about 1000 I/Os but uses very little CPU. To begin with, we note that we would expect relatively long response times (only about 40 random I/Os can be performed each second when successive I/O requests in a query plan must wait for the previous I/O to complete). We would probably need to purchase a large number of disks to provide the needed I/O access rate under this workload, although we could get along with a relatively inexpensive CPU. We normally have a good deal of freedom in choosing larger or smaller CPU systems; IBM mainframe computers, for example, have a linear price scale-up with increasing CPU power.

All of these purchases need to be worked out in advance, of course, which is why the DBA attempts to get some estimate of workload even before an application is implemented. Each query in the workload, depending on its peak frequency and resource utilization, translates to a specific dollar cost in computer hardware, using the "fair rent" on the equipment utilized. A high response time has a cost as well, in that the company needs to hire more employees to get the work done (employee time waiting for a response is usually wasted), and with long delays we might expect to see a high turnover rate as employees quit in frustration. Looking at it this way, it is clear that if we can improve the set of alternatives available to the query optimizer to make a better choice among alternative access plans, an immediate cost saving will result. This is an extremely important area of study for the DBA.

Gathering Statistics

A query optimizer of any sophistication needs to have knowledge about the statistics of the various tables, columns, and indexes it deals with. For example, recall the query:

```
select * from customers
    where city = 'Boston' and discnt between 12 and 14;
```

If the customers table contains only three rows on a single data page, the query optimizer should certainly ignore any indexes that might exist and perform a table scan, a direct search of the rows, to qualify the two predicates. On the other hand, if there are 100,000 rows on 10,000 data pages, the query optimizer would almost certainly save resources by using an index on `city` or one on `discnt`, if such indexes exist. In order to evaluate resource costs at this point, the query optimizer would want to be able to estimate, for example, how many `customers` rows exist with `city` = 'Boston'. If it turns out there is only one value for the `city` column (with the value 'Boston'), then all rows have this `city` value and the query optimizer learns that this index is not of any use after all. We will consider specific statistics and their uses in the sections that follow.

Statistics are not automatically gathered when a table is loaded or an index is created. A special command must be given by the DBA, a utility command that gathers the needed statistics and puts the results in system tables. Later updates on the table can cause changes that are not reflected in the statistics, which then become out of date, and inappropriate decisions by the query optimizer may result without sufficiently frequent reissuance of the statistics-gathering command.

In **DB2** the utility known as RUNSTATS is used to gather statistics. The details of statistics gathered for **DB2** are covered in the following sections. In **INGRES** a command from the operating-system level is used, known as Optimizedb. **ORACLE**, starting with version 7, uses the Analyze command to collect statistics into the data dictionary. Prior to version 7 **ORACLE** did not have any statistics gathering capability, which is to say that the query optimizer was quite unsophisticated.

Retrieving the Query Plan

A query optimizer builds an access plan out of a sequence of *procedural access steps,* or simply *procedural steps* or *access steps.* These procedural steps are peculiar to the specific database system and are put together like a series of instructions in an object program created by a compiler to carry out the logic of a higher-level program (the non-procedural SQL query, in our case). In the following sections we will discuss the access steps available in **DB2**, including

Table space scan
Index scans
    Equal unique index lookup
    Unclustered matching index scan
    Clustered matching index scan
    Index-only scan

Most database systems have analogous procedural steps with different names, although the steps may also have somewhat different effects and thus require different procedural flow, quite analogous to distinct machine instruction sets. **DB2** has an extremely sophisticated set of procedural steps and supports most access concepts available in other systems, with a number of additional special variations. Lack of hashed access is one of the few deficiencies of **DB2**.

The DBA is generally able to access the query plan for a given query by using a command provided by the database system. In **DB2**, the DBA uses a special SQL statement of the form:

```
explain plan [set queryno = n] for explainable-sql-statement;
```

This statement inserts into a user-created **DB2** table, known as the `plan_table`, one row for each individual access step in the plan created for `explainable-sql-statement`. The `queryno` referenced is a column of `plan_table` that can be used for later retrieval with the integer value n specified. Thus, for example, the DBA could give the statement:

```
explain plan set queryno = 1000 for
    select * from customers
        where city = 'Boston' and discnt between 12 and 14;
```

To retrieve all rows of `plan_table` associated with this query, the DBA (or interested user who owns the plan created) could then submit the statement:

```
select * from plan_table where queryno = 1000;
```

The `plan_table` in **DB2** (which we sometimes refer to simply as the "plan table") contains a large number of columns, an almost overwhelming number on first encounter. We will explain the significance of many of these columns as they become relevant, but as an introduction we mention one important column named ACCESSTYPE. When a table space scan is performed in **DB2** to answer a query on a single table (meaning that each row from the table is examined to validate the condition of the **where** clause, what we previously called a table scan), we see an R in the ACCESSTYPE column of `plan_table`, which we symbolize by writing ACCESSTYPE = R. Of course another column gives the name of the table on which the scan is being performed. Note that while the original Select statement might refer to view table names in the **from** clause, the access plan refers only to physical base tables. Most of the early plans we introduce consist of only a single step, and thus a single row appears in the plan table. (Each single-access plan step refers to only a single table, so a multi-step plan is required when more than one table is mentioned in the **from** clause.) A second type of plan exists where a single index is used to qualify rows of the table for retrieval—for example, a cityx index used to retrieve all rows satisfying the predicate "`city = 'Boston'`," while remaining conditions in the **where** clause are validated after qualified rows are accessed; for this type of plan we see ACCESSTYPE = I in the plan table.

Query Plans in ORACLE and INGRES

In **ORACLE** the plan for a specific query can be placed in the default PLAN_TABLE using the following statement:

```
explain plan [set statement id = 'id-string']
    for explainable-sql-statement;
```

The use of this statement is explained in detail in the *ORACLE SQL Language Reference Manual* [7]. For information on how to interpret the execution plan, refer to the *ORACLE RDBMS Performance Tuning Guide,* Chapter 7, "Performance Diagnostics Tools" [6].

In **INGRES** the user can enter a mode of interactive use where the *query execution plan,* known as a QEP, prints out to the terminal, and the query itself is not executed. To enter this QEP listing mode in the terminal monitor, the user types two commands in succession:

```
set optimizeonly;
set qep\g
```

The Embedded SQL forms can also be used—for example, `exec sql set optimizeonly`. For information on how to interpret execution plans, refer to *INGRES Technical Notes,* Note #4 [4].

8.2 | Table Space Scans and I/O

To begin our study of procedural access steps, we consider the table space scan step in **DB2**. Recall that the row in the plan table representing a table space scan has the letter R in the ACCESSTYPE column, which we write as ACCESSTYPE = R.

> **EXAMPLE 8.2.1 Table Space Scan Step.**
> A *table space scan* step in **DB2** is an algorithmic step wherein all the data in a table (the relevant data pages of a tablespace) is scanned and the rows are restricted by a search_condition of a **where** clause. In the **DB2** architecture there are situations in which rows from different tables can be mixed on common extents of a tablespace, which is why this is called a table space scan rather than a table scan. However, in what follows we assume that all pages referenced in a table space scan contain only rows from a single table.
>
> Assume that we are given an employees table with 200,000 rows, each row 200 bytes in length, and that data pages have been loaded just 70% full. (In **DB2**, the **pctfree** specification that determines how full data pages are loaded is given in the Create Tablespace statement.) We assume that each 4-KB page uses roughly 96 bytes for overhead, leaving 4000 bytes, and with data pages loaded 70% full we have 2800 available bytes, so 14 rows will fit on each page. Thus the total number of data pages needed for 200,000 rows is CEIL(200,000/ 14) = 14,286 pages. Now consider the following query:
>
> ```
> select eid, ename from employees where socsecno = 113353179;
> ```
>
> where an employee with a given Social Security number is to be retrieved. If we don't have an index on socsecno, then our only alternative is to scan the whole table with a table space scan, looking for all rows that fit the **where** clause description (we assume there is only one such row, but the query optimizer probably won't know this since socsecno has no index, and statistics gathering usually doesn't include such detail for all columns). Note that the data scan step is in fact the whole of the access plan, since the result of this step completely answers the query. There are 14,286 data pages in this table, so the I/O cost of this plan, $COST_{I/O}(PLAN)$, is 14,286R—that is, 14,286 random I/Os. Recall that we do not try to estimate $COST_{CPU}(PLAN)$, but assume that the total cost is normally proportional to the I/O cost. ∎

The table space scan is also known under other names with other products, such as a *direct search, data scan,* or *table scan.* We have spoken before, for instance in Example 7.4.1, about the elapsed time required to perform a large number of random I/Os. But now it is time to examine some of the assumptions we use in estimating elapsed time, and to introduce some new types of I/O, known as sequential prefetch I/O and list prefetch I/O.

Assumptions about I/O

What implications can be drawn from an I/O cost of 14,286R for the query plan of Example 8.2.1? To begin with, recall that a random I/O on a normal disk takes an expected elapsed time of approximately 0.025 seconds (1/40 of a second), as we saw in Section 7.2. But of course that doesn't necessarily mean that 14,286 random I/Os in succession will require a total elapsed time of 14,286/40 = 357.15 seconds. Quite possibly, these 14,286 data pages could be spread out over (say) ten different disks, and the system could then enlist the service of all ten disk arms moving simultaneously, so that each disk reads only one-tenth as many pages into memory (1429 pages per disk), in one-tenth the elapsed time (35.7 seconds). This approach to having multiple disk arms acting simultaneously in a query plan is known as I/O *parallelism*. Since the CPU time in a query plan is often much smaller than the elapsed time required for disk I/O, we expect the CPU to be able to keep up with retrieving appropriate rows from the data pages as quickly as the pages can be read from disk into memory buffers, overlapping CPU efforts with a large number of simultaneously moving disk arms. Certainly such read parallelism requires no additional CPU, and it significantly lowers the elapsed time for the query.

I/O Parallelism and Disk Striping

I/O parallelism is indeed perfectly possible, and it is a feature offered by a number of database systems. For example, some systems offer the ability to *stripe* the data pages across (say) ten different disks, page 1 on disk 1, page 2 on disk 2, . . ., page 10 on disk 10, then page 11 on disk 1, page 12 on disk 2, and so on, with page N lying on the disk number $((N - 1)\%10) + 1$. ("X%Y" is the C language expression for "X MOD Y". See Figure 8.3.) When we stripe the pages in this way, the system reading successive pages from a table can make multiple I/O read requests into the future and thus keep all involved disk arms busy most of the time. Since we can easily predict future tablespace page requests when performing a table space scan, we merely need an architecture that supports striping, translating logical

530

page addresses into physical device addresses on multiple disks and passing along future I/O requests to the appropriate devices. This is not at all difficult, since allocated extents in such a striping architecture must span multiple disks in a well-defined way.

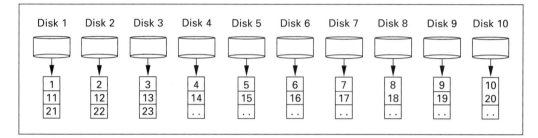

Figure 8.3 Successive Disk Pages on Striped Disks

Given all this, the reader may be surprised to realize that some database systems do not offer a striping capability. Some products that offer a feature called striping do not actually pass along future I/O requests in the manner required to gain I/O parallelism and thus save overall elapsed time in a table space scan. A system that waits for a single I/O at a time, delaying the next I/O request until the prior request has been filled, cannot have multiple disk arms in motion at the same time and thus gains no parallelism from striping. There are a number of reasons why striping for parallel I/O is not more commonly used. Certainly it requires extra effort on the part of the DBA, who must allocate equivalent amounts of space on multiple disks. Balancing the disk arm load to gain maximum parallelism is also a complex problem: if one of the ten striped disks is extremely busy doing other I/O in a workload, that disk will become a bottleneck for a parallel access and possibly cause other disks in the striped tablespace to be underutilized. Also, many systems do not have enough disk devices or a large enough application, requiring parallel scans to make tuning of this kind possible.

Another point is that disk striping doesn't actually save any computer resource cost. We require the same total *number* of random I/Os, even though the workload is split up among several different disk devices. If we estimate the I/O cost of the 14,286 random I/Os of Example 8.2.1 by charging a fair rent on the disk devices during the time they are dedicated, then parallelism has no effect whatsoever on this cost; we are simply using more devices for a shorter time, paying the same ultimate rent. The saving we achieve with a reduced elapsed time for the query has to do with the employee costs mentioned earlier, reducing wasted time and turnover caused by the frustration of waiting for query responses. Because I/O parallelism is still relatively rare, we assume in the following discussion that we are always dealing with the alternative, sequential I/O, where one I/O request must be complete before a second request is made in a plan, unless we specify otherwise. Sequential I/O still has an unrevealed trick to offer, however, known in **DB2** as sequential prefetch I/O, that will actually save a large amount of resource cost in performing a table space scan.

Sequential Prefetch I/O in DB2

We have been assuming implicitly that 14,286R (random I/Os) when performed one after another will require 14,286 times as long as a single random I/O. In Section 7.2, we derived the fact that a single random I/O took an expected average time of about 0.025 seconds, broken down as follows (we make very slight modifications for the 4-KB pages of **DB2**).

Seek time	.0155 seconds
Rotational latency	.0080 seconds
Transfer time	.0015 seconds (for 4 KB of transfer)

TOTAL	.0250 seconds

Figure 8.4 Breakdown of Random I/O Elapsed Time for **DB2**

Now let us return to the consideration of performing 14,286 random I/Os in a table space scan. Because of the way extents are allocated on disk media, we will generally find that successive data pages in a table are contiguous on disk, successive pages on the same track. This seems to imply that successive data page I/Os from a table usually have no seek time component during which a disk arm must move from one cylinder to another. Recall from the discussion at the beginning of Section 7.2 that the seek time of about .016 seconds is an average time for disk arm seek, where it is assumed that successive accessed pages are scattered at random between the two extreme cylinder positions. In our case there is usually no distance to move at all, and we should expect the seek time to completely disappear. In fact, at first glance it would seem that the rotational latency should disappear as well, since we normally retrieve one disk page after another in sequence. In fact there seems no reason why the normal time for bringing successive data pages into memory buffers can't proceed at the speed of full transfer rate, .0015 seconds per 4-KB page. See Figure 8.5 for a tabulation that reflects this idea.

Seek time	.0000 seconds (successive data pages on same cylinder)
Rotational latency	.0000 seconds (successive data pages often contiguous on a track)
Transfer time	.0015 seconds (for 4 KB of transfer)
TOTAL	.0015 seconds (at least in the most common case)

Figure 8.5 Conceptual Elapsed Time for Successive Data Page I/O (**INVALID**)

However, the idea underlying Figure 8.5 turns out to be incorrect. The fact that the seek time goes to zero (.0000) is essentially correct in most cases, but the rotational latency would actually go *up* for **DB2** and most other I/O systems when successive pages are retrieved. The reason for this is that the disk controller device that reads the disk page into the appropriate memory buffer can be pictured as having a small refractory period after it completes this disk page read, during which it is unable to act on another request quickly enough to start reading the next page in sequence on the disk track before the initial edge of the page rotates past the read position. Because of this the disk controller reads one disk page in .0015 seconds, just misses the next page, and must wait until the disk makes one complete rotation back to the appropriate position. Recall that the disk platters rotate at 60 rps, so in this case the longest possible rotational latency of $1/60 = .0167$ seconds takes place.

Seek time	.0000 seconds (successive data pages on same cylinder)
Rotational latency	.0167 seconds (one full rotation)
Transfer time	.0015 seconds (for 4 KB of transfer)
TOTAL	.0182 seconds (this is the most common case)

Figure 8.6 Actual Elapsed Time for Successive Data Page Random I/Os

A number of products have tried placing successive disk pages in an interleaved fashion on disk to overcome the refractory period of the controller. That way the system doesn't have to wait for the disk to perform a full rotation between accessed pages. Although this approach usually has an important speedup effect, it is not as dependable as we would like. In many systems the disk arm can be pulled away to an entirely different region of the disk between successive reads of interleaved pages, and the speedup effect is thus obviated. In what follows, we assume that no interleaving is performed (we have a better method in mind), and the total elapsed time of Figure 8.6 is therefore valid. An elapsed time of .0182 seconds is quite close to the average elapsed time of .025 seconds we have been assuming. We therefore treat such reads from successive data pages as normal random I/Os in what follows and approximate the elapsed time as .025 seconds, rather than ask the reader to remember another I/O rate. Thus we normally say that all random I/Os take .025 seconds.

The **DB2** system offers another type of I/O paradigm, however, known as *sequential prefetch* I/O (also called *multi-block* I/O in other systems). The idea of sequential prefetch I/O is that the system specifies a large number of data pages in sequence to be read in from disk, most commonly 32 pages. This sequence of requests is then communicated to the disk controller *in a manner that allows the disk controller to read successive pages on a track,* avoiding the refractory period problem mentioned earlier by knowing in advance the succession of actions to be performed. As a result, **DB2** is able to perform 32 page reads in sequence at the full rotational transfer rate of the disk, therefore at a much lower cost in terms of elapsed time during which the disk arm is employed. See Figure 8.7 for a comparison between a sequential prefetch of 32 disk pages in sequence and 32 random I/Os. (We assume the .025-second elapsed time for these random I/Os.)

	Random I/O (in seconds)	Sequential prefetch I/O (in seconds)
Seek time	0.016	0.016
Rotational latency	0.008	0.008
Transfer time	0.0015	0.048 (32 times)
Total	0.025	0.072
Total for 32 pages	0.800	0.072

Figure 8.7 Comparison of Sequential Prefetch and Random I/O of 32 Pages

The figure of 0.800 seconds (or somewhat less) for 32 random I/Os is approximately ten times as large as the figure of 0.072 seconds for a sequential prefetch of 32 pages. In what follows, we use the rough rule of thumb that sequential prefetch, in situations where it can be applied, proceeds ten times as fast as random I/O, at a rate of 400 I/Os per second.

EXAMPLE 8.2.2 Table Space Scan with Sequential Prefetch.

Recall the *table space scan* of Figure 8.3, where the given Select statement has an I/O cost of 14,286R. Under standard assumptions of random I/O (no parallelism) we later calculated that the elapsed time for this query, during which one disk arm is completely utilized, is 14,286/40 = 357.15 seconds. On a lightly utilized computer, the elapsed time will actually be quite close to this calculated I/O time, because the small CPU time required to perform the select will probably overlap with waits for I/O.

Now in **DB2** sequential prefetch is available for a table space scan, and the query optimizer would certainly make use of this capability, resulting in $COST_{I/O}$ (PLAN) = 14,286S. The letter S (for sequential) at the end of the number of pages to be read indicates that sequential prefetch is to be employed. The resulting elapsed time for this query is 14,286/400 = 35.72 seconds. This is a real I/O cost saving, since the time spent by the disk arm has actually been reduced by a factor of ten, and the rent on the device is therefore reduced by a similar factor. Putting this a different way, we can perform ten times as many queries of this kind using sequential prefetch on the same disk equipment as we could with random I/Os. ∎

A query plan might make use of both sequential prefetch and random I/O. We use the elapsed time for total I/O as the best common measure, since the rental cost on a disk arm is directly proportional to the elapsed time the arm is in use, and in this important sense sequential prefetch I/Os are about ten times more effective than random I/Os.

This is a good time to introduce another column of the **DB2** plan table, the PREFETCH column. When sequential prefetch is selected for a given access step, we see the letter S in the PREFETCH column for that row of the plan table, and we designate this by writing PREFETCH = S. Thus the table space scan step of Example 8.2.2 would be designated in the **DB2** plan table by ACCESSTYPE = R, PREFETCH = S. The plan table listing only these two columns is given in Figure 8.8.

ACCESS TYPE	PREFETCH
R	S

Figure 8.8 Plan Table for Example 8.2.2

List Prefetch

There is also another kind of prefetch available in **DB2**, known as *list prefetch*, in which the disk controller is provided in advance with a list of pages (usually 32) that need to be read in to memory buffers, but the pages are not necessarily in contiguous sequential order as with sequential prefetch. With list prefetch, the disk arm is programmed in advance with the most efficient possible sequence of movements to perform successive reads, so that the I/Os occur much more efficiently than they would with random I/O requests. The elapsed time for such a list prefetch does not follow a simple general rule, however, and the 0.072 seconds elapsed time given in Figure 8.7 for a sequential prefetch is generally an unattainable optimum for a list prefetch. List prefetch is more efficient than random I/O (which we are assuming performs 40 I/Os per second) and less efficient than sequential prefetch I/O (which we are assuming performs 400 I/Os per second). The actual speed is determined by how far apart the pages are on disk, but as a rule of thumb in the problems that follow we will assume that list prefetch proceeds at 100 I/Os per second. We will use these approximate rates for random, sequential prefetch, and list prefetch I/Os a good deal in what follows, so Figure 8.9 tabulates the rules of thumb just mentioned. Although these are rather rough figures, they usually give a reasonably good estimate for queries that occur in practice.

An access step in the plan table using list prefetch would be designated by PREFETCH = L—that is, a letter L in the PREFETCH column, analogous to the letter S when sequential prefetch is to be used. An access step that uses neither sequential prefetch nor list prefetch would have a blank value in the PREFETCH column.

Random I/O	Sequential prefetch I/O	List prefetch I/O
40 pages/sec	400 pages/sec	100 pages/sec

Figure 8.9 Rules of Thumb for I/O Rates

More about Prefetch

We have mentioned that the number of pages read in by a sequential or a list prefetch is usually 32. In fact, this number is dependent on the number of page buffers available to **DB2**. (There are four different buffer pools possible, but we ignore that for now.)

Buffer pool size	Pages read by refetch
<= 223	8
224–999	16
1000+	32

Since a 1000-page buffer requires only about 4 MB of memory, a relatively small amount by current standards, we generally assume in the calculations that follow that prefetch I/Os involve 32 pages. Of course this assumes that at least 32 pages exist on disk that need to be read into memory, and that the necessary preconditions exist to allow sequential or list prefetch to be used. In the case of sequential prefetch, the preconditions are that the pages to be read lie in contiguous order on disk, and that the query optimizer is able to recognize this fact. The precondition for list prefetch is a good deal more subtle. Essentially, the query optimizer must be able to generate a list of RID values for data rows that need to be read in.

NOTE: We present a number of examples in the following sections to solidify these concepts. However, we do not consider list prefetch until we have had a chance to explain the **DB2** preconditions for list prefetch in Section 8.6. Until then, we act as if table rows are always read in from disk using random or sequential prefetch I/Os.

There are also a number of special cases involving prefetch I/O. When the number of pages that needs to be read from disk is less than 32, a prefetch I/O is still possible; indeed, a prefetch can be performed to read in as few as 4 pages. Naturally such small transfers will adversely affect the I/O rate given in Figure 8.9 since we have reduced the number of pages to amortize the seek time and rotational latency, but in the calculations that follow we generally ignore such effects. However, any time that 3 or fewer pages must be read in from disk, the reader should assume that random I/O is used, even if the preconditions for sequential or list prefetch are met.

It is clear that sequential and list prefetch are important capabilities. This is especially true because CPU costs are still declining at a precipitous rate while disk drive costs are not. Query optimization features that can reduce disk costs give a product an advantage in the database downsizing efforts that are now being undertaken by most large database users to save costs. However, we have mentioned only **DB2** in relation to prefetch I/O, and **DB2** operates only on large IBM mainframe computers. It would seem that all important commercial database systems would by now have intro-

duced a comparable feature, several years after the initial offering of this
feature by an early **DB2** version. However, as of early 1994, several UNIX
database products have only recently begun to support I/O capability to
read 8 pages of 2 KB each in a single sequential prefetch type request.
Many database systems offer no such feature. (This appears to be the case
even with the new DB2.2 database product, which operates on the OS/2
PC operating system.) It is possible to change the size of all I/Os on most
products, so that each I/O by the system brings several normal-size pages
into memory buffers. But one of the important things about sequential
prefetch in **DB2** is that the system has the freedom to choose whether to
read in a single page with a normal random I/O or 32 such pages with a
prefetch I/O. Any attempt to compromise, say on an 8-page read for all
purposes, will penalize some applications while it helps others. There is no
value, for example, in reading in 8 pages around a B-tree node when all the
desired information has been carefully placed on a single page node.
Indeed such behavior penalizes everyone by wasting memory buffer space
that should be applied to keeping other popular information in buffer.
More serious attention to the sequential prefetch capability by commercial
database systems is seriously overdue.

8.3 Simple Indexed Access in DB2

As we noted in Chapter 7, columns of tables referenced in a Select statement can take part in indexes, and a query plan for the Select statement
can sometimes make use of those indexes to limit rows selected and make
the query execution more efficient. In the next several sections we consider
basic indexed access step capabilities. To begin with we will consider only
Select statements having a single table named in the **from** clause and no
new tables named in the search condition of the **where** clause, thus avoiding considerations of join processing. We also confine our attention to the
DB2 query optimizer unless otherwise stated, and we refer to variations in
the **INGRES** and **ORACLE** products only parenthetically. In what follows,
we use example of tables designated by T1, T2, . . ., and columns within
these tables designated by C1, C2, C3, C4, ...

EXAMPLE 8.3.1 Matching Index Scan, Single-Column Index.

Assume that an index C1X exists on the column C1 of table T1 (this is always a B-tree index in **DB2**), and that the following query has been posed:

```
select * from T1 where C1 = 10;
```

This query is implemented in **DB2** by an access step known as a *matching index scan*. In execution, the B-tree index on column C1 is traversed down to the leaf level for the leftmost index entry that has the value 10 (recall the exercise to find the leftmost entry as a variation of the binsearch algorithm of Example 7.3.1). Then the row from table T1 pointed to by that entry is retrieved into the answer set. Following this, successive entries are retrieved from the leaf level of the index while the index value remains 10, passing from left to right in the entries and from one leaf node to the next, following leaf sibling pointers when necessary. For each entry, the corresponding row pointed to in T1 is retrieved into the answer set. When the index value first exceeds 10, the matching index scan is complete. Note in particular that only one traversal of the B-tree down to the leaf level was required. The rows retrieved during this scan may or may not have been found in clustered order by C1; we have made no assumption as to whether C1 is a clustered index. ■

A matching index scan is a single-step query plan, sharing this property with the table space scan: when the step is complete the query has been answered. In the plan table, three columns of which are shown in Figure 8.10, a matching index scan such as that seen in Example 8.3.1 has ACCESSTYPE = I (this represents an index scan), ACCESSNAME = C1X (the name of the index being scanned), and MATCHCOLS = 1. MATCH-COLS gives the number of matching columns in the index; this value can be at most 1 for an index scan on an index with a single column.

ACCESS TYPE	ACCESS NAME	MATCH COLS
I	C1X	1

Figure 8.10 Plan Table for Example 8.3.1

Now consider the following query:

[8.3.1] `select * from T1`
`        where C1 = 10 and C2 between 100 and 200 and C3 like 'A%';`

Recall that the search condition of a **where** clause is made up of a number of logical predicates, listed in Figure 3.17 of Section 3.8, connected by logical operators such as **and, or,** and **not,** as defined in Figure 3.18. The Select statement of (8.3.1) contains three predicates connected by logical operators **and:** (1) a comparison predicate involving the column C1 (this is a special type of comparison predicate known as an *equal match predicate*), (2) a **between** predicate involving the column C2, and (3) a **like** predicate involving the column C3. In each of these cases an index on the associated column can be used efficiently in a **DB2** query plan to limit the rows considered for retrieval. These predicates are said to be *indexable* in **DB2.** Not all predicates are indexable, however, which means that although it might still be possible to use an index to limit the rows retrieved, the index will not be used efficiently. For example, the predicate C1 <> 10 is not indexable, and the query

```
select * from T1 where C1 <> 10;
```

while it *can* use index scan on a C1X index, is more likely to use a table space scan, which is always available as a fallback. We give a detailed list of indexable and non-indexable predicates later in this section. For now, we want to study how multiple predicates in a **where** clause such as we see in the Select statement of (8.3.1) might all be used simultaneously to restrict the rows retrieved.

EXAMPLE 8.3.2 Matching Index Scan, Single Column Index, Additional Predicates to Be Verified.

As before, assume that an index C1X exists on the column C1 of table T1, but this time the query of (8.3.1) has been posed:

```
select * from T1
    where C1 = 10 and C2 between 100 and 200 and C3 like 'A%';
```

We assume that there are no indexes involving the columns C2 and C3. As before, this query is implemented in **DB2** by a single *matching index scan* access step. The B-tree index on column C1 is traversed down to the leaf level for the leftmost index entry that has the value 10; the entries at the leaf level with index value 10 are traversed left to right. Successive rows from table T1 pointed to by these entries are then accessed, and tests are performed on the rows to validate the other two predicates: "C2 between 100 and 200," and "C3 like 'A%'". Rows that pass these tests are retrieved into the answer set. ∎

The matching index scan step introduced in Examples 8.3.1 and 8.3.2 is defined as a step where a *single index* is used to retrieve all the rows from a table that satisfy some (set of) predicates in a **where** clause. In the case of an index on a single column, a matching index scan usually represents a single contiguous range of column values, corresponding to exactly one predicate such as "C1 = 10" (with an index C1X on C1), "C2 between 100 and 200" (with an index C2X on C2), or "C3 like 'A%'" (with an index C3X on C3). A noncontiguous set of column values can also be retrieved with a special case of the matching index scan, known as an *in-list index scan,* on a predicate such as "C4 in (1, 2, 3)" (with an index C4X on C4). It is also possible to satisfy several predicates at once through a single index in a matching index scan. Consider the index C123X, created with the following Create Index statement:

```
create index C123X on T1 (C1, C2, C3) . . .;
```

In the Select statement of Example 8.3.2, we notice that the two later predicates do not reduce the number of rows accessed from T1. Only the index C1X is available, so we can only use the first predicate to limit to rows with C1 = 10, and then access each of these rows from the table to validate the other predicates. But with the index C123X available, we would be able to retrieve all three predicates at once (C1 = 10 and C2 between 100 and 200 and C3 like 'A%') by recourse to this single index. To give an analogy, it is as if we were looking in a library catalog for all books with the last name James (C1 = 10), first name beginning with the letters H through K (C2 between 100 and 200), and title beginning with the letter A (C3 like 'A%'). It should be obvious that we will be able to restrict the number of books to retrieve quite effectively by examining the cards alone.

In a second type of situation there exist separate indexes on each of the columns under discussion. Thus we might have an index C1X on C1, an index C2X on C2, and an index C3X on C3. The method by which three different indexes of this sort can be employed to answer the query of Example 8.3.2 may not be immediately obvious. By analogy, it involves extracting a list of catalog cards from *each* associated catalog that satisfies *one* of the given predicates, sorting each list of cards in order by call number (RID), and then performing a merge-intersect of the three lists of cards so that we end up only with books that obey all three predicates. This multiple-step approach is known as *multiple index access;* we cover it in detail after we have had a chance to look at some of the more basic concepts of indexed access.

Equal Unique Match Index Access

Experience shows that many readers tend to picture columns that have unique values when first introduced to indexed retrieval. This is actually a relatively uninteresting case, but we give an example to place the situation in context.

EXAMPLE 8.3.3 Index Scan Step, Unique Match.
Consider the `employees` table introduced in Example 8.2.1, with a unique index, eidx, on the column `eid`. We are given the following SQL query:

```
select ename from employees where eid = '12901A';
```

If we assume a **DB2** index (see Figure 7.14) with **freepage** = 0 and **pctfree** = 70, we have about 2800 bytes on each page of the index available for index entries. Say the `eid` column requires 6 bytes. Since we know the RID requires 4 bytes, we can assume 10 bytes per entry. Thus there are 2800/10 = 280 entries on each index page, and with 200,000 rows, we require CEIL(200,000/280) = 715 pages at the leaf level, CEIL(715/280) = 3 pages at the next directory level up, and a single root page above this. To access the unique row with a given `eid` value requires an access through three levels of B-tree nodes and then an access to one of the 14,286 data pages to retrieve the `ename` value from the designated row. Therefore it seems that the I/O cost of this Select statement is 4R. But recall that we keep popular disk pages in memory buffers to reduce the number of real disk I/Os. The COSTI/O(PLAN) figure calculated by the query optimizer is meant to be in terms of **real** I/Os; a page that is already resident in memory buffer entails only a minor CPU cost for lookaside. As we explain in detail in Chapter 9 (see Example 9.10.2), it is the economically correct decision to purchase enough memory to keep in memory all disk pages that are accessed again within a few minutes (we assume 120 seconds, to be specific on the IBM **DB2** platforms). That's what we mean when we say we are keeping popular pages buffer resident.

Now we need to ask how often the eidx B-tree index is accessed. If the answer is once each second with a random `eid` value, then we should expect to find the root node of the tree and all three nodes at the next directory level already buffered in memory. On the other hand, the expected time between accesses to leaf-level nodes is 715 seconds, more than the 120-second threshold, so we would *not* expect to find the leaf nodes of the B-tree in buffers. Clearly we would also not expect to find the 14,286 data pages buffer resident. Thus the proper I/O cost for this query plan, under reasonable buffering assumptions, should be 2R, representing the I/Os to read from disk the leaf node of the B-tree and the data page. Note that all the foregoing analysis has assumed a perfect world—that the proper amount of memory has been purchased and that the buffering scheme will keep all the B-tree directory nodes in memory buffers accessible to different terminal users. (A number of rather primitive database buffering schemes do not share buffers between different terminal processes, but this is not a problem with **DB2**.)

The row of the plan table corresponding to this unique match index scan has ACCESSTYPE = I (implies an index scan), ACCESSNAME = eidx (the name of the index being scanned), and MATCHCOLS = 1. The plan does not mention that a unique match is expected; this is a property that we can predict by noting that the eid column was defined to be unique. ∎

Clustered versus Non-Clustered Indexing

We introduce a table named *prospects* for use in examples that follow. The prospects table is modeled on tables used by organizations that perform direct-mail applications (mail advertising). The prospects table has 50 million rows corresponding to people in the United States who are potential customers for new products. Information on prospects is often gathered from warranty questionnaires (it is assumed that people who fill out such warranties expect to have their demographic data kept on record for possible future mailings). The rows of the prospects table are clustered in **DB2** by an index, addrx, representing the address of the prospect:

```
create index addrx on prospects (zipcode, city, straddr) . . .
    cluster . . .;
```

Note that the index columns are normally ordered as successively more restrictive items of the address. The zip code determines the state (zip codes do not cross state boundaries). Many direct mailings, such as sales announcements at area stores, are to small geographical districts consisting of a few zip code regions, and we will see that clustering by addrx permits extremely efficient queries.

We assume that **pctfree** = 0 for the prospects table and all indexes, because we don't expect any inserts, or even updates, to the prospects table during its lifetime. New households are added to the prospects table infrequently. Typically, new prospects would be added only once a month by doing a complete reload of the table to ensure optimal retrieval efficiency. Given that rows of the prospects table contain 400 bytes, we can fit 10 rows on each 4-KB page, and a 50-million-row table requires 5 million pages.

At the leaf level of the addrx index B-tree, we assume that the zipcode column can be represented as an integer in 4 bytes, city requires 12 bytes, straddr 20 bytes, and of course the RID for each entry requires 4 bytes. Thus an entry in the addrx index requires 40 bytes. (We assume for simplicity that there are no duplicate index values—that is, two or more prospects with the same address. We thus avoid needing to take into account the type of **DB2** index compression covered in Figure 7.19.) We can fit 100 40-byte entries in a 4-KB page that is 100% full. With 50 million total entries, this means 500,000 node pages at the leaf level of the tree. The next directory level up contains 5000 nodes, the one above that contains 50 nodes, and the root page lies above that. This is a four-level B-tree.

The prospects table also has a large number of non-clustering indexes. Consider one possible index, on the attribute hobby, provided by the prospect on the questionnaire as a hobby of major interest.

```
create index hobbyx on prospects (hobby);
```

Assume that 100 distinct hobbies are listed in the form the prospect filled out (. . . card games, chess, coin collecting, . . .). We say that the *cardinality* of the hobby column, the number of different attribute values, is 100:

CARD(hobby) = 100

This is a type of statistic used by **DB2** in calculating the I/O cost of a query plan, and it also gives us an idea of the amount of index compression present in the hobbyx index. In the same way, we can assume that there are 100,000 distinct zipcode values in the addrx index, from 00000 to 99999. (This is actually an overestimate used for simplicity.) Basically, the small number of hobbies means that we can assume that the length of the hobby column is irrelevant for leaf-level index entries, because from the **DB2** index compression of Figure 7.19 we see that the index key appears only once for every few hundred RID values. Thus the leaf-level entries can be taken as being 4 bytes in length, 1000 entries per page. This is because we have about 500,000 prospects rows for every one of the 100 hobbyx values, and **DB2** index compression can be applied in its most effective form, 255 RIDs amortizing each key value. With 50 million entries at the leaf level and 1000 entries fitting on a page, we have 50,000 leaf pages. At the next level up the index key separators appear with each entry (there is no compression). If we assume entries of 12 bytes, we fit 333 entries to a page and thus have 50,000/333 = 151 nodes. The next level up is the root. These calculations are summarized in Figure 8.11.

prospects table	addrx index	hobbyx index
50,000,000 rows	500,000 leaf pages	50,000 leaf pages
5,000,000 data pages	5,000 level 3 nodes	151 level 2 nodes
	50 level 2 nodes	1 root node
	1 root node	
	CARD(zipcode)= 100,000	CARD(hobby)=100

Figure 8.11 Some Statistics for the prospects Table

We are now ready for a few more illustrative examples.

EXAMPLE 8.3.4 Matching Index Scan Step, Unclustered Match.
Consider the following SQL query:

```
select name, straddr from prospects where hobby = 'chess';
```

To answer this query, the query optimizer considers an index scan step on the index hobbyx. This is comparable to the matching index scan step of Example 8.3.1, except that this time we will be making I/O estimates. The root node of the hobbyx B-tree is read first, followed by the next node down along the proper path, and then the leaf node is read corresponding to the leftmost of the hobbyx entries with value = 'chess'. The next step is to retrieve successive entries from the leaf level until the hobbyx value that follows 'chess' is encountered. As noted earlier, there are only 100 different values for hobbyx. If we assume that each of the values is equally likely, this means that there are 500,000 entries corresponding to the value 'chess'. To traverse across 500,000 entries with 1000 entries per leaf node requires 500 leaf page I/Os, and these I/Os can be performed using sequential prefetch I/O. Now for each of these 500,000 'chess' index entries we must perform a random page I/O to access the appropriate row of the prospects table and return the name and straddr values. With 5,000,000 data pages and 500,000 rows, we expect each row to be on a separate page (this is case 1 of the "N darts in M slots" problem, discussed in Section 7.6). In any event, we have no reason to think that rows retrieved are close together on data pages, since hobbyx is an unclustered index. Thus each row retrieval requires its own random I/O, and the total number of I/Os needed to resolve this query is

2R for index directory nodes, 500S for index leaf nodes, and 500,000R for data pages.

The elapsed time to read 500 pages with sequential prefetch at 400 pages a second is 500/400 = 1.25 seconds; the elapsed time to read 500,000 pages using random I/O, at 40 I/Os per second, is 500,000/40 = 12,500 seconds, or about 3½ hours. Clearly the I/Os to descend the hobbyx B-tree and even to traverse the entries at the leaf level are insignificant by comparison with the data page I/Os.

■

In exercises involving elapsed time for I/O, you should generally assume that index directory pages are buffer resident and that index leaf pages are not, unless instructed otherwise. You may ignore index I/O in your answers when these sum to less than 10% of the total. However, you should be careful to include index I/O calculations, to demonstrate why you consider them insignificant.

Considering the query of Example 8.3.4 being performed with a table space scan, we see that to retrieve 5,000,000 pages using sequential prefetch I/O (see Figure 8.9) requires 5,000,000/400 = 12,500 seconds elapsed time—*nearly the same elapsed time as required by the index scan.* This is a fairly surprising result, and demonstrates the value of a query optimizer to compare costs of competing plans. Basically what is happening is that with sequential prefetch I/O, approximately ten times as many pages can be read in the same amount of time as is the case with random I/O. Since the unclustered index scan of this example reads 500,000 pages to retrieve the same number of prospects with a single hobby, and the data scan reads 5,000,000 pages with prefetch I/O, the two methods are actually quite close in elapsed time and indeed in I/O disk arm rent. If we had more hobbies for our prospects table, and thus a smaller number or rows per index value, the unclustered index scan would certainly be used, and with fewer hobbies a data scan would probably be more appropriate.

In Example 8.3.4 we used the fact that CARD(hobby) = 100 to conclude that the predicate "hobby = 'chess'" retrieves about 1/100 of the rows of the prospects table. This fraction is known as the *filter factor* of the predicate; we will meet such filter factors a great deal in what follows.

EXAMPLE 8.3.5 Matching Index Scan Step, Clustered Match.
Consider the following SQL query:

```
select name, straddr from prospects
    where zipcode between 02159 and 03158;
```

Recall that there are 100,000 distinct zipcode column values that make up the first component of the addrx index on which the data rows are clustered. The index scan step here performs its search by reading down to the leftmost entry of the addrx B-tree having `zipcode` 02159 (other values in the concatenated key value are immaterial), then examining entries from left to right until the first `zipcode` value outside the range is encountered. We see that approximately the same number of leaf-level index entries are processed here as were processed from the hobbyx index of the last example. The "filter factor" of `hobby =` `'chess'` was 1/100, but here we are retrieving a range of 1000 values from the `zipcode` index with 100,000 distinct values. While the filter factor of "`zipcode = 02159`" would be 1/100,000, the factor for the range predicate with 1000 values permitted is 1000/100,000 = 1/100. The number of leaf-level pages of addrx that is read in with 500,000 entries, at 40 bytes per entry, 100 entries per page, is 5000; and since sequential prefetch can be used, this means an I/O cost of 5000S. (A simple check on this is that the number of pages at the leaf level of addrx, as shown in Figure 8.11, is 500,000, and we will be processing 1/100 of these pages.)

Now we will retrieve the same number of rows from the `prospects` table, or 500,000 rows, as we did in Example 8.3.4. However, since the rows in `prospects` are *clustered* by `zipcode`, where they were not by hobbyx, the 500,000 rows in the contiguous retrieved range of `zipcode`s are *packed together* in the table data pages, 10 to a page. We can therefore assume that we need to retrieve only 50,000 table pages, and that we can accomplish this using sequential prefetch I/O, so the I/O cost is 50,000S. (Note that we required 5,000S to retrieve an equivalent number of addrx entries, 40 bytes in length, and these rows are 400 bytes in length, so this is a check on our work.) The total elapsed time for 5,000S + 50,000S is 55,000/400 = 137.5 seconds, a little over 2 minutes, compared to the 3½ hours of the previous example. This is a dramatic example of the advantage of clustering. ∎

Looking at Example 8.3.5, we note that the query optimizer chooses to examine each index entry in the range before retrieving the row indexed, even though the rows themselves are clustered by the index values. It might seem to be an I/O saving to ignore the index entries once the left end of the range of rows has been located, and thereafter look only at the rows within the sequence of data pages for the range selected. However, this is not done in **DB2**. One important reason that index entries are always examined is that the clustering property breaks down after a number of new row inserts have filled up data pages. When this occurs, future rows inserted in a range of values are placed on data pages that lie entirely out of the local data page sequence, and the only way to retrieve such rows in a range is to examine the index entries. Although we do not intend to insert new rows into the `prospects` table until the table is reorganized, **DB2** is unaware of this and therefore always examines index entries before retrieving the rows.

Index-Only Retrieval

Another interesting observation from Example 8.3.5 is that the index entries retrieved in the desired range entail an I/O cost of 5000S and the data rows retrieved entail an I/O cost of 50,000S. Since the index entries involved are 40 bytes in length and the data rows are 400 bytes in length, the multiple of ten in I/O cost seems natural. This observation, together with some of the other examples we have seen, allows us to categorize the retrieval advantages of index entries over data rows in terms of the following properties:

[1] The index has a directory structure that allows us to retrieve a range of values efficiently.

[2] Index entries are always placed in sequence by value, and therefore the system can use sequential prefetch I/O to achieve low retrieval cost.

[3] Index entries are shorter than data rows and require proportionately less I/O.

We could conceivably place a directory structure on clustered rows, where the rows take the place of entries at the leaf level of a B-tree, as is done with the Modify command of **INGRES**, and thus duplicate properties 1 and 2. Of course we can only cluster the rows by one set of values, while we can create numerous indexes for different indexing values. Recall that **INGRES** provides a feature to include non-key columns in an index with the Create Index syntax, Figure 7.15. We see a special advantage from property 3 in the following example.

EXAMPLE 8.3.6 Concatenated Index, Index-Only Scan.
Consider again the SQL Select statement:

```
select name, straddr from prospects
    where zipcode between 02159 and 03158;
```

Recall that the addrx index was used in Example 8.3.5 to access rows of the prospects table in the desired range of zipcodes, where addrx was created with the statement:

```
create index addrx on prospects (zipcode, city, straddr) . . .
    cluster . . .;
```

But now let us assume—for the current example only—that an alternative index, naddrx, has been created with the statement:

```
create index naddrx on prospects (zipcode, city, straddr, name)
    . . . cluster . . . ;
```

As we will see, the fact that the index naddrx is a *clustered* index for the `prospects` table is not crucial to this example, since the Select statement at the beginning of this example can be answered by reference to components of the values in naddrx *without any reference to the* `prospects` *table.* The concatenated key value of the naddrx index has the form:

```
naddrx key value: zipcodeval.cityval.straddrval.nameval
```

Each of the individual component values can be read out of an index entry retrieved in the desired range and retrieved into the target list of the Select statement. To answer the Select statement, the index entries of naddrx in the range of `zipcode` are accessed as they were in Example 8.3.5; but then instead of referencing the associated row pointed to by the entry RID, the *name* and *straddr* values in the target list of the Select statement are retrieved from the fourth and third components respectively of the naddrx key value. This type of index scan is known as an *index only scan.*

What is the I/O cost of this retrieval? Assume that the index entries in naddrx are 60 bytes in length, three-halves as long as the 40-byte addrx entries because of the addition of the *name* column. In Example 8.3.5, the addrx index entry retrieval had an I/O cost of 5000S, so we would expect the naddrx cost to be 7500S with these larger entries. Since there is no other I/O cost in this index only retrieval, we would expect an elapsed time for this query of 7500/400 = 18.75 seconds. This compares to the elapsed time of 137.5 seconds for the same query in Example 8.3.5. ∎

Index only retrieval occurs for a Select statement when the elements retrieved in the target list can be generated from the entries of the index used, without recourse to data rows. Note in particular that any Select statement from a single table, where "count(*)" is the only element of the target list, can be performed with index only retrieval if an index scan is possible at all; the entries retrieved only need to be counted to supply the answer returned to the target list. When EXPLAIN is used to generate query plan steps in the plan table, an index only scan step is characterized by the plan column ACCESSTYPE = I, and by a new column we mention for the first time, INDEXONLY = Y. In previous examples we have had INDEXONLY = N.

Example 8.3.5 demonstrates a valuable advantage in using concatenated indexes to permit index only retrieval (and an even greater advantage compared with non-clustered index retrieval). However, it is often difficult to create a set of concatenated indexes to foresee all query needs. For example, consider what would happen in the query of Example 8.3.6 if we wished to retrieve some other prospects attribute into the target list as well:

```
select name, straddr, age from prospects
    where zipcode between 02159 and 03159;
```

Then the concatenated index naddrx would be insufficient to answer the query with an index only scan, and it would be necessary to read in the table rows after all, except that now the naddrx index to be used requires more I/O than the simpler addrx index we started with. If we try to foresee all needs in a single concatenated index, the index entries become longer and longer, until we are receiving less advantage over reading in the rows (at least in the clustered case). Furthermore, it costs something to create multiple indexes. For one thing, there is increased disk media cost, although this is often not the major cost bottleneck. Another overhead occurs in situations where new rows are commonly inserted to the table, because the inserts take more resources to update additional indexes. Even in the read-only database case, there is additional cost in the initial load time, a nontrivial consideration for large tables such as prospects. Still, the reader should be aware that there are numerous examples of read-only tables—such as the prospects table—where nearly all single columns of the table have a corresponding index.

8.4 Filter Factors and Statistics

As we pointed out in the introduction to Example 8.3.3, indexed retrieval on a column with unique values is actually a relatively uninteresting case. Indeed, an extremely important feature introduced in relational query languages such as SQL that was missing from earlier database models is the capability to retrieve information based on compound (usually ANDed) predicate conditions. Clearly if a predicate such as "C1 = 10" were to identify a unique row of the containing table, there would be no point in considering compound predicates such as "C1 = 10 and C2 between 100 and 200." If the first predicate identifies a unique row, the second predicate can only rule out that row and return an empty answer set. In what follows, we usually assume instead that a single predicate restriction, such as "C1 = 10," results in a large subset of rows from the table, and the second predicate, "C2 between 100 and 200," filters that set, bringing the number down to a smaller quantity for row retrieval. We speak of the *filter factor* of a predicate P, *FF(P)*, as the fraction of rows from a table resulting from the predicate restriction P. We normally estimate the filter factor of a predicate by making a number of statistical assumptions, including uniform distribution of individual column values and independent joint distributions of values from any two unallied columns.

For example, in Figure 8.11 we said that the number of distinct zipcode values was assumed to be 100,000, symbolized by CARD(zipcode) = 100,000. Assuming that all zipcode values are equally represented in the prospects table (the uniform distribution assumption), we can estimate the filter factor of an equal match predicate, zipcode = const, as follows:

```
FF(zipcode = const) = 1/100,000 = .00001
```

The same assumption allows us to estimate the filter factor of the **between** predicate of Example 8.3.5:

```
FF(zipcode between 02159 and 03158) = 1000·(1/100,000) = 1/100 = .01
```

Similarly the cardinality of the hobby column in Figure 8.11 CARD(hobby) = 100, together with the uniform distribution assumption, gives us:

```
FF(hobby = 'chess') = 1/100 = .01
```

The joint distribution of values from two unallied columns is taken to be independent, meaning that the filter factors for compound ANDed predicates multiply, so that:

```
FF(hobby = 'chess' and zipcode between 02159 and 02658) =
    (1/100)(500/100,000) = .00005
```

A set of predicates, each with a relatively nonrestrictive (large) filter factor, can have significant effect in ANDed combination.

EXAMPLE 8.4.1 Filter Factor Calculation.

Consider a query that might be used by a police department in tracing a car involved in a serious hit-and-run accident: find all drivers who own red 1992 Oldsmobile Toronados that are registered in Ohio:

```
select * from autos where license = 'Ohio' and color = 'red'
    and year = 1992 and make = 'Olds' and model = 'Toronado';
```

Under quite reasonable assumptions, we can expect that the predicates of this clause will filter the number of rows retrieved from an autos table of 40 million rows down to a much more manageable set of a few hundred rows. This would occur if 1/50 of all autos are registered in Ohio, 1/10 of all cars are red, 1/8 have year 1992, 1/6 have make Olds, and of these 1/8 have model Toronado. Except for the dependent pair olds-toronado, we assume that these properties are independent—for example, that driving an Olds Toronado does not predispose the owner toward buying a red car—and we multiply the filter factors for each of the predicates to arrive at the filter factor for the entire **where** clause search condition:

```
FF(search_cond) = (1/50)•(1/10)•(1/8)•(1/6)•(1/8) = 1/192,000
```

The number of rows retrieved by the Select statement is therefore approximated statistically by (1/192,000) • (40,000,000) = 208.33, or roughly 208 rows. Given a solution set of this size, it is reasonable to take the investigation further by speaking with the car owners and inspecting the cars for physical signs of damage. ∎

The filter factor terminology is from **DB2**, which bases its query optimizer estimates on statistics gathered by the RUNSTATS utility.

DB2 Statistics

Figure 8.12 lists some of the statistics gathered by the RUNSTATS utility that are used by the **DB2** query optimizer for access plan determination. For each statistic we list (1) the name of the **DB2** catalog table (name) in which it appears, and (2) the statistic name, which is the column name under which the statistic appears in the specified catalog table. Each of these statistics also has a default value for cases when RUNSTATS has not yet been run. Note that a number of the index statistics assume a concatenated index of several components, which we assume to be the columns (C1, C2, C3).

Catalog name	Statistic name	Default value	Description
SYSTABLES	CARD NPAGES	10,000 CEIL(1+CARD/20)	Number of rows in the table Number of data pages that contain rows of the table
SYSCOLUMNS	COLCARD HIGH2KEY LOW2KEY	25 N.A. N.A.	Number of distinct values in this column Second highest value in this column Second lowest value in this column

SYSINDEXES	NLEVELS
	NLEAF
	FIRSTKEY-CARD
	FULLKEY-CARD
	CLUSTER-RATIO
		0
		CARD/300
		
		25
		
		25
		0% if CLUSTERED = 'N'
		95% if CLUSTERED = 'Y'
			Number of levels of the index B-tree
			Number of leaf pages in the index B-tree
			Number of distinct values in the first
			  column, C1, of this key
			Number of distinct values in the full key,
			  all components—for example, C1.C2.C3
			Percentage of rows of the table that are
			  clustered by these index values

Figure 8.12 Some Statistics Gathered by RUNSTATS Used for Access Plan Determination

Refer back to Figure 8.11 for statistics of the prospects table. Within SYSTABLES, we see a row for the prospects table, as follows, after RUNSTATS has been executed.

SYSTABLES

NAME	CARD	NPAGES
. . .	. . .	. . .
prospects	50,000,000	5,000,000
. . .	. . .	. . .

Within SYSCOLUMNS, rows for the hobby and zipcode columns described before Figure 8.11 would have NAME column values 'hobby' and 'zipcode'. Since column names are not unique across tables, the containing table name for these columns is given in the TBNAME column.

SYSCOLUMNS

NAME	TBNAME	COLCARD	HIGH2KEY	LOW2KEY
. . .	. . .	. . .	. . .	. . .
hobby	prospects	100	Wines	Bicycling
zipcode	prospects	100,000	99998	00001
. . .	. . .	. . .	. . .	. . .

Finally, in SYSINDEXES (below), we see rows for the two indexes listed in Figure 8.10.

For the `zipcode` column, which makes up the first column in the hobbyx index, we assume values from 00000 to 99999, so COLCARD = 100,000, LOW2KEY (the second-lowest value) is 00001, and HIGH2KEY = 99998. (This is inaccurate, but assumed for simplicity.)For the addrx index, FIRSTKEYCARD = 100,000 and FULLKEYCARD = 50,000,000, since we assumed in the paragraph preceding Figure 8.11 that addrx key values have unique RIDs.

SYSINDEXES

NAME	TBNAME	NLEVELS	NLEAF	FIRSTKEY CARD	FULLKEY CARD	CLUSTER RATIO
. . .	. . .	. . .	. . .	. . .	. . .	. . .
addrx	prospects	4	500,000	100,000	50,000,000	100
hobbyx	prospects	3	50,000	100	100	0
. . .	. . .	. . .	. . .	. . .	. . .	. . .

The CLUSTERRATIO is a measure of how well the clustering property holds for the rows of a table with respect to a given index: the closer this value is to 100%, the more we see row retrieval through the index appearing as in the bottom diagram of Figure 7.20. Recall that an index created with a **cluster** clause may cease to have a high CLUSTERRATIO value after updates have caused a significant number of rows to be moved or inserted out of cluster order on the data pages. The significance of this statistic for the query optimizer is that an index scan will use sequential prefetch to retrieve data pages through an index exactly when the CLUSTERRATIO value is 80% or higher for that index.

Filter Factors in DB2

Figure 8.13 contains a list of predicate types and the corresponding formulas for filter factory calculations performed by the query optimizer.

Note that no filter factor calculations are given here for predicates involving Subselects. In fact, predicates involving noncorrelated Subselects can be used for indexed retrieval, but their filter factors are not predictable by a simple formula. We will deal with Subselects later in the chapter, at the same time that we cover joins.

Predicate type	Filter factor	Notes
Col = const	1/COLCARD	"Col <> const" same as "not (Col = const)"
Col $\propto$ const	Interpolation formula	"$\propto$" is any comparison predicate other than equality; an example follows
Col < const or Col <= const	$\dfrac{(\text{const} - \text{LOW2KEY})}{(\text{HIGH2KEY} - \text{LOW2KEY})}$	LOW2KEY and HIGH2KEY are estimates for extreme points of the range of Col values
Col between const1 and const2	$\dfrac{(\text{const2} - \text{const1})}{(\text{HIGH2KEY} - \text{LOW2KEY})}$	"Col not between const1 and const2" same as "not (Col between const1 and const2)"
Col in list	(list size)/COLCARD	"Col not in list" same as "not (Col in list)"
Col is null	1/COLCARD	"Col is not null" same as "not(Col is null)"
Col like 'pattern'	Interpolation formula	Based on the alphabet
Pred1 and Pred1	FF(Pred1) • FF(Pred2)	As in probability
Pred1 or Pred2	FF(Pred1) + FF(Pred2) – FF(Pred1) • FF(Pred2)	As in probability
not Pred1	1 – FF(Pred1)	As in probability

Figure 8.13 Filter Factor Formulas for Various Predicate Types

It is commonly pointed out that the uniform distribution assumption explained earlier is not always valid. For example, consider a sex column on a table containing residents at a boy's school. Although there are occasional residents with sex = 'F', staff and faculty members for example, it is clear that a filter factor calculated in terms of $1/(\text{CARD}(\text{sex})) = 1/2$ is misleading, and a query optimizer that uses this assumption may very well make incorrect decisions. For this reason, **DB2** and a number of other database systems, such as **INGRES**, provide statistics on individual column values that deviate strongly from the uniform assumption. In the interest of brevity, however, we will not discuss these statistics further, and assume in what follows that the uniform distribution assumption is generally applicable.

8.5   Matching Index Scans, Composite Indexes

Assume that a **DB2** index named mailx has been created for the `prospects` table, using the command:

```
create index mailx on prospects (zipcode, hobby, incomeclass, age);
```

This is an index that we might construct to handle common types of mailing requests efficiently (we will see what this means shortly), and we assume that it is not a clustered index. Here `incomeclass` is a smallint variable defining a range of income, with 10 values from 1 to 10, distributed approximately equally on the `prospects` rows (thus equal match predicates have a filter factor of 1/10), and `age` is a smallint variable with (say) 50 values from 16 to 65. Given the CARD of each column, we can therefore calculate the potential number of distinct key values for this index as

```
CARD(zipcode)•CARD(hobby)•CARD(incomeclass)•CARD(age) =
     100,000•100•10•50 = 5,000,000,000
```

Since we have only 50,000,000 rows, we can picture the assignment of rows to mailx values as placing 50,000,000 darts in 5,000,000,000 slots. Very few slots will have two darts, and so we can assume essentially unique key values (FULLKEYCARD = 50,000,000), with no index compression at the leaf level of the kind in Figure 7.19. Now the entries in the mailx index have length given by 4 (integer `zipcode`) + 8 (`hobby` attribute) + 2 (`incomeclass`) + 2 (`age`) + 4 (RID) = 20 bytes. We can therefore fit FLOOR(4000/20) = 200 entries per page. The leaf level of the index then has 50,000,000/200 = 250,000 leaf pages (NLEAF = 250,000). The next level up has 1250 nodes, the next level up has 6, and above this is the root (NLEVELS = 4). The relevant column values in the SYSINDEXES row for the mailx index are shown in the following table.

SYSINDEXES

NAME	TBNAME	NLEVELS	NLEAF	FIRSTKEY CARD	FULLKEY CARD	CLUSTER RATIO
...	...	...	...	...	...	...
mailx	prospects	4	250,000	100,000	50,000,000	0
...	...	...	...	...	...	...

EXAMPLE 8.5.1 Concatenated Index, Matching Index Scan.

Consider the SQL query:

```
select name, straddr from prospects
    where zipcode = 02159 and hobby = 'chess' and incomeclass = 10;
```

Although the concatenated index mailx doesn't enable us to resolve the query in index only, as in Example 8.3.6, it still offers an important advantage in that all three predicates in the **where** clause, zipcode = 02159, hobby = 'chess', and incomeclass = 10, can be resolved in this single index. Filter factors of the three equal match predicates are each calculated as 1/COLCARD and give 1/100,000 = .00001 (for zipcode = 02159), 1/100 = .01 (for hobby = 'chess'), and 1/10 = 0.1 (for incomeclass = 10). The three ANDed attributes together give a filter factor (1/100,000)(1/100)(1/10) = (1/100,000,000), so we expect there will be (1/100,000,000) • 50,000,000 = 0.5 rows selected. (For example, one row might be returned half the time and no rows the other half.) We estimate that the I/O cost for data access is 0.5R, requiring an elapsed time of 0.5/40 = .0125 seconds.

The index scan step performs its search by reading down to the leftmost entry of the B-tree with zipcode = 02159 and hobby = 'chess' and incomeclass = 10, then reading entries from left to right, following leaf sibling pointers if necessary, until the last entry with these values has been processed. You need to convince yourself that all desired entries (even if there are more than one) are in one contiguous scan of the leaf level of the mailx index. We only expect 0.5 entries of this kind, so we expect all entries to lie on a single index leaf page. Assuming that the top two levels of the index are kept in buffer, we estimate the I/O cost of the index scan to be 2R for the third-level index page and the leaf page. ∎

The query of Example 8.5.1 is being performed with a matching index scan on a composite index. What *matching* means is that the predicates in the **where** clause match the *initial* attributes in the index. Whenever we are dealing with equal match predicates on initial attributes, the portion of the index in which selected RID values are found is a contiguous subrange of the whole index leaf level. By analogy, assume that in the metropolitan New York telephone directory, subscribers are alphabetized by lastname, firstname, borough or town, and finally street. Then the query of Example 8.5.1 is like looking up a telephone number by lastname and firstname, without knowing the street, borough, or town.

EXAMPLE 8.5.2 Concatenated Index, Matching Index Scan.
Consider the SQL query:

```
select name, straddr from prospects
    where zipcode between 02159 and 04158
    and hobby = 'chess' and incomeclass = 10;
```

Again, all three predicates in the **where** clause, zipcode between 02159 and 04158, hobby = 'chess', and incomeclass = 10, can be resolved in this single index. We calculate the filter factor for the predicate "zipcode between 02159 and 04158" by using an interpolation formula (see filter factor for the **between** predicate in Figure 8.13):

```
(04158-02159)/(HIGH2KEY-LOW2KEY) = 2000/99,998
```

which we approximate as 2/100 = .02. The other two predicates are approximated by 1/COLCARD as before, and give 1/100 = .01 (for hobby = 'chess') and 1/10 = 0.1 (for incomeclass = 10). The three ANDed attributes together give the filter factor (2/100) • (1/100) • (1/10) = (1/50,000) = .00002. Thus there will be (2/100,000) • 50,000,000 = 1000 rows selected. Because the index is not clustered, the I/O cost for data access is 1000R, requiring an elapsed time of 1000/40 = 25 seconds.

The index scan step performs its search by reading down to the leftmost entry of the B-tree with zipcode = 02159 and hobby = 'chess' and income-class = 10, then reading in leaf pages from left to right following the sibling pointers until the last entry with values satisfying this **where** clause has been processed. However, in this case it is *not* true that all desired entries are in one contiguous scan of the leaf level of the mailx index. There will be entries with other hobby values, for example, intervening between index entries with "zipcode = 02159 and hobby = chess" and entries with "zipcode = 02160 and hobby = chess." This is still a matching index scan, but the only index component matched from the concatenated index is the zipcode range, "zip-code between 02159 and 04158." This means that we need to read 2000/100,000 = 1/50 of the leaf level from the mailx index, or (1/50) • (250,000) = 5000 pages. We can do this with sequential prefetch at a cost of 5000S in elapsed time 5000/400 = 12.5 seconds. The total elapsed time for the query is therefore 12.5 seconds for index scan + 25 seconds for data page retrieval = 37.5 seconds. ∎

Example 8.5.2, in terms of the analogy we used earlier, looks up everyone in the New York metropolitan telephone directory with last name starting with "Sm" and first name "John." There are a lot of entries to scan to retrieve this set of subscribers. But things can get even worse. If the attributes in the **where** clause don't include the initial attribute of the index, we need to consider a *non-matching* index scan. This is comparable to finding everyone with the first name "John" in the borough of the Bronx from the New York metropolitan telephone directory with no idea of the last name, a difficult task. We can't use the alphabetical order of the directory to any effect, since we never know under what last name the first name "John" might show up, and thus we have to look through the whole directory. Still, it is probably preferable to use the telephone directory for such a search (a non-matching index scan) than to go out and canvas the entire town from door to door looking for everyone named John who owns a phone (a table scan, to stretch the analogy somewhat).

EXAMPLE 8.5.3 Concatenated Index, Non-Matching Index Scan.

Again we assume that the mailx index exists. Consider the SQL query:

```
select name, straddr from prospects
    where hobby = 'chess' and incomeclass = 10 and age = 40;
```

We recall that the cardinality of the hobby column is 100, the incomeclass column is 10, and the age column is 50, so we calculate the filter factor of the compound selection predicate as $(1/100)(1/10)(1/50) = (1/50,000) = .00002$. This is the same filter factor we calculated in Example 8.5.2, so we still retrieve 1000 rows from prospects at an I/O cost of 1000R, in a 25-second elapsed time. But the index scan situation is totally different. Because this is a non-matching index scan, we need to read in every one of the 250,000 mailx leaf pages. The I/O cost is 250,000S, and the elapsed time is $500,000/400 = 625$ seconds, over 10 minutes. ∎

Definition of a Matching Index Scan

We have mentioned the idea of an indexable predicate before, when we studied single-column indexes. It is time to give a careful description of what it means to perform a matching index scan. This requires a series of definitions.

DEFINITION 8.5.1 A *matching index scan* retrieves rows from a table after matching a number of predicates to column components of a single index. At least one indexable predicate must refer to the initial column of the index; this is known as a *matching predicate*. A set of indexable predicates can match a *sequence* of initial columns of a composite index, and they are all then known as matching predicates. ∎

For example, consider index C1234X on table T, a composite index on columns (C1, C2, C3, C4). The following compound predicate matches all columns of the C1234X index:

```
C1 = 10 and C2 = 5 and C3 = 20 and C4 = 25
```

The compound predicate

```
C2 = 5 and C3 = 20 and C1 = 10
```

matches the first three columns of C1234X (note that the predicates don't need to be in the same order as the columns). This is analogous to the matching index scan we saw in Example 8.5.1, three ANDed equal match predicates on the first three columns of a four-column composite index, mailx. The compound predicate

```
C2 = 5 and C5 = 22 and C1 = 10 and C6 = 35
```

has two matching predicates on the first two columns of C1234X. The columns C5 and C6 are not part of the index and therefore cannot be matching. The compound predicate

```
C2 = 5 and C3 = 20 and C4 = 25
```

is not a matching index scan, since it has no matching predicates. This is analogous to the situation we saw in Example 8.5.3, three ANDed equal match predicates on the second, third, and fourth columns of a four-column composite index.

Note that in Example 8.5.3, where there were no matching predicates, this doesn't mean that the filter factors of the non-matching predicates have no effect. As we saw in that example, the predicates still have the role of filtering 50,000,000 rows down to a 1000-row answer set. Because this was a non-matching scan, however, the entire index needed to be examined to perform this filtering. In a matching index scan, by comparison, we usually end up with only a small contiguous range of leaf-level entries in the index that need to be considered. (As we will see, there is an exception with the **In-List** predicate, but this is rather special.)

When **DB2** makes use of the filter factors of *non-matching predicates,* as in Example 8.5.3, it ranges through a large number of leaf-level entries of the index before it accesses any data rows, and it discards entries that do not obey the predicates. This practice is known as *predicate screening,* and the non-matching predicates involved are known as *screening predicates.* As we saw in Example 8.5.3, this can lead to a situation where the elapsed time to perform disk I/O reading index entries is much larger than the elapsed time to read in rows in the answer set. The difference between screening predicates and matching predicates is an important one; as we will see, there are situations in index access where predicate screening is not performed by **DB2**. However, matching predicates are always used.

This whole concept of matching index scans is rather complex, so let's review what we have covered up to now. Assume that we are given a composite index C1234X on columns (C1, C2, C3, C4) and a compound predicate involving predicates P1, P2, . . . , Pk.

DEFINITION 8.5.2 Basic Rules of Matching Predicates.

[1] A *matching* predicate must be an *indexable* predicate.

Figure 8.14 gives a list of indexable predicates: equal match and comparison predicates, **between** predicates, **like** predicates, **In-list** predicates, and **is null** predicates are indexable. In general, attaching the *not* logical operator to an indexable predicate gives a non-indexable result.

[2] Matching predicates must match successive columns C1, C2, . . . of an index.

Here is a procedure to determine them. Look at the index columns from left to right. For each column, if there is at least one indexable predicate on that column, we have found a *matching column* and a *matching predicate.* If no matching predicate is found for a column, this terminates the procedure. (There are other rules as well, covered in Definition 8.5.4.)

[3] A non-matching predicate on a column in an index can still be a
     screening predicate.

There might be a matching index scan on one index to answer a
query and a non-matching index scan on a different index with a
much better filter factor that is more efficient. The query optimizer
must consider all index possibilities in arriving at the access plan.

■

In the case of a matching index scan on the leading K columns of an
index such as C1234X, the EXPLAIN command creates a plan table row
with ACCESSTYPE = I, ACCESSNAME = C1234X, and MATCHCOLS =
K. In particular, for a non-matching index scan, we see MATCHCOLS = 0.
    From point 1 of Definition 8.5.2, we see that a matching predicate
must be an indexable predicate. In fact, the term "indexable predicate"
means exactly this and no more.

DEFINITION 8.5.3 An *indexable predicate* is defined as a predicate that can
be used to match a column in a matching index scan, currently the set of
predicates in Figure 8.14.   ■

The term "indexable predicate" is rather confusing, since it seems to imply
that predicates that are not indexable cannot be used in an index to filter
the rows to be retrieved. But this is not true; non-indexable predicates can
still be used as screening predicates in an index scan—they simply cannot
be used for matching. A better term to replace "indexable predicate"
would be "matchable predicate," but unfortunately the earlier term is
firmly embedded in the database vocabulary at this point.

Predicate type	Indexable	Notes
Col ∝ const	Y	"∝" stands for >, >=, =, <=, < But "<>" is NOT indexable
Col between const1 and const2	Y	Must be last in matching series (see rules of matching)
Col in list	Y	But only for one matching column (see rules of matching)
Col is null	Y	
Col like 'pattern'	Y	No leading "%" in pattern
Col like '%xyz'	N	Not with leading "%"
Col1 ∝ Col2	N	Col1 and Col2 from same table
Col ∝ *Expression*	N	For example, C1 = (C1 + 2)/2
Pred1 and Pred2	Y	Pred1 and Pred2 both indexable, refer to columns of the same index
Pred1 or Pred2	N	Except "(C1 = 3 or C1 = 5)", which can be thought of as "C1 in (3, 5)"
not Pred1	N	Or any equivalent: not between, not in list, <>, not like "pattern"

Figure 8.14 Indexable Predicates on a Single Table

In the case of a single-column index, a non-indexable predicate that functions as a screening predicate is unusual, but not impossible. The possibility depends on whether the filter factor makes the query optimizer think it is worthwhile. Since a common non-indexable predicate is "Col <> const", with a filter factor $(1 - 1/\text{COLCARD})$, the filter factor is likely to be close to 1 and to offer very little cost saving in reducing the number of rows retrieved to make up for the cost of reading through a large fraction of the index.

Things get a bit more complex in matching columns when we deal with indexable predicates that are not equal match predicates. We repeat the prescription of the second point of Definition 8.5.2 and add a number of other rules.

DEFINITION 8.5.4 Advanced Rules of Matching Predicates.

[1] Look at the index columns from left to right. For each column, if at least one indexable predicate is found for that column, it is a *matching column* with a *matching predicate*.

[2] If no matching predicate is found for a column, this terminates the search. However, the search may terminate earlier for a number of reasons.

[3] When a matching *range predicate* (comparison of the form <, <=, >, >=, **like** predicate, or **between** predicate) is used for a column, the search terminates thereafter.

[4] At most one **In-list** predicate can be used in a set of matching predicates.   ■

If we assume that the idea of a matching index scan is to end up with a contiguous range of leaf-level index entries, it is easy to see why a range predicate terminates the search for matching predicates. Recall that in Example 8.5.2, the three ANDed predicates of the query refer to the first three columns from the mailx index. However, the predicate on the first column, "zipcode between 02159 and 04158," is a range predicate and thus the remaining predicates are not part of the matching index scan. The reason is that once we limit to the index entries for the range predicate, the entries that satisfy the remaining two predicates appear in 2000 separated intervals, satisfying "hobby = chess and incomeclass = 10" for each of the 2000 zipcode values 02159, 02160, 02161, . . . , 04158. The index scan simply finds it easiest to scan through all entries that obey the range predicate and treat the remaining two predicates as screening predicates. Thus we have a relatively large index scan to perform, requiring an elapsed time of 12.5 seconds even with sequential prefetch, compared to a relatively small row I/O cost of 25 seconds with random I/O.

The **In-list** predicate is the only one that breaks the rule of requiring the final range of leaf-level index entries to be contiguous. Given the C1234X index and the compound predicate

[8.5.1]   C1 in (6, 8, 10) and C2 = 5 and C3 = 20

we have a matching predicate on all three columns, even through we do not end up with a single contiguous range of leaf-level entries. Instead there are three contiguous ranges, one for the leading column selection C1 = 6, one for C1 = 8, and one for C1 = 10. You can picture a matching index scan with an **In-list** predicate in just this way, as a series of scans with equal match predicates substituted for the **In-list**. But **DB2** stops short of allowing a second **In-list** predicate into the matching scan. Thus the compound predicate

[8.5.2]   C1 in (6, 8, 10) and C2 = 5 and C3 in (20, 30, 40) and C4 = 25

would have only two matching predicates. Matching stops before the second **In-list** predicate on C3. When an **In-list** predicate is used in a matching index scan, the plan table row contains a special value, ACCESSTYPE = N. We would have MATCHCOLS = 3 for the first such compound predicate above, and MATCHCOLS = 2 for the second.

EXAMPLE 8.5.4 Query Optimization and Composite Index Scans.

Assume that we are given a table T with columns C1, C2, . . . and the indexes C1234X on (C1, C2, C3, C4); C56X on (C5, C6); and C7X, a unique index on the key column C7. Consider the following queries:

(1) select C1, C5, C8 from T where C1 = 5 and C2 = 7 and C3 <> 9;

This results in a matching index scan on the two columns C1 and C2. The predicate C3 is not indexable (but it would be used as a screening predicate). In the plan table we see ACCESSTYPE = I, ACCESSNAME = C1234X, MATCHCOLS = 2.

(2) select C1, C5, C8 from T where C1 = 5 and C2 >= 7 and C3 = 9;

We see a matching index scan on the two columns C1 and C2. Although the third predicate is indexable, we stop short because the predicate on C2 is a range predicate. The plan table is the same as (1).

(3) select C1, C5, C8 from T
         where C1 = 5 and C2 = 7 and C5 = 8 and C6 = 13;

There is a type of multiple index use we haven't seen yet in which we can combine filter factors of predicates from more than one index; this approach would be used here. If that alternative were not present, the query optimizer would consider a choice between using a matching index scan of two columns on C1234X and a matching index scan of two columns on C56X. We would learn what happens from the plan table, ACCESSTYPE = I, ACCESSNAME = C56X, MATCHCOLS = 2.

```
(4) select C1, C4 from T
        where C1 = 10 and C2 in (5, 6) and (C3 = 10 or C4 = 11);
```

This is a matching index scan on the first two columns. ACCESSTYPE = N (because of the **In-list** predicate), ACCESSNAME = C1234X, and MATCHCOLS = 2. The third predicate, (C3 = 10 or C4 = 11), is not indexable, but it would be used as a screening predicate in the scan. (We do not see screening predicates mentioned in the plan table, but all predicates of the query must be used to filter, and predicates that involve columns of the index chosen are certainly used for screening.) The scan would also have INDEXONLY = Y, a very important factor in determining the cost.

```
(5) select C1, C5, C8 from T
        where C1 = 5 and C2 = 7 and C7 = 101;
```

Because the C7X index is unique, the query optimizer would certainly choose ACCESSTYPE = I, ACCESSNAME = C7X. The plan table does not reveal that this retrieval is unique (or possibly null).

```
(6) Select C1, C5, C8 from T
        where C2 = 7 and C3 = 10 and C4 = 12 and C5 = 15;
```

This query can be handled either by a non-matching index scan on C1234X, columns C2, C3, C4, or by a matching index scan on C56X, column C5. (For reasons to be covered shortly, multiple-index use mentioned in (3) above is not an alternative.) We might see the following result in the plan table: ACCESSTYPE = I, ACCESSNAME = C1234X, MATCHCOLS = 0. ■

Indexable Predicates and Performance

Pattern-match search. A *pattern-match search*, "C1 like 'pattern'," with a leading "%" wildcard in the pattern, is comparable to a non-matching scan of a concatenated index. The predicate may have a small filter factor, but the search is analogous to using a normal dictionary to look up all words that end in "action." An index on the column C1 must be totally scanned to retrieve the set of RIDs pointing to the appropriate rows. Special dictionaries exist that alphabetize words in reverse, and a DBA having a workload with a large number of pattern-match searches with leading "%" wild cards should consider creating indexed columns with reverse spellings. Thus if column C2 is created to contain the text of C1 spelled backwards, the specification "%action" on C1 becomes "noitca%" on C2, a much easier search.

Expressions. The non-indexable predicate, Col ∝ *Expression* given in Figure 8.14, is only one example of a class of non-indexable predicates. Basically, any comparison involving an expression is non-indexable. For example, consider the query:

```
select * from T where 2 * C1 <= 56;
```

The query optimizer is unable to use an index to resolve this predicate. However, you can rephrase the predicate

```
select * from T where C1 <= 28;
```

(dividing both sides by 2), and now the index can be used.

One-fetch access. A certain class of queries is particularly efficient in **DB2**, providing what is called *one-fetch (index) access,* with ACCESSTYPE = I1 in the plan table. An example of such a query is

```
select min(C1) from T;
```

where an index exists with leading column C1. Clearly the query optimizer in this case can simply search down to the leftmost entry at the leaf level of the index and retrieve the C1 value, which is why this is termed "one-fetch access." It is possible to apply this principle in a more general situation. Assume that we have an index C12D3X on T, with columns (C1, C2 DESC, C3). Then, for example, the following queries can be answered by a one-step access step:

```
select min(C1) from T where C1 > 5;
```

(Note that C1 > 5 doesn't necessarily mean that the min value for C1 is 6. Index use is important here.)

```
select min(C1) from T where C1 between 6 and 10;
select max(C2) from T where C1 = 5;
select max(C2) from T where C1 = 5 and C2 < 30;
select min(C3) from T where C1 = 6 and C2 = 20 and C3 between
   9 and 14;
```

Each successive matching equal match predicate reduces the range of values for the index key. In the final example above, **DB2** walks down the C12D3X index to find the first entry key value >= 6.20.9.

8.6 Multiple Index Access

Assume that the following indexes are the only ones defined on the table T: C1X on (C1), C2X on (C2), and C345X on (C3, C4, C5). Now consider the following query:

[8.6.1]   `select * from T where C1 = 20 and C2 = 5 and C3 = 11;`

With the matching index scans we have studied up to now, the query optimizer would need to choose a single one of the three indexes, each of which matches only one of the three predicates in query (8.6.1). Thus we would have the benefit of only one of the three predicate filter factors to extract RID values from an index before retrieving rows from the data, and the query plan would need to test the truth of the remaining two predicates to restrict the rows retrieved.

But this could be a tremendously inefficient course of action. If we assume that each of the predicates has a filter factor of 1/100 and the table T contains 100 million rows, then a single predicate only reduces the number of rows retrieved to 1 million. All three predicates together would have a combined filter factor of 1/1,000,000 and reduce the number of rows retrieved to 100. We ask therefore if there is a way to combine the filter factors of predicates matching different indexes before retrieving the rows selected.

There is in fact a way to do this, and it provides our first example of a multiple-step plan. Basically this approach extracts lists of RIDs from each index that satisfy the matching predicate. Then the lists of RIDs for the distinct indexes are intersected (ANDed), so that the final RID list corresponds to rows that satisfy all predicates indexed. The sequence of steps from the **DB2** plan table resulting from an EXPLAIN of query (8.6.1) might be the plan displayed in Figure 8.15. (Only selected columns of the plan table are shown.)

TNAME	ACCESSTYPE	MATCHCOLS	ACCESSNAME	PREFETCH	MIXOPSEQ
T	M	0		L	0
T	MX	1	C1X	S	1
T	MX	1	C2X	S	2
T	MX	1	C345X	S	3
T	MI	0			4
T	MI	0			5

Figure 8.15 Plan Table Rows of a Multiple Index Access Plan for Query (8.6.1)

The following paragraphs provide descriptions for steps of Figure 8.15.

♦ **MIXOPSEQ = 0.** This plan row with *ACCESSTYPE* = M indicates that multiple index access processing is about to begin on table TNAME = T. The PREFETCH = L value means that list prefetch I/O (which we covered near the end of Section 8.2) is used to retrieve rows from that table T, after the final RID list has been generated.

♦ **MIXOPSEQ = 1.** This plan row with *ACCESSTYPE* = MX indicates that the entries of the index with ACCESSNAME = C1X that satisfy the matching predicates of the query are to be scanned, using sequential prefetch I/O. In this case MATCHCOLS = 1, and the matching predicate in query (8.6.1) is C1 = 20. As the entries from C1X are encountered, the RIDs are extracted and placed into what we call an RID *candidate list* (or simply an RID *list),* in a memory area known as the RID *pool.* At some point after all RIDs have been extracted from this C1X access step, the RID candidate list is placed in sorted order to make the later intersection step easier to perform.

♦ **MIXOPSEQ = 2 and MIXOPSEQ = 3.** These steps perform the same MX function on the indexes C2X and C345X as in MIXOPSEQ = 1, generating their own RID candidate lists for the matching predicates of these indexes. We can think of successive generated RID candidate lists as being pushed on a stack as in a reverse Polish calculator: lists generated more recently are closer to the top of stack and are acted on first by calculator operations.

♦ **MIXOPSEQ = 4.** The *ACCESSTYPE* = MI indicates that an *RID candidate list intersection (AND)* will take place. The two most recently generated RID lists are popped from the top of stack (first the list generated from C345X, then the list generated from C2X); they are intersected to provide a new RID list (an intermediate result that **DB2** names IR1) and this list is pushed back on the stack. Since the RIDs of both lists are in sorted order, the intersection is easily performed by creating two cursors pointing to the initial RID in each list, then repeatedly advancing the list cursor pointing to the lower-valued RID. Whenever a tie occurs we have found an intersection element. We place this RID value into the IR1 list, then advance one of the two cursors to look for the next intersection element. The process is complete when the cursor being advanced goes off the end of the list.

◆ **MIXOPSEQ = 5.** This final step also has ACCESSTYPE = MI, and this pops the top two RID lists from the stack, IR1 and the list generated from C1X. The lists are intersected to form a new RID list named IR2 that is pushed back on the stack, and this is the *final RID list* generated. This final RID list is then used to retrieve rows from the table T, using list prefetch I/O, as mentioned in the initial M step of the plan.

There is one other type of access step used in multiple index access. A row with *ACCESSTYPE = MU* indicates a step that will pop the two RID lists on the stack, perform an *RID candidate list union (OR)* of the two lists, and push the new intermediate result back on the stack. For example, with the same table and index assumptions seen above, EXPLAIN applied to the query given in (8.6.2) might result in rows of the plan table of Figure 8.16.

[8.6.2]   select * from T where C1 = 20 and (C2 = 5 or C3 = 11);

TNAME	ACCESSTYPE	MATCHCOLS	ACCESSNAME	PREFETCH	MIXOPSEQ
T	M	0		L	0
T	MX	1	C1X	S	1
T	MX	1	C2X	S	2
T	MX	1	C345X	S	3
T	MU	0			4
T	MI	0			5

Figure 8.16   Plan Table Rows of a Multiple Index Access Plan for Query (8.6.2)

Figure 8.16 differs from Figure 8.15 only in the row with MIX-OPSEQ = 4, where an MU step is performed to take the union (OR) of the RID lists for predicates C2 = 5 and C3 = 11 instead of intersecting (ANDing) them. This union is then ANDed with C1 = 20 in the final step with MIXOPSEQ = 5.

Note that in both Figures 8.15 and 8.16, successive steps of multiple index extraction into RID lists have been generated to follow the physical order of predicates in the query. Naturally the order of evaluation is independent of the query syntax. The multiple index access steps are actually generated by the query optimizer in an order that uses the RID pool most efficiently, and this *usually* means that there are a minimum number of RID lists in existence at any one time; that is, operations to combine RID lists are executed as early as possible to minimize memory use. What this implies for the query of (8.6.2) is a rearrangement of the rows in Figure 8.16 to the plan of Figure 8.17.

TNAME	ACCESSTYPE	MATCHCOLS	ACCESSNAME	PREFETCH	MIXOPSEQ
T	M	0		L	0
T	MX	1	C2X	S	1
T	MX	1	C345X	S	2
T	MU	0			3
T	MX	1	C1X	S	4
T	MI	0			5

Figure 8.17 More Efficient RID Pool Plan for the Query Given in (8.6.2)

The plan in Figure 8.17 has the same effect as the one in Figure 8.16, but it has the property that there are never more than two RID lists in existence at once.

EXAMPLE 8.6.1 Multiple Index Access.

Consider the prospects table and the hobbyx and addrx indexes with the statistics outlined in Figure 8.11, and assume that the only other indexes available on prospects are the agex index on the *age* column and the incomex index on the *incomeclass* column. A little thought will convince you that these indexes have nearly the same statistics as the hobbyx index, since there is so much index compression at the leaf level that the length of the index key is superfluous in the entry length dominated by multiple RID entries of 4 bytes (thus

8.6 Multiple Index Access

NLEAF is the same); and at higher levels where the key length is more relevant there will be not enough variation to change the NLEVEL statistic. Now consider the query that we dealt with in Example 8.5.1:

```
select name, straddr from prospects
    where zipcode = 02159 and hobby = 'chess' and incomeclass = 10;
```

In that example, we had a concatenated index mailx on which an index scan was performed. With the single indexes assumed above, this query can be performed with the multiple index access plan outlined in Figure 8.18.

TNAME	ACCESSTYPE	MATCHCOLS	ACCESSNAME	PREFETCH	MIXOPSEQ
T	M	0		L	0
T	MX	1	hobbyx	S	1
T	MX	1	addrx	S	2
T	MI	0			3
T	MX	1	incomex	S	4
T	MI	0			5

Figure 8.18   Plan Table Rows of Multiple Index Access Plan (Illustrates Example 8.6.1)

Let us calculate the I/O cost of the step with MIXOPSEQ = 1. This step scans the hobbyx index for the predicate "hobby = 'chess'". Since FF(hobby = 'chess') = 1/100, and NLEAF for hobbyx = 50,000, this entails a scan across 1/100 of the 50,000 leaf-level pages (ignoring the I/Os to walk the directory), at an I/O cost of 500S. This list of RIDs from these leaf-level entries is extracted and pushed on the stack.

For MIXOPSEQ = 2 we scan the addrx index to resolve the predicate "zipcode = 02159" and extract the RID values into a list. Since FF(zipcode = 02159) = 1/100,000 and NLEAF = 500,000 for addrx, the number of leaf pages scanned from left to right to resolve this predicate is (1/100,000) · (500,000) = 5S. With MIXOPSEQ = 4 the predicate "incomeclass = 10" has a filter factor of 1/10, and with 50,000 leaf-level pages the I/O cost to extract the RIDs is 5000S.

Now the ACCESSTYPE = MI list intersection steps in MIXOPSEQ = 3 and 5 require no I/O, since all RIDs are already memory resident. Multiplying the filter factors of the three predicates as we did in Example 8.5.1, we see again that we expect only 0.5 rows to be retrieved from the table. This is a probabilistic estimate, of course.

However many rows are retrieved, they most likely all lie on separate disk pages, and the system retrieves them with a list prefetch (as we saw in MIX-

OPSEQ = 0, where PREFETCH = L). List prefetch programs the disk arm to retrieve up to 32 distinct pages in order by the most efficient predetermined disk arm movements. The I/O cost for retrieving 0.5 pages by list prefetch is designated by 0.5L. As we mentioned in the rule of thumb for I/O rate in Figure 8.8, list prefetch proceeds at 100 I/Os per second. A list prefetch of 0.5 pages is below the lower limit of this rule of thumb approximation (4 pages), but we assume here that it can still be used, since the time involved is insignificant.

The total elapsed time for the query, based on I/O cost, is therefore calculated from 500S + 50S + 5000S + 0.5L as (5550)/400 + 5/100, or about 13.9 seconds. ∎

EXAMPLE 8.6.2 Multiple Index Access.

Under the index assumptions of Example 8.6.1, we examine the query considered earlier in Example 8.5.2:

```
select name, straddr from prospects
    where zipcode between 02159 and 04158
    and hobby = 'chess' and incomeclass = 10;
```

For this query, the **between** predicate on zipcode causes a matching index scan on addrx with a filter factor of (2000/100,000) = 1/50. Since NLEAF = 500,000 for addrx, the scan to extract RID values for this predicate entails a cost of 10,000S. The costs of resolving the predicates on hobby and incomeclass are unchanged from Example 8.6.1, 500S and 5000S.

The total number of rows retrieved by this query is calculated in the same way it was done in Example 8.5.2: (1/50)(1/100)(1/10)(50,000,000) = 1000 rows, likely to all be on separate pages. The total I/O cost for this query is therefore given by 10,000S + 500S + 5000S + 1000L, and the elapsed I/O time is 15,500/400 + 1000/100 = 38.75 + 10 = 48.75 seconds. This compares to the 37.5 seconds we derived in Example 8.5.2, where we assumed that the 1000 data page I/Os were retrieved using random I/O (1000R) and therefore took 25 seconds elapsed, rather than list prefetch I/O (1000L), which takes 10 seconds elapsed. ∎

List Prefetch and the RID Pool

If list prefetch is more efficient than random I/O, why would we ever perform random I/O? The answer, as we suggested at the end of Section 8.2, is that certain rather special preconditions need to be met before list prefetch can occur in **DB2**, conditions that are presented in this subsection as "Rules for RID List Use." However, before proceeding it seems appropriate to make a disclaimer to prevent possible misunderstanding.

Up until now, most of the query access principles we have introduced have been quite general purpose, and although our examples have referred to **DB2** features, we expect to see equivalent features now or in the near future in most relational database products. For example, all relational products you are likely to encounter in education or industry have query optimizers that make use of data statistics, calculate and compare filter factors, and generate query access plans that contain steps such as table scans and various types of index-aided scans. The idea of matching scans on composite indexes and the specific types of predicates that can be matched or used for screening are usually implemented in a less sophisticated form on most non-**DB2** products. (*Matching scan* is actually **DB2**-specific nomenclature.) The same goes for the multiple index access feature and for the concept of a memory-resident RID list. The *ideas* are implemented on many (not yet all) relational products, but generally with less flexibility. The topic of the current subsection, list prefetch and its dependency on RID list rules, crosses the border from general principle to product-specific design. These concepts are important for a good understanding of **DB2** query optimization, but the reader should be warned that there is nothing fundamental about them; indeed a number of the rules are somewhat arbitrary, and it is quite likely that other database products might choose a different (and perhaps superior!) approach in determining whet RID lists to materialize in memory.

To return to the topic at hand, what limits the use of list prefetch in **DB2**? The rule is that list prefetch is only performed when retrieving rows from data pages, when indexing allows the query evaluator to predict rows that will need to be accessed well into the future. For a list prefetch to be possible, the RIDs for the rows to be retrieved must already have been extracted from an index scan into a memory storage area known as the RID pool, then sorted into ascending page number order (implied by ascending RID order). The list prefetch mechanism needs such an RID list so it can program the disk arm to retrieve blocks, up to 32 pages at a time, by the most efficient predetermined movements. As we mentioned in Example 8.6.1, we assume a rate of 100 I/Os per second as a rule of thumb for list prefetch, although the rate actually varies depending on the proximity of the pages fetched.

List prefetch is always used to access data pages in multiple index access (which we sometimes refer to as MX access for short), since the sorted RID list must exist during the plan. In composite index scans, such as the scan of Example 8.5.2 where 1000 rows are retrieved, it would seem that we are also likely to use list prefetch so as to speed up the data page retrieval. The limiting factor in choosing list prefetch is usually a matter of space in the RID pool, and since each RID is 4 bytes in length, a list of 1000 RIDs will take up only 4000 bytes, about the size of one disk page in memory buffer. But there are other limitations on the use of RID lists, which are discussed in Definition 8.6.1.

The size of the RID pool memory area is based on the size of the buffer pools chosen by the DBA (there are actually four different buffer pools in **DB2**, but for simplicity we usually refer to a single pool and assume that other pools are not used). The size of the RID pool is equal to half of the combined sizes of the buffer pools, except that it cannot exceed 200 MB. (This does *not* mean that the RID pool is part of the buffer pool! They are distinct memory areas!) The RID pool is provided for concurrent use by a number of different processes performing queries, and it is doled out rather parsimoniously. Every effort is made to minimize the use of the pool space by the following restrictive rules.

DEFINITION 8.6.1 Rules for RID List Use. The following rules govern the use of RID lists by the query optimizer.

[1] When the query optimizer constructs a plan for a query (this is known as *bind time*) involving RID list generation, the predicted number of RIDs active at any time in the plan cannot require more than 50% of the RID pool. If it does, then an alternate plan is created that does not call for the creation of RID lists. If predictions of RID use turn out to be wrong at runtime, after RID list extraction has already begun, so that RID list generation is actually inappropriate, the plan is aborted and another access method used to answer the query.

[2] The size of any single RID list that can be extracted from an index scan is limited to 16 million RIDs.

[3] No screening predicates can be used in an index scan that extracts an RID list.

[4] An **In-list** predicate cannot be used in an index scan that extracts an RID list. ∎

EXAMPLE 8.6.3 RID List Size Limit.

Consider again the `prospects` table with the indexes of Example 8.6.1, addrx, hobbyx, and incomex. We add a new index, called sexx, on a column of `pros-pects` named *sex*, with two values, 'M' and 'F', where we assume that the two column values appear with equal frequency. Consider the query

```
select name, straddr from prospects
    where zipcode between 02159 and 04158
    and incomeclass = 10 and sex = 'F';
```

Because of index compression, we see that the leaf level of the sexx index must contain approximately 50,000 pages, the same as the hobbyx index. To review this reasoning, there are 50,000,000 rows in `prospects`, and the average leaf-level entry (because of compression of duplicate key values) takes up approximately 4 bytes for the RID. Therefore 1000 entries fit on a leaf page, and 50 million entries require 50,000 leaf pages. Now consider the size of the RID list we would extract from the index sexx to satisfy the matching predicate, with FF($sex = 'F'$) = 1/2. This scan would traverse half of the 50,000-page leaf level and extract all the RIDs, a 25,000-page RID list, since nearly all of the space on the leaf level is made up of RIDs. But by rule 1 of Definition 8.6.1, we would not be able to construct a 25,000-page RID list unless we had a 50,000-page RID pool—that is, 200 MB, the absolute limit. Given that there must be another RID list from the plan in existence at the same time to intersect with, we see that the predicate "$sex = 'F'$" probably cannot have its RID list extracted. An even more obvious point mitigating against an RID list for the predicate "$sex = 'F'$" is rule 2, which disallows an RID list of more than 16 million RIDs. Since we suppose that "$sex = 'F'$" extracts RIDs for half of the 50 million rows of the `pros-pects` table, it is clear that we cannot have an MX step for this predicate. The multiple index plan must make do with the other two predicates and their filter factors, and proceed from there to retrieving the data rows. ■

Even in simple matching index scans, list prefetch access is not always a foregone conclusion.

EXAMPLE 8.6.4 RID List Size Limit, Again.

Consider again the `prospects` table with the hobbyx index and the query evaluated in Example 8.3.4:

```
select name, straddr from prospects where hobby = 'chess';
```

Since FF($hobby = 'chess'$) = 1/100, the dominating I/O cost of Example 8.3.4 was to retrieve (1/100)(50,000,000) = 500,000 rows in unclustered order from the `prospects` table. The cost of 500,000R in elapsed time is 500,000/40 = 12,500 seconds, or about 3½ hours. Clearly list prefetch would be enormously preferable, since 500,000L would be performed in 500,000/100 = 5000 seconds, about an hour and 23 minutes. But in order for list prefetch to take place, the RID list for this predicate must be extracted into the RID pool. There are 500,000 entries scanned, resulting in 500,000 RIDs, which take up 2 MB in the RID pool. This means there must be a 4-MB RID pool by rule 1 of Definition 8.6.1, since any plan can use only half of the RID pool. Because the RID pool is half the size of the buffer pool, a disk buffer size of 8 MB (containing 2000 4-KB disk pages) must be present. If the buffer pool is smaller than that, list prefetch cannot be used for this query. ∎

The RID rules given use rather coarse heuristics to set resource bounds. The number of users active in the system is not taken into account, and if we had a single user performing this query of Example 8.6.4 with a buffer pool size of 7 MB, it seems inappropriate to limit ourselves to using only half of the 3.5-MB RID pool and fail to perform list prefetch when there is no other user competing for the RID space. On the other hand, if there were several users active at once performing queries of this kind, we note that the queries do not result in large sets of popular pages requiring buffering, and thus we would like to be able to "convert" some of the buffer space into RID space to support more list prefetch.

A very important limitation on RID lists is rule 3, which states that index screening cannot be performed at the same time. In particular, a non-matching index scan cannot result in list prefetch in the data row retrieval phase. We will discuss this further after an example.

EXAMPLE 8.6.5 List Prefetch and Index Screening.

Recall the query of Example 8.5.2, where only the mailx index (zipcode, hobby, incomeclass, age) was present on prospects, and how this query was repeated in Example 8.6.2 with different indexes:

```
select name, straddr from prospects
    where zipcode between 02159 and 04158
    and hobby = 'chess' and incomeclass = 10;
```

With the mailx index, the index scan was matching on the zipcode column but not on the later columns hobby and incomeclass, so that "hobby = 'chess'" and "incomeclass = 10" were used as screening predicates. It was calculated that the index scan of mailx would traverse (1/50)(250,000) = 5000 leaf pages of the index, at a cost of 5000S and an elapsed time of 5000/400 = 12.5 seconds, and that 1000 data pages would be retrieved at a cost of 1000R and an elapsed time of 1000/40 = 25 seconds. Since screening predicates were used to achieve this small composite filter factor, we cannot extract an RID list for these 1000 pages (because of rule 3). It is impossible to perform these 1000 data page reads using list prefetch. Therefore a data page I/O of 1000L in 10 seconds elapsed, as we saw in Example 8.6.2, is not possible using this concatenated index. ∎

There doesn't seem to be any theoretically important reason why filter predicates and **In-list** predicates cannot be used for RID list extraction, as stated in rules 3 and 4, except that the RID list would be in use for a somewhat extended period while the filtering was carried out on a large set of index pages. Presumably the designers were looking for limitations on RID list extraction to preserve the valuable RID pool space for more deserving applications and hit on these rules, which hold for version 2.3. Various details of query optimization can change from one release to another, however.

Point of Diminishing Returns in Multiple Index Access

Another rule about RID list extraction in multiple index access is not so much a limitation as a rule of optimization. A scan on an index, with an I/O cost for leaf page traversal, will only be performed if it will pay for itself by reducing the I/O cost of data page retrieval by a larger amount. To determine the indexes that will be scanned with an MX step in a multiple index access plan, the query optimizer follows steps something like the ones that follow.

DEFINITION 8.6.2 Steps to Determine the Point of Diminishing Returns in MX Access.

[1] List indexes with matching predicates in the **where** clause of the query. For simplicity, we assume in what follows that each index has a disjoint set of matching predicates.

[2] Place the indexes in order by increasing filter factor value for matching scans. We will choose an initial sequence of indexes on which MX steps will be performed, with smallest filter factors first. This means we start by considering predicates with smaller index I/O costs and larger effects on saving data page I/O, and the approach can be proved to have optimal results.

[3] For successive indexes listed, perform MX steps only if the I/O cost for the index scan to extract the RID list will pay for itself with a reduced cost of data page scan for final row retrieval. The simplest formulation of this rule is that once we are down to a few rows, we don't read several hundred pages of a new index to get the number of rows down to one! ■

Actually, things are somewhat more complex than this. For example, in step 3 the first index considered may not pay for itself in I/O savings compared to a table space scan, so the procedure might have to consider using two indexes before a saving is evident. As an example, a filter factor of 1/20 for the first index doesn't save much I/O if there are 20 rows on a page. However, a second index with filter factor 1/15 results in a large I/O saving.

EXAMPLE 8.6.6

We refer again to the prospects table with the indexes addrx, hobbyx, agex, and incomex. Consider the query:

```
select name, straddr from prospects
    where zipcode between 02159 and 02658
    and age = 40 and hobby = 'chess' and incomeclass = 10;
```

We assume that multiple index access is used, and try to figure out which predicates will pay for themselves. The filter factors of these clauses are as follows (in ascending order):

(1) FF(zipcode between 02159 and 02658) = 500/100,000 = 1/200

(2) FF(hobby = 'chess') = 1/100

(3) FF(age = 40) = 1

(4) FF(incomeclass = 10) = 1/10

Applying the filter factor for predicate (1) to 50 million rows, we get (1/200)(50M) = 250,000 rows retrieved, unclustered of course, thus likely all to be on distinct pages of the 5 million data pages, and retrieved with list prefetch. The elapsed time for 250,000L is 2500 seconds. We ignore the index cost.

Applying predicate (2) after predicate (1), the scan of the index hobbyx for the predicate "hobby = 'chess'" entails a number of leaf page I/Os, calculated by (1/100)(50,000) = 500, so the cost is 500S, taking elapsed time 500/400 = 1.25 seconds. As a result, we reduce the number of data pages scanned from 250,000 (resulting from the previous step) to (1/100)(250,000) = 2500, and 2500L takes elapsed time 2500/100 = 25 seconds. With an investment of 1.25 seconds for the hobbyx index scan we have gone from a data scan of 2500 seconds to one of 25 seconds, obviously worthwhile.

Applying predicate (3) after predicates (1) and (2), the scan of the agex index (discussed in Example 8.6.1) for "age = 40" entails a number of leaf page I/Os, calculated by (1/50)(50,000) = 1000, at cost 1000S, taking elapsed time 1000/400 = 2.5 seconds. As a result, we reduce the number of data pages scanned to (1/50)(2500) = 50, and 50L takes elapsed time 0.5 seconds. With an investment of 2.5 seconds for the agex index scan we have gone from a data scan of 25 seconds to one of 0.5 seconds, obviously worthwhile.

Applying predicate (4) after predicates (1), (2), and (3), the scan of the incomex index for "incomeclass = 10" entails a number of leaf page I/Os, calculated by (1/10)(50,000) = 5000, so the cost is 5000S, taking elapsed time 5000/400 = 12.5 seconds. As a result, we reduce the number of data pages scanned to (1/10)(50) = 5, and 5L takes elapsed time 0.05 seconds (approximately). With an investment of 12.5 seconds for the agex index scan we have gone from a data scan of 0.5 seconds to one of 0.05 seconds. This is *not* worthwhile, and the incomex index will not be scanned with an MX step in the multiple index access plan. ∎

8.7 Methods for Joining Tables

In this section we study three algorithms currently used by **DB2** for joining two tables. The algorithms are known as *nested loop join, merge scan join,* and *hybrid join.* Each of these methods has performance advantages in a certain class of situations that can arise in performing a join. Other methods have been developed for performing joins that are not used by **DB2** but nevertheless provide performance advantages in special circumstances—for example, the method known as *hash join*—but we will restrict our attention to the join methods provided by **DB2**. The terminology used to describe **DB2** join methods is fairly universal, and some of these concepts are implemented in most database products.

We define a *join* of two tables to be a process in which we combine rows of one table with rows of another to answer a query. By this definition, a join occurs whenever two or more tables appear in the **from** clause of a Select statement. Even if we are taking a simple Cartesian product of rows from the two tables (a table *product*), we refer to it as a join. As we will see, a Select statement with a single table in the **from** clause, and a **where** clause that contains a Subselect from a different table, is often converted by the query optimizer to an equivalent query statement that joins tables. To begin with, we consider only the situation where exactly two tables appear in the **from** clause.

A join of two tables in **DB2** usually occurs in two steps. During the first step, only one table is accessed; this is referred to as the *outer table*. In the second step, rows of the second, *inner table* are combined with rows of the first, outer table. Other predicates, involving columns of the two tables that have not been retrieved through an index, are used to qualify rows as they are retrieved. As a result of all this, a *composite table* is generated that contains all the qualified rows of the join. If a join with a third table is now necessary, the composite table becomes the outer table for the succeeding join step. Otherwise, specified columns of the composite table provide the answer to the query. Although it is simplest to think of the composite table result of a join being fully materialized in a disk workfile, it is important to realize that we may be able to avoid such wasteful materialization. For example, if a user is only likely to look at the first 20 or 30 rows of the resulting output, it would be terribly inefficient to materialize a million-row composite table. Thus in Embedded SQL, when a cursor on a join query is first opened and the first row is retrieved, we avoid materializing tables where possible.

Nested Loop Join

Consider the following query:

[8.7.1] `select T1.C1, T1.C2, T2.C3, T2.C4 from T1, T2`
`where T1.C1 = 5 and T1.C2 = T2.C3;`

In a nested loop join, the table referred to as the *outer table* corresponds to the "outer loop" in a nested pair of loops, as we see in the pseudo-code of Figure 8.19. Assuming that the table T1 in the Select statement of (8.7.1) is the outer table, the first step of the nested join determines rows in T1 that satisfy the relevant predicate(s) on T1—in this case, T1.C1 = 5. If we assume that an index C1X exists on column C1 of table T1, then the first step of the join would give rise to a row in the plan table with the following relevant column values:

PLAN NO	METHOD	TAB NO	ACCESS TYPE	MATCH COLS	ACCESS NAME	PREFETCH	SORTN_ JOIN
1	0	1	I	1	C1X	L	N

This row of the plan table indicates the following. We are employing the first step of a multi-step plan (PLANNO = 1). No join method has yet been employed (METHOD = 0), and we are extracting rows from the first table of the join (TABNO = 1), using an Index scan step with one matching column on index C1X. We are able to retrieve rows from the table T1 using list prefetch.

Now that the rows of the outer table have been determined (they have not actually been extracted yet), a loop is performed to retrieve each of these rows. For each qualified row of the outer table, a retrieval is performed on the second, *inner* table, T2, and all rows of T2 are retrieved that satisfy the join predicate that connects the two tables, T1.C2 = T2.C3. Note that because the row of T1 is fixed for this retrieval, we can treat the value T1.C2 as if it were a constant, K. Then the rows retrieved from T2 are exactly those that satisfy a predicate of the form "T2.C3 = K", and an index C3X on column C3 of table T2 will make this retrieval efficient. This second step of the nested loop join, using the C3X index, has the following row in the plan table:

PLAN NO	METHOD	TAB NO	ACCESS TYPE	MATCH COLS	ACCESS NAME	PREFETCH	SORTN_ JOIN
2	1	2	I	1	C3X	L	N

This row of the plan table indicates the second step of a multi-step plan (PLANNO = 2). The join method being employed is nested loop join (METHOD = 1); we are extracting rows from the second table of the join (TABNO = 2), using an Index scan step with one matching column on index C3X. The second table is in fact T2, and we are retrieving rows from this table using list prefetch. Figure 8.19 contains procedural pseudo-code for the two-step method just explained.

```
R1:  FIND ALL ROWS T1.* IN THE OUTER TABLE T1 WHERE C1 = 5;
     FOR EACH ROW T1.* FOUND IN THE OUTER TABLE;
R2:      FIND ALL ROWS T2.* IN THE INNER TABLE WHERE T1.C2 = T2.C3;
         FOR EACH ROW T2.* FOUND IN THE INNER TABLE
             RETURN ANSWER: T1.C1, T1.C2, T2.C3, T2.C4;
         END FOR;
     END FOR;
```

Figure 8.19 Pseudo-Code for Nested Loop Join (Illustrates Query (8.7.1))

Figure 8.20 illustrates the method of nested loop join for query (8.7.1), using specific tables T1 and T2.

Note that the R1 and R2 labels of Figure 8.19 designate retrievals in the join processing. Additional predicates limiting the rows of either table can be added to the relevant retrievals. Either retrieval can be performed using an index scan (which we have assumed above) or a table scan. The outer table has only one retrieval, while the inner table has a number of retrievals equal to the number of qualifying rows in the outer table. The I/O cost of the join is therefore given by the following formula:

$$COST_{I/O}(\text{NESTED LOOP JOIN}) = COST_{I/O}(\text{OUTER TABLE RETRIEVAL}) +$$
$$\text{NUMBER OF QUALIFYING ROWS IN OUTER TABLE } *$$
$$COST_{I/O}(\text{INNER TABLE RETRIEVAL})$$

For the nested loop join to be an appropriate algorithm to join large tables, we would normally expect to see an index on the matching columns of the inner table, to guarantee efficient retrieval. Nested loop join is particularly efficient when only a small number of rows qualify from the outer table after limiting predicates are applied, or when the inner table is small enough that all index and data disk pages become resident in memory buffers after being accessed once during the join.

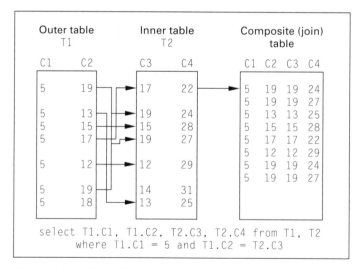

Figure 8.20 Nested Loop Join (Illustrates Query (8.7.1))

EXAMPLE 8.7.1

Assume that we are given two tables, TABL1 with columns C1 and C2, and TABL2 with columns C3 and C4, each with 1 million rows of 200 bytes each. We wish to estimate the I/O cost of the following query performed using a nested loop join:

```
select T1.C1, T1.C2, T2.C3, T2.C4 from TABL1 T1, TABL2 T2
    where T1.C1 = 5 and T2.C4 = 6 and T1.C2 = T2.C3;
```

We assume that a non-clustering index C1X exists on column C1 of TABL1, and on TABL2 we have the index C3X on C3 and C4X on C4. Assume also that the filter factors for these predicates are given as follows: FF(C1 = const) = FF(C4 = const) = 1/100; FF(C2 = const) = 1/250,000; and FF(C3 = const) = 1/500,000. We start with the question, How many rows are retrieved by this query? It turns out that it is best to have a specific join method in mind before we try to answer this question, as we see in the following analysis of I/O cost.

We will evaluate the I/O cost in terms of elapsed time for a possible nested join plan to answer this query, where the outer table is T1 (referring to the shorter alias for TABL1) and the inner table is T2 (the alias for TABL2). The plan we consider consists of the following steps. (1) Using the C1X index, retrieve all rows from T1 where T1.C1 = 5. (2) For each row retrieved from the outer table T1, think of T1.C2 as a constant, renamed K. Using the C3X index, retrieve all rows in the inner table T2 such that T2.C3 = K. As the rows from this index scan are retrieved, further restrict the rows by verifying the predicate T2.C4 = 6. (Note that there is no way to use the index C4X here since, as we explain below, we are only retrieving two rows with the T2.C3 = K clause, and a further use of the C4X index would hit the point of diminishing returns.) (3) Print out T1.C1 and T1.C2 from the outer table row and T2.C3 and T2.C4 for the qualified inner table row.

The following table shows the rows in the plan table for this strategy.

PLAN NO	METHOD	TAB NO	ACCESS TYPE	MATCH COLS	ACCESS NAME	PREFETCH	SORTN_ JOIN
1	0	1	I	1	C1X	L	N
2	1	2	I	1	C3X	L	N

Using the filter factor and the number of rows in T1, the number of rows retrieved from T1 in step (1) is about (1/100)(1,000,000) = 10,000 rows, likely to be all on different pages. The row for PLANNO = 1 tells us that list prefetch is being used. The index I/O cost for this retrieval is assumed to be insignificant next to the data page I/O cost. We therefore assume that $COST_{I/O}$(OUTER TABLE RETRIEVAL) = 10,000L, with elapsed time of 10,000/100 = 100 seconds.

For each outer table row qualified, we assume that the value T1.C2, renamed K, is in the range of values for the column T2.C3. Since FF(C3 = const) = 1/500,000, we expect to retrieve 2 rows out of a table of 1 million rows. This requires for each new value of T2.C3 one random I/O to the leaf level of the C3X index (assuming that upper-level directory nodes are in memory buffers) and then two I/Os (average) to retrieve the two pages containing the two rows. Thus the I/O cost for the 10,000 different inner loop steps is 10,000 * (1R + 2R). We would normally perform a list I/O to retrieve the data pages in this situation, but recall that it is quite misleading to think of a list prefetch of two pages as taking place in 2/100 seconds, since there are too few pages retrieved to amortize the arm seek time and rotational latency. It is much more reasonable to think of this retrieval as equivalent to 2R, and therefore the elapsed time for the inner loop is calculated from 10,000 * (3R), or 30,000/40 = 750 seconds. The elapsed time, then, is 100 seconds + 750 seconds = 850 seconds.

Now to determine how many rows are retrieved in the query, we see that there are 10,000 rows retrieved from T1 and for each row in T1 there are two rows joined to it (on the average) from table T2. Therefore there are about 20,000 rows retrieved at this point, after which a qualification test takes place to see if T2.C4 = 6 for the rows retrieved. With a filter factor of 1/100, the final number of rows retrieved is (1/100) 20,000 = 200. ∎

Merge Join

Merge join is also known in other texts as *merge scan join or sort merge join*. Consider again the query of Example 8.7.1, with the same index assumptions.

[8.7.2]   `select T1.C1, T2.C2, T1.C3, T2.C4 from TABL1 T1, TABL2 T2`
            `where T1.C1 = 5 and T2.C4 = 6 and T1.C2 = T2.C3;`

The merge join method scans two tables only once, in the order of their join columns. In the Select statement of (8.7.2), **DB2** would start by applying the non-join predicates and creating intermediate tables. We first evaluate "select C1, C2 from T1 where T1.C1 = 5 order by C2," placing the output rows in an intermediate table IT1 with columns C1 and C2, and rows sorted in order by C2. Then we evaluate "select C3, C4 from T2 where C4 = 6 order by C3," to get an intermediate table IT2 with columns C3 and C4 and rows sorted in order by C3. Note that these intermediate tables, IT1 and IT2, are usually too large to hold in memory. They are written to disk workfiles as temporary tables, and the sort of the rows is a disk base sort, explained later.

We are now prepared to perform the merge process from which the merge join algorithm takes its name. To perform a merge join on IT1 and IT2, we associate a pointer with each intermediate table, pointing initially to the first row of each. As the algorithm proceeds, the two pointers move forward in such a way that any matching C2/C3 values for rows in the two tables are detected. Except for cases where multiple identical C2 values in IT1 match multiple identical C3 values in IT2, both pointers move steadily forward through the rows of both tables, and detect all matching values IT1.C2 = IT2.C3 that exist. In the pseudo-code of Figure 8.21 the C2 value of the row in table IT1 pointed to by pointer P1 is represented by P1 –> C2, and similarly for P2 –> C3 in table IT2.

```
        CREATE TABLE IT1 AS: SELECT C1, C2 FROM T1 WHERE C1 = 5 ORDER BY C2;
        CREATE TABLE IT2 AS: SELECT C3, C4 FROM T1 WHERE C4 = 6 ORDER BY C3;
        SET P1 POINTER TO FIRST ROW OF IT1;        /* OUTER TABLE           */
        SET P2 POINTER TO FIRST ROW OF IT2;        /* INNER TABLE           */
   MJ:  WHILE (TRUE) {                             /* LOOP UNTIL EXIT MJ LOOP */
            WHILE (P1 -> C2 > P2 -> C3) {       /* IF P2 NEEDS TO ADVANCE  */
                ADVANCE P2 TO NEXT ROW IN IT2;/* ADVANCE IT               */
                IF (P2 PAST LAST ROW) EXIT MJ LOOP;/* OUT OF ROWS, EXIT   */
            }
            WHILE (P1 -> C2 < P2 -> C3) {       /* IF P1 NEEDS TO ADVANCE  */
                ADVANCE P1 TO NEXT ROW IN IT1;/* ADVANCE IT               */
                IF (P1 PAST LAST ROW) EXIT MJ LOOP;/* OUT OF ROWS, EXIT   */
            }
            IF (P1 -> C2 == P2-> C3) {             /* FOUND MATCH ON JOIN   */
                MEMP = P2;                         /* REMEMBER P2 START POINT */
                WHILE (P1 -> C2 == P2 -> C3) {/* LOOP                      */
                    RETURN ANSWER: IT1.C1, IT1.C2, IT2.C3, IT2.C4;
                    ADVANCE P2 TO NEXT ROW IN IT2; /* ADVANCE P2          */
                }   /* LOOP CONTINUES IF P2 -> C3 IS UNCHANGED            */
            }                                      /* DONE WITH JOIN MATCH  */
            /* SINCE FELL THROUGH, P2 -> C3 IS NEW OR BEYOND END OF TABLE */
            ADVANCE P1 TO NEXT ROW IN IT1;     /* ADVANCE P1               */
            IF (PAST LAST ROW) EXIT MJ LOOP;   /* OUT OF ROWS, EXIT        */
            IF (P1 -> C2 == MEMP -> C3)        /* IF NEXT P1-> C2 IS SAME  */
                P2 = MEMP;                     /* START OVER WITH P2        */
        }                /* END OF MJ LOOP                                 */
```

Figure 8.21   Pseudo-Code for Merge Join (Illustrates Query (8.7.2))

Figure 8.22 illustrates the method of merge join for query (8.7.1), using specific tables T1 and T2.

Once a match is found in the pseudo-code of Figure 8.21, we keep P1 fixed and advance P2 through all duplicate values. Then we advance P1; if we find a duplicate, this is the only situation in which a pointer moves backward, where we set P2 = MEMP to run through all duplicates of P2 again. Clearly if there are a lot of occurrences where C2 and C3 have the same value, a large number of rows will be joined, and this innermost loop will have an enormous effect. However, it is more common that there will be only a small number of rows in one table matching more than one row with another, since we don't normally perform joins on columns with a large number of duplicate values (see the section in Chapter 5 on lossy and lossless decompositions). In any event, the query optimizer can determine the likely number of duplicates facing each other using existing statistics, and it is likely that most computer resources will be used in finding any match at all.

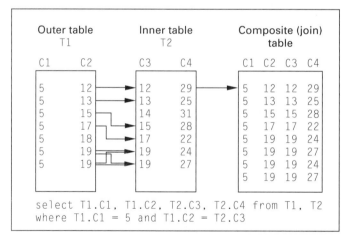

Figure 8.22 Merge Join (Illustrates Query (8.7.2))

EXAMPLE 8.7.2

We repeat the join query of Example 8.7.1 using a merge join:

```
select T1.C1, T1.C2, T2.C3, T2.C4 from TABL1 T1, TABL2 T2
    where T1.C1 = 5 and T2.C4 = 6 and T1.C2 = T2.C3;
```

We have all the same assumptions: non-clustering indexes C1X still exists on column C1 of TABL1, with C3X and C4X on C3 and C4 of TABL2. The tables both contain 1 million rows of 200 bytes each, and we still have filter factors FF(C1 = const) = FF(C4 = const) = 1/100, FF(C2 = const) = 1/250,000, and FF(C3 = const) = 1/500,000. In the nested join of Example 8.7.1, we used the indexes C1X and C3X.

The strategy for answering query (8.7.1) with a merge join consists of the following steps: (1) Using the index C1X, retrieve all rows from T1 where T1.C1 = 5 (again there will be 10,000 rows), output the C1 and C2 values to IT1, and sort the result by C2 value. (2) Using the index C4X, retrieve all rows from T2 where T2.C4 = 6 (10,000 rows also), output the resulting C3 and C4 values to IT2, and sort them.

Then perform the merge-join step, following the pseudo-code above. The merge join plan is shown in the following table. Note the SORTN_JOIN column which shows that a sort is required to achieve IT1 and IT2.

PLAN NO	METHOD	TAB NO	ACCESS TYPE	MATCH COLS	ACCESS NAME	PREFETCH	SORTN_ JOIN
1	0	1	I	1	C1X	L	Y
2	2	2	I	1	C4X	L	Y

As before, step (1) requires a read of 10,000 entries from the T1.C1 leaf-level index, which we treat as insignificant, followed by an I/O cost of 10,000L to retrieve the indexed rows from the data pages. If we assume that each of the C1 and C2 values extracted requires 10 bytes, the materialized table IT1 requires 200,000 bytes, or about 50 pages. It is appropriate to think of this sort taking place completely in memory, so the total I/O cost of step (1) is 10,000L. The same considerations apply to step (2). The total cost for the plan is therefore 20,000L, with an elapsed time of 200 seconds, an improvement over the nested loop sort of Example 8.7.1, which required 850 seconds. The advantage comes from using index C4X in merge join for more efficient batch retrieval from TABL2.   ■

Note that it is not always necessary to extract the rows from a table such as T1 into an intermediate table IT1. If there were an index on T1 that allowed us to qualify the rows of T1 with the predicate "T1.C1 = 5" and still access the qualified rows in order by T1.C2, **DB2** would certainly take that option. This would be possible, for example, if T1 had an index C12X on (C1, C2): the matching scan through the index with the given predicate would provide rows of T1 in order by C2. The same considerations hold for T2.

The merge join is not always a superior strategy.

EXAMPLE 8.7.3

Consider the following join query:

```
select T1.C5, T1.C2, T2.* from TABL1 T1, TABL2 T2
    where T1.C5 = 5 and T1.C2 = T2.C3;
```

We assume that indexes C2X, C3X, and C5X exist on the corresponding columns of tables T1 and T2, with filter factors as in Examples 8.7.1 and 8.7.2, FF(C2 = const) = 1/250,000 and FF(C3 = const) = 1/500,000, and a new filter factor FF(T1.C5 = const) = 1/1000. Thus the I/O cost for a nested loop join with T1 as the outer table can be calculated as follows. With 1000 rows to look up in T1 having T1.C5 = 5, we have an index lookup cost of 1R (for index) + 1000L (for data pages). For each row in the outer table T1, we set T1.C2 = K, then look up rows in the inner table having T2.C3 = K, about two rows, requiring 1R for the index leaf entry lookup and 2R for the row retrievals. The I/O cost for the inner loop is calculated as 1000 * (3R) = 3000R. Thus the total nested loop join cost is 3001R + 1000L, with elapsed time of 3001/40 + 1000/100, or approximately 85 seconds.

For merge join, we calculate costs as follows. We can easily calculate that the extraction of IT1 requires 10 seconds for I/O, but as we will see, this is insignificant in comparison to elapsed time for the loop join. Since there were no independent limiting predicates on T2 such as we had in Example 8.7.2 (T2.C2 = 6), we have a choice between accessing the rows from T2 in order by the index C3X to perform the merge, or materializing and sorting the entire table T2 as intermediate table IT2. In the first case, we would access all rows of T2 through an unclustered index, at a cost for data page access alone of 1,000,000R, clearly not a good strategy. (We can't use prefetch I/O here, because we don't want to retrieve the rows in RID order.) In the second case, we need to materialize a table IT2 with 1 million rows of 200 bytes each (note that all columns of T2 are in the target list) and sort the resulting rows by C3. We defer consideration of disk sort, but it is reasonable to point out that a disk sort of these rows would probably require two passes through the disk pages, writing out the results of the first pass and then reading in these results for the second pass, an I/O cost of over 100,000S, with an elapsed time of 100,000/400 = 250 seconds. Clearly the nested loop strategy is superior. ∎

Hybrid Join

The hybrid join method, METHOD = 4 in the IBM taxonomy, is used less frequently than nested loop join and merge join, and for brevity we merely give a verbal description of the algorithm used.

Description of the Hybrid Join Algorithm. A hybrid join of two tables has an outer and an inner table, just as the nested loop and merge join algorithms do. The first step is the same as that of merge join for the outer table. The table is scanned once in join column order, either through an index or after extracting a set of rows restricted by some predicates into an intermediate table IT1. As rows of the outer table are being scanned in join column order, matching join column values of the inner table are looked up through an index on the join column. The rows of the inner table are not accessed yet, however; instead the rows from the outer table, with an additional column giving the RID value of each matching join row in the inner table, are written to an intermediate table IT2. Rows of IT2 are then sorted in RID order, and list prefetch is used to pick up rows from the inner table to join with outer table rows.

> ### EXAMPLE 8.7.4
> Consider again the join query of Example 8.7.3:
>
> ```
> select T1.C5, T1.C2, T2.* from TABL1 T1, TABL2 T2
>     where T1.C5 = 5 and T1.C2 = T2.C3;
> ```
>
> As in Example 8.7.3, we assume that indexes C2X, C3X, and C5X exist on the corresponding columns of tables T1 and T2, with filter factors as in Examples 8.7.1 and 8.7.2, FF(C2 = const) = 1/250,000, FF(C3 = const) = 1/500,000, and FF(T1.C5 = const) = 1/1000. The I/O cost for a hybrid join with T1 as the outer table can be calculated as follows. With 1000 rows to look up in T1 having T1.C5 = 5, we see an index lookup cost of 1R (for index) + 1000L (for data pages). We only need to extract C2 and C5 from T1 for each of these 1000 rows to write into IT1, about 8000 bytes, so creating IT1 and the following sort by C2 should cost no I/O. For each row in the outer table IT1, we set T1.C2 = K, then look up index entries in the C3X index for T2.C3 = K, requiring 1R of index leaf I/O for each entry, at a cost of 1000R.
>
> As we perform this lookup, we create rows of the form (T1.C2, T1.C5, RID) in intermediate table IT2. This table will contain about 2000 rows of 12 bytes each, about 24,000 bytes or buffer space for six disk pages, so once again we assume that no I/O is needed for creating IT2 and the following sort by RID values. Finally, we pass through the rows of IT2, using the sorted RID values in IT2

as a kind of RID list to retrieve the rows from the inner table T1, and matching the C5 and C2 values of T1 with all columns of T2 to generate the target-list rows. We are retrieving 2000 rows from T2, likely all to be on separate pages, at an I/O cost of 2000L. Therefore the total I/O cost for this method is 1000L (extracting rows from T1) + 1000R (index entries from C3X) + 2000L (extracting rows from T2). The elapsed time is (1000 + 2000)/100 + 1000/40 = 10 + 20 + 25 = 55 seconds, an improvement on the nested loop join calculated in Example 8.7.3, which was superior to merge join. ■

The advantage gained over nested loop join arises from the fact that all row retrievals from the inner table can be performed using list prefetch I/O with large blocks.

Multiple Table Joins

In **DB2** and most database systems, joins of three or more tables are performed by joining two tables at a time; the composite result of the first two joins is written to an intermediate table and then joined with the third table. The resulting composite may be joined with a fourth table, and so on. The order of joins is not determined by the non-procedural SQL Select, but is left up to the query optimizer. The proper choice is very important.

Consider a three-table join of the form:

[8.7.3]   select T1.C1, T1.C2, T2.C3, T2.C4, T2.C5, T3.C6, T3.C7
from T1, T2, T3
where T1.C1 = 20 and T1.C2 = T2.C3 and T2.C4 = 40
and T2.C5 = T2.C6 and T3.C7 = 60;

The query plans available for such a join have a number of different degrees of freedom. We can start by performing either of the joins T1 ⋈ T2 or T2 ⋈ T3. Assuming that we start with T1 ⋈ T2, we can use a nested loop join or a hybrid join with either T1 or T2 in the outer loop, or a merge join (the decision on inner and outer tables in the merge join is immaterial). Once the table T4 := T1 ⋈ T2 has been (at least conceptually) materialized, we need to perform the join T4 ⋈ T3, once again using either a nested loop join, a hybrid join, or a merge join. The query optimizer needs to consider all such plans to discover the most efficient one, and it is here that efficient algorithms for query optimization begin to become important. For joins involving multiple tables, query optimization can require a great deal of computational effort.

Note that in the plan just mentioned, joining T1 and T2 to create T4, then joining T4 to T3, if the query optimizer decides to perform the join T4 ⋈ T3 by a nested loop algorithm, the intermediate table T4 := T1 ⋈ T2 does not need to be physically materialized before starting the final join step. As each row of T4 is generated from T1 ⋈ T2, the next iteration of the nested loop join of T4 ⋈ T3 can be immediately performed. The technique whereby successive rows output from one step of an access plan can be fed as input into the next step of the plan is known as *pipelining*. Pipelining minimizes the physical disk space needed for materialization. Even more important, in cases where only a small fraction of initial rows from the query are ever required (perhaps because the terminal user ceases scrolling through the cursor after getting a look at a few screens of information), minimal materialization by pipelining often saves a great deal of effort. However, pipelining is not always possible: if the query optimizer chooses a merge join to evaluate T4 = T1 ⋈ T2, and then another merge join to evaluate T4 ⋈ T3, where the T4 ⋈ T3 join columns dictate a different sort order than the join columns output from T1 ⋈ T2, then the intermediate table T4 must be fully materialized before the initial sort of the next join step can be performed.

Transforming Nested Queries to Joins

It is possible to transform most nested queries into equivalent queries involving only table joins. This is an important technique for the query optimizer.

EXAMPLE 8.7.5
Consider the query:

```
select * from T1 where C1 = 5
    and C2 in (select C3 from T2 where C4 = 6);
```

Conceptually we think of this query as being performed in two steps. First the subquery is evaluated, extracting a set of values for the C3 target list into an intermediate table IT1, then the outer query, "select * from T1 where C1 = 5 and C2 in IT1," is evaluated, with a condition on the C2 column that it have a value in the IT1 list just created. The most efficient way to do this, given that there is no index created on IT1, is probably as a merge join: "select * from T1 where C1 = 5" is extracted into an intermediate table IT2, the rows are ordered by the T1.C2 value, and then the merge join process of Figure 8.21 is performed between IT2 and IT1. Possible duplicate rows must now be removed, as explained below. This procedure puts us in mind of the following "join form":

```
select distinct T1.* from T1, T2
    where T1.C1 = 5 and T2.C4 = 6 and T1.C2 = T2.C3;
```

The Subselect query at the beginning and this join query give identical results, and the equivalent join form allows the query optimizer to use other algorithms that are not obvious in the nested form. For example, it is now possible to perform a nested loop join with T2 as the outer table.

The need for the **distinct** keyword in transforming nested query to join;in the join form arises from the following observation. If a row r1 of T1 obeys the condition of the join query, then r1.C1 = 5 and there must exist a row r2 in T2 so that r2.C4 = 6 and r1.C2 = r2.C3. But nothing is said about the columns C3 and C4 forming a relational key of T2, so it is perfectly possible that there is a second row r3 in T2 that has the same values for C3 and C4 as r2. Then in the target list of the join query without a **distinct** keyword, the row r1 would appear twice. This would clearly not happen in the original nested form of the query, since each single row of T1 is conceptually considered only once and qualified or not by the predicates "C1 = 5" and "C2 in IT1." Thus the **distinct** keyword in the join form merely casts out duplicates that would not appear in the nested form. ∎

The value of a transformation such as this is that it reduces the number of different types of predicates the query optimizer needs to consider to achieve optimal efficiency. Once the nested query of Example 8.7.5 has been rewritten as an equivalent join query, it is reduced to a problem previously solved, and the query optimizer can use any of the join methods we have already introduced. The next example considers the case of a correlated subquery.

EXAMPLE 8.7.6

Consider the query:

```
select * from T1
    where C1 = 5
    and C2 in (select C4 from T2 where C5 = 6 and C6 > T1.C3);
```

Because this nested form contains a correlated subquery, it is not possible to evaluate the subquery until the outer product row is fixed so that T1.C3 can be evaluated. From this consideration, it seems that the only valid approach is to start by looping on rows of T1, then for each row in T1 find all rows in T2 through an index on C4, where T2.C4 is equal to the outer T1.C2, and then resolve the clause T2.C6 > T1.C3. Now notice that the nested query above gives the same result as the join query:

```
select distinct T1.* from T1, T2
    where T1.C1 = 5 and T1.C2 = T2.C4 and T2.C5 = 6 and T2.C6 > T1.C3;
```

It is much easier to picture the strategy of performing a merge join with the query in this form. Extract rows from T1 where T1.C1 = 5 into intermediate table IT1, and sort by T1.C2. Then sort T2 in order by column C4 into table IT2. Now merge join IT1 and IT2 on matching values for T1.C2 and T2.C4 (casting out duplicates), and qualify rows matched by making them obey the predicate T2.C6 > T1.C3. This strategy might be superior to the nested loop join that seemed most natural for the query in nested form. ∎

Theorem 8.7.1 gives a general form covering the cases described above.

THEOREM 8.7.1 The following two query forms give equivalent results:

```
select T1.C1 from T1 where [Set A of predicates on T1 and] T1.C2
    is in (select T2.C3 from T2 [where Set B of predicates on T2, T1]);
```

and

```
select distinct T1.C1 from T1, T2
    where T1.C2 = T2.C3 [and Set A of predicates on T1]
    [and Set B of conditions on T2, T1];
```

Note that Set A of conditions can be empty, as can Set B. Note too that if no conditions in Set B from the nested query refer to table T1 in the outer query, the entire nested query is non-correlated. The forms given above can be generalized to multiple tables in the outer and inner queries. ∎

DB2 performs this transformation only under certain conditions, including the following.

[1] The subquery target list is a single column, guaranteed by a unique index to have unique values.

[2] The comparison operator connecting the outer query to the subquery is either **in** or **=any** (with the same meaning).

Thus, for example, all nested queries involving the **not exists** predicate are not transformed into join predicates. But most nested queries have equivalent join forms, and it turns out that the **DB2** query optimizer usually finds a more efficient execution plan if the query is posed in the join form. This is true even if the transformation into a join plan doesn't take place under **DB2** rules of transformation and implies that the person writing queries should make some effort to create a join form rather than the equivalent nested form query if possible. Given that a nested form query is used, it is possible to tell from the output of the EXPLAIN command if a transformation into join form has been performed. A join is indicated by a METHOD column value of 1, 2, or 4.

8.8 Disk Sorts

There are a number of situations in query processing in which a sort of some set of objects too large to fit in memory must be performed. Recall that RID lists are assumed to lie completely in memory in the RID pool. As a result, the method used to sort the RIDs can be any one of the efficient memory sorts you have probably already encountered in a data structures programming course, such as merge sort. However, when the set of objects being sorted does not fit entirely in memory, the problem becomes a good deal more difficult. The database system needs to use methods that minimize disk I/O, a problem that probably never arose in earlier programming courses. We refer to a sort of data, some of which must be disk resident, as a *disk sort*. In the analogy of keyed lookup, the most efficient lookup structure for memory-resident data (allowing arbitrary inserts and range finds) is a balanced binary tree or 2-3 tree, whereas for data that is disk resident the most efficient structure is the B-tree.

DB2 must be ready to employ an efficient disk sort during merge join and hybrid join processing, where the intermediate tables IT1 and IT2 are sorted by join column or by RID. (Sorts must be performed unless an index is used for accessing the original tables that already has the right order.) These tables are often small enough to retain in memory, but **DB2** cannot depend on that, and so a disk sort is used. The disk sorts used in merge join and hybrid join processing are assumed to take place during the second step of these two step join plans (PLANNO = 2, METHOD = 2 or 4), and the sort is reflected in the plan row by two new column values,

SORTN_JOIN = Y and SORTC_JOIN = Y. There are a number of other plan table columns that are used to indicate when disk sort steps are being performed, and for what purpose. These plan columns include SORTC_ORDERBY (generally triggered when an **order by** clause is used in the Select statement); SORTC_GROUPBY (to gather terms together in response to a **group by** clause); and SORTC_UNIQ (generally used when a **distinct** keyword is used in the target list). The columns contain value 'Y' when the sort is being performed and otherwise contain value 'N'. Note that there are three columns in the plan table that are never used in the current release of **DB2**, and therefore always contain the value 'N'; these columns are SORTN_GROUPBY, SORTN_UNIQ, and SORTN_ORDERBY.

The N-Way Merge Disk Sort Algorithm

In what follows we refer to a *table* of *rows* to be sorted by some *sortkey* column. Note that we are not necessarily referring to a relational table, but to any list of record-structured objects that the database system cannot hold entirely in memory. A disk sort takes place in a series of *passes*. In each pass the algorithm makes progress toward producing a sorted result on disk, as much progress as possible given the limitations of memory space in comparison to the total size of the table to be sorted. If by chance the table to be sorted and all temporary sort information can be held totally in memory during the sort, then a single pass will produce a completely sorted list. Otherwise, the first pass sorts the largest possible fraction of the table into ascending order and writes this out to disk as a sorted block, then repeats this process until all rows in the table have been written out in a sequence of sorted blocks. Each successive pass performs successive *merges* of N blocks into new, longer blocks containing sequences of ordered rows, until all rows are sorted. The N-way merge sort is a generalization of the memory-resident two-way merge sort often taught in data structures classes, in the same way that a B-tree is a generalization of a binary tree, and for the same reason. By increasing N we can greatly reduce the number of passes, where each pass must read all information in the table from disk and write it back again. Thus the I/O is minimized.

To be more specific, assume that we are given a table of short rows of data to be sorted that takes up a number D of disk pages (we assume that the disk pages are contiguous on disk, so that sequential prefetch I/O can be used), and that we have M+1 disk buffer pages of memory, $M \leq D$, that we are allowed to use during our sort. We wish to illustrate the procedure of an N-way merge sort. As we will see, if $M \geq D$, then we can perform the sort entirely in memory. It turns out that the exact length of the rows isn't important, as long as all rows always lie entirely within some disk page (rows cannot cross pages). To have some numbers to work with for purposes of illustration, let us assume that $D = 10,000$ pages and $M = 2$ pages. In what follows we will perform an M-way merge sort—that is, since $M = 2$, a two-way merge sort. All calculations that follow can be generalized back to arbitrary values for D and M.

To begin with, we say that the rows to be sorted are originally stored on 10,000 contiguous disk pages known as area A1, and for simplicity we assume that we have a second disk area of 10,000 contiguous pages known as area A2. Successive *passes* in the merge sort move pages from A1 to A2 and back again. In reality we don't need so much extra space, but the algorithm is easier to explain with these two distinct areas. We start by assuming that there is no order whatsoever to the rows and proceed to describe pass 1 of the M-way merge sort. Note that in describing passes of the M-way merge sort, we won't consider any sequential prefetch I/O optimizations. Later, when sequential prefetch I/O is considered, we will describe a slightly more general N-way merge sort, with $N < M$.

Pass 1. The sort module reads the first block of M pages of the table to be sorted, represented as pages $1, 2, \ldots, M$, from disk area A1 into memory; sorts the rows within the buffered area by a method to be described later (we assume that the sorted rows can be placed on M pages again after sorting so that no row laps across a page boundary—this is simple if all rows have the same length); and writes out these M pages as a *sorted block* to the corresponding positions on area A2, pages $1, 2, \ldots, M$. This process is repeated with successive blocks of M pages (possibly less for the final block, if M does not divide D). The module reads from area A1 the pages numbered $M \cdot i + 1, M \cdot i + 2, \ldots, M \cdot i + M$, sorts the rows in this block, and writes the resulting pages out to area A2, block B_{i-1}. Since we have fixed on the value $M = 2$ (an unrealistically small number, used for purposes of illustration), we can schematically picture the result of the first pass written to area A2 as follows:

Page	1 2	3 4	5 6	7 8	9 10	11 12	13 14	15 . . .	. . .	D–1 D
Block	B_0	B_1	B_2	B_3	B_4	B_5	B_6	B_7		$B_{(D-1)/2}$

The pages are numbered 1, 2, 3, 4, . . . , D–1, D, and they are blocked into pairs by blocks B_0, B_1, . . . , meaning that within each block (consisting of a pair of pages) all rows are in sorted order. We assume here that D is even, and the last two pages in area A2, D–1 and D, are odd and even respectively. If instead the last disk page D were an odd number, then the final block $B_{(D-1)/2}$ would be only a single disk page in length. In pass 1 we have initialized the disk sort process, but successive passes are where actual merges takes place.

Later passes. Each merge pass reads in initial pages from groups of (up to) M blocks from the most recent pass completed and merges these blocks into a larger block, writing out one page at a time to the new block on the alternate area not containing input. As an example, pass 2 for the M = 2 example above takes the output from pass 1 on area A2, merges pairs of blocks containing two pages each, and writes the resulting ordered sequence of rows to blocks four pages in length on area A1.

Page	1 2 3 4	5 6 7 8	9 10 11 12	13 14 15 . . .	. . .	. . . D–1 D
Block	B_1	B_2	B_3	B_4		$B_{(D-1)/4}$

Consider carefully how the I/O for this merge takes place. The merge pass begins by reading in the first page of block B_1 and the first page of block B_2. Both B_1 and B_2 are in sorted order, so it is clear that we only need to look at the first page of each block to find the smallest row contained in the two blocks. In fact, once these initial block pages have been read into memory, we only have to look at the initial row on each of these pages, comparing the two sortkey values to find the smallest row in sort order. Now we merge the two blocks to a larger output block, moving merged rows to a sort output page in buffer and performing disk reads and writes as necessary.

In the general case, we read in the first page from each of M blocks from the previous pass and place cursors pointing to the initial row in each page. We then determine the smallest row under any cursor and place it at the beginning of a buffer page set aside for sort output. (Recall that there are M + 1 pages of buffer available, one for a page in each block being merged and one for output.) At this point it is necessary to advance the cursor pointing to the row just merged to the next row in that block. If there are no more rows in the current page, we read in the next page from the containing block. If there are no more pages in the block, we drop this cursor and continue merging rows from the remaining cursors until all rows have been merged. Whenever the sort output page fills up, we write it out to the next page of the output block. At the end of this process, all rows in the M input blocks, b pages in length, have been merged into sort sequence on a new output block containing M • b pages. We continue merging M blocks at a time from the prior pass, until all rows have been merged into new longer blocks and the pass is complete. We perform successive passes until the size of the block output by a pass would exceed D; at this point the sort is complete. ∎

EXAMPLE 8.8.1 Example of a Two-Way Merge Sort.

Assume a sequence of 2000-byte rows, two on each disk page, to be sorted in order by the key values of the following sequence, which represents the initial order of the rows.

57 22 99 64 12 29 46 7 91 58 69 17 65 36 33 28 77 6 54 63 88 95 38 44

After pass 1 of a two-way merge sort, we have (four rows to each two-page block):

22 57 64 99	7 12 29 46	17 58 69 91	28 33 36 65	6 54 63 77	38 44 88 95

After pass 2, we have (four-page blocks):

7 12 22 29 46 57 64 99	17 28 33 36 58 65 69 91	6 38 44 54 63 77 88 95

After pass 3, we have (eight-page blocks; the final block has no pair to merge with):

7 12 17 22 28 29 33 36 46 57 58 64 65 69 91 99	6 38 44 54 63 77 88 95

And finally, after pass 4, we have the sorted sequence:

6 7 12 17 22 28 29 33 36 38 44 46 54 57 58 63 64 65 69 77 88 91 95 99

∎

It is clear that all nonterminal blocks increase by a factor of M in size during each pass of an M-way merge sort. Each page from blocks of the prior pass needs to be read in only once, and an equivalent number of pages written out during the pass to create these longer blocks. Thus pass 1 requires 2 • D page I/Os, and each successive merge pass requires 2 • D pages also. Figure 8.23 gives output block sizes and I/Os required for successive passes of the two-way merge algorithm, assuming 10,000 pages of data.

Pass number	Block size	I/Os in pass
1	2	20,000
2	4	20,000
3	8	20,000
4	16	20,000
5	32	20,000
6	64	20,000
7	128	20,000
8	256	20,000
9	512	20,000
10	1024	20,000
11	2048	20,000
12	4096	20,000
13	8192	20,000
14	16,384	20,000

Figure 8.23 Sequence of Passes for Disk Sort of 10,000 Pages Using Two-Way Merge Sort

Recall that when the block size exceeds the number of pages in the table, the table has been successfully sorted. This means that the table has been successfully sorted with pass 14, using 14 • 20,000 = 280,000 I/Os. More generally, after K passes, we have achieved a block size of 2^K, and we complete our sort when $2^K \geq D$, or in other words when K = CEIL($\log_2(D)$). Thus the total number of I/Os required to perform a two-way merge sort of D pages is 2 • CEIL($\log_2(D)$) • D.

Pass number	Block size	I/Os in pass
1	4	20,000
2	16	20,000
3	64	20,000
4	256	20,000
5	1024	20,000
6	8192	20,000
7	32,768	20,000

Figure 8.24 Sequence of Passes for Disk Sort of 10,000 Pages Using Four-Way Merge Sort

The two-way merge sort is not an optimal disk sort, of course, given that a reasonably large amount of buffer space exists. An M-way merge sort increases block length by a factor of M with each pass. Thus we will complete our sort after K passes, where $M^K \geq D$, or in other words where $K = CEIL(\log_M(D))$. Each pass still requires only 2 • D page I/Os, so the total number of I/Os required for an M-way merge sort of D pages is 2 • $CEIL(\log_M(D))$ • D.

Pass number	Block size	I/Os in pass
1	100	20,000
2	10,000	20,000

Figure 8.25   Passes for Disk Sort of 10,000 Pages with 100-Way Merge Sort

This change, from $\log_2(D)$ to $\log_M(D)$ as a factor of the needed I/Os, is quite important. Figure 8.24 gives output block sizes and I/Os required for successive passes of the 4-way merge algorithm, assuming 10,000 pages of data. Figure 8.25 gives these figures for a 100-way merge sort.

EXAMPLE 8.8.2 Example of a Three-Way Merge Sort.
Given the same sequence as that of the previous example, demonstrate a three-way merge sort. We start with the initial order:

57 22 99 64 12 29 46 7 91 58 69 17 65 36 33 28 77 6 54 63 88 95 38 44

After pass 1, we have three-page blocks:

12 22 29 57 64 99	7 17 46 58 69 91	6 28 33 36 65 77	38 44 54 63 88 95

After pass 2, we have

6 7 12 17 22 28 29 33 36 46 57 58 64 65 69 77 91 99	38 44 54 63 88 95

And with pass 3, the same sorted order that we got with a two-way merge sort:

6 7 12 17 22 28 29 33 36 38 44 46 54 57 58 63 64 65 69 77 88 91 95 99

■

EXAMPLE 8.8.3 Two-Step Plan Requiring Sort.

Recall Example 8.3.6, in which we used the naddrx index for the prospects table, created by the command

```
create index naddrx on prospects (zipcode, city, straddr, name) . . . ;
```

and needed to find a plan for the query (modified slightly here to require a sort):

```
select name, straddr from prospects
    where zipcode between 02159 and 04158
    order by name, straddr;
```

The query plan performs an INDEXONLY step, where the range of leaf-level entries with zipcode values from 02159 to 04158 is accessed using sequential prefetch, and the name and straddr values are extracted. Given that FF(zipcode between 02159 and 04158) is approximately 2/100, the index scan step to extract these values needs to access 1 million entries of 60 bytes each, 15,000 disk pages, so the I/O cost is about 15,000S, requiring 15,000/400 = 37.5 seconds.

A sort must be performed to place the output (name, straddr) rows into the proper order for output, so we begin by finding the length of the temporary table IT1 created to hold these rows. We have assumed that both the name and straddr columns are 20 bytes in length, so the rows are 40 bytes long and can fit 100 on a page. We need to materialize a table of 500,000 rows, requiring 5000 disk pages.

Assume that we can only spare 11 memory buffer pages to perform the sort (an unrealistically small number, used for purposes of illustration). We can therefore perform a ten-way merge sort. After pass 1 we have blocks of size 10; after pass 2, size 100; after pass 3, size 1000; after pass 4, size 10,000; after pass 5, size 100,000, and we are done. Now it is important to realize that there is no opportunity to perform sequential prefetch I/O in the I/Os we are performing during block merge I/O. Therefore passes 1 through 4 each require 5000 page reads and 5000 writes, a total of 4 • 2 • 5000 = 40,000R. The final pass does not need to perform disk writes, since the rows are now in the right order to be returned to the user. We will materialize the rows in the final pass on buffered pages and output them as quickly as possible to the user, then deallocate the pages so the final writes are not needed. Therefore the I/O cost of the final pass is 5000R, and the total I/O cost for the sort is 45,000R, requiring 45,000/40 = 1125 seconds.

Note that the final pass of the sort step never has a cost for page writes unless a subsequent step requires a materialized table for input. It is much more common to pass off the output from one step to the input of the next step without materializing the rows passed. You should be sensitive to this "end-game" efficiency in the last pass of a sort. ■

In modern database systems the number of buffer pages available for a sort is large enough so that a two-pass sort is probably the longest anyone will see. We make a rough assumption that 100-page sorts occur entirely in memory and all other sorts occur in two passes.

8.9 Query Performance Benchmarks: A Case Study

A *software benchmark* is a prescription for a set of measurements to evaluate some category of software capability, usually performance. A good benchmark allows an administrator to make a purchase decision for a hardware/software platform based purely on cost-performance considerations. Alternatively, if the purchase is to be made based on other considerations, such as compatibility with existing systems, the administrator may wish to ensure that there are no cost-performance problems serious enough to alter this decision. Benchmarks also offer a good quality assurance test for software developers, allowing them to plan and implement their new product releases to improve performance in critical areas.

The *Set Query benchmark* presented in the next few sections measures database system performance for a wide range of queries. The queries are defined in terms of SQL, but can be implemented in other query languages as well and are meant to be portable to as many platforms as possible—for example **DB2** on an IBM system/390 mainframe, **ORACLE** on a Pyramid UNIX system, or FoxPro on MS DOS 486 PC. The measurements reported here resulted from a benchmark in which **DB2** version 2.3 was run on a small IBM system/390.

It is hoped that these concrete results, and the accompanying discussion of the query plans from which they arose, will solidify in the mind of the reader an appreciation for the way **DB2** performs queries that could not be achieved by discussion of theory alone. However, a great deal of detail is reported in the following sections, and mastery of these details may not come easily. The reader is encouraged to proceed with care to avoid confusion, to take the details that follow one at a time, and to refer to the exercises at the end of the chapter for a test of understanding. All of the basic principles needed to follow the discussion have already been presented, but frequent references to earlier sections for supporting details may be necessary.

Note that the Set Query benchmark has a difficult task comparing database performance of the many different architectures with which it must deal, and it achieves this comparison by imposing a simple unifying criterion, rating each platform with a single figure: dollar cost per query per minute (abbreviated $/QPM). The dollar cost of the system represents the cost for hardware, software, and maintenance over a five-year period. (Software and maintenance are often licensed on a monthly or yearly basis, even when the hardware is purchased all at once. At the end of five years, it is common to assume that the system is totally depreciated and to replace it with a newer, faster, and cheaper one.) The "query per minute" (QPM) rating for the system is a measurement of throughput for a specific query *workload* (see Section 8.1), all queries of the benchmark receiving equal weight. Although this may seem rather limiting, a more sophisticated approach is possible where the QPM rating for an arbitrary workload can be derived from published detailed timings, required by the benchmark, for each of the individual queries measured. This is an extremely flexible capability, and theoretically it allows the DBA to compare performance on different platforms for the specific workload for which the DBA is responsible.

In the Chapter 9 we will cover a different benchmark, known as the TPC-A benchmark, which measures database performance for update transactions; but for now we concentrate on **DB2** query performance to round out our coverage of query optimization.

The BENCH Table

The Set Query benchmark performs all its queries on a single table, known as the BENCH table, which is specified in great detail so that everyone performing the benchmark will get the same results. The default BENCH table contains 1 million rows of 200 bytes each, and the disk pages containing the rows should be loaded 95% full. (A BENCH table with more than 1 million rows is possible within the framework of the specification, but we do not consider this variation in what follows.) To offer indexed predicates with a range of filter factors, the BENCH table has 13 indexed columns with integer values, assumed to be 4 bytes in length. To start with, we have the KSEQ column, a key column with values 1, 2, . . ., 1,000,000, in the same order as the loaded rows. We see best performance if KSEQ is a column with perfect clustering, meaning that the rows in sequence by KSEQ, and the pages on which the rows lie, are all blocked together in successive order on disk. This can usually be achieved, even with database products that do not support clustering indexes, by using a freshly initialized disk to hold the data and sorting the rows in KSEQ order before loading them. All the other columns contain natural integer values with cardinality suggested by their name; for example, column K2 has only values 1 and 2, K4 has values 1, 2, 3, and 4. Figure 8.26 gives a list of all indexed columns in the BENCH table.

Column name	Range of values contained in the column
KSEQ	1, 2, . . . , 1,000,000 in sequential order
K2	1, 2 at random
K4	1, 2, 3, 4 at random
K5	1, 2, 3, 4, 5 at random
K10	1, 2, . . . , 10 at random
K25	1, 2, . . . , 25 at random
K100	1, 2, . . . , 100 at random
K1K	1, 2, . . . , 1000 at random
K10K	1, 2, . . . , 10,000 at random
K40K	1, 2, . . . , 40,000 at random
K100K	1, 2, . . . , 100,000 at random
K250K	1, 2, . . . , 250,000 at random
K500K	1, 2, . . . , 500,000 at random

Figure 8.26 Indexed Columns of the BENCH Table

Note that the letter K appearing at the end of a column name, as in "K40K," represents a factor of 1000. Thus K40K has values from 1 to 40,000. All indexed columns of the BENCH table other than the KSEQ column have randomly generated integer values in the appropriate range specified in Figure 8.26. The random number generation function assigning values to the columns is provided in the benchmark specification to ensure identical results for different sites performing the benchmark. Of course the numbers are only pseudo-random, since they are generated by a simple function. The effect, however, is that each column seems to have random values in the appropriate range. See Figure 8.27 for a tabulation of the indexed columns of the first ten rows of the BENCH table. The random nature of these columns allows us to give a rather precise statistical prediction of the result of many queries. For example, consider the query:

```
select count(*) from BENCH where K5 = 2;
```

Since there are five different values for K5, the filter factor for the predicate K5 = 2 is 1/5 = 0.20, and with 1 million rows in the BENCH table we expect to retrieve a number close to 200,000. (The actual number retrieved is 200,637.)

KSEQ	K500K	K250K	K100K	K40K	K10K	K1K	K100	K25	K10	K5	K4	K2
1	16808	225250	50074	23659	8931	273	45	4	4	5	1	2
2	484493	243043	7988	2504	2328	730	41	13	4	5	2	2
3	129561	70934	93100	279	1817	336	98	2	3	3	3	2
4	80980	129150	36580	38822	1968	673	94	12	6	1	1	2
5	140195	186358	35002	1154	6709	945	69	16	5	2	3	2
6	227723	204667	28550	38025	7802	854	78	9	9	4	3	2
7	28636	158014	23866	29815	9064	537	26	20	6	5	2	2
8	46518	184196	30106	10405	9452	299	89	24	6	3	1	1
9	436717	130338	54439	13145	1502	898	72	4	8	4	2	2
10	222295	227095	21610	26232	9746	176	36	24	3	5	1	1

Figure 8.27 Indexed Column Values for the First 10 Rows of the BENCH Table

The 13 indexed columns have a total length of 13 • 4 = 52 bytes. To make up the additional 148 bytes of a 200-byte row, the BENCH table has eight character columns that are never used in retrievals: S1 (char 8) and S2 through S8 (char 20). The decision to avoid queries by non-indexed columns is reasonable, considering the resource cost of a table space scan, which we will see shortly.

The rows contain 200 bytes of user information but are actually a bit longer because of necessary overhead information. With rows exactly 200 bytes in length, we would expect to be able to fit 20 rows on a 4-KB disk page loaded 100% full. With 1 million rows this would mean 1,000,000/ 20 = 50,000 pages for data rows. Because of the extra row length and the fact that pages are only 95% full, there are actually 18 rows to a page in **DB2** (version 2.3), and the number of data pages is CEIL(1,000,000/18) = 55,556. See Figure 8.28 for **DB2** statistics on the BENCH table.

All indexes are also loaded 95% full, one for each indexed column (there are no indexes that concatenate different columns), and index names are based on the corresponding column name with the letter X affixed; thus column K100 has index K100X. Indexes with an extremely large number of duplicate values, such as K2 through K100, have index entries averaging about 4 bytes in length because of index compression performed by **DB2**. Thus we should be able to fit about 1000 entries on each leaf page (if the pages were 100% full), and about 1000 index leaf pages would be needed to contain all entries. In Figure 8.28 we provide the actual measured values for the number of disk pages (NLEAF) for each index. For indexes with fewer duplicates, the compression becomes less valuable and the effective length greater, so that more disk pages are needed. There is no compression possible with KSEQ, and compression doesn't help with K500K, so NLEAF is largest for these indexes.

Note in Figure 8.28 that the COLCARD value for each column is what you would expect in all the low-cardinality columns, but it is surprisingly deficient in large-cardinality columns. For example, K500K has a COLCARD value of only 432,419, a good deal less than the 500,000 values possible. The reason for this becomes immediately apparent if we consider the random generation of column values and picture throwing 1 million darts into 500,000 slots. By formula (7.6.4), the expected number of slots hit is

$$M (1 - e^{-N/M}) = 500,000 (1 - e^{-2})$$

Working this out on a calculator, we get 432,332, close to the actual value observed.

	CARD	NPAGES
BENCH table	1000000	55,556

	COLCARD	INDEX NLEAF
KSEQ	1000000	2080
K500K	432419	2168
K250K	245497	1682
K100K	99996	1303
K40K	40000	1147
K10K	10000	1069
K1K	1000	1053
K100	100	1051
K25	25	1051
K10	10	1051
K5	5	1051
K4	4	1051
K2	2	1051

Figure 8.28   Statistics for the BENCH Table in **DB2** Version 2.3

Load Measurements

The measurements reported in what follows were taken running **DB2** version 2.3 on an IBM 9221 model 170 mainframe, with 1200 4-KB memory buffer pages (the buffer space required by the benchmark) and two 3390 disk drives (any number is permitted, but the greatest efficiency comes when one disk drive is used for data pages and one for indexes).

The elapsed and CPU times for loading the BENCH table and executing RUNSTATS to gather statistics are given in Figure 8.29, together with the disk storage required to hold the table and indexes.

	Elapsed time (secs)	CPU time (secs)	Disk MB
LOAD	10,170	3186	
RUNSTATS	5082	1535	
Disk space used			296

Figure 8.29   BENCH Table Load Measurements, **DB2** Version 2.3, IBM 9221 Model 170

8.10 Query Performance Measurements

In the following section we present measurements from running suites of queries labeled as Q1, Q2A, Q2B, Q3A, Q3B, Q4A, Q4B, Q5, Q6A, and Q6B. The reader is again warned to proceed with care, to take the details that follow one at a time. Each suite of queries normally consists of a set of measurements of a single SQL query form, with predicate variation to use a number of different indexed columns and provide a spectrum of filter factor characteristics. (See, for example, Figure 8.30 for query Q1 results.) Paired queries such as Q2A and Q2B have comparable but slightly different SQL forms.

For each query measured we provide the elapsed time in seconds (that is, wall clock time waiting for response), CPU time in seconds, and count of pages requested, broken down into random I/Os, sequential prefetch I/Os, and list prefetch I/Os. (Any two of these I/O counts can be zero.) These numbers are extracted from a standard MVS logging facility by the DB2PM product (**DB2** performance monitor), which is licensed separately and priced in Section 8.11. The random I/Os reported are designated *sync I/Os* in DB2PM reports. Note that all queries reported here are submitted as Embedded SQL statements from a program, and the elapsed and CPU times reported are slightly less than what you would see submitting ad hoc queries from the standard user interface (SPUFI). We also try to make the I/O measurements consistent by flushing the memory buffers in advance of each query suite, so that disk pages to be accessed are not likely to be already resident. The process used to flush the buffers is to perform a long query of a different kind, so some small overlap is possible as in normal use. We explain the results from each query as we progress, in terms of the EXPLAIN results from **DB2**.

Query Q1

Query Q1 has the form:

```
For each KN ∈ {KSEQ, K100K, . . ., K4, K2}
    select count(*) from BENCH where KN = 2;
```

As indicated by the set notation preceding the Select statement, the symbol "KN" stands for any one of the indexed columns KSEQ, K100K, ..., K4, K2. Each of these cases represents a query with measures given in Figure 8.30, and together they make up the Q1 query "suite."

Note that Q1 is a typical early query in text retrieval applications (see Example 3.10.7). A user searching for all published journal articles with a specific keyword in the abstract might well start by asking how many articles contain that keyword, and then later refine the search further until the number of articles counted is small enough to retrieve the full abstracts of the documents. Clearly the filter factor of the keyword might vary dramatically and unexpectedly from one keyword to another (keyword = 'experiment%' vs. keyword = 'ruthenium'), and this motivates having KN range over various column cardinalities.

KN	Elapsed time (secs)	CPU time (secs)	Get page requests	Random I/O count	Sequential prefetch I/O count	List prefetch I/O count
KSEQ	1.33	0.07	3	3		
K100K	0.59	0.08	3	3		
K10K	0.89	0.07	3	3		
K1K	0.67	0.09	4	4		
K100	0.83	0.19	14	2	2	
K25	1.73	0.58	44	25	3	
K10	2.20	1.34	107	54	5	
K5	3.47	2.55	214	46	9	
K4	5.09	3.13	265	57	10	
K2	7.73	6.17	528	48	18	

Figure 8.30 Q1 Measurements

The EXPLAIN command applied to all queries in the Q1 suite shows that the appropriate KN index is used (for example, in the case where KN represents K100, ACCESSTYPE = I, and ACCESSNAME = K100X), and also that the query is resolved entirely in the index without recourse to the data (INDEXONLY = Y). Thus in the top row of Figure 8.30, where KN represents KSEQ (we symbolize this in what follows by KN ≡ KSEQ), we see that three random I/Os are performed to access the three levels of the

KSEQX index down to the unique entry at the leaf level. Recall that the buffer has been flushed of most useful pages, so the maximum number of I/Os is usually performed.

In all cases with duplicate values, the predicate KN = 2 is resolved in index by walking down to the leftmost value 2 in the appropriate index leaf level, then progressing from left to right until there are no more entries with value 2. For the predicate K100K = 2, this means that approximately ten entries are traversed; for K10K, 100 entries; and so on. (The precise number of rows retrieved for most queries in the Set Query benchmark is given in Appendix C.) Since nearly 1000 entries fit on each leaf page, we would not expect more than three I/Os for the two predicates just mentioned (the leaf-level traversal will probably not cross pages), and perhaps four for K1K = 2, with 1000 entries (where the traversal is practically guaranteed to cross from one leaf page to another). With the predicate K2 = 2, we would expect to traverse approximately 500,000 entries at the leaf level, and this implies about 526 leaf pages, or half of NLEAF for the K2X index (see Figure 8.28). We see from the number of Get Page requests, G = 528, that these 526 leaf pages, and an additional two index pages are accessed. We also see that 18 sequential prefetch I/Os are performed and 48 random I/Os. We can calculate the total number of pages accessed through prefetch as (528 − 48) = 480, and the average number of pages read in each prefetch as (480)/18 = 26.7. Note that **DB2** uses 18 sequential prefetch I/Os of 26.7 pages each, rather than the maximum prefetch size of 32 pages. The reasons for this are technical and are of little interest, but note that short prefetch I/Os of this kind appear on several rows of measurements for Q1.

Most of the elapsed time for the longer queries arises from CPU time, however, rather than I/O wait time. We can roughly calculate the elapsed time for I/O using our rule of thumb. In the K2 case, 480S at 400S per second gives 1.20 seconds, and 48R at 40R per second gives 1.20 seconds, so the total I/O elapsed time is 2.40 seconds. Adding a CPU time of 6.17 seconds, we come up with 8.57 elapsed seconds. Since the elapsed time was only 7.73 seconds, we conclude that some of the I/O time overlapped with CPU time, a perfectly reasonable effect that we continue to see in queries that follow. The range of CPU time measurements is well predicted by a linear function of the number of leaf-level entries traversed. If the predicted CPU time is represented by T and the number of entries traversed is N, then we can write:

$$T = .0000122 \cdot N + 0.07$$

This linear form has a maximum error of 0.05 seconds across the entire range of measurements. Here the constant 0.07 seconds represents a relatively constant startup cost, and the constant .0000122 seconds represents the time needed to deal with (that is, count) each leaf-level entry, not counting overhead for I/O and other operations that are less significant. Given that this is a 6.5 MIPS CPU, the actual number of instructions executed for each entry is (6,500,000) (0.0000122) = 79, an important improvement over past releases, but still somewhat large when we consider that all that is being done is to count successive entries in a long list. Much more efficient counting methods exist; the original Set Query paper measured performance of a database product known as MODEL 204, which performed Q1 queries 20 to 30 times more efficiently. But most relational database products are not as efficient as **DB2** in terms of CPU.

Query Q2A

Query Q2A has the form:

```
For each KN ∈ {KSEQ, K100K, . . ., K4}
    select count(*) from BENCH where K2 = 2 and KN = 3;
```

The measurements are shown in Figure 8.31a.

KN	Elapsed time (secs)	CPU time (secs)	Get page requests	Random I/O count	Sequential prefetch I/O count	List prefetch I/O count
KSEQ	0.38	0.08	4	4		
K100K	1.27	0.09	14	4		1
K10K	2.27	0.14	100	4		4
K1K	12.46	0.39	969	7		31
K100	71.33	2.29	9167	17	3	287
K25	108.41	7.59	28,935	45	4	903
K10	125.83	14.35	47,248	47	5	1474
K5	135.19	21.05	54,792	61	8	1706
K4	133.27	26.90	55,559	56	1737	

Figure 8.31a   Q2A Measurements

Q2A is another typical early query in text retrieval application, searching for journal articles with two properties, one with a low filter factor (date > '65/01/31' and keyword = 'Plutonium'). Query Q2A might also be used in direct-marketing applications to estimate the number of prospects with a given pair of qualities (sex = 'M' and hobby = 'Tennis'). One of the reasons this query type was included in the benchmark was to measure how well a database product performs in combining RID lists from two separate indexes. As we have learned, the **DB2** product has the capability to combine such RID lists by using the MX type plan explained in Section 8.6. Having combined the two indexes, there is no need to ever access the data rows, since the target list contains only a count(*) function that can be satisfied by counting the final RID list.

However, the EXPLAIN command for this suite of queries shows that an MX plan is never used, and the reason is quite illuminating. Recall that a single RID list can use only 50% of the RID pool, and the RID pool space is half the size of the disk buffer pool. Since there are 1200 pages in the disk buffer pool allowed by the benchmark, the RID pool contains 600 pages worth of space, or about 2400 KB. Now consider the predicate K2 = 2. We expect to find 500,000 rows that satisfy this predicate, and 500,000 RIDs, at 4 bytes each, take up 2000 KB—more than the 50% of the 2400 KB of the RID pool. Therefore the predicate K2 = 2 cannot be extracted in an MX-type plan, and an alternative plan must be used.

The EXPLAIN command for the Q2A suite reveals that **DB2** uses two different plans for different queries. In cases where KN does not represent K4 (KN ≠ K4), **DB2** uses the predicate with the smaller filter factor (KN = 3) in a matching index scan (ACCESSTYPE = I) to retrieve rows from the data, then tests each row to resolve the remaining predicate, counting the rows that satisfy both conditions. In the case where KN ≡ K4, however, a table space scan is used (ACCESSTYPE = R) to solve the query. In the bottom row of Figure 8.31a, where KN ≡ K4, we see 1737 sequential prefetch I/Os and 56 random I/Os performed. The total number of pages read in is 55,559 (note that in Figure 8.28, NPAGES = 55,556). Sequential prefetch I/O reads (55,559 − 56) = 55,503 pages, and we see 55,508/1737 = 32 pages per sequential prefetch. Our rule of thumb says that the elapsed time required for 55,503S is 55,503/400 seconds = 138.76 seconds, and the 56R adds a relatively insignificant 1.4 seconds. Obviously this gives a slight overestimate of about 5%—138.76 + 1.4 = 140.16 seconds compared to the measured time of 133.27 seconds. We can assume that the CPU time of 26.90 seconds completely overlaps with I/O during this heavily I/O-limited query.

Now consider the predicates on the other randomly generated columns referenced in suite Q2A, $KN = 3$ where $KN \in \{K100K, K10K, K1K, K100, K25, K10, K5\}$. The measurements for random and sequential prefetch I/Os for the corresponding rows of Figure 8.31a correspond to the resources used to scan through the appropriate index and compare quite closely to the INDEXONLY measures of Q1. (For example, the resources to evaluate the predicate $K5 = 3$ in Figure 8.31a are eight sequential prefetch I/Os and 61 random I/Os. In Figure 8.30, the index I/O resources to evaluate the predicate $K5 = 2$ are nine sequential prefetch I/Os and 46 random I/Os.) The list prefetch I/Os appearing in Figure 8.31 are used exclusively to access the desired rows. In the case of $K100K = 3$, there are about ten rows retrieved—probably all on separate disk pages—and there is one list prefetch I/O. A list prefetch I/O can access *up to* 32 pages, but in this case it accesses only about ten. Similarly, in the case $K10K = 3$, there are about 100 rows retrieved—probably on 100 distinct disk pages—and four list prefetch I/Os. Consider the case where $K100 = 3$. The number of rows retrieved is about 10,000. To see the number of disk pages retrieved, picture this as the problem of throwing 10,000 darts randomly into 55,556 disk pages and asking how many pages are hit. Formula (7.6.4) gives us

$$E(\text{No. Pages Hit}) = M\,(1 - e^{-N/M}) = 55{,}556\,(1 - e^{\,(-10{,}000/55{,}556)}\,) = 9152$$

Now to calculate the number of list prefetch I/Os needed to pick up 9,196 disk pages, we take $CEIL(9{,}152/32) = 286$, quite close to the 287 list prefetch I/Os performed.

The fact that an MX-type plan cannot be used for this query suite is a serious problem. If we could combine indexes without going to the data, the maximum elapsed times for Q2A would probably compare best to the Q1 time for $K2$ plus some other time in Q1 to extract the RID list of KN, a maximum of less than 20 seconds. Instead, we see numerous much larger elapsed times. Note that **DB2** had enough RID pool space in most cases to handle the Q2A queries (the final case might not fit), but an inflexible rule made it impossible to take advantage of this. This is not the behavior we might expect from a query optimizer. Still, **DB2** has a good deal of flexibility, and the lesson to take from this is that *the DBA should always plan a buffer pool as large as possible, and order more memory if necessary.*

614

Query Q2B

Query Q2B has the form:

```
For each KN ∈ {KSEQ, K100K, . . ., K4}
    select count(*) from BENCH where K2 = 2 and not KN = 3;
```

See Figure 8.31b for the measurements of this query suite.

KN	Elapsed time (secs)	CPU time (secs)	Get page requests	Random I/O count	Sequential prefetch I/O count	List prefetch I/O count
KSEQ	142.73	30.07	55,569	56	1737	
K100K	137.83	30.24	55,568	63	1737	
K10K	137.45	30.12	55,569	47	1737	
K1K	140.33	30.42	55,569	59	1737	
K100	141.73	30.17	55,569	59	1737	
K25	144.65	30.25	55,569	60	1737	
K10	139.72	29.82	55,569	53	1737	
K5	142.73	30.07	55,569	56	1737	
K4	135.29	29.13	55,562	48	1737	

Figure 8.31b Q2B Measurements

Q2B is a variant of Q2A that was suggested when the Set Query benchmark was originally being tested with a group of commercial users. It represents a query type that finds use in cases where it can be efficiently executed (MODEL 204 users can usually get a response to this query in less than a second). In the case of **DB2**, a number of problems arise for efficient indexed use. We would like to see the query optimizer perform a non-matching index scan to extract an RID list for the predicate "not KN = 3" and then perform MX processing with the predicate K2 = 2, thus avoiding accesses to all the table rows. However, the RID list for K2 = 2 cannot be extracted, as we saw in the discussion of Q2A, because of the limited size of the RID pool. Even if there were no limitation on the RID pool, another factor rules out MX processing, since **DB2** will not perform a non-matching index scan on KN to extract an RID list. With the KN index ruled out, a simple index scan on the predicate K2 = 2 does not have sufficient filtering power to exclude any disk pages from consideration (there are 17 rows per page), so the query optimizer chooses a table space scan for all queries of the Q2B suite. Measurements compare to the K4 row of Q2A.

Query Q3A

Query Q3A has the form:

```
For each KN ∈ {K100K, K10K, K100, K25, K10, K5, K4}
    select sum(K1K) from BENCH
        where KSEQ between 400000 and 500000 and KN = 3;
```

Figure 8.32a contains measurements of this query suite.

KN	Elapsed time (secs)	CPU time (secs)	Get page requests	Random I/O count	Sequential prefetch I/O count	List prefetch I/O count
K100K	1.84	0.09	24	8		1
K10	2.06	0.14	110	8		4
K100	14.43	3.12	5778	200	184	
K25	14.89	3.37	5778	202	184	
K10	15.35	3.73	5778	199	184	
K5	15.07	4.17	5778	208	184	
K4	15.01	4.24	5778	197	184	

Figure 8.32a   Q3A Measurements

Query Q3A was created to model a direct-marketing type of application, where rows of a prospects table within a range of zip codes (in a given geographical area) and having some other property (hobby = 'tennis') must be examined in detail. Up to now, all queries considered have been ones that could be satisfied by examining only index information. (Although **DB2**'s rules make this impossible in Q2A and Q2B, MODEL 204 is able to satisfy these queries in index only, with much faster response times.) In the Q3A case, however, the set function sum(K1K) cannot be satisfied in index, since the K1K values do not appear in any index used in the **where** clause. (Note that Figure 8.32a has no entry for KN ≡ K1K, so the INDEXONLY case is avoided.) Therefore the rows selected must be accessed in order to sum the K1K values. Although Query Q3A retrieves only a single set function value, it does most of the work of a query that retrieves a column value from each row.

The EXPLAIN command reveals that there are two different types of query plans used in performing this suite. For KN ≡ K100K and KN ≡ K10K, a matching index scan is performed on K100K and K10K respectively, and the predicate on KSEQ is then tested for the rows retrieved. In Figure 8.32a the random I/Os are used to retrieve the index entries, and the list prefetch I/Os are used to retrieve the rows, approximately ten rows with one prefetch in the K100K case and 100 rows with four prefetches in the K10K case. It turns out that with a maximum of 100 rows to retrieve using random I/O, there is no advantage to be gained in performing multiple index access, extracting an RID list from KSEQ to save some of those row accesses—we have reached the point of diminishing returns seen in Section 8.6.

For low-cardinality columns, KN ∈ {K100, K25, K10, K5, K4}, the **between** predicate on KSEQ is used in a matching index scan, and the predicate on KN is tested for the rows retrieved. For each of these cases, Figure 8.32a shows that 5778 pages are read in. Most of these represent about 10% of the index leaf pages and 10% of the data pages to evaluate the predicate "KSEQ between 400000 and 500000," and we can calculate this from the statistics of Figure 8.28 as NLEAF/10 + NPAGES/10 = 208 + 5556 = 5764 pages. We see that 184 sequential prefetch I/Os are used to retrieve 5778 − 200 = 5578 pages (in the KN ≡ K100 case, relatively representative I/O use for the low-cardinality columns), and this means that the average number of pages read in sequential prefetch I/Os is about 30.3.

DB2 performs extremely well in this query suite, beating MODEL 204 and all other current products by a wide margin, because of the unique prefetch I/O capability that is part of the **DB2** bag of tricks, aided by intelligent disk controllers.

Query Q3B

Query Q3B has the form:

```
For each KN ∈ {K100K, K10K, K100, K25, K10, K5, K4}
    select sum(K1K) from BENCH
        where (KSEQ between 400000 and 410000
        or KSEQ between 420000 and 430000
        or KSEQ between 440000 and 450000
        or KSEQ between 460000 and 470000
        or KSEQ between 480000 and 500000)
        and KN = 3;
```

Figure 8.32b lists the measurements of this query.

KN	Elapsed time (secs)	CPU time (secs)	Get page requests	Random I/O count	Sequential prefetch I/O count	List prefetch I/O count
K100K	2.01	0.09	17	5		1
K10K	2.23	0.14	109	7		4
K100	7.57	2.48	714	34	12	18
K25	10.66	3.66	1934	57	7	55
K10	14.37	5.93	3068	79	14	88
K5	57.76	47.33	5430	250	173	
K4	57.77	47.58	5430	235	173	

Figure 8.32b Q3B Measurements

Query Q3B was created as a variant of Query Q3A after experience with direct-marketing applications showed that prospects in a given geographical area do not normally fall within a single range of zip codes, but in a union of different ranges. In addition, the query is a good one to evaluate advanced capabilities of the query optimizer. Note that the **between** predicates, connected by ORs in this query, together make up 60% of the single range covered in Q3A (a total 6% of the KSEQ range and clustered data range).

The EXPLAIN command shows three different types of query plans used to perform the Q3B suite. As with Q3A, when KN ≡ K100K or KN ≡

K10K a matching index scan is performed on K100K and K10K respectively, and the predicates on KSEQ are then tested for the rows retrieved to determine if one of them holds. The measurements for these cases are very similar to those of Q3A. For the two lowest-cardinality columns, KN ≡ K5 and KN ≡ K4, EXPLAIN shows a plan with ACCESSTYPE = I, ACCESSNAME = KSEQX, and MATCHCOLS = 0; in other words, a non-matching index scan on KSEQ. What seems to be happening is that the KSEQ index values ranging from 400,000 to 500,000 are examined, and for each value the KSEQ predicates are tested to determine that one of them holds. With the resulting RIDs, rows from the BENCH table are read in (sequential prefetch I/O is used, because the data is clustered by KSEQ), and the remaining KN = 3 predicate is tested. We see that a somewhat smaller number of sequential prefetch I/Os are being used in this case than in the Q3A results, since a smaller number of rows is being retrieved. The fact that the reduced number of sequential prefetch I/Os in Q3B exceeds 60% of the number in Q3A is not fully explained. Note that in these two cases, the CPU resources used (and resulting elapsed times) are extremely large compared to the CPU resources used in comparable cases of Q3A. This seems to arise from the necessity to test a number of **between** predicates on all values extracted from index in the non-matching index scan, and represents a serious resource cost.

ACCESSTYPE	MATCHCOLS	ACCESSNAME	PREFETCH	MIXOPSEQ
M	0		L	0
MX	1	K100X	S	1
MX	1	KSEQX	S	2
MX	1	KSEQX	S	3
MU	0			4
MX	1	KSEQX	S	5
MU	0			6
MX	1	KSEQX	S	7
MU	0			8
MX	1	KSEQX	S	9
MU	0			10
MI	0			11

Figure 8.33 EXPLAIN Plan for Q3B, in the Case KN = K100

For intermediate-cardinality columns, KN ∈ {K100, K25, K10}, MX
processing is used to take the union of RID lists from the different **between**
predicates on KSEQ, then intersect the result with the RID list from the
predicate KN = 3. For example, the plan for the case KN ≡ K100 is given in
Figure 8.33. In Figure 8.32b you should assume that sequential prefetch I/O
is being used to access the KN and KSEQ index values, and then list prefetch
is being used to access the data pages. The **DB2** query optimizer probably
makes a mistake in this query suite using a non-matching index scan in the
two cases of lowest-cardinality columns, judging by the large jump in CPU
use for these cases. Nevertheless, performance is quite good compared to
most other products.

Queries Q4A and Q4B

The two variant query suites Q4A and Q4B have the form:

```
select KSEQ, K500K from BENCH
    where <constraint with 3 (Q4A) or 5 (Q4B) ANDed predicates>;
```

Queries in suite Q4A have three predicates and queries in suite Q4B have
five predicates chosen from the sequence of ten predicates given in Figure
8.34. The filter factor for each predicate is given in a column on the right.

No.	Predicate	FF	No.	Predicate	FF
(1)	K2 = 1	1/2	(6)	K4 = 3	1/4
(2)	K100 > 80	1/5	(7)	K100 < 41	2/5
(3)	K10K between 2000 and 3000	1/10	(8)	K1K between 850 and 950	1/10
(4)	K5 = 3	1/5	(9)	K10 = 7	1/10
(5)	(K25 = 11 or K25 = 19)	2/25	(10)	K25 between 3 and 4	2/25

Figure 8.34   Predicate Sequence, with Filter Factors FF, for Suite Q4

Predicates used in a query are chosen in sequence within the 1–10
order, with a given starting point and wraparound from predicate 10 back
to predicate 1. For example, a query from suite Q4A with three predicates
and starting point 5 will have predicates in the range 5–7 (that is, {5, 6, 7}),
with the following form:

```
select KSEQ, K500K from BENCH
    where (K25 - 11 or K25 = 19) and K4 = 3 and K100 < 41;
```

A query in suite Q4B with five predicates and starting point 7 will have predicates in the range 7–1 (that is {7, 8, 9, 10, 1}), and the following form:

```
select KSEQ, K500K from BENCH
    where K100 < 41 and K1K between 850 and 950 and K10 = 7
    and K25 between 3 and 4 and K2 = 1;
```

A query of the kind measured in Q4A and Q4B is representative of a final form query resulting from document retrieval search (for example, limiting articles by keywords, journal where they appeared, period of appearance, etc.) or direct-mail applications (for example, retrieving name and address for prospects in a given salary range, sex, hobby, geographical location, etc.). The measurements for query suites Q4A and Q4B are given in Figures 8.35a and 8.35b, respectively.

Predicate sequence range	Elapsed time (secs)	CPU time (secs)	Get page requests	Random I/O count	Sequential prefetch I/O count	List prefetch I/O count
1–3	109.04	32.29	17,321	102	14	531
2–4	62.10	26.91	4409	155	22	121
3–5	107.29	16.50	17,112	111	14	525
4–6	134.55	27.02	54,802	72	8	1706
5–7	156.67	39.47	55,834	126	1747	
6–8	127.00	30.42	47,378	73	5	1477
7–9	83.07	14.94	9393	115	11	287
8–10	22.74	10.69	1097	154	16	25

Figure 8.35a Q4A Measurements

EXPLAIN tells us that the queries of Suite Q4A all use either index scans or MX processing. Certain predicates from the sequence of Figure 8.34 are never used for indexing: predicate (1) with FF = 1/2, predicate (7) with FF = 1/5, and predicate (5) requiring a non-matching index scan, which is not allowed in RID processing, or else an MU step to achieve FF = 2/25. In addition, predicate (6), with FF = 1/4, is only used for the query with predicate range 5–7, where otherwise there would be no indexable predicate (since (5) and (7) are ruled out). Presumably the unused predicates are not used because of diminishing returns, as explained in Section 8.6. All query plans use all other predicates in the given range for indexing. This implies, for example, that the query with predicate range 1–3 performs MX processing on predicates (2) and (3) (predicate (1) is never used); the query with predicate range 5–7 is solved by a matching index scan on predicate (6), and the only place where this predicate is ever used, since predicates (5) and (7) are ruled out; finally, the query with predicate range 8–10 performs MX processing on all three predicates, (8), (9), and (10), since none of these is ruled out.

Knowing the predicates used, it is possible to estimate the number of rows accessed in the table and to confirm the reported number of I/Os. For example, with range 8–10, the product of the filter factors with the number of rows in the BENCH table gives (1/10) (1/10) (2/25) (1,000,000) = 800. This is also the total number of rows retrieved, since no other predicates exist, and from Appendix C we see that the precise number of rows retrieved in this case is 785. Sequential prefetch I/Os are generally used to access index data, and list prefetch I/Os to access data pages. Since the 785 rows to be retrieved lie on (to a first approximation) nearly 785 data pages, they can be brought into memory with CEIL(785/32) = 25 list prefetch I/Os, the number listed in Figure 8.35a for range 8–10.

Predicate sequence range	Elapsed time (secs)	CPU time (secs)	Get page requests	Random I/O count	Sequential prefetch I/O count	List prefetch I/O count
1–5	63.17	21.06	416	127	22	121
2–6	62.06	20.90	4416	165	22	121
3–7	109.02	15.72	17,377	160	24	525
4–8	109.60	15.82	17,613	180	23	532
5–9	84.30	10.48	9658	175	21	287
6–10	22.64	9.59	1092	161	16	25
7–1	22.96	9.71	1090	157	16	25

Figure 8.35b Q4B Measurements

More predicates are available from among the five used for queries in suite Q4B, so we expect consistent MX processing throughout and much smaller answer sets. EXPLAIN tells us that the queries of suite Q4B all use MX processing with three predicates, and that the predicates used are always the ones with the smallest filter factors, except that predicate (5), requiring a non-matching index scan or MU processing, is never used. Thus, for example, the query with predicate range 4–8 performs MX processing on three of the predicates (4), (6), (7), and (8), with FF values 1/5, 1/4, 2/5, and 1/10, respectively, and chooses the three predicates with smallest values, (4), (6), and (8). For another example, we note that the query with predicate range 7–1 has predicates (7), (8), (9), (10), and (1) to choose from, and selects the three predicates with smallest FF values, (8), (9), and (10), the same as the query having predicate range 8–10 in suite Q4A. As a result, the I/Os for these two queries of Q4A and Q4B are nearly identical. The number of rows in the solution set for the Q4B query, however, is reduced from that of the Q4A query (785 from the discussion earlier), as a result of the filter factors of the two additional predicates, (1) and (7), so that the answer set is approximately (1/2) (2/5) (785) = 157. From Appendix C, we see that the exact number of rows retrieved in this Q4B query is 152.

Query Q5

Query Q5 has the form:

```
For each pair (KN1, KN2) ∈ { (K2, K100), (K10, K25), K10, K25) }
    select KN1, KN2, count(*) from BENCH
        group by KN1, KN2;
```

The measurements for query suite Q5 are given in Figure 8.36.

KN1, KN2	Elapsed time (secs)	CPU time (secs)	Get page requests	Random I/O count	Sequential prefetch I/O count	List prefetch I/O count
K2, K100	242	219	55,896	81	1737	
K4, K25	230	208	55,802	34	1737	
K10, K25	248	223	55,903	87	1737	

Figure 8.36 Q5 Measurements

This query suite is representative of an application known as *crosstabs,* used in decision support systems to calculate the effect of one factor on another in a population. For example, a department store might have a table of `customers`, with columns containing information on `hobby` and `incomeclass`, and one giving levels of purchase totals (1–10, like incomeclass) in various store departments—for example, `sportsw_purchases` in the sportswear department. A crosstabs analysis of type Q5 can be used to see if there is some correlation between `hobby` and any desired category of purchases:

```
select count(*) from customers
    group by hobby, sportsw_purchases;
```

If some hobbies, such as sailing, show a high concentration of high-level purchases, then this group is a good choice to receive a mailing announcing a coming sale in the sportswear department.

EXPLAIN shows that queries in suite Q5 are implemented in two-step plans. In the first step (PLANNO = 1), a table space scan (ACCESSTYPE = R) goes through all the data pages and extracts the column pairs (KN1, KN2) into a temporary table. Certain I/Os to perform writes into this temporary table are not shown in Figure 8.36, because they are not reported. (Page writes do not generally occur as part of the plan, but later as the buffer pool runs out of space and must write changed pages out to disk to make room; the pages for this data are only used temporarily, however, and may escape being written out to disk entirely.) In the second step (PLANNO = 2), a sort step is performed on this temporary table (METHOD = 3, SORTC_GROUPBY = Y) on both columns KN1 and KN2, with the result that all identical terms are collected together, and in the output from this sort the number of pairs (KN1, KN2) of each identical type is counted and put out to the answer set. We see in Figure 8.36 the signature of a table space scan, 1735 sequential prefetch I/Os, that we have seen before. The CPU time makes up a large proportion of the elapsed time for these queries.

Query Q6A

Query suites Q6A and Q6B exercise joins of two tables. Q6A has the form:

```
For each KN ∈ {K100K, K40K, K10K, K1K, K100}
    select count(*) from BENCH B1, BENCH B2
        where B1.KN = 49 and B1.K250K = B2.K500K;
```

The measurements for query suite Q6A are given in Figure 8.37a.

KN	Elapsed time (secs)	CPU time (secs)	Get page requests	Random I/O count	Sequential prefetch I/O count	List prefetch I/O count
K100K	0.95	0.10	65	12		1
K40K	1.00	0.14	115	7		1
K10K	3.75	0.29	393	22		4
K1K	16.05	1.68	2313	15	36	31
K100	83.31	13.35	111,510	45	48	290

Figure 8.37a Q6A Measurements

Although the BENCH table plays two roles in this query, as B1 and B2, there is no advantage gained thereby over the case where two distinct tables exist, except for a very minor improvement in buffer residence. EXPLAIN tells us that all queries of suite Q6A are implemented as two-step plans performing nested loop join. In step 1 (PLANNO = 1) we use a matching index scan loop on KN to extract an RID list for rows to be extracted from the outer table (TABNO = 1—that is, rows with B1.KN = 49). For each row retrieved from B1 in the outer loop, the value B1.K250K has a fixed constant value, which we designate by K. In step 2 the nested loop join (METHOD = 1), assuming a fixed row from the outer table B1, retrieves the count of rows in B2 where B2.K500K = K. A matching index scan on K500K is used for this, and since only a count is retrieved, the step has INDEXONLY = Y. Note that for each row found in the outer table, we expect to find about two rows in the inner table, since B2.K500K = K is true for about two rows of B2, as long as K lies in the range 1, 2, . . ., 500,000; and since K is extracted from B1.K250K this is certainly the case. Thus with KN ≡ K100, for example, we expect to find 10,000 rows in the outer table and a total of about 20,000 rows after the join with matching columns, which determines the total number of rows in the final answer from the inner table. From Appendix C, we see that the precise count retrieved is 19,948.

In this case, KN ≡ K100, approximately 10,000 rows from B1 must be accessed in the outer loop. As we calculated earlier in analyzing Q2A, these lie on approximately 9152 data pages, and the page reads are accomplished with 290 list prefetch I/Os. Most of the remaining I/Os are used to retrieve leaf-level entries from the K500K index to perform the final count.

Query Q6B

Query Q6B has the form:

```
For each KN ∈ {K40K, K10K, K1K, K100}
    select B1.KSEQ, B2.KSEQ from BENCH B1, BENCH B2
        where B1.KN = 99 and B1.K250K = B2.K500K and B2.K25 = 19;
```

The measurements for query suite Q6B are given in Figure 8.37b.

KN	Elapsed time (secs)	CPU time (secs)	Get page requests	Random I/O count	Sequential prefetch I/O count	List prefetch I/O count
K40K	2.66	0.27	161	97		1
K10K	11.03	0.91	720	418		4
K1K	77.27	6.68	5164	2842	36	31
K100	191.59	27.59	38,646	86	67	1190

Figure 8.37b Q6B Measurements

Query Q6B is similar to Q6A except for the new restriction on table B2 (B2.K25 = 19) and the fact that data, rather than just a count, is retrieved from columns in both tables. The EXPLAIN command shows that nested loop join (METHOD = 1) is used for queries in suite Q6B with KN ∈ {K40K, K10K, K1K}, but a merge join (METHOD = 2) is used when KN ≡ K100.

To start with discussion of the nested loop join processing, the plan is very similar to the one used for all queries in suite Q6A. A matching index scan on KN is used to extract rows from the outer table, with B1.KN = 99. For each row retrieved from B1 we designate the fixed constant value B1.K250K by K. In the inner loop, instead of just retrieving a count from the K500K index, we retrieve rows in B2 where B2.K500K = K. These rows are then qualified by testing that B2.K25 = 19, and the resulting rows are joined with the row from outer table B1. Note that for each row found in the outer table, we expect to find about two rows in the inner table with B2.K500K = K, as explained in the Q6A discussion. This time, however, the resulting row lies in the answer set only if B2.K25 = 19, and so the number of total rows in the join is shrunk by a factor of 1/25. In the case where KN ≡ K1K, we would expect 1000 rows in the outer table B1 and 2000 rows retrieved from B2, but only $(1/25)$ (2000) = 80 rows in the final join. As we see from Appendix C, the precise number is 81 rows. Note that the I/Os for this case in Figure 8.37b are nearly identical to the I/Os that take place in the comparable case for Q6A, except that there are 2827 more random I/Os. We would expect accesses through to rows in B2 through the predicate B2.K500K = 19 to require about three I/Os (one index leaf and two data pages) for each of the 1000 rows found in the outer table, and the somewhat smaller number 2827 no doubt arises because of buffer hits on the K500K index leaf pages.

In the Q6B case where KN ≡ K100, a merge join takes place. In step 1, all the rows in B1 with B1.K100 = 99 are selected with an index scan on K100 and projected onto two column rows, (B1.KSEQ, B1.K250K), placed in a temporary intermediate table IT1. Similarly, the rows in B2 with B2.K25 = 19 are selected with an index scan on K25 and projected onto rows (B2.KSEQ, B2.K500K) in a temporary table IT2. Both tables IT1 and IT2 are sorted, IT1 by sortkey B1.K250K and IT2 by sortkey B2.K500K. Then IT1 and IT2 are joined on B1.K250K = B2.K500K with the forward moving cursor procedure of Figure 8.5.3. Considering I/O resources, we see that the index scan on B1.K100 requires a sequential prefetch I/O to retrieve the relevant index and then a number of list prefetch I/Os to retrieve approximately 10,000 rows. These 10,000 rows will lie on a number of pages calculated in the discussion of Q2A, $58,824 \cdot (1 - e^{(-10,000/58,824)}) = 9196$. Thus the number of list prefetch I/Os required to access these rows is CEIL(9196/32) = 288. The index scan on B2.K25 requires about two sequential prefetch I/Os to retrieve the relevant index and then a number of list prefetch I/Os to retrieve approximately 40,000 rows. The approximate number of pages needed to retrieve these rows is $58,824 \cdot (1 - e^{(-40,000/58,824)}) = 29,023$. This implies that we will need CEIL(29,023/32) = 907 list prefetch I/Os. For a total number of list prefetch I/Os, we arrive at 288 + 907 = 1195, rather close to the measured number, 1190.

8.11 Cost-Performance Assessment

The Set Query benchmark provides a rating for a hardware/software platform in terms of dollar cost per query per minute ($/QPM). Because all platforms are provided with the same data and respond with the same query answers, the dollar cost to provide these answers is considered a fair measure. The QPM rating for the platform is easily calculated. There are 69 queries in the benchmark, all weighted the same. If we say that the elapsed time to measure all the queries of the benchmark is T minutes, then we are running at a rate of 69/T queries per minute. Adding up the elapsed times for all queries of Section 8.10, we get 4492.24 seconds, or 74.87 minutes, so the QPM rating is 69/74.87 = 0.9216 queries per minute.

The dollar cost of the system represents the cost for hardware, software, and maintenance over a five-year period. The platform for the queries measured in Section 8.10 was an IBM 9221 model 170, running **DB2** version 2.3 on the MVS XA 2.2 operating system. The five-year price for this system is based on the retail prices from October 1993 given in Figure 8.38. The DASD (IBM's name for disk) costs are an exception, representing used prices, since the devices are no longer sold by IBM. Note that monthly maintenance costs are free during the first year of hardware ownership, so only 48 months are charged. Software cannot normally be purchased and the first 2 months are free, so prices are for monthly license (a small initial fee is charged for the MVS operating system).

Priced item	Purchase price	Monthly charges (5 years)		
		Charges	Months	Total
IBM 9221 model 170	$252,350	$775	48	$37,200
Ancillary hardware				
1 Channel group	$35,450	None		
Rack enclosure	$3820	$4	48	$192
DASD controller 3880-E23	$3000	$158	48	$7584
DASD device 3380-AE2	$1500	$256	48	$12,288
MVS license	$585	$10,662	58	$618,396
DB2 license	None	$3675	58	$213,150
DB2PM license	None	$405	58	$23,490
TOTAL	$296,705			$912,30

Figure 8.38 Price Calculations for **DB2** System Measured

The total dollar cost for the **DB2** system measured is $296,705 + $912,300 = $1,209,005. This supports a QPM rate of 0.9216, and we calculate the final rating by dividing the dollar cost by the QPM rating. The final rating for the Set Query benchmark on this platform is therefore $1,209,005/0.9216 = 1,311,854 $/QPM.

Elapsed Time versus CPU Time Rating

We used an elapsed time measure in the above rating. However, this may not lead to a true estimate of *query throughput* in a multi-user system. Assume for a moment that we require 10 elapsed minutes to run all the queries of the Set Query benchmark on some platform, but use only 1 minute of CPU time in doing so—the longer elapsed time is a result of waiting for I/O. But if we have a lot of users waiting to get queries performed, couldn't we overlap some of those users, time-share the CPU so that we get a lot more queries run every minute? The answer is yes, provided we have several disks holding the data, so that disk I/O doesn't become the bottleneck and overlapping queries on the CPU can find overlapping disks to retrieve needed data. Given all this, it might seem to be more sensible to use CPU time rather than elapsed time in arriving at the rating.

The only problem in taking this step is that the Set Query benchmark has been run as a single-user benchmark. If we were to run multiple simultaneous users with multiple disks on the system, we would be more justified in generalizing in this way, but as it stands we can't be absolutely sure there isn't some kind of system interference between concurrent user queries that makes this sort of multi-user scenario a pipe dream. There isn't any theoretical reason for such interference—there are no exclusive row locks or other complications that we encounter with update transactions in Chapter 9. But we still have to be careful in coming to the conclusion that we can use all the CPU time in the system. For one thing, as the CPU resource comes closer and closer to being 100% utilized, users form longer and longer *queues* waiting for CPU service, and this has a bad effect on response time. We can only hope to use (perhaps) 90% of the CPU on a reasonably balanced production system. Note that if we calculate the elapsed time for the 69 queries of the Set Query benchmark on the **DB2** platform measured in the last few seconds, we arrive at 74.87 minutes, whereas if we calculate the total CPU time, we arrive at 24.77 minutes. This is a gap of about three to one, not large enough to cause a great deal of concern. If concurrent queries can be performed without interference on a multi-user system (and we have reason to believe from other measurements that this is the case with **DB2**), then the multi-user rating might be reduced from 1,311,854 $/QPM to as little as 500,000 $/QPM. At some point it is appropriate to consider a multi-user test, to see if the queries can be effectively overlapped on the CPU.

Customizing the Rating

It is possible to reinterpret the measurements of the Set Query benchmark to estimate the behavior of a tested platform on a specific query workload. The benchmark query suites have been chosen to span most types of query work, so that it should be possible to equate a given custom workload to a specific weighting of queries from the benchmark. Admittedly, some sophisticated flexibility is required if the workload to be estimated contains query forms not included in the Set Query suites. A workload of concurrent update transactions with conflicting data accesses cannot be modeled in this way. We will meet a benchmark for a specific workload of update transactions, the TPC-A benchmark, in Chapter 9.

Assume that we can determine a set of weights, W_i, to represent the relative workload frequency of the benchmark query Q_i, where i ranges from 1 to 69, and assume that all weights are non-negative (some may be zero) and sum to 1.0. The rules of the Set Query benchmark say that all query ratings must be reported in detail, so we always have the elapsed time, the CPU time, and the various types of I/O for each query. Now if we assume that query Q_i takes T_i elapsed minutes to complete, we can calculate the weighted elapsed time period by the formula:

$$E = \text{Elapsed time period for a weighted query} = \sum_i W_i \cdot T$$

The weights W_i sum to 1.0, so the quantity E can be thought of as the elapsed time in minutes required for a *single* query that sums up the effects of all queries in the benchmark. Therefore the number of queries per minute, Q_m, for this weighting is given by 1/E. If C is the dollar cost for the platform on which the benchmark has been run, then the custom rating in units of $/QPM is arrived at by dividing C by Q_m, or equivalently, multiplying C by E.

$$\text{Final weighted rating} = C \cdot E = \sum_i W_i \cdot T \text{ (in units \$/QPM)}$$

630

To test that this makes sense, note that a *larger* rating represents *inferior* performance, since the cost goes up or the QPM rating goes down. Sure enough, if the cost C of the platform in the final weighted rating goes up, say because the vendor raises the price of the platform, a larger rating reflects a lower cost-performance value. The same thing happens if a single one of the T_i values with a positive weight increases, indicating that some query now takes longer.

Note that all the considerations of replacing elapsed time with CPU time, mentioned in the last subsection, still hold in the custom workload. The advantage of performing a standalone set of measurements is that it is possible to customize by using different query weights in a workload. In a multi-user test the usual course is to choose a specific workload and measure the total elapsed time. Individual measures for the different queries are therefore not available, and a custom rating cannot be derived. However, if the hypothesis of noninterference between concurrent queries holds, we can derive an approximate custom multi-user rating under carefully limited circumstances.

Suggestions for Further Reading

The standard SQL reference manuals for most database products give little guidance in understanding query optimization. However, the *DB2 Administration Guide* [1] has quite good coverage. Some **INGRES** details are to be found in the *Technical Notes* [4]. **ORACLE** has coverage in the *Database Administrator's Guide* [5] and the *Performance Tuning Guide* [6]. The Set Query benchmark is presented in more detail in *The Benchmark Handbook* [3]. Goetz Graefe's paper on query evaluation techniques [2] introduces a number of principles we have not had space for here, principles that in many cases have not yet been implemented in commercial database systems, but that will probably appear in the future.

[1] *DB2 Administration Guide*. See Chapter 4, "Designing a Database," and Chapter 7, "Performance Monitoring and Tuning."

[2] Goetz Graefe. "Query Evaluation Techniques for Large Databases." In *ACM Computing Surveys* 25(2), June 1993, pp. 73–170.

[3] Jim Gray, editor. *The Benchmark Handbook (for Database and Transaction Processing Systems)*, 2nd ed. San Mateo, CA: Morgan Kaufmann, 1993.

[4] *INGRES Technical Notes*. Alameda, CA: ASK Group.

[5] *ORACLE RDBMS Database Administrator's Guide*. Redwood Shores, CA: Oracle.

[6] *ORACLE RDBMS Performance Tuning Guide*. Redwood Shores, CA: Oracle.

[7] *ORACLE SQL Language Reference Manual*. Redwood Shores, CA: Oracle.

Variations in DB2, INGRES, and ORACLE

Note that specific limitations on index use vary with new releases of all database products. As of release 6 **INGRES** is unable to combine indexes to perform AND and OR processing. As of release 7 **ORACLE** cannot combine any predicates except equal match and also cannot use an index for the predicate C1 is null. In general, it is fair to say that **DB2** currently has the most advanced bag of tricks for query optimization.

Exercises

Exercises with solutions at the back of the book in "Selected Solutions to Exercises" are marked with the symbol •.

In exercises involving elapsed time for I/O, you should generally assume that index directory pages are buffer resident and that index leaf pages are not, unless instructed otherwise. Ignore index I/O in your answers when these sum to less than 10% of the total. However, you should normally be careful to include index I/O calculations, to demonstrate why you consider them insignificant. The following exercises assume **DB2** architecture except as otherwise mentioned—that is, pages of 4 KB, compression at the leaf level of a B-tree, and so on.

[8.1] We have been assuming that **DB2** is able to choose to use sequential prefetch I/O in one part of an index scan (as in reading from the index) and not in another (in reading data pages in the unclustered case of Example 8.3.4 based on the RIDs found in the index). In this problem, we assume instead that we must choose between performing random I/Os of 4 KB pages, or else prefetch I/Os of 8-page blocks, and make this choice uniformly for all the I/Os of a given WORKLOAD. There is no flexibility for how I/Os can be performed within a query, that is available to the query optimizer. The current exercise demonstrates the disadvantage of such inflexibility.

(a)• Use the values in Figure 8.4 for the components making up an I/O to calculate the time required for an 8-page sequential prefetch I/O.

(b) Calculate the elapsed time taken by the unique match query of Example 8.3.3:

(i)   Under assumptions of 8-page prefetch.

(ii)   Under assumptions of single-page random I/Os.

You can continue to assume that the top two levels of the B-tree index are buffer resident, but not the leaf level. Note that performing uniform 8-page sequential prefetch I/O hurts elapsed time performance in this case.

(c)• Recalculate the time taken for Example 8.3.5:

(i)   Under assumptions of 8-page prefetch.

(ii)   Under assumptions of single-page random I/Os.

In this case, 8-page sequential I/O helps elapsed time performance.

(d) Consider a WORKLOAD of some number W1 of queries of the kind mentioned in (b) (type (b)), and W2 of queries of the second mentioned in (c) (type (c)). Type (b) queries have an elapsed time disadvantage when prefetch I/Os are required, and type (c) queries have a disadvantage when random I/Os are required.

(i)   Choose the weights W1 and W2 so that the total elapsed time due to I/Os in the workload is the same for both choices, random I/O or 8-page prefetch. We are assuming that type (b) queries are much more frequent than type (c) queries.

     (ii)   Now calculate the total elapsed time for each query when   **633**
we have flexibility in different queries to choose between
prefetch and random I/Os.

[8.2]   This problem duplicates the mathematical derivation given in Section 7.6. If you have had a course in elementary probability, you should have no trouble justifying your answers. You have the option to generate your results by doing a program simulation with a random number generator.

  (a)• Consider the Unique Match query of Example 8.3.3, with an `employees` table that has 100,000 rows of 400 bytes each. Assume that both the data pages and the eidx index (10-byte entries) have **pctfree** = 0, and thus show that there are 10,000 data pages and a depth 2 eidx B-tree index with 250 leaf pages.

     Now assume that we have a set of memory buffers that is kept populated by an algorithm that drops a page from buffer when it has not been referenced for exactly 125 seconds. Assume that our WORKLOAD performs two queries of the type in Example 8.3.3 each second, with a *randomly chosen* `eid` value, and that this is the only query type in the workload that references the `employees` table or eidx index. Each time one of these queries is performed, the root node of the eidx B-tree is referenced, so the root node clearly stays in buffer. Note that if the `eid` values referenced were properly selected to circulate uniformly through the eidx leaf nodes, then after 125 seconds every one of the 250 leaf nodes would be referenced, and they would all stay in buffers. That's not likely to happen, of course, since the `eid` values are chosen at random.

  (b)• (i)   What is the probability, P(leaf), that a given leaf node is referenced on any given query?

     (ii)   Give a formula for the probability that a given leaf node is *not* referenced by a given query.

     (iii)   Give a formula for the probability that a given leaf node is not referenced by some number N of queries in a row. (Hint: there is a power involved.)

(iv)   Using a calculator, give the probability that a leaf node from the eidx B-tree has not been referenced for the last 250 queries, 125 seconds, and therefore is not present in buffers.

(v)   What is the expected number of leaf nodes present in buffers?

(vi)   State this problem in terms of throwing N darts at M random slots, as in Section 7.6. Perform the calculation of the exponential form for part (v) from that section.

(c)   (i)   Repeat all the steps of part (b) for the data pages of the `employees` table.

(ii)   How many actual database page references take place in the last 125 seconds, counting index root page and all others? How many references have there been to index leaf pages? To data pages?

(iii)   Approximately how many index leaf pages have been referenced during that time? How many data pages have been referenced? (Some pages have been referenced two or more times, but count each page only once.)

(iv)•   Explain why the number of leaf pages remaining in buffer is smaller than the number of data pages.

(d)   What is the approximate number of pages, B, that need to be present in buffers, counting both B-tree and data pages, in order to keep all pages referenced in the last 125 seconds buffer resident?

(e)   The LRU buffering algorithm, the most common type in use, works with some well-defined pool of P buffer pages: LRU brings each newly referenced page into the pool and makes room for it by discarding the buffer page that has gone the longest time without reference. Give an estimate of the number of pages P that must be present for queries of the type we have been dealing with so far, in order to guarantee that each page referenced has a life of *approximately* 125 seconds. Explain your answer.

(f)• Assume that a page in buffer results in an I/O cost of 0 (zero) when it is referenced, whereas a page out of buffer results in a cost 1 (we have to fetch it from disk—simple units here). What is the I/O cost per second resulting from the query WORK-LOAD assumed here? (You can estimate this from the results of parts (b) and (c).)

(g) Assume that we extended the lifetime of pages in buffer from 125 seconds to 250 seconds. Calculate how this would affect problems (b), (iv) and (v), (c) (i), (d), (e), and (f). What we are doing here is reducing the I/O (disk arm) cost by purchasing extra memory to hold more buffer pages.

(h)• What would the I/O cost per second be if we had exactly 251 buffer pages and we kept the eidx root page and all eidx leaf pages in buffer and dropped all data pages? Conclude from this that the idea of keeping all pages around a fixed length of time is not optimal.

[8.3] Write a program to simulate the buffering situations of Exercise 8.2. The program should be callable as a function.

(a) Input a number N of leaf pages and M of data pages. (We would use N = 250 and M = 10,000 in the situation of Exercise 8.2.) Now input K to represent the number of seconds a page must go unreferenced before it is dropped from buffer. (Note that this is *not* an LRU approach.) Assume that two queries are performed each second, referencing some leaf page and data page. Define a function to be called for each query that returns the number of distinct leaf pages and data pages that remain in buffer after the query. Use a random number generator to generate random references to a leaf page and a data page for the query. If you average a long sequence of query results (calling the function 100 or so times in a row, once the system is warmed up), you should get the same sort of answers you derived in Exercise 8.2(b) (v) and 8.2(c). (Note that the hard part in writing this program would be to perform efficient lookup to see if a new page referenced is already in buffer, and if not, to determine which page should be dropped from buffer. However, it is not necessary to write efficient code for this exercise. The easiest way is to keep reference times for all M+N page, in two big arrays.)

(b) With N and M as in part (a), write a simulation of LRU buffering with a given fixed buffer size input as B. The query function should return the number of pages *not* found in buffer on each new query (values 0, 1, or 2) and the age of the page being dropped from buffer. The caller of the query function should print out the sequence of ages starting when the system is warmed up. Check the result of Exercise 8.2(e) by looking at this list of ages. Average a long series of returned values to estimate the average I/O cost of a query, and check the calculation of Exercise 8.2(f) and (g).

[8.4] Assume that we have a table T with 100 million rows, each containing 200 bytes, loaded 90% full. Assume that we have an index C1234X on T with columns (C1, C2, C3, C4), and that the table T is clustered by this index. We also have an index C5678X on T with columns (C5, C6, C7, C8), and after running EXPLAIN we find that CLUSTERRATIO for C5678X is 20. Assume that *each column*, C1, C2, C3, C4, C5, C6, C7, C8 is 4 bytes in length.

CARD(C1) = 100, CARD(C2) = 200, CARD(C3) = 50, CARD(C4) = 10,
CARD(C5) = 10, CARD(C6) = 1000, CARD(C7) = 20, CARD(C8) = 5000

Assume that for each column Ck, the values populating the column go from 1 to CARD(Ck) with uniform distribution.

(a) Give a table where you calculate the following statistics. Explain your reasoning.

(i) For the table T, CARD and NPAGES.

(ii) COLCARD, LOW2KEY, and HIGH2KEY for C2, C3, C6, and C7.

(iii) For each of C1234X and C5678X, FIRSTKEYCARD and your best estimate of FULLKEYCARD (explain your reasoning).

(iv) Using FULLKEYCARD and reasonable assumptions about **DB2** index compression (*important*), calculate NLEAF for each index, then NLEVELS for each. Please show work.

(b)• Consider the following query.

```
select C10 from T where C1 <= 10 and C2 between 100
    and 110 and C3 = 4;
```

(i)   Give the relevant columns you would see in the plan
       table after an EXPLAIN of this query.

(ii)   Say explicitly what range of index entries must be
       retrieved in order to answer the query given in (b). How
       many leaf pages is this? Can we use sequential prefetch?
       What is the approximate elapsed time for this step?

(iii) Calculate the filter factor for the compound predicate for
       the query in (b).

(iv)   How many rows are retrieved? Explain why these rows
       are *not* contiguous and why sequential prefetch can *not*
       be used. What is the elapsed time for this data-page
       access step?

(v)   Specify (from (ii) and (iv)) the total I/O and elapsed time
       for this index step.

(c) Repeat the same steps as in (b) for *each of* two plans that sug-
    gest themselves on the two indexes of T, for the query:

```
select C7 from T where C7 = 3 and C1 = 99 and C2 = 55;
```

Which of these plans is of lower cost in terms of elapsed time
for I/O?

[8.5] Consider again the table T and associated indexes and columns of
       Exercise 8.4.

(a) Name the matching columns of the following search condi-
    tions, and give reasons why the matching stops where it does if
    all predicates don't match.

(i)•   select * from T where C1 = 7 and C2 >= 101 and C3 in
       (1,5) and C4 in (2,4,7);

(ii)   select * from T where C1 in (1,3,5) and C2 = 6 and C4 = 7;

(iii)• select * from T where C1 <> 6 and C2 in (1,3,5) and C3 = 5;

(iv) `select * from T where C1 in (1,3,5) and C2 = 7 and C3 = 6 and C4 in (3,6,8);`

(v)• `select * from T where C1 = 7 and C2 in (1,5) and C3 like '%abc' and C4 in (2,4,7);`

(vi) `select * from T where C1 in (1,3,5) and C4 > 3 and C3 = 7 and C2 = 6;`

(vii)• `select * from T where C1 = C4 + 6 and C2 in (1,3,5) and C3 = 5;`

(b) Show your work in providing answers to the following questions.

(i)• What is the composite filter factor for the matching predicates of the query of part (a) (i)?

    `(select * from T where C1 = 7 and C2 >= 101 and C3 in (1,5) and C4 in (2,4,7);)`

(ii) What is the filter factor for the *whole* search condition?

(iii)• What is the number of pages accessed for index lookup for this query? What kind of I/O is performed (R or S or L)?

(iv) What is the number of data pages accessed, assuming that we used the screening predicates? What kind of I/O (R or S or L)?

(v)• What is the total elapsed time to perform these I/Os?

[8.6] In this exercise, assume that the `prospects` table and the indexes addrx, hobbyx, agex, and incomex, as used in Example 8.6.1 and preceding.

(a)• Explain under what circumstances the predicate "`income-class = 10`" can be a matching predicate for an MX step in a multiple index scan.

(b) Is it possible to use the predicate "`age = 40`" in an MX step for a multiple index scan? Explain.

(c)• Is it possible to use the predicate "`age between 20 and 39`" in an MX step for a multiple index scan?

(d)   Is it possible to use the predicate "age between 40 and 44" in an MX step for a multiple index scan?

(e)• Explain why it is not possible to use the predicate "age in (40, 43, 45)" in a single MX step for a multiple index scan.

(f)   Is there a way to create a compound predicate with the same effect as the one in (e) that can be used in an MX step sequence?

[8.7]   For the following exercise, add the index mailx, defined in Section 8.5, to the indexes considered for Exercise 8.6. Consider the search condition "zipcode between 02139 and 02238 and income-class = 10 and age = 40."

(a)• Consider a matching index scan on mailx for this compound predicate, and specify relevant column values in the plan table. In particular, what is MATCHCOLS?

(b)   What is the filter factor that will result from the matching scan on mailx:

(i)   If an RID list is *not* used?

(ii)   If an RID list *is* used? Explain why there is a difference.

(c)• In case (b)(ii), we can consider making this scan of mailx an MX scan in a multiple index access. In that case we can use other indexes as well.

(i)   Can we perform an MX step on incomeclass = 10?

(ii)   Show the plan table for the multiple index steps we can use.

(iii) What is the filter factor for the full search condition in this case?

(d)   Calculate the I/O elapsed time for the full plan that is characterized in (b)(i). (You need to calculate index and data page I/O times. Be sure you use the right kind of I/O—random, list prefetch, or sequential prefetch.)

(e)• Calculate the I/O elapsed time for the full plan that is characterized in (c)(ii).

[8.8] Assume that the prospects table has indexes addrx, hobbyx, incomex, sexx (of Example 8.6.4), agex, and mailx.

(a)• Is it possible to have the predicate "sex = 'F'" in an MX step of a multi-index access plan?

(b) Consider the query:

```
select * from prospects where zipcode between 02139
    and 07138 and hobby = 'chess' and age = 20;
```

(i)• It is possible to resolve this query with an index scan of mailx. Name the matching predicates in the above and the screening predicates.

(ii) It is also possible to perform multi-index access. Place the predicates in order by descending filter factor. Then give the plan table that would be used for this MX-type plan, where smallest filter factors come first and we maintain as few RID lists as possible at once.

(iii)• What is the number of rows retrieved in both parts (i) and (ii), and how many data pages are involved? What kind of I/O is used (R, L, or S), and what is the elapsed time for data page access in both cases? Please show work.

[8.9] Assume indexes mailx, hobbyx, incomex, and agex for the following. Consider the query:

```
select * from prospects
    where zipcode between 02159 and 04158 and
    (age = 40 or age = 44) and hobby = 'tennis'
    and incomeclass = 7;
```

(a)• Explain why we cannot simply use a matching index scan on mailx to resolve all these predicates. However, we can perform a matching scan with screening predicates figuring into the filter factor. Analyze elapsed time for I/O for such a plan, including index I/O and calculating the number of rows that will be retrieved, and the I/O type for them. Give the total elapsed time.

(b) Now determine the plan for multiple index access to match as many of the predicates of the query as seems reasonable. Start by placing the predicates in order by decreasing filter factor. Calculate the I/O cost for index for each predicate RID extraction, the filter factor after each predicate is used, and whether the predicate pays for itself. Follow the pattern of Example 8.6.8. At the end of this determination, write the multi-step index plan columns, as in Figure 8.18, that follow the order of evaluation you have calculated and minimize the number of existing RID lists in the stack at any one time. What is the total elapsed time for this multi-step plan?

(c)• Which wins, (a) or (b)? As a general rule, when we have one composite index with a search condition matching only the first column and a group of other single column indexes on later columns of the composite index, the composite index scan is still the winner. Justify this rule.

[8.10] Consider Examples 8.7.1, 8.7.2, and 8.7.3. We have the same tables TABL1 and TABL2, but we use some new columns and indexes. There are 1 million rows, 200 bytes each, and the columns are 4 bytes long; we also assume that no space is wasted on the index pages or the data pages. We have the query:

```
select * from TABL1 T1, TABL2 T2
    where T1.C6 = 5 and T1.C7 = T2.C8
    and T2.C9 = 6;
```

Assume that we have indexes C6X, C7X, C8X, and C9X, FF(T1.C6 = const) = 1/20, FF(T2.C9 = const) = 1/400, the column T1.C7 has values ranging from 1 to 200,000, uniformly distributed, and T2.C8 also has values ranging from 1 to 200,000, uniformly distributed. There is no recognizable correlation between values of T1.C7 and T2.C8 by row number or anything else. They are independently random.

(a)• Derive the expected number of rows retrieved from this query.

(b) There are three possible plans to consider for this query: (i) nested loop join where T1 is the outer table, (ii) nested loop join where T2 is the outer table (these are different), and (iii) merge join. Work out the total elapsed I/O time for each case and declare which is the winner. In the case of merge join, where a sort is necessary, assume that a sort of no more than 50 pages will not require disk I/O, but that for more than 50 pages each page must be written out and then read back in, using sequential I/O to write but random I/O to read in again. (The reason for this has to do with the disk sort algorithm.)

[8.11] As in Example 8.8.1, assume a sequence of 2000-byte rows, two to a page, to be sorted in order by the values of the following sequence, which represents the initial order of the rows.

67 12 45 84 58 29 76 7 91 81 39 22 65 96 33 28 77 4 54 13 41 32 1 59

(a)• Perform a two-way merge sort on these numbers, as in Example 8.8.1. Show all intermediate results.

(b) Repeat the sort of part (a), now as a three-way merge sort.

(c) Now assume that the rows given are 4000 bytes in length and therefore one to a page. Perform a four-way merge sort on these numbers.

[8.12] Answer the following questions about the Set Query benchmark, referring to **DB2** measurements in all cases. How many rows of the BENCH table would you expect to retrieve with each of the following **where** clauses?

(a)• K2 = 2 AND K10 = 7.

(b) KSEQ BETWEEN 400000 AND 410000 OR KSEQ BETWEEN 480000 AND 500000.

(c)• Conditions 1 through 4 of the Predicate Sequence list of Figure 8.34.

(d) (i) In Q1, assuming that all **DB2** prefetch I/Os are sequential prefetch, how long would the I/Os take in the K2 case? In the K10 case?

(ii) Argue that **DB2** is CPU-bound in the K2 case.

(iii) How many pages are being brought into memory in the K10 case? Give details of how many pages *must* be looked at to perform the query plan.

(e)• Consider query Q2A. Some of the cases clearly use sequential prefetch in blocks of 32 pages. Name one such case. How long does sequential prefetch I/O take, and how does that jibe with the rule of thumb we've been using?

(f) Look at Query Q4B, detailed in Figure 8.35b.

    (i) What indexes are being used in condition sequence 5–9?

    (ii) Give the count of rows you expect to retrieve from the table after combining these indexes.

    (iii) Using the darts in slots formula to calculate the number of pages on which the rows of (ii) lie, compare this to the number of pages brought into memory as reported in Figure 8.35b.

(g)• In Query Q6B, in the K100 case, perform a calculation, explaining your reasoning, to estimate the total number of rows (joined) that will be retrieved. How does this compare to the number actually retrieved? (Where do you find those numbers?)

[8.13] Consider the following query on the BENCH table of the Set Query benchmark.

```
select B1.KSEQ, B2.KSEQ from BENCH B1, BENCH B2
    where B1.K100 = 22 and B1.K250K = B2.K100K and B2.K25 = 19;
```

(a)• Calculate the number of rows that you would expect to see retrieved. Please show your work.

(b)• Calculate the elapsed time for I/O on the *two different nested loop joins possible,* and declare which plan wins.

[8.14] Consider the following query on the BENCH table of the Set Query benchmark.

```
select B1.KSEQ, B2.KSEQ from BENCH B1, BENCH B2
    where B1.K100 = 22 and B1.K250K = B2.K250K and B2.K100 = 19;
```

(a) Calculate the number of rows that you would expect to see retrieved. Please show your work.

(b) Calculate the elapsed time for I/O with a *nested loop join* (both are equivalent) and then with a *merge* join. Please show your work and declare which plan wins.

[8.15] Consider the BENCH table and the indexes on it. In the following exercise, assume that the BENCH table and all indexes are loaded with pages 100% full. Use standard assumptions for **DB2** in the calculations that follow, and show your calculations.

(a)• After running RUNSTATS, give a Select statement to retrieve from the appropriate **DB2** system catalog table the number of data pages on which rows of the BENCH table sit.

(b) Calculate the number of data pages you would expect to find, with the assumption that pages are loaded 100% full.

(c)• Calculate the number of leaf pages you would expect to find in the K2X index with the assumption that pages are 100% full. Don't forget leaf-level index compression.

(d) Assume that we delete the row in BENCH with KSEQ = 300,000. Is it true or not that we can proceed directly to the index entry in K2X for this row in order to delete it? (That is, do we have a way to "look up" the entry in the directory structure?) Give a reason for your answer (if possible, cite a reference in the text).

Update Transactions

In Section 4.4 we introduced the concept of a *transaction*. We now wish to review the ideas introduced there, starting with a definition.

DEFINITION 9.1 A *transaction* is a means by which an application programmer can package together a sequence of database operations, so that the database system can provide a number of guarantees, known as the *ACID properties* of a transaction (explained later in this section). When the operations making up a transaction consist of both reads (that is, Selects) and updates, they represent an attempt by the application programmer at a consistent *change of state* in the data; when they consist only of reads, they represent an attempt at a consistent *view* of the data. ∎

There is no Begin Transaction statement in standard SQL; a transaction begins whenever there is no active transaction in progress and an SQL statement is performed that accesses the data (for example, Select, Update, Insert, Delete, etc.). While a transaction is in progress, any updates it makes are not visible to concurrent users, and data read cannot be concurrently updated. Recall that in standard SQL there are two statements bearing on transactional execution. The first is the *Commit* statement:

```
exec sql commit work;
```

The programmer uses this statement to inform the system that the ongoing transaction has successfully completed; all updates made by the transaction become permanent in the database and visible to concurrent users.

The second statement that bears on transactional execution is the *Rollback* statement:

```
exec sql rollback work;
```

This statement indicates that the ongoing transaction has ended unsuccessfully; all data updates made by the transaction are reversed, and prior versions of the data are put back in place and become visible again to concurrent users. A rollback action that ends a transaction, whether initiated by the program or the system, is often referred to as an *abort*.

In Section 4.4 we introduced the concept of a transaction only in sufficient depth to motivate the need for including a Commit or Rollback statement in an application program, and to suggest the need to handle aborts resulting from deadlock in transactional locking. In the current chapter we propose to treat the transaction concept in much greater depth. Even so, this chapter is just an introduction to a complex and important field. Many hardware and software vendors that offer database system products have created a separate development group, sometimes even in a different physical location, to develop transaction system capabilities. Database system features in the area of query processing are extremely far removed from what is needed to support transactions, and the reader should be prepared to encounter a change of mind-set in this chapter.

Starting in the 1950s, transactions were developed to solve a number of problems that early systems designers faced in writing large database applications. One such application was to support banking activities, allowing a large number of bank tellers to simultaneously read and make changes to customer accounts. In dealing with such an application, early developers faced the following problem areas.

1. Creating an inconsistent result. What are we to do about the following situation? Our application is transferring money from one account to another (the accounts are two different records lying, in general, on different disk pages). After the first account has had money subtracted from its balance and this change has been recorded on disk, the system crashes because of a power failure. When we bring the machine back up, our application doesn't remember what logic it was executing; the only permanent memory is on disk, and the application has destroyed money with the single account record update it made.

2. Errors of concurrent execution. Concurrent (simultaneous) process executions can interfere with one another in a number of ways if no control is placed on records being read and written. One such type of interference is known as *inconsistent analysis*. Assume that teller 1 is transferring money from account A to account B of the same customer while teller 2 is trying to add up the two account balances to perform a credit check. If the application acting on behalf of teller 1 subtracts the transfer amount from account A and then teller 2 adds up the two account balances before teller 1 can add the transfer amount to account B, then teller 2 sees the customer as having less money than is true in reality. As a result, the customer may fail a credit check that should have been passed.

3. Uncertainty as to when changes become permanent. Recall that we normally buffer popular pages in memory to save on disk I/Os. This means that an extremely popular record, such as the one containing the balance for the bank branch, remains in memory for an extended period. As we mentioned in problem 1, after a crash we can only remember what has been written to disk, so this seems to mean that either we must always write out all buffered records after they change (and thus we are not saving many I/Os by buffering after all) or else updates don't get out to disk very frequently (and this makes us nervous about handing out money for customer withdrawals, for fear the withdrawal won't be recorded before a computer crash occurs). Can we be confident of updates being recorded without performing a disk write for every record change?

To solve these problems, the systems analysts came up with the concept of a transaction (although the idea did not start to be formalized until the mid-1970s). With these concrete problems in mind, the analysts defined a *transaction* to be a grouping of a series of reads and updates to a database that is logically one piece—for example, a transfer of money spanning a number of accounts (involving both reads and updates), or a credit check involving a number of accounts (involving a series of reads only). Application programmers decide what set of reads and updates logically make up a transaction, and then the database system makes the following four *transactional guarantees* to solve the problems listed above, known as the *ACID guarantees*, or *ACID properties*. The term *ACID* is an acronym for the four properties atomicity, consistency, isolation, and durability.

Atomicity. This property guarantees that a set of record updates that are part of a transaction is indivisible (the old meaning of atomic, before atomic fission was discovered). Thus either all updates of a transaction occur in the database, or none of them occurs. This guarantee continues to hold even in the event of a system crash (see "Durability," below). A procedure known as *database recovery* is performed after a crash to bring the disk-resident database to a state where it will reflect either all or none of the row updates for any transaction that was in progress at the time of the crash. Thus problem 1, the problem of creating an inconsistent result, is solved. The system provides this atomicity guarantee by writing notes to itself on disk in advance of any changes made on disk to the actual data. In the event of a crash the system can figure out what it was in the midst of doing and decide to either back out all transactional disk changes (so the database reflects none of these changes), or else apply all transactional changes that didn't make it out to the disk (so the transaction is completed).

Consistency. This is another property commonly named as a transactional guarantee made by the system; it is defined a bit later. We do not give consistency the same prominence as the other ACID properties because consistency is not logically independent of the other properties. In fact it is implied by the existence of the isolation guarantee (following), which seems to be more fundamental.

Isolation. That transactions are *isolated* means that one can only affect another as it would if they were not concurrent, if their operations were not interleaved in time. Another name for this property is *serializability,* meaning that any schedule of interleaved operations permitted by the system is equivalent to some *serial schedule,* where transactions are scheduled one at a time, and all operations of one transaction complete before any operation of another transaction can start. For performance reasons (explained later in the chapter) we need to have interleaved operation schedules, but we want everything to seem as if we were executing transactions in series. This guarantee solves problem 2, errors arising from concurrent execution. As we have already mentioned, in Section 4.4, this guarantee is usually accomplished in commercial systems by having transactions lock data items they access to exclude certain concurrent operations on those same data items by other transactions.

Durability. The last property guaranteed by the system is this: when the
system returns to the program logic after a *Commit Work* statement, the
transaction is guaranteed to be recoverable. At this point, for example, an
ATM (automatic teller machine) can disburse money to a customer without fear that the record of the withdrawal will be lost, a solution to problem 3. We name this transactional guarantee *durability*—that is, a
transaction that is *durable* is resistant to a crash. The system uses the same
notes to itself on disk to provide durability as were mentioned in regard to
the atomicity guarantee. At the same time, the number of I/Os to guarantee
durability of a large number of record updates is much reduced, because
the system can write out a lot of notes at once with a single disk write,
involving many record updates on distinct pages, that otherwise would
require multiple disk accesses.

Clearly the properties of atomicity and durability are trivially satisfied
in a read-only transaction, where no updates occur; the only transactional
property that has an effect in this case is isolation, and it guarantees that
the rows read by a read-only transaction do not contain any data changes
made by uncommitted transactions. If such a thing were allowed, the problem of inconsistent analysis could arise, where teller 2 adds up the balances
of account A (after the still uncommitted transaction of teller 1 has
changed it) and account B (which will be changed by teller 1 before its
transaction commits). The three transactional guarantees given prominence above, atomicity, durability, and isolation, require a good deal of
study, because they interact in complex ways. In Section 9.1 we begin with
a study of isolation (that is, serializability). Later sections deal with atomicity and durability.

The property mentioned above as being implied by isolation is known
as consistency. We alluded to it when we spoke of inconsistent analysis in
problem 2. *Consistency* is a logical property based on some consistency
rule, such as "Money should neither be created nor destroyed by a banking
transaction transferring money between accounts." Such a rule is an
injunction to the programmer, for one thing, that the logic of the money
transfer program should not make unbalanced updates to accounts within
transaction boundaries. Then, given that the program logic does what it
should (acting in isolation), the consistency property says that the system
should guarantee that consistency continues to hold during concurrent execution. However, it turns out that the isolation property already guarantees this, since isolation guarantees that transactions acting concurrently

affect one another only as they would if their operations were not interleaved in time. Clearly if the program logic acts consistently in isolation, it will continue to do so in concurrent execution given the isolation guarantee, so in what follows we exclude the consistency property from consideration in the list of guarantees offered by a database system. Note, however, that a test of the consistency property in a database system application is a good test that isolation has been properly implemented. We see this in the TPC-A benchmark of Section 9.10.

In the following sections, we take a rather rigorous approach to transaction concepts, with definitions and theorems and so on. We have taken this kind of approach before in Chapter 2, when we introduced the concept of the relational model, and in Chapter 5, when we studied database design. One reason for such an approach is that the concepts being covered are somewhat difficult to grasp, and a rigorous approach is a good pedagogical method to communicate ideas in the most explicit possible way. Another reason is historical: the field of transactional systems, which began in the 1950s, gave rise to a good deal of publishing activity in rigorous computer science journals starting in the mid-'70s. Why transactions developed as they did is rather revealing, and it constitutes an interesting motivation for rigorous development that the reader may not have heard before.

The transactional systems being planned in the 1950s were expected to generate tens of millions of dollars in hardware and software sales. (A bargain for the banks and the millions of bank clerks, chained to the terrible drudgery of keeping account books.) Today, money spent on transactional systems by industry amounts to nearly 6 *billion* dollars *per year*. Naturally the cost to develop systems sold into these markets was a good fraction of the revenue realized. When computer companies start making this kind of investment in new systems, they want to be sure that the underlying concepts used in program implementation will result in something that will not have any nasty surprises. Top-level management listened carefully to systems programmers and designers for these projects, and asked how they could be sure that the proposed multi-million-dollar development plan would result in a working system that would do what it was supposed to do. Everything was subject to question. Do we know all the problems that can arise (problems 1–3 above)? Does the approach solve all the problems that we know about? Are there any other problems we haven't thought of? How can we be sure?

Rigorous proof is created to answer just this kind of question, at least in those areas of endeavor where the problems are simple enough to axiomatize. The journal articles didn't come first, of course. An early set of rough-and-ready principles was created and justified, and then the first transactional systems were built. As these principles continued to be developed, a set of founding papers was eventually published, often written by programmers who had not been involved in journal publishing before. These papers founded the transactional field, codifying all the explicit assumptions and problems, and proving the principles that underlay the solutions adopted. Most of these principles are still used today in commercial systems.

9.1 Transactional Histories

The need for the transaction isolation concept is present whenever two or more users can perform interleaved operations of read and write on the database. When we speak of reads and writes, we are referring to the most primitive possible operations, from which the more "set-oriented" SQL statements are constructed. To "read" means to access a data item, such as an individual row of a table or an index entry in the database; to "write" means to change or update a data item in the database. We normally refer to reads and writes of data items rather than reads and updates, because the term update has a more powerful implication from SQL. We use the notation $R_i(A)$ to mean that a transaction, given an identification number i by the database system and denoted by T_i, performs a read of data item A. Consider a table T1 with two columns, *uniqueid* and *val*. Then $R_i(A)$ can usually be pictured as transaction T_i performing the following SQL statement:

```
select val into :pgmval1 from T1 where uniqueid = A;
```

We also use the notation $W_j(B)$ to mean that a transaction T_j performs a write on data item B, and this can be pictured as transaction T_j performing the following SQL statement:

```
update T1 set val = :pgmval2 where uniqueid = B;
```

These examples are a bit simplistic. There is actually more than one data item read by the Select statement given, and the same might be said of the Update statement. In both statements, a **where** clause predicate has been evaluated to determine the row in T1 with the given `uniqueid` value. We can picture this predicate evaluation information as being a data item in its own right. In a later section we will see that this observation has important ramifications. Note that we are not specifying the actual values read and written with the notation above, but if we wish we can expand $R_i(A)$ to be $R_i(A, pgmval1)$ and $W_j(B)$ to be $W_j(B, pgmval2)$. The value read or written is the second argument (the column name "`val`" is not mentioned), and we would normally simply specify constants for these values—for example, $R_i(A,50)$ or $W_j(B,80)$. The Select and Update statements for $R_i(A)$ and $W_j(B)$ we have just given are the simplest possible examples; reads and writes actually arise in much more complicated situations. For example, instead of reading or updating a single column value of a uniquely identified row, a read or write could involve all the columns of that row. More generally, assume that transaction T_1 were to execute the SQL statement on a set of rows:

[9.1.1]   `update tbl set val = 1.15*val`
         `where uniqueid between :low and :high;`

In this case a large number of different reads and writes might be generated by this one statement. The first operation performed by T_1 would be $R_1(\text{PREDICATE})$, meaning that the set of rows satisfying the predicate in the **where** clause, with uniqueid values between the program variables :low and :high, must be determined by some means, such as an index lookup. After taking note of the list of rows that fall in the given range, the Update statement of (9.1.1) performs a sequence of reads and writes, $R_1(\text{uniqueid}_k, value_k)$ and $W_1(\text{uniqueid}_k, 1.15^*value_k)$, k = 1 to n, for all uniqueid_k values in the :low to :high range. The fact that none of these row values is returned in a program variable doesn't matter. They all represent data from which the program logic (conceptually) receives information, and on which it acts to change data items in the database. In this case the program logic enlists the non-procedural aid of the SQL Update statement, but the logic is specified by the application itself.

In what follows, we assume that each user performs all reads and writes within some transaction (in the SQL standard, each read and write operation is part of a transaction—a read or write begins a new transaction if none is in progress—and the transaction ends only when the commit work statement is encountered). The database system intercepts each transaction initialization (the first read/write operation after a prior transaction ends) and assigns a number i to it. For now, we assume that all database activity performed by any transaction can be modeled as a series of reads $(R_i(A))$ and writes $(W_j(B))$, together with commits (C_i) arising from the commit work statement and aborts (A_j) arising because of the rollback work statement or because of deadlock, as in Section 4.4. We ignore row inserts and deletes until later. The reads represent all information taken in by the transaction, and the writes represent all update activity the transaction performs.

An "interleaved" series of read and write operations for two transactions, T_1 and T_2, looks like this:

[9.1.2] $\ldots R_2(A)\ W_2(A)\ R_1(A)\ R_1(B)\ R_2(B)\ W_2(B)\ C_1\ C_2 \ldots$

A sequence of operations such as this is known as a *history,* or sometimes a *schedule.* In the history of (9.1.2), we see that transaction T_2 first reads the data element A, then transaction T_2 writes back a new value of A, after which T_1 reads the resulting value of A, and so on, with the final operations C_1 and C_2 representing commits by transactions T_1 and T_2 respectively. This history results from a series of calls submitted by simultaneously executing transactions at the application program level (see Figure 9.1) and eventually transformed into the form of (9.1.2) at the level of the database *scheduler.*

654

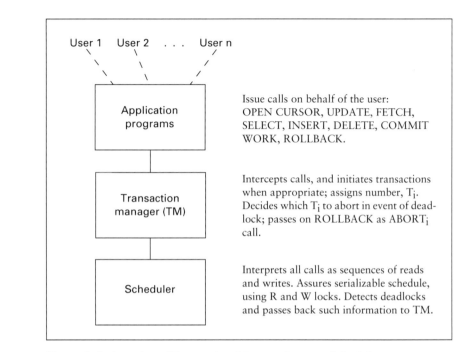

Figure 9.1 Layering of Transactional System Down to Scheduler

To give a hint of what is to come in the next few sections, we intend to show how a database scheduler, as pictured in Figure 9.1, processing a sequence of interleaved operations of the kind we see in the history given in (9.1.2), can act in such a way that the history actually allowed by the scheduler is *equivalent* in effect to some serial schedule. In this way we are always guaranteed that each of the transactions is isolated from the others—that is, we provide the isolation guarantee. The scheduler accomplishes this task by delaying some submitted operations when it sees that allowing them to occur in the order submitted would break the isolation guarantee; in some special cases, the scheduler declares a *deadlock* and (as we saw in Chapter 4) aborts one of the transactions involved. As a matter of fact, the history given in (9.1.2) represents an illegal series of operations from a serializability standpoint, and the database scheduler will not allow it to occur in this form. The reason this history is illegal is that we can think of a situation in which a series of operations in this order will give an inconsistent result. We call this an *interpretation* of the history.

EXAMPLE 9.1.1

We give an interpretation of the history in (9.1.2), to see how we could arrive at an inconsistent result. To do this, we give specific values to the data items read, postulate an underlying purpose to the logic that determines the values that are written by the transaction based on its input values, and then specify a consistency rule that the series of operations will break. Assume that the data elements A and B are two accounts held by a bank customer, and that their initial values are A = 50 and B = 50. As in Examples 4.4.1 and 4.4.2, the inconsistent analysis example we gave to motivate the need for isolation, transaction T_1 is simply adding up the values in the two accounts and printing out the net worth of the customer who owns these accounts to provide a credit check. Transaction T_2 is transferring money from one account to another, moving 30 units from account A to account B. Both transactions operate under the consistency rule that they neither create nor destroy money. However, because the operations of the two transactions are "interleaved" in a way the scheduler should not allow, an inconsistency can arise. Here is a restatement of the history of (9.1.2) with the given value assumptions added.

[9.1.3] ... $R_2(A,50)\ W_2(A,20)\ R_1(A,20)\ R_1(B,50)\ R_2(B,50)\ W_2(B,80)\ C_1\ C_2$...

We see in this history that transaction T_1 reads the value of A after transaction T_2 has acted on it (and therefore sees the value 20), but it reads the value of B before transaction T_2 has changed it (and therefore sees the value 50). The sum of the two accounts that T_1 sees is 70, which is incorrect either before or after the updates made by transaction T_2. Such an inconsistent view can clearly lead to an inappropriate failure of a credit check. The reason for the inconsistency is that T_1 has somehow seen "partial" results of the T_2 transaction. The two transactions are not properly isolated from one another. ■

This viewing of partial results could never have occurred if transaction operations weren't interleaved. Consider the following two "serial" histories, histories in which all the operations of one transaction must be complete before any operations of a different transaction can begin, shown in Figure 9.2.

... $R_1(A, 50)\ R_1(B, 50)\ C_1\ R_2(B, 50)\ W_2(B, 20)\ R_2(A, 50)\ W_2(A, 80)\ C_2$ ...

... $R_2(B, 50)\ W_2(B, 20)\ R_2(A, 50)\ W_2(A, 80)\ C_2\ R_1(A, 80)\ R_1(B, 20)\ C_1$ ...

Figure 9.2 Two Serial Histories for (9.1.2)

Note that in both of these serial histories, transaction T_1 gets a consistent view of the data elements A and B. In the first case, T_1 sums 50 and

50 to get 100, and in the second it sums 80 and 20 to get 100. Money has never been created nor destroyed. It should be clear that if all transactions obey the consistency rule that money is neither created nor destroyed by a transaction, then in any serial execution each transaction starts with a consistent view: the same amount of total money in the system. However, if money is to be transferred, then it must be created or destroyed at some intermediate point in a sequence of transactional updates, since we can't subtract from one row and add to another row in a single W operation. The problem with viewing partial results of an update transaction, then, is that it may become possible to view an inconsistent state of the data. But if transactions operate only in a serial history, in which all operations of one transaction complete before another transaction can start its operations, then no inconsistencies of the kind shown in (9.1.3) can arise.

In what follows, we use the idea of serial execution as a touchstone of what we consider correct. We say that a history of interleaved transactional operations is *serializable* if it can be shown to have the same effect as some serial history in any possible set of circumstances; we say that two histories such as this are *equivalent*. But how do we judge that a history like the one in (9.1.2) is or is not equivalent to some serial history? Consider again the reasoning we followed in Example 9.1.1. We say that we created an *interpretation* of a history, H (such as in (9.1.2)), when we specified a consistency rule (money is neither created nor destroyed) and postulated a purpose for the underlying transactions, leading to a sequence of specific values for the reads and writes of H (as in (9.1.3)). When an interpretation of a history, H, can be shown to break the consistency rule (T_1 sees a total balance that cannot exist despite program logic that is correctly written), then it is *not* equivalent to any serial history. We will see a number of such examples in what follows.

At this point it is reasonable to review the four defining properties of a transaction, known as the ACID properties, that we met in the introduction to this chapter. We say that transactions are

Atomic. The set of updates contained in a transaction must succeed or fail as a unit.

Consistent. Complete transactional transformations on data elements bring the database from one consistent state to another. For example, if money can neither be created nor destroyed, then successive states must all have the same balance totals.

Isolated. Even though transactions execute concurrently, it appears to each successful transaction that it has executed in a serial schedule with the others. (Some transactions might be aborted to guarantee isolation; they are not successful, but can be *retried*.)

Durable. Once a transaction commits, the changes it has made to the data will survive any machine or system failures.

The properties of atomicity, isolation, and durability are all guaranteed by the database system to make the programmer's job easier. The idea of consistency is a logical property that the programmer must maintain in writing the logic for individual transactions acting under isolated circumstances. By guaranteeing the isolation property, the system also guarantees that consistency is maintained, even in the presence of interleaved operations and system failure.

9.2 Interleaved Read/Write Operations

We have just learned that a serial history, in which all operations of one transaction must complete before any operations of another can be executed, is not prey to the inconsistencies arising from interleaved operations of read and write. Why then do we interleave operations from different transactions? Why not execute all transactions in a strict serial schedule? This approach can be thought of as a very simple rule of behavior that the scheduler can impose on an arriving series of transactional operations: after one transaction, T_i, has executed a single data access operation (R_i or W_i) to begin its transaction, we say that T_i is *active,* or *in process.* if another transaction, T_j, operating on behalf of a different user, now submits an initial transactional operation (R_j or W_j) to the scheduler, the scheduler makes transaction T_j WAIT until T_i has completed its sequence of operations—that is, until T_i has either aborted (A_i) or committed (C_i). If more than one transaction is forced to WAIT, then when the scheduler sees that a transaction has completed, it allows the next transaction to begin (execute its first operation), using a first-come-first-served order.

The reason most database systems do not impose a strict serial schedule of transactional operations—normally allowing interleaved operations—is simple: interleaved transactional operations offer a chance for greatly improved system performance. The freedom to have several transactions in process at one time means that while one transaction is performing I/O, another transaction can be using the CPU, thus increasing the *throughput* of the system, a measure of the number of transactions that can finish in any given period of time. Since I/O takes a long time, throughput is most enhanced when the system has several disk drives and several transactions in process at once.

EXAMPLE 9.2.1

Assume that a large number of users are awaiting service from a transactional application, and that each transaction uses CPU and I/O resources in the following sequence: (CPU use) $R_i(*)$ (CPU use) $W_i(*)$ C_i, where the operations $R_i(*)$ and $W_i(*)$ represent disk I/O. We assume that the system has a single CPU, that the resource use of the commit action is zero, that each CPU use interval is 5 ms (.005 seconds), and that the I/O to perform $R_i(*)$ or $W_i(*)$ (read or write of some unknown data element) requires a wait time of 50 ms. (As we have seen, an I/O that is immediately serviced requires 25 ms, but we assume that a "waiting line" or "queue" is slowing down the service. We begin the following discussion with a single transaction thread, but this is merely a preparation for discussing a situation with a number of concurrent users, where queuing delays are common.) We can picture the sequence of events that occur when a series of transactions is serviced according to a strict serial schedule with the schematic diagram of Figure 9.3.

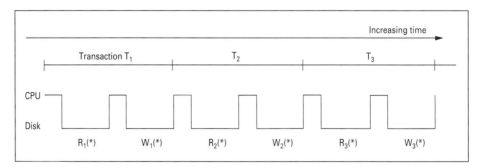

Figure 9.3 Sequence of Events in a Serial Transactional Schedule

In this figure the resource use of the system is symbolized by the step function graph, with intervals of resource use alternating between CPU and disk (I/O use). Each disk use is labeled with the transactional access operation being performed, such as $R_1(*)$ or $W_1(*)$. We see that each transaction spends the first 5 ms using CPU, then performs a 50 ms $R_i(*)$, then 5 ms more of CPU and a 50 ms $W_i(*)$. The time to perform C_i is taken to be zero, so the next transaction starts immediately. Each complete transaction therefore takes an interval 110 ms, and we have a throughput of one transaction every 110 ms, a rate of 9.09 transactions per second (9.09 TPS). The CPU is underutilized with this schedule, active for only 10 ms out of each 110 ms, or 9.09% active, but the disk is rather well utilized, active 100 ms out of each 110 ms.

Figure 9.4 shows a schedule in which two transactions interleave operations, but the system still has only one disk. Although we have two labels for CPU and disk on the left, in order to graph resource use for two concurrent transaction processes (also known as transaction threads), the two CPU labels stand for the same thing as do the two disk labels.

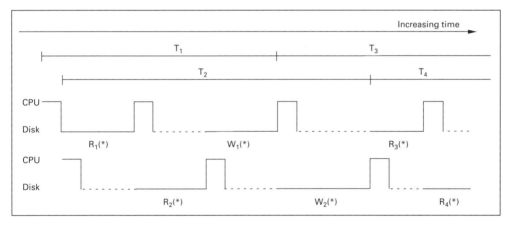

Figure 9.4   Sequence of Events with Two Interleaved Transactions, One Disk

In Figure 9.4 we see that the two transaction threads spend most of their time waiting for each other to finish access to the disk so they can get their turn. However, the schedule does succeed in overlapping CPU with I/O. Each transaction requires 100 ms of disk access, and the disk is now fully utilized instead of being unused for 10 ms out of every 110 ms, as it was earlier. In the long run, therefore, since I/O is the gating factor, we have a throughput of one transaction every 100 ms, or 10 TPS. The specific schedule shown in the figure may be a bit confusing, however, so we work it out in detail. At the very beginning of the example, we see that transaction T_1 uses 5 ms of CPU, then 50 ms for $R_1(*)$, then 5 ms of CPU, waits 45 ms for $R_2(*)$, to complete, then 50 ms for $W_1(*)$ and completes, requiring $5 + 50 + 5 + 45 = 105$ ms. This is unusually fast because T_1 gets a head start on resource use. From that point on, however, all subsequent transactions T_i spend 5 ms on CPU, wait 45 ms for disk, spend 50 ms for $R_i(*)$, 5 ms for CPU, 45 ms waiting for disk, 50 ms for $W_i(*)$, and complete, requiring $5 + 45 + 50 + 5 + 45 + 50 = 200$ ms. Thus, in the long run, each thread runs one transaction every 200 ms, and the two threads together run one transaction every 100 ms, or 10 TPS.

In Figure 9.5 we see two transaction threads interleaving operations, with odd-numbered transactions performing I/O access on disk 1, while even numbered transactions use disk 2. (Of course it wouldn't happen so neatly on a real system, but we will consider this point later.) We see that both threads proceed without waits (except in the very first 5 ms, where T_1 uses the CPU and T_2 waits for it.) In successive CPU use, the offset established in the beginning assures that even-numbered transactions never overlap with odd-numbered transactions. (This too is unrealistic for a real system.) Just as in Figure 9.3, each transaction thread performs one transaction each 110 ms, a rate of 9.09 TPS, and the two threads together execute transactions at twice that rate; 18.18 TPS. In this case the CPU in utilized for 10 ms out of each 55, about 18.18% utilized.

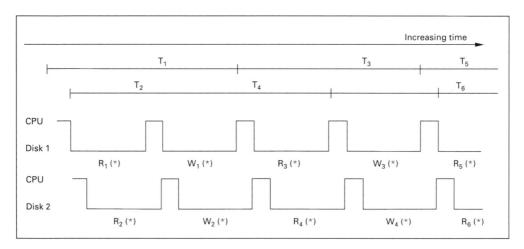

Figure 9.5 Sequence of Events with Two Interleaved Transactions, Two Disks

In order to increase the utilization of the CPU even further, we add more disks and more transactional threads to overlap operations. Figure 9.6 gives a schematic picture of resource use when 11 disks are available and there are 11 transactional threads, and we assume that resource overlap is perfect. In this case we have 11 threads running at full speed. Each transaction requires 110 ms as in the first case above, but with 11 transactions running simultaneously, we have a throughput of 11 transactions every 110 ms, or 100 TPS. The CPU is 100% utilized because of the unrealistically perfect resource overlap assumed. ■

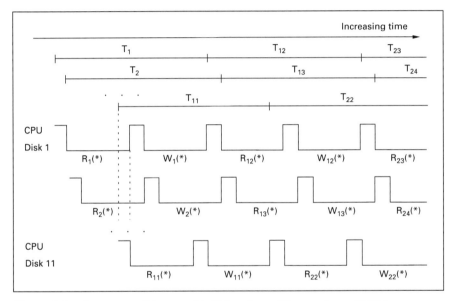

Figure 9.6   Sequence of Events with 11 Interleaved Transactions, 11 Disks

The ratio of 5 ms of CPU use to 50 ms of disk I/O is quite common in transactional systems. As less expensive computers become faster with new advances in technology the ratio can be expected to become even more extreme, since CPU rates are advancing faster than disk I/O rates. For this reason, many transactional systems will be configured to run with a large number of disks.

Naturally, concurrently executing transactions are not always guaranteed to access distinct disks and to perfectly overlap their CPU time, as they do in Figure 9.6. Let us consider the approach a DBA would normally take to configure for the workload of Example 9.2.1, where each transaction uses 10 ms of CPU and 50 ms of disk. (In the following analysis we consider only the actual utilization of the disk arm, 25 ms per I/O instead of 50 ms, because the decisions we make will affect the waiting time for disk service.) If we pose this problem properly, it is an exercise in a mathematical discipline known as *queuing theory,* a field that incorporates a good deal of hard-won intuition. It is difficult to provide an explanation of the principles involved without the mathematical background, but we try to provide a feel for what happens. A sensible configuration with a ratio of 5 to 1 in I/O elapsed time to CPU time, given above, is to use a good deal more than five disks, say ten disks, and then run more than ten simultaneous transaction threads, say 20. The data to be read and written by the transactions should be divided evenly over the disks, so that any $R_i(*)$ or $W_i(*)$ operation of an arbitrarily chosen transaction is equally likely to access any one of them. Clearly, as we increase the number of disks there is more and more chance that any thread, as it completes its CPU interval and requires data from disk, will find the data it wants on a disk that is not already occupied seeking data for another thread. Thus it will not have to wait in line, or queue. What we are doing here is shortening the average disk service time in comparison to the CPU time by adding more disks. Although the disk service time was specified as 50 ms in the examples we considered above, the time actually depends on the number of disks available to reduce the queue lengths for a given rate of random service requests. It has a lower limit of 25 ms.

Now the DBA also needs to minimize hardware cost by not buying more disks than are required to properly utilize the CPU resource. This means that there will still be a good deal of disk collision, where I/O requests of two different threads are sent to the same disk at nearly the same time; we certainly won't achieve the perfect interleaving that we saw in Figure 9.6. This would be an extremely serious problem if we continued to run only 11 threads, as in that example with an average disk service time of 50 ms, since I/O requests would have to be filled in a nearly perfect interleaved pattern to keep the CPU occupied. But with 20 concurrent threads available, we can conceivably have as many as 20 transactions running in parallel. We can picture at any given instant that some of the transactions are waiting for CPU or running the CPU (these transactions are said to be in the CPU queue) and some transactions are waiting for one of the disks or running one of the disks (these are said to be in one of the different disk queues). In order to achieve high CPU utilization, we merely need to guarantee that the CPU queue rarely becomes empty (whereupon

the CPU would have no transaction to execute), and this is achieved if we
guarantee a long average CPU queue. Now it should be clear that we can
do this if we can keep an average of nearly five out of the ten disks running
at all times. It is one of the basic principles of queuing theory that if
requesters (transactions) leave one part of the system (the disk part) and
make requests of another part (the CPU) faster than they can be serviced,
then the queue for the overloaded resource provider will grow arbitrarily
long. (Because the disk to CPU service time ratio is 25 ms on each disk to 5
ms on the sole CPU, when more than five disks are being kept in service
simultaneously on the average, the CPU will be unable to keep up.)

By permitting a large number of threads, we give the system more to
do in the event that some subset of disk requests collide. Even though several threads are tied up waiting for disk service, the CPU can run other
transactional threads and put out more disk requests. With enough
requests, we will be relatively certain to place requests to more then five of
the ten disks, and as a result we will keep the CPU heavily utilized. Note
that we don't *have* to run 20 simultaneous transactions just because we
have that number of threads, and in fact everything we have explained so
far is part of a feedback process. As new transactions enter the system, they
are assigned to distinct threads, so that up to 20 can run concurrently.
However, transactions may run to completion at too high a rate for 20
simultaneous transactions to ever be in existence—the more transactions
that run concurrently, the higher the throughput rate, and we shouldn't
normally need maximum thread concurrency. We wouldn't normally
expect to see 100% CPU utilization either, but rather 80% or 90%. On the
other hand, if the CPU utilization falls too low, so that the workload is not
being handled at the needed throughput rate, then more transactions enter
the system to run concurrently up to the maximum of 25, and this
increases the disk and CPU utilization. (Additional transaction starts after
the 25 threads are occupied have to wait in another queue to be assigned
threads.)

Thus we depend on statistical behavior to increase the CPU utilization
as more disks and threads are added. Readers interested in how this sort of
process can be numerically balanced should read one of the standard introductory texts on queuing theory.

9.3 | Serializability and the Precedence Graph

In this section we derive a criterion that allows us to say when a given history of transactional operations (such as the one we saw in (9.1.2)) is *serializable*. This means that the history is *equivalent* to some serial schedule (where all operations of one transaction must complete before any operations of another can be executed), and therefore the history can be accepted by a system scheduler that supports the property of transaction *isolation*. We begin with a discussion to demonstrate what it means when two transactions with interleaved operations in a serial history H have *conflicting operations*. We say that read and write operations by different transactions *conflict* if they reference the same data item and at least one of them is a write (the other can be either a read or a write). This concept is stated with more precise notation in Definition 9.3.1. Now when two operations by different transactions conflict in a history, the order in which they occur is important, and we can say that two different histories containing the same transactional operations in a somewhat different order are nevertheless *equivalent* if all pairs of conflicting operations lie in the same order in both histories. With this background, we now define a history to be *serializable* if it is equivalent to some serial history. In Theorem 9.3.4 we demonstrate a criterion for determining when a history is serializable.

To begin to motivate some of these concepts, let us assume that we are given a history H of transactional operations of the kind we saw in (9.1.2). Now assume that in the history H, one transaction reads a data item A and at a later point in time a second transaction updates (writes) the same data item. Thus the two operations shown in (9.3.1) appear in H, with ellipses (. . .) representing arbitrary intervening operations of the history.

[9.3.1]   . . . $R_1(A)$ . . . $W_2(A)$ . . .

When we say that an update is performed by operation $W_2(A)$ in the history H, we simply mean that a new value overwrites the current value of data item A. We are not necessarily implying the kind of update performed by the SQL Update statement, since there is no implied read of the data item A on which to base the new value written (of course, there is also nothing saying that there is no such read). If we had meant to imply a prior read, we would have written . . . $R_2(A)$ . . . $W_2(A)$ . . . in place of . . . $W_2(A)$ . . ..

Now we want to try to come up with an *equivalent* serial history to the history H that contains the two operations of (9.3.1) in the order specified. There may be more than one equivalent serial history, but we denote a representative one by S(H). Then in any equivalent serial history S(H), we claim that all the operations of transaction T_2 must come later in time than all the operations of transaction T_1. This is because transaction T_1 in the history H reads a value for the data item A (say 50) that existed prior to the write performed by T_2; this write might have changed the value of A, say to 20. We can certainly construct an *interpretation* where this happens. Since it seems necessary that in an "equivalent" serial history all transactions read the same data as they do in history H, it seems obvious that T_2 must follow T_1 in serial order in both cases. We use the notation

$$R_1(A) <<_H W_2(A)$$

to mean that $R_1(A)$ comes before $W_2(A)$ in the history H, and we claim that this means that the same order must be preserved in an equivalent serial history S(H) (there may be more than one). We denote this by

$$R_1(A) <<_{S(H)} W_2(A)$$

More generally, since all operations for a transaction T_i occur together in a serial history, we can denote the set of all operations performed in T_i by the notation T_i itself, and write

$$T_1 <<_{S(H)} T_2$$

Now in an entirely different situation, if the transaction T_2 updates (writes) a data item B prior to a read of this data item by transaction T_1 in the history H:

$$W_2(B) <<_H R_1(B)$$

then we claim that transaction T_2 must precede T_1 in an equivalent serial history S(H), or $T_2 <<_{S(H)} T_1$. What we have determined so far is this: two operations $X_i(A)$ and $Y_j(A)$, by different transactions T_i and T_j in a history H, are said to *conflict* if, when one occurs before the other in the history H, the same order must be maintained for the corresponding transactions in

665

an equivalent serial history. The operations $R_i(A)$ and $W_j(A)$ are conflicting operations in a history in whatever order they might occur.

To put it loosely, we have determined that reads conflict with writes. There are only two types of operations, four types of operation pairs, so let us now ask if reads conflict with reads—that is, do $R_i(A)$ and $R_j(A)$ conflict? We maintain that two reads do not conflict in and of themselves. If we had a sequence . . . $R_i(A)$ . . . $W_k(A)$ . . . $R_j(A)$ . . . in the history H, we could conclude that $T_i <<_{S(H)} T_k$ and $T_k <<_{S(H)} T_j$ because of the two pairs of conflicting R-W operations, and thus by transitivity $T_i <<_{S(H)} T_j$. However, the reads themselves are guiltless: a history H that has $R_i(A)$ $R_j(A)$ and a history H' that has $R_j(A)$ $R_i(A)$ are the same, so long as no other operations intervene between the two reads.

The pair of operations $W_i(A)$ and $W_j(A)$, on the other hand, *are* conflicting. It should be clear that the order of these two operations is crucial, since if the two writes update the data element A to different values, the final resulting value of data element A will be determined by the specific write that comes last. Clearly two histories cannot be identical that give different final results. Figure 9.7 illlustrates the three pairs of conflicting operations we have found.

---

(1) $R_i(A) \rightarrow W_j(A)$ (meaning, in a history, $R_i(A)$ followed by $W_j(A)$)

(2) $W_i(A) \rightarrow R_j(A)$

(3) $W_i(A) \rightarrow W_j(A)$

Figure 9.7 The Three Types of Conflicting Operations

These three pairs of operations, together with the pair $R_i(A)$ and $R_j(A)$, which we concluded did not conflict, make up all possible pairs of operations between two transactions T_i and T_j that can occur on the same data element. By contrast, any pair of operations on *different* data elements are *not* conflicting: $R_i(A)$ does not conflict with $W_j(B)$, for example, since the order in which these operations are performed doesn't seem to matter. If two different transactions act on totally distinct data items, the order in which they execute is irrelevant. Again, as with the $R_i(A)$ and $R_j(A)$ example, we can conceive of a third transaction T_k, which would conflict with $R_i(A)$ and $W_j(B)$ and force a specific order on T_i and T_j by transitivity; but we are claiming that $R_i(A)$ and $W_j(B)$ are not conflicting in themselves. To sum up the foregoing discussion, we give a number of definitions.

DEFINITION 9.3.1 Two operations $X_i(A)$ and $Y_j(B)$ in a history are said to *conflict* if and only if the following three conditions hold. (1) A = B. Operations on distinct data items never conflict. (2) $i \neq j$. Two operations conflict only if they are performed by distinct transactions. (3) One of the two operations X or Y is a write, W, while the other may be either a R or a W. ■

This definition of conflicting operations in a history seems like many mathematical definitions at first: we wonder what application it has. To see what we can do with this concept, we need a few examples. Recall the history given in (9.1.2), which we designate as H1.

$$H1 = R_2(A)\ W_2(A)\ R_1(A)\ R_1(B)\ R_2(B)\ W_2(B)\ C_1\ C_2$$

Recall that in Example 9.1.1 we gave an interpretation of this history that showed that it was not serializable.

DEFINITION 9.3.2 An interpretation of an arbitrary history H consists of three parts. (1) A description of the purpose of the logic that is being performed by the transactions involved in the history. (2) A specification of precise values of data items being read and written in the history. (3) A consistency rule, a statement of a logical property that we can demonstrate must be preserved by isolated transaction executions of the logic described in (1). In the case where a history is being shown to be nonserializable, we demonstrate that the consistency rule is broken by some transaction in the history, where this is clearly impossible in any serial execution.   ■

EXAMPLE 9.3.1
To repeat the interpretation of Example 9.1.1, we concluded that the given history H1 was not serializable because of the following interpretation:

$$\ldots R_2(A,50)\ W_2(A,20)\ R_1(A,20)\ R_1(B,50)\ R_2(B,50)\ W_2(B,80)\ C_1\ C_2 \ldots$$

Here T_1 is doing a credit check, adding up the balances A and B, T_2 is transferring money from A to B, and the consistency rule is that neither transaction creates or destroys money. But this schedule is not serializable because T_1 sees an *inconsistent result,* the sum 70 of the two balances A and B, rather than the balance of 100 that would be seen in any serial execution.

The concept of conflicting operations we have introduced gives us a more direct way to check for serializability. Note that the second and third operations in H1 consist of a conflicting pair: $W_2(A) <<_{H1} R_1(A)$. According to what we have said about conflicting operations, we must therefore have in any equivalent serial history S(H1), $T_2 <<_{S(H1)} T_1$. At the same time, the fourth and sixth operations of the history H1 give us $R_1(B) <<_{H1} W_2(B)$, and therefore we see that $T_1 <<_{S(H1)} T_2$. Clearly these two facts lead to a contradiction, since it is impossible to create a serial history where at the same time $T_1 <<_{S(H1)} T_2$, and $T_2 <<_{S(H1)} T_1$. We conclude from this that no equivalent serial history can exist. ∎

If you consider the two facts that led to this conclusion, you will see that Example 9.3.1 supports the reasons we gave that the order of the conflicting operations in an arbitrary history H must be preserved in S(H). The reason for the inconsistency is that (1) T_1 reads the data item A *after* it has been written by T_2, and (2) T_1 reads the data item B *before* it has been written by T_2, two conflicting pairs with opposite orientation. As a result, the explicit values used in the interpretation show that T_1 encounters a sum that could not be produced in any serial execution of the logic, and the reason is precisely this: in any proper serial execution, one of the conflicting pairs would be reversed in order.

EXAMPLE 9.3.2

Consider the history H2, given by

$$H2 = R_1(A) \ R_2(A) \ W_1(A) \ W_2(A) \ C_1 \ C_2$$

This is an example of transactional inconsistency known as *lost update,* or sometimes *dirty write,* where each transaction reads a data item and then writes it back without realizing that the other transaction is doing the same. As an Interpretation, assume that A is a bank balance starting with the value 100 and that T_1 tries to add 40 to the balance at the same time that T_2 tries to add 50. The result would be

$$\ldots R_1(A, 100) \ R_2(A, 100) \ W_1(A, 140) \ W_2(A, 150) \ C_1 \ C_2 \ldots$$

and the final value for A is 150. However, going by the intentions of the two transactions, we should have A = 190 in any serial schedule. Therefore this schedule cannot be serializable! In fact, we see that the first operation in this history, $R_1(A)$, conflicts with the fourth operation, $W_2(A)$, giving us $R_1(A) <<_{H2} W_2(A)$, and therefore $T_1 <<_{S(H2)} T_2$. Also, the second operation in the history, $R_2(A)$, conflicts with the third operation, $W_1(A)$, giving us $R_2(A) <<_{H2} W_1(A)$, and therefore $T_2 <<_{S(H2)} T_1$. Thus, as in Example 9.3.1, there is no equivalent serial history. This example demonstrates that two conflicting pairs, $R_i(A) <<_H W_j(A)$ and $R_j(A) <<_H W_i(A)$ of type (1) from Figure 9.7, are together sufficient to result in the nonserializability that can be demonstrated by interpretation.   ∎

EXAMPLE 9.3.3

Consider the history H3, given by

$$H3 = W_1(A)\ W_2(A)\ W_2(B)\ W_1(B)\ C_1\ C_2$$

This example demonstrates that a conflicting pair of type (3) can cause nonserializability as well. Clearly, since there are no reads involved, conflicting pairs type (1) and (2) cannot be involved. Since the first two operations give $W_1(A) <<_{H3} W_2(A)$, we have $T_1 <<_{S(H3)} T_2$. Since the third and fourth operations give $W_2(B) <<_{H3} W_1(B)$, we have $T_1 <<_{S(H3)} T_2$, and so—as in the two previous examples—no equivalent serial history is possible. How would we create an interpretation to demonstrate this fact? Assume that there are two accounts A and B, with balances starting with a sum of 90, and that we are dealing with only one type of transaction in this history that "tops up" the two accounts, resetting the sum of the balances to 100. We have a consistency rule that the sum of the two balances never exceeds 100. Note that a transaction that sets the sum of the two balances need not read the original values—it can simply perform "blind writes" (writes without preceding reads) to A and B so that the two sum to 100. Now consider the following specification of the values for H3:

$$W_1(A,50)\ W_2(A,80)\ W_2(B,20)\ W_1(B,50)\ C_1\ C_2$$

Both of the transactions obey the consistency rules (each one in isolation would give a sum of 100 for the two accounts A and B), but the result of the inter-leaved schedule gives a sum of 130, and the consistency rule is broken.   ∎

The Precedence Graph

To generalize the serializability argument we have seen in these three examples, that certain configurations of conflicting operations are impossible in any serial schedule, we define something called a *precedence graph*. A precedence graph is a structure, created from a history H, that remembers the order of transactions implied by conflicting pairs in the history.

DEFINITION 9.3.3 The Precedence Graph. A precedence graph for a history H is a directed graph denoted by PG(H). The vertices of the precedence graph correspond to transactions that have committed in H—that is, transactions T_i for which the Commit operation C_i exists in the history H.

An edge T_i -> T_j exists in the graph whenever two conflicting operations X_i and Y_j occur in that order in the history H. The edge T_i -> T_j should be read to mean that T_i comes before T_j in any equivalent history $S(H)$—that is, that $T_i <<_{S(H)} T_j$. ∎

Whenever a pair of operations conflicts in a history, we can draw the corresponding directed arc in the precedence graph. The precedence graphs for the histories considered in Examples 9.3.1, 9.3.2, and 9.3.3 are all identical, with the structure shown in the following illustration.

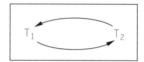

As we can see, this graph has a circuit, and it is for this reason that we argue that no equivalent serial history exists. Any serial history would have to place either T_1 or T_2 earlier in time, say $T_1 <<_{S(H)} T_2$, and then at least one edge of the precedence graph would point backward in time, from T_2 to T_1. Now an edge exists in PG(H) because of conflicting operations between the two transactions, and the direction in which it points is the original order of occurrence in the history H. To have an edge of PG(H) pointing backward in a serial history means that we have reversed the order of two conflicting operations from the original history H, and therefore that the order in the serial history is not equivalent to the original history H. It should be clear then that if PG(H) has a circuit, there can never be a serial history equivalent to H, since at least one edge of PG(H) must always point backward in any serial order of transactions. (The proof of this is given as an exercise, below.) In what follows, we prove that if the precedence graph PG(H) does not have a circuit, then there is a serial execution of the transactions that is equivalent to H.

THEOREM 9.3.4 The Serializability Theorem. A history H has an equivalent serial execution $S(H)$ if and only if the precedence graph PG(H) contains no circuit.

PROOF. We leave the *only if* proof for the exercises at the end of the chapter, and show here that if PG(H) contains no circuit, then there is a serial ordering of the transactions so that no edge of PG(H) ever points from a later to an earlier transaction. Let us assume that there are m transactions involved, and renumber the transactions of PG(H) if necessary, so that they are denoted by $T_1, T_2, \ldots, T_m$. We are trying to find some reordering of these transactions to form a desired serial history $S(H) = T_{i(1)}, T_{i(2)}, \ldots, T_{i(m)}$, where $i(1), i(2), \ldots, i(m)$ is some reordering of the integers $1, 2, \ldots,$ m. We start by assuming a lemma, to be proven later, that in any directed graph G with no circuit there is always at least one vertex with no edge entering it. This means that the precedence graph PG(H) has at least one vertex, T_k, with no edge entering it. We choose that transaction, T_k, to be $T_{i(1)}$, the first transaction in the serial history S(H). Notice that it has an important qualifying property, that no other transaction T_m chosen from the remaining vertices of PG(H), which will be placed to the right of $T_{i(1)}$, has an edge in PG(H) pointing backward to $T_{i(1)}$. We now remove the vertex just placed, T_k, from the graph PG(H), as well as all edges leaving T_k, and call the resulting graph $PG^1(H)$, where the superscript 1 means that one vertex has been removed from the original. Note that $PG^1(H)$ also has the property that it contains no circuits (no edges have been added to PG(H), so no circuit could have appeared). By our lemma, this means there is a vertex T_k^1 in $PG^1(H)$ that has no edges entering it in $PG^1(H)$. We choose this vertex to be the second element of S(H), $T_{i(2)}$. Note that there might be an edge from $T_{i(1)}$ to $T_{i(2)}$ in PG(H), but there is no edge entering $T_{i(2)}$ in $PG^1(H)$. That means there will never be an edge going from right to left to point at $T_{i(2)}$ in the serial schedule yet to be determined from the remaining vertices of $PG^1(H)$. Proceeding inductively, we define $PG^{r-1}(H)$ with T_k^{r-1} removed to be $PG^r(H)$, and while $PG^r(H)$ is non-empty, choose T_k^r to be a vertex of $PG^r(H)$ with no edge entering it, setting T_k^r to be element $T_{i(r+1)}$ in S(H). By construction, no edge of PG(H) will ever point backward in the sequence S(H), from $T_{i(m)}$ to $T_{i(n)}$, m > n. The algorithm used to determine this sequence, known as a *topological sort*, is described in a number of algorithmic texts. ■

We now have only to prove the lemma mentioned.

LEMMA 9.3.5 In any finite directed acyclic graph G, there is always a vertex v with no edges entering it.

PROOF. Choose any vertex v_1 from G. Either it has no edge entering it or there is an edge entering it from a vertex v_2. Now v_2 either has no edge entering it or there is an edge entering it from vertex v_3. Continuing in this way, we find that the sequence either ends with some vertex v_m, so that v_m has no edge entering it, or the sequence continues forever. But if the sequence continues forever, then at some point some vertex must be relabeled, since there are only a finite number of vertices in G. Assume that when we label v_n, we find for the first time that this is equivalent to some previously labeled vertex v_i, $i < n$. But then we have a circuit, $v_n \rightarrow v_{n-1} \rightarrow v_{n-2} \rightarrow \ldots \rightarrow v_{i-1} \rightarrow v_i = v_n$. We have specified that the graph G is acyclic, so this is impossible. This means that the sequence specified doesn't continue forever and there must be a last vertex v_m with no edge entering it, which is what we wished to show. ∎

9.4 Locking to Ensure Serializability

Examine Figure 9.8, which is identical to Figure 9.1, to follow the discussion below.

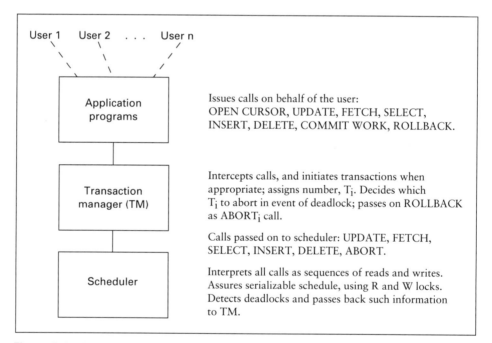

Application programs	Issues calls on behalf of the user: OPEN CURSOR, UPDATE, FETCH, SELECT, INSERT, DELETE, COMMIT WORK, ROLLBACK.
Transaction manager (TM)	Intercepts calls, and initiates transactions when appropriate; assigns number, T_i. Decides which T_i to abort in event of deadlock; passes on ROLLBACK as $ABORT_i$ call. Calls passed on to scheduler: UPDATE, FETCH, SELECT, INSERT, DELETE, ABORT.
Scheduler	Interprets all calls as sequences of reads and writes. Assures serializable schedule, using R and W locks. Detects deadlocks and passes back such information to TM.

Figure 9.8   Layering of Transactional System Down to the Scheduler

In a transactional database system there are normally a large number **673** of users at terminals trying to get work done—users who are unaware of such things as transactions or database calls made on their behalf. In the normal course of execution, an application program issues an operation on behalf of some user, and the database initiates a transaction and assigns a number, i, to the transaction. The module of the database system that does this is known as the *transaction manager,* or *TM,* as we see in Figure 9.8. The TM passes on such calls as UPDATE, FETCH, SELECT, INSERT, and DELETE to the scheduler.

It is the job of the *scheduler* to assure that the "interleaved history" of all the transactional operations is serializable. It does this by forcing some transactional operations to WAIT and allowing others to proceed, so that the resulting history of operations is a serializable one. When a transactional operation is forced to WAIT, the corresponding user is required to wait as well; but since the time period is typically a small fraction of a second, the user will never notice.

One simple approach we have already mentioned can be used by the scheduler—to impose a strict serial history discipline on the transactional operations, insisting that all operations of one transaction be complete (including a final commit or rollback), before operations from the next transaction are allowed to begin. As we saw in Section 9.2, requiring strict serial execution is usually a very bad idea from the standpoint of performance. In this section we explain how a scheduler that works on the basis of locking can guarantee a serializable schedule with a good deal of interleaving of operations.

The locking discipline used to assure transactional consistency in commercial database systems is known as *two-phase locking,* abbreviated *2PL.*

DEFINITION 9.4.1 Two-Phase Locking, or 2PL. Three rules determine how locks are taken and released in 2PL.

[1] When transaction T_i attempts to read a data item, $R_i(A)$, the scheduler intercepts this call and first issues a call on its behalf to *read lock* the data item, $RL_i(A)$. Similarly, when T_i attempts to write (update) a data item, $W_i(A)$, the scheduler first issues a call on its behalf to *write lock* the data item, $WL_i(A)$.[1]

---

[1]Although read locks and write locks are logically sufficient, many modern database systems impose a number of other types of locks, known as *granular locks* or *multigranular locks* or *intention locks*, that are outside the scope of this text. See references [1] and [2] at the end of this chapter.

[2]   Before granting a lock on a data item, the scheduler requires the requesting transaction to WAIT until no *conflicting lock* on the data item exists. (Conflicting locks are for what we have been calling conflicting operations, as defined below. Example 9.4.2 shows how such a WAIT affects the history execution.)

Two locks on the same data item are said to *conflict* if and only if they are attempted by different transactions and at least one of the two locks is a write lock.

[3]   There are two phases to locking: the *growing phase,* during which locks are acquired, and the *shrinking phase,* during which locks are released. The scheduler must ensure that after the shrinking phase begins, no new locks are acquired; it is forbidden for a transaction to release a lock and then acquire another lock at a later time.   ∎

The rules for 2PL theoretically allow locks to be released by a transaction before the transaction commits, as long as no new locks will be requested later. Most commercial systems, however, release all locks at once at the last stage of the COMMIT process. We assume that this is what occurs in the discussion that follows except when an unlock action is explicitly performed prior to commit. Two locks by the same transaction never conflict—in particular, a transaction with a read lock on a data item can acquire a write lock so long as no other transaction has a lock on the item. A transaction with a write lock on a data item need not acquire a read lock; we say that a read lock is less powerful than a write lock, and the request $RL_i(A)$ on a data item A on which T_i already has a write lock immediately returns successfully.

The definition of conflicting locks is clearly intended to guarantee that two transactions performing conflicting operations will be "serialized," so that a circuit in the precedence graph can never occur. When two transactions have conflicting operations on a data item A, the transaction that accesses the data item first gets a lock and forces the other transaction to "come later" in any equivalent serial history. If the second transaction already holds a lock that the first transaction needs at a later point in its execution, this results in a deadlock, and one of the transactions must abort. The operations of the aborted transaction are then "removed" from the history, so that the result is serializable. Thus the 2PL discipline guarantees a serializable history. We need to deal with the issue of deadlocks before we can show this rigorously.

First, however, we want to demonstrate the importance of locking rule 3 of Definition 9.4.1, which states there must be a growing phase followed by a shrinking phase in locking. This "two-phase rule" is crucial if locking is to have the desired effect of guaranteeing serializability.

EXAMPLE 9.4.1

Recall that history H1 was shown not to be serializable in Example 9.3.3.

$$H1 = R_1(A) \; R_2(B) \; W_2(B) \; R_2(A) \; W_2(A) \; R_1(B) \; C_1 \; C_2$$

We demonstrate that if we allow the two-phase rule to be broken in this history, we can perform locking that satisfies all the other rules, but allows the nonserializable history H1 to execute. In what follows, we add a number of new types of operations to illustrate locking operations in an "extended" history H1. The operation designated by RL signifies that a read lock is taken, WL signifies that a write lock is taken, RU signifies that an unlock operation is performed to release a read lock, and WU means that an unlock operation releases a write lock. Thus, for example, $RL_1(A)$ signifies that transaction T_1 takes a read lock on data item A, and $WU_2(A)$ that transaction T_2 unlocks a write lock on data item A. As usual, all locks held by a transaction are implicitly released at commit time. Here is the extended history H1:

$$RL_1(A) \; R_1(A) \; RU_1(A) \; RL_2(B) \; R_2(B) \; WL_2(B) \; W_2(B) \; WU_2(B) \; RL_2(A) \; R_2(A) \; WL_2$$
$$(A) \; W_2(A) \; RL_1(B) \; R_1(B) \; C_1 \; C_2$$

In this extended history each transaction takes the appropriate lock, RL or WL, just before performing the operation R or W, respectively. Thus rule 1 of 2PL Definition 9.4.1 is obeyed. Furthermore, rule 2 is obeyed, since there is never a conflicting lock held on the data item by another transaction when a requested lock is granted. The third operation, $RU_1(A)$, releases the lock that would conflict later with the request of the eleventh operation, $WL_2(A)$, and similarly the eighth operation, $WU_2(B)$, releases the lock that would conflict with the thirteenth operation, $RL_1(B)$. Thus the only rule broken in this extended history is the two-phase rule, since both operations acquire new locks after they release one. This demonstrates the necessity of the two-phase rule of locking to guarantee serializability. ■

The Waits-For Graph

The *waits-for graph* is a directed graph, maintained by many transactional locking schedulers, with vertices consisting of all current transactions in process and an edge from vertex T_i to vertex T_j, $T_i \rightarrow T_j$, exactly when T_i is currently waiting for a lock on some data item that is held by transaction T_j. The scheduler keeps a waits-for graph up to date as new transactions start (a new vertex is added to the graph), transactions are forced to WAIT (a new edge is added to the graph), or old transactions commit (a node is deleted, locked data items are released, and the first transaction in the waiting line for each data item is given the lock; this may now result in other transactions being required to wait on the new transaction holding the lock, but the algorithm by which this is done is relatively efficient). We say that a *deadlock* occurs whenever a circuit appears in the waits-for graph.

The scheduler tests for a circuit in the waits-for graph at regular intervals after the graph changes. If a circuit is found, the scheduler chooses some transaction in the circuit as a *victim* to abort. The criterion used to select the victim can be of various kinds: abort youngest transactions first, abort transactions that have performed the least amount of work, and so on.

> **EXAMPLE 9.4.2**
>
> We refer once again to history H1, which was shown in Example 9.3.3 not to be serializable. What will happen when the 2PL discipline is applied?
>
> $H1 = R_1(A) \, R_2(B) \, W_2(B) \, R_2(A) \, W_2(A) \, R_1(B) \, C_1 \, C_2$
>
> History H1 gives rise to the following sequence of events when a locking discipline is applied:
>
> $RL_1(A) \, R_1(A) \, RL_2(B) \, R_2(B) \, WL_2(B) \, W_2(B) \, RL_2(A) \, R_2(A) \, WL_2(A)$ (conflict with earlier $RL_1(A)$—T_2 must WAIT) $RL_1(B)$ (conflict with earlier $WL_2(B)$—T1 must WAIT—there is now a circuit in the waits-for graph, so we must abort some transaction—choose T_1 as victim) A_1 (locks by T_1 released, so now $WL_2(A)$, which caused a WAIT, is successful) $W_2(A) \, C_2$ (assume retry by T_1 code, renamed T_3) $RL_3(A) \, R_3(A) \, RL_3(B) \, R_3(B) \, C_3$
>
> The scheduler, by forcing WAITs and aborting one transaction, has permitted both transactions to eventually succeed. ∎

THEOREM 9.4.2 Locking Theorem. A history of transactional operations that follows the 2PL discipline is always serializable. ∎

We start by proving a necessary lemma.

LEMMA 9.4.3 Let H be an extended history of transactional operations that follows the 2PL discipline (we call this a 2PL history). If the edge $T_i \rightarrow T_j$ is in the precedence graph for H, PG(H), then there must exist a data item D and two conflicting operations $X_i[D]$ and $Y_j[D]$ in H, such that $XU_i[D] <<_H YL_j[D]$. ∎

PROOF. Since $T_i \rightarrow T_j$, by the definition of precedence graph and conflicting operations, there must exist two conflicting operations $X_i[D]$ and $Y_j[D]$ such that $X_i[D] <<_H Y_j[D]$. By the definition of two-phase locking, there must be locking and unlocking operations on either side of these operations, with $XL_i[D] <<_H X_i[D] <<_H XU_i[D]$ and $YL_j[D] <<_H Y_j[D] <<_H YU_j[D]$. (The unlocking operations might be implicit in commit operations for the two transactions, but we choose to make them explicit in the history H, occurring just prior to the commit operations.)

Now for operations occurring in the range of operations $XL_i[D] <<_H X_i[D] <<_H XU_i[D]$, the X lock is held on D by transaction T_i, and for operations occurring in the range $YL_j[D] <<_H Y_j[D] <<_H YU_j[D]$, the Y lock is held on D. Since X and Y conflict, the locks conflict, and the two intervals cannot overlap. But since $X_i[D] <<_H Y_j[D]$, this means that the locking intervals around these two operations must occur in this order:

$$XL_i[D] <<_H X_i[D] <<_H XU_i[D] <<_H YL_j[D] <<_H Y_j[D] <<_H YU_j[D]$$

and the desired result of the lemma is proved. ∎

Given this result, we can prove Theorem 9.4.2.

PROOF OF THEOREM 9.4.2 We wish to show that every 2PL history H is serializable. But assume for purposes of contradiction that a 2PL history H has a precedence graph PG(H) that contains a cycle $T_1 \rightarrow T_2 \rightarrow \ldots T_n \rightarrow T_1$. By lemma 9.4.3, for each pair of connected transactions $T_K \rightarrow T_{k+1}$ in PG(H) there is a data item D_K such that $XU_K[D_K] <<_H YL_{K+1}[D_K]$. We can write all these facts on successive numbered lines, as follows:

1. $XU_1[D_1] <<_H YL_2[D_1]$
2. $XU_2[D_2] <<_H YL_3[D_2]$

        . . .

n–1. $XU_{n-1}[D_{n-1}] <<_H YL_n[D_{n-1}]$

n. $XU_n[D_n] <<_H YL_1[D_n]$

But by the two-phase property, all locks must be performed in a transaction T_i before any unlocks are performed. Therefore, considering the transaction T_2, $XL_2[D_1] <<_H YU_2[D_2]$, we can conclude from facts on lines 1 and 2 and transitivity that

$$XU_1[D_1] <<_H YL_3[D_2]$$

That is, some data item is unlocked by transaction T_1 before some other data item is locked by transaction T_3. Continuing to arrive at conclusions in this way, by induction through line n, we conclude that

$$XU_1[D_1] <<_H YL_1[D_n]$$

But this contradicts the two-phase property that all locks are performed by transaction T before any unlocks are performed. Since we assume this was a 2PL history, we have arrived at a contradiction, and we conclude that no circuit can exist in PG(H). Therefore H must be serializable. ∎

9.5   Levels of Isolation

Theorem 9.4.2 tells us that a scheduler can guarantee serializable histories by imposing a two-phase locking discipline. This means that before any read or write of a data item, the scheduler attempts to take a read lock or write lock on behalf of the transaction performing the access, and the scheduler retains all locks achieved until the transaction that owns them completes, either with an abort or a commit. Remember that property 3 of 2PL assures us that a transaction won't release a lock and later acquire a different lock. We have to hold all locks until there are no remaining new data item accesses to come. (In fact, we are assuming that we hold all locks until the transaction commits.)

However, scheduling that guarantees perfect serializability can be very intrusive on performance. As we add more threads and concurrent transactions, especially when transactions deal with a large number of data items that are highly popular, transactional accesses begin to overlap on data items, and lock conflicts mean that more and more transactions find themselves in a WAIT state. The number of deadlocks also increases with greater concurrency, and the aborts and subsequent retries of transactional victims that the scheduler chooses seem to waste computer resources. But the most serious problem arises because, with large numbers of simultaneously active transactions, more and more transactions go into WAIT because of locking conflicts. This effect is so pronounced that in certain circumstances, if we increase the number of threads for concurrent transactions, we actually *reduce* the number of transactions that are concurrently active and not blocked in WAIT state (the *effective concurrency level*). The performance problem that arises is not because CPU is wasted on abort retries, but rather because the CPU can never be fully utilized since we can never get a high enough effective level of concurrency.

Because of this sort of problem, it was suggested a number of years ago that database system schedulers might weaken the rules of two-phase locking to reduce the number of transactional access conflicts that cause WAITs and thus increase effective concurrency. Of course with weaker rules, we don't have such a strong guarantee of isolation, and it is possible that transactions with overlapped operations will produce effects on one another that wouldn't be possible with strict serial schedules. Nevertheless, various weakened forms of locking are now a fact, with SQL-92 offering a feature known as *isolation levels*. Note that the SQL-92 definition of isolation levels differs in important ways from an earlier definition of *degrees of isolation*, 0°, 1°, 2°, and 3°, still used in some products. We cover only the SQL-92 syntax here.

It is possible in SQL-92 syntax to set the isolation level, immediately before executing an SQL statement that initiates a transaction (any data access), with something known as a *Set Transaction* statement. The four isolation levels provided in SQL-92, in increasing restrictiveness and level of guarantee to the programmer, are known as

[1] Read Uncommitted (known elsewhere as "dirty reads")

[2] Read Committed (known in **DB2** and elsewhere as "cursor stability")

[3] Repeatable Read

[4] Serializable

For example, we can include the following statement in an Embedded SQL program to guarantee that subsequent transactions are executed under the most stringent isolation level, Serializability, equivalent to serializability defined in Theorems 9.3.7 and 9.4.4.

```
exec sql set transaction serializable;
```

Alternatively, a Set Transaction statement could be used to set the isolation level to any of the other types listed. What we need to do next is discuss each of these other levels and indicate how they differ from perfect serializability, isolation level 4.

Whenever a transaction reads or writes a data item, it must take a *short-term lock* in most systems, also known as a *latch,* an exclusive lock to guarantee that the read or write is *atomic.* Clearly we need to ensure that no other transaction writes on or moves the data item while the first transaction is in the midst of accessing it, since such an overlap could lead to problems. However, a question arises after the access to the data item is complete: Should a read or write lock continue to be held on this data item until the requesting transaction completes with an abort or commit—that is, should we make this a *long-term lock*? The two-phase locking variant we have been using would say yes, the locks should be held long term. But with lower isolation levels, we sometimes decide to release the locks immediately, holding them only short term. Figure 9.9 lists which locks should be held long term for each of the isolation levels of SQL-92. Note that we differentiate between taking locks on data items that are rows of tables and taking locks on predicates occurring in **where** clauses. This point is explained below.

	Write locks on rows of a table are long term	Read locks on rows of a table are long term	Read and write locks on predicates are long term
Read Uncommitted (dirty reads)	N.A. (read only)	No	No
Read Committed (cursor stability)	Yes	No	No
Repeatable Read	Yes	Yes	No
Serializable	Yes	Yes	Yes

Figure 9.9 Long-Term Locking Behavior of SQL-92 Isolation Levels

Notice that it is possible for a scheduler to support concurrently executing transactions of different isolation levels in the same transactional workload. This is why SQL-92 allows programs to perform Set Transaction statements programmatically, resetting the level of isolation for subsequent transaction executions.

Read Uncommitted Isolation Level

From the first row of Figure 9.9, we see that transactions operating under the isolation level of Read Uncommitted take no long-term locks whatsoever. This would seem to mean that the phenomenon of dirty writes can occur (see Example 9.3.2), a write by one transaction at this level can be overwritten by another transaction based on an earlier read value, and therefore an update to an account balance can be lost because of a concurrent update to the same balance. However, this turns out not be a problem because a transaction at the Read Uncommitted isolation level is not permitted by SQL-92 to perform updates. A feature of the Set Transaction statement allows for announcing that subsequent transactions will be either *Read Only* or *Read Write*. Certain special capabilities can be provided by database systems for transactions that are Read Only, so it is considered a good idea to declare this intention: a Read Only transaction receives an error return if it attempts to execute any SQL Update statement. The usual default for transactions when no Set Transaction statement has been issued is Read Write, but in the case of the Read Uncommitted isolation level, the only possible setting is Read Only. Thus the dirty write problem does not occur. However, dirty reads certainly do occur. A transaction reading through the accounts and summing up balances in a bank branch ignores all other transaction locks and is able to view uncommitted data. (Notice that the short-term exclusive lock taken to hold the data item constant during access ignores transactional write locks.) As a result, the balance sum arrived at by the transaction is likely to have a value that was never valid at that branch. Certainly this will not satisfy an auditor, who wants an accounting that is exact to the penny. It may satisfy the reporting requirements of the bank manager, however, who simply wants to see a statistical idea of the branch balances once a week.

Read Committed Isolation Level (Cursor Stability)

In the second row of Figure 9.9, we see that the Read Committed isolation level holds write locks (on rows) long term, but not read locks. This excludes two of the three pairs of conflicting operations (for rows) by concurrently active transactions that we saw in Figure 9.7, (2) $W_i(A) \rightarrow R_j(A)$ and (3) $W_i(A) \rightarrow W_j(A)$. A transaction at this isolation level cannot read or write rows that have been written by another transaction until that transaction commits. (In particular, it cannot read uncommitted dirty data. It can only read data written by transactions that have already committed. This explains the name of this isolation level, Read Committed, and also the name of the previous level, where reading uncommitted (dirty) updates of data is possible.) The only conflicting operation on rows that can occur between concurrently executing transactions with the Read Committed isolation level is (1) $R_i(A) \rightarrow W_j(A)$. What sort of anomalies can a user see with this isolation level that would not occur with strict serial executions? The next two examples illustrate two such anomalies.

EXAMPLE 9.5.1 Nonrepeatable Read Anomaly.

Consider a transaction that opens a cursor on a set of rows, fetches successive rows and reads them, then later opens the cursor again to read the rows a second time. We find with the Read Committed isolation level that the record values read may not be the same the second time through the cursor. A read lock is held on the row under the cursor, but as soon as the cursor has left a row behind, the row can be updated by concurrently executing transactions. This anomaly is known by the name Nonrepeatable Read. ∎

This type of anomaly is not necessarily a problem for many database applications. In fact, **DB2** and a number of other products have offered this isolation level for some time, calling it *cursor stability,* with the aim that customers might want to use it for greater concurrency. The name "cursor stability" comes from the fact that a type of lock comparable to a read lock is held on rows selected by the cursor up to and including the time that each row is fetched; when the fetch moves on to the next row of the cursor, a write lock is kept on the prior row if it has been updated (the cursor must have been declared **for update**), but otherwise any locks on this row are dropped. As a result of this locking behavior, if we were come back and read the row again with a Select statement later in the same transaction, we might find that the row had been changed by another transaction. Row values were not kept "stable" by transaction locks after the cursor fetch passed it by. However, there is no lost update with the code sequence of Figure 9.10 that gives everyone at the SFBay branch a 10.00 bonus, because a lock is always held on the current row of the cursor.

```
exec sql declare cursor deposit for select balance from accounts
    where branch_id = 'SFBay' for update of balance;
exec sql open c;
(loop through rows in cursor)
    exec sql fetch c into :balance;
    balance = balance + 10.00;
    exec sql update account set balance = :balance
        where current of deposit;
(end of loop)
exec sql close deposit;
exec sql commit work;
```

Figure 9.10   Logic with No Lost Update under Isolation Level Read Committed

We can also achieve this update with the single statement update of Figure 9.11 in a transaction of isolation level Read Committed with no lost update, since once again the update occurs while the lock is held on the current row.

```
exec sql update accounts set balance = balance + 10.00
    where branch_id = 'SFBay';
exec sql commit work;
```

Figure 9.11   Alternate Logic with No Lost Update under Isolation Level Read Committed

However, the code sequence of Figure 9.12 to update a single row might result in a lost update. This is because no lock is held on the row after it is read by the first statement, and before it is updated by the second statement.

```
exec sql select balance into :balance from accounts
    where acct_id = 'A1234';
balance = balance + 10.00;
exec sql update accounts set balance = :balance
    where acct_id = 'A1234';
exec sql commit work;
```

Figure 9.12 Logic with Possible Lost Update under Isolation Level Read Committed

Another problem that arises in the Read Committed (or cursor stability) isolation level is much more serious than what is implied by the name "Nonrepeatable Reads."

EXAMPLE 9.5.2 Non-Audit-Balanced History.
Consider the following history, legal under Read Committed isolation.

$R_1(A, 50)$ $R_1(B, 50)$ $R_2(A, 50)$ $R_2(B, 50)$ $W_2(B, 60)$ $W_2(C, 110)$ C_2 $R_1(C, 110)$ C_1

In this history, we assume the consistency rule that the balances in rows A and B must always add up to give the balance in row C. T_1 is going through rows A, B, and C and simply checking that the rule holds, printing out a serious error message to the head teller if it does not. T_2, on the other hand, is adding 10 to the balance at row B and correcting the sum at row C. The problem, of course, is that T_1 holds no long-term read locks, so T_2 gets to make its update to B and then correct the balance C that T_1 hasn't seen yet. After T_2 commits, T_1 reads the incorrect balance and prints out an error message. ∎

It does not seem likely that all programmers using this isolation level are aware of the anomalies that can arise. A good DBA should make a special effort to ferret out programs that can fail for this reason.

Repeatable Read Isolation Level

The third row of Figure 9.9 shows that the Repeatable Read isolation level supports all the discipline of two-phase locking, as long as we consider only locks on rows of tables. This level solves all the problems we have mentioned that arise in the Read Uncommitted level. In particular, it solves the problem of Example 9.5.1, that reading through the rows of a cursor might not be repeatable with the same values the second time the cursor is opened. Hence the name "Repeatable Read." Since long-term read locks are held on all records accessed, the other problems of lost updates in Figure 9.12 and the non-audit-balance of Example 9.5.2 are also solved.

True Serializability, the isolation level on row four of Figure 9.9, supplies all the guarantees of Repeatable Read plus the guarantees associated with *predicate locking*, which we have not yet discussed. As it turns out, this allows interleaved transaction executions to avoid isolation anomalies known as *phantoms*, or *phantom updates*. This is a fairly subtle problem, which we deal with in the next subsection.

Serializability and Phantom Updates

We provide an example of an isolation anomaly that can arise with the Repeatable Read isolation level, very much like the one given earlier for cursor stability.

EXAMPLE 9.5.3 Phantom Update Anomaly.

Consider a transaction at the Repeatable Read isolation level that opens a cursor on the set of accounts rows at a given branch of a bank, fetches successive rows and sums their balances, then tests that the sum of these balances equals the balance of a special-purpose row in the `branch_totals` table with `branch_id` equal to that same branch id, and prints out an error if it is not. This might be accomplished by the following logic:

```
exec sql select sum(balance) into :total from accounts
    where branch_id = :bid;
exec sql select balance into :bbal from branch_totals
    where branch_id = :bid;
if (bbal <> total)
    (print out serious error);
exec sql commit work;
```

The phantom problem is reminiscent of Example 9.5.2, where we saw an anomaly arise in the Read Committed concurrency level. If the transaction executing the above check is T_1, then in Example 9.5.2 we saw another update transaction, T_2, that was able to slip in and update one of the account balances after T_1 had read it, then update the branch balance and commit before T_1 got to read this (now changed) balance. This problem could only arise because T_1 didn't hold any read locks long term.

However, a different sort of anomaly can occur because of an operation type that has not been considered up to now: an insert of a new rows. We use the terminology $I_i(A)$ to indicate that an insert of data item A has been performed by transaction T_i. When we wish to specify column values for the insert, we do so with a notation of the following sort: $I_i(A, \text{branch} = \text{SFBay}, \text{balance} = 50)$. (Recall that A is taken to be the field value that gives a unique identifier for the row in question, such as acct_id in the accounts table.) Now consider the following history.

> R_1(predicate: `branch_id` = `'SFBay'`) R_1(A1,100.00) R_1(A2, 100.00)
> R_1(A3,100.00) I_2(A4, `branch_id` = `'SFBay'`, balance = 100.00)
> R_2 (`branch_totals`, `branch_id` = `'SFBay'`, 300) W_2 (branch_totals,
> branch_id = `'SFBay'`, 400) $C_2 R_1$(`branch_totals`, `branch_id` = `'SFBay'`, 400)
> (Prints out error message) C_1

In words, what is happening is that transaction T_1 first determines what rows of the accounts table have branch_id equal to 'SFBay', and finds that the rows in question have acct_id values A1, A2, and A3. The three balances of these accounts are read, and they sum to $300.00. At this point another transaction T_2 comes along and creates a new account with acct_id value A4 at the SFBay branch (it certainly needs new accounts). T_2 then updates the `branch_totals` row with SFBay as acct_id to reflect the added account balance for that branch. But now when T_1 reads the SFBay account balance, it sees an impossible value, $400.00, where the three accounts it had added summed to only $300.00. ■

There is nothing stopping T_2 from adding this new account A4, and the change it makes to the branch balance for SFBay is valid by the consistency rule that the branch balance must equal the sum of the balances of accounts within the branch. No row locks are ignored by this logic, but an anomaly still arises. The reason is that a new row, A4, comes into the picture after T_1 has evaluated the predicate "`branch_id` = `'SFBay'`," presumably as an index range in the `accounts` table. T_1 would certainly have taken a lock on A4 if it had a chance to notice it, but A4 is added too late.

Does this mean that there is some problem with the serializability theorem, that 2PL does not imply true serializability? No. It only means that we haven't been taking a lock on enough objects, that we cannot restrict ourselves to table rows. Serializability requires that *all* information accessed by a transaction must figure into the precedence graph of Definition 9.3.3. When T_1 reads the predicate "`branch_id` = `'SFBay'`," it must take a read lock on that information—that is, on the information consisting of the set of balance rows, {A1, A2, A3}, that exist at that branch. When T_2 inserts a new row A4 into that branch, it is implicitly taking a write lock on that same predicate, since it is going to change the information available when the predicate is evaluated. Extending the history of Example 9.5.3 to include the appropriate read and write locks, we get the following:

> RL_1(predicate: `branch_id = 'SFBay'`) R_1(predicate: `branch_id = 'SFBay'`) RL_1(A1,100.00) R_1(A1, 100.00) RL_1(A2,100.00) R_1(A2,100.00) RL_1(A3, 100.00) R_1(A3,100.00) WL_2(A4, `branch_id = 'SFBay'`) (prepare to perform the insert I_2(A4, `branch_id = 'SFBay'`, balance = 100.00), but this conflicts with the earlier RL_1 on this predicate, so T_2 must WAIT) R_1(`branch_totals`, `branch_id = 'SFBay'`, 300) (sum is correct, no error) C_1 (now locks are released, so) I_2(A4, branch_id = 'SFBay', balance = 100.00) R_2(`branch_totals`, `branch_id = 'SFBay'`, 300) W_2(`branch_totals`, `branch_id = 'SFBay'`, 400) C_2

The execution is now totally serializable. As we showed in Figure 9.9, the SQL-92 isolation level known as Serializable takes long-term read and write locks on predicates. Thus the phantom update anomaly of Example 9.5.3 is avoided, and histories with this locking protocol are totally serializable. The reader should not take the idea of locks on predicates too literally, however. Any type of locking that guarantees that one transaction can't be examining an aggregation of rows based on some predicate while another transaction adds a different row to that aggregation will serve to eliminate phantom updates. Some database systems lock entire tables to achieve this, a coarse locking granularity that unnecessarily reduces concurrency level, but guarantees the Serializable isolation level with simple system logic.

We also mention a rule of SQL-92, that if a database system wishes to comply with the standard but doesn't support one of the isolation levels, it must provide one *at least* as secure as the one requested in a Set Transaction statement. For example, if the database system doesn't have a Read Committed isolation level, but does have Repeatable Read, then when the following statement is executed:

```
exec sql set transaction read committed;
```

the system must impose a Repeatable Read isolation level.

9.6 │ Transactional Recovery

As we have previously pointed out, the data in a database normally resides on disk, which is a *nonvolatile* storage medium. The fact that it is nonvolatile means, for example, that a sudden power loss will not cause the data to be lost. By contrast, data stored in memory disappears when power is lost, and memory storage is therefore termed *volatile*. A number of other conditions can also cause memory to become undependable—for example, a system crash resulting from imperfect bulletproofing of an operating system or database system. Bugs like this are thought by most systems designers to be inevitable, and such bugs can make it nearly impossible to trust that memory contents will remain stable over an extended period (months or years). If we could, we would leave data on disk at all times so as not to have to worry about memory volatility.

However, as you will recall from the discussion in Section 7.2, disk access is very slow compared with memory access. We need to read disk pages into memory buffers so the data will be available for high-speed random access by normal computer instructions. Once the page has been read into memory buffer, we make every attempt to keep it there in the hope that it will be referenced again in the near future, and we will then save on disk I/O. To support buffering we use an approach known as *lookaside,* which allows the system responding to a disk page read request to first try to hash to an entry for that page in the *lookaside table.* If such an entry is found, this tells the system that the page is already in a memory buffer; otherwise it needs to be read in from disk. Naturally the pages we most want to keep in memory buffers are the ones that are the most "popular," and this has historically been achieved with a method known as *LRU buffering* (LRU stands for least recently used). The idea is that database pages that have been read from disk into memory buffers will remain in memory until a new page being read in from disk requires space, and all buffer pages are already occupied. At that point, some page must be dropped from buffer to make room; that will be the page, among all those in buffers, that has not been referenced for the longest time—the least recently used page.

Just as we want to keep popular pages in memory to be read over and over by different transactions, we also don't want to have to write a page back to disk every time it is updated by some transaction. If it is a popular page for update, containing a set of rows with bank branch balances for example, we might be able to allow hundreds, or even thousands, of updates without writing out the page in question. This is one of the most important optimizations for a common class of transactional applications. To repeat: *We don't want to write out all pages updated by a transaction as soon as the transaction updates them and commits.* Instead we generally allow popular pages to remain in buffer until either they become less popular and *drift out* of buffer on their own because LRU needs their buffer place (note that updated pages must be written back to disk before they can be replaced in buffer), or else we force them to be written back to disk after some period of time has passed. We will talk about forcing disk pages to be written back to disk a bit later; however, most of the time we don't do this, we just depend on LRU. A page in buffer is said to be *dirty* if it has been updated by some transaction since the last time it was written back to disk. We normally allow dirty pages to remain in buffer long after the transaction that originally dirtied them has committed. (We will see some problems in the exercises on buffer-page reads and writes under LRU.)

But now we have a problem. Suppose we suddenly lose power or have a system crash. Some of the pages on disk might be terribly out of date because they were so popular that they haven't been written out from buffer during the last thousand updates that took place. But if all those updates existed only in memory, then it would seem they are now totally lost. How can we handle this problem, and be able to *recover* these lost updates, without going back to the approach of writing out every update as soon as it happens?

The answer is that as each row update occurs the system writes a note to itself, known as a *log entry,* into a memory area known as a *log buffer.* These log entries contain sufficient information about updates to remind the system how to perform the update again, or to reverse the update if the transaction involved needs to be aborted. At appropriate times the log buffer is written out to disk, into a sequential file known as a *log file,* that contains all the log entries created for some interval of time into the past. In this way, if memory is lost at some point, the recovery process will be able to use the sequential log file to recover updates of rows that are out of date on disk. One reason that this log method is preferable to writing out each update as it happens is that it is more efficient—the system only needs to write the log buffer out to disk at infrequent intervals; it is usually able to batch together a large number of page updates and thus save I/Os.

We also see a bit later that the system needs these notes to itself to perform recovery at all. Even if all disk page updates were written out to disk as soon as they occurred at no cost in system resources, this would not be sufficient to allow the system to perform recovery. If the system were to crash in the middle of a transaction, it could leave the database in an inconsistent state (for example, money has been created or destroyed because the compensating update has not yet been executed), and since we have lost memory contents, we have also lost our place in the program logic that knows how to complete the compensating update. It is important not just to recover every page update, but also to recover a consistent set of updates up through the most recent transaction that committed before the crash. To accomplish this, a log file is needed.

This general introduction to the idea of recovery covers most of the guarantee we have in mind when we refer to the durability of ACID transactions, mentioned earlier in the chapter. (One remaining aspect of durability that guarantees against loss of data on stable media such as disks is covered briefly in Section 9.9.) We now proceed to discuss the kinds of notes a normal database system writes to itself in the log file to protect against memory loss, and the way the system uses these notes when it performs a recovery procedure after a system crash.

9.7 Recovery in Detail: Log Formats

Consider the following history H4 of operations as seen by the scheduler:

[9.7.1] $H4 = R_1(A,50) W_1(A,20) R_2(C,100) W_2(C,50) C2 R_1(B,50) W_1(B,80)$
$C_1 \ldots$

Because of the LRU buffering scheme explained in the previous section, we notice that the updated values of the data elements A, B, and C might not be written out to disk in the order in which the updates occur in this history. If a crash were to occur at some time in the future, we might find the following values on disk: A = 50 (the update $W_1(A,20)$ was never written out because A was on a popular disk page), C = 100 (the update of C never got out to disk), and B = 80 (the update of B *did* get out to disk). It should be clear that while we depend on the LRU buffering scheme to write out updates in a manner that minimizes disk resource use, we cannot expect consistent results to be on disk as a result of LRU buffering. The bank account withdrawal of $50 carried out by transaction T_2 didn't get out to disk even though the transaction committed and, presumably, the customer walked away with the money. At the same time, the customer who transferred \$30 from account A to account B has somehow gained \$30 on the deal. (Banks don't like this kind of behavior.)

However, as we mentioned earlier, a system that performs updates to disk as soon as they occur wouldn't solve the problem. (Even if the system tried to perform all writes to disk at commit time, this would not be a solution.) Assume that we are operating under a discipline where we perform writes to disk as soon as the page is updated in buffer, and that a system crash occurred immediately after the operation C_2 in history H4. Then the second update performed by transaction T_1 would not make it out to disk. When we restarted the system after the crash, we would find on disk that A = 20, C = 50, and B = 50. The sum of A and B should be 100, since T_1 never intended to create or destroy money, but instead we see that money has been destroyed. The problem with trying to perform all writes to disk at commit time is that a crash might still occur between one page write and the next, so the same example shows that this approach doesn't solve the problem.

The problems we have just raised are addressed by two of the transactional guarantees mentioned at the beginning of this chapter, atomicity and durability. Recall that atomicity guarantees that a set of data item updates that make up a transaction is indivisible; either all updates of the transaction occur in the database or none of them occurs. This guarantee continues to hold even in the event of a system crash, when it is referred to as durability. Durability says that when the system returns to the program logic after a Commit Work statement, the transaction is durable, so that the updates are remembered after a system crash. As we have already mentioned, these guarantees are achieved when the system writes notes to itself in a log file. A procedure known as *database recovery* is performed after a crash that uses the log entries written earlier and brings the disk-resident database to a state where it will reflect either all or none of the row updates for transactions that were in progress at the time of the crash.

Note an important assumption of recovery that we mentioned in passing in the previous section: *a transactional system, after being restarted following a crash, will never remember the intentions of the transaction logic that was running when memory was lost.* Such program states are considered too subtle to recapture. All the recovery process can depend on is that there is information in nonvolatile storage that will allow it to bring the database back to a consistent state. What is the proper consistent state in the case of the system crash we just explained, immediately after operation

C_2 in history H4? It is this: since T_2 performed a commit, we should be able to recover the final results of that transaction; but since T_1 failed to perform one of the updates it intended, and therefore certainly did not commit, *all* the updates performed by T_1 should be rolled back! This would give us the results A = 50, C = 50, B = 50, a consistent state.

We now rewrite the operations of history H4 in Figure 9.13, and list beside these operations schematic log entries that are written into the log buffer in memory for the recovery method presented here. (We emphasize that log entries are placed in a *memory-resident* log buffer. The occasions when the contents of this log buffer are written out to the disk-based log file are mentioned as special events in Figure 9.13.) Note that the details presented here are not based on the recovery architecture of any specific commercial database system. Instead we are offering a simplified and easy-to-follow recovery approach that captures the spirit of what recovery is expected to do in most systems. An actual recovery architecture of a commercial database system would be quite complex and detailed by comparison.

Operation	Log entry
$R_1(A,50)$	(S, 1)— Start transaction T_1 log entry. No log entry is written for a read operation, but this operation is the start of T_1.
$W_1(A,20)$	(W, 1, A, 50, 20)—T_1 write log for update of A.balance. The value 50 is the before image (BI) for the balance column in row A, 20 is the after image (AI) for A.balance.
$R_2(C,100)$	(S, 2)—Another start transaction log entry.
$W_2(C,50)$	(W, 2, C, 100, 50)—Another write log entry.
C2	(C, 2)—Commit T_2 log entry. (*Write log buffer to log file.*)
$R_1(B,50)$	No log entry.
$W_1(B,80)$	(W, 1, B, 50, 80)
C_1	(C, 1)—Commit T_1. (*Write log buffer to log file.*)

Figure 9.13 Operations from History H4 and the Corresponding Log Entries

Recall that the second operation in Figure 9.13, $W_1(A, 20)$, is assumed to represent an update by transaction T_1, changing the balance column value to 20 for a row in the accounts table with acct_id = A. In the same sense, in the write log (W, 1, A, 50, 20) of Figure 9.13, the value 50 is the before image for the balance column in this row, and 20 is the after image for this column. In more sophisticated log entries, a unique identifier for the row would be used (perhaps the ROWID) and the list of columns changed with all before and after image values. The log entry types appearing in this figure are all that we will consider for now. Log entries also exist for insert and delete operations, for example, but we will simplify our discussion by ignoring them. We see two events in Figure 9.13 where the contents of the log buffer are written out to the sequential log file. The log buffer is normally written out to the log file under only two circumstances in our simple scheme: (1) when some transaction commits; and (2) when the log buffer becomes too full to hold more entries, if that should occur first. (So as not to slow down other work, we expect the system to do a "double-buffered disk write," meaning that it has a second log buffer in memory into which it continues to write log entries, while the first log buffer is being written to disk "asynchronously.")

Now we want to prove to ourselves that there is enough data in these log entries to permit the system to recover after a system crash. We see that two different kinds of problems may have occurred. First, we may have written to disk page updates of transactions that never completed. We say that we need to *UNDO* updates of this kind on disk, and it is for this reason that we include before images in the log entries. We may also find that some page updates of transactions that have committed never got to disk. We say that we need to *REDO* updates of this kind, to write the new values out to disk, and it is for this purpose that after images occur in the log entries.

Now assume that a system crash occurs immediately after the operation $W_1(B, 80)$ has completed, in the sequence of events of Figure 9.13. This means that the log entry (W, 1, B, 50, 80) has been placed in the log buffer, but the last point at which the log buffer was written out to disk was with the log entry (C, 2), and this is the final log entry we will find when we begin to recover from the crash. At this time, since transaction T_2 has committed while transaction T_1 has not, we want to make sure that all updates performed by transaction T_2 are placed on disk and that all updates performed by transaction T_1 are rolled back on disk. As we explained just before Figure 9.13, the final values for these data items after recovery has been performed should be A = 50, B = 50, C = 50.

After the crash the system is reinitialized and the system operator gives a command that initiates recovery. (This is normally known as the RESTART command, and we often refer to the recovery process as

RESTART.) The process of recovery takes place in two phases, *ROLL-BACK* and *ROLL FOWARD*. In the ROLLBACK phase, the entries in the sequential log file are read in reverse order back to system startup, when all data access activity began. (We assume here that this system startup happened just before the first operation, $R_1(A,50)$, of history H4.) In the ROLL FOWARD phase, the log file is read forward again to the last entry. During the ROLLBACK step, recovery performs UNDO of all the updates that should not have occurred, because the transaction that made them did not commit, and also makes a list of all transactions that have committed. During ROLL FOWARD, recovery performs REDO of all updates that should have occurred, because they were legal updates by transactions that have committed. Recall that we are presenting a simple recovery architecture for purposes of illustration, and in it we assume that the ROLLBACK phase occurs first and the ROLL FOWARD phase afterward. This is the order that was used by IBM's System R, a prototype precursor of **DB2**, but the reader should be aware that most modern databases perform these phases in the opposite order. This is not important for our illustrative introduction, however.

Figures 9.14 and 9.15 list all the log entries encountered and the actions taken during these two phases of recovery. Note that the steps of ROLLBACK are numbered on the left. This numbering is continued during the ROLL FORWARD phase of Figure 9.15.

Log entry	ROLLBACK action performed
1. (C, 2)	Put T_2 into the committed list.
2. (W, 2, C, 100, 50)	Since T_2 is on the committed list, we do nothing.
3. (S, 2)	Make a note that T_2 is no longer active.
4. (W, 1, A, 50, 20)	Transaction T_1 has never committed (its last operation was a write). Therefore system performs UNDO of this update by writing the before image value (50) into data item B. Put T_1 into the uncommitted list.
5. (S, 1)	Make a note that T_1 is no longer active. Now that no transactions were active, we can end the ROLLBACK phase.

Figure 9.14 ROLLBACK Process for History H4, Crashed Just after $W_1(B,80)$

We need to explain the steps taken in these two figures. During ROLL-BACK the system reads backward through the log entries of the sequential log file and makes a list of all transactions that did and did not commit. This is easy, because the last operation performed by any such transactions is either a commit or some other operation that indicates that no commit took place, and the system encounters this last operation first. The list of committed transactions is used in the next phase, ROLL FORWARD, but the list of transactions that did not commit is used to decide when to UNDO updates. Since the system knows which transactions did not commit as soon as it encounters (reading backward) the final log entry, it can immediately begin to UNDO write log changes of uncommitted transactions by writing before images onto disk over the row values affected. Naturally, disk buffering is used during recovery to read in pages containing rows that need to be updated by UNDO or REDO steps. We see an example of an UNDO write in step 4 of Figure 9.14. Since the transaction responsible for the write log entry did not commit, it should not have any transactional updates out on disk. It is possible that some values given in the after images of these write log entries are *not* out on disk (they never got there), but in any event it is clear that writing the before images in place of these data items can't hurt—we eventually return to the value such data items had before any uncommitted transactions tried to change them. The attention that is paid to the Start Transaction log entries during ROLLBACK is not strictly necessary, because we are guaranteed that when we reach the beginning of the log file, corresponding to system startup time, no transactions were active. In a slightly more general case, however, ROLLBACK will need to know what transactions were still active in order to decide when to terminate.

During the ROLL FORWARD of Figure 9.15, the system simply uses the list of committed transactions gathered during the ROLLBACK phase as a guide to REDO updates of committed transactions that might not have gotten out to disk. (We see an example of REDO in step 9.)

Log entry	ROLL FORWARD action performed
6. (S, 1)	No action required.
7. (W, 1, A, 50, 20)	T_1 is uncommitted—no action required.
8. (S, 2)	No action required.
9. (W, 2, C, 100, 50)	Since T_2 is on the committed list, we REDO this update by writing after image value (50) into data item C.
10. (C, 2)	No action required.
11.	We note that we have rolled forward through all log entries and terminate recovery.

Figure 9.15 ROLL FORWARD Process, Taking Place after ROLLBACK of Figure 9.14

At the end of this phase the data we find on disk should have the right values. All updates of transactions that committed will be applied, and all updates of transactions that did not complete will be rolled back. Indeed, we note that in step 4 of ROLLBACK we write the value 50 to the data item A, and in step 9 of ROLL FORWARD we write the value 50 to data item B. Recall that the crash occurred just after the operation $W_1(B,80)$ in H4. Since the log entry for this operation didn't get to disk (as we see in Figure 9.13), we cannot apply the before image for A during recovery. We need to depend on the fact that the update for A to the value 80 also did not get out to disk. Basically we need to be sure that if an update of an uncommitted transaction got out to disk, the needed log entry to UNDO that update also got out to disk. We consider this in the next subsection. Given that we can depend on the fact that the new value, B = 80, did not get out to disk, the values for the three data items mentioned in H4 are A = 50, B = 50 (the initial value), and C = 50, the proper values that recovery was to put in place.

Guarantees That Needed Log Entries Are on Disk

How can we be certain that all the log entries needed for proper recovery are out on disk? To begin with, it is important to realize that the operating system offers a guarantee when data is written out to disk, comparable to the guarantees that ACID transactions offer to application programmers. Writes to disk are carried out in an atomic fashion, meaning that even if a crash occurs while a disk write is in process, later reads of the block that was just written will be able to tell immediately if the write was successful; if so, then the block can be depended on to contain exactly the data that the database system logic intended to write. When a disk write is performed, the I/O subsystem normally tests the resulting disk image by reading it again immediately after it is written, and then performs the write again if there is any error. A serious error return to the operation system occurs if a write is not successful after a given number of retries. Thus the normal logic that continues after a successful disk write will never regain control if there is a write error. For example, if a log file is being written out triggered by a transaction commit, the commit will fail when there is an error return in attempting the disk write. If the write-read retry sequence is interrupted by a crash so that an erroneous block reaches disk to be read after RESTART, the error in the block will be detected when a disk read occurs. Thus we have a guarantee that there will be no undetected error; the guarantee is supported by sensitive "error detection encoding" of the data stored on disk, and a "read after write" protocol in performing disk writes that is built into the disk head. All of this error detection is performed at a very low level of the I/O subsystem, transparent even to the operating system.

The guarantee that there will be no undetected errors for disk writes carries over to situations where no crash occurs. When the system is notified of successful completion of a disk write, this carries a high probability guarantee that future reads of the block will be successful (unless the entire disk is lost, as explained in Section 9.9). Thus, when the logic in the database system writes out the log buffer to the log file (it actually does this to two different disks at once on systems with serious recovery concerns, for extra guarantee of durability), it can safely consider the commit that triggered this write to be successful.

Now, given that we can trust log writes to disk, we still have to assure ourselves that the logic of recovery is correct: that we will always be able to find needed log entries in the log file to achieve the kind of recovery we have outlined. Recall that we can break down the tasks we need to perform into two kinds, UNDO and REDO. Consider first the need to REDO all updates of transactions that have committed. We know that a commit log is a trigger for writing out the log buffer, and the transaction is not considered to have successfully completed until this log buffer write has been successful. (For example, if the transaction were a bank withdrawal, we would not actually hand out the money until the buffer write was complete.) Since the commit log must get out to disk, clearly all earlier write logs for that transaction are out to disk (they were placed into the log buffer in sequential order, and the commit log came last), so we are assured that the REDO task can be performed successfully.

The second task we need to carry out during recovery is to UNDO all updates of transactions that have not committed in the log file. We have not previously been provided any guarantee that all log entries for updates of uncompleted transactions will get out to disk. For example, the final write log entry in the recovery example of Figures 9.13 through 9.15, (W, 1, B, 50, 80), was written to the log buffer but did get out to disk before the crash occurred (we do not write the log buffer out to the log file until the (C, 1) log event in Figure 9.13). We need to ask ourselves whether any problems could arise as a result of this. Could a needed UNDO not take place during recovery because the associated log entry didn't go out to disk? It should be clear that this could happen only if the page updated drifted out to disk through the LRU buffer before the log buffer containing the associated write log entry was written to the log file. (If this page had not drifted out, the UNDO operation would not be needed in recovery, as we saw earlier in considering the value of data item B.) It seems that the updated data page could beat the associated write log entry to disk, for example, if there were an enormous amount of page read activity of new pages after a page write, without any intervening commits to force the log buffer out. The read activity could eventually force the buffering scheme to reuse the page on which the updated row sits.

This is a perfectly reasonable scenario, and so we need to offer some special guarantee to ensure that it does not happen. One possibility is to subvert LRU page replacement in some way, so that an updated page will not drift out to disk until the transaction that has written on it has committed. Such a buffering scheme has in fact been proposed, where all pages dirtied by a transaction in buffer will remain in buffer until the transaction commits. With this scheme, in fact, no UNDO processing is ever needed at all during recovery, and therefore before images are not needed in the logs. However, in cases where an arbitrarily large number of updates might be performed by a single transaction, we cannot guarantee to keep all pages in memory buffers until the transaction commits (we might run out of memory). A more sophisticated scheme is required, one that allows a transaction to say it is finished with a page before the transaction commits. For example, when a FETCH from a CURSOR on a table finishes with a given page, we can say that the transaction is finished with that page and it need not be kept in buffer. (Of course, a transaction at the Serializable isolation level must retain its lock on any row it has read or updated, whether the row is on a page in buffer or not.)

Thus we come back to the case where an updated page might drift out to disk through the LRU queue before the associated log buffer is written out to disk, leading to a problem in UNDO recovery. To guard against this, the system makes a guarantee that relevant logs will be written out to disk prior to dirty buffer pages reaching disk that might be subject to UNDO recovery at a later time. This is often referred to as the *write ahead log* (WAL) guarantee. To implement it, database systems usually create something called the *log sequence number* (LSN), a sequentially increasing integer value associated with every entry written into the log buffer. We keep track of the smallest LSN of any entry in the log buffer that has been created since the log buffer was last written out to disk; we call this LSN_BUFFMIN. (This is a global value for the database system, if we assume that there is only one system page buffer in memory.) Additionally, for every disk page in buffer, we note the most recent LSN of an action that has performed an update on a data item in that page, and call this value LSN_PGMAX. Finally, we institute a rule that a disk page cannot be written out to disk from the LRU buffer unless its associated LSN_PGMAX is smaller than the global LSN_BUFFMIN value. This guarantees that the associated page never gets written out to disk until the log buffer with the relevant log entry has been written out to disk, and so solves the UNDO problem. With this definition we have the following theorem, which we offer without proof.

THEOREM 9.7.1 Simple Recovery. Given these guarantees on logs getting to disk, the recovery procedure outlined will perform valid recovery on any transactional history as of a given crash point. The transactions committed as of the time of the crash will have all their updates reflected on disk, and the transactions with partial results that have not yet committed will have all their disk updates backed out. ∎

9.8 Checkpoints

In the recovery example of Section 9.7, we performed ROLLBACK to the time of system startup. This is an obvious choice, since at that time the database was completely consistent, no dirty pages were sitting in cache buffers, and indeed all transactional data updates lay in the future. We can picture that the ROLLBACK process is attempting to restore the database to this pristine state (except that some updates of transactions committed later remain on disk), and the job of ROLL FORWARD is to go forward from that point and REDO all the changes that were performed by transactions that completed before the system crash.

But the length of time needed to perform recovery grows with the length of the log file that we need to read through in our ROLLBACK-ROLL FORWARD phases. In each phase we have to actually read rows in from disk and update them, and in the worst case this might take just as much elapsed time as it originally did to run the applications that executed the updates in the first place. If we assume that most transactions are relatively short-lived (a few seconds), then the ROLLBACK phase quickly becomes quite efficient as it reads backward through the log file, since we only need to UNDO row updates for transactions that were still active at the time of the crash. ROLL FORWARD, however, entails a large effort through most of the length of the log, since we need to REDO all updates of transactions that have committed (presumably, most of them). The elapsed time to perform ROLL FORWARD might even take longer than the original applications that executed these updates, if the recovery process is naive about using concurrent threads of recovery. What we would like is the ability to reestablish the state we had at system startup after a reasonable amount of time has passed, so that recovery does not have to ROLL FORWARD all the way from the beginning of time, but only from this new point (which we call a *checkpoint*). Naturally we want to be able to guarantee that recovery will still work, that it will be able to ignore all the transactions and page updates that occurred before this checkpoint.

There are three distinct approaches to creating a recovery checkpoint for a database system. In order by increasing sophistication and complexity, these three methods are known as *commit-consistent checkpointing*, *cache-consistent checkpointing*, and *fuzzy checkpointing*. With the more complex checkpointing methods, the system gains the ability to maintain a smoother flow of transactional throughput, so as users we prefer complex checkpointing schemes if the system designers have been able to implement them properly. No system would have any reason to support two different methods at the same time. We start by describing the simplest type of checkpoint that can be taken in the midst of running a transactional system, a *commit-consistent checkpoint*.

The Commit-Consistent Checkpoint

To begin with, the system makes the decision that it is time to initiate a checkpoint (perhaps because the count of log events since the last checkpoint has exceeded some limit). Now the system enters a "performing checkpoint state" with the following steps.

DEFINITION 9.8.1 Commit-Consistent Checkpoint Procedure Steps. After the performing checkpoint state is entered, we have the following rules.

[1] No new transactions can start until the checkpoint is complete.

[2] Database operation processing continues until all existing transactions commit, and all their log entries are written to disk.

[3] The current log buffer is written out to the log file, and after this the system ensures that all dirty pages in buffers have been written out to disk.

[4] When steps 1–3 have been performed, the system writes a special log entry, (CKPT), to disk, and the checkpoint is complete. ■

Steps 1–3 of Definition 9.8.1 also define the precise process we would use for an orderly shutdown of the system, so that we would not need to perform recovery when we next start up. The final state is equivalent to what we have been thinking of as system startup, when the log file has zero length. As a result, it should be clear that we can now modify the recovery process of the previous section, so that it rolls back only until it encounters a log entry of the form (CKPT), instead of continuing until nothing earlier is left in the log file. We have a guarantee that there are no transactions running at this point and that all earlier transactions have completed all their operations to disk, so that there are no earlier operations of importance in the log file. The benefit we receive from performing the checkpoint is that we have greatly shortened the length of time needed to perform recovery.

Motivation for Other Kinds of Checkpoints

As we mentioned, the checkpoint procedure given in Definition 9.8.1 requires exactly the same effort as an orderly shutdown of the system. No new transactions can start until the system has been "drained" of active transactions and all dirty pages in buffer have been written out to disk. This may require a long period of time. We tend to think of transactions as being rather short, in the sense that they probably take only a few seconds to complete, but this is not guaranteed in all computer sites. It is perfectly possible on most database systems for transactions to last minutes, or even hours, performing reads and updates throughout this period. While such long transactions are in process a commit-consistent checkpoint is almost impossible, unless we are willing to shut down the system to users for this extended period. (As we said in step 1 of the definition, no new transactions can be accepted while the checkpoint procedure is in process.) To speak of writing out the buffers, consider that if we had 200 MB of memory devoted to disk buffering of 4-KB pages, and half of these pages were dirty and had to be written out, we would have about 100M/4K = 25,000 pages to write out. Since each page takes about 1/40 of a second to write to disk using a single disk arm, the total time required would be 25,000/40 = 625 seconds, divided by the average number of disk arms being kept busy. As memory prices continue to drop, such scenarios will become more common.

To avoid these problems of halting system operations during a checkpoint procedure, more sophisticated checkpoint schemes have been devised. The type of checkpoint we outlined in Definition 9.8.1 is known as a *commit-consistent checkpoint* because all transactions must commit and the dirty cache buffers must be flushed to disk. The next stage of sophistication is known as the *cache-consistent checkpoint*. With this scheme, transactions are allowed to continue active through the checkpoint process, and we only require that all dirty pages in buffer (and associated write log entries) be forced out to disk. Disk buffer space in memory is also known as disk cache, and this explains the name of the checkpoint procedure. While a cache-consistent checkpoint is in process, the transactions that remain active must WAIT; in particular they can perform no new I/Os. However, this still represents a great advantage over being required to drain the system of active transactions for a commit-consistent checkpoint, which may take a very long time when long-lived transactions are permitted. We next outline the recovery procedure associated with a cache-consistent checkpoint. We simply mention at this point that there also exists a yet more sophisticated type of checkpoint covered below, known as a *fuzzy checkpoint*, which allows a checkpoint to be taken even without forcing out all pages in cache. (This checkpoint is not considered complete until all pages in cache get out to disk, but useful work is allowed to continue in the meantime.)

The Cache-Consistent Checkpoint

Here is the procedure the system follows when a cache-consistent checkpoint has been initiated.

DEFINITION 9.8.2 Cache-Consistent Checkpoint Procedure Steps.

[1] No new transactions are permitted to start.

[2] Existing transactions are not permitted to start any new operations.

[3] The current log buffer is written out to disk, and after this the system ensures that all dirty pages in cache buffers have been written out to disk.

[4] Finally a special log entry, (CKPT, List), is written out to disk, and we say that the checkpoint is complete. The List in this log entry contains a list of active transactions at the time the checkpoint is taken. ■

The recovery procedure when cache-consistent checkpoints are used differs from the procedure when commit-consistent checkpoints are employed in a number of ways.

EXAMPLE 9.8.1 A Log File and Recovery Using a Cache-Consistent Checkpoint.

Here is a new history of events to illustrate the features of cache-consistent checkpointing. We will outline the log entries written to the log buffer and the recovery process performed after a crash during this history. First, the history:

$R_1(A, 10)$ $W_1(A, 1)$ C_1 $R_2(A, 1)$ $R_3(B, 2)$ $W_2(A, 3)$ $R_4(C, 5)$ CKPT $W_3(B, 4)$ C_3 $R_4(B, 4)$ $W_4(C, 6)$ C_4 CRASH

Here is the series of log entry events resulting from this history. The last one that gets out to disk is the (C, 3) log entry.

(S, 1) (W, 1, A, 10, 1) (C, 1) (S 2) (S, 3) (W, 2, A, 1, 3) (S, 4)(CKPT,
(LIST = T_2,T_3,T_4)) (W, 3, B, 2, 4) (C, 3) (W, 4, C, 5, 6) (C, 4)

At the time we take the cache-consistent checkpoint, we have these values out on disk: A = 3, B = 2 , C = 5. (The dirty page in cache containing A at checkpoint time is written to disk.) We assume that no other updates make it out to disk before the crash, and so the data item values remain the same. The following diagram illustrates the time scale of the various events. Transaction T_k begins with the (S, k) log and ends with (C, k).

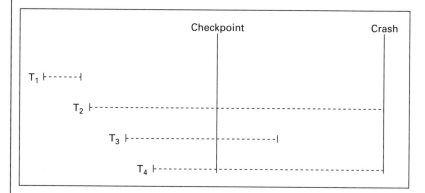

Now we outline the actions taken in recovery, starting with ROLLBACK.

ROLLBACK

1. (C, 3)	Note that T_3 is a committed transaction in active list.
2. (W, 3, B, 2, 4)	Committed transaction, wait for ROLL FORWARD.
3. (CKPT, (LIST = T_2, T_3, T_4))	Note active transactions T_2, T_4 not committed.
4. (S, 4)	List of active transactions now shorter: {T_2}.
5. (W, 2, A, 1, 3)	Not committed. UNDO: A = 1.
6. (S, 3)	Committed transaction.
7. (S, 2)	List of active transactions empty. Stop ROLLBACK.

We see that with a cache-consistent checkpoint, when ROLLBACK encounters the CKPT log entry the system takes note of the transactions that were active, even though we have never seen any operations in the log file. We now take our list of active transactions, remove those that we have seen committed, and have a list of transactions whose updates we need to UNDO. We continue in the ROLLBACK phase until we complete all such UNDO actions. We can be sure when this happens because as we encounter an (S, k) log, rolling backward, we take transactions off the active, uncommitted list. When all such T_k have been removed the ROLLBACK is complete, even though there may be more entries occurring earlier in the log file.

ROLL FORWARD

8. (CKPT, (LIST = T_2, T_3,T_4))	Skip forward in log file to this entry. Committed transactions = {T_3}.
9. (W, 3, B, 2, 4)	ROLL FORWARD: B = 4.
10. (C, 3)	No action. Last entry, so ROLL FORWARD is complete.

In starting the ROLL FORWARD phase, we merely need to REDO all updates by committed transactions that might not have gone out to disk. We can jump forward to the first operation after the checkpoint, since we know that all earlier updates were flushed from buffers. ROLL FORWARD continues to the end of the buffer file. Recall that the values on disk at the time of the crash were A = 3, B = 2 , C = 5. At the end of recovery, we have set A = 1 (step 5) and B = 4 (step 9). We still have C = 5. A glance at the time scale figure (and the fact that the (C,4) log entry was never written) shows that we want updates performed by T_3 and those by T_2 and T_4 to be backed out. No writes performed by T_4 got out to disk, so we have achieved what is necessary for recovery: A = 1, B = 4, C = 5. ∎

The Fuzzy Checkpoint

The aim of a fuzzy checkpoint is to reduce to an absolute minimum the elapsed time needed to perform a checkpoint. A cache-consistent checkpoint, which only needs to flush all dirty buffer pages to disk, is an improvement over a commit-consistent checkpoint, which needs to also allow all transactions in progress time to complete. However, flushing a 40-MB buffer with dirty pages accumulated over several minutes of operation to random positions on disk at 40 writes per second on a small number of disks can still take a good fraction of a minute. Users accustomed to seeing transactional response in a few seconds will be quite sensitive to such a "hiccup," during which no transactional activity can be carried on.

To get around this limitation, fuzzy checkpoint recovery makes use of *two* checkpoint events, the most recent two checkpoints that have been recorded to the log file with the CKPT log notation. The way this works is that each time the system takes a fuzzy checkpoint, $CKPT_N$, it takes note of the set of dirty pages that have accumulated in buffers since the *prior* checkpoint, $CKPT_{N-1}$. The intent is that all of these pages will be written out to disk by the time the *next* checkpoint is taken, $CKPT_{N+1}$. During the period between checkpoints, there is a good opportunity for most of the pages dirty during the first checkpoint to drift out to disk under the normal operation of the buffer manager. When the time for the next checkpoint is close, a background process can be enlisted to force out extremely popular dirty pages before we start the next checkpoint process, so that by the time the checkpoint is performed we have the following guarantee: all the pages that were dirty at the time $CKPT_{N-1}$ was taken have been forced out to disk by the time we complete $CKPT_N$. This allows us to avoid having to do any buffer flushing at the time of $CKPT_N$. We only need to modify the recovery process from the one used with the cache-consistent checkpoint by performing ROLL FORWARD from the time of the *second* most recent CKPT log, $CKPT_{N-1}$, if $CKPT_N$ is the one most recently completed.

DEFINITION 9.8.3 Fuzzy Checkpoint Procedure Steps.

[1] Prior to checkpoint start, the remaining pages dirty as of the previous checkpoint are forced out to disk (but the rate of writes should leave I/O capacity to support current transactions in progress; there is no critical hurry in doing this).

[2] No new transactions are permitted to start. Existing transactions are not permitted to start any new operations.

[3] The current log buffer is written out to disk with an appended log entry, $(CKPT_N, List)$, as in the cache-consistent checkpoint procedure.

[4] The set of pages in buffer that are dirty since the last checkpoint log, $CKPT_{N-1}$, is noted. This will probably be accomplished by special flags on the buffer directory. There is no need for this information to be made disk resident, since it is used only to perform the next checkpoint, not in case of recovery. The checkpoint is now complete. ∎

As explained above, the recovery procedure with fuzzy checkpoints differs from the procedure with commit-consistent checkpoints only in that ROLL FORWARD must start with the first log entry following the *second-to-last* checkpoint log. See the exercises for an illustration.

9.9   Media Recovery

Up to now we have been making the assumption that data in memory might be lost as a result of power failure or a system crash, but data that has gone out to disk is dependable, in the sense that everything on disk will be available after a crash. This is not the whole story. It is possible for a disk unit and all the data it contains to be lost, for example, as a result of a "head crash" where the disk medium is physically scored in the way that an old-fashioned record might be scratched by a phonograph needle. When such an event occurs a special type of recovery, known as *media recovery,* must be performed. We need to take this into account in our general recovery strategy. In this section, we indicate the approach that is taken to solve this problem.

When there is a system crash that does not involve any of the disk media, we perform recovery following the methods outlined in Sections 9.7 and 9.8, where we trust disk media to be correct. If a disk is lost during transactional operation the system will crash, with an advisory to the operator as to which disk has been lost, and it will be clear that there is a need to perform media recovery. The simplest version of media recovery is this. Before system startup, it is standard practice to perform a bulk copy of all disks being run on a transactional system. The copies are made to duplicate disks or to less expensive tape media, and we refer to *backup copies* of the online disks. When a disk has been lost in a system crash, we replace it with a backup disk (still keeping a backup in case a new problem arises), and run the normal recovery process. During this recovery, however, we perform ROLLBACK all the way to system startup, since we can't depend on the backup disk to have any updates that were forced out at the last checkpoint. Then we run ROLL FORWARD from that point to the time of system crash. We can simply pretend that the new disk is the same one that just crashed on the system, except that all the data elements on that disk were *very* popular and never drifted out to disk since the time of system startup. With this viewpoint, it is clear that normal recovery will allow us to recover all updates on this backup disk.

Stable Storage

Now that we know that disk media can fail, the question arises, What happens if the log file is on the disk that fails? The answer is that we foresee such an eventuality and handle it by writing out two copies of the log file to separate devices (tape is common). This practice is often referred to as *log mirroring*. We attempt to ensure that the two devices receiving mirrored logs have *independent failure modes;* we take pains to ensure that an accident that might cause us to lose data on one of the two devices does not affect the data on the other device. For example, the two devices are on separate power services (or at least have separate power backup), and they are separated so that a physical jolt will not affect both of them at once. Storage that has been duplicated on two independent devices (whether it is used for logs or not) is also referred to as *stable storage,* as compared with *nonvolatile* storage for a single copy on disk and *volatile storage* for memory.

9.10 Performance: The TPC-A Benchmark

Let us review the performance-related issues that have been discussed so far in Chapter 9. In Section 9.2 we explained how high levels of concurrency allow us to overlap operations of different transactions to keep multiple disk arms busy at one time. As a result, we get much better CPU utilization and improved transactional throughput. In Section 9.5 we explained how insisting on perfect transaction serializability could hurt the throughput of a system by reducing the *effective concurrency level* when too many transactions enter WAIT state, and introduced the idea of *isolation levels,* provided by SQL-92. In Section 9.6 we began to deal with durability issues arising from buffering disk pages in memory; of course performance is the motivating factor for buffering to reduce I/O elapsed time and save on disk arm resource requirements.

At the same time, however, we have avoided discussing a number of rather complex implementation issues that have a tremendous influence on transactional performance. The ACID guarantees offered by transactional systems require a good deal of CPU and I/O resource overhead at runtime, to the point where it is almost meaningless to compare a transactional system with a simpler disk access file system that doesn't provide such guarantees. To gain some idea of the runtime overhead, consider the following scenario of a transaction execution.

Assume that a transaction begins with an SQL call that accesses a row through an index. A series of I/O calls are generated and passed to the transaction manager (see Figure 9.8), which must establish a transaction number for this thread and then pass calls along to the scheduler. The predicate for index lookup must be locked by the scheduler, involving a check that this lock doesn't conflict with previous ones in existence, and lookaside must be performed for all I/Os before the actual disk access is performed. Short-term and long-term locks must also be taken on disk pages and rows accessed. If a lock request locates a conflict, a test must be performed that a deadlock has not occurred. Assuming there is no deadlock, the calling thread must be placed in a WAIT state by the scheduler, and some sort of *process switch* must be performed to change the context of the machine to run a different thread. When a deadlock is detected, a victim transaction must be chosen and aborted, with the effect of reversing all data item updates by updating previously modified rows using Before Images. Of course each time an update is performed on a row or index in the normal course of the transaction, a log entry must be created with before images and after images of all data affected, and this entry must be placed in the log buffer. When the transaction commits (in the simple system we've been considering), the log buffer contents must be written out to the log file (two copies, to two stable media devices with independent modes of failure).

We see that a lot of work needs to be done by systems providing the transactional ACID guarantees, and to perform this work numerous design choices must be made. Historically a number of performance bottlenecks in transactional systems arose from naive design features. As time passed and serious system implementers became more sophisticated about how to design for improved performance, various transactional benchmarks were developed to allow users to compare transactional systems from different vendors. The most famous of these developed into something called the *TPC-A benchmark*. This is a benchmark test that has been standardized and carefully specified by the Transaction Processing Performance Council (TPC), an industry consortium of transactional database software and hardware vendors. (As of August 1992, the TPC had 38 members, including, for example, Ingres Corp., Oracle Corp., and IBM). Very few vendors today would think of trying to market a transactional database product without publishing the results of the TPC-A (or a simpler TPC-B) to meet the information demands of potential customers. The reason that the benchmark has been so carefully specified is to ensure that all vendors performing the benchmark are making the same test—that there is no looseness in the rules that one vendor might be able to interpret to its own benefit, so as to report unfairly high transactional throughput numbers.

The TPC-A benchmark gives a good idea of the kind of bottlenecks that can arise in a transactional system to hurt performance. A short description of the benchmark follows.

The TPC-A Benchmark Specification

The TPC-A benchmark models a banking application and requires four tables to be defined, specified in Figure 9.16. (Note that the transactional system under test need not be relational, and instead of a table with a given number of rows we might speak of a *file* with the same number of *records*. ACID properties are required, however, so we can't perform this benchmark on a simple file system.)

Table name	Number of rows	Row size	Primary key
Account	10,000,000	100 bytes	Account_ID
Teller	1000	100 bytes	Teller_ID
Branch	100	100 bytes	Branch_ID
History	Varies	50 bytes	(Account_ID, Time_Stamp)

Figure 9.16 Tables Required for the TPC-A Benchmark (Rating ≤ 100 TPS)

Note that the number of rows specified for each of the first three tables of Figure 9.16, Account, Teller, and Branch, is based on the assumption that the benchmark will result in a transactional throughput of no more than 100 TPS. The number of rows required for these tables actually scales linearly up or down with larger or smaller TPS ratings. For example, for a rating of 200 TPS to be valid, Account would need to have 20 million rows, Teller 2000, and Branch 200. A test that resulted in a smaller rating could use a larger number of rows, but the test engineer might wish to reduce the table sizes to see if this will improve performance (because an increased fraction of the data would be memory-buffer resident for I/O).

In general, a large number of transactions is expected to be in process concurrently during the benchmark period, each transaction requested by an emulated terminal. The transactions are all identical in outline, adding a Delta value (presumed withdrawal) to the Balance field of a number of rows identified by values for a specific Account (Account.Account_ID =

Aid), Teller (Tid), and Branch (Bid). A History row is also written to a History file during this process. Pseudo-code for the logic executed by all transaction executions is provided in Figure 9.17. Only the parameters Aid, Tid, Bid, and Delta vary from one execution to another.

```
(Read 100 bytes from the terminal, including Aid, Tid, Bid, and Delta)
(BEGIN TRANSACTION)
    Update Account where Account.Account_ID = Aid
        set Account.Balance = Account.Balance + Delta;
    Insert to History (50 bytes, include column values: Aid, Tid,
        Bid, Delta, Time_Stamp)
    Update Teller where Teller.Teller_ID = Tid
        set Teller.Balance = Teller.Balance + Delta;
    Update Branch where Branch.Branch_ID = Bid
        set Branch.Balance = Branch.Balance + Delta
COMMIT TRANSACTION
Write 200 byte message to Terminal, including Aid, Tid,
    Bid, Delta, Account.Balance
```

Figure 9.17 Transaction Logic of TPC-A Benchmark

Note that three row updates are performed for each withdrawal transaction, a form of triple-entry bookkeeping to prevent errors. The Aid, Tid, and Bid values in the sequence of transactions used in the benchmark measurement period are randomly generated before runtime in such a way that all of the rows in the Account table are equally likely to be updated by each transaction, and similarly for the Teller and Branch tables. Note that no test is performed at runtime, to ensure that adding Delta to the Account row balance does not reduce the balance below zero (recall that this is a withdrawal, so Delta is negative), but this is a decision made by the TPC committee and is the same for everyone.

A number of tests given in the full benchmark specification are intended to determine that the ACID properties of atomicity, consistency, isolation, and durability are supported by the system. These tests are not part of the timed benchmark interval. A test of the Isolation guarantee listed in Paragraph 2.4.2.1 of the TPC-A Benchmark Specification is given in Figure 9.18. This test has transaction executions using the logic of Figure 9.17. However, it is the responsibility of the test sponsor to demonstrate the full Serializable isolation level of SQL-92 under any mix of arbitrary transactions, not just TPC-A transactions. Tests of durability include causing memory failures in a running system and showing that recovery will recapture changes made by completed transactions up to a consistent point. Durable (stable) media failure recovery is also tested. One important point to note is that the History table mentioned earlier cannot be used for log recovery. Although the History rows seem to have all the necessary information to perform recovery, they are under the control of the application, and might be deleted at any time.

Start transaction 1. (Logic of Figure 9.17)
Stop transaction 1 immediately prior to COMMIT.
Start transaction 2.
Transaction 2 attempts to update the same account record as transaction 1.
Verify that transaction 2 WAITS.
Allow transaction 1 to complete. Transaction 2 should now complete.
Verify that the account balance reflects the results of both updates.

Figure 9.18 Isolation Test for Completed Transactions (Conventional Locking Schemes)

Recall that we are emulating a system with a number of different terminals requesting transactions during the timed interval of the benchmark. To specify the frequency and number of transaction executions requested by these terminals during this interval, we need the following definition.

DEFINITION 9.10.1 The time between successive requests to the system from a single terminal is referred to as the *cycle time,* and is made up two parts—the *response time* (delay by the system) and the *think time* (approximating the time the terminal user spends thinking). ∎

To run a valid TPC-A benchmark, the think times between terminal requests must be randomly generated before the benchmark is run, so that the resulting cycle times average at least 10 seconds. (This is a somewhat difficult problem, because we don't know the precise response time until we perform the benchmark, so we don't know exactly how long the think time should be in order to get a cycle time as close as possible to a 10-second average. We can only determine an accurate think time by a series of approximations.) The point of requiring a cycle time of 10 seconds is that a transactional system that wishes to achieve a rate of 100 TPS must be able to efficiently serve a network of at least 1000 terminals. There is also a condition limiting response time in the benchmark. Most systems measured would give a response time of much less than 1 second when only a single user is being run, but as more and more users are added we begin to see resource queues forming for the disk and CPU, leading to slower response. The official method used to determine the TPS rating of a system is basically this: we start with a given number of terminals and crank up the number, each executing one transaction every 10 seconds, until just before the point where 10% of the transactions executed have a response time of more than 2 seconds. This is the criterion used to ensure that all vendors performing the TPC-A benchmark get approximately the same resource utilization.

DEFINITION 9.10.2 Response-Time Criterion of the TPC-A Benchmark.
During the measurement interval of the benchmark, at least 90% of all executed transactions must have a response time of no more than 2 seconds. ∎

To run the test, there is a warm-up period during which the concurrent transaction stream is run, until the system attains a "steady state" with a sustainable TPS rate. The measurement interval in steady state must extend for at least 15 minutes and no longer than 1 hour, and a checkpoint must take place during this interval. We usually assume that enough disks have been provided for the system under test so that the CPU is over 90% utilized, with the resource queues expected under the response-time criterion. How many disks to use is up to the test engineer, but there is an incentive to economize because one of the two major ratings for a system (other than the TPS rating) is the 5-year system cost per TPS ($COST/TPS).

Database system	Hardware	TPS	$COST/TPS	Date
ORACLE7	VAXcluster 4x 6000-560	425.70	$16,326	5/12/92
UNIFY 2000	Pyramid MIServer 12S/12	468.45	$5971	3/4/92
INFORMIX 4.10	IBM RISC 6000/970	110.32	$2789	7/16/92
SYBASE 4.8.1.1	Symmetry 2000/250	173.11	$2770	3/30/92

Figure 9.19 Some TPC-A Ratings of Commercial Systems

As with the Set Query benchmark (which modeled its $COST/QPM rating on the earlier TPC-A benchmark) the $COST figure is calculated by including all hardware costs (including terminals and network), plus software and maintenance rental for 5 years. (This is a simple sum, without net present value calculations.) To give some idea of ratings that occur, a small number of reported ratings for randomly selected commercial systems is given in Figure 9.19. Notice that a TPC-A TPS rating of hundreds of transactions per second is perfectly possible. As a general rule, the $COST/TPS increases with increasing TPS. The UNIFY 2000 rating in Figure 9.19 is an exception.

Lessons from the TPC-A Benchmark

Bottlenecks are likely to occur in a number of areas in transactional systems if naive design features are used, and the TPC-A benchmark does an excellent job of making these bottlenecks prominent when they exist. To begin with, we note that the TPC-A transactions interleave very simple CPU tasks, theoretically requiring only a few thousand instructions, with requests for I/O, and a relatively small number of update requests are made before the transactions commit. However, the deceptively simple transaction logic exercises three important bottlenecks in three areas that we consider below: (1) data item locking, (2) writes to the log file, and (3) buffering.

Data Item Locking

We note that the rows of the 100-row Branch table and recent portions of the History table are extremely popular during transaction execution. From Figure 9.16 we see that there is 1 row in the Branch table for each transaction executed each second, with the assumed 100 TPS rating. This means that each row of the Branch table is locked on the average of once a second, and since there are certain to be a lot of overlaps we will see a lot of occasions when a transaction is forced to WAIT. Some of the early systems were very inefficient at taking locks and switching context from one process to another under these circumstances, and transactional throughput was held down as a result. We also note that since nearly 10% of the transactions can spend more than 2 seconds before they commit (response time criterion), there can be a real problem getting enough access to the Branch rows, at the rate of once a second, to run the full transaction rate.

This can be thought of as an added requirement—locks on Branch rows must not be held so long that access to the rows becomes a bottleneck.

Historically many database products have taken locks, not on rows of tables, but on the disk pages that contain those rows. (**DB2** is one such product, and no official TPC-A ratings of **DB2** have been published.) Page locking for rows simplifies the locking logic, since page locks are necessary in any event when rows on a page must be reconfigured. Clearly if a transaction takes a lock on the disk page containing a row, so that another transaction attempting to access any row on the same page runs into a conflict on the page lock and has to WAIT, this excludes conflicting pairs of accesses to the same row just as well as row locking. The only problem is that a lot of additional rows are excluded from access at the same time.

There are two tables in the TPC-A benchmark where page locks can be expected to cause a throughput problem: the Branch table and the History table. With no new row inserts to the Account, Teller, and Branch tables during the measured interval of the TPC-A benchmark, we would expect tables to be loaded 100% full, so that Branch rows of 100 bytes fit 40 on a page in **DB2**. History rows are inserted with every transaction in sequential order, but we would normally want to pack the rows as tightly as possible, so that 50-byte rows in the History table will fit 80 on a page. Since locks on Branch rows are already very critical for the level of concurrent access in TPC-A that will support good throughput, a locking protocol that grabs a lock on an additional 39 Branch rows can be expected to cause a serious bottleneck. Similarly, in the case of the History table, each transaction inserts a new History row in sequential order, and this means that new transactions are always making inserts on the last page of the table. We can assume that this page is buffered because of its popularity, but a locking protocol that takes a lock on the containing page will now lock out any concurrent transaction from writing a History row. The lock will be held until the requesting transaction commits, making the system write the log buffer to the log file on disk, and we can expect this to take at least 1/40 of a second (with our rule of thumb for random I/O). As a result, the page-locking protocol can be expected to limit the maximum throughput of a transactional system to 40 TPS.

To get around this sort of bottleneck that arises with page locking, the DBA can do something rather clever, configuring the Branch table and the History table so that in each case only one row falls on each page. There will be a good deal of wasted space as a result, but at least now when the locking protocol takes a lock on the containing page it locks only one row, and presumably the bottlenecks pointed out in the previous paragraph are solved. What this costs us is disk space to hold these relatively empty data pages and memory space to buffer them. The Branch table has only one Branch row for each 1 TPS in the rating, so with 100 TPS we would expect 100 disk pages. This is quite inexpensive in terms of disk cost, and even though all of these popular pages are consistently buffered, it is inexpensive in memory cost as well. By the cost rule of thumb presented in Section 7.2, 100 4-KB pages of disk at $1000 per gigabyte cost approximately $0.40, and 100 pages of memory at $50 per megabyte cost $20.

With the History table we need to keep only a small number of pages buffered, the most recent pages to receive inserts in sequential order, so the memory cost is minimal. But the disk cost is a different story. There is a rule in the cost calculation for the TPC-A benchmark specification (paragraph 9.2.3.1) that the report must include in the $COST of the system enough online storage (disk) to contain history rows for 90 8-hour days at the published TPS rate. That's $90 \cdot 8 \cdot 60 \cdot 60 = 2,592,000$ rows for each 1 TPS. Assuming one row per 4-KB page, a 100-TPS-rated system must pay for 252,200,000 disk pages, or about 1009 gigabytes of disk, at a cost of about $2 million. This compares with a cost of $25,000 if the History table is stored 80 rows to a table page. Such a large cost for History storage will be sure to adversely affect the TPS/$COST rating of the system, and this is the way the TPC-A specification penalizes the relatively primitive page-locking protocol. The satisfying thing about this is that the requirement for 90 days of online storage for the History table is relatively realistic, and the penalty is one that would probably apply in commercial use.

Writes to the Log File

The log file on disk is normally configured as a sequential file, since recovery must read log entries in temporal placement order. As successive transactions commit and the log buffer contents is written to the log file, there is a "refractory period" after one disk write has been started and before the next write can be successful. The rule-of-thumb rate for random I/O we have been using, 40 I/Os per second, is a reasonable estimate of how fast we can perform writes to the log file. Since the system must write out the log buffer to disk with every transaction commit under the simple scheme we have been discussing, this means that we can have only about 40 transaction commits each second, or a maximum rating of 40 TPS. The TPC-A benchmark, with its extremely simple transaction logic, can be expected to find this a bottleneck. As we saw in Figure 9.19, TPS ratings of hundreds per second are quite common. How are these rates achieved, given the limitations on log writes?

One possible way to achieve TPS ratings higher than the log file I/O rate is a somewhat sophisticated design alternative known as *group commit*. The idea is that instead of force-writing the log buffer out to the log file every time a single transaction commits, we allow a *group* of transactions to commit before we force this write. Of course a transaction commit isn't complete until the log buffer has been written to disk (a bank won't hand out money for a withdrawal until it has a durable record of the event), and this means that a transaction that completes must be put in WAIT state until its commit log entry is written out, even though this won't be done immediately. But there is no need to worry about long delays here, since what we are trying to do is achieve a high TPS rate. If it takes a long time for a group of several transactions to complete, then we don't have to wait on writes to the log file after all. We just have to write slowly enough, a maximum of 40 times a second, so that we don't outrun the disk I/O rate. Basically what this means is that with group commit the system writes out the log buffer to disk whenever either of the following two events occurs:

[1] The log buffer in memory fills up with entries.

[2] 1/40 of a second has passed since the last log file write.

The log buffer is typically 16 KB or longer, so it should be able to contain enough log entries for a large number of transactions at high TPS rates before being forced to disk.

Buffering and the 5- Minute Rule

How many real disk I/Os (page requests not found in buffer) for data and index are being performed in running the transactional logic of Figure 9.17? (We are not counting the log write here.) Clearly this depends on which index and data are to be found in buffer once a steady state has been reached in the TPC-A measurement interval. The only thing restraining us from buying enough memory for buffers to contain all the data in the TPC-A benchmark is that this will add to the $COST for the system, and even if the TPS rating is somewhat improved, this could adversely affect the $COST/TPS rating reported. It turns out to be cost effective to purchase enough memory for I/O buffers so that the Branch and Teller rows are always buffer resident. However, it is *not* cost effective at present to keep the entire Account table memory resident.

To make the determination of what data is cost effective to keep buffered in memory we use the 5-minute rule, introduced by Jim Gray and Franco Putzolu in 1987 [3]. They pointed out that the reason for buffering disk in memory is to reduce the need for disk arm movement to perform data accesses that cannot be found in buffer. More memory buffers reduce the number of disks we need to buy (we assume that we can place the same data on fewer disks), and for this we are willing to invest money to buy more memory for buffering. In this tradeoff we are spending more money on memory, keeping more and more popular pages memory resident, and saving on disk cost. With a given workload and known costs for disks and memory, there is a specific point in reduced popularity where we stop investing in new buffer space. Popularity of a disk page is measured in time between accesses: the more frequent the accesses, the more popular the page. What Gray and Putzolu showed was that the time between accesses that characterizes the marginal utility point, where we stop buying more memory for buffers, is about 5 minutes—hence the 5-minute rule. But the time interval was arrived at under slightly different assumptions than we want, and we will derive our own.

EXAMPLE 9.10.1 The 5-Minute Rule.
For simplicity we assume that we buy disks or memory for an unchanging workload over a 5-year period, so we don't have to worry about a rental rate for short time intervals. In purchasing disks, we can achieve a high rate of disk accesses per second, for each page of resident data, by loading a smaller amount of data under each disk arm than would be possible if we used all the capacity of the disk. (Note that some disks have multiple arms serving distinct regions, and it is the capacity served by the arm that is important.) This will cost more, of course. For example, the Account table in a system with a 100 TPS rating for TPC-A contains 10 million rows of 100 bytes each, or 1 gigabyte of data (we ignore the index for now). Commercially available disks at present service between 1 and 2 gigabytes with each disk arm, at a maximum access rate of 40 I/Os per second. We assume 1 gigabyte, and that the cost of the disk is $2000. At 100 TPS we will see 100 read and 100 write I/Os per second to the Account tables. With a nominal rate of 25 I/Os per second for each disk arm (less than the maximum rate of 40 I/Os per second because with 100% utilization the disk

queue will grow too long), this implies a need for at least eight disk arms to perform the I/Os to the Account table. Since the Account table contains 1 gigabyte, and the 8 disk arms we need sit over 8 gigabytes of disk medium, we see that the capacity of the disks is only about 12% utilized. The cost for eight disks to hold the Accounts table is $16,000. If we could buffer this data entirely in memory instead of leaving it on disk, we could reduce the need for disk arms, placing the entire Account table on a single disk, and save $14,000 of the disk cost.

The cost to keep 1 gigabyte of data in memory at $100 per MB is $100,000, so it is not appropriate to place the entire Account table into memory to save $14,000. But if the price for memory were to go down to $1 per MB while the disk price stayed the same, it would be appropriate to keep the Account table on a single disk, at a cost of $1000 for memory, saving $14,000 in disk costs. From this it becomes clear that there is a tradeoff between disk and memory prices in our decision of how much data to buffer. ∎

EXAMPLE 9.10.2 More about the 5-Minute Rule.
Under the same assumptions as Example 9.10.1, we derive the marginal reference frequency for a disk page, where the price of being buffered in memory is the same as the price of being kept on disk. Assume that this rate is represented by X, in accesses per second for a page, 4 KB of data. The cost of keeping this 4 KB of data in memory at $100 per MB is about $100/256 (1M/4K = 256) or

Cost for memory residence = $100/256 = $0.39

On the other hand, we can perform X accesses per second by using a fraction of a disk arm given by X/25, since a disk arm supplies 25 I/Os per second. Since the cost of a disk arm is $2000, this means that the cost for X accesses per second when the page is on disk is

Cost for disk residence = $2000 • (X/25) = X • $80

At the marginal reference frequency, we see that the cost to keep the page in memory is the same as the cost of keeping it on disk, so we need to solve the following equation for X:

$0.39 = X • 80$

The solution is X = .004875, in references per second, or taking 1/0.004875 we get about 205 seconds per reference, the *marginal access interval*. Pages that are referenced more frequently than once every 205 seconds have a larger value for X, and we see that the cost of disk residence goes up while the cost for memory residence remains the same. Thus these more popular pages should remain in memory. The converse is true for less popular pages, referenced less than once every 205 seconds. ∎

Note that 205 seconds is slightly less than 4 minutes, so we see that the 5-minute rule is not inappropriate as a name. However, memory components are going down in cost faster than disk components, and as memory becomes cheaper relative to disk the marginal access interval for popular pages becomes longer. In another 20 years the marginal access interval will probably be much longer.

In performing buffering for the TPC-A benchmark, it is interesting to note that we are not particularly concerned about response time. Our transactions can take up to 2 seconds, while an additional disk I/O takes only about 50 ms, and for practical purposes we can ignore it. What we are concerned with is good buffering behavior to minimize the $COST of the system. A good transactional system under the TPC-A benchmark displays a real I/O rate to disk reflecting just a bit over two I/Os per transaction for data tables. Hashing should be used for the Account table index if possible, since otherwise the leaf level of a B-tree might not be buffer resident and would increase the I/O to over three per second. The Teller and Branch tables are much more frequently referenced than the Account table, and remain in memory buffers for long periods, while being updated with every referencing transaction. Clearly it is important that we do not write pages out to disk whenever they are updated. The History table only needs to be written out to disk about once every 40 transactions, assuming that History rows are packed as fully as possible on the page.

Data that is referenced with high frequency is said to possess *heat*. When data is sufficiently popular that it should be buffered in memory, it is known as *hot* data. The Branch and Teller tables are examples of this. When data should not be buffered, but must be stored on disk in a way that does not use the full storage capacity in order to provide faster disk-arm service, we say that it is *warm* data. We saw this behavior with the Account table. Transactional systems commonly deal with warm data. On the other hand, it is often the case with query systems that there are very large storage requirements and relatively low concurrent use requirements, so that storage capacity becomes the gating factor in cost-performance, and we say that the data is *cold*. The History table represents cold data, except for the tail that is buffered to receive inserts, because there are no real-time references to the History records after they are written (at least none that are modeled in the TPC-A benchmark).

Suggestions for Further Reading

We recommend two books that contain more details about transactions: a text by Bernstein, Hadzilacos, and Goodman (BHG), and a text by Gray and Reuter. The BHG text concentrates mainly on proofs of correctness for some of the approaches mentioned in the current chapter, although it goes into some implementation detail on the technique of fuzzy checkpointing. A number of concurrency methods and recovery approaches that were not covered here are presented in detail, such as multiversion concurrency and shadowing. (These methods find little current use in commercial systems, but this situation might change in the future.)

The Gray and Reuter text, on the other hand, provides a fascinating compendium of system-implementation details needed to support the database features we have been discussing, as well as a myriad others. Proofs are provided, but the main concentration is on how to make database systems work. This is a seminal work, and no serious transactional system practitioner can afford to be without it.

[1] P. A. Bernstein, V. Hadzilacos, and N. Goodman. *Concurrency Control and Recovery in Database Systems*. Reading, MA: Addison-Wesley, 1987.

[2] Jim Gray and Andreas Reuter. *Transaction Processing: Concepts and Techniques*. San Mateo, CA: Morgan Kaufmann, 1993.

[3] Jim Gray and Franco Putzolu. "The 5 Minute Rule for Trading Memory for Disc Accesses and the 10 Byte Rule for Trading Memory for CPU Time." In *SIGMOD '87 Proceedings,* pp. 395-398. Umeshwar Dayal and Irv Traiger, eds. New York: ACM, 1987.

Exercises

Exercises with solutions at the back of the book in "Solutions for Selected Exercises" are marked with the symbol •.

[9.1] For this exercise, assume that each transaction requires 10 ms for each CPU block and 50 ms for each I/O, as a variation from the 5 ms CPU and 50 ms I/O assumed in Example 9.2.1 and the discussion following that example.

(a)• Taking the approach of Figure 9.6, draw the equivalent graph of resource usage with the maximum number of disks and the maximum number of simultaneous transaction "threads" that give optimal throughput with perfect resource overlapping. What is the resulting throughput, in TPS?

(b) Consider the more realistic case where we have statistical allocation of resources, with random allocation of data on 10 disks. Assume 20 concurrent transactions as of a given time, with 5 transactions in queue for CPU and 15 in queue for disk I/O.

(i) With the model of throwing 15 darts at 10 disks, calculate the expected number of disks that do *not* have moving disk arms, and thus the disk utilization (percentage of disks busy). Do not use an approximation.

(ii) With the model that a queue of five transactions for CPU is like an average queue length of five in hashing, calculate the percentage of CPU we expect to be utilized.

[9.2] Draw the precedence graph for the histories:

(a)• $W_3(A) R_1(A) W_1(Z) R_2(B) W_2(Y) W_3(B)$ C1 C2 C3

(b) $W_3(D) R_1(D) W_1(F) W_2(F) R_2(G) W_3(G)$ C1 C2 C3

[9.3] • Consider the following history:

$R_1(A) W_1(A) R_2(A) R_2(B) C_2 R_1(B) W_1(B) C_1$

There is a circuit in the precedence graph (draw it), yet we can argue that nothing inconsistent could have occurred if we go by the effect of this history on the database alone. Transaction T_2, it is true, may have seen a partial result of transaction T_1, but it took no action and therefore had no effect on any data in the database. Transaction T_1, on the other hand, has seen only consistent data, since T_2 made no changes. Therefore we ask why we must say that this history is *not* serializable, since the only nonserializable view of data had no effect. (The flaw in this reasoning is that T_2 *might* have taken some other action if it had seen a consistent view of the data.)

Explain, and give an interpretation for this history where such an inconsistency can cause problems.

[9.4] Prove that if PG(H) contains a circuit, there is no ordering of transactions that doesn't have an edge of PG(H) pointing from right to left. (This is the part of the serializability theorem that was left as an exercise.)

[9.5] • Show how the following series of calls would be handled by the locking scheduler. Take the approach of Example 9.4.2.

$$R_1(A) \ R_2(A) \ W_1(A) \ W_2(A) \ C_1 \ C_2$$

[9.6] As in the previous exercise, show how the locking scheduler would handle the following sequences of transactional operation requests. Draw the waits-for graph at any point where a deadlock would occur.

(a)• $W_3(A) \ R_1(A) \ W_1(Z) \ R_2(B) \ W_2(Y) \ W_3(B) \ C1 \ C2 \ C3$

(b) $W_3(D) \ W_1(F) \ R_1(D) \ W_2(F) \ R_2(G) \ W_3(G) \ C1 \ C2 \ C3$

[9.7] We consider cache buffering of disk pages in memory, under the assumption that to begin with the cache buffer disk pages are empty, and that the maximum number of pages that can be held in cache is four (an unrealistically small number to test understanding). Assume in the history that follows that each of the data items A, B, C, D, E, F accessed in the history lies on a distinct page.

$H = R_1(A,1) \ R_2(B, 2) \ W_1(A, 3) \ R_3(C, 4) \ W_2(B, 5) \ C_2 \ W_3(C, 6) \ R_4(D, 7)$

$R_5(E, 8) \ W_5(E, 9) \ R_6(B, 5) \ R_6(A, 3) \ R_3(F, 10) \ W_3(F, 11) \ W_4(D, 12)$

(a)• Name the first operation where an existing page in buffer must be dropped in order that another page can be read in.

(b) Pages in buffer are called *dirty* if they have been updated in buffer but not yet written back out to their place on disk. What are the dirty pages in buffer at the time of the operation named in (a)?

(c)• Assume that we are using an LRU scheme, and that each page is in use only for the duration of the read or write that accesses it. What page will be dropped from buffer at the time of the operation named in (a)?

(d) Can we simply drop the page mentioned in (c) at that time, forgetting its value, or must some other event take place first? Why?

(e)• When C_2 occurs in the history above, does this force out the page with the data item updated by T_2?

(f) List all of the operations above and the set of all data-item pages that are in buffer at the conclusion of each operation, together with their values. Also list values of these data items on disk, when they are different. For example,

Operation	Data items in buffer	Different on disk
$R_1(A,1)$	A=1	
$R_2(B, 2)$	A=1, B=2	
$W_1(A, 3)$	A=3, B=2	A=1

[9.8] In the following histories, assume that there are no prior transactions in existence at the beginning of this history, and that each transaction starts with the first operation listed here, as in Example 9.8.1. For each history, provide the following.

(1) Write down the log entries that this series of operations would create in the log buffer under cache-consistent checkpointing.

(2) Write down the cache-safe ROLLBACK and ROLL FORWARD sequences, starting from the last entry that would be found in the log file on disk.

(3) Draw a timescale for the duration of these transactions, as in Example 9.8.1.

(a)• $H_1 = R_2(A,1)\ R_1(B, 2)\ W_1(B, 3)\ R_3(C, 4)\ W_2(A, 5)\ W_3(C, 6)$ CKPT R_4 (D, 7) $R_2(E, 8)\ W_2(E, 9)\ C_2\ R_3(B, 10)\ W_4(D, 11)$ Crash

(b) $H_2 = R_1(A, 1)\ W_1(A, 3)\ R_2(D, 2)\ R_3(B, 4)\ C_1\ W_2(D, 5)\ W_3(B, 6)$ CKPT $R_3(C, 7)\ R_2(E, 8)\ W_2(E, 9)\ C_2\ R_3(B, 10)\ W_3(C, 11)$ Crash

[9.9] • Here is a timescale for a cache-consistent checkpoint followed by a crash, on which we claim that all possible transaction durations are exemplified. Argue why this is true, then consider each case and explain why the recovery process we have outlined does the right thing for each. This is how you would prove to yourself and others that such an algorithm works.

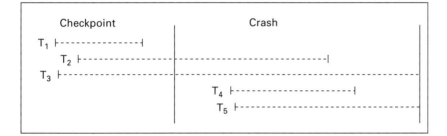

[9.10] Is it possible for a transaction to continue active through more than one cache-consistent checkpoint? If not, explain why not. If so, explain why recovery will still work.

[9.11] •Give an example of a serializable history H with operations from at least the three transactions T_1, T_2, and T_3, having the following properties: (1) every operation in T_1 precedes every operation in T_2, which precedes every operation in T_3; (2) in SG(H), we have $T_3 \nrightarrow T_2$ and $T_2 \rightarrow T_1$. Write down the equivalent serial history. (Hint: you will need two other transactions, T_4 and T_5, and the ordering in SG(H) is by transitivity.) Note that no locking scheme is specified here, so you are free to design the serializable history independent of the temporal sequencing that a locking scheme would force on the system.

[9.12] Recall the phantom problem of Example 9.5.3, where a new row is placed in an aggregate collection (account rows with a given branch) by one transaction, and another transaction performing an aggregation on these rows gets an inconsistent result. Explain how predicate locking solves this problem. Assume that T_1 needs to count the employees in the math department and that T_2 needs to add a new employee.

(a) Show how the phantom problem could occur without predicate locking.

(b) In predicate locking, what is locked by T_1 and in what mode?

(c) What is locked by T_2 and in what mode?

(d) How does this solve the phantom problem?

Parallel and Distributed Databases

In the preceding chapters we introduced most of the concepts that have been developed for traditional database systems, but the discussion of these concepts has been simplified by restricting consideration to a relatively old-fashioned computer environment: a single CPU database system architecture. In this environment we have pictured multiple terminals connected to a powerful computer having a single CPU and a relatively large number of connected disk drives. See Figure 10.1 for a schematic diagram of this architecture. We have not gone into much detail about this, but we have assumed that the single CPU is performing *time-shared* computing, running a number of different terminal processes (or *threads)* in a time-sliced manner to execute independent streams of application logic. Twenty years ago this picture of the standard database environment would have been accurate, but today competing database system architectures are replacing the old standard in most commercial applications. For a number of reasons, most new systems today operate in an environment where multiple CPUs are working in parallel to provide database services.

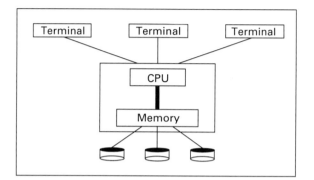

Figure 10.1 A Single CPU Database System Architecture

In this chapter we describe briefly a number of different types of database system architectures that support multiple CPUs. Some of these architectures assume CPUs sharing equal responsibility for database services that are all physically close together, in the same building communicating at very high speed, while others assume that the CPUs are geographically distributed, in different cities communicating relatively slowly by telephone lines. Database systems with multiple CPUs that are physically close together are generally said to have a *parallel architecture* and to be *parallel systems,* while systems that are geographically distributed are generally said to be *distributed systems.* Architectures can vary in numerous other ways; indeed there are sufficient variations that consistent naming of the different types is becoming a bit of a problem. As we will learn, many of the most basic concepts of database operation are fundamentally dependent on these architectural variations. A thorough coverage of the various architectures is beyond the scope of this text. In the following sections we give a short introduction to the most fundamental concepts, and then list several references that deal with these architectures in more detail.

10.1 Some Multi-CPU Architectures

In this section we delineate three multi-CPU database architectures in which the CPUs bear equal responsibility for database services, and one called *client-server* in which different CPUs have differing responsibilities.

New types of systems are still being invented, and our list is nowhere near complete; however, the architectures listed exemplify most of the basic principles.

As explained earlier, database systems with *parallel* architectures have multiple CPUs that are physically close together, while *distributed* systems have multiple CPUs that are geographically far apart. These two types of architecture actually arose from different needs. Parallel systems represent an attempt to construct a faster (and less expensive) centralized computer, while sidestepping the need to always have to construct a faster CPU. As we will see in the next section, it is more economical to purchase several smaller CPUs that together have the power of one large CPU. Distributed systems, on the other hand, arise from the need to offer local database autonomy at geographically distributed locations—for example, local branches of a large company. The distributed database approach developed as it became possible to allow these distributed systems to communicate among themselves, so that data could be effectively accessed between machines in different geographic locations. We start by describing three system architectures, beginning with the most closely coupled CPUs in the parallel architecture category and proceeding along a spectrum to the most loosely coupled distributed systems.

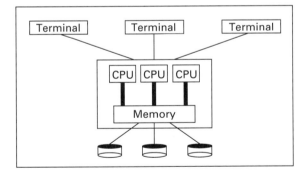

Figure 10.2   A Shared-Memory Multiprocessor Architecture

The first type of parallel database system is known as a *shared-memory multiprocessor,* where a computer has several simultaneously active CPUs that share access to a single memory and a common disk interface. See Figure 10.2 for a schematic picture. This is the type of parallel architecture that is closest to the traditional single-CPU processor, and the design challenge is to get N times as much work performed with N CPUs as can be performed with a single CPU of the same power. However, the design must take special precautions that the different CPUs have equal access to the common memory, and then that data retrieved by one CPU is not unexpectedly modified by another CPU acting in parallel. Because memory access uses a very high-speed mechanism that is difficult to partition without losing efficiency, these shared-memory access problems become more difficult as the number of CPUs increases. The largest IBM 3090 mainframe currently has only eight parallel CPUs. (Another type of developing architecture, known as *massively parallel,* allows hundreds of CPUs to share access to a common memory, but this requires some special design variations that we do not cover here.)

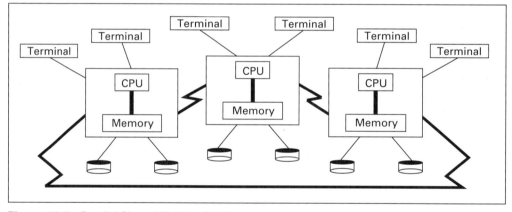

Figure 10.3   Parallel Shared-Nothing Architecture

The second type of system falls in the category of *parallel shared-nothing* architecture, where a number of physically proximate CPUs acting in parallel each have their own memory and disk. We sometimes refer to this generically as a *parallel database system,* when there is no chance of confusion. CPUs sharing responsibility for database services in this type of configuration usually split up the data among themselves and perform transactions and queries by dividing up the work and communicating by messages over a high-speed network, at a communication rate measured in megabits per second. In Figure 10.3 this high-speed network is represented by thick jagged connecting lines between the different CPU/memory packages, known as *system sites,* or simply *sites,* in what follows.[1] Such high-speed networks are limited in size, because of speed-of-light considerations, and this leads to the requirement that a parallel architecture has CPUs that are physically close together. Such networks are known as *local area networks,* or *LANs.*

The third type of system, a *distributed database system,* is also an example of shared-nothing architecture, since memory, like high-speed networks, cannot be shared between CPUs separated by great distance. Once again the system database is partitioned between the different autonomous sites, so that queries and other data manipulation statements must be performed independently at the different sites and partial results communicated between the CPUs involved. However, network communication between CPUs in different cities is currently limited to telephone-grade lines for most purposes, with a relatively low communication rate measured in tens of kilobits per second (on *wide area networks,* or *WANs*). See Figure 10.4, where the jagged connecting lines between CPUs are thin in comparison to those in Figure 10.3. Otherwise, the design of distributed systems and parallel shared-nothing systems is identical.

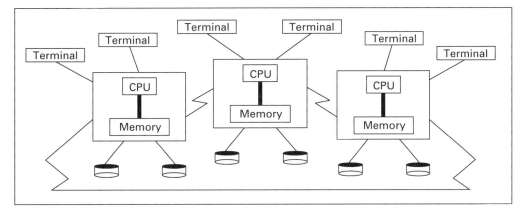

Figure 10.4 Distributed (Shared-Nothing) Architecture

---

[1]The term *sites* is more commonly used for the physically removed CPUs and memories of a distributed database system (see the next architecture description), but we find it useful not to differentiate between a distributed system and a parallel shared-nothing system.

Parallel database systems are usually designed from the ground up to provide best cost-performance, and they are likely to be quite uniform in site machine architecture. Distributed database systems, on the other hand, often arise out of a need to tie together preexisting systems in different locations. As a result, the different site machines are quite likely to be *heterogeneous,* with entirely different individual architectures: an **ORACLE** system on Pyramid UNIX hardware at one site, **DB2** on a 3090 MVS machine at another, and SQL Server on an NT machine at a third. Such machines often have different systems of data representation (for example, of floating point numbers) as well as varying SQL syntax (motivating the common X/OPEN syntax when queries must be communicated between sites). Cooperation between site machines in a parallel system is usually achieved at the level of the transaction manager module of a database system (see Figure 9.8), but this is not generally possible in an architecture that combines heterogeneous sites with widely varying database systems. For this reason, a new type of software system known as a *TP monitor* is often used to tie such sites together. The TP monitor sits above the individual database systems on the various sites and uses them locally to provide needed services. The TP monitor provides threads for user execution and *remote procedure calls* (*RPCs*) to allow application logic to make requests to remote sites; the monitor supplies the needed data representation conversion in the act of communicating parameters of such calls. TP monitors are extremely sophisticated systems that are outside the scope of this text; they are investigated in great detail in the text by Gray and Reuter [5].

In the architectures of Figures 10.2, 10.3, and 10.4, all CPUs pictured are equally responsible for database services delivered by the system. In the shared-nothing architectures, data is partitioned between the disks at the distinct sites, and queries that reference data on multiple sites must have the cooperation of all the CPUs involved, communicating partial results back to the site with the terminal that made the request. Clearly these architectures have important implications for database system design. How is query optimization affected when tables of a database are partitioned on disks in different cities? How are update transactions affected when one CPU doesn't have all the data affected in a transaction under its control? These significant problems are still being investigated by database implementors.

Client-Server Architectures

The motivation for the parallel architectures of Figures 10.2 and 10.3 is the relative economy of small CPUs in comparison to large ones. But there is an alternative to the types of architecture in which the CPUs share responsibility equally for all database services. With the *client-server* architecture, small client CPUs (usually personal computers, costing about a thousand dollars) take responsibility for interaction with the user, providing presentation services and deciding what data is needed to answer user requests. The client machines do not have most of the needed data on local disks, however, and to respond to user needs the client machines pass high-level data requests (SQL-level requests or else programmatic *remote procedure calls)* to a *centralized server* machine, often a shared-memory multiprocessor. It is also possible to have client machines deal with more complex parallel servers, or even multiple servers on a network. The major characteristic of a client-server system is the division of labor between the client CPUs, which take responsibility for presentation services, and the server CPUs, which take responsibility for database services.

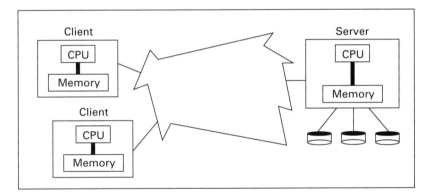

Figure 10.5   Client-Server Architecture

10.2   The Curve of CPU Cost versus Power

We have mentioned that a major motivation for parallel database architectures, pictured in Figures 10.2 and 10.3, is cost-performance. Let us expand on this point.

We define the *$Cost* of a specific CPU as the cost in dollars for which one CPU can be purchased at wholesale. Note that most PCs costing over $1000 have CPUs that cost less than $100; the extra cost is for the casing, disk drive, software, etc. We define the *power* of the CPU as the number of instructions the CPU can execute in 1 second, and assume that this is reported in *millions of instructions per second, or MIPS.* It is important to realize that this definition of power is badly flawed; there are a lot of different types of work a CPU can perform (scientific computation, graphics display, various types of commercial database applications), and benchmarks need to be devised to allow us to measure any one kind accurately. Once such benchmarks have been designed, they become targets for partisan vendor representatives performing "benchmarketing." For certain well-known benchmarks, computer designers have created special operations and compiler modifications for the sole purpose of achieving high ratings on that benchmark. In many cases these ratings drop sharply when minor realistic modifications are made in the benchmark logic. Also, in many cases the people measuring the performance ratings of a machine are the same ones who want to sell the machine, and this leads to a self-serving inflation of ratings. It is certainly the case that a PC with a 50 MIPS rating is a good deal less powerful than an IBM mainframe with a 50 MIPS rating. IBM has not supported MIPS ratings for some time because of the difficulties just mentioned and a number of others.

Still, everyone likes a simple answer, so in what follows we act as if there is a simple MIPS rating that can be determined for different CPUs, and that this MIPS rating reflects the type of CPU work that needs to be performed in all database system applications. Then the most important fact driving computer architecture for the last 10 years or so is the curve presented in Figure 10.6, representing the relationship between *$Cost* and *power* for a range of CPUs. We do not claim that the specific numbers shown are accurate (prices and CPU technology are constantly changing), but the general shape of the curve is valid.

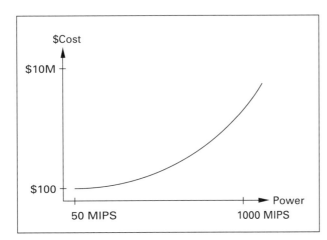

Figure 10.6   Relationship between CPU $Cost and Power

What this curve shows is that $Cost is a function of power that grows at a super-linear rate. That is, if 50 MIPS in a single CPU costs $100, then 20 MIPS in a single CPU will cost a good deal *more* than $200. By the time we get to a 1000-MIPS CPU, with power 20 times as great as that of the CPU we started with, the $Cost is $10 million, *100,000 times as much as the 50 MIPS CPU!* The reason for this extraordinary growth in cost is basically this: as the CPU speed goes up we are getting closer and closer to the upper limits of the technology, and we have to pay more and more for the sophisticated means needed to gain more speed. It's like the difference between sending a letter to Europe by two-day mail (cheaply) and hiring a courier to fly on the Concorde and deliver it personally. It's faster, but it costs a *lot!*

What is the lesson to the database industry? Simply this: *lots of little CPUs are cheaper than one big CPU!* If a commercial company owns a powerful old-style mainframe machine that is spending most of its time in time-shared mode giving interactive service to a group of terminal users, the company should probably buy a PC for each user to give the needed interactive service. Then it can connect all the PCs as client machines to a central server, and that server can be a much smaller machine, now that it doesn't have to deal with presentation services for a lot of terminals. With this design the server is doing the work that large machines are best at, accessing data on a large number of disks and communicating simple answers to clients. Thus we see that the $Cost/power curve of Figure 10.6 is the motivation for the client-server architecture. Indeed it provides the motivation for all the types of multiple-CPU database architectures mentioned above: we need to learn how to make several small CPUs do the work of one big CPU.

It is extremely simple to parallelize certain types of work that are naturally divisible. An example of such a type of work is when word processing is being performed by a group of technical writers who don't need to communicate except by passing printed text to each other for review. In this case the proper solution is to buy all the users PCs and some single-user word processing software. This work environment provides all needed parallelism and an important cost saving over using a time-shared computer for word processing (which was actually done at one time, at extremely high cost).

But with database applications there are numerous requirements for communication that make it less straightforward to run applications on a group of distinct CPUs, even when these CPUs communicate over a high-speed network. A good deal of thought must go into a system architecture that will support database applications, and without great care the communication overhead for such applications can add back the cost that we are saving by using smaller computers. In addition, a database system has a significant investment in online data access devices, such as disk drives (as much as 50% of the cost on modern workstation systems), and a careless approach to storage will also make an architecture uneconomical. Thus we see that CPU cost scalability isn't the only cost factor in a distributed database system. The battle to find the best parallel database system architecture is still being fought, and we try to give some idea of the problems that can arise in the following section.

10.3 Shared-Nothing Database Architecture

The usual idea of a shared-nothing database architecture, as pictured in Figures 10.3 and 10.4, is as follows. For reasons of either cost-performance or geographical distribution, it is not considered feasible to provide all database services on a single mainframe computer, so the data is partitioned and placed on disks of a number of different low-cost computers with separate memories. These different systems (we call them *sites* or *site machines)* must then cooperate to perform database work, and this entails a need to communicate between sites.

EXAMPLE 10.3.1 The TPC-A Benchmark.

The TPC-A benchmark was described in Section 9.10, with no mention of the possiblity of implementing the benchmark on a multi-CPU shared-nothing database system. However, such an implementation was foreseen by the benchmark designers (the TPC), and certain rules were laid down to make sure that the benchmark test will be realistic. To run TPC-A on a shared-nothing system, the data must be partitioned on a number of machines. Assume that there are ten site machines and that we are measuring for a 100 TPS rating, therefore with 100 rows in the Branch table. Now each of the tellers and accounts (rows in the Teller and Account tables) is associated with a specific branch: there are ten tellers and 100,000 accounts in each "home" branch. In order to use each of the site machines of the distributed database system equally to support the TPC-A workload, it is necessary to *partition* the tables among the ten sites. The normal way to do this is to give each site its own Branch, Teller, and Account table, except that the Branch table contains only 10 rows at each site (we are dividing, or partitioning, the 100 rows of the Branch table among the ten site machines); then the Teller and Account tables are also partitioned among the ten site machines, and the tellers and accounts belonging to local branches are the only ones that have rows in a local site.

Now to recapitulate the transaction logic for TPC-A, each transaction represents an account holder (Aid) coming into a bank branch (Bid) to some teller (Tid) at random, and making a withdrawal (Delta) from the holder's account balance; this withdrawal is reflected in the Branch balance and Teller balance as well. Where, we wonder, does the communication requirement between the site machines come in? If an account holder enters the local bank branch and makes a withdrawal, there seems to be no need for communication to access data from other sites. Ah, but we have failed to mention another requirement. Of the randomly generated (Aid, Tid, Bid, Delta) messages, 85% can represent Aid values that belong as home accounts to the Bid listed, but another 15% of the messages must have randomly chosen Aid values from all Account_ID values that are held at *foreign* branches. Since the Bid value determines the local site machine that processes the message, the need for communication now becomes clear. About 15% of the transactions will be drop-in account holders making withdrawals on accounts from foreign branches. Since there are ten branches at each site, about 90% of these foreign branch drop-ins will require communication with a different site. Remember that the transaction needs to add Delta to the Branch balance (local site) and to the Teller balance (local site), but it also needs to add Delta to the Account balance, and this implies an update to an Account row at a different site as part of the same transaction that updates the local Branch and Teller rows. As we will see, this means that we need to revisit our ACID properties to make sure that this *distributed transaction* is properly handled. ∎

At first the communication overhead suggested by Example 10.3.1 doesn't appear very serious; it seems that we have to send a message and make an update at a foreign site about 15% of the time. The problem is that different rows to be updated in a single transaction now appear in distinct memories, the locks are held on separate processors, and it is therefore not possible to coordinate the transaction commit as we have done in the traditional centralized database architecture. Presumably we need to start another transaction at that foreign site to make that update, and then coordinate the commits of the two transactions. This is rather vague, but on the whole it seems like a fairly simple requirement. On closer examination, however, it turns out that a number of complex problems arise in executing distributed transactions. We treat several of these in the following subsections.

Two-Phase Commit

Consider the idea mentioned earlier of starting another transaction when a local transaction must suddenly access data at a remote site and become distributed. For example, in TPC-A on a shared-nothing system, consider the situation when an account holder at a branch handled by the site 2 machine drops in to a foreign bank branch handled by the site 1 machine. From the transaction logic of Figure 9.17, we see that the first data access is at site 2, while the teller-terminal interaction is at site 1. Therefore a distributed transaction T_D is immediately initiated, coordinated at site 1, with a local transaction component at site 2, which we call rather simplistically T_2. The second data access to the History table is on the local machine at site 1, so the distributed transaction T_D now also has a local transaction component T_1 at site 1. When the logic of the TPC-A transaction commits, the two transactions T_1 and T_2 must commit in a coordinated fashion to successfully complete the distributed transaction T_D.

In most shared-nothing database systems with homogeneous sites, access to remote data is transparent to the application logic; it is normally handled by the transaction manager (TM) component of the database system, which has a global picture of how the database is partitioned on the various site machines. See Figure 9.8 and the discussion that follows for a schematic picture of the TM and its place in the transactional system. In a shared-nothing architecture, the TM decides which sites should start local component transactions, forwards scheduler calls for data access and manipulation to the appropriate site and awaits replies, and takes responsibility for the distributed transaction commit. The TM might eventually find when it comes time to commit (or abort) that the transaction has read and updated a large number of different data items at several different sites (although the TPC-A transaction is too simple to involve more than two sites).

We say that the site transactions of a distributed transaction are *coordinated* if they are all guaranteed to commit or abort together. Given this coordination, the distributed transaction inherits the ACID properties from its site components. If two-phase locking is used whenever some data item is accessed at any site by a distributed transaction, this provides isolation for all distributed data items accessed as a package. (The locking theorem, 9.4.2, still holds in a distributed transaction.) Isolation then implies consistency, as we explained earlier. As far as the ACID property of durability is concerned, we need to consider what will happen if a single site crashes. A distributed transaction that has committed will have written the commit log at all local sites (remember we assume that all participating site transactions commit or abort together), and so we conclude that the system will be able to perform REDO recovery when the crashed site comes back to life. Naturally a new level of recovery logic is needed to handle recovery of a distributed transaction when one site out of several crashes, but this presents no difficulty.

The only hard part in all this comes with our assumption that all site transactions of a distributed transaction can be coordinated, so that they all commit or abort together. This can also be thought of as the ACID guarantee of atomicity for the distributed transaction; all updates of the transaction are performed (all sites commit) or none are performed (all sites abort). It turns out to be impossible to coordinate different site transactions in this way with the type of local transactional behavior we have dealt with up to now, which we call *basic transaction* behavior. As we have described it, a basic transaction that has been initiated by a scheduler has only three states in which it can exist. These basic transaction states are

Active   A transaction becomes *active* on being initiated by the scheduler in response to a data access request by some application thread. A transaction can pass from the active state to either the committed or the aborted state. In the event of a system crash and subsequent recovery, a transaction in the active state enters the aborted state.

Committed	An active transaction becomes *committed* as a result of a commit request by the application thread. There is no way to leave the committed state.
Aborted	An active transaction becomes *aborted* as a result of a rollback request by the application thread or because of various other conditions that can arise in the system, such as transaction deadlock or system crash and recovery. There is no way to leave the aborted state.

Figure 10.7 gives a schematic picture of the basic transaction states and the possible transitions between them. Note carefully that while an active transaction can enter either the committed or the aborted state, once either of these states is entered no further change of state is possible. When a transaction commits, it loses the ability to back out the effects of its data item updates that it possessed as an active transaction. This is because the commit causes locks to be released (we have to let them go sometime), and the effects of the updates become visible to other transactions; with the loss of isolation, we can no longer roll back. At the same time, an abort arising for any reason also causes locks to be released. Finally, it is important to understand that the system never has any guarantee that a basic transaction in any other state will enter the committed state. If the site where the transaction is active crashes, even if recovery is almost instantaneous, an active transaction will have UNDO recovery performed on all its updates and enter the aborted state. The aborted state is entered in this case because it is normally impossible for the system to recover enough context to continue the transaction through a successful commit. Only the original application logic can do that by performing a *retry*. Finally, we note that in our model there is no way to guarantee against crashes at a given site.

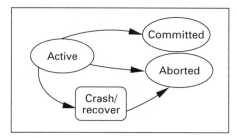

Figure 10.7 Basic Transaction State Transition Diagram

It turns out that this combination of properties of the basic transaction states makes coordination of site transactions (so that they are always guaranteed to abort together or commit together) an impossible task. To see this, assume that as before we initiate two basic transactions on different sites, with the intention of performing the distributed TPC-A logic of Example 10.3.1. Denote by T_1 the action at the "local" branch, site 1, where Delta (a negative number) is added to the Branch and Teller balances, and denote by T_2 the "remote" transaction where Delta is added to the balance of an account at a foreign branch, site 2. Now let us assume that TM at site 1 acts as a *coordinator,* attempting to schedule the two site transactions so that they commit or abort in lockstep. How is the coordinator to act?

One possibility is for the coordinator to start by committing the local transaction T_1, and after succeeding locally sending a message to commit the remote transaction T_2. But if site 2 has crashed by the time it receives this message, then T_2 will abort when recovery takes place. See Figure 10.8 for an illustration of this series of events.

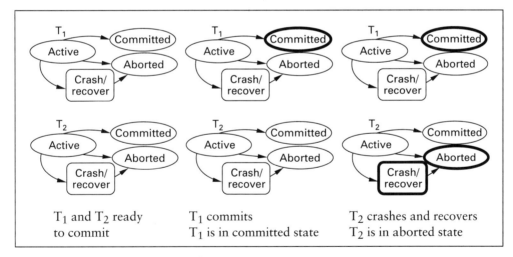

T_1 and T_2 ready to commit

T_1 commits T_1 is in committed state

T_2 crashes and recovers T_2 is in aborted state

Figure 10.8 Failed Coordination of a Distributed Transaction

After site 2 has recovered, the request to commit T_2 will be unsuccessful since T_2 has irrevocably entered aborted state. Because T_1 has committed and T_2 has aborted, money has been destroyed in the bank records (it was taken out of the branch and teller by T_1, but not given to the account holder by T_2).

A second possibility (not pictured) is that the coordinator starts by sending a message to site 2 to commit transaction T_2 and after receiving successful return notification attempts to commit T_1. This approach can also go wrong. The commit at site 2 may be successful but then site 1 may crash before it receives the successful return notification so the coordinator can commit T_1. After recovery T_1 will be aborted and T_2 committed, so the foreign account balance will have money taken out but there will be no compensating changes in branch and teller (and presumably the account holder has not received any cash). Finally, the coordinator could forget about waiting for successful notification and try to perform both commits "at the same time" by sending out both commit requests one after another. But of course it is still possible for either of the two sites to crash, causing an abort, while the other succeeds in committing.

There is no way to get around the fact that an arbitrary site in a distributed transaction can crash at an inopportune time. Our problem with coordination arises when one site transaction aborts and another commits; both site transactions have entered irrevocable states, and these states conflict. In the situations we have been considering, the aborted state is entered because an active transaction in a crashed site is forced into an aborted state by recovery. What we need is some new state that has more flexibility than this. We introduce something called the *prepare request* that can be made by a coordinator to cause site transactions to enter a state we call the *prepared state*. Here is the definition.

Prepared	A transaction becomes *prepared* as a result of a request by a distributed transaction coordinator (a TM) making a *prepare* request. From a prepared state, the transaction can enter either the committed state or the aborted state. In the event of a system crash and subsequent recovery, a transaction in a prepared state returns to prepared state. (Some practitioners refer to this as the *hardened* state.)

When a prepare request is received at a site for an active site transaction, a process is performed to *make the current flexible active state durable*. Note that all transactional logic has been completed before prepare is called.

Now a *prepare log* is placed into the log buffer and the buffer is force-written to the log file, after which we say that the transaction has entered the prepared state. In the event of a crash and subsequent recovery, the current state of the transaction is reconstructed; from this recovered prepared state, we can still perform either a commit or an abort (see Figure 10.9). In order to maintain this flexibility, we could, after a site crash, REDO all updates of the transaction and maintain all before image log entries in the log file after recovery is complete. All data item locks held by the transaction in its active state must also be reestablished after recovery.

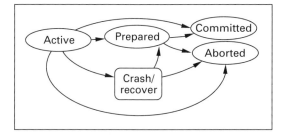

Figure 10.9 Transaction State Transition Diagram with Durable Prepared State

With this new prepared state, a distributed transaction coordinator can overcome the problem of inopportune aborts in participating sites. In the example just presented of the distributed TPC-A transaction, symbolized as T_D, with T_1 at site 1 and T_2 at site 2, the coordinator at site 1 can perform the logic of Figure 10.10. The method employed is known as a *two-phase commit* (2PC) protocol, and it is a standard approach used by commercial database systems to achieve a coordinated commit of distributed transactions. Notice that the initial request to PREPARE(T_2) in Figure 10.10 may fail for a number of reasons. An abort may occur at the site for some reason, such as to break a deadlock, and in this case a response of "unsuccessful" is returned by site 2. Alternatively, the site might crash or become disconnected from the network, and we treat this in the same way as we treat a return message of "unsuccessful": in every case we presume that T_2 will abort. This is certainly the proper course if a crash occurs, since an active transaction is aborted by recovery. If a network failure has occurred, we make a rule to abort an active transaction after some timeout period. On the other hand, if the PREPARE request did reach site 2 before the site or network failure, we have a more durable state. Since the coordinator got no response, it aborts T_1, writes "ABORT T_D" to the local log file, and transmits the message to site 2 with an appropriate distributed transaction identifier for T_D. We assume that this message is delivered to site 2 when it recovers, so site 2 will know enough to abort T_2, which was a participant in T_D.

```
BEGIN
    REQUEST PREPARE(T2)               /* requires message to site 2      */
    IF RESPONSE IS "UNSUCCESSFUL"     /* site 2 crashed, network failed  */
        ROLLBACK T1, WRITE "ABORT TD" /* abort distributed transaction   */
    ELSE IF (T1 is "ACTIVE")          /* T1 hasn't aborted while waiting  */
        COMMIT(T1, TD)                /* no going back now                */
        REQUEST COMMIT(T2)            /* will succeed eventually          */
    ELSE                              /* T1 has aborted                   */
        WRITE "ABORT TD"              /* abort distributed transaction    */
        REQUEST ABORT(T2)             /* message to site 2                */
END
```

Figure 10.10 Two-Phase Commit for Two-Site Distributed Transaction

On the other hand, if the response from site 2 is "successful," the coordinator commits the local transaction T_1, together with the distributed transaction T_D, writing log entries to the log file. This is the point of weakness in distributed transaction coordination that we explained earlier. After one transaction has committed the other site crashes, and on recovery the other basic transaction has aborted. But that can't happen here, because T_2 has been prepared. If a crash occurs at site 2, this will only mean a delay, since on recovery T_2 will return to the prepared state. After committing T_D and T_1 locally, the coordinator sends a COMMIT message to site 2, and eventually this will be delivered to an operational site with T_2 in the prepared state and succeed. If site 1 crashes after T_D is committed, recovery will bring it back up with a list of participating site transactions and another commit message will be sent to site 2 (a second one won't hurt). This sequence of events is pictured in Figure 10.11.

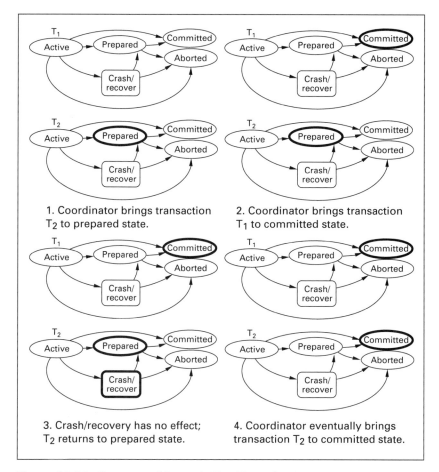

1. Coordinator brings transaction T$_2$ to prepared state.

2. Coordinator brings transaction T$_1$ to committed state.

3. Crash/recovery has no effect; T$_2$ returns to prepared state.

4. Coordinator eventually brings transaction T$_2$ to committed state.

Figure 10.11   Sequence of Events in Two-Phase Commit

Two-phase commit also works for transactions at more than two sites. An outline of the multi-site 2PC protocol follows.

Phase 1. Coordinator sends messages to all involved foreign sites asking them to prepare site transactions that participate in this distributed transaction.

If any of these sites respond "unsuccessful," then the coordinator rolls back the local site transaction and sends messages to all sites in doubt to tell them to abort as well.

Phase 2. If all prepare requests result in "successful" responses, the coordinator commits the distributed transaction T_D, and the local transaction component, and then starts sending commit messages to each of the participating site transactions. Sooner or later these messages will all be delivered.

Further Problems with Shared-Nothing Architecture

The two-phase commit protocol isn't very easy to implement (**DB2** has spent several years in development), and a number of other complexities arise as well. We list some of them below.

Distributed deadlock. Assume that distributed transaction T_{D1} updates data item A on site 1, then attempts to update data item B on site 2, but finds it locked, and therefore goes into WAIT. Now assume that the lock on data item B at site 2 is held by distributed transaction T_{D2}, which attempts to update data item A at site 1. Clearly this is a deadlock. But how is the deadlock going to be detected? Recall that we are dealing with site CPUs that do not have common memory or any knowledge of locking tables for data items on foreign machines. No single site machine knows enough to trace a WAITSFOR circuit that might extend over several sites. The simplest solution to this problem is to give up on deadlock detection and use *timeout abort*. When a distributed transaction is waiting for a lock on a foreign data item so that distribute deadlock is possible, then after a certain waiting period (a few seconds), the transaction aborts and retries. It is important that different transactions choose randomly different timeout periods. That way they don't get into a "chatter" mode of giving up and retrying together so that they run into each other again.

Transaction blocking. A transaction is said to be *blocked* if it must wait for recovery from some sort of long-term failure before it can proceed. Since the blocked transaction might be holding locks on popular data items (12-oz. cans of Pepsi in a soft-drink wholesale business), this can be a serious problem. Blocking can occur with the two-phase commit protocol we have just presented in the following way. Assume that a coordinator at site

1 makes a prepare request for transaction T_2 at site 2, and then crashes before sending the final message to site 2 that it should commit (or abort if the local transaction T_1 has aborted for some reason). We assume that either outcome is possible and because of this, transaction T_2, which is in the prepared state, cannot make a choice on its own under the protocol. It must hold itself in readiness for whatever decision the coordinator announces after it recovers. This might take quite some time, however, and if T_2 is holding a lock on the PEPSI_12_OZ row that is normally referenced by 50 orders a second, such an outage is unacceptable. There is no good solution to this. A different protocol known as *three-phase commit* has been designed to avoid blocking under most circumstances, but it involves another round of messages to arrive at a commit, and it has not been commercially adopted. (Remember the fear that communication overhead was going to cost enough to lose back the cost advantage of smaller CPUs?)

Replicated data. Leslie Lamport, a well-known researcher, is said to have remarked, "A distributed system is one where the failure of some computer I've never heard of can keep me from getting my work done." The problem, of course, is that we have partitioned the data, and if a lot of transactions need data from several machines (not a problem with TPC-A transactions because they're so simple), this greatly increases the chance of failure. If we have a group of CPUs that individually fail only once a month (assuming 8-hour days and 5-day weeks), and we put a hundred of them into a distributed database, one of them will fail every 1.7 hours! (Added to this is the problem that inexpensive CPU hardware has inferior mean time to failure (MTTF) ratings when compared to large mainframe CPUs.) To overcome this problem, the standard approach is to *replicate* all the data in the database, so that data is not simply partitioned but stored at a minimum of two different sites. The bad side of this replication is that any data updates must then be communicated to at least two sites and take place in lockstep. Once again we have the problem of communication and other types of overhead increasing the cost of a distributed database.

Notwithstanding all these complexities with update transactions, shared-nothing database systems are the coming thing. The economies and ease of use that arise are just too compelling for any complexities to daunt the practitioners designing new database systems, and new approaches are being tried constantly.

10.4 Query Parallelism

Up to now we have been concentrating on how to use multiple CPU architectures to support update transactions, and most of the complexity we have seen has revolved around the need to perform updates. But there are a growing number of application systems where online updates rarely occur, queries are the common requests, and new data is added infrequently in a merge of old data with new that happens offline. For example, large department store chains commonly study past customer buying habits to determine locations to hold sales and customers who should receive mailing announcements. Almost all merchandisers use existing sales data to drive their reordering. The reorders are executed as row inserts, a particularly simple kind of update that can be processed in update transactions at a later time, but the determination of *what* to order is query based. And the queries used can be quite complex, since marketing specialists are not merely reordering what has been purchased before. Careful analysis can determine new products that should be ordered, seasonal items such as snow chains that need to be stocked, or how to change the layout of a store to improve visibility of items that should be selling better. A system like this is known as a *decision-support system* (DSS). A number of large companies (for example, drug wholesalers) provide this kind of analysis as a value-added service to their customers. Systems that support mainly queries in normal use are also provided by libraries, book and audio stores, state license agencies for police inquiries, and so on.

With query-only distributed systems, it is clear that we don't have the problems associated with two-phase commit (there are no updates to coordinate), transaction blocking (there are no write locks), or distributed deadlock. If data is replicated for availability in case of failure, it simply remains in place, and there is no concern about updating multiple copies simultaneously. Our major challenge is to come up with an architecture that allows us to decompose a query into parts that can act in parallel, usually at several different sites. This is sometimes known as *intra-query parallelism*.

Intra-Query Parallelism

Here is a classical picture of a shared-nothing query system. The tables to be queried are partitioned among K different sites, comparable to what we saw with the TPC-A earlier, the Account table being partitioned into Acct1 at site 1, Acct2 at site 2, . . . , AcctK at site K. The site machines do not share memory or disk, but communicate among themselves by messages over a communication network. Now assume that we wish to answer the following query, submitted let us say at site 1, to list the senior citizen account holders:

[10.4.1] `select Account.name, Account.phone from Account`
`        where Account.age >= 65;`

Now there is no single Account table in our architecture, and the straightforward way to accomplish this task is to have the system decompose query (10.4.1) into K different queries Q_J, of the form:

```
select AcctJ.name, AcctJ.phone from AcctJ
    where AcctJ.age >= 65;
```

Here J ranges from 1 to K. The query coordinator needs to send messages for each query Q_J, communicating the request to site J. Each site then answers the query from data in its local table AcctJ and communicates the answer back to the coordinator, let us say at site 1. Site 1 has the task of accepting rows from each of the participating sites and putting them together to form the answer.

Note that the query coordinator's job could become somewhat more complicated, for example, if an **order by** clause were affixed to query (10.4.1), such as ". . . order by Account.name". The same clause would then be affixed to each of the Q_J queries, so that participating sites would return their rows in the appropriate order, but it is still left to the coordinating site to merge these different streams into a single ordered sequence of rows. As with the queries we have already seen, there might be good reason to limit the materialization of the answer if there is any suspicion that only an early set of rows in the answer will be considered, and this feature creates slightly more complexity for the coordinator. Another alternative arises when we consider a modification to query (10.4.1):

[10.4.2] `select count(*) from Account where Account.age >= 65;`

This query too will be decomposed into site-component queries, and the coordinator must now know enough to *add* the responses from the various sites to arrive at the final answer.

The most difficult problem of all arises as a result of a query that requires a join to take place between tables at different sites. Consider a design where individuals can have multiple bank accounts at different branches, but one of the accounts is considered to be *primary*. The Account table contains a column named acct_type that has value *primary* or *secondary*; rows that are secondary have a column value Pracct_ID, which gives the value of Account_ID for the corresponding primary account. (Rows that are primary have a null value for Pracct_ID.) Now consider the following query to bring together all multiple account balances of multiple account holders:

```
[10.4.3] select A1.Account_ID, A1.balance, A2.Account_Id, A2.balance
         from Account A1, Account A2
         where A2.acct_type = 'secondary'
             and A2.pracct_id = A1.Account_ID;
```

Consider how this query will be executed in a multi-site database of the kind we have been discussing. We can fragment the query into different queries QJ for communication to sites J, varying from 1 to K, where secondary accounts are positioned:

```
[10.4.4] select A1.Account_ID, A1.balance, A2.Account_Id, A2.balance
         from Account A1, AcctJ A2
         where A2.acct_type = 'secondary'
             and A2.Pracct_ID = A1.Account_ID;
```

But we note that the Account table for primary accounts taking part in the join is still multi-site resident. A join between different sites is unavoidable under these circumstances. One possible query execution plan when query (10.4.4) is executed at site J is to retrieve all Account_ID values from AcctJ into a set X:

```
[10.4.5] select A1.Pracct_ID into X
         from AcctJ A2
         where A2.acct_type = 'secondary';
```

We can now have database site J partition X into sets $X_1, X_2, \ldots, X_K$, where set X_M consists of Pracct_ID values that match with Account_ID values at site M (the system knows where the different rows of the Account table are stored by primary key value). Now site J sends messages to the different sites M asking for solutions to the query:

[10.4.6] ```select A1.Account_ID, A2.balance
        from AcctM A1
        where A1.Account_ID in X```$_M$```;```

When the answers to these queries are returned from the different sites M to the requesting site J, a join can then be performed to answer query (10.4.4). The results of the various queries of the form (10.4.4) can now be communicated back from the different sites J to answer the original query (10.4.3).

Queries on a multi-site shared-nothing database can have extremely complex query plans, involving multiple levels of intra-site messaging. Clearly a set of distributed sites with slow communication over a wide area net is at a severe disadvantage for plans of this kind, involving *dataflow* between different sites. An excellent overview of shared-nothing queries of this kind is given in a paper by DeWitt and Gray [2].

Suggestions for Further Reading

Distributed database system design, with all the variant problems that can arise, is well presented in the text by Ozsu and Valduriez [7]. The Bernstein, Hadzilacos, and Goodman text [1] gives a good rigorous grounding for distributed transactions, and Gray and Reuter [5] give a superb introduction to the design and implementation issues that arise. The Gray and Reuter text is also the best introduction to TP monitors. The text by Khosafian, Chan, Wong, and Wong [6] is a good basic introduction to writing client-server applications in SQL on a number of systems. Parallel queries are discussed in the paper by DeWitt and Gray [2], the chapter of *The Benchmark Handbook* [4] dealing with the Wisconsin benchmark, and several papers of the Stonebraker text [8], which also reprints founding papers on distributed database systems.

752

[1] P. A. Bernstein, V. Hadzilacos, and N. Goodman. *Concurrency Control and Recovery in Database Systems.* Reading, MA: Addison-Wesley, 1987.

[2] D. J. DeWitt and J. Gray. "Parallel Database Systems: The Future of High-Performance Database Systems." *Comm. of the ACM,* 35, 6 (June 1992), p. 85.

[3] Goetz Graefe. "Query Evaluation Techniques for Large Databases." *ACM Computing Surveys,* 25, 2 (June 1993), pp. 73–170.

[4] Jim Gray, editor. *The Benchmark Handbook for Database and Transaction Processing Systems,* 2nd ed. San Mateo, CA: Morgan Kaufmann, 1993. See Section 4.3, "Benchmarking Parallel Database Systems Using the Wisconsin Benchmark."

[5] Jim Gray and Andreas Reuter. *Transaction Processing: Concepts and Techniques.* San Mateo, CA: Morgan Kaufmann, 1993.

[6] Setrag Khosafian, Arvola Chan, Anna Wong, and Harry K. T. Wong. *A Guide to Developing Client/Server SQL Applications.* San Mateo, CA: Morgan Kaufmann, 1992.

[7] M. Tamer Ozsu and Patrick Valduriez. *Principles of Distributed Database Systems.* Englewood Cliffs, NJ: Prentice-Hall, 1991.

[8] Michael Stonebraker, editor. *Readings in Database Systems,* 2nd ed. San Mateo, CA: Morgan Kaufmann, 1994. See original research papers: Chapter 7, "Distributed Database Systems," and Chapter 8, "Parallelism in Database Systems."

Exercises

[10.1] •Answer true or false for the following questions and explain your answers.

(a) Two-phase commit is required in order to guarantee a coordinated transaction on a shared-memory multiprocessor.

(b) Distributed deadlock is not possible on a shared-nothing DSS system where only queries are performed.

(c) The server in a client-server architecture cannot be a shared-nothing parallel database system.

(d) According to Figure 10.6, five CPUs with a 60 MIPS rating should cost less than one CPU with a 300 MIPS rating.

(e) A transaction in a prepared state can still commit after the site machine on which it lives has crashed and later recovered.

Introductory Tutorial

A.1 | Setting Up the CAP Database in INGRES

This tutorial explains the skills you need to perform Exercise 3.2.1 of Chapter 3, a computer assignment to exercise SQL *data definition statements* to create database tables duplicating the customers-agents-products (CAP) database of Figure 2.2. Specifically, you will learn in this tutorial how to create and later destroy a database (if database creation hasn't already been done for you by the DBA); how to enter the database from the operating system; how to load data from an operating system file into an already defined table of the database; and how to interact with the **INGRES** terminal monitor. The **INGRES** terminal monitor has a number of commands that allow you to compose SQL statements, execute them, edit them, save them to operating system files, then read them back, and so on. As explained in Section 3.2, you first need to get an account on your operating system—an OS user ID and password to log in to the computer—and a separate account on the database system itself to give your OS user ID privilege to enter the database system. Your instructor should be able to advise you how to do this at your installation.

Creating the CAP Database

Once you have an **INGRES** account of the proper privilege, you can create a database by entering the *createdb* command at the operating system level:

[A.1.1] `createdb` *dbname*

where *dbname* is the name of the database you want to create. A database is like a directory that contains a set of tables with related information; an example is the `customers-agents-products` (CAP) database of Figure 2.2. Once the database is created, you receive a message from **INGRES**: `exiting createdb`. You can now enter **INGRES** and proceed with the creation of the database tables. To erase a database created in error, you can use the analogous operating system command:

[A.1.2] `destroydb` *dbname*

where *dbname* is the name of the database you wish to erase.

Entering INGRES

To enter **INGRES**, give the operating system command:

[A.1.3] `sql` *dbname*

where *dbname* is the name of the database you created earlier using the **createdb** command, or else the database created for you by the DBA. After giving this command, you see a new kind of prompt:

```
    *
```

which means that you are talking to the **INGRES** terminal monitor. This terminal monitor environment has a number of commands (basically, *editor* commands) that are explained in the next section, but for now we concentrate on the SQL statements you will want to create. These SQL statements are really *directives* to the **INGRES** system (rather than to the terminal monitor, which you are just using to compose them) that allow you to create tables, load them, pose queries, and so on. As discussed in

general terms in Section 3.2, to create the CUSTOMERS table of the CAP
database in **INGRES**, you would issue the Create Table statement. Using
INGRES datatypes and the lowercase table name customers, the desired
statement is

[A.1.4] ```* create table customers (cid char(4) not null, cname varchar(13),```
      ```* city varchar(20), discnt float4); \g```

The SQL Create Table statement given in (A.1.4) is understood by
INGRES version 6; earlier versions of **INGRES** may not understand certain
clauses used, such as **not null**. The result of the Create Table statement is
the creation of an empty customers table with the column names (or
attributes) cid, cname, city, and discnt. The *type* of each attribute
(also known as the *domain* of the attribute) follows each attribute name
specified; thus cname is of type varchar(13) (meaning a variable length
character string of maximum length 13) and discnt is of type float4.
Refer to Section 3.2 for further explanation and to Section A.3,
"Datatypes," for a complete list of **INGRES** datatypes.

The *Copy* statement is another **INGRES** SQL directive (it is not valid in
other database systems) that is used to load a table such as customers
from data that sits in a standard operating system file and has been prepared in advance using a regular system editor. For example, to load the
customers table in **INGRES**, we submit the following statement:

[A.1.5] ```* copy table customers(cid=c0, cname=c0, city=c0, discnt=c0) from```
      ```* 'custs.in';```

The string in single quotes on the second line represents the name of the
text file custs.in, which contains a set of individual lines (with no initial
spaces or tabs) of the form:

```
c001,Tiptop,Duluth,10.0
c002,Basics,Dallas,12.0
c003,Allied,Dallas,8.00
. . .
```

and so on. Note that this name for the file assumes that custs.in is in the
current directory being used when **INGRES** was entered. Otherwise a more
complete directory pathname might be used. For example, in UNIX a file

custs.in in the poneil user directory, ingres subdirectory might be represented in the Copy command by '/usr/poneil/ingres/custs.in'. This is referred to generically as 'full pathname of custs.in'. The formatting specification, (cid=c0, cname=c0, city=c0, discnt=c0), in the Copy command specifies the layout of the data in the file custs.in. The column specification c0 means that the individual column values are separated by commas. If instead we listed column values in known character offset starting positions, allowing fixed lengths for each column, 5 characters for the cid value, 12 characters for the cname value, etc. (note that these are not necessarily the same lengths as in the table definition), we could use a different specification, (cid=c5, cname=c12, . . .). Note too that even though the column named discnt is of type float4 in the Create Table Definition, the Copy command uses a format specification of c0; this is because we expect the number to appear in the file cust.in as a character string, which will require conversion to the internal computer representation for float4.

The Copy statement can also be used to dump the contents of a table in **INGRES** out to a file understood by the operating system. The full format of the Copy statement that we use in this text is

[A.1.6] copy table tablename (colname=format {, colname=format})
            [into | from] 'full-path-filename [,text]';

The terms in this definition in boldface are meant to be entered, exactly as written. Thus every command of this form begins with the words "copy table . . . ," while the "tablename" word is not actually entered and should be filled in with some table name, such as "customers". When a bar (|) occurs within a sequence of terms surrounded by brackets ([ ]), it means that only one of the terms is to be used. Thus we can either copy a table *from* a file or *into* a file—we can't do both at once. When a single phrase occurs in brackets ([ ]), it means that the phrase is optional. Thus the clause [,text] can be used to restrict the Copy command to consideration of text-type files. When a phrase occurs in braces ({ }), it means that the phrase can be repeated any number of times (zero or more). Thus we can use an arbitrary number of clauses of the form {, colname=format} to stand for however many columns in the table that are to be read from the operating system file. Look again at the Copy statement in (A.1.5) for an example of the definition of (A.1.6). Note that we state that the full format of the Copy statement used in the current text is given in (A.1.6). We do not always specify all possible options for **INGRES** SQL statements or text format statements; we refer the reader to the *INGRES SQL Reference Manual*. More complete forms of some statements are given in Appendix B.

Now that you have seen how to create a table and how to load it, you need to know how a table is to be destroyed (deleted from the database, as a file is deleted from a directory). As explained in Section 3.2, for this purpose we use the command:

[A.1.7] `drop table tablename;`

Using the INGRES Terminal Monitor

Recall that you entered **INGRES** by giving the operating system command on the line numbered (A.1.3) above:

`sql dbname`

where *dbname* is the name of a database created earlier. After giving this command, you see a new kind of prompt:

`*`

which means that you are talking to the **INGRES** terminal monitor. The **INGRES** terminal monitor has a number of commands that allow you to compose SQL statements, edit them, save them to operating system files, then read them back, and so on. The following is a short introduction to the commands of the terminal monitor.

You can type in any SQL statements you want, free-form with multiple carriage returns, as you would write a program in which lines end with semicolons. These statements go into the monitor *buffer;* like an editor buffer—every keystroke gets remembered. However, the monitor won't *do* anything with what you enter until you type in a character string of the form "\ç<CR>", a backslash, "\", followed by some known character represented here by "ç", and then a carriage return. As an example, to create the table `customers` you could type:

```
*create table customers (cid char(4) not null, cname varchar(13),
*city varchar(20), discnt float4);
*\g
```

Notice that every time you press Return, you see a new prompt symbol, "$*$". The terminal monitor doesn't attempt to pass the Create Table statement on to the **INGRES** interpreter, which will not act on it until it sees the "\g" command, which can be interpreted to mean **\go**. The "\g" command doesn't need to sit alone on a new line; you could type instead:

```
*create table customers (cid char(4) not null, cname varchar(13),
*city varchar(20), discnt float4);\g
```

Once you type "\g" to execute the statements in the buffer, and the execution is successful, the default assumption is that you are finished with the buffer contents. If you now enter a new line of text, the effect is to erase the prior buffer contents. To keep the buffer from being cleared, type "\a" immediately after execution; this causes successive text to be **\appended** to the existing buffer.

```
*\a copy table customers(cid=c0, cname=c0, city=c0, discnt=c0) from
*'full-pathname-of-file-custs.in';
```

If you're unsure of the contents of the buffer at any time, you can type "\p" to **\print** it to your terminal screen. You can also force the buffer to be cleared by typing "\r" for \reset at any time.

The value of the monitor buffer shows up most clearly when you have a long sequence of statements to compose. For example, by typing "\e" for **\edit** you can enter a system editor to edit the lines in the buffer so far; exiting the editor brings you back to the terminal monitor environment. Here is a complete list of terminal monitor commands:

```
\g          "go", Execute the contents of the buffer workspace
\p          "print", print (to terminal screen) contents of buffer
\a          "append", append (after \g) newly entered text to old
\r          "reset", clear buffer (empty it)
\e          "edit", drop into editor to edit current buffer contents
\w fname    "write", write contents of buffer to named file
\i fname    "include", bring named file into buffer
\q          "quit", leave INGRES
```

There are two commands left to discuss. You can **\write** the contents of the buffer to a named file at any time, using the "\w" command, or **\include** a named file, reading it into the buffer, with the "\i" command. Once you've got a working sequence of command in your buffer (and you've tested it), you can save this sequence as a procedure named proc1 to be run again later, by typing

```
\w proc1
```

You will then be able to bring it into the buffer again later, using the \i command. Note that neither the \w nor the \i command expects the file fname that follows to be enclosed in any kind of quotes. This differs from the usage of the Copy command.

As an example, you could create a file named "makecusts" before entering **INGRES**, with the following lines of text:

```
drop table customers;
create table customers (cid char(4) not null, cname varchar(13),
city varchar(20), discnt float4);
copy table customers(cid=c0, cname=c0, city=c0, discnt=c0)
    from 'custs.in';
```

The effect of this procedure is first to drop the current customers table (we assume that it was improperly loaded earlier, but if the table does not already exist we will see a warning message with no ill effect on what follows), then to re-create the table, and finally to load it from the file custs.in. Thus at a later time you can use the following sequence of commands:

```
*\i makecusts
*\p          (check that the lines are there)
*\g          (execute them)
```

You have just used the \i command to "include" the precreated procedure makecusts, then printed out the lines now in the buffer with the command \p, and then executed this procedure using the \g command. **INGRES** prints back messages after the \g command executes, hopefully indicating success in creating and loading the table customers. You can now execute the simplest possible SQL Select statement to check your success, asking that all rows of the customers table be printed out to the terminal screen.

```
*select * from customers;\g
```

The monitor, as usual, doesn't try to submit this statement to **INGRES** until it hears the command \g at the end of the line. Then, if everything has worked properly, you should see the entire table contents printed out to your terminal screen.

INGRES also provides a few "help" commands that may be of value. Typing

```
*help\g
```

gives a list of tables present in the database—for example, customers, agents, products, and orders. Then typing

```
*help customers\g
```

gives the information about the column names for the customers table (or whatever other table is used after help). You can also use the statement

```
*help help\g
```

to see a list of the topics on which help is available. One such topic is "copy"; if you then type

```
*help copy\g
```

INGRES prints out to the screen the general form of the Copy statement. You should experiment with the help facility to see what is available, although the main value of help is to remind you of the syntax of commands that you already understand from your other reading.

Once the data is available in files custs.in, agents.in, prods.in, and ords.in, the creation and load of all four tables can be performed by the following statements. It is crucial that the datatypes of columns that will be joined should agree across tables; implicit conversion of datatypes is often *not* performed.

```
drop customers;
create table customers (cid char(4) not null, cname varchar(13),
    city varchar(20), discnt float4);
copy table customers (cid=c0, cname=c0, city=c0, discnt=c0)
    from 'custs.in';

drop agents;
create table agents (aid char(3) not null, aname varchar(13),
    city varchar(20), percent smallint);
copy table agents (aid=c0, aname=c0, city=c0, percent=c0) from 'agents.in';

drop products;
create table products (pid char(3) not null, pname varchar(13),
    city varchar(20), quantity integer, price float4);
copy table products (pid=c0, pname=c0, city=c0, quantity=c0,
    price=c0) from 'prods.in';

drop orders;
create table orders (ordno smallint not null, month char(3),
    cid char(4), aid char(3), pid char(3), qty smallint, dollars float);
copy table orders (ordno=c0, month=c0, cid=c0, aid=c0, pid=c0,
    qty=c0, dollars=c0) from 'ords.in';
```

A.2   Setting Up the CAP Database in ORACLE

This section explains the skills you need to perform Exercise 3.2.1 of Chapter 3, a computer assignment to exercise SQL *data definition statements* SQL data definition; to create database tables duplicating the `customers-agents-products` (CAP) database of Figure 2.2. Specifically, you will learn in this tutorial how to enter the database from the operating system, how to load data from an operating system file into the database, and how to deal with the SQL*Plus interactive environment. SQL*Plus has a number of commands that allow you to compose SQL statements, edit them, save them to operating system files, then read them back, and so on. As explained in Section 3.2, you first need to get an account on your operating system—an OS user ID and password to log in to the computer—and an **ORACLE** name and password to enter the database. Your instructor should be able to advise you how to do this at your installation.

In **ORACLE** there is usually one monolithic database owned by the database administrator. Unlike **INGRES**, individual users in **ORACLE** do not normally create their own databases. In order to keep different users' data separate, the database administrator grants each user access to a private *tablespace* in the database. A tablespace is like a directory that contains a set of tables. We will still informally refer to a group of related tables as a "database"; an example is the customers-agents-products (CAP) database of Figure 2.2.

Creating the CAP Database

To enter **ORACLE**, give the operating system command:

[A.2.1] sqlplus

ORACLE then prompts you for your database username and password, which your DBA should have given you. If your username and password are accepted, you see a new kind of prompt:

```
SQL> _
```

which means that you are now in the SQL*Plus interactive environment. This environment has a number of commands (basically *editor* commands) that are explained in the next subsection, but for now we concentrate on the SQL statements you will want to create. These SQL statements are really *directives* to the **ORACLE** system (rather than to the interactive environment, which you are just using to compose them) that allow you to create tables, load them, pose queries, and so on. As explained in Section 3.2, to create the CUSTOMERS table of the CAP database in **ORACLE**, using the lowercase table name customers, you would issue the statement:

```
SQL> create table customers (cid char(4) not null, cname varchar(13),
    2 city varchar(20), discnt real);
```

Notice that after performing a carriage return on the first line, the system prints out a prompt for the second line, "2". The prompt for the third line would be 3, and so on. There is no limit to the number of lines you can type. The system doesn't attempt to interpret what you have written until you end a line with a semicolon (;).

The result of the Create Table statement is the creation of an empty customers table with the column names (or attributes) cid, cname, city, and discnt. The *type* of each attribute (also known as the *domain* of the attribute) follows each attribute name specified; thus cname is of type varchar(13) (meaning a character string of variable length of up to 13 characters) and discnt is of type real. Refer to Section 3.2 for further explanation and to Section A.3, "Datatypes," for a complete list of **ORACLE** datatypes.

Now that we have a table, we can load data into it. To do this, we leave SQL*Plus by typing **exit** at the SQL prompt, and then run the SQL*Loader utility.

Using the SQL*Loader

The SQL*Loader is a utility program that reads operating system text files and converts the contents into fields in a table. To do this, it must be told what format it should expect the external data to be in. This description is stored in a control file, which usually has the filename extension ".ctl". For example, the control file cust.ctl should look like this:

```
load data
replace
into table customers
fields terminated by ","
(cid, cname, city, discnt)
```

The data file, typically having the extension ".dat", contains the data to be loaded into the table. It should be in the format described in the control file. For example, cust.dat should look like this:

```
c001,Tiptop,Duluth,10.0
c002,Basics,Dallas,12.0
c003,Allied,Dallas,8.00
. . .
```

To run the loader, type the operating system command:

```
sqlload control=cust.ctl
```

The SQL*Loader then prompts you for your **ORACLE** username and password. If you prefer, you may put these in the command line:

```
sqlload username/pas control=cust.ctl
```

Note that this command assumes that `custs.ctl` is in the current directory when the command is entered. Otherwise a more complete directory pathname would be needed. For example, in UNIX a file `custs.ctl` in the poneil user directory, oracle subdirectory would be represented in the Copy command by `'/usr/poneil/oracle/custs.ctl'`. In either case, the SQL*Loader requires write-permission in the directory containing the control file, so that it can create log files and bad files. Log files, ending with the filename extension ".log", contain a detailed report of the loading process. The bad file, ending in ".bad", contains any records that could not be properly read. You will need to copy cust.ctl and cust.dat from your instructor to one of your own directories before you can use them properly; sqlload will fail if it attempts to create the log file and the bad file in your instructor's directory, since you are only allowed to read that directory.

Now that you have seen how to create a table and how to load it, you need to know how a table is to be destroyed (deleted from the database, as a file is deleted from a directory). As explained in Section 3.2, for this purpose we use the command:

[A.2.2] `drop table tablename;`

All the tables can be created by the use of one file of statements, here named create.sql, and provided as input to sqlplus as follows:

```
sqlplus username/password @create.sql
```

The file create.sql has the following content. (Note that we drop tables before creating them, in case there are old versions in the database.)

```
/* create.sql: Oracle file for table creation
    Use command form: sqlplus username/password @create.sql */

drop table customers;
create table customers (cid char(4) not null, cname varchar(13),
    city varchar(20), discnt real);

drop table agents;
create table agents (aid char(3) not null, aname varchar(13),
    city varchar(20), percent number(6));

drop table products;
create table products (pid char(3) not null, pname varchar(13),
    city varchar(20), quantity number(10), price real);

drop table orders;
create table orders (ordno number(6) not null, month char(3),
    cid char(4), aid char(3), pid char(3),
    qty number(6), dollars float);
```

After the above commands are executed, the tables can be loaded by sql-load as follows:

sqlload username/password **control=cust.ctl**
sqlload username/password **control=agents.ctl**
sqlload username/password **control=prods.ctl**
sqlload username/password **control=orders.ctl**

To automate the job fully, put the sqlplus command and the four sqlload commands in a command file—for example, dbload.bat for MS DOS or dbload.cmd on some other systems—and then the simple command line "dbload" (@dbload on VMS) does the whole job.

Using SQL*Plus

SQL*Plus is the environment you enter by typing sqlplus from the operating system level. To begin with you see the prompt:

```
SQL> _
```

You can type in any SQL statement you want: if it doesn't fit on one line, you may continue onto the next line. SQL*Plus prints the line number of each new line as a prompt at the beginning of the line; for example:

```
SQL> select * from customers
    2 where cname = 'Tiptop'_
```

SQL*Plus won't try to interpret this statement until you terminate it with a semicolon:

```
SQL> select * from customers
    2 where cname = 'Tiptop';
```

After a carriage return on line 2, SQL*Plus prints out the row that matches this query and returns you to the SQL> prompt. It is also possible to enter a command but not execute it; the usefulness of this feature will become apparent shortly. To terminate a command without executing it, simply enter a completely blank line; you then return to the SQL> prompt. The text of the command (whether executed or not) is saved in the "buffer." We can always view the current contents of the buffer by typing the command "l" or "list":

```
SQL> l
    1   select * from customers
    2*  where cname='Tiptop'
SQL> _
```

SQL*Plus commands that operate on the buffer, such as "l", are not saved in the buffer; that would severely limit their usefulness!

In the above example, the star after the 2 indicates the current line in the buffer, which is used by several SQL*Plus commands. To change the current line, simply enter the line number at the SQL prompt:

```
SQL> 1
    1* select * from customers
SQL> _
```

To alter a small part of the current line, rather than retyping the whole thing you may use the "c" or "change" command, which replaces an old sequence of text with a new sequence of text. For example:

```
SQL> c /customers/agents
    1* select * from agents
SQL>  _
```

the slashes (/) are called "separating characters." You may use any non-alphanumeric character for separating characters; for example, the command "c &customers&agents" would be equivalent to the example above. To delete a substring of the current line, simply replace it with an empty string:

```
SQL> c /agents/
    1* select * from
SQL> _
```

To replace the contents of an entire line, type the line number, followed by the new contents:

```
SQL> 1 select * from customers
```

To re-execute the (possibly modified) contents of the buffer, use the command "/"; the command "r" lists the contents of the buffer and then executes them.

You can delete the current line in the buffer by using the command "del".

You can insert lines after the current line in the buffer with the "i" command. This command can be used in two different ways: you can either insert a single line of text following the i command:

```
SQL> i where cid = 'c001'
SQL> _
```

or, to enter several lines of text, type i with no arguments:

```
SQL> i
    2 where cid
    3 = 'c001';
```

In this mode, SQL*Plus behaves as if you are simply continuing to add to the previous command (or insert after a given line in a large buffer). A terminating semicolon, as in this example, executes the entire buffer contents.

We use these commands to correct a typical spelling error. Assume that you type

```
SQL> sellect * from customers
    2 where cname = 'Tiptop' _
```

and then realize your spelling error. You can correct it by ending command entry (entering a blank line), selecting the line to modify, replacing the misspelled word with the correct spelling, and executing the buffer:

```
SQL> sellect * from customers
    2 where cname = 'Tiptop'
    3
SQL> 1
    1* sellect * from customers
SQL> c /sell/sel
    1* select * from customers
SQL> /
```

This is the equivalent of simply retyping the command, but it requires fewer keystrokes.

The "edit" command is a trapdoor to your system editor. With no arguments, it invokes the editor on the contents of your buffer; or you can specify a filename to edit.

To execute an SQL command file from within SQL*Plus, use the command "@", followed by the command file's name. To simply load a command file into the buffer, use the command "get", followed by the filename.

To save the contents of the buffer to a file, use the command "sav" or "save", followed by the filename.

To summarize, here is a table of commands available in the SQL*Plus
environment:

```
c /old/new       change first occurrence of old string to new string
                 in current line
l                list contents of buffer
del              delete current line from buffer
i new line       insert a new line after current line in buffer
i                begin interactively inserting lines after current
                 line
                 in buffer
/                execute statements in buffer
r                list and then execute statements in buffer
edit filename    edit file using default operating system editor
edit             edit buffer using default operating system editor
@filename        execute SQL statements stored in file named
get filename     load file named into buffer
save filename    save buffer to file with given name (overwrites old)
5 new line       replace line 5
5                set current line to 5
host command     do the operating-system command as specified
```

If the edit command does not work, you need to issue the sqlplus command "define _editor = 'editor_name'". There are automatic
startup files to do such setup, but their description is beyond the scope of
this summary.

A.3 Datatypes

The datatype for each column named can be chosen from the list of types
shown in Figure A.1.

INGRES	ORACLE	DB2	Range	C equivalent
char(n)	char(n)	char(n)	$1 \leq n \leq 254$	char array[n+1]
varchar(n)	varchar(n)	varchar(n)	$1 \leq n \leq 254$	char array[n+1]
smallint	number(6)	smallint	$-2^{15} \leq x \leq 2^{15} - 1$	short int
integer	number(10)	integer	$-2^{31} \leq x \leq 2^{31} - 1$	long int
float4	real	real	$-10^{-38} \leq x \leq 10^{38}$ 7-digit precision	float
float	float	double precision	$-10^{-38} \leq x \leq 10^{38}$ 15-digit precision	double

Figure A.1 Legal Datatypes for the Create Table Statement

The char(n) datatype contains fixed-length strings of n characters. Thus in (3.2.1) the `cid` column is defined to have datatype char(4) and is perfect for strings such as 'c001', but a value such as 'c1' (which we do not have in our tables) would be filled in with blanks at the end, "c1$\Delta\Delta$", where the symbol "Δ" represents a blank character. For columns with highly varying string length values, it saves storage space to use a datatype varchar(n). For example, the attribute `city` has the datatype varchar(20), allowing varying character strings of *up to 20 characters*. Here short character strings don't require long terminal sequences of blank characters, and common short `city` names such as 'Troy' and 'Austin' use up less storage space than long ones such as 'Oklahoma City' and 'San Francisco'. We would use a smallint datatype in place of integer for the same reason: to save storage space in cases where the integer value in question will never exceed 32,767 in absolute value.

Individual database products often have additional datatypes not listed in Figure A.1.—for example, the *long varchar* datatype in **DB2**, or simply *long* datatype in **ORACLE**, which supports character string values up to 65,535 characters in length. **INGRES** has a different upper limit of 2000 characters instead of 254 for char(n) and varchar(n). Another datatype supported by **INGRES** is the *money* datatype, which displays with a dollar sign and decimal point for dollars and cents, supporting accuracy of 10^{16}. Numerous other datatypes are specified in the SQL reference manuals for each of the standard products, but for our purposes the datatypes of Figure A.1 are sufficient. In defining the CAP database, you should use the double datatype for the cost and dollars columns. If you are using **INGRES**, you may use the money datatype at the instructor's discretion.

Statement Syntax

809tThis appendix gathers together in alphabetical order the syntax definitions of the standard Embedded SQL statements presented in this text. The statements covered are listed in Figure B.1. Note that there are a large number of statements in various product dialects of SQL that are not covered in the current text.

Alter Table	Add or delete columns or constraints on an existing base table
Close	Close a cursor
Commit Work	Bring current transaction to a successful conclusion
Connect	Connect to a database
Create Index	Create an index on a base table
Create Table	Create a base table
Create Tablespace	Create tablespace (in **ORACLE**)
Create View	Create a view table
Declare Cursor	Define a cursor
Delete	Delete rows from a table
Describe	Get information about dynamic prepared columns

Figure B.1   Embedded SQL Statements Presented in this Text

(continued next page)

Disconnect	Disconnect from a database
Drop	Destroy (delete) a table, view, or index in a database
Execute	Execute a prepared dynamic statement
Execute Immediate	Execute an SQL statement in a host variable character string
Fetch	Advance a cursor and fetch values from the next row
Grant	Grant privileges on a table
Insert	Insert rows into a table
Modify	Create a primary access structure for a table or index (**INGRES**)
Open	Open a previously declared cursor
Prepare	Prepare a Dynamic SQL statement for execution
Revoke	Revoke privileges on a table
Rollback	Bring current transaction to an unsuccessful conclusion
Select	Retrieve desired table values
Update	Update values in a table

Figure B.1 Continued

B.1   Alter Table Statement

The Alter Table statement was introduced in Section 6.1, with variant X/
OPEN and **ORACLE** forms in Figures 6.6 and 6.7. The Alter Table statement allows the DBA to alter the structure of a table originally specified in
a Create Table statement, adding or deleting columns of the table, and with
many products adding or deleting various constraints as well. This statement is intended to apply to tables that already have existing columns, and
this brings up a number of new considerations of disk storage. The Alter
Table statement is not specified in the ANSI/89 SQL and ISO standards,
and the X/OPEN standard provides only the capability to add new columns, not to delete old columns or to add or drop constraints.

Alter Table Statement in X/OPEN

```
[exec sql] alter table tablename
    add columnname data-type
    | add (columnname data-type {,columnname data-type})
```

Figure B.2 X/OPEN Alter Table Syntax

Alter Table Statement in ORACLE

The **ORACLE** product provides many features that do not exist in the X/OPEN standard.

```
[exec sql] alter table tablename
    [add (columnname data-type [col_constr]
        {, columnname data-type [col_constr]}
        {, table_constr} ) ]
    [modify (columnname data-type [col_constr]
        {, columnname data-type [col_constr]})]
    [drop constraint constr_name]
    [disk storage and update transaction clauses (not covered, or
    deferred)]
```

Figure B.3   ORACLE Alter Table Syntax

The only action not permitted is to **drop** an existing column from the table.

Alter Table Statement in DB2, INGRES, and SQL-92

The **DB2** product offers approximately the same capabilities as the **DB2** Create Table form, except that a new column cannot be specified as **unique** and the constraints that can be added or dropped are limited to **primary key** (which is, of course, unique for the table) and **foreign key** . . . **references**, which is the only named constraint in the **DB2** syntax.

As of release 6.4, **INGRES** does not provide the Alter Table statement.

See the *SQL Reference Manual* for the specific product you are working with to determine the exact form of Alter Table statement available. The SQL-92 standard provides a very large set of features. All constraints are given names, and all columns and constraints can be added or dropped. See the Melton-Simon SQL-92 reference at the end of Chapter 6.

Alter Table Syntax: General Discussion

See the Create Table syntax discussion for an explanation of most syntax elements.

If a new column is added by an Alter Table statement, it must be created as all nulls or all default values. Therefore it cannot be specified as **not null**, unless, in **DB2**, it is **not null with default**. An added constraint that does not originally hold, such as **not null** for a column containing nulls, normally results in a restrict action—that is, the statement will not succeed. In SQL-92, when a column is to be dropped a [**cascade** | <u>**restrict**</u>] action defines whether constraints in other tables that depend on this column are to be dropped or whether the action to drop the column is to be restricted.

Adding new columns to a table definition has important implications for the physical storage of the rows, which may now be expanded in size to a point where they do not fit in their current disk area. Most products allow the DBA to alter the table and assume null values in new columns without moving all rows of the table to a new disk area at that time, a task that can require tremendous computer resources for very large tables. There is a good deal of variation among the different database products in treating physical storage considerations.

B.2 Close (Cursor) Statement

The statement to close a cursor has the form:

```
exec sql close cursor-name;
```

This statement closes the cursor so that the active set of rows is no longer accessible. It is always performed from within a program, since cursors are not open in ad hoc SQL. It is an error to close a cursor that is not open.

B.3 | Commit Work Statement

The statement to commit a transaction has the form:

```
exec sql commit work;
```

This statement causes the transaction to finish successfully; all row updates made during the transaction become permanent in the database and visible to concurrent users. All rows read during the transaction become once again available to concurrent users for update.

B.4 | Create Index Statement

The Create Index statement was introduced in Chapter 7, with a number of variant forms introduced in Figures 7.1 (X/OPEN), 7.7 and 7.13 (**ORACLE**; the two figures have identical syntax, but the **pctfree** clause is not explained until Figure 7.13), 7.14 and 7.21 (**DB2**; the syntaxes of these two figures are different and are amalgamated here), and 7.15 (**INGRES**). See also the Modify statement in this appendix for the **INGRES** command that creates a primary and secondary index access.

Create Index Statement in X/OPEN

Here is the X/OPEN standard specification of the Create Index statement.

```
[exec sql] create [unique] index indexname
    on tablename (columnname [asc | desc] {, columnname [asc | desc]);
```

Figure B.4 X/OPEN Syntax for the SQL Create Index Statement

The table specified by tablename in the Create Index syntax must be a base table that already exists at the time that the statement is issued. The statement of Figure 7.1 creates a set of *index entries* of the form (keyval, rowid), one for each of the N rows of the table. Index entries look like rows of a table with two columns: the *index key,* consisting of the concatenation of values from the columns named in the Create Index statement, and a "pointer" to the disk position of the row from which this specific entry was constructed, represented here by a rowid. The index entries are then placed on disk in sorted order by index key (hashed access is not supported in the standard), with **asc** or **desc** order for each component column, as in the **sort by** clause of the Select statement. Lookup through an index locates a sequence of index entries with a given key value or range of key values, and it generally follows the entry pointers to the associated rows. Note that entries of the index automatically respond to changes in the table after the Create Index statement has been performed. When a row is inserted in the table, a new index entry is created in the index and placed in the appropriate index structure position for efficient lookup; similarly, row updates that change the index key value are reflected by a change in the associated index entry.

Create Index Statement in ORACLE

Here is the **ORACLE** syntax for the Create Index statement.

```
[exec sql] create [unique] index indexname on tablename
    (columnname [asc | desc] {, columnname [asc | desc]})
    [tablespace tblspacename]
    [storage ([initial n] [next n] [minextents n] [maxextents n]
        [pctincrease n] ) ]
    pctfree n
    [other disk storage and transactional clauses not covered]
    [nosort]
```

Figure B.5   ORACLE Create Index Statement Syntax

The tablespace clause specifies the tablespace on which the index is to be created. See Figure 7.3 for a schematic picture of **ORACLE** data storage structures. The **storage** clause options are explained in the text following the Create Tablespace statement syntax of Figure 7.4. The **nosort** option indicates that the rows already lie on disk in sorted order by the key values for this index; thus index entries are extracted in that order and the effort of the sort step can be saved. **ORACLE** checks that the key values extracted are actually in increasing order and returns an error if the order is not as promised. The value of n in the **pctfree** clause can range from 0 to 99, and the value determines the percentage of each B-tree node page (recall that a page is known as a *block* in **ORACLE**) that is *left unfilled* when the index is originally created. This space is then available for new index entry inserts when rows are inserted to the underlying table. The default value for **pct-free** is 10, and larger values permit more row insertions before node splits occur. A comparable parameter for leaving free space in index nodes is provided by **DB2**. Indeed **ORACLE** makes an effort to remain compatible with **DB2** syntax, so we can expect identical naming conventions when differences in disk storage architecture don't require variations.

Create Index Statement in DB2

Here is a simple version of the **DB2** Create Index statement syntax.

```
[exec sql] create [unique] index indexname on tablename
    (columnname [asc | desc] {, columnname [asc | desc]})
    [using . . .]
    [freepage n]
    [pctfree n]
    [additional clauses not covered]
    [cluster . . . ];
```

Figure B.6   Simple Version of **DB2** Create Index Statement Syntax

The **using** clause of the **DB2** Create Index statement specifies how the index is to be constructed from disk files (called *datasets* in IBM nomenclature), and it takes the place of the **tablespace** and **storage** clauses of the **ORACLE** Create Index statement. The **pctfree** clause in **DB2** is identical in meaning to the **ORACLE** form, but **DB2** adds another free storage specification with the **freepage** clause. The integer n of the **freepage** clause specifies how frequently an empty free page should be left in the sequence of pages assigned to the index when it is loaded with entries by a **DB2** utility. One free page is left for every n index pages, where n varies from 0 to 255. The default value for n is 0, meaning that no free pages are left. A value of n = 1, however, means that alternate disk pages are left empty. The intention here is to leave some free pages for node splits in the B-tree, so that newly split nodes can remain as close as possible on disk to the immediate sibling nodes from which they split. **DB2** makes extremely efficient use of contiguous disk storage when doing index range retrievals, so it is especially important to keep leaf nodes as close as possible on disk.

The **DB2 cluster** clause has no arguments, except in the case that the index being created is a partitioned index, a variation we do not cover. Only one index for a table can be identified as a **cluster** index. After an index is identified as a clustered index in an empty table that is about to be loaded with new rows, the **DB2** LOAD utility causes rows to be sorted into the appropriate order when they are placed on disk. Existing rows of a table are not rearranged immediately into a clustered sequence after a clustered index is defined, however. A special utility, known as the REORG utility, must be run to cause the reordering of the rows to match this clustered index. The result in **DB2** looks like the tree structure at the bottom of Figure 7.20, a B-tree index conceptually lying above a sequence of table rows placed in data pages in the same order. Indeed the entire structure looks a bit like a B-tree with an extra level, with the data rows in order by key value at the new leaf level and the former leaf level of the index acting as a higher-level directory to the rows (not just the data pages, as it would be for a true directory to the leaf level of a B-tree).

This analogy is somewhat inaccurate because of the behavior of the structure as new rows are inserted. **DB2** advises the table creator to leave free space on the data pages for the table, and successive row inserts are directed by **DB2** to the free slots on the appropriate data page to maintain the clustering order whenever feasible. However, when a data page runs out of slots and new rows are inserted that would normally be placed on such a page, the B-tree approach of *splitting* the leaf node does not take place on the data pages. Instead, a new data page is allocated in the current extent, probably far removed from the clustered page position, and newly inserted rows are placed on this data page in rather arbitrary order as the original clustered data pages fill up. The longer we proceed with new inserts, the less clustered the index becomes because of latecomer rows that are entirely out of clustered sequence. Eventually the index can lose much of its clustering property, and the user is advised to run the REORG utility again to cause the rows to be resorted in appropriate order.

Create Index Statement in INGRES

Here is the Create Index statement in **INGRES**. (See also the **INGRES** Modify statement in this appendix for an explanation of index access structure.)

```
[exec sql] create [unique] index indexname on tablename
        (columnname {, columnname})
    [with       /* commas separate clauses following*/
        [location = . . . ]
        [structure = btree | isam | hash | . . . ]
        [key = (columnname {, columnname})]
        [fillfactor = n]
        [nonleaffill = n]
        [additional clauses not covered] ]:
```

Figure B.7 INGRES Create Index Statement Syntax

Note that the **asc** | **desc** descriptor for columnnames of the index is missing, but this is not visible to the SQL user, who can still specify ascending or descending columns in the **order by** clause of a Select statement. The **with** keyword must be present if any of the later comma-separated clauses appear. The **location** clause specifies how the index is to be constructed from disk files and takes the place of the **tablespace** and **storage** clauses of the **ORACLE** Create Index statement. The **structure** clause is unique to **INGRES**, and names the access structure that the index will be assigned when it is created. See the discussion in the Modify statement of this appendix and following Figure 7.22 in the text. The **key** clause indicates that the index key value will be constructed from the columnnames listed, a subset of the columnnames on the second row of the syntax, listed in the same order. Columns appearing on the second row that are not part of the **key** clause are available to the **INGRES** Query Optimizer to perform an efficient type of index-only retrieval, as explained more fully in Chapter 8. The **fillfactor** and **nonleaffill** parameters of the **INGRES** Create Index statement compare to the **pctfree** parameters of the **DB2** and **ORACLE** statements, except that where **pctfree** gives the percentage of node space that should remain *unfilled* during the initial creation of the index, **fillfactor** and **nonleaffill** give the percentage of the node space that should be *filled*: fillfactor gives the percentage for what we can think of as leaf nodes of the index, and **nonleaffill** the percentage for non-leaf nodes.

    INGRES pictures indexes rather differently than other products do, and this difference is somewhat subtle. Recall that a B-tree index entry consists of a pair of values (keyval, rowid). **INGRES** pictures the index as a *table in its own right*, containing two-column rows of the form (keyval, tid), but a special form of table because the system uses it for lookup and users are not allowed to update the table (that is, index) directly. **INGRES** always defines something called a *structure* for all its tables. A structure determines the way in which rows are stored on disk and often also determines a *primary index* lookup directory for keyed access to the table; it is often set using the Modify statement.

B.5 Create Table Statement

The general Create Table statement was introduced in in Section 6.1, with a number of variant forms for X/OPEN, **ORACLE**, **DB2**, and **INGRES** introduced and explained throughout the section. The form of the **ORACLE** Create Table statement given below was originally presented in Figure 7.5, and it assumes a knowledge of storage allocation clauses explained in the **ORACLE** Create Tablespace statement.

Create Table Statement in X/OPEN

Here is the X/OPEN standard specification of the Create Table statement.

```
[exec sql] create table tablename
    (columnname data-type [default {defaultvalue|null|user}]
        [col_constr]
    {, columnname data-type [default {defaultvalue|null|user}]
        [col_constr]}
    {, table_constr})
The col_constr form that constrains a single column value follows:
[not null [unique]]
[references tablename [(columnname)] ]
[check (search_condition)]
The table_constr form that constrains multiple columns at once
follows:
unique (columnname {, columnname})
| check (search_condition)
| primary key (columnname {, columnname})
| foreign key (columnname {, columnname})
| references tablename [(columnname {, columnname})]
```

Figure B.8 Full X/OPEN Standard Create Table Syntax

The ANSI/89 and ISO standards for Create Table syntax are basically
identical to the X/OPEN standard. This syntax is accepted by **ORACLE**,
largely supported by **DB2** version 2.3 (with some minor variations) and not
at all closely supported by **INGRES** as of release 6.4.

The Create Table command of Figure B.8 begins by naming the table
being created and then lists in parentheses a comma-separated sequence of
columnname definitions. Each columnname definition contains columnname and datatype, and an optional **default** clause. This clause specifies
the default value that the database system supplies for the column if the
SQL Insert statement does not furnish a value. (Note that bulk-load commands such as Load and Copy are not covered by the SQL standard and
are therefore not constrained to provide this value.) The default value supplied can be a constant of appropriate datatype supplied as "defaultvalue,"
or **null**, or **user**. The keyword **user** represents a character string whose
value is the current user name.

Each columnname definition is optionally followed by a list of *column
constraints*, symbolized in Figure B.8 by col_constr, which consists of a
sequence of optional clauses. At the end of the list of columnname definitions, a comma-separated list of *table constraints*, symbolized by
table_constr, is appended before the defining parentheses are closed.

We explain the column constraint clauses before moving on to the
table constraints.

Column Constraints

The **not null** condition means that null values cannot occur in this column.
Only if **not null** is specified can **unique** be added, and the column is then
constrained to contain a different value on every row inserted in the table.
Basically this means that the table creator wants this single column to function as a *candidate key*. If **not null** appears in a col_constr, then the **default**
clause cannot specify **null**; if neither the **default** clause nor the **not null**
clause appears in a column definition, then **default null** is assumed.

For a column defined with a **references** clause, each row is constrained
to contain in this column one of the values that appears in the tablename
referenced, either in the columnname specified or, if no columnname is
specified, in the single column primary key of that table. This constraint is
a means of defining a column to be a *foreign key* referencing the primary
key, or possibly a candidate key, of a different table. In the case of a multi-

column foreign key, we need a somewhat more general definition (see the following definition of table constraints).

If the **check** clause appears, then each row is constrained to contain a value in this column that satisfies the specified search_condition. In the X/OPEN standard this search_condition is only permitted to contain references to constant values; no other column references or set functions are permitted.

Table Constraints

The **unique** clause has the same meaning as **unique** in the case of a col_constr, except that it is possible to specify a set of columns that must be unique in combination (the col_constr form is merely a special case of the table_constr from). Therefore this is a way to specify a multi-column candidate key for a table. Every column that participates in a **unique** clause must be defined to be **not null**.

The **check** clause as a table constraint is similar to the column **check** clause and limits acceptable values for a set of columns; the search_condition can refer to any column values in the same table, on the same row for which an Update or Insert statement is in process. As in the column analog, no Subselects or set functions are allowed in the X/OPEN standard. This limitation is removed in SQL-92, and the expanded power is extremely significant, but most database products currently maintain the limitation of an X/OPEN search_condition.

The **primary key** clause specifies a non-empty set of columns to be a primary key—that is, a candidate key referred to by default in another table in a **references** clause (see below). Every column that participates in a **primary key** clause must be defined to be **not null**. There can be at most one **primary key** clause in any Create Table statement.

The **foreign key** and **references** clauses always occur together (although because they are independent optional clauses in the Create Table syntax, they can occur in any order). The **foreign key** columnname list specifies a set of columns in the table being created whose values on each row are constrained to be equal to the values of a set of columns on some row of another table, as specified by the associated **references** clause. When the columns in the other table being referenced form the primary key, the **references** clause does not specify a list of columns. A detailed discussion of the concepts of primary key, foreign key, and referential integrity is presented in Section 6.1, starting with Example 6.1.5.

Note that the **primary key** clause has much the same effect as the **785** unique clause; the only added factor is that a **references** clause from another table will reference the primary key by default if no columns are specified. This means that a **unique** specification for a column is considered redundant with the **primary key** specification; only one of the two clauses will be accepted by many products.

Create Table Statement in ORACLE

The form of the **ORACLE** Create Table statement shown below was originally presented in Figure 7.5, and it assumes a knowledge of storage allocation clauses explained in the **ORACLE** Create Tablespace statement (given in this appendix). The **ORACLE** Create Table statement accepts all of the integrity constraint clauses (col_constr and table_constr clauses) of the X/ OPEN standard syntax in Figure B.8. However, if you are using an **ORACLE** release prior to version 7.0, most of these clauses are merely accepted syntactically by the Create Table statement, with no power to actually enforce constraints on later update statements.

The **ORACLE** Create Table statement is given in Figure B.9. Note that this statement contains a number of clauses that define how rows of the table are stored on disk. For further details of the **ORACLE** Create Table statement, refer to the *ORACLE SQL Language Reference Manual* and *Database Administrator's Guide* (see references at the end of Chapter 6).

```
[exec sql] create table tablename
    (columnname datatype [default {defaultvalue|null|user}]
        [col_constr]
    {, columnname data-type [default {defaultvalue|null|user}]
        [col_constr]}
    {, table_constr} )
    [tablespace tblspacename]
    [storage ([initial n] [next n] [minextents n] [maxextents n]
        [pctincrease n] ) ]
    [pctfree n] [pctused n]
    [other disk storage and transactional clauses not covered]
    [as subselect]
```

Figure B.9   ORACLE Create Table Statement Syntax

The **ORACLE** product provides an optional constr_name for every specified constraint for later reference. The Create Table form of Figure B.9 with the **as** subselect clause allows the user to create from existing tables a table containing the result of a Subselect. The columnnames of the table created and the elements of the target list of the Subselect must be in one-to-one correspondence, and column names of the new table may be inherited from the target list as long as they are unique in the new table. Note that the column definition elements following the columnnames are left out of the Create Table syntax when the **as** subselect clause is used, because the column datatypes are determined from the Subselect. Furthermore, column and table constraints are not included in that syntax; such constraints can be added to the table at a later time using the Alter Table statement.

The optional storage clauses of this Create Table syntax allow the creator of a table to override the parameters for extent allocation associated with the tablespace in which the table is defined.

The **pctfree** and **pctused** clauses together determine how much space on each disk page can be used for inserts of new rows, as opposed to how much space must be set aside for future expansion in the size of existing rows. The **pctfree** value must be an integer n from 0 to 99, where a value of 0 means that all page space can be used for new row inserts. The default is 10, meaning that new inserts to the page will stop when the page is 90% full. The **pctused** value specifies where new inserts to the page will start again if the amount of space used by stored rows falls below a certain percentage of the total. This value must be an integer n from 1 to 99; the default value is 40. Note that the sum of the **pctfree** and **pctused** values must be less than 100, and together they determine a range in which the behavior with respect to inserts on the disk page remains stable, depending on the last percentage value encountered.

Create Table Statement in DB2

The **DB2** format is somewhat complex, and we do not consider a number of features. For further details the reader is referred to the *IBM DB2 SQL Reference Manual* and the *DB2 Administrator's Guide* (see references at the end of Chapter 6).

The **DB2** Create Table statement has fewer constraints that are specific
to a column. The **DB2** Create Table format that we cover is the following:

```
[exec sql] create table tablename
    (columnname data-type [col_constr] {, columnname data-type
        [col_constr]}
    {, table_constr} )
```

The col_constr form for **DB2** is:

```
[not null [unique | with default
| fieldproc program-name (const {,const})]]
```

The **not null unique** phrase means what the same phrase would mean
in the X/OPEN standard. If **not null with default** is chosen, a null will
never appear in this column; but if an Insert statement leaves this column
unspecified, it will be replaced with a default value determined in advance
for each specific type—for example, 0 (zero) for numeric type and a string
of length zero for varchar.

A **fieldproc** option names a program containing a set of functions, one
of which will be called to examine a char or varchar datatype value that is
about to be placed in this column (for example, by an SQL Update statement) and encode it before it is stored. Similarly, any values read from this
column (for example, by a search_condition) are first passed to a function
in this program and decoded. The *const* arguments of the program are
passed to a function of the program at the time of the Create Table statement. Clearly the **fieldproc** option offers a great deal of power to deal with
inserted char or varchar values, allowing the DBA to create a flexible analog to the **check** clause, for example, or to perform sophisticated types of
data compression and decompression.

The table_constr form for **DB2** follows:

```
unique (columnname {, columnname})
| primary key (columnname {, columnname})
| foreign key [constr_name] (columnname {, columnname})
        references tablename
[on delete {restrict | cascade | set null}];
```

DB2 supports the **primary key** and **foreign key** table_constr clauses of the X/OPEN standard. The columns making up a foreign key must always match in value the primary key columns, left to right, in the referenced tablename. The optional constr_name attached to the foreign key definition is used in any error messages associated with this constraint, and also in the Alter Table statement to drop such a foreign key constraint.

The optional **on delete** clause specifies an "action" that should take place when some update would break the foreign key integrity constraint. For example, consider the foreign key, cid, in the orders table that references the primary key of the customers table. What action should be taken in response to a Delete statement that removes a row from the customers table whose cid value is referenced as a foreign key from rows of the orders table? The three actions permitted are **restrict, cascade,** and **set null.** With the **restrict** effect, the delete of the customers row would be rejected. With the **cascade** effect, when the customers row with a given cid value was deleted, all orders rows referring to that customer cid would also be deleted, and deletes would continue recursively for other rows, with a cascaded foreign key dependency on other rows deleted. With the **set null** effect, the customers row would be deleted and cid values in the orders table that refer to that row would be set to null. (The column cid in orders must therefore not be created with the **not null** specification.) If the **on delete** clause is missing from this **foreign key** specification, then the **on delete restrict** option is assumed. The **on delete restrict** action is also the default action assumed by the SQL standards where no **on delete** clause is provided.

Create Table Statement in INGRES

The **INGRES** Create Table statement has only one column constraint clause and no table constraint clauses. The Create Table syntax is

```
[exec sql] create table tablename
    (columnname datatype [not null [with default | not default]
        | with null]
    {, columnname datatype [not null [with default | not default]
        | with null]})
    [with_clause]
| create table tablename (columnname {, columnname})
        as subselect
        [with_clause]
```

The optional **with null** clause means that nulls are supplied for updates
that do not supply a value for this column; **not null with default** means that
INGRES supplies a default value instead; **not null not default** means that
the Update statement must supply a value for this column or encounter a
runtime error. If no clause at all is provided, **with null** is assumed. If only
not null is provided, **not null with default** is assumed.

The optional with_clause specifies details of disk placement and transactional conventions (not covered in this text; see the *INGRES SQL Reference Manual* cited in "Suggestions for Further Reading" at the end of
Chapter 6). The with_clause also allows for an **INGRES** guarantee of Relational RULE 3, which states that duplicate rows cannot exist in the table.
The form, used after all columns have been defined in parentheses, is the
following:

```
with noduplicates
```

Even when this clause is used, the guarantee that rows will not be duplicated does not hold unless a primary index structure is imposed on the
table to provide efficient reference through some column values. (This is
known in **INGRES** as an indexed *storage structure*, imposed through the
Modify statement, presented separately in this appendix.)

INGRES has no **unique** keyword. Unique values for columns and combinations of columns are supported separately by creating a unique table
storage structure on these columns with the Modify command. **INGRES**
has no **check** clause to constrain columns or combinations of columns, but
it provides this function with a Create Integrity statement, explained
below. As of release 6.4, **INGRES** does not support any **primary key** clause,
foreign key clause, or **references** clause, for either a single column or set of
columns. However, **INGRES** supports a form of procedural constraint
known as *database rules,* similar to the **SYBASE** triggers capability
described a bit later in this section. By creating appropriate database rules
(not covered in this text), it is possible to simulate the referential integrity
constraint imposed by the X/OPEN Create Table statement.

Check Clause Integrity Constraints in INGRES

The Create Integrity statement in **INGRES** creates an integrity constraint
comparable to a **check** clause in the standard Create Table command. A

discussion of its use is given in Section 6.1, starting with Example 6.1.4. The general form of the Create Integrity statement in **INGRES** is

```
[exec sql] create integrity on tablename [corr_name]
    is search_condition;;
```

The search_condition here can refer only to column values in the same table, on the same row for which an Update statement is in process. No Subselect or aggregate set functions can be used. When an attempt is made to create an integrity constraint on a table that initially disobeys this constraint, a runtime error is returned.

To get a list of all constraints imposed on a table with the Create Integrity statement, the interactive Help Integrity statement is used, with the general form:

```
help integrity tablename;
```

The response from this statement is a list of integers, known as *integrity numbers*. In a programmatic setting the equivalent function can be accomplished with a query from the iintegrities catalog table, with the structure given at the end of the *INGRES SQL Reference Manual*. To drop integrity rules from a table, the Drop Integrity statement is used with a list of integrity number integers. The general form is

```
[exec sql] drop integrity on tablename integer {, integer };
```

Integrity constraints are implemented on **INGRES** by an application of an approach known as *query modification*, as explained in the text.

Integrity Constraints in SQL-92

The SQL-92 standard has a number of new integrity features, most of which are not yet available on commercial database products. We give only skimpy coverage of this standard in our text; the interested reader is referred to the SQL-92 text by Melton and Simon (see "Suggestions for Further Reading" at the end of Chapter 6).

Check Clause in SQL-92

One of the more important modifications is in the optional **check** clause of the Create Table statement:

```
check (search_condition)
```

In SQL-92 this form accepts any valid search_condition form. In the X/OPEN **check** clause described above and in most current database products, the search_condition of the **check** clause can refer only to column values in the same table, on the same row for which an Update or Insert statement is in process, with no Subselects or set functions allowed. This is quite a strong limitation, a form known technically as a *restriction predicate,* and it should be obvious that there are many business rules we might wish to impose that cannot be provided without more powerful search_conditions. A discussion of this is given in the text, starting with Example 6.1.8.

Create Assertion Statement in SQL-92

As explained in the text, there is a rather strange side effect that the **check** constraint of a Create Table statement is always true for an empty table. This provides motivation for another new feature of the SQL-92 standard, the *Create Assertion* statement. This statement has the syntax:

```
create assertion constraint constr_name check (search_condition);
```

The way an assertion search_condition differs from the search_condition in the **check** clause of a Create Table statement is that the assertion is not associated with any specific table (it is meant to span multiple tables), and therefore the constraint test is not automatically true if the associated table is empty. The use of the Create Assertion statement is explained in the text of Section 6.1, starting with Example 6.1.10.

Other Constraints: Create Trigger Statement in SQL3

Relatively powerful triggered procedures are currently available in the **SYBASE** commercial database product, and somewhat less powerful forms are in a number of other products, such as Interbase and the Microsoft SQL server. SQL-92 offers no standard for triggers, but most vendors have simply gone beyond SQL-92 and used triggers as the basis for their implementation. The SQL3 Create Triggers syntax given in Figure B.10 is not final, because the standard has not been released, but it gives some idea of the capabilities.

```
create trigger trigger_name before | after
    insert | delete | update [of columnname {, columnname}
    on tablename [referencing_clause] [when (search_condition)]
    (statement {, statement}) [for each row | for each statement]
```

Figure B.10 SQL3 Create Trigger Statement Syntax

The Create Trigger statement creates an object named trigger_name. The name is used in error messages and in a later request to drop this trigger from currency: Drop trigger_name. The trigger is *fired* (executed) either before or after one of the events listed (**insert, delete,** or **update** optionally limited to a set of named columns) takes place to the table given by tablename. If the trigger is fired, the optional search_condition, if present, is executed to determine if the current row or set of rows affected should cause further execution. If so, the triggered *action,* a program given by the comma-separated list of statements in parentheses, is executed. The *granularity* of the action is either **for each row** or **for each statement** (the default), and this determines how frequently the action is executed, once for each row affected or else at the end of the statement. (Clearly we might have a multi-row update, delete, or insert, so there can be an important distinction here.) In the case of a triggered **update** event, the sequence of statements in the action program may wish to distinguish between values in each row affected *before* the update and values *after* the update occurs. To achieve this we have an optional referencing_clause in the Create Trigger syntax, of the form:

```
referencing [old [as] old_corr_name]
    [new [as] new_corr_name]
```

The two correlation names used to qualify a column name identify whether the column value comes from the old table (before update) or the new table (after update). Either the old or the new correlation name specification clause may be left out, but not both.

Because a trigger causes a series of statements to be executed, the comma-separated list we call the *action,* a trigger is said to implement a *procedural constraint.* The DBA can specify a sequence of statements to perform the constraint-implementing program action. The exact forms of statements permitted in the action program of the trigger will probably be subject to a good deal of further discussion before a final syntax is determined. Certainly all standard SQL statements will be included among the statements provided. In addition, most current database products (**SYBASE**, **ORACLE**, **INGRES**) have a number of procedural extensions to the SQL language that provide local memory-resident variables, permit if-then-else logic, and offer a means to return errors to the caller. Examples of trigger use with an imaginary set of statements of this kind are given in Section 6.1, starting with Example 6.1.11.

793

B.6   Create Tablespace Statement in ORACLE

Figure B.11 contains the complete syntax form for the Create Tablespace statement in **ORACLE**. A more complete description of **ORACLE** database storage structure elements is given in Section 7.2, with a diagram of these structures in Figure 7.3.

```
[exec sql] create tablespace tblspacename
    datafile 'filename' [size n [K|M]] [REUSE]
        {, 'filename' [size n [K|M]] [REUSE]}
    [default storage ([initial n] [next n] [minextents n]
        [maxextents n] [pctincrease n] ) ]
    [online | offline];
```

Figure B.11   ORACLE Create Tablespace Statement Syntax

The tablespace is constructed from a set of operation system files named in the **datafile** clause. The **reuse** keyword specifies that existing filenames should be reused, thereby destroying any information contained. If the **size** keyword is omitted, the file must already exist. A tablespace is created **online** by default, meaning that it is immediately available for use by the database system. The tablespace can be brought **offline** and **online** again by the DBA for various purposes with the Alter Tablespace statement (not covered in this text). The **default storage** clause of Create Tablespace allows the tablespace creator to specify default parameters governing how allocation of disk extents is to be handled in contained segments. Here are explanations of these parameters:

initial n
: The integer n specifies the size in bytes of the initial extent to be assigned. The default is 10240.

next n
: The integer n specifies the size in bytes of the next extent numbered 1; the size of subsequent next extents may increase (but not decrease) if a positive **pctincrease** value is specified. The default is 10240.

maxextents n
: The integer n specifies the maximum number of extents, including the initial extent, that can ever be allocated. The default is 99.

minextents n
: The integer n specifies the number of extents to be allocated initially when the segment is created. Since extents must be contiguous, this allows for a large initial space allocation, even when the space available is not contiguous. The default is 1.

pctincrease n
: The integer n specifies the percentage by which each successive next extent grows over the previous one. If the integer is zero, there is no increase. The default of 50 causes successive next extents to grow one and a half times over the prior next extent.

All extent sizes are rounded to an integral multiple of a block (page) size. The minimum size for an extent is 4096 bytes; the maximum is 4095 MB.

B.7 | Create View Statement

The complete description of the Create View statement used in this text is

```
[exec sql] create view viewname [(columnname {, columnname})]
       as subselect [with check option];
```

Recall that a Subselect, first defined in Figure 3.11, is missing the **union** and **order by** clauses of the full Select statement, so this imposes a limitation on view tables we can define. (SQL-92 adds the ability to use a **union** clause.) The Create View command is legal within a program as an Embedded SQL statement; however, the Subselect statement of the view must not contain any host variables or any dynamic parameters. The user creating the view becomes the *owner* of the view and is given update privileges on the view, assuming that the view is updatable (as explained in Section 6.2 of the text, beginning with Figure 6.11) and that the user has the needed update privileges on the base table on which the view is defined (there will be only one such table).

The optional **with check option** clause specifies that inserts and updates performed through the view to result in base table changes should not be permitted if they result in rows that would be invisible to the view Subselect. Note that the **with check option** clause is not a part of the X/OPEN standard and may not currently exist in all database products. However, it is offered by **ORACLE**, **DB2**, and **INGRES**, and is part of the SQL-89 standard. If the optional *columnname* list in the Create View syntax is not specified, then the columns of the new view table will inherit names of single columns in the target list of the Subselect statement. However, names must be provided when any view columns represent expressions in the target list. Also, qualifiers that result in unique columnnames in the target list will be absent in the inherited view, so we need to create specific column names for a view if the original column names of a target list would become identical without qualifiers.

B.8   Connect Statement

The Connect statement is used in an Embedded SQL program to connect to a database. It has the following syntax:

```
exec sql connect vendor_defined_argument;
```

Examples of the vendor_defined_argument forms used in **INGRES** and **ORACLE** are given in Section 4.1. To disconnect from the database when accesses have been completed, the program should use the Disconnect statement, discussed in this appendix.

B.9 | Declare Cursor Statement

The full syntax of the Declare Cursor statement is given in Figure B.12. The Subselect form used in B.12 is defined in the general Select statement syntax of Figure 3.11. The Declare Cursor syntax is quite close to the syntax of Figure B.12; however, most database system products do not provide a column alias for an expression retrieved in the target list: such a feature is less valuable because there is no default table display in the embedded case (although it is sometimes used to provide a named column for use in the **order by** clause).

```
exec sql declare cursor_name cursor for
    Subselect
    {union Subselect}
    [order by result_column [asc | desc] {, result_column [asc | desc]}
    | for update of columnname {, columnname}];
```

Figure B.12 Embedded SQL Declare Cursor Syntax

In **DB2**, as in Figure B.13, it is necessary to choose only one of the two final clauses in this syntax, **order by** or **for update of**. However, both **INGRES** and **ORACLE** allow both forms to be used simultaneously. In the X/OPEN SQL specification, the **for update** clause must be included with the cursor declaration if the program logic attempts to update or delete a row through the cursor; more on this below.

Note that a Fetch statement is used to retrieve selected rows from a cursor, but the cursor can only move forward through a set of rows. This limitation will disappear when SQL-92 features become generally available, because of the new scrollable cursor feature that is part of the SQL-92 standard. Until that time, however, the programmer needs to close and reopen a cursor in order to fetch a row for a second time. The same cursor may be opened and closed successive times in a single program. It generally must be closed, however, before it can be reopened (**ORACLE** permits an exception to this rule).

Declare Cursor Statement in SQL-92

SQL-92 provides important generalizations of the Declare Cursor and Fetch statements. First, the new Declare Cursor statement is given in Figure B.13.

```
exec sql declare cursor_name [insensitive] [scroll] cursor for
    Subselect
    {union subselect-form}
    [order by result_column [asc | desc] {, result_column [asc | desc]}
    [for read only | for update of columnname {, of columnname}];
```

Figure B.13   The SQL-92 Declare Cursor Statement Syntax

Basically the two new syntax elements are the keywords **insensitive** and **scroll**. When the **scroll** keyword is used in a cursor definition the cursor is said to be *scrollable,* and the new capabilities of the SQL-92 Fetch statement can be exercised. This Fetch statement is discussed later in this appendix. When the **insensitive** keyword is present, the cursor is said to be *insensitive;* this means that the rows pointed to by the cursor will *not* change as a result of a Searched Update or Searched Delete outside the cursor itself. The effect is as if the system took a snapshot of rows under the cursor when the cursor is opened. (This would be an inefficient way to implement it, however.) Now the program logic can look at rows that are no longer there, but if an attempt is made to perform a Positioned Update or Positioned Delete (using **where current of cursor** syntax), then an error to show that the row no longer exits is returned. If the **insensitive** keyword is left out of a Select statement that complies to this SQL-92 feature, then updates and deletes outside the cursor are immediately reflected in the rows retrieved in the cursor.

B.10   Delete Statement

There are two forms of the Delete statement, a *Positioned Delete* that deletes the current row (most recently fetched row) of a cursor, and the

Searched Delete that has the same sort of form we have already seen in interactive SQL Delete, in Section 3.9. Here is syntax that describes the two forms:

```
[exec sql] delete from tablename [corr_name]
    [where search_condition];
```

Figure B.14   Interactive or Embedded SQL Searched Delete Syntax

```
[exec sql] delete from tablename [corr_name]
    [where current of cursor_name];
```

Figure B.15   Embedded SQL Positioned Delete Syntax

The Positioned Delete statement of Figure B.15 uses a special "**current of** cursor_name" syntax. Only one of the two **where** forms can be used; if neither is used, all rows of the table will be deleted. The corr_name is for use in the search_condition and may cause a runtime error condition in some products if used with a Positioned Delete. Following a Searched Delete, the long int variable sqlca.sqlerrd[2] will contain the number of rows affected. If no rows are affected, the **not found** condition of the Whenever statement will arise.

In the Positioned Delete, after the delete is executed the cursor points to a new position, following the row deleted but just preceding the next row, if any. This is in the same sense that after an **open** of a cursor, the cursor points to a position just before the first row in the Select; this behavior is carefully chosen to work well with loops (see Example 4.3.1). If the cursor is not pointing to a row when a delete is executed (that is, it is pointing just before some row, or else Fetch has already returned a **not found** condition and is pointing to a position after all rows), a runtime error is returned. In order for the positioned delete to work at all, the cursor stipulated in the delete must already be open and pointing to a real row, and the **from** clause of the delete must refer to the same table as the **from** clause of the cursor select. In addition, the cursor select must have been declared **for update** in order for the delete statement to work (it suffices to specify any column names at all in the declare cursor **for update** clause).

B.11   Describe Statement

When the Prepare statement is called to prepare a Dynamic Select statement in a sqltext[ ] string, the compilation process calculates the number and types of the column values to be retrieved. For the program to learn this information, it must now call a new Dynamic SQL Describe statement, which places the information for all columns retrieved into the SQLDA variable struct. Here is the syntax of the Describe statement:

```
exec sql describe statement_identifier into sqldavar_pointer;
```

Examples of Dynamic Select statements are given in Section 4.6, starting with Figure 4.24. Note that the SQLDA structure is quite different in **INGRES** than it is in **ORACLE**.

B.12   Disconnect Statement

The Disconnect statement is used in an Embedded SQL program to disconnect from a database, and it has the following syntax:

```
exec sql disconnect;
```

Examples of its use are given in Section 4.1.

B.13   Drop {Table | View | Index} Statement

There is a standard SQL statement used to delete a table, view definition, or index from the system catalogs, and in the case of table and index to free up any allocated space. The complete description of the Drop statement is

```
[exec sql] drop [table tablename | view viewname | index indexname];
```

Only the owner of a table, view, or index (usually the original creator) is authorized to drop it. Most products use the Drop statement to delete other types of objects from the system catalogs as well (tablespaces, aliases, etc.), but these three objects are all part of the X/OPEN standard.

Note that when a view or table is dropped, there is some question of what happens to other objects whose definitions depend on it. The X/OPEN standard actually adds an optional choice after the tablename and viewname, [<u>cascade</u> | **restrict**]. If **cascade** is included, then other objects depending on the object to be dropped are also dropped; and if **restrict** is used, then the object cannot be dropped while other dependencies exist. **ORACLE**, **INGRES**, and **DB2** currently do not offer this option. Rather unexpectedly, compared with referential integrity constraints, **cascade** behavior is presumed with the Drop statement.

B.14 Execute Statement

After the Prepare statement has been called to prepare a Dynamic SQL statement from a sqltext[ ] string, the Execute statement is used to associate needed parameter values with dynamic parameters (of the form "?") in the string and to execute the prepared statement. Here is the syntax of the Execute statement:

```
exec sql execute statement_identifier
    using :host_variable {, :host_variable};
```

Examples of Execute statement use are given in Section 4.6, starting with Figure 4.23. Note that the Dynamic SQL statement may or may not be a Dynamic Select statement (examples start with Figure 4.24).

B.15 Execute Immediate Statement

An Execute Immediate statement performs a Dynamic SQL statement contained in a sqltext[ ] string, without need for a previous Prepare statement. The general form of the Execute Immediate statement is this:

```
exec sql execute immediate :host_string;
```

Note that no dynamic parameters of the kind handled by the Prepare and Execute statements are needed, since each execution with Execute Immediate is one of a kind. The character string contents of the host_string must represent a valid SQL statement, including any of the following types: Alter Table, Create Table, Delete (either Searched or Positioned), Drop (Table, View, or Index), Grant, Insert, Revoke, and Update (either Searched or Positioned). Other statements may be possible in specific products.

B.16   Fetch Statement

The statement to fetch a row from an active set of an opened cursor (dynamic or not) has the form:

```
exec sql fetch cursor_name
    into :host_variable {, :host_variable}
    | using descriptor :sqldavar_pointer;
```

The sqldavar_pointer is used with a dynamic cursor and the host_variable list is used otherwise to receive the values retrieved by the Fetch. Executing the Open statement positions the cursor, cursor_name, just before the first row of an active set of rows. Each successive Fetch statement repositions cursor_name to the next row of its active set and assigns column values from that row (named in the Declare Cursor statement) to the **into** or **using** target named in the Fetch statement. For examples of dynamic cursor use, see Section 4.6, Figures 4.24 and 4.25. In order for a Fetch statement to work, cursor_name must already be open and the number of target variables must match the number of columns in the target list of the define cursor. The **not found** condition of the Whenever statement arises when a Fetch statement is executed on an active set of rows that is empty, or when the cursor is positioned after the last active row.

Fetch Statement in SQL-92

The syntax of a Fetch statement of a nondynamic cursor in SQL-92 is shown in Figure B.16.

```
exec sql fetch
    [{next | prior | first | last
    |{absolute | relative} value_spec} from ]
    cursor_name into host-variable {, host-variable};
```

Figure B.16 The SQL-92 Fetch Statement Syntax

The specification of position movement (**next, prior, . . .**) is known as *orientation.* The current standard behavior is the default, **next,** meaning "Retrieve the next row in sequence following the current position in the cursor." The **prior** orientation means, "Retrieve the row in sequence prior to the current position." The orientations **first** and **last** retrieve the first or last row within the cursor sequence. The **absolute** orientation, with value_spec given by an integer from 1 to the number n of rows in the cursor, retrieves that numbered row in the cursor sequence: **absolute** 1 is equivalent to **first.** Negative numbers can also be used, from -1 down to -n, and **absolute** -1 is equivalent to **last.** The **relative** orientation means to retrieve the row an integer number of rows away from the current position. Thus **relative** -1 is the same as **prior, relative** 1 is the same as **next,** and **relative** 0 retrieves the row just retrieved a second time. Note that a scrollable cursor of this general capability is already available in the SYBASE and Microsoft SQL Server products, and it is part of the ODBC standard.

B.17 Grant Statement

The Grant statement is an SQL command issued by the owner of a table (base table or view table) to authorize various kinds of access (select, update, delete, or insert) to the table by another user or class of users. It is a form of table access security, but column access can also be implemented through views. The other user must already be able to enter the database containing the table, an authorization provided by the database administrator.

The general form of the Grant command in the SQL-89 standard (slightly more general than the X/OPEN standard) is

```
[exec sql] grant {all privileges | privilege {, privilege}}
    on tablename | viewname
    to {public | user-name {, user-name} } [with grant option]
```

The Grant command either grants *all* types of access privileges or else a comma-separated list of privileges from the following set:

```
select
delete
insert
update [columnname {, columnname . . . }]
references [columnname {, columnname . . . }]
```

The privileges named (**select, delete, . . .**) give authorization to all present and future users (in the case of **public**) or else to the list of user names specified to use the corresponding SQL statement with this tablename/viewname as an object. The references privilege (supported in **ORACLE** but not in **INGRES, DB2**, or **SYBASE**) gives a user authorization to create a foreign key constraint in another table that refers to this table. If the columnname list is not specified with the update privilege, then authorization is given to update *all* present or future columns in the table. The optional **with grant option** clause provides the user(s) receiving these privileges the additional authority to grant other users these same privileges. Note that the **grant option** clause is not included in the X/OPEN SQL standard, and in particular it is not supported by **INGRES**, although **DB2** and **ORACLE** allow it. A Grant statement can be issued in Embedded SQL.

The owner of a table automatically has all privileges, and they cannot be revoked. To grant privileges on a viewed table to other users, the granter must own the viewed table (and have necessary privileges on all tables from which the view is derived) or else must have been granted these privileges with a **with grant option** clause. To grant the insert, delete, or update privilege on a viewed table, the table must be updatable.

B.18   Insert Statement

The Insert statement is identical in Embedded and Interactive SQL, presented in Sections 3.9 and 4.3. There are two insert forms, one that inserts a single row with specified values and one that may possibly insert multiple rows, derived from a general Subselect statement as specified earlier in this section. Following an insert derived from a Subselect, the long int variable sqlca.sqlerrd[2] will contain the number of rows affected. If no rows are affected, the **not found** condition of the Whenever statement will arise.

```
[exec sql] insert into tablename [(columnname {, columnname})]
        { values (expression {, expression}) | [subselect] };
```

A newly inserted row usually cannot be placed into a table at a designated position, but only at a position determined by the disk structure of the table.

B.19 | Modify Statement in INGRES

The **INGRES** database system provides the Modify statement to create an access structure that places the rows of the table in position by index key value. The general form of the Modify command in **INGRES** is given in B.17, and the non-hash structures are discussed at length in Section 7.4. The Modify statement with hash structure target is discussed in Section 7.5.

```
[exec sql] modify tablename | indexname
    to [btree | isam | hash | heap | . . . ]
        | [merge | relocate | reorganize | truncated ]
    [unique] [on columnname {, columnname)]
    [with        /* commas separate clauses following
        [location = ...] [, newlocation = ...] [, oldlocation = ...]
        [minpages = n] [, maxpages = n]
        [fillfactor = n]
        [leaffill = n]
        [nonleaffill = n] ];
```

Figure B.17   INGRES Modify Statement Syntax

Recall that **INGRES** pictures an index as a table with rows of two columns, (keyval, tid), and a default isam-type directory. More generally, **INGRES** creates such a directory on an arbitrary table when the Modify statement is applied to the table with structure type btree or isam. Refer to Figures 7.15 and 7.16 for the directory structures btree and isam on an arbitrary table, except that after the Modify statement used above the table rows at the bottom layers are also in clustered order, as in the bottom tree of Figure 7.20. These structures are what we refer to as *clustered indexes*. (Structure type *heap* is simply a structure with no directory where new inserts are placed left to right on new pages of new extents; heap is the normal default structure for newly created tables.)

When the Modify statement is issued to create btree or isam structures, all rows of the named table are immediately sorted in order by key value and placed on data pages, and the clustering index is created with no name; it is simply the primary means of access to the rows of the table. Note too that an indexname can be given as the object of a Modify command in order to provide the index with a new structure. For example, an existing index with structure isam can be given a new btree structure. If instead of a structure name in the Modify command, one of the verbs **merge, relocate, reorganize,** or **truncated** is specified, the action specified is relative to an already existing structure type for the table. The **merge** action, for example, performs a minor reorganization of a btree directory structure (only this structure is affected), spreading the information evenly on the nodes at all levels. The **truncated** action deletes all the rows of the table, releases the disk space used, and converts the resulting empty table to the heap structure.

The **location** clause specifies how the modified table is to be constructed from disk files. The **oldlocation** and **newlocation** clauses are appropriate only when the **relocate** verb is used, which specifies how the table is to be moved to a new location on disk. The **minpages** and **maxpages** clauses are relevant only for hash structures, and we therefore defer consideration. The **fillfactor** parameter determines how full each data page is with rows during the initial reorganization to this structure, with a value n varying from 1 to 100. The **leaffill** and **nonleaffill** parameters determine how full the leaf-level nodes of a B-tree (immediately above the data-page level) and higher-level directory nodes (non-leaf nodes of a B-tree or isam structure) should be with index entries during the initial reorganization. In considering the Create Index statement, we referred to the **fillfactor** parameter as controlling how full the leaf nodes of the index should be initially, identifying data pages of an index with leaf nodes of other B-tree indexes we had been discussing, and left out consideration of the **leaffill** parameter under the assumption that the index would have an isam structure.

Hash primary indexes exist in **INGRES** and are discussed in Section 7.5. The general form of the Modify command to give a table a hash structure leaves out many of the parameters of Figure B.17, as shown in Figure B.18.

```
[exec sql] modify tablename | indexname
    to hash [unique] [on columnname {, columnname}]
    [with
        [location = . . . ]
        [minpages = n] [, maxpages = n]
        [fillfactor = n] ];
```

Figure B.18 INGRES Modify Statement to Create a Hash Index

As with isam and btree, we do not insist on unique key values unless the keyword **unique** is present. If no columnnames are specified in the Modify command, the index key defaults to the first column mentioned in the Create command for the table. The meaning of the parameters **fillfactor**, **minpages**, and **maxpages** is discussed at length in Section 7.5, in the explanation of Figure 7.24.

B.20 Open (Cursor) Statement

The statement to open a previously declared nondynamic cursor has the form:

```
exec sql open cursor_name;
```

When the Open statement is executed, the database system evaluates expressions in the **where** clause of the cursor specification for cursor_name and identifies a set of rows that become the active set for subsequent fetch operations. Any host variables used in the cursor definition are evaluated *at the time the open statement is executed*. If these values change later, this does not affect the active set of rows. For many database products the cursor cannot be opened again if it is already open. **ORACLE** allows an exception to this rule; since an already open cursor can be reopened, redefining the active set of rows.

The statement to open a dynamic cursor has the form:

```
exec sql open cursor_name
    using :host_variable {, :host_variable}
    | using descriptor :sqldavar_pointer;
```

The host variables or descriptor values are provided to substitute for dynamic parameters in the **where** clause of the previously prepared SQL Select string associated with the cursor.

B.21   Prepare Statement

A Prepare statement is used in Embedded SQL to prepare a Dynamic SQL statement contained in a sqltext[ ] string for execution. (See the Execute statement, as well as the Execute Immediate statement, which combines the effect of the two statements Prepare and Execute.) The Prepare statement has the following form:

```
exec sql prepare statement_identifier from :host_string;
```

The character string contents of the host_string must represent a valid SQL statement, including any of the following types: Alter Table, Create Table, Delete (either Searched or Positioned), Drop (Table, View, or Index), Grant, Insert, Revoke, and Update (either Searched or Positioned). Other statements may be possible in specific products.

B.22   Revoke Statement

The SQL statement to revoke privileges on a table has the following general form in X/OPEN standard SQL:

```
[exec sql] revoke {all privileges | privilege {, privilege . . .} }
    on tablename | viewname
    from {public | user-name {, user-name . . .} }
    [cascade | restrict];
```

The Revoke statement can revoke a subset of privileges earlier granted to a user. Unlike the Grant statement, the Revoke statement cannot specify specific columnnames in revoking update privileges. The owner of a table automatically has all privileges, and they cannot be revoked. The Revoke statement can be issued in Embedded SQL, and an attempt to revoke privileges that were not previously granted results in an sqlwarning condition, not an sqlerror.

Note that neither **ORACLE** nor **DB2** implements the optional [cascade | restrict] clause, and **INGRES** doesn't support the syntax of the Revoke statement at all, as explained below. The effect of the **cascade** option is to revoke privileges or drop views that depended on the privilege currently being dropped (to create a view, one must have a **select** privilege on an underlying table), while the **restrict** option retains those objects, created in the past, that are dependent in this way. If neither **cascade** nor **restrict** is specified, effects of this kind differ between different commercial database system products.

INGRES does not have the Revoke statement. In **INGRES** one can interactively list all privileges that have been granted on a table with the command:

```
help permit tablename\g
```

A numbered list of privileges (permits) on this table is printed. A privilege can be revoked by typing

```
drop permit on tablename integer [, integer];
```

where the command lists all integers that number permits retrieved through the Help Permit command.

B.23 Rollback Statement

The Rollback statement is used in an Embedded SQL program when an active transaction must be aborted—that is, terminated unsuccessfully. The Rollback statement has the following format:

```
exec sql rollback work;
```

When the Rollback statement is executed, all row updates made during the transaction are reversed and the prior version of these rows is put in place and becomes visible again to concurrent users. All rows read during the transaction become once again available to concurrent users for update. If neither a Commit nor a Rollback statement is executed for a transaction in progress before a program terminates, a product-dependent default action (Commit or Rollback) is performed.

B.24 Select Statement

The full general form of the Interactive Select statement is given in Figure B.19.

```
Subselect general form
      select [all|distinct] expression {, expression}
      from tablename [corr_name] {, tablename [corr_name]}
      [where search_condition]
      [group by column {, column}]
      [having search_condition]

Full Select general form
      Subselect
      {union [all] Subselect}
      [order by result_column [asc|desc]
           {, result_column [asc|desc]}]
```

Figure B.19 Full Interactive Select Statement Syntax

The various clauses and syntactic elements of the Interactive Select statement are described in great detail in Chapter 3, culminating in Section 3.8, where this general form is introduced. As we see in this general form, the **union** and **order by** clauses are not allowed to appear in Subselect statements.

Embedded SQL Select Statement

Recall that a Select statement can be executed in an Embedded SQL program only when no more than one row is to be retrieved (zero or one rows are permitted); otherwise a cursor must be defined. If more than one row is found by an Embedded SQL Select statement, a runtime error is returned. The syntax of this statement in Embedded SQL is given in Figure B.20.

```
exec sql select [all | distinct] expression {, expression}
    into host-variable {, host-variable}
    from tablename [corr_name] {, tablename [corr_name])
    [where search_condition]
    [group by column {column}]
    [having search_condition;]
```

Figure B.20   Embedded SQL Select Statement Syntax

Because only a single row can be retrieved by an Embedded Select statement, the interactive SQL **union** and **order by** clauses are not included in this general form. This means that the Select statement of Figure B.20 is identical to the Subselect general form of Figure B.19 (except for the **into** clause of Figure B.20, which establishes host variables as targets for the Select). The Embedded Select statement will change in the future, since it has been noted that a union of several Subselects can sometimes be known to contain only a single row (as when a product row is known to appear in exactly one of several regional tables), and so the **union** clause is permitted in the Embedded Select of SQL-92. The variables named in the **into** clause must be in one-to-one correspondence with the expressions retrieved, and they must have an appropriate type. If the Select statement results in no row being retrieved, the **not found** condition of the Whenever statement is raised.

Dynamic Select Statement

The concept of a Dynamic Select statement, which can be constructed as a character string within an Embedded SQL program at runtime, compiled, and executed in a cursor form, is covered in detail in Section 4.6. Dynamic SQL statements involved are Prepare, Describe, and special forms of Open and Fetch. The SQLDA descriptors into which retrieved values of a Select statement are retrieved vary in structure a good deal between products: see Figures 4.24 through 4.28 in Section 4.6 for illustrations of **INGRES** and **ORACLE** formats. An attempt is being made with SQL standards to solve this problem, starting with the X/OPEN standard, in which a number of standard descriptor-manipulation statements are added to SQL: Allocate Descriptor, Deallocate Descriptor, Get Descriptor, and Set Descriptor. We do not cover these concepts in the current text since they have not yet been implemented in most commercial products.

B.25 | Update Statement

As with the Delete statement, there are two versions of the Update statement: a *Searched Update*, a multi-row Update statement that can be executed either interactively or in Embedded SQL, and a *Positioned Update*, which acts through a cursor and can be executed in Embedded SQL only. The format of the Searched Update statement is illustrated in Figure B.21.

```
[exec sql] update tablename [corr_name]
    set columnname = expression {, columnname = expression}
    [where search_condition];
```

Figure B.21 Searched Update Statement Syntax

Following a Searched Update, the long int variable sqlca.sqlerrd[2] contains the number of rows affected. If no rows are affected, the **not found** condition of the Whenever statement arises. The Positioned Update statement has the following form, as shown in Figure B.22.

```
exec sql update tablename
    set columnname = expression {, columnname = expression}
    where current of cursor_name;
```

Figure B.22 Embedded SQL Positioned Update Syntax

For the Positioned Update statement to work properly the cursor must be open, the tables named in the **from** clause of the Update and in the Declare Cursor statement must be identical, and the cursor must be pointing to a valid row (rather than to a position just before or after some row). In addition, the cursor must be declared **for update** on all the columns changed by the Update statement. If any of these conditions are not valid, a runtime error will be returned from the Positioned Update statement execution.

Set Query Counts

The following list shows the number of rows selected (with different values in a few cases) for each of the queries Q1 through Q6B of the Set Query benchmark. This list is an aid to the practitioner attempting to run the benchmark. If the data has been properly generated and loaded on any platform, these numbers should be duplicated.

Query	Case	Row Count
Q1	KSEQ	1
--	K100K	8
--	K10K	98
--	K1K	1003
--	K100	10,091
--	K25	39,845
--	K10	99,902
--	K5	200,637
--	K4	249,431
--	K2	499,424

Query	Case	Row Count	Sum
Q2A	KSEQ	1	
--	K100K	5	
--	K10K	58	
--	K1K	487	
--	K100	5009	
--	K25	19,876	
--	K10	49,939	
--	K5	100,081	
--	K4	125,262	
Q2B	KSEQ	499,423	
--	K100K	499,419	
--	K10K	499,366	
--	K1K	498,937	
--	K100	494,415	
--	K25	479,548	
--	K10	449,485	
--	K5	399,343	
--	K4	374,162	
Q3A	K100K	1	434
--	K10K	9	5513
--	K100	991	496,684
--	K25	3989	1,978,118
--	K10	9920	4,950,698
--	K5	20,116	10,027,345
--	K4	24,998	12,499,521
Q3B	K100K	1	434
--	K10K	6	3300
--	K100	597	299,039
--	K25	2423	1,209,973
--	K10	5959	2,967,225
--	K5	12,000	5,980,617
--	K4	15,031	7,496,733

Query	Case	Row Count	
Q4A	1–3	10,059	**815**
--	2–4	4027	
--	3–5	1637	
--	4–6	4021	
--	5–7	7924	
--	6–8	10,294	
--	7–9	4006	
--	8–10	785	
Q4B	1–5	161	
--	2–6	86	
--	3–7	142	
--	4–8	172	
--	5–9	77	
--	6–10	76	
--	7–1	152	
Q5	K2=K100=1	4962	
--	K4=K25=1	9970	
--	K10=K25=1	4049	
Q6A	K100K	23	
--	K40K	55	
--	K10K	239	
--	K1K	2014	
--	K100	19,948	
Q6B	K40K	3	
--	K10K	4	
--	K1K	81	
--	K100	804	

Solutions to Selected Exercises

Chapter 2 Solutions

[2.1] (a) A and B are both keys, since they are singleton attributes having unique values in each row. No other key can contain either A or B. Neither C nor D distinguishes all rows singly, but as a pair they do. Therefore the three candidate keys for T1 are A, B, and CD.

(c)

A	B	C	D
a1	b1	c1	d1
a2	b1	c1	d1
a1	b2	c1	d1
a1	b1	c2	d1

Clearly D is not a part of any key, and ABC is a superkey. None of the single columns, A, B, or C, can be a key, since in each column we have three equal entries. No pair of columns AB, BC, or CA can be a key because of duplicate entries. Therefore ABC is the only key.

[2.2] (a) The three candidate keys are `ssn`, `name information-no`, and `name address city zip`.

[2.4] (a) `(ORDERS where qty >= 1000)[ordno,pid]`.

The parentheses are necessary because of the high precedence standing of projection.

(c) `(ORDERS where dollars < 500 JOIN CUSTOMERS) [ordno,cname].`

There is only one attribute in common between ORDERS and CUSTOMERS, so the join matches that one column and extends the ORDERS table to include customer information, of which we project down to just the ordno and cname. Equally well, we could project out the unnecessary ORDERS columns before joining:

```
((ORDERS where dollars < 500)[ordno,cid] JOIN CUSTOMERS)
    [ordno,cname]
```

(e) `((ORDERS where month = 'mar' JOIN CUSTOMERS)[ordno,cname,aid]`
`    JOIN AGENTS)[ordno,cname,aname]`

NOTE: Unlike the previous two exercises, here the first projection is necessary to prevent unwanted matching in the join based on the city attribute: because it appears in (ORDERS where month = 'mar' JOIN CUSTOMERS), and also in AGENTS, only rows with the matching customer city and agent city would appear in the result unless we do the first projection to throw out the city.

(g) `(PRODUCTS where city = Duluth JOIN ORDERS`
`    where month = 'jan')[pname].`

Again, additional projections before the join are harmless unless they remove the pid.

[2.5] **(a)** `(((CUSTOMERS TIMES AGENTS) TIMES PRODUCTS)`
`    where CUSTOMERS.city = AGENTS.city`
`    and AGENTS.city = PRODUCTS.city)[cid,aid,pid]`

Because Cartesian product is associative, the following solution that specifies the product of three tables without saying which product goes first is preferable:

```
((CUSTOMERS TIMES AGENTS TIMES PRODUCTS)
    where CUSTOMERS.city = AGENTS.city
    and AGENTS.city = PRODUCTS.city)[cid,aid,pid]
```

(c) `((CUSTOMERS TIMES AGENTS TIMES PRODUCTS)`
`    where CUSTOMERS.city <> AGENTS.city`
`    and AGENTS.city <> PRODUCTS.city`
`    and PRODUCTS.city <> CUSTOMERS.city)[cid,aid,pid]`

Do you see why you need the third condition? $x <> y$ and $y <> z$ does not imply $x <> z$. For example, $x = c$, $y = k$, $z = c$.

(e) `((ORDERS JOIN (CUSTOMERS where city = 'Dallas')[cid] JOIN`
`    (AGENTS where city = 'Tokyo')[aid] JOIN PRODUCTS)[pname]`

Projection of the CUSTOMERS and AGENTS tables is needed at some point to remove the city columns so they will not be counted in the join. Also we are taking the JOIN of four tables without specifying order with parentheses because JOIN, like Cartesian product, is associative.

(g)
```
A1 := AGENTS, A2 := AGENTS
((A1 X A2) where A1.city = A2.city and A1.cid< A2.cid)
    [A1.aid, A2.aid]
```

This is like the example in the text where we want to list only distinct pairs of agents, exactly once.

(i) This is very hard if you've never seen the trick before. Let
```
C1 := CUSTOMERS, C2 := CUSTOMERS
X(cid1,cid) := ((C1 TIMES C2) where C1.discnt >= C2.discnt)
    [C1.cid, C2.cid].
```

Now the answer is exactly those `cid1` values on the left that are paired with *all* `cid` values on the right—that is, with `discnt >=` *all* `discnts`—so the answer is
```
X DIVIDEBY C2[cid].
```

To find customers who have the smallest discount, change ">=" to "<=" in the above.

(k)
```
(ORDERS where ORDERS.aid = 'a03')[pid]
    -(ORDERS where ORDERS.aid = 'a06')[pid]
```

(m) We can start by finding all the agents T who do not place orders for any product in Newark:
```
T := all agents - agents who order products in Newark
= AGENTS[aid] - (O JOIN PRODUCTS where city = Newark)[aid]
```

Now `(T JOIN AGENTS)[aid,aname]` adds on the `aname` information, and we can finally select on those `aname`s:
```
(T JOIN AGENTS) [aid,aname] where aname >= 'N' and aname <'O'
```

The final result is obtained by substitution.

(o) Let P1 = all products ordered by customer C002, that is `P1 :=` `(ORDERS where cid = c002)`. Then we need the agents who place orders for all of P1. Their `aid`s are
```
ORDERS[aid,pid] DIVIDEBY P1
```

so the answer by substitution is
```
((ORDERS[aid,pid] DIVIDEBY (ORDERS where cid = c002))
    JOIN AGENTS)[aname]
```

Here the double use of "ORDERS" looks suspicious, but in fact causes no problem: an alias is required only in cases where the two tables' column names are used at the same point in the computation.

(q) CUSTOMERS TIMES AGENTS TIMES PRODUCTS - CUSTOMERS JOIN AGENTS
JOIN PRODUCTS

(s) ((ORDERS where dollars > 500)[aid,cid] JOIN CUSTOMERS
where city = Kyoto)[aid]

[2.6] **(b)** In Definition 2.7.9, if there are no columns in common, then
the columns B1 through Bk in the two tables do not exist (k =
0). Thus in the definition of when a row t is in the table R
JOIN S, we should ignore references to columns Bi. Then the
remainder of the definition reduces to Definition 2.6.7, for the
product R TIMES S, with appropriate column-name substitution. Another argument you could give is that in Theorem
2.8.2, which expresses JOIN in terms of other operators, if we
remove references to columns Bi, then the first part of the definition reduces to T := R TIMES S. The second part defining T_2
simply renames columns to remove qualifiers.

[2.7] By Exercise 2.6, R JOIN S is identical to R TIMES S when R and S
have no attributes (columns) in common. Let r be a row in R. It is
enough to point out that the row r is paired with *all* rows of S on
some row of R TIMES S. This being the case, if we divide by S, we
get back the row r. This shows that every row of R is in (R JOIN S)
DIVIDEBY S. But if another row u were to show up in (R JOIN S)
DIVIDEBY S, this would mean that u must be paired with all rows
of S in (R JOIN S)—that is, in (R TIMES S). But by the definition of
TIMES, such a row u must be in R because only such rows are
paired with rows of S and placed in R TIMES S. A fully rigorous
proof would codify the loose meaning of phrases such as "the row r
is paired with ALL rows of S," by using the form of Definition
2.6.7: "for every pair of rows u and v in R and S respectively, there
is a row t in R TIMES S such that t(R.Ai) = u(Ai) and . . ."

[2.8] **(a)** Let N_A be the constant table with one row all nulls and heading consisting of the attributes that are in A but not in B, and
similarly let N_B be the table with nulls for attributes of B that
are not in A. Then

$$A \bowtie_0 B = A \bowtie B \cup N_A \times (B - (A \bowtie B)[Head(B)]) \cup (A - (A \bowtie B)[Head(A)]) \times N_B$$

[2.9] **(a)** With three tables R, S, and T, there are various ways that
attributes can be in common between tables: they can be common between R and S, or S and T, or T and S, and some of
these could be in common to all three. R JOIN S selects for
rows that agree on the attributes in common to R and S. Then
(R JOIN S) JOIN T selects among those for rows that also

agree on attributes in common between those of T and R JOIN S—that is, between T and R and also between T and S. Clearly the result requires agreement on any of the three sets of attributes in R – S, S – T, and T – S. Similarly R JOIN (S JOIN T) can be shown to require that same agreement. In all cases, the rows are selected from R × S × T, projected to squeeze out duplicated or triplicated columns.

[2.11] The table "S where C" contains all rows of S that obey condition C. Thus

r is in (S where C) iff r is in S and C is true for r.

r is in ((R where C1) where C2) iff r is in (R where C1) and C2 is true for r.

(R where C1) is the set of rows in R for which C1 is true.

Thus r is ((R where C1) where C2) iff r is in R and C1 and C2 are true.

Similarly the other expressions can be reduced to the same elementary form.

[2.13] By a previous exercise, the join of compatible tables is just the intersection of the tables. Consider any x in R INTERSECT T. Since R is a subset of S, R INTERSECT T is a subset of S INTERSECT T.

Consider any x in U DIVIDEBY S. This means that (x,s) is in U for all s in S. But then (x,s) is in U for all s in R, since R is a subset of S. Thus x is in U DIVIDEBY R.

Consider any x in R DIVIDEBY V. This means that (x,v) is in R for all v in V. But then (x,v) is in S for all v in V, since R is a subset of S. Thus x is in S DIVIDEBY V.

Consider any x in (R where C). Then x is in R and C is true for x. Then x is in S and C is true for it. Thus x is in (S where C).

[2.15] (b) For any x in (R ∪ S)[H], there is some (x,x') in R ∪ S, so (x,x') is in R or in S. When these are individually projected, x is seen to be in R[H] or in S[H], and thus in their union. Similarly, any x in R[H]∪ S[H] is in R[H] or in S[H], and thus there is some (x,x') in R or in S—that is, in R ∪ S—with projection x. Thus x is in (R ∪ S)[H].

Chapter 3 Solutions

[3.1] (a) ```
select c.cid, a.aid, p.pid
    from customers c, agents a, products p
    where c.city = a.city and a.city = p.city;
```

(c) ```
select c.cid, a.aid, p.pid
    from customers c, agents a, products p
    where c.city != a.city and a.city != p.city
    and c.city != p.city;
```

Note that even if two of these conditions are true, the third one may fail, so an **and** of all three conditions is called for.

(e)
```
select pname from products where pid in
   (select pid from orders where
   cid in (select cid from customers where city = 'Dallas') and
   aid in (select aid from agents where city = 'Tokyo'));
```

This demonstrates that we can use two "in" conditions in the same **where** clause. Alternatively, we can do this all with a join.

```
select distinct pname
   from products p, orders o, customers c,agents a
   where p.pid = o.pid and o.cid = c.cid and c.city = 'Dallas'
   and o.aid = a.aid and a.city = 'Tokyo';
```

(g)
```
select al.aid, a2.aid from agents al, agents a2
   where al.city = a2.city and al.aid < a2.aid;
```

(i)
```
select cid from customers
   where discnt >=all
   (select discnt from customers);
```
```
select cid from customers
   where discnt <=all
   (select discnt from customers);
```

(k)
```
select distinct pid from orders where aid = 'a03'
   and pid not in (select pid from orders where aid = 'a06');
```

(m) The following would appear to suffice:
```
select distinct a.aid, a.aname from agents a, orders o
   where aname like 'S%' and a.aid = o.aid
   and o.pid not in (select pid from products
     where city = 'Newark');
```

But in fact this only lists agents who placed orders. The complete solution is

```
select a.aid, a.aname from agents a where a.aname like 'S%'
   and a.aid not in
     (select o.aid from orders o where o.pid in
     (select pid from products where city = 'Newark'));
```

(o)
```
select aname from agents a where not exists
   (select * from orders x where x.cid = 'c002' and not exists
   (select * from orders y where y.aid = a.aid
     and x.pid = y.pid));
```

(q)
```
select cid, aid, pid from customers c, agents a, products p
   where c.city != a.city or c.city != p.city
   or a.city != p.city;
```

(s)
```
select aid from customers c, orders o
   where c.cid = o.cid
   and o.dollars > 500 and c.city = 'Kyoto';
```

Solutions to Selected Exercises

[3.2] (a)
```
select aid from agents where percent >any
    (select percent from agents);
```

(c) The quoted query returns the same result as (a) only as long as the minimum commission is 5, which may not continue to be true in the future.

This is what we mean when we say that Figure 2.2 represents "the content as of a given moment," and illustrates what was meant in Example 2.7.6 by a content dependency: the fact that two queries have the same result for a table of a given content is not sufficient to guarantee that the two queries are equivalent.

[3.3] (a) We know that 'x in y' is the same as 'x =any y', where y is a set of values returned by Subselect and x is a simple value. Now 'x not in y' is the same as 'not (x in y)', but 'not (x =any y)' is *not* the same as 'x <>any y'. This is because 'x <>any y' is true if there exists a value in y that doesn't equal x, but 'not (x =any y)' is true only if x is not equal to any value of y; this condition is stated by the SQL predicate 'x <>all y'. Thus **not in** is the same as **<>all**, but not the same as **<>any**.

(c) The query to retrieve exactly those rows not retrieved by the query of Example 3.4.7:
```
select aid from agents where percent >any
    (select percent from agents);
```

[3.4] (a)
```
select distinct cid from orders, agents
    where orders.aid = agents.aid
    and (agents.city = 'Duluth' or agents.city = 'Dallas');
```

(c)
```
select A1,...,An from S, T where S.A2 = k and
    S.A1 = T.B1 and T.B2 = c and T.B3 = S.A3;
```

[3.6] (a)
```
INITIALIZE LIST L to EMPTY
FOR T FROM ROW 1 TO LAST OF TABLE T (No alias)
    IF (T.B1 = c)
        Place B1 on LIST L;
END FOR T;
FOR S FROM ROW 1 TO ROW LAST OF TABLE S
    IF(A2 = k and A1 an element of LIST L)
        Place (A1,...,An) on SOLUTION LIST M
END FOR
PRINT OUT UNIQUE ROWS ON SOLUTION LIST M
```

[3.7] (a)
```
select * from R union select * from S;
```

(c) Consider a row w in (R UNION S) MINUS T. It is in R or S but not in T. Suppose it is in R. Then it is in R but not in T. Likewise, if it is in S, then it is in S but not in T. Thus it is in R −T or in S – T; that is, it is in (R – T) UNION (S – T), and this expression can be written in SQL using the results of 3.7(a):

```
(select * from R where not exists (select * from T
    where R.A₁ = T.A₁,R.A₂ = T.A₂, ... ,R.Aₙ = T.Aₙ))
UNION
(select * from S where not exists (select * from T
    where S.A₁ = T.A₁,S.A₂ = T.A₂,....,S.Aₙ = T.Aₙ))
```

(e) By Theorem 2.8.3,

```
R DIVIDEBY S = R[A₁,...,Aₙ] - ((R[A₁,...,Aₙ] TIMES S)
  - R)[A₁,...,Aₙ]
```

Here **R** is `"select cid,aid from orders"` and S is `"select aid from agents where city = 'New York'."` $HEAD(R) = A_1 \ldots A_n B_1 \ldots B_m =$ `cid aid` and $S = B_1 \ldots B_m =$ `aid`, so we see that $n = 1$, $A_1 =$ `cid`, $m = 1$, $B_1 =$ `aid`, and `R[cid] TIMES S` is **V** defined as follows:

```
V = select o.cid,a.aid from orders o, agents a
    where city = 'New York'
```

We need as a final result `R[cid] - (V-R)[cid]`. By MINUS of part (d),

```
(V-R) = select o.cid, a.aid from orders o, agents a
    where city = 'New York' and not exists
    (select * from orders x
        where x.aid = a.aid  and x.cid = o.cid)
```

`(V-R)[cid]` is the same, with `a.aid` dropped from the selection list. Finally the answer is, using MINUS once more from part (d):

```
select cid from orders y where not exists
    (select o.cid from orders o, agents a
        where city = 'New York'
            and not exists
            (select * from orders x
                where x.cid = o.cid and x.aid = a.aid)
                and y.cid = o.cid);
```

In fact this returns the result duplicated several times, so `select distinct` is called for.

[3.8] **(a)** `select aid, pid, sum(qty) from orders group by aid, pid;`

(c) `select a.aid from agents a where not exists`
`    (select o.* from orders o, customers c, products p`
`        where o.aid=a.aid and o.cid=c.cid and o.pid=p.pid`
`        and c.city='Duluth' and p.city ='Dallas');`

(e) select distinct cid from orders o
        where aid in ('a03', 'a05') and not exists
        (select * from orders x where
            o.cid = x.cid and x.aid not in ('a03', 'a05'));

(g) select aid from agents
        where percent = (select max(percent) from agents);

(i) update agents set percent = 11 where aname = 'Gray';
    select * from agents;
    update agents set percent = 6 where aname = 'Gray';
    select * from agents;

(k) select cid, sum(dollars) from orders where aid = 'a04'
        and cid not in (select cid from orders
        where aid != 'a04') group by cid;

(m) select o.pid from orders o, customers c, agents a
        where o.cid = c.cid and o.aid = a.aid and c.city = a.city;

[3.9] (a) select discnt from customers where city = 'Duluth';

Output (**ORACLE**):
```
+------+
|discnt|
+------+
|    10|
|     8|
+------+
(2 rows)
```

select percent from agents where city like 'N%';

Output:
```
+------+
|percen|
+------+
|     6|
|     6|
|     6|
+------+
(3 rows)
```

select city from customers where discnt >=all
    (select discnt from customers where city = 'Duluth');

Output:
```
+-------+
|city   |
+-------+
|Duluth |
|Dallas |
+-------+
(2 rows)
```

```
select city from agents where percent >any
    (select percent from agents where city like 'N%');
Output:
+--------+
|city    |
+--------+
|Tokyo   |
+--------+
(1 row)

select city from customers where discnt >=all
    (select discnt from customers where city = 'Duluth')
    union
    select city from agents where percent >any
        (select percent from agents where city like 'N%');
Output:
+--------+
|city    |
+--------+
|Dallas  |
|Duluth  |
|Tokyo   |
+--------+
(3 rows)
```

[3.10] **(a)** By definition, a superkey is any set of columns whose values uniquely identify each row: no two rows have identical values in these columns. Thus, if we select columns that include the superkey from a table, our result has no two rows that are identical.

(c) It is false. The query given by

```
select count(*) from table group by <key>;
```

where <key> is a comma-separated list of columns containing any superkey of the table, invariably produces a table of the same length as the original table, with a single column of ones, all identical.

[3.11] **(a)** `select * from customers where cname >= 'A' and cname < 'B';`

[3.12] **(a)** In an outer join, a row should appear for an agent who takes no orders, and a row should appear for an order by an `aid` that has no corresponding `aname` in the `agents` table:

```
select a.aname, a.aid, sum(x.dollars) from agents a, orders x
    where a.aid = x.aid group by a.aid, a.aname
union
select aname, aid, 0 from agents
    where aid not in (select aid from orders)
union
```

```
select 'null', aid, sum(x.dollars) from orders x
    where aid not in (select aid from agents) group by aid;
```

[3.13] (a) Answer: They form a distinct group.

```
Output:
+------+
|percen|
+------+
|     5|
|     6|
|     7|
|      |
+------+

(4 rows)
```

(c) (i) "Get names of agents whose commission is at least as large as all Geneva-based agent's commissions." Comparisons with null return UNKNOWN, so this returns 0 rows.

```
Output:
+-------+
|aname  |
+-------+
+-------+

(0 rows)
```

In the case that there are no agents at all in Geneva, the answer would list all agents (see Exercise 3.14). Thus the existence of a null value can greatly change results.

[3.14] (a) This query returns all customer IDs.

Chapter 4 Solutions

NOTE: Most of the programs use prompt.c and its header file, prompt.h. Each should be built by "cc prog.c prompt.c" where prog.c is the C program produced by the Embedded SQL preprocessor from the Embedded SQL program, and prompt.c contains functions prompt1 and prompt2 of Figures 4.2 and 4.3. Here is prompt.h:

```
/* prompt.h: include file for functions prompt1 and prompt2  */
/* prompt1: prints prompt, reads user input into tk1, of max length
    max1. Returns 0 on success, -1 on failure. */
int prompt1(char *prompt, char *tk1, int max1);
/* prints prompt, reads tokens into tk1 and tk2, of max length max1 and
    max2, respectively. Returns 0 on success, -1 on failure. */
int prompt2(char prompt[], char x[], char y[]);
/* maximum length of input lines */
#define LINELEN 255
```

[4.2] /* 4.2, **INGRES** version: program to report on product quantities by agent for spec. cid and pid */

```
#define TRUE 1
#include <stdio.h>
#include <string.h>
#include "prompt.h"
exec sql include sqlca;

main()
{
    char prompt[] = "PLEASE ENTER CUSTOMER ID AND PRODUCT ID: ";

    exec sql begin declare section;
        char cust_id[5], product_id[4], agent_id[4];
        int total_qty;
    exec sql end declare section;

    exec sql whenever sqlerror stop; /* error trap condition */
    exec sql declare agent_qty cursor for /* declare cursor */
        select aid, sum(qty) from orders
            where cid = :cust_id and pid = :product_id
                group by aid;

    exec sql connect poneilsql; /* INGRES format: connect to
        database */
    exec sql whenever not found goto fetchdone; /* set up for loop
        termination  */
    while ((prompt2(prompt, cust_id, 4, product_id, 3)) >= 0) {
        exec sql open agent_qty; /* first set cid, then open cursor*/
        while (TRUE) { /* loop forever to fetch rows */
            exec sql fetch agent_qty into :agent_id, :total_qty;
            printf("%s %d\n", agent_id, total_qty); /* display row */
        }
    fetchdone:
        exec sql close agent_qty;/* close cursor when done with
            fetches  */

        exec sql commit work; /* release read locks on rows accessed*/
    }   /* end of prompt loop: repeat */
    exec sql disconnect; /* disconnect from database */
}

/* 4.2, ORACLE version: program to report on product quantities by
agent for spec. cid and pid */
#define TRUE 1
#include <stdio.h>
#include <string.h>
#include "prompt.h"
exec sql include sqlca;
main()
{
    exec sql begin declare section;
```

```
        VARCHAR username[20],password[20];
        VARCHAR cust_id[5], product_id[4], agent_id[4];
        long total_qty; /* summing shorts, sum may need long */
    exec sql end declare section;
    char prompt[] = "PLEASE ENTER CUSTOMER ID AND PRODUCT ID: ";

    exec sql whenever sqlerror stop; /* error trap condition */
    exec sql declare agent_qty cursor for /* declare cursor */
        select aid, sum(qty) from orders
            where cid = :cust_id and pid = :product_id
            group by aid;

    strcpy(username.arr, "scott") ;/* set up username and password */
    username.len = strlen(username.arr); /* as varchar strings */
    strcpy(password.arr, "tiger"); /* for Oracle login */
    password.len = strlen(password.arr);
    exec sql connect :username identified by :password;

    while (prompt2(prompt, cust_id.arr, 4, product_id.arr, 3) >= 0) {
        cust_id.len = strlen(cust_id.arr); /* turn C string into
            VARCHAR */
        product_id.len = strlen(product_id.arr); /* for cursor*/
        exec sql open agent_qty; /* open cursor */
        exec sql whenever not found goto fetchdone;
        while (TRUE) { /* loop forever to fetch rows */
            exec sql fetch agent_qty into :agent_id, :total_qty;
            /* turn into C string for printf-- */
            agent_id.arr[agent_id.len] = '\0';
            printf("%6s %d\n", agent_id.arr, total_qty); /* display
                row */

        }

    fetchdone:
        exec sql close agent_qty;  /* close cursor when done with
            fetches */
        exec sql commit work; /* release read locks on rows
            accessed */
    }   /* end of prompt loop: repeat */
    exec sql disconnect; /* disconnect from database */

}
```

(d) If a commit is done after the reads, those quantities may change before the updates are made, and cause just the problems the checks were supposed to prevent—for example, keeping inventory amounts non-negative. No, there are no valid places here for additional commits.

[4.10]
```
/* 4.10. Ingres version: Histogram of dollar amounts of orders */
#define TRUE 1
#define RANGE 500.0
#include <stdio.h>
```

```
                  exec sql include sqlca;
                  main()
                  {
                      exec sql begin declare section;
                          float dollars;
                      exec sql end declare section;
                      float range_start = 0;
                      float range_end = range_start + RANGE;
                      double range_sum = 0.0;
                      exec sql declare dollars_cursor cursor for
                          select dollars from orders
                              order by dollars;
                      exec sql whenever sqlerror stop;
                      exec sql connect poneilsql;
                          exec sql open dollars_cursor;
                          exec sql whenever not found goto fetchdone;
                          printf("%-17s %-8s\n"," range","total orders");
                          while (TRUE) { /* loop over orders table */
                              exec sql fetch dollars_cursor into :dollars;
                              if (dollars <= range_end) {
                              range_sum += dollars; /* point in same old range */
                              } else { /* point beyond end of this range */
                              while( dollars > range_end) { /* --and possibly several
                                  ranges */
                                  printf("%8.2f-%8.2f %8.2f\n",range_start,range_end,
                                  range_sum);
                                  range_sum = 0;
                                  range_start = range_end; /* step range */
                                  range_end += RANGE;
                              }
                              range_sum += dollars; /* found new range that fits
                                  point */
                              }
                          }    /* end while loop on aid values */
                  fetchdone:
                      if (range_sum)
                          printf("%8.2f-%8.2f %8.2f\n",range_start,range_end,
                              range_sum);
                      exec sql close dollars_cursor;
                      exec sql commit work; /* release locks */
                      exec sql disconnect;
                  }

                  /* 4.10, ORACLE version: Histogram of dollar amounts of orders */
                  #define TRUE 1
                  #define RANGE 500.0
                  #include <stdio.h>
                  exec sql include sqlca;
                  exec sql begin declare section;
```

```
    VARCHAR username[20], password[20];                              831
exec sql end declare section;
main()
{
    exec sql begin declare section;
        float dollars;
    exec sql end declare section;
    float range_start = 0;
    float range_end = range_start + RANGE;
    double range_sum = 0.0;
    exec sql declare dollars_cursor cursor for
        select dollars from orders
            order by dollars;
    exec sql whenever sqlerror stop;
    strcpy(username.arr, "scott"); /* set up username and password */
    username.len = strlen(username.arr); /* as varchar strings */
    strcpy(password.arr, "tiger"); /* for Oracle login* /
    password.len = strlen(password.arr);
    exec sql connect :username identified by :password;
    exec sql open dollars_cursor;
    exec sql whenever not found goto fetchdone;
    printf("%-17s %-8s\n"," range","total orders");
    while (TRUE)    { /* loop over orders table */
        exec sql fetch dollars_cursor into :dollars;
        if (dollars <= range_end) {
            range_sum += dollars; /* point in same old range */
        } else { /* point beyond end of this range */
            while( dollars > range_end) { /* --and possibly several
                ranges */
                printf("%8.2f-%8.2f %8.2f\n",range_start,range_end,
                range_sum);
                range_sum = 0;
                range_start = range_end; /* step range */
                range_end += RANGE;
                }
                range_sum += dollars; /* found new range that fits point */
            }
        }    /* end while loop on aid values*/
fetchdone:
    if (range_sum)
        printf("%8.2f-%8.2f %8.2f\n",range_start,range_end,
            range_sum);
    exec sql close dollars_cursor;
    exec sql commit work; /* release locks */
    exec sql disconnect;
}
```

[4.12] (a)
```
exec sql begin declare section;
      char city[21];
exec sql end declare sections;
```

(b)
```
exec sql declare cc cursor for
    select distinct a.city from agents a, orders x, products p
        where a.aid = x.aid and x.pid = p.pid and p.price < 1.00;
```

An alternative form with Subselect is of course possible. It is a common error to fail to list products at all, using the condition x.dollars < 1.00, but of course this doesn't answer the question posed.

(c)
```
while (1){   /* or while TRUE, assume TRUE = 1 */
    exec sql whenever not found goto fetchdone;
    exec sql fetch cc into :city;
    printf ("%s", city);
}
fetchdone:  ...
```

[4.13] (a)
```
if(sqlca.sqlcode == 100) goto error_handle;
```

(b)
```
if(sqlca.sqlcode < 0) goto error_handle;
```

[4.14] (a)
```
select c.city, cid, aid, pid from customers c, agents a,
    products p
        where c.city = a.city and a.city = p.city order by c.city;
```

It is a common mistake to write "group by c.city," but of course that isn't legal since the other elements of the target list are not single-valued for individual values of c.city. Ordering by c.city assures that rows occur one after another when they are from the same city.

(b) $30 \times 10 \times 20 = 6000$

(c) The idea here is to avoid printing out 6000 lines for New York. We want to print out "New York" and then three simple lists (without repetition) of cid values, then aid values, then pid values for customers, agents, and products that have city = New York. We want to do this for all cities, one after another. We don't have to write perfect C (pseudo-code is OK), but we have to show how to use Embedded SQL to accomplish this. Start by showing the cursors we need, where in pseudo-code we leave out the "exec sql."

```
declare cities cursor for select distinct c.city
    from customers c, agents a, products p
    where c.city = a.city and a.city = p.city;
declare cids cursor for select cid from customers
    where city = :city;
```

```
declare aids cursor for select aid from agents
    where city = :city;
declare pids cursor for select pid from products
    where city = :city;
open cities;
while ( rows remain in cities); { /* loop to fetch citynames */
    fetch cities into :city; /* city value to open other
        cursors */
    print cityname header;
    open cids;
        loop to print out cid values of cursor cids;
    open aids;
        loop to print out aid values of cursor aids;
    open pids;
        loop to print out pid values of cursor pids;
}   /* loop while cities remain*/
```

It is a common mistake to use a single cursor, something like

```
declare ccs cursor for select c.city, cid, aid, pid
    from customers c, agents a, products p
    where c.city = a.city and p.city = a.city order by c.city;
```

and then use logic of the following kind:

```
open ccs;
fetch first row of ccs into :city, :cid, :aid, :pid;
remember city name as oldcity;
print city name header;
start printing columns of cid, aid, pid values
while (rows from ccs remain) {
    if latest city does not match oldcity{ /* start new
        oldcity */
        remember new city name as oldcity;
        print new city name header;
        start printing columns of cid, aid, pid values;
    }
    else{   /* same oldcity name */
        print out new values of cid, aid, pid in columns;
    }
}   /* next row of ccs */
```

But this doesn't do what we want, to restrict the amount of information (number of rows), because there are still 6000 rows to print out. (The problem is that the list of cid values for New York, for example, has a *lot* of duplicates.)

[4.15] (a)
```
exec sql declare topsales cursor for
    select pid, sum(dollars) from orders
    group by pid
    order by 2 desc;
```

(**b**)
```
count = 0; /* count 10 rows to print out */
while (1){
    fetch topsales into :pid, :doltot: dolind;
    if(sqlca.sqlcode == 100) break; /* if run out of rows,
    exit loop */
    if(dolind != -1){ /* not a null value, so count it */
        if(++count >= 10) break; /* have already printed 10
        rows */
        printf("pid value is %s, total dollar sales is %s ",
        pid, doltot);
    }   /* end if */
}   /* end loop */
```

[4.16] We don't really need to test for deadlock after the *first* access, since there can't be one (although there's no harm in doing so). The important thing is to drop *all* locks if we run into one, and it is a common error to simply loop back and try to make the *second* access again, without doing a rollback.

```
        exec sql whenever sqlerror continue; /* other action will
            interfere */
        count = 0;
begintx:
        exec sql update orders
            set dollars = dollars - :delta
            where aid = :agent1 and pid = :prod1 and cid = :cust1;
        if (sqlca.sqlcode < 0) goto handle_err; /* can't be deadlock
            yet */
        exec sql update orders
            set dollars = dollars + :delta
            where aid = :agent1 and pid = :prod1 and cid = :cust1;
        if (sqlca.sqlcode == -4700){
            if(count++ < 2) {
                exec sql rollback; /* need to drop locks held */
                goto begintx;
            }
            else{
                exec sql rollback;
                goto skip;/* give up entirely */
            }
        if (sqlca.sqlcode < 0) goto handle_err; /* other error? */
        exec sql commit work; /* if not, commit */
skip :/* and out of loop */
```

[4.17] (**a**) `if(sqlda -> sqld >= 2) goto ge2;`

(**b**) `if(*(sqlda -> sqlvar[1].sqlind) == -1) goto null_back;`

Note that the condition to detect a null is to test if the indicator is equal to −1.

(**c**) `if(sqlda -> sqld == 0) goto not_select;`

Chapter 5 Solutions

[5.1] Of the four possibilities, min-card = 0 or 1, max-card = 1 or N, only two of these are actually constraints: min-card = 1 (we are not allowed to have 0) and max-card = 1 (we are not allowed to have more than 1). If an example breaks such a constraint, then we know that the constraint does not hold universally. Thus, in Figure 5.6(a), we can be sure that min-card(E,R) = 0, since this is the case here, and that min-card(F,R) = 0, but we can't be sure about the max-card in either case. In (b), we can be sure that min-card(E,R) = 0 and max-card(E,R) = N, but we can't be sure about card(F,R), because no real constraint is broken. In (c), we see that min-card(E,R) = 0, max-card(E,R) = N, min-card(F,R) = 0, and max-card(F,R) = N; that is, that no real constraints hold, since all possible constraints are broken by the example.

[5.2] See Figure 6.2 for an acceptable E-R diagram. Note that the labeled cardinalities of the attributes are all somewhat arbitrary in the min-card value, except for the primary keys that must be labeled (1,1). We try to place the entity E that relates to F by a verb rel to the left or above the entity F; thus `Orders ships Products` and `Orders` is to the left, `Agents places Orders` and `Agents` is above.

[5.4] (a) Legal.

(c) Violates (3).

[5.5] Let us start by considering FDs with a single attribute on the left. In addition to the identity functional dependencies, we have the following. (a) All values of the A column are the same, so it can never happen for any other column X that $r1(X) = r2(X)$ while $r1(A) \neq r2(A)$. Thus we see that B –> A, C –> A, and D –> A. At the same time, no other column X is functionally dependent on A since they all have at least two distinct values, and so there are always two rows r1 and r2 such that $r1(X) \neq r2(X)$ while $r1(A) = r2(A)$. Thus A $\nrightarrow$ B, A $\nrightarrow$ C, and A $\nrightarrow$ D. (b) Because the C values are all different, in addition to C –> A, above, we also have C –> B and C –> D. At the same time, C is not functionally dependent on anything else since all other columns have at least two duplicate values: B $\nrightarrow$ C, and D $\nrightarrow$ C are the new FDs derived. (c) We have B $\nrightarrow$ D (because of rows 1 and 2) and D $\nrightarrow$ B (because of rows 1 and 3). Therefore we can list all FDs with a single attribute on the left (with a letter in parentheses keyed to the paragraph above that give us this fact).

(a) A $\nrightarrow$ B	(a) B –> A	(a) C –> A	(a) D –>A
(a) A $\nrightarrow$ C	(b) B $\nrightarrow$ C	(b) C –> B	(c) D $\nrightarrow$ B
(a) A $\nrightarrow$ D	(c) B $\nrightarrow$ D	(b) C –> D	(b) D $\nrightarrow$ C

This gives us nontrivial FDs: (1) C –> ABC, (2) B –> A, and (3) D –> A. Now consider pairs of columns on the left. (d) Since C determines all other columns, clearly any pair of columns containing C also determines all others, but these are all trivial results. (e) The column A, combined with any other column X on the left, still functionally determines only those columns already determined by X (because no new row pairs are different when A is added). Now the only pair that does not contain A or C is BD, and since BD has distinct values on each row (see the table T again), we have that BD –> everything. We already know from nontrivial FD (2) that B –> A, and it is trivial that BD –> BD, so the only new FD that comes out of this is (4) BD –> C. If we consider now triples of columns, it is clear that any triple that does not contain C (and therefore functionally determines all other columns) must contain BD (and therefore funtionally determines all columns). The complete list of nontrivial FDs follows:

(1) C –> ABC,   (2) B –> A,   (3) D –> A,   (4) BD –> C

[5.7]   (a) No, the last row never figures in the discussion and can be dropped.

[5.9]   Union rule: If X –> Y and X –> Z, then X –> YZ. XX –> YX by given X –> Y and augmentation. But XX = X, so X –> XY. Similarly, augment X –> Z by X and get X –> XZ.

Next, augment by Y, obtaining XY –> XYZ. Then X –> XY and XY –> XYZ give X –> XYZ. But YZ is a subset of XYZ, so by inclusion XYZ –> YZ, and by transitivity X –> YZ.

Decomposition: If X –> YZ, then X –> Y and X –> Z. YZ –> Y and YZ –> Z by inclusion, and X –> YZ and YZ –> Y, then X –> Y by transitivity, and similarly for X –> Z.

Pseudotransitivity: If X –> Y and WY –> Z, then XW –> Z. X –> Y gives XW –> YW by augmentation, and this with WY –> Z gives XW –> Z by transitivity.

[5.11]   (a) Suppose that X$^+$ does not equal X. Then there is an attribute A in X$^+$, not in X, such that X –> A (otherwise we can never leave X by following FDs). This FD must be covered by F, so A is contained in the right-hand side of some element of F, with left-hand side X$_i$. Since X does not contain any of these left-hand sides, there is some nontrivial set B of attributes in X$_i$ but not in X. Then X$_i$ = BX, BX –> A, and also X –> A. But this means that X$_i$ is not minimal; specifically, B can be dropped in step 3 of the minimal cover algorithm. Contradiction.

[5.12] Here is a list of Armstrong's Axioms and results of Theorem 5.6.8 for use in proving the desired results. Let W, X, Y, and Z be arbitrary sets of columns.

[1] **Reflexivity:**   If Y is a subset of X, then X –> Y.

[2] **Augmentation:**   If X –> Y, then WX –> WY.

[3] **Transitivity:**   If X –> Y and Y –> Z, then X –> Z.

[4] **Union:**   If X –> Y and X –> Z, then X –> YZ.

[5] **Decomposition:**   If X –> YZ, then X –> Y and X –> Z.

[6] **Pseudotransitivity:** If X –> Y and WY –> Z, then XW –> Z.

(a) D –> ABCD

Steps numbered. (1) By reflexivity, since D is a subset of D (both singleton sets), D –> D. (2) Since D –> ABC (by FD (3) given) and D –> D, by union, D –> ABCD.

[5.14] (a) Step 1. H = {A–>B, C–>B, D–>A, D–>B, D–>C, AC–>D}.

Step 2.

1. A–>B. J = H – {A–>B}, X$^+$ under J: X[0] = A, X[1] = A, X$^+$ = A, not containing B, so keep A–>B; that is, H remains the same.

2. C–>B. J = H – {C–>B}. X[0] = C, X[1] = C, so X$^+$ = C, not containing B, so same H.

3. D–>A. J = H – {D–>A}. X[0] = D, X[1]= DBX, X[2] = DBX, so X$^+$ = DBX, not containing A, so same H.

4. D–>B. J = H – {D–>B}, X[0]= D, . . . , X$^+$ = DABC, containing B, so drop this FD.

New H = {A–>B, C–>B, D–>A, D–>C, AC–>D}.

5. D –> C. J = H – {D–>C}. X$^+$ = DAB, not containing C, so same H.

6. AC–>D. J = J – {AC–>D}. X$^+$ = AC, not containing D, so same H.

Resulting H = {A–>B, C–>B, D–>A, D–>C, AC–>D}.

Step 3. Only AC –> D could possibly be reduced on the left-hand side. Loop over B in its left-hand side:

1. B = A, Y = C , J = {A–>B, C–>B, D–>A, D–>C, C–>D}. (Y$^+$ under J) = CBDA, (Y$^+$ under H) = CB, not same, so keep H same.

2. B = C, Y = A, J = {A–>B, C–>B, D–>A, D–>C, A–>D}. (Y+ under J) = ABDC, (Y$^+$ under H) = ABC, not same, so keep H same.

Note how the proposed (but rejected) changes make too many attributes reachable in the closure.

Step 4. M = { A->B, C->B, D->AC, AC->D}.

[5.15] Let Y^+_H stand for Y^+ determined under H. Then we need to show that $Y^+_H = Y^+_J$ implies $H^+ = J^+$. Here J = (H − {x->A}) UNION {Y->A}, and Y = X − {B}. J has the same FDs as H except for one FD that has one less attribute on the left-hand side, making it imply more than the one it replaces, so clearly H^+ is a subset of J^+. We claim that if they are actually different, then Y->A, clearly in J^+, is not in H^+. For if Y->A is in H^+, then all FDs in J are in H^+ by its definition, so that H^+ covers J, and thus covers J^+, so J^+ is a subset of H^+. But we already knew that H^+ is a subset of J^+, so $H^+ = J^+$. Contradiction.

So far we have shown that if H^+ and J^+ differ, then Y->A is not in H^+. But if Y->A is not in H^+, then A is not in Y^+_H, and we know that Y->A is in J^+; that is, A is in Y^+_J, so the sets Y^+_H and Y^+_J are different. The contrapositive is the desired result.

[5.17] (b) Here we will work independently of part (a) until we actually need its results to explain things. A slightly neater approach would be to use the results of (a) from the start. We start with the table T = (A, B, C, D, E, F, G). What is the primary key for this table? B and C are not on the right-hand side of any FD and therefore must be in any key, since a key functionally determines all other columns. Now given BC, we get A (from (1) and (5)); E (from (2)); and since we have A, by transitivity we get F (by (3)). Then (4) gives us G, and (5) gives us D. So we have (accumulating from the left) BC, A, E, F, G, and D, which is all of them. Thus BC is a superkey for T, and since B and C must be in any key, BC is the key. All the given FDs lie in this one table.

Now D is not fully functionally dependent on BC, but dependent on C alone, making C->D a proper-key-subset FD. Therefore even for 2NF we need to factor out a table, and we have two tables: T_1 = (B, C, A, E, F, G) and T_2 = (C, D), with keys BC and C, respectively. T1 contains all the given FDs except (5), which lies in T_2, and (1), which appears to cross tables. However, if we adopt the minimal cover FD set computed in A, we see that all but one are contained entirely in T_1 and one is contained entirely in T_2. FDs A -> F and F -> G are transitive dependencies. Thus T_1 and T_2 form a 2NF decomposition.

(d) Algorithm 5.8.8 with F = {BC–>AE, A–>F, F–>G, C–>D}

S = nullset. Loop through all FDs in F:

BC–> AE. Nothing is S yet, so nothing can contain BCAE, so add it to S: S = {{BCAE}}.

A–>F. AF is not contained in BCAE, so add it to S: S = {{BCAE},{AF}}.

F–>G. FG is not contained in either set so far, so add it: S = {{BCAE},{AF},{FG}}.

C–>D. CD is not contained in any set so far, so add it: S = {{BCAE},{AF},{FG},{CD}}.

Here the only candidate key is BC, and it is contained in BCAE, so the second loop does not add anything to S. The resulting table design is the same as we had before.

[5.19] FDs for banking problem: Each account has a unique type, balance, and branch, so we have `acctid –> acct_type acct_bal bno`. Each branch has a city and each customer has a name, so the set is

```
acctid -> acct_type acct_bal bno
bno -> bcity
ssn -> clname cfname cmidinit
```

T = (acctid, acct_type, acct_bal, bno, bcity, ssn, clname, cfname, cmidinit). Since `ssn` and `acctid` appear only on the left of the FDs, they must be in any key, and in fact all the other attributes are in the closure of {ssn,acctid}, so this is in fact the key of T. Now the first and third FDs are key-subset dependencies, and the second one is a transitive dependency, but since the normal level of decomposition is 3NF, we don't really care about this difference, and just decompose three times—for example, as follows:

```
1. T1 = (acctid, acct_type, acct_bal, bno, bcity), T2 = (acctid,
ssn, clname, cfname, cmidinit).
2. T1 = (acctid, acct_type, acct_bal, bno), T2 = (bno, bcity), T3
= (acctid, ssn, clname, cfname, cmidinit).
3. T1 = (acctid, acct_type, acct_bal, bno), T2 = (bno, bcity), T3
= (ssn, clname, cfname, cmidinit), T4 = (acctid, ssn) Final
result, in 3NT form.
```

Note that along the way we have extracted all the non-key attributes from T, leaving T4 = (acctid, ssn) as a skeletal remain of the original universal table. But in fact it represents an important fact about this design: there is a true binary relationship between accounts and customers. This design is the same as the second proposed design in Exercise 5.3. We can now justify that second design, over the first one, with more confidence. Design 1 of Exercise 5.3 is not fully factored. Look at its result:

```
accounts = (acctid, acct_type, acct_bal)
branches = (bno, bcity)
customers = (ssn, clname, cfname, cmidinit)
has_account_at = (ssn, acctid, bno)
```

We have asserted that acctid -> bno, and this means that the last table has a key-subset dependency and is not even 2NF.

Chapter 6 Solutions

[6.1] **(a)**
```
create table agents (aid char(3) not null unique,
        aname varchar(13), city varchar(20),
        percent integer check(percent >= 0 and percent <= 10)
        primary key aid);

create table products (pid char(3) not null unique,
        pname varchar(13), city varchar(20),
        quantity integer check(quantity > 0),
        price real check(price > 0.0));
```

[6.3] See Figure 6.2 for most of them. There should be exactly one product for each line item, but possibly many line items, or none at all, for each product, so the connection between for_prod and Products should be labeled (0,N) and the connection between for_prod and Line_items should be labeled (1,1).

As in Section 5.4, we start with tables for the entities and then add foreign keys and/or relationship tables to complete the relational design.

Starter entity tables, using just what we see in Figure 5.11, plus entity IDs, for simplicity:

```
customers = (cid)
orders = (ordno)
agents = (aid)
line_items = (ordno,lineno)
products = (pid)
```

The relationship requests is N–1, and thus is implemented with a foreign key:

```
orders = (ordno,cid)
```

Similarly, `places` and `has_item` are also N–1, so orders becomes:

```
orders = (ordno,cid,aid,lineno)
```

Finally, `for_prod` is also N–1, so `line_items` becomes

```
line_items = (ordno,lineno, pid);
create table customers (cid char(4) not null, primary key (cid));
create table orders (ordno integer not null, cid char(3) not null
references customers, aid char(3) not null references
agents,lineno integer not null references line_items, primary key
(ordno));

create table agents (aid char(3) not null, primary key (aid));
create table line_items (ordno integer references orders, lineno
integer not null, pid char(3) not null references products,
primary key (ordno, lineno));
```

[6.4] (a) Yes, make its foreign key "not null references...."

(c) No.

[6.5] (b)
```
create view agentview (aid, aname,city,percent)
    as select aid,aname,city,percent from agents
    where percent> = 0 and percent<=10 with check option;
```

(d)
```
create view vproducts as
    select pid, pname, city, quantity from products;
grant select, update (city, quantity) on vproducts to beowulf;
```

[6.6] (a) False by the definition of the primary key clause in Definition 6.1.3.

(c) False. No subselect is allowed in the **check** clause in X/OPEN.

(e) True.

(g) False. This is a grouped view and the select contains a **where** clause.

[6.7] (a) Restrict, cascade, set null. (**DB2**)

[6.8]
```
create table customers (cid char(4) not null, cname varchar(13),
    city varchar(20) references discounts, discnt float4);
create integrity on customers is discnt <= 15.0;
create unique index cidx on customers (cid);  (See Example 7.1.2)
```

[6.10] (a) The view referred to, `agentords`, is identical except for name to the one given in Example 6.2.1:

```
create view agentords (ordno, month, cid, aid, pid, qty,
    price, aname, acity, percent)
  as select ordno, month, cid, a.aid, pid, qty, price,
      aname, acity, percent
      from orders o, agents a where o.aid = a.aid;
```

The view `agentorders` would not be updatable in X/OPEN by the rules of Figure 6.11 (and similarly in SQL-92, but SQL3 allows updates in more circumstances). In general, inserts, updates, and deletes on `agentords` rows can be thought of as the same operations on `orders` rows with which `agentords` rows are in one-to-one correspondence. `Agents` rows are generally in correspondence with many rows of `agentords`, but it is defensible to argue that updates to the `agents` table should also be allowed to take place as long as they make sense.

Insert with a new `aid` value. It looks like we are inserting a new `agent` row and a new `orders` row, both at the same time: the order refers to the new agent. We allow this. Of course all existing integrity constraints must still hold, so for example the order must refer to an existing product `pid`, and the `ordno` cannot duplicate one that already exists.

Insert with an old `aid` value. This is an insert of a new order with an existing `aid`. The only thing that could go wrong is if this insert specifies an existing `aid` with the "wrong" values for other `agents` columns, such as `aname`. Since `aid` is supposed to be the primary key for agents, `aid` functionally determines all other columns, and giving a different `aname` value, for example, would break an integrity constraint, and thus should fail. It seems reasonable to allow an insert with dependent `agents` columns left unspecified, with the default being the functionally determined values.

MACHINE ASSIGNMENTS

[6.12] INGRES script—

```
* help integrity customers\g
Executing . . .

Table customers has no integrities constraints on it

continue
* create integrity on customers is discnt <= 12.0\g
Executing . . .

E_USODA4 INTEGRITY on customers: constraint does not initially
hold.
      (Sat Mar 6 17:48:53 1993)
```

```
continue
* update customers set discnt = 10.0 where cid = 'c001'\g
Executing . . .

(1 row)
continue
* create integrity on customers is discnt <= 12.0\g
Executing . . .

continue
* update customers set discnt = 16.0 where cid = 'c001'\g
Executing . . .
(0 rows)

continue
* select * from customers\g
Executing . . .

+-----+---------+------------+---------+
|cid  |cname    |city        |discnt   |
+-----+---------+------------+---------+
|c001 |Tiptop   |Duluth      |   10.000|
|c002 |Basics   |Dallas      |   12.000|
|c003 |Allied   |Dallas      |    8.000|
|c004 |ACME     |Duluth      |    8.000|
|c006 |ACME     |Kyoto       |    0.000|
+-----+---------+------------+---------+

(5 rows)
continue
* help integrity customers\g
Executing . . .

Integrity constraints on customers are:
Integrity constraint 1:
create integrity on customers is discnt <= 12.0

continue
* drop integrity on customers 1\g
Executing . . .

continue
* abort\g
Executing . . .

continue
* update customers set discnt = 16.0 where cid = 'c001'\g
Executing . . .

(1 rows)
continue
```

```
* select * from customers\g
Executing . . .

+-----+---------+----------+---------+
|cid  |cname    |city      |discnt   |
+-----+---------+----------+---------+
|c001 |Tiptop   |Duluth    |  16.000|
|c002 |Basics   |Dallas    |  12.000|
|c003 |Allied   |Dallas    |   8.000|
|c004 |ACME     |Duluth    |   8.000|
|c006 |ACME     |Kyoto     |   0.000|
+-----+---------+----------+---------+

(5 rows)
continue
```

[6.13] (a) **INGRES** script—

```
* insert into orders (ordno, month, cid, aid, pid, qty, dollars)
* values (1031, 'jul', 'c001', 'a01', 'p01', 1000, 450.0)\g
Executing . . .

(1 row)
continue
* create view returns (ordno, month, cid, aid, pid, qty, dollars,
*          discnt, percent, price)
*   as select ordno, month, o.cid, o.aid, o.pid, qty, dollars,
*       discnt, percent, price
*   from orders o, customers c, agents a, products p
*   where c.cid = o.cid and a.aid = o.aid and p.pid = o.pid\g
Executing . . .

continue
* help\g
Executing . . .

        Name          Owner        Type
        agents        poneil       table
        customers     poneil       table
        employees     poneil       table
        orders        poneil       table
        ords          poneil       table
        products      poneil       table
        returns       poneil       view

(7 rows)
continue
* help view returns\g
Executing . . .

View:           returns
Owner:          poneil
Check option: off
```

```
View Definition:
create view returns (ordno, month, cid, aid, pid, qty, dollars,
discnt, percent, price) as select ordno, month, o.cid, o.aid,
o.pid, qty, dollars, discnt, percent, price from orders o,
customers c, agents a, products p
where c.cid = o.cid and
a.aid = o.aid and p.pid = o.pid
continue
```

(c) INGRES—

```
* select ordno, qty, dollars, discnt, percent, price,
*    qty * price - discnt / 100 * price * qty from returns \g
Executing . . .
+-----+-----+---------+--------+------+--------+---------+
|ordno| qty |dollars  | discnt |percen|price   |col7     |
+-----+-----+---------+--------+------+--------+---------+
| 1011| 1000|  450.000| 10.000|   6  |  0.500|  450.000|
| 1012| 1000|  450.000| 10.000|   6  |  0.500|  450.000|
| 1016| 1000|  500.000|  0.000|   6  |  0.500|  500.000|
| 1021| 1000|  460.000|  8.000|   5  |  0.500|  460.000|
| 1024|  800|  400.000|  0.000|   5  |  0.500|  400.000|
| 1031| 1000|  450.000| 10.000|   6  |  0.500|  450.000|
| 1031| 1000|  450.000| 10.000|   6  |  0.500|  450.000|
| 1019|  400|  180.000| 10.000|   6  |  0.500|  180.000|
| 1013| 1000|  880.000| 12.000|   7  |  1.000|  880.000|
| 1017|  600|  540.000| 10.000|   5  |  1.000|  540.000|
| 1026|  800|  704.000| 12.000|   5  |  1.000|  704.000|
| 1018|  600|  540.000| 10.000|   7  |  1.000|  540.000|
| 1014| 1200| 1104.000|  8.000|   7  |  1.000| 1104.000|
| 1015| 1200| 1104.000|  8.000|   7  |  1.000| 1104.000|
| 1023|  500|  450.000| 10.000|   6  |  1.000|  450.000|
| 1022|  400|  720.000| 10.000|   5  |  2.000|  720.000|
| 1020|  600|  600.000|  0.000|   7  |  1.000|  600.000|
| 1025|  800|  720.000| 10.000|   5  |  1.000|  720.000|
+-----+-----+---------+--------+------+--------+---------+
(18 rows)
continue
```

Chapter 7 Solutions

[7.1] (a) Since minextents is 3, $3 \cdot 20{,}480 = 61{,}440$ bytes.

   (b) Since maxextents is 8, $8 \cdot 20{,}480 = 163{,}840$ bytes.

[7.2] (a) We have 2048 bytes in a page, and for 512 slots we would need $512 \cdot 2 = 1024$ bytes for the row directory. This leaves $2048 - 1024 = 1024$ bytes for rows, and we have $1024 / 512 = 2$ bytes for each row.

   (c) We can allow $2^{23} = 8{,}388{,}608$ pages/table.

[7.4] (a) We need about 102 bytes per row (2 for the directory offset) and we have nearly $0.75 \cdot 2048 = 1536$ usable bytes/page. Now 1536 bytes/page / 102 bytes/row = 15 rows/page. 200,000 rows / 15 rows/page = 13,334 pages.

(d) We will need one disk access for the root of the index, and one for the next level directory. We are searching through 10,000 leaf-level entries, and at 148 entries/page this means about CEIL(10,000/148) = 68 accesses for leaf node pages. Since the rows are not clustered and assuming buffering is negligible, retrieving 10,000 rows will take 10,000 disk I/Os. Therefore the number of disk I/Os is $(1 + 1 + 68 + 10,000) = 10,070$ disk accesses. At 40 accesses/second, we require about 252 seconds.

(f) To *count* the number of rows, the query optimizer only needs to count the number of entries, not go down and pick up the rows themselves, so the number of accesses is $(1 + 1 + 68) = 70$, and at 40 I/Os/second, this is 1.75 seconds.

[7.6] (a) (i) False. **DB2** does allow the use of 32-KB pages when 4 KB is too small.

(iii) True. See Example 7.3.2.

(v) True. There will be 1000 pages in the buffer, out of 1,000,000, so 1 in 1000 will be in the buffer.

[7.7] (b) 75% of 2000 is 1500 bytes usable on a page. The entry contains the `rowid`, 6 bytes; the `keyval`, here 7 bytes; and 1 byte of overhead, a total of 14 bytes. Then 1500/14 = 108 entries/page. 400,000 entries/(108 entries/page) = 3704 leaf-level pages.

(e) With a clustered index, the same number of index pages is used, but the 20,000 data rows are adjacent on disk, in 20,000/8 = 2500 pages. Thus the total is only 2689 disk-page I/Os.

[7.8] (b) This table is 50% full, so for each slot we have the approximate result

$$\text{Pr(collision chain of length 21)} = (.5)(.5)^{20} = 5 \times 10^{-7}$$

There are 20 slots in a page, each independently capable of this event, so together the probability is 20 times the individual figure, or approximately 10^{-5}.

[7.9] (a) Here N = 128 and M = 10,000. $E(S) = 10,000*(1-.9999^{128})$

$.9999^{128} = .9999^{2*2*2*2*2*2*2} = ((((((.9999^2)^2 ...^2) = .9873$
$E(S) = 10,000* .0127 = 127$

Using 7.6.4, $10,000*(1-\exp(-128/10,000)) = 10,000(1-.9873) = 127$

Yes, both show that only one collision is expected.

[7.10] (a) The probability that all the darts will be in different slots, for 2 darts, is 364/365, because the first dart can go into any slot and the second dart must miss the first in 364 out of 365 ways. Then for 3 darts the probability is $(364/365) \star (363/365)$. For N darts, it is $364 \star 363 \star \ldots \star (365 - N + 1)/365^{N-1} = .5$ at the desired value of N. $(1 - 1/365)(1 - 2/365)\ldots(1 - (N-1)/365) = .5$. Expanding the product and neglecting terms with multiple factors of 365 in the denominator, we have approximately $1 - (1 + 2 + 3 + \ldots + (N-1))/365 = .5$, or $1 + 2 + \ldots + (N-1) = 365/2$. The sum of the numbers is about $(N-1)^2/2$, so $(N-1)^2 = 365$ or $N = 20$, approximately. By doing it numerically, we find that $N = 23$ has the closest to .5, at .493, so the neglected terms have some effect.

Chapter 8 Solutions

[8.1] (a) Seek time .016 seconds + rotational latency .008 seconds + transfer time .012 seconds (8 times .0015) = .036 seconds.

(c) (i) In this case, sequential prefetch of 8 pages at a time *helps*. To read in 5000 index pages in P8 blocks, we calculate $5000/8 = 625$ blocks, so about $625 \star 0.036$ seconds elapsed time, or 22.5 seconds. (We have no rule of thumb here, as in the case where we say that sequential prefetch proceeds at a rate 400 I/Os per second, so we need to calculate more carefully.) We also have 50,000 clustered data pages, and $50,000/8 = 6250$, $6250 \star 0.036 = 225$ seconds. So total elapsed time is $22.5 + 225 = 247.5$ seconds.

(ii) In the case where random I/Os are used, 50,000R + 5000R takes 55,000/40 seconds, or 1375 seconds.

[8.2] (a) With pctfree = 0, we can fit 10 rows of 400 bytes each on a 4-KB disk page. Thus 100,000 rows require $100,000/10 = 10,000$ data pages. The eidx index, with 10-byte entries, fits 400 entries on a leaf page; thus with 100,000 entries at the leaf level, there are $100,000/400 = 250$ leaf pages. At the next level up, with entries the same size, we fit 400 entries per page, and the 250 entries needed clearly fit in a single page, a root.

(b) (i) P(leaf) = 1/250.

(ii) (1 – P(leaf)) = 249/250.

    (iii) Call this event NOT-leaf-N. We require a conjunction of N independent events, each with probability 249/250. P(NOT-leaf-N) = (249/250)**N (Nth power).

    (iv) (249/250)**250 = 0.367. (You might be interested to note that this is a good approximation to exp(−1), 0.368 since the formula we are calculating is $(1 − 1/x)**x$, for a large x, and in the limit as x approaches infinity this formula approaches exp(−1).)

    (v) A fraction 0.367 will have fallen out of buffers because they were not referenced in the last 125 seconds, so the number we expect to see remaining in buffers is (1 − 0.367) ⋆ 250 = 158.25. (You can recast this in terms of the definition of "expectation" if you want. For each specific leaf, P(leaf in buffer) = 1 − 0.367 = 0.633. Expected number of leaves remaining in buffer = number of leaves ⋆ 0.633 = 158.25.)

    (vi) Here we have N = 250 darts and M = 250 slots, so the expected number of slots hit is approximately $E(S) = M(1 − e^{−N/M}) = 250(1 − e^{−1}) = 158$.

(c) (iv) Since there are fewer leaf pages than data pages, they are rereferenced more often. We see that only 250 − 247 = 3 data pages were rereferenced in the 125 seconds, while 250 − 158 = 92 index leaf pages were rereferenced in the period (ignoring double rereferences). Thus fewer *different* index leaf pages were referenced in the period and remain in the buffer.

(f) Here we have two queries per second. The fraction of the data pages not available in buffer (10,000 − 247)/10,000 = .975, so we have an I/O cost of 2 ⋆ 0.975 or 1.950. A root page is never out of buffer. The leaf pages have a probability 0.367 to be out of buffer (from part (b)), and so this adds an I/O cost for two queries, or 0.734. Total I/O cost is then 1.950 + 0.734 = 2.684 per second.

(h) I/O cost would be 2, for the data pages. Clearly this is a superior strategy to LRU, since we use less memory and have a lower I/O cost.

[8.4] **(b)** (i) ACCESSTYPE = I, ACCESSNAME = C1234X, MATCH-COLS = 1, (INDEXONLY = N).

    (ii) We must retrieve all index entries with C1 having values from 1 to 10. This is 1/10 of the whole range of C1234X, which has NLEAF = 150,151, so the number of leaf pages retrieved is 15,015. Sequential prefetch can be used, so elapsed time is 15,015/400 = 37.54 seconds.

(iii) The filter factor for this compound predicate is (1/10)(1/20) (1/50) = 1/10,000.

The number of rows retrieved is (1/10,000)(100,000,000) = 10,000. Rows of T are contiguous by the index C1234X. Here there are 10 values of C1 selected, each subdivided into 200 regions of C2 values, of which we select 10 adjacent. But each of these 10 is further subdivided into 50 regions of various C3 values, of which we select one. Thus there are 100 separate regions of the index in use here, separated by parts of the index not in use. The 10,000 rows are distributed across these 100 ranges, so there are about 100 rows that are contiguous in each range, but the whole set is far from contiguous. But DB2 cannot take advantage of these little contiguous ranges, because it will find them while processing screening predicates. (List prefetch will not be used either, because no filtering is allowed in extracts into an RID list.) Therefore elapsed time is 10,000/40 = 250 seconds.

15,051S + 10,000R, with elapsed time 37.54 + 250 = 287.54 seconds.

[8.5] (a) (i) C1 and C2 are matching columns. The matching stops at C2 because of part 3 of Definition 8.5.7.

(iii) No columns are matching, because C1 <> 6 is not an indexable predicate.

(v) C1 and C2 are matching columns. The matching stops before C3 because "C3 like '%abc'" is not indexable.

(vii) No columns are matching because C1 = Expression is not indexable.

(b) (i) FF(C1 = 7) = 1/100 = .01, FF(C2>=101) = 100/200 = .5, so the composite FF = .01 $\star$ .5 = .005.

(iii) .005 $\star$ 100,000,000 = 500,000 index entries. Recall that all columns are 4 bytes in length. For C1234X, the key value length is 16 bytes. There is a certain amount of compression at the leaf level, with each block of duplicates containing 1 key value (16 bytes), 4 bytes block overhead, and 10 RIDs of 4 bytes each; this means a total of 60 bytes for 10 entries, or 6 bytes per entry. We can fit FLOOR(4000/6) = 666 entries per page. Thus there are 500,000/666 = 750 pages at leaf level, and these can be read by sequential prefetch (S). The index has another level above the leaf level, but only one page of it is accessed on the original lookup of the very first access. This page would require random access (R).

(v) 750S + 600R = 750/400 + 600/40 = 16.875 seconds.

[8.6] (a) Here we have 50 million rows and FF(incomeclass = 10) = 1/10, so this RID list extraction from incomex will result in 5 million RIDs, below the absolute maximum of 16 million. 5 million RIDs require 20 million bytes, and this must be below 50% of the RID pool, so the RID pool must be at least 40 million bytes. Since the RID pool is half the size of the buffer pool, this means the buffer pool must be at least 80 million bytes. Thus the system must have enough memory to accommodate 120 million bytes for buffer and RID pools.

(c) FF(AGE between 20 and 39) = 2/5: there will be .4 * 50 million = 20 million agex index entries, above the absolute maximum for RID lists, so it is not possible.

(e) It is not possible because of rule 4 of Definition 8.6.3, excluding in-list predicates.

[8.7] (a) ACCESSTYPE = I, ACCESSNAME = mailx, MATCHCOLS = 1. We stop matching columns left-to-right with the zip code component for two reasons: (1) the next column in mailx, hobby, is not matched, (2) always stop matching when come to **between** predicate.

(c) (i) Yes, under the memory conditions found in Exercise 8.6(a), We can use an MX step on incomeclass = 10, using the incomex index.

(ii)

ACCESS TYPE	MATCH COLS	ACCESS NAME	PRE FETCH	MIXOP SEQ
M	0		L	1
MX	1	mailx	S	2
MX	1	agex	S	3
MI	0			4
MX	1	incomex	S	5
MI	0			6

Note that the predicates are ordered from smaller to larger by filter factor, and intersection takes place as often as possible to avoid having more than one RID list at once on the imaginary stack. Other orders are also usable.

(iii) 1/50,000.

(e) As in (d), start with index scan of mailx to extract RID list for **zipcode** predicate, taking 6.25 seconds. Then extract RID list for **age** predicate from agex with NLEAF = 50,000, so (1/50)(50,000), I/O cost is 1000S, elapsed time, 1000/400 = 2.5 seconds. Finally, extract RID list for **income** predicate from incomex with NLEAF = 50,000, so (1/10)(50,000), I/O cost is 5000S, elapsed time 12.5 seconds. Finally, 1000 rows on 1000 data pages, but this time we can use list prefetch, 1000L, elapsed time 1000/100 = 10 seconds. Total elapsed time: 6.25 + 2.5 + 12.5 + 10 = 31.25 seconds. The fact that they come out the same is an accident.

[8.8] (a) No. It would have 25,000,000 RIDS, over the absolute maximum.

(b) (i) "zipcode between 02139 and 07138" is matching, the rest are screening.

(iii) For either method, we expect FF ⋆ 50,000,000 = .01 ⋆ .02 ⋆ .05 ⋆ 50,000,000 = 500 rows, not clustered. For method (i), the RIDs are found during screening, and thus entail random I/O, at 500R = 500/40 = 12.5 seconds. For method (ii), we obtain a RID list and thus can use list prefetch, for 500L = 500/100 = 5 seconds.

[8.9] (a) The only matching column is zipcode, because by Definition 8.5.7, a **between** predicate terminates the search for matching predicates. The index I/O we perform for the zip code between predicates will scan (2000/100,000)(250,000 leaf pages) = 5000 leaf pages, with sequential prefetch used, and 5000S requires an elapsed time of 5000/400 = 12.5 seconds. The combined filter factor for all predicates, including screening predicates, in order by predicate clauses as they appear is (200/10,000)(1/50 + 1/50)(1/100)(1/10) = (1/50)(1/25)(1/100)(1/10) = 1/1,250,000. With 50,000,000 rows in prospects, this means that we expect to retrieve (1/1,250,000)(50,000,000) = 40 rows. With random I/O (we can't use list prefetch because we didn't extract an RID list, since we used screening predicates), 40R take elapsed time 40/40 = 1 second. The total elapsed time is 13.5 seconds.

(c) (a) wins with 13.5 seconds elapsed time, versus (b) with 22.75 seconds. The reason for this general rule is that the matching scan of the first column, in the case where screening predicates are used, must be duplicated in the case of MX retrieval, along with other index scans as well, so the MX case pays more for index I/O. It is *just possible* that this deficit will be made up at the end by the fact that the MX approach allows list prefetch in data page retrieval.

[8.10] (a) With T1.C6 = 5, we limit the 1,000,000 rows of T1 down to 1/20 as many, or 50,000 rows. Now each value of T1.C7 is matched by a value of T2.C8, and for each of the 50,000 rows selected in T1, we have a constant value K for T1.C7. We ask how many rows in T2 match—that is, what is the selectivity of T1.C7 = K? Clearly the answer is 1/200,000, and there are (on the average) 5 rows that match. Therefore each of the 50,000 rows in T1 matches 5 rows in T2, and we have 250,000 rows in the join so far. Now we have to limit T2.C9 = 6, with filter factor = 1/400, and the resulting number of rows in the join is (1/400)(250,000) = 625.

[8.11] (a) After pass 1:

12 45 67 84 l 7 29 58 76 l 22 39 81 91 l 28 33 65 96 l 4 13 54 77 l l 1 32 41 59

After pass 2:

7 12 29 45 58 67 76 84 l 22 28 33 39 65 81 91 96 l l 4 13 32 41 54 59 77

After pass 3:

7 12 22 28 29 33 39 45 58 65 67 76 81 84 91 96 l l 4 13 22 4` 54 59 77

After pass 4:

1 4 7 12 13 22 28 28 32 33 39 41 45 54 58 59 65 67 76 77 81 84 91 96

[8.12] (a) (1/2)(1/10)(1,000,000) = 50,000.

(c) For K2 = 1, 1/2. For K100 > 80, 1/5. For K10K between 2000 and 3000, 1000/10,000 = 1/10. For K5 = 3, 1/5. So (1/2)(1/5)(1/10)(1/5)(1,000,000) = (1/500)(1,000,000) = 2000.

(e) As explained in the text, a table space scan is being used in the K4 case, and 1737 prefetch I/Os gives 1737 * 32 = 55,584 pages. Recall that the BENCH table has 58,556 pages, so this is very close. Our rule of thumb would mean that 55,584S takes 55,584/400 = 138.96 seconds. In fact, we see 125.83 seconds elapsed, so we are reading in a bit faster than that. Note that the CPU time of 14.35 seconds does not get subtracted from 125.83

seconds before we start timing the I/Os: I/O and CPU overlap, so basically all of the elapsed time has I/O taking place.

(g) We use a nested loop join as the basis for calculation, as in Exercise 8.4 (a). Limit B1 by B1.K100 = 99, so 10,000 are rows retrieved. For each one of these, B1.250K is a constant K, and we ask how many rows in B2 have B2.500K = K? Average 2. Thus we now have 20,000 rows in the join. Now limit with B2.K25 = 19, FF of 1/25, and (1/25)(20,000) = 800. The actual number retrieved (Appendix C) is 804.

[8.13] (a) B1.K100 = 22 selects for 10,000 rows of B1, and for each of these, B1.K250K is a constant between 1 and 250K, so that B1.K250K = B2.K100K selects for nothing at all if the constant is over 100K, and 10 rows of B2 if it is not over 100K. This happens 40% of the time. Of the 10 rows, only 1/25, or .4 on average, are selected by B2.K25 = 19. Thus we expect .4 * .4 * 10,000 = 1600 rows in the join.

(b) B1 the outer table. Here the 10,000 value-22 index entries of the K100 index are read into an RID list, allowing list prefetch of the 10,000 rows of B1 needed to determine B1.K100K and B1.KSEQ; this datapage access has I/O cost 10,000L. The index entries are all duplicates, so they take 4 bytes each, or 40,000 bytes in all, or 10 pages, accessible by sequential prefetch at I/O cost 10S. Then for each of the 10,000 rows the inner loop accesses either about 10 rows of B2 (40% of the cases), using list prefetch, or 0 rows (60% of the cases), depending on whether B1.K250K is below or above 100,000 in value. The 10 rows are further screened by the B2.K25 = 19 predicate, resulting in .4 rows in the join. But this happens only in 40% of the 10,000 cases—that is, in 4000 cases, so the I/O cost is 4000 * 10L = 40,000L. The total I/O cost is then 10S + 50,000L = 50,000/100=500 seconds.

B2 the outer table. Here the 40,000 value-19 index entries of the K25 index are read into an RID list, allowing list prefetch of the 40,000 rows of B2 needed to determine B2.K100K and B2.KSEQ; this datapage access has I/O cost 40,000L. The index entries are all duplicates, so they take 4 bytes each, or 160,000 bytes, or 40 pages, accessible by sequential prefetch at I/O cost 40S. Then for each of the 40,000 rows, the inner loop accesses about 4 rows of B1 via the match on B1.K250K = B2.K100K (all cases, since here the B2.K100K value is always in-range for K250K). Now 4 is a bit small for list prefetch, but we have been allowing it, so we count this as 40,000 * 4L = 160,000L. These rows are further screened by predicate B1.K100 = 22. The total I/O cost is 40S + 200,000L = 2000 seconds.

[8.15] (a) `select npages from systables where name = 'bench':`

(See Figure 8.12.)

(c) The K2X index is almost all duplicates, so there are 4 bytes/ entry, or about 2000 entries/page. There are 1,000,000 entries, so 500 pages at leaf level.

Chapter 9 Solutions

[9.1] (a)

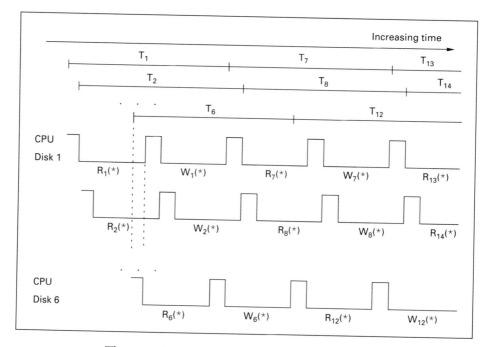

There are 6 transactions in 120 ms, or 50 TPS.

[9.2] (a) T2 $\longrightarrow$ T3 $\longrightarrow$ T1

[9.3]

	$R_1(A)$	$W_1(A)$	$R_2(A)$	$R_2(B)$	C_2	$R_1(B)$	$W_1(B)$	C_1
Operation number:	1	2	3	4		5	6	

Operations 2 and 4 give $T_1 \rightarrow T_2$, and operations 4 and 6 give $T_2 \rightarrow T_1$. The precedence graph is

To answer the second part of the question, assume that A and B are accounts that normally see only deposits, and that T_1 has the job of seeing that account A doesn't get over 100 — if A is over 100, T_1 brings the value of A down to 50 and moves the excess, adding it to account B. We assume that the job of T_2 is to check the sum of accounts A and B, and if the sum is more than 200 to bring the sum down to 150 by subtracting from A and B and adding the excess to a third balance, C. Now assume to start that A = 120 and B = 140. Since T_1 doesn't change the sum of of A and B, we see that any serial execution will have T_2 subtracting from A and B and adding to C. However, what we see instead is

$R_1(A,120) \ W_1(A,50) \ R_2(A,50) \ R_2(B,140) \ C_2 \ R_1(B,140) \ W_1(B,210) \ C_1$

We note that T_2 sees A + B as *at most* 50 + 140 = 190. Since that is less than 200, T_2 makes no changes. This could not have occurred in any serial schedule.

[9.5] This is the "dirty write" example, where each transaction writes back a new value for A that fails to take the other's update into account. The locking scheduler translates this into the following sequence of events.

$RL_1(A) \ R_1(A) \ RL_2(A) \ R_2(A) \ WL_1(A)$ (conflict with earlier $RL_2(A)$ – T_1 must WAIT) $WL_2(A)$ (conflict with earlier $RL_2(A)$ – circuit in WAITS-FOR Graph - choose T_2 as victim) A_2 ($WL_1(A)$ now successful) (T_2 now retries as transaction T_3) $RL_3(A)$ (conflict with $WL_1(A)$ – T_3 must WAIT) $W_1(A) \ C_1$ ($RL_3(A)$ now successful) $R_3(A) \ WL_3(A) \ W_3(A) \ C_3$

and we see that the operations for T_1 and T_2 (renamed T_3) occur in serial order.

[9.6] (a) $WL_3(A) \ W_3(A) \ RL_1(A)$ (conflict with earlier $WL_3(A)$ – T_1 must WAIT for T_3) $RL_2(B) \ R_2(B) \ WL_2(Y) \ W_2(Y) \ WL_3(B)$ (conflict with earlier $RL_2(B)$ – T_3 must wait for T_2) C_2 (releases lock on B, so $WL_3(B)$ is successful) $W_3(B) \ C_3$ (releases lock on A so $RL_1(A)$ is successful) $R_1(A) \ WL_1(Z) \ W_1(Z) \ C_1$

$W_3(A)$	$R_1(A)$	$W_1(Z)$	$R_2(B)$	$W_2(Y)$	$W_3(B)$	C1 C2 C3

Operation number:

1	2	3	4	5	6

Note from operations 1 and 2 that $T_1 \rightarrow T_3$ in the waits-for graph. Next, from 4 and 6, we have $T_3 \rightarrow T_2$. No other pairs of operations act on identical data elements. Therefore there are no other conflicting pairs, and the waits-for graph never has a cycle, so there is no deadlock. The waits-for graph after operation 6 is this.

$$T_1 \longrightarrow T_3 \longrightarrow T_2$$

[9.7] (a) $R_5(E,8)$, since before this the pages with A, B, C, and D have been accessed and fill the 4 pages of the cache buffer.

(c) The page with data item A will be dropped by the LRU scheme, since it has the longest interval since reference.

(e) No, it only forces out the log data on this transaction. The actual dirty page may linger in the buffer until a convenient time to write it.

[9.8] (a) (i) Here is the series of log entries written as a result of this history:

(S, 2) (S, 1) (W, 1, B, 2, 3) (S, 3) (W, 3, A, 1, 4) (W, 3, C, 4, 6) (CKPT, LIST = T1, T2, T3) (S, 4) (W, 2, E, 8, 9) (C, 2) (W, 4, D, 7, 11)

(ii) The last write will not get out to the log file, since no Commit forces it. Now we outline the actions taken by recovery:

Rollback

1.	(C, 2)	Place T2 as committed on active list.
2.	(W, 2, E, 8, 9)	No action.
3.	(S,4)	No action.
4.	(CKPT, LIST = T1, T2, T3)	Active list = (T1(NC), T2(C), T3(NC)).
5.	(W, 3, C, 4, 6)	UNDO: C=4.
6.	(W, 3, A, 1, 4)	UNDO: A=1.
7.	(S, 3)	Active list = (T1(NC), T2(C)).
8.	(W, 1, B, 2, 3)	UNDO: B=2.
9.	(S, 1)	Active list = (T2(C)), only committed, end of rollback.

Roll forward (Jump to first log entry after checkpoint)

10.	(S, 4)	No action. Active committed transactions: T2.
11.	(W, 2, E, 8, 9)	REDO: E=9.
12.	(C, 2)	No action. No more active committed transactions. End of roll forward.

(iii)

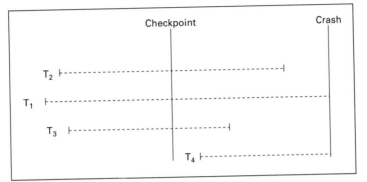

[9.9]   First we argue why these are all possible cases of transaction durations. Every transaction must start and stop, start must come before
stop, and there are three times possible: (1) before the final checkpoint taken (in the next exercise we show that there is no difference if
it started two checkpoints ago), (2) after the final checkpoint and
before the crash, and (3) at the time of the crash (at least a stop can
happen at this time). Therefore the set of start-stop times that covers
all possibilities would seem to be (1–1), (1–2), (1–3), (2–2), (2–3),
and (3–3). But (3–3) is really impossible, and each of the other cases
is covered by one of the transactions T_1 through T_5, in that order.

Now we argue that each of these cases is appropriately recovered
by the recovery process with cache-consistent checkpointing.

(1–1) Both the start and stop for the transaction took place before
the last checkpoint. In recovery we don't perform any UNDO or
REDO of any of these data items, since the transaction was not
active at the time of the checkpoint, and of course performed no
write operations after the checkpoint took place. In fact, all update
operations for this transaction took place before the last checkpoint, and that checkpoint forced every "dirty" data item out to
disk. Thus all updates from this transaction are out to disk, and we
don't do anything to change them in recovery.

(1–2) The transaction started before the last checkpoint and ended
after the last checkpoint. Note that we see the Commit log entry
first during rollback, and therefore perform no action on write logs
until roll forward. With roll forward, starting after the checkpoint,
we REDO all write log entries for this transaction to data items on
disk. Any updates which occurred before the checkpoint are
already out to disk.

(1–3) The transaction started before the last checkpoint and ended as a result of the crash. Since the transaction aborted, we should UNDO all writes that it performed. Note that during rollback, we will either start by seeing a write log (and not a Commit) or by seeing at the time of the last checkpoint that the transaction was still active (and since we saw no Commit log, it was uncommitted). We must UNDO all write entries for the transaction. If a write log entry occurred after the last checkpoint, we see that it is an uncommitted transaction immediately, and are able to UNDO the action for that same log entry. If it leaves no trace with a write log entry after the checkpoint, we will still see that it was active at the time of the checkpoint, and will continue rollback until we see the transaction Start log; UNDO will be performed for all write logs back to that point.

(2–2) The transaction started after the last checkpoint and ended after the last checkpoint. Note that we see the Commit log entry first during rollback, and therefore perform no action on write logs until roll forward. With roll forward, starting after the checkpoint, we REDO all write log entries for this transaction to data items on disk. This is just what is desired.

(2–3) The transaction started after the last checkpoint and ended as a result of the crash. Since the transaction aborted, we should UNDO all writes that it performed. Note that during rollback we will start by seeing a write log (and not a Commit), and since we saw no Commit log, it was uncommitted. When we see a write log entry, we see that it is an uncommitted transaction immediately, and are able to UNDO the action for that same log entry, and all other write log entries back to the Start log.

There is one final point to consider. Is it possible that we perform two different actions on the same data element, UNDO-UNDO, UNDO-REDO, or REDO-REDO which interfere with one another, so that the wrong data element eventually ends up in place? If we consider performing an UNDO action first, we see that this action occurs during rollback, because the transaction that performed an update on the data item never completed and must now abort. By locking, if we assume we hold all locks until Commit, we see that no other transaction could have updated this data item at a later temporal point. Further UNDO actions could only be performed by the same transaction and ultimately put in place the earliest value this transaction saw. Any future REDO actions on the data item (if there are any) must occur earlier in time, and it is clear that the last REDO action (if there is one) will leave the same value in place that the earliest UNDO action put in place. Therefore all committed transactions have completed their updates on this data item (there can only be one) and any uncommitted transaction has had no effect. If we consider performing a REDO action first, by locking we see that there can be no earlier UNDO action; therefore the final REDO action has put into place the final value. We depend on the serializability of histories under the locking discipline to see that this was the right value.

[9.11] $H = W_4(A)\ R_1(A)\ C_1\ W_2(B)\ R_4(B)\ W_5(C)\ R_2(C)\ C_2 W_3(D)\ R_5(D)\ C_3\ C_4\ C_5$

$$T_4 \rightarrow T_1 \qquad T_2 \rightarrow T_4 \qquad T_5 \rightarrow T_2 \qquad T_3 \rightarrow T_5$$

$PG(H) = T_3 \rightarrow T_5 \rightarrow T_2 \rightarrow T_4 \rightarrow T_1$

Thus $PG(H)$ contains no circuits, and H is serializable by Theorem 9.3.4. The equivalent serial history $S(H)$ is

$W_3(D)\ C_3\ W_5(D)\ C_5\ W_2(B)\ R_2(C)\ C_2\ W_4(A)\ R_4(B)\ C_4\ R_1(A)\ C_1$

(Note that locking would put T_1, then T_4, T_2, and T_5 into waits, so only T_3 would be running at the time of C_3, which would release T_5, and so on.)

Chapter 10 Solutions

[10.1] (a) False. The master lock table and master transaction table can be in shared memory, so locks and transaction states are system-wide synchronous and two-phase commit is not needed.

(b) True, assuming that the queries take only read locks. No other read-only process needs to wait for such locks.

(c) False. The server can carry out a service via messages to the various processors.

(d) True. A CPU of 60 MIPS would have a point on the graph and the 300-MIPS CPU would be a point 5 times farther out on the horizontal axis. Five 60-MIPS CPUs would be a point on the ray through the origin and the first point, extended until it reaches the 300-MIPS mark. Since the curve bends up more and more, the 300-MIPS CPU would be the higher point.

(e) True. See Figure 10.9, where crashed state feeds back into the prepared state.

Index

The Morgan Kaufmann Series in Data Management Systems
Series Editor, Jim Gray